THE UNDERGROUND LAWYER

by
Michael Louis Minns
Attorney at Law

Gopher Publications, Inc. • Katy, Texas

GOPHER PUBLICATIONS
870 Mason Road, Suite 104-813
Katy, Texas 77450

Second Printing 1990

PRINTED IN THE UNITED STATES OF AMERICA

Library of Congress Cataloging-in-Publication Data

Minns, Michael Louis

The Underground Lawyer
ISBN 0 929801 00 8
1. Law 2. Government 3. History. 4. Politics. 5. Taxation,
Taxpayer's Bill of Rights. 6. Torts, Injuries. 7. Divorce.
8. Education. 9. Insurance. 10. U.S. Constitution.
11. Judges. 12. Jury System. 13. Legal Research.
14. Income. 15. Banking

Cover photography by C. Michel Feray
Collation management by Michelle M. Minns
Cover concept by Richard L. Minns
Cover Design Copyright © 1989 Gopher Publications
The gopher symbol is a registered trademark of Gopher Publications.

LIST OF ILLUSTRATIONS

ABOUT THE AUTHOR

by L. R. Robertson, *Member of the State Bar of Texas, Legal Assistant's Division*

"I was impressed by Minns' personal characteristics: honesty, courage, commitment to justice and his desire to make his life worthy because some day he would stand before God."

Michael Louis Minns, the author, was named in part after his father Richard Louis Minns, the founder of a chain of health studios, who in turn had been named in part after his father George Richard Minns of England.

George Minns, a boxer and merchant soldier, married Ethel Goldberg after a whirlwind two week courtship in Temple, Texas. Friends had told him not to do it, but George always did what he was told not to do.

On the author's maternal side, great grandfather Fish came from Poland with his family to the United States through New York, eventually settling in Indian territory in Oklahoma. During the immigration process in the New York harbor, Fish changed his name when he was told that "Fish" sounded silly in English and was also clearly a Jewish name in a new land where the Irish, Italians, Jews, and Poles were hated. He changed his name to the tribal name "Levy" believing no one would know he was Jewish. His son, Sam Levy, married Russian immigrant, Esther. Their daughter Miriam, married Richard Minns. In 1951, in Houston, Texas, they gave birth to the author.

In 1965, the 14 year old Minns engaged in his first contractual dispute. A snow cone truck he had purchased (which was older than he was) had defects. The former owner had guaranteed it to be "like new." The idealistic Minns thought the guarantee should mean something. The seller did not agree. David Komiss, now a prominent Houston attorney, represented Minns in his lawsuit, which was successfully settled. At 15, Minns worked for Seymour Lieberman and Komiss as a legal assistant. Two years later, he founded a new business enterprise: a pool hall. Minns was also an outstanding athlete, proficient in swimming, water skiing, weightlifting, and boxing, in which he won the Golden Gloves championship at age 17. After high school, he enrolled in Washington University in St. Louis, Missouri.

At 20, he got married while putting himself through the last year of college, earning a bachelor's degree in English. Then, as a ditch digger, welfare worker and school teacher, he supported his wife and two children while attending law school at night. In law school he won the Corpus Juris Secundum Award, as an outstanding sophomore, earned a position on the school's successful International Moot Court team, and won several other scholarship awards.

On June 13, 1977, he received his first law license from the Texas Supreme Court, and on the following Monday tried his first case as a licensed lawyer. Following that case, he went seven years without a professional defeat. The defeat that broke up his string of legal wins was the famous Arkansas trial of five defendants accused of harboring the fugitive Gordon Kahl. He represented Irene and Ed Udey. Irene was the only defendant to be acquitted.

Details of this case are related in Chapter XI B, and the full story is the subject of several books, including, *"There Was a Man, Kahl,"* by Professor Bruce Boals and publisher Ajay Lowery.

The author currently lives in Katy, Texas, with his wife, Michelle, and three children—Jourdan, 15; Rain, 14; Michael, 13;—2 chow dogs, Chu and Nemo; 40 fish; 3 turtles; a cat called TC; and Tam Tara, a two-year old Arabian filly; and Jubalene, a ten-year old expecting Arabian mare.

Since his first license and trial in June, 1977, Minns has been practicing law continuously and has acquired an additional 25-plus licenses in jurisdictions spanning the continental United States. Shepard's, one of the nation's largest law book publishing companies, brags in an advertisement about one of its author's credentials: 12 licenses. Fewer than 1% of the lawyers in the United States have 10 licenses.

Minns maintains a broad general law practice covering a large and varied spectrum of the legal field: local, state, federal (including the U.S. Supreme Court) and international. He has handled criminal matters from misdemeanors to capital murders. His civil law cases have included landlord-tenant disputes to million dollar real estate transactions; corporate and contract litigation, personal injury suits, bankruptcy; and consumer complaints of deceptive trade practices. He has handled both civil and criminal federal income tax matters.

I have worked with him continuously since April 22, 1985 and am personally familiar with more than a third of the stories in this book, having been a central character in many of them. I've participated in cases that took Mr. Minns to such diverse places as London, Switzerland, Hawaii, New York and Alaska.

I met the author in March, 1985, when he placed an employment ad in a local newspaper seeking a "Legal Assistant Trainee." My education at Lehman College of the City University of New York, from which I graduated Magna Cum Laude in 1969, had been geared toward early childhood and elementary education. My recent work experience had been as a teacher and curriculum developer at several pre-schools since 1980. However, growing up as the daughter of an executive secretary at a prosperous New York City law firm had provided me with an early taste of the law profession. I had amassed the equivalent of three years' experience as a legal secretary working summer jobs in the late sixties and early seventies.

I sent my resume to Mr. Minns, took a written test and eventually had two interviews. I was impressed by the plethora of certificates adorning his office walls, showing that he had been admitted to practice law in about two dozen different jurisdictions. Never, in any other law office, had I seen so many achievement and license certificates with the same name on them. Most other lawyers proudly displayed membership designations in various professional clubs; not Minns. With the licenses and scholarship awards, the walls had no room for them! I noticed the office's extensive law library and the modern computer system. Most of all, however, I was impressed by Minns' personal characteristics: honesty, courage, commitment to justice and his desire to make his life worthy because some day he would stand before God. This concept fit in well with my Christian principles.

When I accepted his offer of employment, he coined a new name for me: "L.R.," to avoid confusion between me, his secretary, Linda A.V. de Gastelum, and an investigator, also named Linda. I readily accepted this new nomenclature, especially since those had been my lifelong initials.

We help a lot of people, including some whom can find help no where else, and some whom can buy any legal services they choose, rich and poor.

My career has become a major priority in my life, ranking in importance only behind my love for God and for my family. My family consists of my husband, Richard (Dick) Robertson, a Ph.D. chemical engineer and computer consultant, our children—Donald, 16; David, 15; George, 13 and Doris,10—4 cats, 2 gerbils and our 2 beagles: Liberty Belle and Justice Fur All. Natives of New York and New Jersey, we transplanted our roots to Texas in 1977.

To further my career development, I became a member of the State Bar of Texas Legal Assistant's Division and have attended numerous continuing education seminars.

This year, I will turn 40 years old. Only God knows whether the future for me includes law school or just further enrichment of my legal assistant role. Whatever happens, I will be proud and happy to continue my professional association and personal friendship with the author of this book, Michael Louis Minns.

"Traditionally Government has feared the power of the jury as an absolute veto over its misuse of power. However, when the government controls the powerful jury system, it's no longer a free force, but a pet of the government."

*"I hope the reader will often concur with me,
occasionally be convinced by me, and sometimes—
in the spirit of the First Amendment
to the Constitution—
openly disagree with me."*

MICHAEL LOUIS MINNS

CHAPTER I
INTRODUCTION & BACKGROUND

"...Benjamin Franklin, would not be pleased if he thought the heirs of this document, after having celebrated the 200th anniversary of our Constitution, would not fight to keep it, or even read it."

A. INTRODUCTION TO THE CONSTITUTION OF THE UNITED STATES OF AMERICA—THE SUPREME LAW OF THE LAND

Prior to the mid-Eighteenth Century, England had accumulated the largest area of land holdings in the world. Proud British subjects bragged that because the Union Jack flew all over the globe, the sun never set on British soil. However, on July 4, 1776, the 13 original American colonies declared themselves fully independent of Great Britain. The sun would soon start setting on the great British Empire.

Shortly thereafter, the colonies drew up, adopted and were governed by the Articles of Confederation. For various reasons, the Articles didn't work.

In 1787, a diverse group of men assembled in Philadelphia to consider revising that governing document. Some were aristocrats like Madison and Jefferson: men of principle, money, and formal education devoted to enlightenment and human rights. Some were self-made capitalists and entrepreneurs like Roger Sherman, W. Livingstone, Alexander Hamilton, and A. Baldwin. Some were military men like the powerful, yet soft spoken commander Washington. They were tax protesters, all, operating under the influence of men of radical wisdom like Thomas Paine. Some of them were seldom more than a few steps away from prison.

Although these philosophers, these moral idealistic visionaries, met for the purpose of amending the Articles of Confederation, they abandoned this goal after determining it was necessary to create a new governing document. On September 17, 1787, they finished and signed the Constitution of the United States of America. Shortly thereafter, the Bill of Rights was unanimously added to the Constitution—forming the most significant advancement in human rights and freedoms since Mosaic law and adding the first new dimension to the spirit of the jury trial since Magna Carta.

The delegates, having achieved their historical mission, rushed out, but an enterprising young reporter managed to stop the 81-year-old senior conventioneer for a question:

"What kind of government is it to be?"

The delegate, the inventor of the bi-focals he was wearing, developer of the indoor cooking stove, discoverer of electricity, journalist, self-made millionaire, self-taught multi-linguist, and originator of *Poor Richard's Almanac*, looking a little radical with his long, stringy moppish hair falling from the three sides of his nearly bald pate, replied with a twinkle in his eye:

"A Republic, if you can keep it."

This wise old gentleman spoke novels with that short, simple answer. It was a promise and a warning. The reporter was eager to read this new document. So was the new nation.

The old gentleman, Benjamin Franklin, would not be pleased if he thought the heirs of this document, after having celebrated the 200th anniversary of our Constitution, would not fight to keep it, or even read it.

B. INTRODUCTION TO THE UNDERGROUND LAWYER

A client and friend of mine strolled into our conference room to browse through the first rough draft of this book. He read the preceding short discussion on the United States Constitution and said, "Hey, sounds interesting, but what's it got to do with the law?"

A copy of the United States Constitution is included in the back of this book. It is entitled: "The Supreme Law of the Land."[1] If there is such a thing as law, the Constitution matters. Franklin would have it no other way; neither should you. Like the directions to a recipe, if you don't read

---

"A copy of the United States Constitution is included in the back of this book. It is entitled: "The Supreme Law of the Land."[1] If there is such a thing as law, the Constitution matters."

---

it, it won't do you any good. In fact, it might as well not exist for you.

My original purpose for this book was simply to teach my legal assistant trainee, L.R., how to do legal work under my supervision. I drafted 10 to 15 pages a day. She read them, and worked. I subsequently decided to prepare a manual to train other legal assistants working in my office. I intended to call it the Legal Assistant's Manual. While preparing that manual, I won the first significant case against the Unauthorized Practice of Law Committee in Texas—a case involving the use of legal assistants by my former law partner. After this experience, I decided to enlarge the scope of the manual to reach to the very limits of what legal assistants are allowed to do and to touch on trends for the future. The new book then would be of use to other offices using legal assistants and would be valuable to prospective legal assistants. I intended to enliven the manual with examples and anecdotes from real cases, to escape the dull tone of many instructional publications.

As I practiced law over the years in courtrooms across the country, I've seen non-lawyers being pushed around by their opponent's lawyers, by their own lawyers (sometimes for their benefit, sometimes against their best interests), and by the system itself. A few words of straightforward advice often would have made all the difference in the world. Would a book with some of this advice have value?

Because many of my friends and clients said "yes," *The Legal Assistant's Manual* became *The Legal Assistant: An Introduction to American Law.* My goal changed to help not only those persons who chose a career in the legal field, but to inform the average citizen who wanted to learn more about the way our system really works.

When the capital murder charges against Norma Ginter were dismissed, I received a flood of lecture invitations from numerous patriot groups throughout the country. Literally thousands of concerned Americans were publicly asking questions and openly expressing their grievances concerning the shortcomings in our judicial system. These people wanted to know the legal rules, and they wanted to know why lawyers seemed to have absolute control over that system. They were often curious about what went on during confidential negotiations between opposing lawyers and what was whispered up at the bench, between judges and lawyers, veiled from public scrutiny.

We all know the system isn't working properly. We all know it should. Whenever a lawyer is licensed before a state or federal bar, he is required to swear an oath to protect the Constitution of the United States; yet he is not required to read it.

The Constitution—like the Magna Carta, the works of Thomas Paine, Thomas Jefferson, Roger Sherman and George Washington—has gone the way of the Holy Scriptures: people worship it but they do not read it. A similar phenomenon occurs with the rest of the developing body of the law: people talk about it and express their opinions, but seldom read it in print, or watch it being interpreted in court.

In the past when I heard people say "Lawyers are crooks," as a member of the bar myself I thought I should defend the profession. It was easy to do. The lawyers, bar associations, and newspapers were on "our side." However, after a while I realized that many, many lawyers actually were crooks. I concluded that God hadn't put me on earth to defend those "bad" lawyers at the cost of my own integrity, so I stopped. There are good lawyers and bad lawyers, good judges and bad judges, good laws and bad laws, honesty and dishonesty. When you practice law, you form opinions.

Our American heritage is to hate slavery, plundering and taxation. Our heritage is to distrust government and judges, to demand our historic common law rights of jury nullification of bad government laws. Now, however—like sheep herded to the slaughterhouse—Americans pray to judges, worship laws that steal from workers and give to plunderers and let politicians tell them how to live, how to die and how to pray. Our system returns murderers and rapists to the streets while jailing people who file tax returns late. Our government pays farmers not to grow food, and then takes their farms away in the name of bank and government-created inflationary debt.

In this topsy-turvy, nightmare world, a man who calls for public redress of his grievance after reading the First Amendment to the Constitution may be jailed, and those responsible for his jailing are given lifetime pensions which equal their income after 20 years on the job.

We are being conditioned to think of "work" as one of those four-letter words. The industrious person is diagnosed as having a new disease and is labeled a "workaholic." We punish him with heavy taxes.

Our politicians were once part-time patriots who came to Congress a

---

"The Constitution—like the Magna Carta, the works of Thomas Paine, Thomas Jefferson, Roger Sherman and George Washington—has gone the way of the Holy Scriptures: people worship it but they do not read it."

short time each year. Now they live in the capital and commute home on jets we pay for. They are full-time government employees. Each Congressman hires more helpers than the entire executive staff under George Washington. They spend mega-millions on beautiful monuments to their worthlessness, with extensive senatorial privileges that would have made the Roman senators blush. We free sovereign citizens are called upon to work for a quarter of each year to pay for plush living and expensive toys for these Washington lords.

REMEMBER:

Bastiat's warning that law is force; Lincoln's admonition that the love of free government money is a danger greater than slavery; and Jefferson's reminder that government is the enemy of freedom. All are forgotten slogans!

The new official language of the monstrous bureaucracy and the legal system is Orwell's 1984 double-speak. Our legislators smile benignly on laws too complicated to understand. Judges interpret laws that make no sense because the people who voted for them didn't read them, and the various tacked-on provisions, known as riders, often conflict.

Moses and Socrates would roll over in their graves if they could see our current system in which juries are not sworn to obey the Constitution or moral law, but rather they are told to do only as the judge orders them! Who is the judge? A mere politician.

The jury system was intended to be a veto against government suppression and authority, and unclear laws of the king. When properly utilized, the system works.

This book is intended to get the reader's feet a little wet by wading into the somewhat murky waters of the American legal system, and to help the reader assist lawyers, resist lawyers, or understand them. A little knowledge can be a dangerous thing. You might get into more trouble knowing something, than not knowing anything at all. The alternative could be slavery.

Justice Learned Hand eloquently declared, "Liberty lies in the hearts of men and women; when it dies there, no constitution, no law, no court can save it."

In order to address these concerns, I have added a history of our judicial system, have documented my observations concerning the rapid destruction of our sacred jury system, and have offered suggestions for change. To emphasize the importance of each section, I have used real cases as examples—usually cases that I tried.

As this book progressed, I talked and lectured throughout the country and learned that there was widespread disenchantment and confusion concerning the complexity of the law, politics, and the truth about the legal profession, of which few non-lawyers are knowledgeable. The scope of the book widened again. Finally, the title emerged out of an all-night telephone rap session: *The Underground Lawyer*.

MY PURPOSES ARE:
   1) To teach a little law to non-lawyers.
   2) To use this book as a text for training my future legal assistants.
   3) To encourage people to read the Constitution.
   4) To urge more people to question government authority.
   5) To publicly redress our government for change and exercise freedom of press and speech.
   6) To give non-lawyers a tour of the legal sewers, so they will not be so helpless.
   7) To make an honest buck selling this book.

All the characters in this book are either real or composites of real people. For the most part, I have used real names. If a name is changed to protect the guilty or foolish, I've said so. If a client did not give permission to use his name, it was deleted. I did not seek the permission of adversaries. Even the cartoons and similar sketchings are composites of real people.

Don't burn your law books! Don't trade this book for legal advice. It is not intended to convey legal advice—only to open a few doors, expose a few sewer rats and share a few tales. I do not want to get you in trouble. Legal advice does not come in instant capsules, spray cans or even between the pages of a single volume. Good legal advice must be given to a person eyeball-to-eyeball on a one-to-one basis. This book is not legal advice. It does contain information previously sold to hundreds of clients for large sums of money. It's not for sale as a program tailored for specific individuals, but for the general information of readers.

This book is filled with my subjective opinions. I hope the reader will often concur with me, occasionally be convinced by me, and sometimes—in the spirit of the First Amendment to the Constitution of the United States—openly disagree with me.

C. DISCLAIMER

THE AUTHOR DISCLAIMS THE FOLLOWING:

A. That this book has any value;

B. That this book will help anyone regardless of race, color, or creed other than the author;

C. That anyone, including the reader or the author, is competent to or should practice law;

D. That if said person chooses to practice law anyway, he will never become competent enough to do law, whatever that means;

E. That law has anything to do with justice; and

F. That my use of the generic "he" is evidence of male chauvinism. My office forms read he/she/it (to cover the sexes and corporations), but it just does not read well in a book; "he" means everyone and everything unless otherwise indicated. When the author uses both, it's only because it reads well or is an attempt to change the pace.

THE AUTHOR DOES WARRANT:

A. That he has more licenses on one wall than he has ever seen in any other law office in the world, and that the licenses were legitimately acquired;

B. That the author has successfully entered courthouses in more than a score of locations, has had legal confrontations in many of them, and has pleased more of his own clients than he has displeased; and

C. That law may be hazardous to your health.

D. ACKNOWLEDGMENTS

The most significant contribution from any helper or employee came from my legal assistant Linda Roderick (L.R.) Robertson. She worked on this book thousands of hours and was the reason I began it.

Ajay Lowery, publisher of the nationally circulated newspaper, The Justice Times, who insisted that someone should write a book to provide patriots with some basic insights into the law was a driving force behind this project.

My law office staff members typed the first draft as the demands of their normal workload permitted. As the original manual evolved into this book, my sister Cathy sent me one of her students, named Joy—who turned out to be a real joy to work with and who spent a month typing and re-typing the book at super-speed with enthusiasm.

The task of juggling my time, juggling my files, organizing people in and out of the office to keep the book progressing fell on my efficient office manager, Linda V. de Gastelum, and super-secretary, Tracie Porcheddu. The third version was retyped by my sister Cathy, an expert in word processing and the author of three books on the subject.

The photography, layout, and production of the cover along with the text design were completed by C. Michel Feray.

My Deepest thanks goes to my father, Richard L. Minns, who designed the cover of this book and gave me advice, support and direction throughout this endeavor.

Special thanks go to newspaper reporter and editor Gene Nail, formerly of the *Arkansas Democrat*, who has attempted to guide me in developing the finer points of writing and who has spent many hours—along with others—editing the final draft of this book.

The book's name came to me at 2 o'clock one morning while I was on the phone with L.R. and her husband, Dick.

Without a decade's worth of clients and friends who referred those clients to me, this book would not have been possible.

Without the influence of Underground Lawyers like my grandfather, father, Ajay Lowery, Peggy Christensen, Cathy and others, the concept would not have materialized. I did not create The Underground Lawyer. He was around before I was born. I just identified him and gave him a name.

Without good judges who let cases finish and jurors deliberate, this book would not have been possible. Without competent lawyers to learn from and with, I would not have been able to practice law. Many of the stories are based on interactions with competent peers and adversaries.

However, without rude, incompetent and often corrupt judges, and without dishonest, frequently stupid and lazy attorneys, this book would have been boring. My acknowledgments to all.

E. HOW TO USE THIS BOOK

If you examined the cover, you used this book. The law has become mystical; rites are spoken in Latin; "secrets" are controlled by a select few. *The Underground Lawyer* has emerged to bring law, truth and light to the average person on the street, as well as to clean up some garbage.

I've spent over a decade in the legal sewers. I'm sharing some of the trade secrets with you. If you've got courage and an eighth-grade education, hold on to your nose and jump in, cover to cover.

If you prefer a varied approach, I suggest:

A. Scan the Table of Contents.

B. Read any specific chapters that interest you.

C. Please read Chapter IV, for a survey on the legal labor unions and a tour of the sewers.

D. To further explore what you have learned in a chapter, consult the footnotes in the Addendum, find and read some of the sources.

E. If you want to try your hand at research, to work for a law office, against a law office, or for yourself, read the research section and the specific topics you need, then read other sources and proceed with extreme caution. Be prepared to lose. You don't have to become a pro at research to profit from this chapter. Many lawyers can't do professional research.

F. Read and examine the cartoons. If you don't understand one, read the nearest chapter, then re-examine the cartoon. Many of the cartoons tell stories children can understand.

G. Order 10,000 copies of this book and give them to your friends, relatives, neighbors and community groups. Lobby for some reasonable changes.

H. Four copies of this book stacked on top of each other are suitable for lifting an average 3 1/2-year-old from an average chair up to an average table. Warning: author cannot guarantee safety. This book does not pass federal coefficient of friction standards to limit slip and fall accidents.

I. If you start a chapter and don't like it, then skip it. Most chapters will stand on their own. Some readers will have no interest in research or jury history—fine, skip those.

F. WHO IS THE UNDERGROUND LAWYER ANYWAY?

The Underground Lawyer is a non-conformist. You can't necessarily pick out The Underground Lawyer by just looking at him or her. He could be in a three-piece suit with an Ivy League briefcase; she could be in a Rockefeller blazer jacket with a conservative not-too-revealing business-like gray skirt and tie; but The Underground Lawyer could also be a homemaker with a flour-stained apron over her housedress or a construction worker in mud-caked jeans.

The Underground Lawyer might be a licensed attorney-at-law; or he might not be. The Underground Lawyer is anybody involved in the legal system who is also seeking honesty and efficiency. The Underground Lawyer may be licensed in 20 or more courts or may be a next door neighbor telling you how she beat a traffic ticket. Clarence Darrow was an Underground Lawyer. He often protested, "That's not fair." The legal system isn't fair today. Many people who stumble onto this basic truth are compelled to become Underground Lawyers. People who champion constitutional rights for constitutional reasons are usually Underground Lawyers. Lawyers who fight the system or who get disbarred from various legal unions may be Underground Lawyers; unless the sanction was precipitated by some morally questionable act, such as stealing money from a widowed client after having drawn up the will which left the lawyer himself in charge of managing the estate. Most lawyers who steal from their clients are considerably safer from the bar's disciplinary hand than those who rebel against the bar or scream "That's not fair" too loudly. Lots of legal clinics are run by Underground Lawyers.

You can't always tell an Underground Lawyer by the things he does, but some things do indicate a person might be an Underground Lawyer. Wearing jeans and tennis shoes in your law office is an Underground Lawyer type of thing to do. When I see Jerry Spence—an attorney who has won many multi-million dollar cases—wearing a cowboy hat, I think of him as a financially successful Underground Lawyer.

Underground Lawyers practice law, but they're not necessarily licensed. The individual who represents himself is an Underground Lawyer. He usually is not violating any laws, but he is violating labor union rules and he's going against the system. This person, who may know law better than many licensed lawyers, helps out friends and family after hours. Many Underground Lawyers are considered insane by the mainstream. Some of them are. The one qualification, above all others, is that he or she is a unique individual. There are very few boring Underground Lawyers.

The Underground Lawyer frequently has the need to remain inconspicuous and unnoticed. An Underground Lawyer who files a lawsuit against the Internal Revenue Service—bringing to the agency's attention the fact that he or she hasn't filed a tax return in 25 years—will often find herself in some unwanted limelight.

People who teach others how to practice law without a license and who may be violating laws in many states are underground lawyers. Some operate above the street while others choose the subterranean environment. The Underground Lawyer often is economically unsuccessful. Although some Underground Lawyers are extremely rich, many are too involved in law to run a business.

Actually, it is easier to specify what an underground lawyer is not, because there are some absolute signs that are easy to see. An Underground Lawyer never works in a law firm which has more than 25 lawyers in it. He or she would be too establishment. Underground Lawyers do not look like H.R. Haldeman. It is nearly impossible, slightly rarer than unicorns, to find Underground Lawyers sitting as judges. Underground Lawyers almost never work for the FBI. It is absolutely, unconditionally, unacceptable for an Underground Lawyer to be an IRS agent, although some very competent and interesting Underground Lawyers are former IRS agents.

Underground Lawyers are almost never politicians and are even more rarely, successful politicians. Their innate desire for truth precludes them from most public offices. Thomas Jefferson was an Underground Lawyer who did succeed in winning a public office. Teddy Roosevelt was a successful politician, who nevertheless was imbued with the spirit of an Underground Lawyer.

G. THE MAKING OF A FEW UNDERGROUND LAWYERS

I am an attorney in large part because of the work and persistence of the late George Richard Minns, known to my brother, sisters, cousins and me as "Granddad." He was married to Ethel Goldberg, known to us as "Granny." Granddad stood five-foot, one-inch tall, but was a giant when it came to standing up for causes that he believed in. An ex-boxer, sensitive about his height, he once answered someone who asked how he tall he was with, "Tall enough for my feet to reach the ground." When the inquirer pursued the same line of questioning, Granddad responded, "I look a lot taller when you're looking at me from the ground." The inquiry stopped. My great grandparents came to Texas and started the first bee farm in the United States about 100 years ago. Granddad's father came to Texas because of his lung condition. He had been told that the climate would be healthy for him. As it turned out, he ended up in a humid, dusty area with atmospheric conditions that hastened his demise. Great Granddad established a thriving general merchandise store. After several years in the United States, he decided to return to England for a visit. He sold his store for $1,000 cash and gave the money to a neighbor for safe keeping.

The neighbor put the money in an old whiskey bottle and stuck it under a shelf. When Granddad and his parents returned years later, the money was still there. This was the way things were done in those days. A handshake meant more than a legal contract does today. There was not a lot of litigation in the old west. There were, however, occasional shootings. An act of dishonesty could easily result in death. Fortunately for the propagation of our early ancestors, it rarely occurred in our family. My Granddad said that the old west was a place of capitalism unhampered by the hand of lawyers.

When they returned to the United States, Granddad was taught by his father to work in the store. He ended up starting his own general store in La Grange, Texas.

At 30 he determined that he would get married and have a big family. He had heard some propaganda that Jewish families were more closely united than many other families. So he declared during a bar discussion that he would go ahead and marry a Jewish woman. Over half a century before it became popular to stand up against racism, my grandfather fought against it in bold and dramatic ways which shocked his neighbors. He went up to the front door of the Goldberg home where old man Goldberg lived with five, single daughters. With flowers and candy in hand, leaving one of the few cars in town parked out front, he asked for a date with the Goldberg girl who was considered the prettiest of the family. She wasn't home. So Granddad, undaunted, extended the invitation to my grandmother, Ethel Goldberg. She accepted, and her whirl-wind courtship began. Flowers and candy arrived twice daily for two weeks: once with the morning milk and again before a scheduled daily date. At the end of this 14-day courtship, they got married. The marriage lasted over 50 years until Granny died.

Grandmother Ethel's family had a high regard for education. Everyone in her family had at least a high school diploma; her four brothers became medical doctors. The fact that Granddad was one of the wealthiest people in town was sufficient reason for the Goldbergs to approve his marriage to their daughter, even though he was not highly educated or Jewish. Granddad, although he'd only had a fifth grade education, could read and write well and, on rare occasions, would practice a little law. In those days, the boundaries of what was the practice of law weren't as carefully guarded.

Granny's influence led to her grandchildren's achieving numerous college degrees. She instilled the love of poetry and literature in my father. These educational aspirations were further influenced by my granddad's unflinching rebellion against anything that he thought was unfair in any way, shape, or form coupled with his even greater love for capitalism. Granddad, always the rebellious capitalist, would later turn this bizarre union into financial advantage and a cause of public friction. The following incident shows Granddad's genius as an underground lawyer who was able to turn a potentially disastrous situation to his advantage.

Granddad's general store became a political statement supporting his right to what was then considered a very mixed marriage. His sense of indignation at all inequalities and prejudices led to a war of sorts. In his day, in many parts of the United States, Latin Americans, blacks, persons of Jewish descent and others were, for the most part, precluded from entering the front doors of retail businesses. The prime stock was sold to "white" people through the front doors. Ethnic minorities either had to pay whites to shop for them or go to the back door. The quality of goods and services minorities were able to obtain was, at best, second class. At worst, the process was degrading. Granddad rebelled, and in the end gained substantial profit as a result of his moral stand. First of all, he began running continuous sales. The Depression created business opportunities. Granddad would go off and buy huge quantities of merchandise from bankrupt stores at five to ten cents on the dollar. He would transport them back to his store and sell them for twenty-five or thirty percent of their fair market dollar value. Next, in a town heavily infested with Ku Klux Klan members, Granddad put up a sign stating "Se habla espanol," (We speak Spanish) and similar signs referring to several other languages: Dutch, French, German, etc. Underneath the sign in big black letters he added, "And we're all Americans." His practice was to let everyone in town enter through the front door of his store. The sign and his front-door policy enabled him to obtain a near monopoly of all minority business in the area. Some Latin and black buyers would travel a hundred miles or more to be treated fairly. For brief periods of time, substantial numbers of caucasians boycotted the store, but after a while they determined that the support of racism was not as important as getting the best price. Since Granddad was able to offer substantial discounts through his shrewd purchasing methods and because he stocked a wide variety of goods, other merchants could not compete with him on price or merchandise selection. The boycott failed.

The community leaders, undaunted in their goals of racial segregation, developed another scheme. A huge cross was burned in Granddad's front yard. Sketched on the cross were the words "Jew Lover, Nigger Lover." To say the least, Granddad and his bride were concerned. Granddad, guilty of both charges and faced with severe repercussions, nevertheless refused to compromise his principles. When friends suggested he leave town, he "capitalized" on their suggestion and implemented his plan. He went to the bank where his credit was honored and his business had always been appreciated and borrowed $1,000, a huge sum in those days, and cheerfully agreed to pay 10% interest, also an incredibly high sum in those days. He withdrew the money and deposited it in a bank in San Antonio. A few days later he returned to the bank, and solemnly told its President "I am dreadfully sorry, but I have bad news. I'm going to have to leave the city, and I'm going to have to renege for the first time in my life on a debt commitment that I made." The banker was horrified. This was a substantial amount of money to lose; litigation would be difficult; the likelihood of a recovery of his entire loan remote. He questioned Granddad about this new problem, "Was business bad?" Granddad replied, saying, "Business is better than ever, or I would not have taken the loan. As a matter of fact, under normal circumstances, I would have no difficulty paying each installment promptly." Granddad's voice then dropped, and in a whisper he confided, "Do you remember a few weeks ago when the Klan burned a cross in my front yard?" Granddad paused waiting for a response. The banker without pause and without blinking replied, "No, I haven't heard anything about it." (The truth of this statement was as suspect as if he had claimed to have never heard of the Civil War). The Banker then addressed Granddad with some annoyance, slightly raising his voice: "Well, after that, why did you feel safe coming here and borrowing the money?" Granddad humbly answered, "I felt that all the problems had blown over and there was nothing to worry about but, I've been hearing a bunch of rumors from a lot of my customers (who asked that their names not be used) that worse things are coming. I guess I should have confided in you. I really don't know much about politics. You would have known what to do."

As a matter of fact, worse things had been occurring daily. Rocks had been hurled through windows; nasty anonymous letters had been delivered; merchandise had been vandalized at the store. Events that were completely out of the ordinary were becoming commonplace.

The Banker's anger subsided. He sat up straight and dignified in his chair and paternally advised, "George, don't make any rash decisions.

Now, I don't know who's been doing this or what's been happening, but I'm a man of considerable influence in this town and I'll look into it. You come back in a couple of days and tell me if this problem has been cleared up or not." For the first time in approximately three weeks nothing happened to any of Granddad's property...and nothing ever happened again. Granddad made certain that he owed the bank money at all times, and he always paid on time. The Banker looked after his 30-year-old prodigy. Granddad's law of capitalistic common sense had worked!

My grandfather had always been interested in the law, and in fact, at one time, had considered becoming a lawyer. At that time, Texas didn't have a law school and no bar examination was required for an aspiring lawyer to gain his credentials. If a candidate could secure a judge's letter of recommendation, the state bar would send him his license. Since Granddad had been practicing law off and on for years, the local judge suggested he become an attorney. Granddad considered the idea, but declined. Granddad was engaged in the sale of general merchandise. He felt that if he became a lawyer, people would not trust him and it would hurt his business. My grandfather drew up his own corporations, submitted the forms to the secretary of state and usually had no problem getting them approved. On rare occasions the papers would bounce, and he would go to a lawyer, pay him a small fee, type the documents out on the lawyer's letterhead and send them back to the secretary of state and they would be accepted.

Grandfather was an underground lawyer. He drafted deeds, filed corporations and gave excellent legal advice throughout his lifetime. He knew more real estate law than most attorneys learn during their careers. In spite of his lack of formal education, he encouraged me to go to law school. He provided moral and emotional support and eased my growing family's tight financial situation with his faithful financial contributions.

My father, Richard Minns, was an underground lawyer. Several of his personal attorneys had him negotiate deals on their behalf because he was more skilled at it than they. His contracts were written better than those of most attorneys. He and I together once drafted a suit for him which made news telecasts and the front pages of our city newspapers.

My sister, Cathy Minns, is an underground lawyer. She handled uncontested divorces by typing them up for people. Her price beat that offered by most attorneys, but being a capitalist, she went on to more profitable work. The Unauthorized Practice of Law Committee of Texas sent her a nasty letter, so she re-opened her "practice" for awhile just to spite them.

She quit because people were starting to identify her as a lawyer, and it offended her. She obviously was Granddad's granddaughter.

A Montana housewife named Peggy Christensen saw her husband convicted because of his principles, and watched lawyers smile and shake hands as he was locked up. She decided to do legal research for herself and others and, over the last decade, has rung up a slew of victories.

An ex-IRS agent blew the whistle on his colleagues who violated civil and constitutional rights or just behaved badly. He was suspended without pay. He did it again. He was again suspended without pay. He did it again. Today, Paul DesFosses assists victims of IRS abuse. When he shows up in a courtroom, Government agents tremble.[2]

Ralph Nader recently wrote an expose showing that the insurance industry's "data" and "propaganda" about its current crisis is a hoax. A lot of people would like to shut him up.

These people are underground lawyers. They often create their own rules. They are universally loved by their admirers and hated by their assorted opponents: the legal unions, many judges, insurance companies, often the IRS, and sometimes even other underground lawyers.

"Whenever a lawyer is licensed before a state or federal bar, he is required to swear an oath to protect the Constitution of the United States; yet he is not required to read it."

CHAPTER II

THE AMERICAN JURY:

A HISTORICAL PERSPECTIVE CONTRASTED WITH THE MODERN SYSTEM

"The theory behind the jury concept is that a random selection of people would more nearly depict the will of the country than any other system..."

A. CONSTITUTIONAL BASIS

What does the Constitution of the United States say about trial by jury?

Article III, Section 2, Part 3 of the Constitution says:

"The trial of all crimes, except in cases of impeachment, shall be by jury, and such trial shall be held in the state where the said crimes shall have been committed; but when not committed within any state, the trial shall be at such place or places as the Congress may by law have directed."

Three amendments further construe trial by jury.

The Fifth Amendment to the Constitution gives you the right to grand jury indictment as well as the right not to incriminate yourself by your own testimony and establishes the concept of "due process":

"No person shall be held to answer for a capital, or otherwise infamous crime, unless on a presentment or indictment of a grand jury, except in cases arising in the land or naval forces, or in the militia, when in actual service in time of war or public danger; nor shall any person be subject for the same offense to be twice put in jeopardy of life or limb; nor shall be compelled in any criminal case to be a witness against himself; nor be deprived of life, liberty, or property, without due process of law; nor shall private property be taken for public use without just compensation."

After indictment by a grand jury, the Sixth Amendment gives you the right to a speedy, public trial by an impartial jury, the right to assistance of counsel and the right to question your accusers in all criminal cases:

"In all criminal prosecutions, the accused shall enjoy the right to a speedy and public trial, by an impartial jury of the State and district wherein the crime shall have been committed, which district shall have been previously ascertained by law, and to be informed of the nature and cause of the accusation; to be confronted with the witnesses against him; to have compulsory process for obtaining witnesses in his favor, and to have the assistance of counsel for his defense."

The Seventh Amendment gives you the right to trial by jury if there's more than $20 at stake in a civil case.

"In suits at common law, where the value in controversy shall exceed twenty dollars, the right of trial by jury shall be preserved, and no fact tried by a jury, shall be otherwise re-examined in any court of the United States, than according to the rules of the common law."

These rights are very clearly, unambiguously created. Many courts today ignore them. The Constitution did not make them optional.

B. SCRIPTURAL ROOTS

Throughout the history of the world, leaders of society have attempted to promulgate sets of rules for their society to live by. One of the earliest known attempts was Hammurabi's Code written in ancient Babylon, centuries before Christ.[1] Although harsh, it was an improvement over the arbitrary whims of previous rulers. Rules and punishments for the violation of those rules were spelled out.

Dearest to many Judeo-Christian hearts is the Law established by God and given to Moses more than 5,000 years ago, the Ten Commandments[2], which include such precepts as: worship no gods other than the one true God; honor thy father and thy mother; do not kill; do not steal; and do not bear false witness against your neighbors. This false witness commandment is the ancestor of our perjury laws which forbid lying under oath.

One could speculate that our Founding Fathers may have been mirroring the Ten Commandments when they drew up the Ten Amendments which constitute our Bill of Rights. In Exodus we find the Hebrew people forced into 400 years of slavery in Egypt.[3] They leave Egypt, and shortly thereafter, for what may be the first time in recorded history, laws are set up to invoke the ultimate abolition of slavery. Slaves cannot be traded, and after seven years all slaves must be freed.[4] This is the great ancestor of our current Thirteenth Amendment prohibiting slavery in the United States.

People often refer to the commandment against "lying." The Ten Commandments did not instruct the chosen people not to lie. It merely instructed them not to bear false witness against their neighbors. It implies a trial or some sort of formal proceeding in which a person bears witness against another in order to make an accusation or to bring forth some type of judicial review. The ancient Hebrews regarded the independent testimony of two men of good standing in the community as binding to establish truth. More than 1,000 years after the Ten Commandments, English feudal witnesses would bear witness and their numbers would be counted and weighed according to their social standing and the truth determined by a judge's calculation.

The Old Testament sets forth a multitude of laws, rules, and regulations for living, eating, praying and doing justice. This portion of the Bible, studied and revered by Jews, Christians and Moslems, has a message which is rather forcefully stated: that "an eye for an eye and a tooth for a tooth" [5] should be the measure of justice and also that "Vengeance is Mine, sayeth The Lord." [6] There are universal beliefs which transcend barriers of race, color, creed and historic background which support the concepts we know as justice, fairness, and equity. The early pagan cultures which gave us the Greco-Roman and the Norse mythologies included stories in which various supreme beings were not always fair or good, and did not always win, but, nevertheless, were answerable to some ideals of justice that should, and ultimately did, prevail.

One of the most interesting parts of the Judeo-Christian Scriptures is the Book of Job, a masterfully written tragedy that unlike the early Greek tragedies has a happy ending. In the epilogue which follows the account of Job's dialogue with his creator, Job is rewarded and justice triumphs, Job's losses are restored two-fold.[7] It is one of the earliest Scriptural accounts which purports to question divine will. The evil one, Satan, is allowed to unjustly inflict injuries upon the righteous Job. In the end, justice

---

"The underlying function of all legal systems is to accomplish orderly rule and to suggest that such rule is just."

prevails. Job's old family is replaced with a new family, and his wealth is returned in excess of what it once was. Job is proclaimed a righteous man. The message is that ultimately justice will prevail; good will triumph over evil—suggesting the rewards of submission to divine will.

The underlying function of all legal systems is to accomplish orderly rule and to suggest that such rule is just. How can one question the righteousness of the leader who claims God is on his side—if one believes the leader?

C. JURISPRUDENCE OF ANCIENT GREECE (SOCRATES)

The Athenian democracy of Plato and Aristotle in 399 B.C. predates us by approximately 2,200 years. One of the greatest arguments and discussions of the legal system in the history of mankind is attributed to the great teacher Socrates written by his pupil Plato in *The Apology*.[8] Socrates was accused of destroying the moral fiber of the youth of Athens and had to stand trial for this "offense." His method was effective criticism of government. His ordeal was the most important clash between an individual's free speech (his right to petition government with grievances) and government in the history of world jurisprudence. A careful reading of *The Apology* reveals a great deal about Athenian justice. Large numbers of citizens were present in the trial room: there were more than 100 jurors hearing Socrates' trial. The concept of legal representation for the accused had not yet evolved. A well-rounded Greek education included the study of "rhetoric" so that citizens would be prepared to defend themselves in legal proceedings. There were obviously citizens experienced in this rhetoric who had developed a special language for trial.

Socrates echoed a very familiar complaint reflected today by observers of American jurisprudence. He did not understand the words that were used in legal proceedings. He begged the Athenian jurors to listen to him anyway and to give him the benefit that they would give someone from another country who did not speak the language but who was seeking justice. Anyone without a legal education who has ever been before a judge or a jury under a complex system of rules described in a strange language can sympathize with Socrates. Socrates was a man of principle. He stated that he was a loyal citizen of Athens, who *has merely dared to*

"Socrates...man of principle...has merely questioned the authority of those persons who claim to be experts."

question the authority of those persons who claim to be experts. Each and every person whom he questioned, he found to be wanting in his particular field. Each and every person who indicated that he is an expert in his field of endeavor failed to adequately answer Socrates' questions. Through Socrates' questions the self-proclaimed experts were made to look foolish. Socrates proves each inadequate in the mastery of his own discipline whether philosophy, making pottery, or tradesmanship. From these experiences, Socrates concludes that he is the wisest of all men because he admits how little he knows; whereas these others, impostors, pretend to have great knowledge. Therefore, he knows what they do not know: the limits of his own knowledge.

In ancient Athens, a mere majority of the jurors' votes was required for conviction, and there was no presumption of innocence. When Socrates was convicted of perverting the youth of Athens, the next stage of trial began.

From the dialogue in *The Apology*, we learn how Athenian judgment was administered once someone is convicted. The accuser offered a penalty. The defendant offered a penalty. The jurors then vote on which penalty should be enforced. Obviously, it was in the interest of the party who won the conviction not to make the penalty too harsh because the jurors would probably not consider it. It was also equally obvious that the defendant, who would not want to face the wrath of the jurors who had just convicted him, would propose a penalty at least severe enough so that it would be considered.

In the case of Socrates, the prosecutor, wisely, did not want to make a martyr out of him. The prosecutor wanted Socrates to admit his crime by suggesting his own punishment. Therefore, the prosecutor offered the jurors the harshest possible penalty: death. In effect, the prosecutor was backing off from his claim against Socrates. It was obvious that death was too severe for the ridiculous charges Socrates had been convicted of. Rather than propose a small fine or "an apology," Socrates placed the onus back on his jurors and refuses to suggest any punishment at all. Socrates let the jurors know that he was an old man and that he was pre-

"Socrates concludes that he is the wisest of all men because he admits how little he knows; whereas these others, impostors, pretend to have great knowledge. Therefore, he knows what they do not know: the limits of his own knowledge."

pared to die. At this late stage in his life, to submit to any type of punishment at all would be a hypocrisy. It would amount to an admission that his life had not been worthwhile, that he had not been honest, and that he had committed a wrongful act. Socrates refused to grant them this victory, and he told the jurors that he would accept no punishment. Since he had done nothing evil, his punishment should instead be a reward. The jurors were faced with either punishing him by death or determining that their vote for conviction was an unfair one and allowing him to go free without penalty. The jurors chose death. The rest is history. Few remember the name of Socrates' accusers today; but the name Socrates is a household word, synonymous with justice and wisdom.

This fascinating jury system clearly and irrevocably left an enormous amount of power with the jury as the ultimate triers of fact and law. It did not, however, provide any appellate protection or constitutional safeguards. There was no First Amendment to protect Socrates' freedom of association and freedom of speech. The jurors in Plato's rendition of the trial of Socrates determined both whether a law had been broken and whether a penalty should be assessed. The members of the audience had an enormous amount to say about this. All citizens of Athens were entitled to vote on juries.

D. JURISPRUDENCE OF EARLY GERMANIC TRIBES

The ancient German people of the post Roman Empire era had one of the more freedom-oriented societies in the history of civilization. The German people were strong, devoted advocates of their own, individual freedom. They despised government power and government control and refused to submit to it. Early government rules were obeyed occasionally and disobeyed frequently. These autonomous German tribes—which were the source of the armies that overthrew the Roman Empire and conquered England where the Magna Carta would be born hundreds of years later—entrusted all power to the jury.

The jury was selected at random from neighbors of the person accused. The jury had absolute power to disregard any law and to make final conclusions regarding the evidence. The jury also set the penalty. A plaintiff

"Few remember the name of Socrates' accusers today; but the name Socrates is a household word, synonymous with justice and wisdom."

and a defendant or the government and the accused had equal access time before this jury panel. In order to deprive someone of their liberty, property, or freedoms, a unanimous jury decision was necessary. Obviously this was not an easy goal to achieve. These free-spirited individuals, these great thinkers and great fighters were not easily persuaded and were even more difficult to convince unanimously for a guilty verdict. No ruler could alter the decision of the jury. No judge sat in the conference room with the jury. The jurors ran and regulated themselves and had a bailiff or law enforcement official available to execute their orders.[9]

Two hundred years before the adoption of the Magna Carta in England, Emperor Conrad of Germany established a guarantee of trial by jury. He declared that "No one shall lose his estate unless according to the custom of our ancestors and according to the sentence (or judgment) of his peers."[10] The jury, not the government, determined civil justice and fairness (due process). After the English king was forced to sign the Magna Carta, the English would slowly develop a jury system resembling their German ancestors, this one coupled with appellate protections.

About 150 years before the Magna Carta, the Normans introduced Trial by Combat to England. The accused challenged his accuser to single combat and staked the question of his guilt or innocence on the result of the duel. Presumably William the Conqueror supported this method of justice which effectively allowed him to legally conquer the Anglos and Saxons.

Trial by Ordeal, which predated trial by combat, forced the accused to submit to various tests—such as taking a hot iron in his hand, walking blindfolded across red hot plow shares, thrusting his arm into boiling water, being thrown with bound hands and feet into cold water, or swallowing excrement. A common expression comes from that hot coal treatment. A bed of hot coals was prepared. The accused had to walk barefoot over the hot coals. If he fell and burned to death or went lame, he was obviously guilty. If he made it across, he was innocent. The phrase "raked over the coals" survives today.[11] The population felt confident that an accused's guilt or innocence was miraculously made known by one's survival or the alternative. The words "combat" and "ordeal" still befit modern trials, but for different reasons.

These types of justice were later replaced by swearing matches. Each litigant would tell his side and then have supporters swear to the truth of their side. There would be no evidence or cross-examination.

The following passage depicts the ancient Germanic society:

"The Government of the Germans, and that of all the northern nations, who established themselves on the ruins of Rome, was always extremely free; and those fierce people, accustomed to independence and inured to arms, were more guided by persuasion than authority in the submission which they paid to their princes. The military despotism of the Roman Empire... was unable to resist the vigorous efforts of the free people, and Europe, as from a new epoch, rekindled her ancient spirit."[12]

In addition to being restricted from exercising power over juries, German monarchs were also not given a free hand to impose taxes on their kingdoms. In discussing the origin and nature of the English Constitution and its Germanic Anglo-Saxon roots, one historian concluded:

"There are but two things the Saxons did not think proper to trust their kings with; for being of like passions with other men they might very possibly abuse them; namely, the power of changing the laws enacted by consent of king and people; and the power of raising taxes at pleasure." [13]

E. NATURAL LAW

Most of us have an innate sense of what is right and what is wrong. We develop this sense of justice at a very early age, usually before we can read, write, or calculate figures. A very small child develops a sense of property rights from experiences such as finding an apple and claiming it as his own. By the age of three or four, youngsters understand that when one of their playmates climbs a tree and picks an apple from the branch, by virtue of this labor the apple has become the property of the child who plucked it. It cannot be removed from the custody of that child without tearful, possibly painful consequences. A child who has been socialized into a system whereby he or she is not allowed to take this apple (or a toy) from the hand of another child rapidly learns this system of fairness and justice. As the child grows older and builds forts or tree houses out of

"Humans possess rudiments of an instinctive knowledge of right and wrong...It is this basic perception of good and evil, and property rights which lies at the heart of the viability of the jury system and allows the system to work."

cardboard boxes or wood, the child maintains a possessory interest over his work-product. The other children understand this. The parents in the community understand this. They have a similar sense of right and wrong, justice and injustice.

Animals also recognize the territorial domain of others of their species. I recall the action of our rather timid, household cat who seldom ventured outside, and on those rare occasions when he did, was clearly afraid of all creatures great and small. When a larger, much stronger, streetwise cat belonging to one of our neighbors entered our house, our cat courageously defended his territory. Strangely enough, the larger cat yielded to our cat's strong demands and backed off. These animals recognized a type of territorial property integrity. It is instinctive.

Humans possess rudiments of an instinctive knowledge of right and wrong, and that knowledge is further refined by the discipline exercised by parents and teachers while socializing children into their culture. It is this basic perception of good and evil, and property rights which lies at the heart of the viability of the jury system and allows the system to work.

According to Lysander Spooner, a Nineteenth Century jury observer and scholar:

"It is not only the right and duty of juries to judge what are the facts, what is the law, and what is the moral intent of the accused; but that it is also their right and their primary and paramount duty, to judge of the justice of the law, and to hold all laws invalid, that are, in their opinion, unjust or oppressive, and all persons guiltless in violating, or resisting the execution of, such laws."[14]

Spooner says that if juries do not judge the law, the facts, and all of the evidence, then they are merely

"...tools, rather than being a barrier against the tyranny and oppression of the government."[15]

"Magna Carta literally means 'great charter.' It was an agreement, providing, among other things, trial by jury for the nobility."

F. THE MAGNA CARTA: ITS IMPACT ON ENGLAND AND AMERICA

After William the Conqueror seized power in England in 1066 the English became subjects of the Norman King. The defeated nobility resented their enforced demotion to secondary status. In 1215 A.D., the heirs of the Anglo-Saxons rose up against the king and demanded certain guarantees of their cherished freedoms and feudal rights.

Those Anglo-Saxons who had maintained control of their lands by resisting or marrying the conquering Normans, and the now Anglicized Normans decided to consolidate their power and achieve a stability not available with trial by combat or dictatorship by a king. Their method was to pressure King John into adopting the Magna Carta in 1215 A.D. Magna Carta literally means "great charter." It was an agreement, providing, among other things, trial by jury for the nobility. No longer would they face the unmitigated wrath of the king's judges.

Trial by jury was theoretically instituted. The jury was to consist of 12

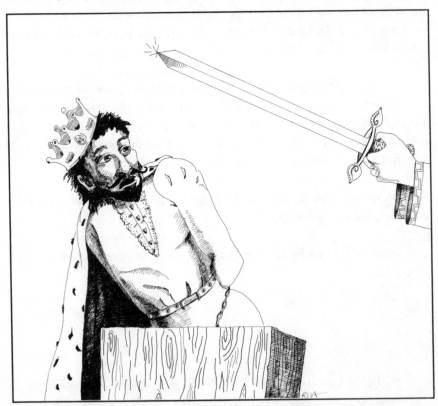

Now that I've reconsidered it, jury trials might be a good idea.

people who were randomly selected from the neighborhood of the accused. In order to convict, these 12 people had to unanimously agree that a crime had been committed, *that the crime was a violation of existing law, that the law was just,* and further, that the prosecution had proven beyond a reasonable doubt that the crime had been committed by the defendant. Once these four essential facts were determined, then the jury could deliberate on the convicted defendant's penalty.

King John signed the charter under duress. It was politically expedient to comply, since the alternative was to have his head separated from his body. This jury system was given the Latin name, "per pais," which means trial by the country. The jurors symbolically represent the country.

The Magna Carta of 1215 was followed by the Great Charter of Henry III, issued in 1216 and again in 1225. The charter was confirmed by his grandson, Edward I in 1297. The power of the jury in England pre-dates the institution of Parliament, which seems originally to have been nothing more than a personal invitation from the king to some barons to a cordial Christmas dinner.

Judges were not present in the courtrooms for trials during the early Magna Carta era. The only officers in attendance were ministerial functionaries: sheriffs, bailiffs and stewards. They were not judicial officers. It was taken for granted that government officials could not give the jurors any reliable, neutral information concerning the law, "It is plain that the juries in these courts must of necessity have been the sole judges of all matter of law whatsoever."[16] It is also unlikely that the jurors were guided by any written law set down by the king, since:

"Few laws were enacted and many of those were not written but only agreed upon in counsel...Not only were the common people unable to read their own language, but at the time of Magna Carta, the laws were written in Latin, language that could be read by few persons except for priests."[17]

Early English jury assembling instructions called for the summoning of:

"Twelve free and legal men, or sometimes twelve knights, to be in the court prepared upon their oaths to declare whether A or B have the greater right to the

"...checks and balances for the preservation of human rights: a process of fairness which we call 'due process.'"

land or other thing in question. By one law, everyone was to be tried by his peers who are of the same neighborhood as himself."[18]

In the centuries that followed the Magna Carta, members of early English juries were judging the law as well as the facts. When there was a judge on the bench, his function was to give the jurors no assistance in determining the matter of fact and only to act in an advisory capacity if the jurors had any doubt among themselves relating to matters of law. The judge would explain a question of law to them, and then the jurors would be free to make up their own minds. They were under no obligation to follow any suggestions the judge might have made. This was the law as late as 1794 in the United States.

In old England the king's judges were so well known to be corrupt and untrustworthy that they were not permitted to sit unsupervised in a jury trial of any importance. Four knights were chosen in each district to keep the judges honest.[19]

Regarding the historical role of jurors on civil suits, Blackstone, the great English law authority, taught:

"They are sworn well and truly to try the issue between the parties and a true verdict to give according to the evidence. At this time they were not told to grant a verdict on the law but on the evidence."[20]

Spooner sets forth the ancient oath of jurors in civil suits: "They would make known the truth according to their consciences."[21] This doctrine sets the jurors above the authority of all legislation. A more modern jurors' oath in England is that they "will well and truly try the issue between the parties and a true verdict give, according to the evidence,"[22] implying similar broad powers. In the United States, in most jurisdictions, jurors are sworn to try the case "according to the law of the land." Spooner states

"There is substantially the same reason why a jury ought to judge of the justice of the laws, and hold all unjust laws invalid, in civil suits, as in criminal ones. That reason is the necessity of guarding against the tyranny of the government."[23]

Without this jury veto over the king's law, or for that matter *any* government's law—the king is absolute. No one has ever explained this better than Spooner who expounded:

"How is it possible that juries can do anything to protect the liberties against the government, if they are not allowed to determine what those liberties are? Any government, that...determines...for the people...its own powers over the people, is an absolute government, of course. It has all the powers that it chooses to exercise." [24]

This fear was unquestionably in the minds of our forefathers when they set up the Constitution, declaring that the government should be of the people, by the people and for the people, but those brilliant patriots went further. The Bill of Rights was intended to protect the people against the government, safeguarding individuals against excessive power of the republic they had set up. These rights are clearly and unequivocally established by people who did not trust government. Thomas Jefferson was a strong foe of government power and man's power over man. His words still ring true today:

"All authority belongs to the people...In questions of power let no more be heard of confidence in man, but bind him down from mischief with chains of the Constitution." [25]

Was Jefferson being consistent? He was opposed to government power but also wanted man's mischief to be controlled. He had helped draft a document forbidding an income tax but still wanted chains on man. Yes, he was entirely consistent. The Constitution clearly chained only men in government and men who would use government to work their will on others.

Government was to be the servant. Juries were supposed to have absolute veto over arbitrary governmental actions, but the Constitution was to be an absolute veto over *both:* arbitrary government and arbitrary jurors. An independent judiciary would exist, with a supreme court—for the purpose of reviewing the decisions of lower courts and protecting defendants, both civilly and criminally. Jefferson's jury sentiments placed severe burdens on government and his presumption of innocence for all who are accused inspired him to proclaim:

"The sword of the law should never fall but on those whose guilt is so apparent as to be pronounced by their friends as well as their foes." [26]

It was our forefathers' blueprint for individual freedom. Constitutional guarantees would be further upheld by an appellate judiciary sworn to defend the Constitution. Never before in any age or country had there been such protection, such ingenius checks and balances for the preservation of human rights: a process of fairness which we call "due process."

The theory behind the jury concept is that a random selection of people would more nearly depict the will of the country than any other system. It was expected that these human beings would exercise that sense of justice that people naturally have and, in case of excess, the appellate process would constitute an additional constitutional check and balance to protect accused persons.

One flagrant example of a government judge enforcing his own agenda during jury selection was the trial of abolitionists Scott, Hayden and Morris, in the United States District Court of Massachusetts in 1851, before Judge Peleg Sprague. The defendants were accused of harboring escaped slaves, in violation of the Fugitive Slave Law.

The judge asked the individual jurors:
"Do you hold any opinions upon the subject of the Fugitive Slave Law, so-called, which will induce you to refuse to convict a person indicted under it, if the facts set forth against him, and the court directs you that the law is Constitutional?"[27]

The question presumably had to be asked, because so many good citizens of Massachusetts hated the institution of slavery. The judge did not allow the jury to determine the justice of the law and decide whether the law was constitutional. He took the power out of their hands. Sprague eliminated all persons with a conscience from the jury panel. Only by lying in his answer to the question propounded by the Court and denying his true feelings on the slavery issue, could a person who was against slavery have stayed on the jury. Furthermore, the court made the determination that only Judge Sprague would decide whether or not the law was Constitutional, not the jurors. The judge's role was not one of added protection for the defendants but as a barrier between them and the potential protection of the jury.

Ideally, random and impartially selected jurors would have heard the case. They would have been able to rule on the following issues: Was the Fugitive Slave Law constitutional and just? If so, did the defendants violate this law? Were the defendants' constitutional rights protected during the time? If all the answers to these questions were positive, the next item for the jury to decide would be: Should the defendants be punished? If their answer was in the affirmative, they would then decide an appropriate punishment. A jury shackled in irons by a repressive judge cannot fulfill its noble purpose.

Another example of judges overturning the decision of conscientious jurors was the infamous Dred Scott case. The matter was litigated on various levels between 1846 and 1857. Dred Scott was a slave who sued his master, in Missouri state court, contending that because he and his master had resided for a period of time in a free state (Illinois) and a free territory (north of Missouri) that he should therefore, in accordance with existing legal precedent, be considered free. In 1850, a St. Louis jury declared Scott to be a free man! However, in 1852, the Missouri Supreme Court through Chief Justice William Scott, reversed the jury's decision and again branded Dred Scott a slave.

Undaunted, Scott filed suit in federal court in Missouri, against the administrator of his now deceased master's estate, John Sandford. Sandford's New York residence now was the key to getting this matter into federal court, which under the Constitution, has jurisdiction over disputes between citizens of different states—diversity jurisdiction. The federal court, under Judge Robert Wells, ruled against Scott.

Scott appealed to the Supreme Court of the United States in 1856. In a shockingly racist opinion, Chief Justice Roger B. Taney ruled that because Dred Scott was a Negro, he could not be a citizen of the United States and could not sue in federal court. Taney precipitated the Civil War by declaring the Missouri Compromise of 1820 to have been unconstitutional, and declared that slavery was legal in all the territories until the territories became states and decided the slavery issue for themselves. Dred Scott would have lived the remainder of his life in slavery, had not some white friends purchased him, and then freed him—no thanks at all to the perversion of the American jury system (the decision of those brave St. Louis jurors who originally upheld Scott's right to freedom had been politically quashed).[28]

Washington, Jefferson, Paine and Franklin were all mercifully dead when judges moved down a treacherous road of judicial usurpation of jury power, refusing to stay within the role defined by the Constitution

Did our forefathers intend all three branches of government to be in constant conflict? Absolutely.

they had sworn to support. Instead of a protective shield for the accused, the judicial process became a whip in the hands of government politicians.

In 1794, the first Chief Justice of the U.S. Supreme Court, John Jay wrote:

"It is presumed that juries are the best judges of fact; it is...presumed that the courts are the best judges of law. But still both objects are within your [the juror's] decision. You have a right to take it upon yourselves to judge both law as well as fact in controversy."[29]

The concept in which the jury rules on both the law and the fact—even to the extent of disregarding the judge's instructions—is popularly known as "jury nullification." Most of the judiciary today do not trust jurors to have this much power.

Oliver Wendell Holmes upheld the jury nullification concept in 1920 when he stated "the jury has the power to bring in a verdict in the teeth of both law and facts." [30]

Again, Spooner's brilliant analysis, says it all:

"If the government can decide who may and may not be jurors, it will, of course, select only those persons who are partisan to its efforts and friendly to its measures...it might also question each person drawn as a juror as to sentiments...before suffering him be sworn on the panel..."[31]

These individuals, then, make their judgments:

"... not by their own judgments of their rightful liberties—but by standards dictated to them by the government. IF THE GOVERNMENT DICTATES THE STANDARD OF TRIAL, IT OF COURSE DICTATES THE RESULTS OF THE TRIAL."[32]

Our government was set up with a system of checks and balances. There is the executive branch which consists of the president, his cabinet, advisors and assistants—who have the authority for carrying out and enforcing laws. The legislative branch consists of both houses of Congress, Senate and House of Representatives, which has the authority to enact the laws. Finally, there is the judiciary, which has the authority to make judgments against the other two branches of government, to interpret the statutes enacted by the legislative branch and to strike down laws which, in its opinions are contrary to the Constitution.

Did our forefathers intend all three branches of government to be in constant conflict? Absolutely. The concept of separation of powers was designed to weaken government not strengthen it. This system—which provides the machinery for vetoes by the president, overriding vetoes by Congress, vetoes by jury nullification, and vetoes by judicial interpretation of constitutional protections—was meant to confound and temper the action of any person or group of persons that might curtail individual freedoms and liberties. We went much further then the mere veto of a Magna Carta jury—we had actually declared the individual citizen a sovereign. Today, when the Supreme Court grants government officials immunity for their wrongful acts, it spits in the face of the intent of our Constitution's framers.

In Switzerland today, the last vestige of the ancient Germanic jury system survives. On important criminal matters, jurors are still instructed that they judge both facts and law. Switzerland also has one of the most law-abiding societies in the world. Our American judiciary doesn't trust us as much as the Swiss judiciary trusts its citizens.

Obviously, our complex system is not as efficient as a monarchy or an oligarchy in which decisions can be made quickly and permanently. Multiple vetoes are inefficient. Our forefathers designed the Constitution to make government cumbersome because they did not trust government, and they wanted government officials to be in constant conflict with each other. They believed that the less power held by any one branch of government, the less harm that government could do. Thomas Jefferson and his compatriots were no fans of government.

The Bill of Rights and the Constitution were not written to protect government. They were written to protect individuals, first against government, and then, against groups of individuals. The jury was to have the greatest power of any of these groups because the jury was a temporary, random collection of individuals who answered to no one and did not profit or suffer by their decision.

G. THE BILL OF RIGHTS: A BLUEPRINT FOR AMERICAN JUSTICE

Four of the first ten Amendments to our Constitution deal directly with trial, juries and the criminal justice system. The Fifth Amendment provides that no one shall be tried for an infamous crime unless previously indicted by a grand jury and that no one should be forced to testify against himself. All citizens have a right to due process. Throughout history, government officials had habits of torturing people into making confessions. The French writer, Michel Foucault, in his book *Discipline and Punishment*[33] addressed the issue of the role of punishment in criminal justice. Prior to punishment, in order to justify the government's actions, there needs to be a finding of guilt. The most effective evidence of guilt is from the accused wrongdoer's own mouth. In many societies, the accused is tortured until a confession is elicited from him in order to prove that he is guilty.

The determination of guilt was extremely important to the system of justice in France prior to its revolution. Torture was commonplace. The Fifth Amendment was incorporated into the Constitution, in part to thwart government agents from eliciting confessions through torture or made under unfair circumstances that denied due process.

The due process requirement has deep roots reaching back to medieval England. By 1345 A.D., the principle was established that:

"No man, of what estate or condition that he be, shall be put out of his land or tenement, nor taken, nor imprisoned, nor disinherited nor put to death, without being brought in answer by due process of law."[34]

The Sixth Amendment states that an accused must be given speedy, public trials by an impartial jury, and the accused must be informed of the nature of the accusation. In Kafka's classic *The Trial*,[35] a human being is accused of some unknown offense. He is subjected to the nightmare of a trial not understanding the crimes he supposedly committed. *The Trial* portrays the individuals' bewildered helplessness against a vast, sinister, impersonal bureaucracy which the reader intuitively knows is evil, but which has its own twisted kind of logic, convincing everyone in the book that the victim must have done something wrong.

There is no doubt in my mind that in the United States today there are some citizens who can readily identify with Kafka's feelings because they believe they were charged with confusing, complex crimes—the nature of which they don't even understand. If an accusation is so intertwined in legalese that no one other than a lawyer or a judge can pretend to understand it, then there is no crime, only an unjust law. No one should be held to be morally accountable for a crime whose nature he cannot understand.

The insane Orwellian "double-speak"[36] principle that "Ignorance of the law is no excuse...unless you are insane" is like the irrational unbirthday party of the rabbit in *Alice in Wonderland*." After Magna Carta, *ignorance of the law was an absolute defense*. If a normal human being could not understand the law, he was to be found not guilty. Justice demands the jury nullify confusing incomprehensible laws. Now, if the law is insane but you aren't, and you can't follow the reasoning of the Mad Hatter, you can go to jail. However, if you're as nutty as a fruitcake and obviously predisposed to commit violent crimes, you may go free. Perhaps, the only rational option for an intelligent defendant who examines this system is to lose his mind.

The Seventh Amendment provides that in common law litigation when more than $20 is in dispute the right of trial by jury shall be mandatory.

The Eighth Amendment states that excessive bond shall not be required, that excessive fines shall not be imposed and that no cruel and unusual punishments are to be inflicted. Sometimes the long, exaggerated trials—which are almost a trademark of the system today—constitute not only a violation of the spirit of the Sixth Amendment right to speedy trial but also cruel and unusual punishment whether the jury convicts or acquits.

H. THE JURY AS "JUDGE OF EVIDENCE"

One of Lysander Spooner's most piercing observations in his *Trial by Jury*, is his concept that the jury must be the judge of the evidence at trial.

"The jury must also judge the laws of evidence. If the government can dictate to a jury the laws of evidence, it can not only shut out any evidence it pleases, tending to vindicate the accused, but it can require that any evidence whatever, that it pleases to offer, be held as conclusive proof of any offense whatever that the government chooses to allege." [37]

It is manifest, therefore, that the jury must hear and try the *whole* case, free from any dictation or imposition of governmental influence. The jury must judge the existence of the law; the justice of the law; and the admissibility and weight of all the evidence offered. Otherwise, the government will have everything its own way. The jury will be mere puppets in the hands of the government, and the trial will be, in reality, a trial by the government and not a *trial by the country*. Spooner's arguments still make a lot of sense. They would have served Dred Scott and would serve us today.

"...the authority to judge...the powers of the government and...the liberties of the people must...be vested in...the government or the people; because there is no third party ..." [38]

"There is no more absurdity in giving a jury a veto upon the laws, than there is in giving a veto to each of these other tribunals. The people are no more...against themselves, when a jury puts its veto upon a statute, which the other tribunals have sanctioned, than they are when the same veto is exercised by the Representative, the Senate, the Executive or the people. When did a government ever fail to determine that all of its acts were within the Constitutional and authorized limits of its power if it were permitted to determine that question for itself?" [39]

"If, now, this government (the three branches thus really united in one), can determine the validity of, and enforce, its own laws, it is, for the time being, entirely absolute and wholly irresponsible to the people." [40]

Spooner's book was written in 1852, almost a decade before the Civil War, the year after Peleg Sprague's jury manipulation in the abolitionist trial. It is an amazing prediction of exactly what happened in the South after the Thirteenth Amendment to the Constitution was passed to avoid the authority of the amended Constitution. "Rules" were set up to determine who could vote. Spooner wrote that he believed that tyrants would try to control the voting, just as the early kings had tried to control the jury system by setting judges over them.

We Americans believe that the erosion of the jury system occurs elsewhere...in some far away, despotic countries where the charades of jury trials are often performed for propaganda value. It's difficult persuading the inexperienced that the "powers that be" in this country implement and enforce laws to keep themselves in power. Yet, everyone knows that something is wrong. The fullness of the revolutionary vision of the jury system as perceived by the English barons in 1215 and expanded by the framers of our Constitution in 1787, has never completely materialized.

The ink had hardly dried on the Bill of Rights when controversy arose between those who favored strong central government and those who championed more local autonomy—the argument over federalism versus states' rights. Government has perpetuated a seemingly never-ending cycle of abuse and disregard for individual sovereignty.

While the mid-Twentieth Century was characterized by some major advances in civil rights, in the final decades of this century individual freedoms are being assaulted from all sides. The files of my decade-plus years of law practice are a catalogue of clients hamstrung by a system seeking to keep itself all-powerful. In the first five years of my practice, one jury decision was thrown out by a Judge. In the last two years it has happened four times, and this does not include Judges who blatantly interfered with the jurors' deliberations.

This is a history of people ensnared in a web of governmental bureaucracy that systematically destroys individual sovereignty. Included in this book are stories of people who struggled against venal judges, disenfranchised juries and public apathy, not in some Third World dictatorship, but right here in the United States!

I. THE NETHERLAND ANTILLES: COMPARISON AND CONTRAST

When I visited Curacao, Netherland Antilles (a colony of Holland), representing a client's corporate interests, I eagerly seized an opportunity to examine the courthouse.

The Dutch possession of the Antilles is very different from its tax haven cousin, the Cayman Islands. The Cayman Islands are an independent nation under the protection of the British government. The Cayman government gets its revenues from investors, branch offices, and subsidiaries of companies all over the world which are set up for the purpose of avoiding national and international taxes. The nation prospers and the people are happy and friendly. There is absolutely no income taxation in Cayman. The revenues are based on usage taxes, licenses and fees. There is almost no crime in Cayman. It's a nice place for a family to visit. Cayman pays no significant financial tribute to its mother country, England. The natives keep the bounty from their labor and their tax-free policies.

There exists the English system of trial by jury which is conducted by Cayman lawyers or individuals in English, the language of Cayman.

In stark contrast to that are the practices of the Netherland Antilles. Their money goes back to Holland. It is controlled by the Dutch Government. The people on the island speak Spanish and Parmienta, a mixture of several African and Latin American dialects. The official language of the court system is Dutch. The native civil litigants or criminal defendants do not even have the ability to understand the trials they may be involved in.

There is no jury.

As I sat in a courtroom gallery spellbound, observing a trial, I gained new, modified, respect for what our system was and had been, and fear of what it could become. The judge and lawyers wore traditional wigs and robes. The effect of this increased formality was to create even more feeling of separation between litigants and the lawyers and judges than is generally felt in the United States. At a long heavy wooden table, the prosecuting attorney sat with the judge. Away from the judge and the prosecuting attorney, at another smaller table, sat the defense attorney.

Although the national languages were Spanish and Parmienta and many natives also spoke English, all of the proceedings were conducted in Dutch only by imported Dutch "bar boys."

The accused stood off to the side, away from all of the lawyers. He was a black man accused of "burglary of premises." He could not speak or understand Dutch. He had only a vague idea of the proceedings that were being conducted against him and that vague idea was expressed with his sad eyes and bent servile body.

I asked an officer what was going on, and he told me, with a stern look, to shut up. When I explained to him that I was an attorney from the United States observing Antilles' justice, he warmed up, and smilingly said "Excuse me, I'll help you if I can. Our system is a lot different than yours." Now, realizing that I apparently was not one of the local spectators either enjoying the modern equivalent of the Romans feeding Christians to the lions or a friend of the soon-to-be-convicted accused, he transformed himself into a friendly guide pointing out the players and their respective roles.

The judges were highly educated, important, carefully selected individuals who were chosen for lifetime service on the bench. These persons judged the law and the facts. Those attorneys aspiring to attain a judgeship were prosecutors. Of course both worked for the government. The less ambitious or less skilled attorneys were the defense attorneys: those sitting farthest away from the center of power. The persons in the courtroom with no skills or assets sat even farther away. This included the accused.

The accused was guilty. After receiving a fair trial, he would be con-

The power to determine what evidence the jury shall see and hear is the power to determine the conclusion of the trial.

victed. "Was the accused ever innocent?" I asked. The answer: not that my guide could remember, but occasionally, very rarely, because of a whim or a holiday or an appeal due to some legal technicality, one might be freed.

The law enforcement officer was testifying by way of a piece of paper. He was not actually present in the courtroom. In the United States or British justice system that type of evidence would be considered hearsay. Hearsay is an out-of-court statement offered in court for the purpose of proving some fact. The problem with hearsay is that the accused can't challenge it. Since the officer whose statement is written on the paper is not present in the court, the defense attorney cannot discuss his testimony with him.

The Sixth Amendment to the Constitution allows a defendant to confront his accuser and examine his testimony vigorously. At the time of Magna Carta, hearsay was admissible, but then the jury could decide whether it was credible or not credible. Today, in the United States, there is a large body of rules which determine whether or not hearsay can be given to the jury or must be kept away from the jury. The judge decides, and his rulings are almost never reversed by appellate courts.

In the Netherland Antilles, hearsay evidence from law enforcement officers is admitted as a credible source. There is nothing to stop a law enforcement officer from writing anything he wants in this evidence. There is no way to cross-examine it. (Examine it vigorously with questions which the witness testifying against the defendant must answer.) The accused can't do anything about it either. He can't even testify. He can't speak Dutch.

I happened to meet a relative of the accused in the back of the courtroom. In an effort to obtain a second opinion of what I was watching, I quietly asked him to render his thoughts and answer my questions by whispering to me. He graciously complied.

An enlightening interpretation was given to me by this individual. The family member pointed out the prosecutor and the judge. He said they were conversing in Dutch to decide what the penalty would be. I asked my companion how they would arrive at a decision. He replied that they would consider such factors as how much they liked the defense attorney and how strong and forceful the hearsay information was.

The defense attorney would speak to the judge on behalf of his client. Since he would not be disputing the law officer's version, he did not need to consult with his client for assistance; besides his client didn't know what was going on and couldn't help much anyway.

The judge and prosecutor would confer with each other and decide the punishment. "What about guilt or innocence?" I asked. "Not relevant in this case," he answered. This defense lawyer apparently only debates punishment. He doesn't achieve a "not guilty" verdict in trial. The defendant could not afford one of the lawyers who did that—if, in fact, that achievement was even possible.

In America or in England we would laugh at such a travesty of justice if it were portrayed on television. However in the United States of America in 1988, the judge can admit hearsay information under many, many different guises. We're not so far advanced from this barbaric feudal and unfair unilateral system of justice. We have absolutely no protections whatsoever. Why? Because the government can create its own hearsay evidence. The judge, who is a government employee, can allow it to be put before the jury, and you may not defend with your own hearsay unless the judge allows you do so. The power to determine what evidence the jury shall see and hear is the power to determine the conclusion of the trial.

I had the opportunity to meet the judge in the Netherland Antilles case. He was kind enough to entertain me during a break after a brief interlude with his bailiff. I asked the bailiff if he would introduce me to the judge. The bailiff explained that I could not meet with the judge. The judge was far too busy to speak with me. I told the bailiff that I was an attorney from the United States, that I had watched the proceedings, that I had many questions, and that I would be grateful if the judge would talk with me. The bailiff said the judge might be interested, and he entered the judge's chambers, returning shortly to tell me that the judge would grant me a five minute audience. I was privileged to be allowed to spend two hours in chambers with the judge.

He was an intelligent, well-educated man, and I personally liked him. I also found him to be a despot. I would have enjoyed discussing a play or a book with him, but I would have recoiled in horror at defending a client in his courtroom or being a litigant under his jurisdiction. He was similar to many American judges I'd known, except that his power was unlimited by either an independent appellate review, a jury or politics. He had an absolute belief in his ability to determine the facts without hearing evi-

"To the defense attorney, all the jurors are cards turned face down."

dence from the accused. He had implicit faith in the truthfulness of the officer's affidavit and no interest in going further. He acknowledged that, at one time, the jury system was necessary but that due to the "high level of training now achieved by judges, juries were a relic of an antiquated and ineffective system." He felt that American judges were poorly educated and boring; American lawyers were peasant-oriented; and American juries were outdated burdens. He, a proper judge, knew all this from a course he had taken. Humility was a quality he neither practiced nor aspired to—humility was for the accused, the defense counsel, and the law enforcement officer, in that order.

A description of the Antilles appellate system was even more enlightening. The trial judges sat as appellate judges on a rotating basis. They were all close personal friends, and they would judge each other's personal decisions. They would decide whether or not to reverse their own decisions. The final appellate decision would go back to Holland. The judge found nothing wrong with this particular system of having his close friends judge him and having the government judge him. As an observation with a possible correlation, I noticed that the Dutch oil company, Shell Oil, appeared to dominate the island. In my discussions with natives, I learned Shell Oil Company almost always won its cases, regardless of their nature. The judge agreed, but attributed Shell's successes to its superb management and well educated lawyers.

Residents of the Netherland Antilles are not as happy and free as those on Cayman. In the Cayman Islands, under the British system, citizens have the right to trial by jury, and they are able to keep the proceeds from their own tax-free enterprises. There is virtually no unemployment or crime in the income-tax-free Cayman society. In the Antilles where there is a very high personal tax structure for the inhabitants, there was rampant unemployment during my visit in 1983—about 30 percent—exceeding the 29 percent peak in the United States during the Great Depression.

Does the unjust legal system somehow disable the spirit of the people of the Netherland Antilles? There is a lesson to be learned by the juxtaposition of the societies of the Cayman Islands and the Netherland Antilles, so geographically and ethnically similar but politically worlds apart. A society that is oppressively taxed and judicially abused will be neither happy nor productive.

"For the government's attorney, the jurors are cards turned face up—particularly in tax-related cases."

J. THE EROSION OF POWER OF THE AMERICAN JURY

Spooner observed that:

"Any government, that can for a day, enforce its own laws, without appealing to the people, (or to a tribunal fairly representing the people), for their consent, is, in theory, an absolute government,irresponsible to the people, and can perpetuate its power at pleasure." [41]

In the early American system of justice (because government was not trusted) another check on government power was designed. The individual defendant was given the right to a certain number of arbitrary strikes—the right to eliminate a potential juror, without giving a reason—from the jury panel prior to selecting the trial jury. This enabled the accused to remove potential jurors whom he felt might be prejudiced against him. Supposedly, these strike privileges helped the accused to select a "jury of his peers."

It wasn't long before the government realized that these strikes tended to prevent the conviction of the accused. The government decided that it wanted to be guaranteed a jury of "its peers" also, and the government was by statute, given arbitrary strikes too. This marked a further diminishing of the protective power of the jury in the United States. It detracted from jury's function as a shield, protecting the accused individual against the powers of the government.

Who is the peer of a government anyway? A king? A popular pamphlet, designed to educated potential jurors, describes citizens as the Kings and Queens of the Jury."[42] Giving the government strikes so that the government can have a fair trial by a jury of its peers upset the balance which our forefathers intentionally established. Our system was established to protect the accused whose liberty is in jeopardy.

In today's trials the government has a distinct advantage over the accused. As a matter of fact, defense attorneys frequently end up playing an unfair game of concentration during *voir dire* (the questioning of prospective jurors during the jury selection process). To the defense attorney, all the jurors are cards turned face down. He or she has a bare minimum of information about jurors: name, address, occupation, etc. In the majority of federal cases, lawyers are not permitted to question the jurors directly or in depth although they may submit questions to the judge who may ask the jurors the questions, either as a panel or individually. The judge also might choose to ignore the questions submitted by the attorneys.

For the government's attorney, the jurors are cards turned face up—particularly in tax-related cases. Ex-IRS agent and whistleblower Paul DesFosses has explained how the IRS utilizes its computers and manpower to examine all of the potential and actual jurors. IRS agents will drive by homes of selected jurors, review their tax returns, and even try to date jurors during trial recesses. No expense in time and labor appears to be unjustified in obtaining an unfair advantage in jury selection and jury evaluation. How many middle-class taxpayers would stoop so low or could even afford to finance such tactics if they wanted to? After being practically hand-picked by the government, jurors are sworn to uphold the law as it is given to them by the judge, who is a government official. Now that the government has sworn in "its" jury, the government carefully monitors what evidence will be heard by the jury and what questions will be submitted to the jury.

This helps explain our government's incredible 95 percent win ratio in tax cases. The rate of conviction in drug cases, where the government often does not have access to IRS agents, is much lower. On the other hand, when the defendant has the resources, utilizes jury selection and evaluation tactics, such as investigators, sociologists and ghost juries, a more equal shot at winning can be purchased.

A personal injury case I tried in January, 1986, exemplifies judicial control over the jury. The owner of a vehicle had allowed his car to be driven by his close personal friend, whom he knew to be an alcoholic, and who had two previous arrests for driving while intoxicated. The car owner's conduct was irresponsible. The inebriated driver struck my client's vehicle from the rear, causing the front of her car to collide with the rear of a vehicle stopped in front of hers, and fled the scene! His conduct showed total disregard for the rights and safety of others. My client, formerly a healthy, athletic young woman, was left with a permanent, painful injury to her neck.

I was not allowed to tell the jury that the driver had been arrested twice for driving while intoxicated, nor was I allowed to tell the jury that the driver was, by his boyfriend's admission, an alcoholic who had not admitted his condition, and who, thus, had not taken the first step toward controlling his drinking problem. I was not permitted to tell the jury that these two men met in a bar and were now "drinking together happily ever after." I was not allowed to tell the jury what it cost to put this case on: approximately $7,000 out of my pocket. I was not allowed to tell the jury

Jurors: Some very important grown up matters will be discussed now. You'll have to go to your room.

that the defendants were covered by a $100,000 insurance policy. The judge did, however, allow the defendants' attorney—who really represented their insurance company—to tell the jury that my client had collected $1,000 from her insurance company due to another auto accident. In fact, my client had not even tried to collect anything from her other accident because she had not sustained any injuries from it. The statement was not true.

The jurors were frequently herded off to the jury room like children banished to the nursery when "adult conversation" was taking place between the lawyers and judge. The judge decided what evidence the jury should hear and what should not be divulged to them. Even though much of the relevant evidence was declared inadmissible, the jury did hear the following facts:

> *"The jurors were frequently herded off to the jury room like children banished to the nursery when adult conversation" was taking place between the lawyers and judge."*

A) My client, a bartender, had the professional expertise to determine that the man who ran into her was drunk; B) The defendant admitted he had been drinking before the accident; C) The occupants of the damaged vehicle in front of my client's car were a retired deputy sheriff and his wife, a retired insurance adjuster. Both of these individuals, experts in their respective fields, corroborated my client's version of the accident. D) The defendant thought my client was driving, and that the road was wet. In fact, my client's husband was in the driver's seat, no one was "driving" at the time of impact because the car was stopped at a red light, and the road was bone dry.

The judge contended that since no one smelled the driver's breath (he hit and ran), there was insufficient evidence to *allow* the jury to consider whether he was drunk or not. The jury was not permitted to consider awarding punitive damages. The jury was also not permitted to rule on the negligent entrustment question (the liability of the owner of the car for lending it to someone who was unfit to drive). We won a verdict for actual damages of $10,000, but the jurors were not allowed to consider punitive damages.

After the trial, the jurors told my co-counsel and me that they were certain the defendant was drunk (even though they were only allowed to hear a limited portion of the evidence) and would have awarded damages of at least six figures if they had been permitted to award punitive damages.

We appealed this case, asking for a new trial for punitive damages only. In June, 1987, the Court of Appeals upheld the trial court's decision, agreeing with the judge's conclusion that there was insufficient evidence of the defendant driver's intoxication and gross negligence. Therefore, the appellate court concluded that there was no negligent entrustment on the part of the owner who lent the vehicle. The appellate court also determined that a bartender's eyewitness account, a former deputy sheriff's eyewitness account, the admission by the driver that he had been drinking, and the fact his pants and shirt were undone and he had hit and run, all meant nothing because no one had smelled his breath.

The trial and appellate courts overlooked the fact that the driver had run away, not permitting anyone to smell his breath or gaze into his eyes to see if they were bloodshot! The appellate court seemed to be endorsing a strange new legal doctrine which I put into the following words on appeal—If you drink, drive and hit, it's wise to make it a hit and run.[43]

We filed a motion for rehearing in the same appellate court, pointing out what we perceived as errors in the court's reasoning.[44] Our motion for rehearing was denied.

In September, 1987, we filed an application for writ of error in the Texas Supreme Court. In December, we received notice that our application was denied, with a finding of no reversible error. The Supreme Court found this judicial usurpation of jury power to be unimportant, and refused to hear the case.

Popular scuttlebutt around the courthouse says that the Texas Supreme Court favors the high-campaign-contribution paying plaintiffs' firms. I disagree. In my opinion, the court is impartial. I believe it favors contributors from either persuasion equally, a friendly green brief is always impressive. I have been the recipient of reversals by this court ruled on without a hearing per curiam, (no judge signs the order, it's just unanimously agreed to.) As this book goes to press in 1989, with a new chief justice and an additional new judge on the highest bench, I'll cross my fingers and hope for change. The Republicans are offering to clean up the judiciary. Unfortunately, they may owe the insurance industry a lot of favors and the "clean up" could come at the expense of the victims. Some of the most well financed judges have taken up the cause of victims of banking and insurance company abuses. These victims are not campaign contributors. They are just victims. In fact, my favorite Texas Supreme Court justice is also said to be the largest recipient of campaign funds.

As of April, 1988, during the 11 years of my legal career having handled hundreds of cases, I have had only two civil trials and four criminal trials in which the jury did not grant a favorable judgment to my clients (this is out of approximately 100 jury trials.) In each of these instances, I believe the result would have been different if I had been permitted to present a full and complete picture to the jury and if the jury had more authority. I have also occasionally enjoyed unfair verdicts on behalf of my clients, because the rules enabled me to cloud the facts. When the name of the game is not truth but persuasion, each side tries to utilize the judge to hide harmful truth from the jury with objections. The jury of course, renders decisions on what it hears and what it thinks it hears.

In cases tried by a jury under Magna Carta precepts, it was intended that the punishment and award be fixed by the jury, not assessed as a matter of law, and certainly not determined by the judge! Our Constitution was not a step back from the Magna Carta, but a step forward. It did not give fewer protections, but increased them.

The oath of the juror at the time of Magna Carta was simply that "They would neither convict the innocent nor acquit the guilty."[45] In the case of convictions, the jury's sentence was not necessarily final. The accused had the right of appeal to the king and his judges and to demand either a new trial or an acquittal if the trial or conviction had been against law. Under the Magna Carta, the judge was more of an administrative functionary, and did not have a modern judge's awesome power over witnesses and lawyers to control the trial.

Lysander Spooner addressed the concept of contempt of court as follows:

"If the judge has power to punish for contempt, and to determine for himself what is a contempt, the whole administration of justice (or injustice, if he choose to make it so) is in his hands. And all the rights of jurors, witnesses, counsel, and parties, are held subject to his pleasure, and can be exercised only agreeably to his will...This arbitrary power, which has been usurped and exercised by judges to punish for contempt, has undoubtedly had much to do in subduing counsel into those servile, obsequious, and cowardly habits, which so universally prevail them and which have not only cost so many clients their rights, but have also cost the people so many of their liberties."[46]

In a recent Texas case, seven decent, God-fearing citizens were sentenced to 30 days in jail because they refused on religious grounds to rise when the judge, presiding over a traffic dispute, entered the room. The Court of Criminal Appeals upheld this sentence! A federal judge was alleged to have commented, "They should be damned glad they weren't in my courtroom, I'd have given them six months!"

One of the very few federal officials to be impeached, U.S. District Judge James Peck of Missouri, was impeached (accused of wrongdoing) in 1830 by the House of Representatives and tried in the Senate for abusive use of his contempt power.[47] The senate acquitted him. No other Federal Judge has ever even been seriously questioned for this type of arbitrary and exessive use of contempt power.

The statement is often made that "Judges define the law and juries decide the facts." Lysander Spooner attacked that division of roles as follows;

"Judges do not even live up to that part of their own maxim which requires jurors to try the matters of fact. By dictating to them the laws of evidence,"[48]

By dictating what evidence juries may or may not hear and by dictating to them rules for weighing such evidence as they are permitted to hear, judges obviously dictate the conclusion that juries will reach. It is clearly impossible, in the nature of things, for a jury to try a question of fact, without reviewing every piece of evidence in support of those facts.

A wider range of powers should rest with the jury, not because the jurors know the law better than the judges, but on the grounds that the judges are untrustworthy. They are exposed to bribes; they are overly fond of power and authority, suffering from a lack of humility; they are sometimes the dependent and subservient creatures of the powerful. To allow them to dictate the law not only places the rights of the parties at risk of being sold for money, but is equivalent to surrendering all the property, liberty and rights of the people unreservedly into the hand of arbitrary power to be disposed of at its pleasure.

It is only since the real power of the juries has been severely limited, and in fact, jurors have often been reduced to mere tools in the hands of judges that they have become "pets" of the government. Public lip service is paid to the grandeur of our jury system because jurors are not normally exposed to dishonest temptations.

In praise of independent jurors, Spooner wrote:

"They are not liable to bribery for they are unknown to the parties until they come into the jury box...twelve men, taken by lot...will (not) all prove dishonest. A jury therefore, ensures to us what no other court does, that first and indispensable requisite in a traditional tribunal, integrity."[49]

The concept of trial by jury emerged in the Athenian city-states as the culmination of thousands of years of legal evolution. It continued to progress through the Germanic enlightenment to the English Great Charter and reached its climax with the adoption of the U.S. Constitution and its Bill of Rights. Each step of the way, however, government intruded and slowed this great progress toward human liberty. Liberty is, and always has been, the enemy of government power and the enemy of democratic tyranny. Ideally, the jury protects citizens against the government. Appellate review protects against juror injustices and even democratically imposed injustices (the majority telling a minority what to do). The ideal is still a visionary dream. We can either start approaching it again, or backslide.

If you walk down the street and are stopped by two immoral ruffians, should they be allowed to vote with you to decide the distribution of the proceeds of your wallet? Of course not. If your resources as a wealthy individual allow you to select and influence, should you be permitted to help yourself to someone else's resources? Of course not. The system of checks and balances properly applied, with a strong jury system checked by constitutional limitations and reviewed by an appellate panel, is the best protection against these and other injustices which may be inflicted either by a judge or a jury or the voting populace.

A thorough evaluation of the judiciary is the next step toward learning appreciation for the jury system.

K. TYPES OF JURIES

Jury—A certain number of men, selected according to law and sworn to inquire of certain matters of fact, and declare the truth upon evidence to be laid before them.[50]

When we hear the word "jury," we customarily think of those 12 people who, in a criminal case, decide guilt or innocence or in a civil case, decide which party owes money and how much. (In some jurisdictions the number can be six or even three.)

This oversimplification fails to differentiate between the various types of bodies of people who are called jurors. Some basic definitions follow.

Grand jury—A body which consists of about 10 to 30 people, usually politically chosen, who listen to evidence provided by the prosecution, and then decide whether there is sufficient evidence to indict an individual for the commission of a crime.

The Fifth Amendment of the Constitution guarantees the right of a person accused of an infamous crime to be indicted by a grand jury. This procedure was intended to be a safeguard against overzealous prosecutors and a protection against an unnecessary trial. The term "infamous crime" has been interpreted as one that could require imprisonment at hard labor. In a less serious crime, if a prosecutor opts not to use the grand jury method, he simply takes the short cut of preparing an "information"—a document charging an accused with an offense. A prosecutors' information is simply a short cut to a formal grand jury. The prosecutor skips the grand jury and takes the accused straight to trial.

The Supreme Court has ruled that the Fourteenth Amendment did not make the grand jury requirement mandatory on the states.[51] Although 32 states have adopted the "grand jury indictment for infamous crimes" standard, in 18 other states the use of grand juries is optional.

Grand juries in theory are made up of impartial, independent citizens. The institution was intended to protect the rights of the accused from unfounded prosecutions. It does serve, in that way, to a very limited extent. If a grand jury had been convened in the Ginters' capital murder case, Norma and Leonard Ginter probably would not have been accused of capital murder. (See Chapter XI B for more details on the Ginter case.) Yet, the way the prosecution now controls most of the grand jury process, the grand jury is reduced to little more than a rubber stamp. The fox is guarding the chicken coop!

The prosecutor usually controls the testimony placed before the grand jury. The defendant has very little control over what happens in front of the grand jury. The defendant is, in all federal cases and in 49 states not allowed to have an attorney in the room. Massachusetts is a rare exception to this rule. In contrast, the government is represented by one who handles many cases, frequently over a period of several months with the same grand jurors and has built up a rapport with them. The government attorney usually acts as though he is the grand jury's lawyer, and they frequently treat him that way. Without fair opposition, the government attorney wins the greatest portion of his contests. The grand jury usually issues what is called an indictment or "true bill." This legally accuses the defendant and forces him to go to trial.

When the grand jury's accusation is read at trial by the judge to the trial jurors, they usually think, ah, something foul's a foot. The "fight" before the grand jury is like a soccer match with only one team on the field and one goal. No goalie guards the goal. The prosecutor keeps kicking at the defendant's goal until he scores or gets bored and wants to accuse someone else. It's usually not much of a match, but it doesn't appear that way to the trial jurors. It seems as though an important decision has already been made. Some jurors ignore it, some don't. With many, the grand jury's accusation creates a presumption of guilt.

Large Jury Panel—On any given day in a metropolitan area, hundreds, sometimes thousands of citizens are randomly selected, generally from voter registration rolls, to serve on juries in various jurisdictions. One presiding judge will tell this large group a little about their duties and then divide them into smaller groups, of about 25 to 30 people, and send them to specific courtrooms for further selection. This judge can, if he wishes, further influence the group of jurors—and the lawyers or parties who are not present at the time will generally not know what is said.

Court Jury Panel—The jury panel of approximately 25 to 30 (depending on the type of trial) is then sent to its courtroom. The judge in this courtroom may give further instructions. In most state courts, attorneys for the parties may speak directly to these jurors and question them about their backgrounds, experiences, and opinons. In federal courts, usually only the judge addresses the jurors for that purpose. This process is called "voir dire" which means, literally, "to speak the truth," which is what the prospective jurors are admonished to do in response to the attorneys' questions. Some jurors are dismissd by the judge at this point.

Afterwards, depending on the jurisdiction, each side gets to kick off a certain number of jurors with arbitrary strikes. The methods of removing them vary from state to state. The federal judiciary also varies its methods from state to state and sometimes from judge to judge. The jurors who remain will hear the case. They are the trial jury.

Trial Jury—This jury is also called petit jury or ordinary trial jury. They range from six to twelve in number. These are the jurors so often seen on television or in the movies, who sit on the sidelines, and are often portrayed as relatively unimportant.

Unfortunately, most modern jurors are unaware of the jury system's proud heritage and the power they still have left. In civil cases, juries are in danger of going the way of the horse and carriage. Vociferous critics argue that juries composed of average lay people cannot possibly understand complex economic or scientific arguments of expert witnesses, and therefore, a "jury of experts" should decide the merits of complex civil cases. In criminal cases, the jury can still say not guilty and let the accused leave the courtroom free.

"Liberty is, and always has been, the enemy of government power and the enemy of democratic tyranny. Ideally, the jury protects citizens against the government."

CHAPTER III

HERE COMES THE JUDGE

"Modern judges are relics of ancient ecclesiastical authorities, who did not determine mere facts but determined 'divine law.' They were priests. They uttered mystical incantations, wore divine robes of office, and sat behind altars."

A. IN OPEN COURT...

All Americans have a right to a public trial. That means no closed doors. The author remembers, with regret, the efforts of Judge Andrew Ponder of Lawrence County, Arkansas to deprive Norma and Leonard Ginter of their public trial rights.

Joe Izen and I, representing Leonard Ginter and Norma Ginter, respectively, went to Lawrence County, Arkansas for a hearing in the capital murder case styled State of Arkansas vs. Ginter. (For more details on the case, see Chapter XI B.) The Ginters were accused of capital murder in the death of Lawrence County Sheriff Gene Matthews. Matthews was becoming a folk hero and a guilty party needed to be found quickly. Norma's husband had been host to a man with a gun and good aim. Under the scapegoat theory of law, that was enough to accuse her of capital murder and get the local prosecutor's name and picture on the front page of local newspapers. The only fact working in her favor was that she was completely innocent of any killing.

Judge Ponder boasted that he had been a judge for 30 years. He was a strict "I-am-the-judge, who-the-heck-are-you?" type. Everyone in the county paid him homage as though he were some kind of feudal lord. On the first day in his courtroom, he took Izen and me into his chambers and told us who he was: The Boss. We had flown from Texas seeking a bond reduction hearing. While Ponder let drug dealers and real killers out on little more than a song and a promise, he held both Ginters, both innocent, without bond.

Although no one in Lawrence County wanted to represent her, and although Norma had asked Ponder to appoint a lawyer because she was indigent, Ponder ruled that she could afford to hire an attorney. Ponder also jailed the couple without bond and without hearing any evidence, although a so-called hearing was recorded by a court reporter. No lawyers had attended and no evidence was introduced. The proceeding was a joke.

The first real bond reduction hearing was postponed so Ponder could leave for a fishing trip. I reminded him that two elderly people were in jail, and that we had flown from Texas to Lawrence County specifically for the hearing. Ponder's reply: "Patience is a virtue." Although Ponder denied it later when he was placed on the witness stand, a local citizen testified at another bond reduction hearing that Ponder said, "Now I've got the S.O.B." (meaning Leonard).

At the bond reduction hearings, the government was not able to prove that Norma was likely to flee. In fact, she was demanding her right to a public trial and wanted to prove her innocence. Norma produced convincing evidence she would not be dangerous or flee, but the judge ignored it.

A third hearing was scheduled. This time Norma's federal harboring trial was over, and the federal government had released her. No additional evidence of her right to bond was put on—only evidence to prove that law enforcement officers had intentionally burned the Ginters' home. Nevertheless, we also asked for a bond reduction. I told Ponder if he disallowed it, we'd get Norma out on a writ of habeas corpus now that federal officials had released her.

At first the press helped initiate public demand for vigilante-like justice against the Ginters. After a few hearings, however, the attitudes of the press changed. *The Justice Times, The New York Times* and *The Arkansas Democrat* began asking important questions. People wanted to know what really was going on. Questions were being asked. How could Norma have killed the sheriff when she had already been arrested and was on her way to jail before he was killed? So, who really killed the sheriff?

Ponder's half-blind, feel-your-way-around-without-evidence-or-law technique was not impressing the papers. The courtroom kitchen was getting too hot. Did Ponder get out of the kitchen? Shucks, no! He moved the kitchen.

Several hundred people were crowded into Ponder's courtroom like sardines for the Ginters' third bond hearing. Always a law unto himself, Ponder puffed away on his cigarettes while his smoke clouded the "No Smoking" sign. The press filled two rows. Ponder quickly announced that the court would take a 30-minute recess, and we were called into his private chambers, the judge's office, across the hall from the courtroom.

The chambers, however, are not generally considered open to the public. Ponder told us he had invited a visiting judge to use his courtroom. He gave us a choice: postpone the hearing—which would mean another wasted flight to Arkansas and that our clients would stay in jail—or finish the hearing in chambers. Both alternatives were inadequate, and the press was furious. Ponder wanted Izen and me to cover for him and tell the press he was holding the hearing in private for our benefit, so our trip wouldn't be wasted. I told Ponder "No" and complained on the record vigorously. The guest judge volunteered, "I don't need the courtroom for my business. It will only take a little time, and my matters are uncontested so we don't need the big courtroom."

Ponder compromised. He wasn't about to inconvenience the visiting judge. We went into his chambers, but left the door open to give the appearance of a public hearing. Three hundred citizens and dozens of reporters filled the hallway between the chambers and the courtroom. Almost 700 eager and ears crammed up against the door, fighting for elbow room. The cameras were pointed every which way. Ponder's bailiff was instructed to keep people from crossing over the threshold into his chambers.

Ponder tried to assume the traditionally relaxed chamber pose while appearing dignified. "I don't mind closing the door if you'd feel more comfortable, Mr. Minns," Ponder offered. "Your Honor," I told him, "I don't think I could feel comfortable in your courtroom."

Meanwhile the huge courtroom sat empty. The visiting Judge had finished his business in a few minutes.

Was this third hearing public or private? It's hard to say. However, it was a strange experience; it was awkward, and it was short. Ponder reduced Norma's bond to $50,000, which was still unreasonably high, although considerably better than denial of bond altogether. Two months later the bond money was raised, and she was released after being held for seven months.

With the case dropped, Ponder was finished with me, and with the publishing of this book, I am finished with Ponder. Judicial immunity protects him from Norma's civil rights action. It didn't however protect him from the voters. "Impeach Ponder" posters went up all over Lawrence County. An election was held, and after 30 years on the throne, Ponder was retired.

Most cases in most courts play to empty or near empty audiences. They are public in the sense that anyone can listen, but as Dicken's said in a *Bleak House*, courtroom scene, "no one cares."

When you are born in the United States, you enter the American legal system with a legal document called a birth certificate. Half of all Americans get a divorce, and 20 percent experience the criminal justice system as a victim or an accused. More than 10 percent either have or cause a personal injury. Nearly half will buy at least one home. These are just some of the legal matters that involve nearly every American at some time. One hundred percent of the people die. (This figure is very accurate.) Death subjects you to the legal system even if—by some miracle—you avoid all the other legal proceedings. What happens behind courtroom doors affects all of us.

A lot of lawyers have never seen a jury trial. I have listened, amused and sometimes distressed, when deskbound lawyers tell clients what a jury will probably do in a given situation and charge a handsome fee for their less than valuable advice. Often these lawyers draw up complex, legal documents that will be interpreted sometime in the future by jurors. If a dispute arises, the client will probably seek out a trial lawyer who will end up with the responsibility of defending the confusing document. The document drafting lawyer is wrong as often as he is right. Expensive joke? You bet! Funny? Not always.

How many trials has your lawyer won? There's no more nitty-gritty confrontation than eyeball-to-eyeball conflict, whether it be in the boxing ring, on the battlefield or in the courtroom. The courtroom is the legal battleground where cherished beliefs are crushed and fair is often only a fairy tale. When trials are not public, they become the exclusive property of judges and lawyers. Don't die without watching a trial. Even watching two wouldn't hurt you.

If you need a lawyer and want to interview one in action, the courthouse is an ideal place to watch. Most lawyers in the courthouse are working lawyers, and are available if the price is right. A lawyer can tell you a dozen times how good he is, but there is a lot to be said for showing it.

"What happens behind courtroom doors affects all of us."

B. PRAYING TO JUDGES

"I became a state supreme court justice ONLY because my grandfather, who had been a United States Senator from West Virginia and governor, had many friends."[1]

Judge Richard Neely, author of *How Courts Govern America* urges: .

"The public must watch trials. Not just sensational murder trials but suits on auto wrecks, because if no one goes into the public courtroom the trial really isn't public."[2]

Anyone who has ever spent time exercising his Sixth Amendment obligations and rights to public trial by watching or participating in a trial knows that the central character in the courtroom is the judge. Court does not even officially begin until the bailiff solemnly intones, "All rise," and the black-robed judge enters.

It was not always thus. In the early Germanic and medieval England, the jury had absolute power and authority in the courtroom subject only to an appeal to the king for review.

Today, we assume it is bad for the jury to have so much authority. In fact, articles are frequently written about runaway juries that give judgment far in excess of their authority or outside the bounds of reason. The jury is shackled with the blame for the medical malpractice crisis. The jury is blamed for rising insurance costs.

Yet, in contrast, homage and respect are paid to the *jury system.* Much of this respect is mere lip service, based more on half-remembered tidbits from high school civics class than from real understanding of the way our system works. Other nations admire the American jury system saying "it is good," and "we wish we had it." Of course, the English speaking countries who have adopted British common law also utilize the jury system and are proud of it, but the American jury system is the most widely publicized legal system in the world.

On television when you watch the jury system in action, however, you see an inaccurate version of it. The only element in these shows that customarily mirrors the truth is that the jury is of minor importance in the

"A lawyer can tell you a dozen times how good he is, but there is a lot to be said for showing it."

scheme of things. They are not considered important except for the one tense moment at the end of the drama in which they go out and people wait for them to make their decision. There is no focus on the individual identities of the jurors. The focus is on the lawyers and the judge.

We don't even wait long for the jury to make its decision because we already know what the jurors will do. They will follow the script. Today judges frequently feed scripts to the jury members. When jurors grant "runaway" verdicts, judges revise them. We accept this. When a judge reverses an award, or grants a new trial, we assume the jury was wrong.

In an exceptional, highly publicized case, a female television news commentator sued her former network for wrongfully firing her, apparently because the network wanted its female commentators to be not only attractive, but also eternally young. A jury awarded her a large sum of money. The trial judge disagreed, and a new trial was granted. A second jury also gave her a large award. Again, the judge ruled against her. Why did she even bother to go for round two? Trial is expensive. Winning by the rules, and having your win taken away by the judge, destroys the petitioner's faith in the system. Unfortunately, the public keeps its faith in the system, accepts the judicial decree as just and goes about its business.

Under early jury systems the jurors were the judge of both law and fact. Our system has degenerated to the point where jurors are not allowed access to the truth. In fact, juries hear small segments of the truth, lies and half versions of the truth. To tell half a truth is to tell half a lie. Jurors are not allowed to know the totality of the circumstances of the case they must decide.

Unless the judge supports jurors, or strong, independent jurors are selected with uncommon perception, the government often uses the jury system as a rubber stamp, because the jurors are only allowed to hear what the government wants them to hear. In the past, kings scorned and condemned the jury system and continuously tried to bring king-appointed judges into the jury system to control the jurors. These efforts at jury control were strenuously fought. It was only after the king was allowed to put a judge—separate from the jury itself—into the system after nearly 500 years of justice, that kings began to show approval for the jury system that had been forced upon their predecessors at the point of a sword.

With this in mind, let's look at our American judges. The very frank and honest statement from Judge Neely at the beginning of this chapter gives us an idea how judges are selected. Harvard law school Professor

Alan Dershowitz, offers an interesting prospective on their moral and intellectual fiber.

He writes:

"Most judges have little interest in justice...It is amazing how many judges— especially, but not exclusively, state judges—lack the basic intelligence to understand a moderately complex legal argument. Some are just plain stupid; others lack the necessary legal education; still others are lazy or impatient."[3]

Modern judges are relics of ancient ecclesiastical authorities, who did not determine mere facts but determined "divine law." They were priests. They uttered mystical incantations, wore divine robes of office, and sat behind altars. Lesser priests could be paid to intercede and offer prayers of sorts to the higher ecclesiastic authorities. Of course the king could usually go to the top priest and offer prayer more directly.

We haven't gone far from that in our current era. A large portion of our judges wear black robes, creating a theatrical aura of power, dignity, and an air of quasi-authority and righteousness. These long, black clerical looking robes imply religious authority. "Legalese" is the mystical tongue spoken to and by them, which the common man does not understand. It is not far removed from the Latin which was spoken hundreds of years ago in England, where the majority of the Anglo-Saxon population did not speak Latin. In fact, beautiful, borrowed Latin phrases permeate the law, almost as though we, the lawyer/priests, subscribe to an ancient, pre-feudal religion, no longer completely understood but nonetheless cherished for its antiquity. As mentioned previously, a similar situation exists today in the Netherland Antilles, where Dutch is used in the court system even though most people do not speak the language, and the actions of the court must be accepted as a matter of faith.

A further indication of the pervasiveness of both the religious authority and feudal lord symbolism connected with the judicial system is the fact that written documents submitted to a judge requesting he do something are known as "pleadings." The very word implies the attitude of a servant groveling at a superior's feet. In the final paragraph of most pleadings, where the writer is asking a judge to make a decision based on statements

"'Legalese' is the mystical tongue spoken to and by them, which the common man does not understand."

contained in that document, the following archaic form is commonly used "WHEREFORE PREMISES CONSIDERED, Plaintiff *prays* for relief." (This means, that because of what I've just said, I beg for help.) This paragraph is known as the prayer. Strict followers of the Ten Commandments may argue this prayer violates the First Commandment not to pray to idols.

Judges are not completely autonomous, they must answer to the authority of the appellate court. Citizens rarely view trials but public attendance is even sparser at the appellate level. Appellate courtrooms are almost always completely empty. Even the parties to the case under consideration usually do not attend appellate hearings. The appellate process is generally carried on by the filings of written briefs. Generally a 10 or 20 minute oral argument is presented by attorneys for each side. The appellate judges sit up on a slightly higher altar (bench) than the trial court judges whose judgment they are reviewing.

It is interesting to note that appeal courts do not judge written decisions of the jury because the jury does not commit its findings to writing. The trial court judge, after listening to the jurors' decision, determines what he will include in his written order and what he will exclude—or whether he will even follow the jury's verdict. Only the judge's final order is ruled on in an appeal.

Who are these judges, and how do they get there? In all situations, the determination for a human being to be a judge is a political determination. No examinations are given to test candidates' understanding of legal complexities. No evidence of exemplary moral character must be presented. Rather, politicians decide. This rule is true for all judiciaries: the federal system and the various state systems, both elected and appointed.

In over a decade of law practice, I have known a few judges who exemplified what a judge should be: humble, sensitive and wise. I have run into more who had some of those qualities but not all, and many with none. If I were allowed to pick only one of the three qualities, I'd choose humility.

We want judges to be human, to care. We want them to be firm. We want speedy justice. We want judges who don't think they are better than we are. Are we asking too much?

If we expect all judges to be equally imbued with humility, wisdom, and sensitivity, then we are asking too much. Solomon was given his great wisdom as a gift from God. When he asked for wisdom, he didn't ask for humility or sensitivity, and some of his brilliant decisions did not show those qualities. He may have shown wisdom in decreeing that a baby disputed between two mothers be cut in half, but he did not show a great deal of sensitivity to a grieving mother's feelings. When he accepted the challenge proposed by the Queen of Sheba, of discerning between the genuine flowers and the artificial, he showed off his cleverness but did not demonstrate humility. Absolute monarchs do not customarily show humility. It's not a requirement of the job. If even Solomon fell short of the ideal, how do our modern American federal and state judges rank?

C. THE GOOD, THE BAD, THE UGLY...AND THE CRAZY

The two worst judges, bar none, that I have ever had the misfortune to encounter are Judge Frank Seay, presiding federal judge of the Eastern District of Oklahoma, at Muskogee, and former Judge Andrew Ponder, who used to preside over the state court in Lawrence County, Arkansas. I call them bad judges.

Seay threatened to jail me for contempt before I had been in his courtroom for 30 minutes, simply because I had the temerity to be a vigorous advocate for my client in a willful failure to file case. When my client's first trial ended with a hung jury after deliberations until 2:30 a.m., this judge unilaterally set the date for a re-trial without asking the prosecutor if he thought it was worth the expense to try this case again.

The second time around, Judge Seay systematically cut the heart out of my client's defense, openly taking sides by not allowing the defendant to present his theory of the case, and by repeatedly trying to discredit me in the presence of the jury. Several years previously, my client had been misled by a disbarred attorney who had incorrectly told him that by setting up a ministry and giving away all of his money (except for necessary living expenses), he would be exempt from federal income tax. The main issue at trial was whether or not my client was trying to "get away with not paying taxes" or whether he, in good faith, had established a church which distributed money to deserving recipients according to my client's religious principles. Was there criminal intent? Had my client really given away his money? By selectively admitting and excluding evidence, Judge Seay allowed the government to show that my client received a certain amount of money and did not file a personal income tax return. The defendant was not permitted to put on witnesses and introduce evidence showing his humble lifestyle and the manner in which he had distributed the funds. As a result, this second trial ended in a conviction. The rumors are that the first jury voted 7-to-5 for acquittal. It's only a rumor because Judge Seay would not allow us to talk to the jurors after the trial was over.

He said that would be jury tampering. No one has yet explained how you can tamper with a jury *after* the trial is over. We are now waiting for the Tenth Circuit Court of Appeals to decide if it is appropriate for the jury to hear both sides.

The conduct and demeanor of Judge Andrew Ponder is described in Chapter III A and Chapter XI B. Since his defeat by voters, Lawrence County, Arkansas is a far better place to live.

Both Seay and Ponder exhibited minimal levels of intellect; both were insecure, and mean. Before each judge, you had to be very careful to explain cases simply but not talk down to the judge—who was always on guard for a slight innuendo of his inability to appreciate the meaning of a case. Homage was very important. In fact, a pious plea for forgiveness over some failure to acknowledge the court's nobility could make the difference between a short or long visit to jail.

With what other attributes could a bad judge be endowed? He could simply be an ugly man. To exemplify the category of ugly, I pick the judge of the Eleventh Judicial District Court of Houston from 1968 to 1988, William Blanton.

Physically, he's a tall, handsome and distinguished looking old man, stiff bearing, and proud with a winning smile. He loves dignity and decorum, and has a quotation from former Supreme Court Chief Justice Warren Burger posted on the bulletin board outside his courtroom:

"Civility is to the courtroom what antisepsis is to the hospital; the best medical brains cannot outwit soiled linen or dirty scalpels, and the best legal skills cannot justify or offset bad manners.

Lawyers and judges who know how to think, but have not learned how to behave courteously are a menace..."

Blanton reads and understands the law. Unlike Ponder and Seay, he's an intelligent man. That's where the potential good stops and the ugly starts. He never had an opponent in twenty years on the bench. He was the Democratic candidate from the party power machine in the old big-firm days and he serves his power-structure master well. The big firms outdo the little ones in his court, nine times out of ten. His friends are given enormous latitude to make mistake after mistake. Those he does not like are abruptly dismissed and often defeated for failing to observe archaic, sometimes nonexistent, local rules he imposes unilaterally to protect those he supports. His local rules aren't simply Houston, Texas, rules, but are often unwritten rules particular only to *his* courtroom. Minorities of all kinds are not on his list of protected parties.

The big law firms, banks, insurance companies and government agencies all find protection under his kind left wing, while he wields a sword with his rigid, angry right arm, striking down the downtrodden, the indigent, and the small practitioner who is fighting institutions. He does so with a regal but nasty disposition, taking pleasure in humiliating those he disfavors. He hates to be called unfair. He is seldom openly criticized, because he abuses his judicial power to strike intemperate slashes at those who dare to question him.

Blanton has announced his planned retirement at the end of 1988, paraphrasing Ecclesiastes, that there is a time for all things, and that now is his time to leave the bench. "Amen." It is an ill wind that does not blow away some of the officious odors of humanity. In the eleven years that I have practiced law, while I have quite often had my differences with judges, only three judges have caused me to hate them: Frank Seay, Andrew Ponder and William Blanton. (MacAfee was too crazy to hate.) I do not stand alone. Those who hate them are legion, Blanton is far worse than a Seay or a Ponder because he had the intellectual gift to be a good judge. However, those who publicly announce it are few. I've been told over and over again it's a dangerous business to speak out about ugly and bad judges. My response: So what? It needs to be done. Can lawyers be disciplined for speaking out against judges? YES! Does it bother me? Yes. However, the First Amendment is too important to sell out for a law license. The following story shows how this judge "Blantonly" disregarded a jury verdict.

During the week I settled my Commonwealth case, which you'll read about in Chapter XVI F, my former partners, Butch Bradt and Joe Izen were fighting Round II of my mother's case against Houston Health Clubs and Health and Tennis Corporation of America. In 1983, the Club tore down my mother's building which they had been leasing, and replaced it with another building. They called it "remodeling." Mom called it destruction! This unconscionable act, along with other breaches of the lease, formed the basis of my mother's suit. The Health Club was represented by Tom Alexander, a self-proclaimed legal guru, who formerly worked for Butler Binion, a large Houston firm, and then branched out on his own to form Alexander and McEvily.

In Round I of the same case, Alexander had lost an $800,000 judgment and his client's $3,000,000 building by default. His clients had failed to file an answer after being served with the lawsuit twice. The Defendants were

Houston Health Clubs, Inc. (corporate name for President's Club) and Health and Tennis Corporation of America (owners of H.H.C. stock). My father started President's Club 30 years ago. When the giants came in, he sold out. They made him an offer he didn't want to refuse. As part of my parents' divorce settlement, Mom got the club building in question and the land it stood on. President's Club was bought by Houston Health Clubs, Inc. (H.H.C.). The stock in H.H.C. was owned by Health and Tennis of America, Inc. (H.T.A.) which owned health clubs all over America. H.T.A. was owned by Bally Manufacturing, publicly organized and traded, and involved in vending machines, gambling casinos and other ventures. Both suits reached the offices of the club's attorneys. Neither lawyer filed a written response. A default judgment was entered against the Health Club chain.

More than six months later, after the judgment was executed, by closing down the Health Club chain, the judge, a personal friend of Tom Alexander's, changed his mind, threw out the final judgment he had previously signed, and ordered a new trial. A related story is found in Chapter V. part C. The Health Club chain was re-opened and the Great Izen and I filed an action against the judge. The First Court of Appeals ordered the original judge to reinstate the judgment. He did. By this time, he had already recused himself (withdrawn from the case) after a hotly disputed hearing.

The "random" lottery system thrust the case into the court of Judge Blanton, who had been a former partner of Alexander when they worked for the firm Butler Binion. We complained to the presiding Judge Thomas Stovall who ordered a new Judge on the case, but Blanton kept it anyway. For a while, it lay dormant, awaiting a ruling from the Supreme Court of Texas. Alexander filed an action against the entire appellate court which had ruled against the first judge. The Supreme Court threw out the final judgment, without a hearing, and ordered a new trial—a victory for Bally and Alexander. Alexander named me as a principal witness, forcing me to withdraw from the case. I had gotten in and out of the case as Mom's other lawyers kept quitting. Although it's tough to represent your own mother, in this situation I had no choice, or she wouldn't have been represented at all. We ran through a series of five other lawyers. Each time one got off, I got back on to fill the gap. The final trial team was 2/3 of the old Minns, Izen, Bradt partnership: Izen and Bradt. I represented both of them in their own cases. They couldn't quit Mom's case and keep me. I also imposed on our friendship to keep them in the saddle. I prevailed on

Butch Bradt to take over my position as lead counsel and try the case with the Great Izen. Simultaneously, I called everyone on the other side and begged for a settlement. The case and its appeals had dragged on for four years. Alexander arrogantly vowed a bloody fight. It was.

The details of this war will have to wait for a future book. However, in the place of the $800,000 verdict thrown out by the Supreme Court, Butch, Joe and Mom won a jury verdict of $2,500,000 in cash and $3,000,000 in property. My mother, Mimi Minns, who resides in Hot Springs, Arkansas, is an underground lawyer of sorts. She has gone through a number of trials as a party and has accumulated a nearly perfect win ratio. Unlike the other non-lawyers in my family who practice law, Mom does not practice law—she practices facts. In this case as in all her other cases, she studied the facts, documented them with correspondence, permits, contracts and pictures and had them ready and organized for immediate use at trial. If Butch had a question, she had the answer documented and available for him. Mom had learned through experience that during the heat of trial, papers can slip through an attorney's hands like water through a sieve. Mom, operating in her own best interest, filled the holes in the sieve and played a significant role in her own victory.

Judge Blanton, ignoring the First Amendment, ordered lawyers on both sides not to discuss the verdict with the press—it could hurt the Health Club's business. Sure could! Members might not buy lifetime memberships to a building no longer in the possession of Bally. Another favor for a friend.

Butch and Joe had done battle in this hostile arena, as a favor to me, for my mother. Under these unfavorable conditions, they had been expected to lose. In fact, they did lose nearly every judicial decision during trial. However *they won the jury's decision!* It's a miracle winning a case when the Judge lets the jury know he wants you to lose.

The jury deliberated for almost four days. Judge Blanton's answers to all of the questions asked by the jury were deliberately designed to force them to rule in favor of the Health Club. Nevertheless, the jury determined that possession of the building should be awarded to my mother again and that the Health Club should pay punitive damages of $2,500,000! But that's not the end of the story. After a delay from the mid-December jury verdict, to late January, Blanton entered the judgment, proposed by his former partner, in direct opposition to the jury's award. He ruled that Mom lost. Like a political puppet, he signed the order drawn up by Tom Alexander against Mom. "Alexander the Great" had

won again! The jury verdict meant nothing. Blanton "blantonly" interfered with the jury system and ruled for the Health Club. During Butch's
trial in which I represented him on his personal auto injury the week before Blanton's final ruling, the opposing counsel told us he had talked to
Blanton and Mom's win would be taken away. He successfully predicted
an astonishing and unlikely future. Some might suspect treachery. The
case is now on appeal. The winner is appealing!

Lest you despair of the possibility of any noble creatures on the bench,
take comfort. There are judges who accept pay cuts, sometimes in the million dollar range, to take the bench; judges who love people, have great
wisdom and sometimes humility to boot. In fact, there are a lot of them.
Here's a picture of some of the very best. I call them good judges.

Judge Walter Stapleton: federal appellate judge; formerly a very successful attorney; a nice guy and a scholar; tall, dark- haired, with an aristocratic bearing. Every decision of his is backed by case law. Court starts at
10 a.m. and recesses around 4:30 p.m. Justice is not rushed. He writes with
the classical skill of a man who has studied the law of other nations and
the past. His dignified bearing and unpretentious quiet confidence demands respect, but he is interested in hearing arguments from both sides
and is not ashamed to change his mind. He is fair. He shows no favoritism
during trial and when he instructs the jury about their constitutional obligations, he does so with strength and sincerity. He believes it.

At the time I met this great man, presiding over a trial in 1984 in the
federal district of Delaware, I had considered quitting the practice of law.
I'd faced so many idiots and crooks on the bench, I felt I could take no
more. After a three-week trial and the influence of Judge Stapleton, I was
refreshed and a believer again. He has since been elevated to the Third
Circuit Court of Appeals by President Reagan. I'd love to see this man on
the Supreme Court.

Judge David O. Belew, Jr.: a big warm bear of a man, with a hearty
handshake and deep Texas drawl. He presides over a federal court in the
Northern District of Texas, (Fort Worth, Texas), and has a lot of that good
ole country horse sense former U.S. Senator Sam Erwin showed to the
country during the Watergate trials. You can't help but like the man, because he likes you. There is a relaxed air in his courtroom. He has the
demeanor of a concerned father, so that both sides, plaintiff and defendant, feel protected. He has an infectious laugh, a strong sense of right and
wrong and a love of justice. His past includes acclaim as a war hero and
success in his law practice. I'd hate to see him put on an appellate bench

because he's the single best trial court judge I've ever been before. He was appointed by former President Carter.

Judge J. Spencer Letts: a graduate of Harvard, formerly from a big law firm, where he did not have a great deal of trial experience. He sits as a federal district judge in the Central District of California. A tall and lanky man, he was a former captain in the Army who was educated in the east and has lived in Texas and California—in California long enough to have picked up the west coast way of accepting many cultures. He is a legal scholar with great sensitivity to human feelings and with great humility.

This man stands when the jury enters the room in a time when most juries are required to stand when the judge enters the room. He's extremely intelligent and very fair. When he talks to lawyers in chambers, he takes off his robe and asks them to relax. Because of his limited trial experience, and his 22 years of association with four large law firms, I would not have selected him for the bench. I'm glad it wasn't my decision to make.

Judge Letts has a consuming intellectual curiosity that compels him to hear both sides of an issue. He loves to review the law, and does so from the point of view of interpreting case law in such a way that justice might prevail.

Prior to taking the bench, Judge Letts drew much larger wages than he now receives, doing corporate securities work with big law firms, handling some of the most complex type of legal problems, and writing numerous outstanding articles, turning difficult areas of law into simple language. The man has a genius about him mixed with the milk of tenderness and compassion. He loves to discuss law and morality and enjoys backing down from his positions—but they are well thought out and convincing. Unlike the judge who tries to bully you into retreat, Judge Letts can actually change your perspective. I found myself occasionally in chambers being persuaded to abandon some of my client's positions, which can be dangerous, because to win, I have to believe in my theory of the case. Some lawyers don't, but I do. Letts simply loves and reveres the jury in a way other judges only pretend. He holds them up on a higher altar than his bench. If you love the jury system, you have to love Letts.

A Texas state judge whom I hold in high regard is Eugene Chambers, a former law librarian. He ran for the office of judge several times and was defeated. He was an expert in legal research. He worked very hard in the law library, and he enjoyed his work. He practiced law on the side for approximately 30 years. As a librarian, he was not treated with any great distinction. He perceived his role to be one of serving lawyers, legal assistants, and members of the public who asked for help in research. This experience helped make an already wise and honest man, humble. He came into his judicial office on the coattails of the Reagan-Republican landslide. He hasn't changed. He is still humble. He has the wisdom of his years and the vast legal knowledge amassed through his service in the law library. When a case is tried in his court, the jury gets to hear both sides. Efforts to keep evidence out are overruled more often than not. Both sides, whether they like the judge or not, usually feel they had a fair shot at justice when the trial is over. He likes to let the jury decide.

A Justice formerly on the First Court of Appeals, Ken Hoyt, is one of less than a handful of black Republicans. At 39, he is young, smart and political. When he ran for the Texas appeals court after less than a year on a trial bench, he ordered the Republican party not to print his picture. Why run as a black, just to help Republicans pick up votes in the black community, when he could run as a successful lawyer, former Republican judge with a good record? His tactic put him on the appellate bench for a six-year term. While Hoyt's written opinions show great skill and promise, his courtesy to the people before him shows something even greater: humanity and love. You cannot help but love this man. He was appointed to the federal bench in 1988, one of Reagan's last appointments, and one of his best. In 10 years, he will be recognized as one of our country's great judges.

Texas Judge Jerry MacAfee was just plain nuts. MacAfee ran for the Republican nomination for judgeship in 1980, when no one in Texas thought a Republican could win. He ran against a sweet but not too bright black woman, Alice Bonner, who—while she did not deal well with legal principles—tried to be fair and seek justice. For that reason, she was better than many. In a race no one watched or thought about, MacAfee became the new judge after the votes were counted.

In one day, I watched MacAfee rewrite the Constitution and the Bill of Rights. A newspaper reporter had written an unfavorable article about him. The judge took action. He wrote out and posted an order that the reporter could not come into the courtroom without giving the judge advance notice so the judge could have a tape recorder present. If the reporter violated the order he was told he faced contempt charges and jail.

On the same day, I watched a lawyer argue that his client's adversary was in bankruptcy but he had to proceed in state court anyway, because his client had ordered him to do so even in the face of certain defeat. His opponent smugly and correctly argued that the Constitution gives the federal court absolute jurisdiction over all civil matters when a citizen is in bankruptcy and only the bankruptcy court can release this litigation back to state court. He told MacAfee he had no jurisdiction.

MacAfee looked to the respondent, who stood behind a sign which said defendant/respondent—signs were put up at the bench to show the lawyers where to stand, sort of like the arrangements you may remember from kindergarten—and asked: "Counselor, what's your response?" The lawyer shrugged his forlorn shoulders and replied: "It's embarrassing judge, but my client demanded I try. I have no law to support my position." He added with a smirk: "Why not overrule 100 years of federal supremacy, judge?" There was a little weak laughter in the courtroom. The magnificent MacAfee ruled: "No reason for the federal courts to bully everyone around. I overrule their jurisdiction and set this case for trial in my court."

Both winner and loser were shocked.

My case came up: Heinz Weber vs. Sarah Desimone. I had never met the client, Mr. Weber. The case had belonged to Joe Izen in the old Minns, Izen, Bradt days and my name had been put on it. Joe's dad, Dr. Izen, was the Plaintiff's doctor and chief witness, so Joe could not try the case. The case had come up for trial, I had been notified and I explained to the Honorable MacAfee it was not really my case—we needed 60 days to get someone else on the case. Judge MacAfee disagreed. "Dr. Minns", he said, (All lawyers were called doctor in his Court, so Joe Izen, Jr., the lawyer was called Dr. Izen, and his dad, Joe Izen, Sr., a medical doctor was called Dr. Izen. If you called another lawyer, counselor or mister, you could be held in contempt of court. If a lawyer could prove he did not have a doctorate in law, but held an LLB, the J.D.'s predecessor, he could apply for permission not to be called Doctor.) "Announce ready for trial now, or I'll dismiss Desimone's case."

"Desimone is the Defendant sir," my opponent volunteered, "you should dismiss Mr. Weber's case."

"Case dismissed," MacAffee ordered.

"I announce ready," a surprised me volunteered.

"I'll set you for..." and we were on our way to trial. I met the client that afternoon.

Mr. Weber had been hit from the rear by Ms. Desimone while on the freeway in stop-and-go traffic. Ms. Desimone said it was his fault, he should have moved out of the way. Mr. Weber had incurred about $150 in medical bills in six years but still had a neckache. The insurance company's lawfirm, Fulbright & Jaworski, the largest firm in Houston, had offered a $1,000 settlement. Mr. Weber demanded $2,500. We were heading for trial over the difference.

During trial, my opponent, Lannie Temple, displayed an incredible knowledge of medicine.

Ms. Desimone backed down from her position on fault—maybe it wasn't Mr. Weber's fault, but it did her no good. The jurors heard her confronted with her deposition testimony taken several years earlier, when she blamed Heinz Webber for the accident. The jurors were annoyed at her previous subterfuge. We could expect some punishment.

Dr. Izen (the medical doctor) took the stand. I asked him a few questions, established the $150 in bills and future *possible* bills, physical pain and turned him over to Dr. Temple (the lawyer). Dr. Temple went from Weber's neck to his spine to his toes to his liver and kidneys and to his knee. After an hour of this, I objected. (I try to let the opposition bore the jurors if they are not hurting my position, but enough is enough.) "Irrelevant, your honor. Objection. This suit has nothing to do with Mr. Weber's knee." The Judge overruled me. "Overruled Dr. Minns. Let Dr. Temple proceed." The jurors thought this "doctor" business was a joke, and they broke up laughing.

During closing arguments, I told the jury they had to pick between Dr. Temple (the lawyer) and Dr. Izen (the medical doctor). My medical recommendation (as Dr. Minns, the lawyer) was to go with Dr. Izen.

They returned a verdict of $13,000. This presented a problem for Sarah Desimone who had only a $10,000 insurance policy. There was an even bigger problem for the law firm which had advised its client against accepting $2,500 settlement offer and had spent another $3,000 (estimate) fighting the case. The insurance lawyer had exposed Ms. Desimore to $3,000 liability because they had been unwilling to settle.

With more than insurance policy limits at stake and not wanting to wait for an appeal, I offered a settlement that no one who cared for Desimone's position could refuse. Give us the policy $10,000, and we'll drop the rest. Fair all around? You bet. No humiliation for the insurance guys and immediate cash for the good guys.

Temple reluctantly told me he could not take any offer until after his Motion to Reduce the Judgment was heard. Ridiculous. He had no legal grounds. Why should we wait? I told him if we got our Judgment finalized, the negotiations were over. He then told me his client had authorized him to settle for $8,600 after the hearing but he couldn't *make* the offer until after the hearing. I was stunned. Why $8,600? Why not $9,620? Why not policy limits?

Solution and answer. Judge MacAfee, after a hearing, lowered the Judgment to $8,600. He told me and my client he was doing this because I had done such a poor job trying the case. Dr. Temple went off to practice law and/or medicine with another firm.

The State Judicial Grievance Committee of Texas finally punished MacAfee. Was it for being crazy? Was it for violating the federal supremacy law? Was it for eliminating free press and public trials in his courtroom? Was it for his strange courtroom signs? Was it for interfering with jury verdicts? No way. He was punished for making lawyers call each other doctor. They said he had to stop doing that. His punishment was that he was told to stop doing it publicly, and he was officially embarrassed. After the punishment, he made the use of the term "doctor" for lawyer optional.

D. THE FEDERAL JUDICIARY

Our federal judges complain that in 1988 dollars, their wages ($89,500 to $125,000) are insufficient to live on. The fringe benefits, lecturing for fees, free travel, excellent medical, and lavish retirement benefits make up in a small way for the insultingly low wages.

Although the popular myth is that "all lawyers are rich," there has never been a shortage of lawyers willing to set aside their private practice and take the bench. The security plums in the legal profession are the lifetime federal bench jobs. Lawyers and state judges stand in line to beg Senators for these appointments. When a federal judge finally gets tired of the measly $100,000 a year salary he receives for government service and retires, bevies of lawyers are waiting in the wings to fill the empty slot. The ex-judge frequently retires to collect political favors from lawyers who previously appeared before him. Many of these judges had trouble feeding their families by the fruits of their former private practices. Some were defeated politicians who called in debts. As judges, they jump up to the top five percent of the country in terms of their income. When they leave the bench, their ante jumps two to five times; retired judges make big bucks.

Thomas Jefferson, argued that when a person takes on a public trust, he should consider himself to be public property.[4] Most judges don't read Jefferson or at least they don't accept his argument seriously. It goes against human nature to consider yourself public property. Judges have vast, nearly unlimited power. Although a lot of younger judges today are disdaining the robes and attempting to be more human, they are not abdicating the power or mystique of their exalted position. Everybody says "Hello, judge. I like you, judge. I admire you, judge." Almost never does someone say, "Judge you're a crook. You're dishonest. I can't stand you, and you're not very bright."

Professors like Alan Dershowitz occasionally do.[5] Occasionally, a rare judge, with integrity and guts, such as West Virginia's former Chief Justice, Richard Neely, will publish a book critical of his fellow justices. He will then suffer the disfavor of his colleagues. Neely writes:

"At the judge's conventions, my observations...are received with the same enthusiasm that the bastard son is received at the reading of the will...Other judges stick up their noses because I insufficiently appreciate the pristine Olympian functions of the judiciary."[6]

As a society, we worship these human beings who have been put on the bench because of their political abilities, not because of their intellectual abilities. These people who earn, without the help of their spouses, four times the national average income, complain about their suffering due to insufficient wages. The salary of a federal judge is accompanied by fringe benefits of virtually unlimited power over other human beings and prestige. This public servant, who is required to suffer on the meager $100,000 a year government salary, does have some alternatives. He can give lectures and accept handsome fees. There are judges who are not shy about accepting these lecture fees. Judges also receive an enormous amount of non-taxable fringe benefits. They have a staff that works for them, helps them and worships them. Most people will probably believe that these judges, if they pinch their pennies, will be able to live comfortably to a ripe old age on their government salary and the other benefits that come with the job.

Federal judges frequently look down upon the state court judges who have to run for re-election, disdaining them as perpetual politicians. Federal judges are removed from the political circus. They are protected from the specter of unemployment. They are removed from the uncertainties of the economy. They are endowed with a lifetime of massive power and above average income. This near total and complete authority is not bal-

"Judges have vast, nearly unlimited power."

anced with a similar level of responsibility because almost no one looks over their shoulders. They are practically immune from public condemnation for their acts. Only two sitting federal judges have ever been convicted in the first 200 years of our history of criminal wrongdoing. Is this wrong?

Let's be reasonable. Since we know our politicians are at least a little less honest than we are, and since all judges are former or current politicians, is it likely only two federal judges in 200 years were crooks, or is it more likely a lot of crooked ones slip through the legal net?

Do many of them retire for higher paying jobs? Yes. After achieving the political influence of a judge and after building up friendships—everyone wants to be the judge's friend—over a decade, these individuals frequently find that they can double, triple, or quadruple their wages upon leaving the judiciary.

There are many very fine, decent, competent honest judges, but it is still a fact of life that a majority of them gain a pay raise when they become federal judges. It is also true most of these judges like their job—because they are good judges or because they enjoy the power. Most of them would not quit if offered double or triple their salary. A $1 million salary would not buy the enormous amount of power federal judges have.

The president appoints all the federal judges in the 50 states. His decision must be confirmed by the Senate. The overwhelming majority, more than 90 percent, of all presidential judicial appointments are confirmed. Occasionally there is some politicking in the Senate over these confirmations, especially if the president's party is outnumbered. Generally the senior senator (of the president's party) from the state with the vacant judgeship will make selection recommendations. If there is no senior senator from that state in the president's party, the recommendation will come from the state governor or some high-ranking official of the president's

---

"Federal judges are removed from the political circus...protected from the specter of unemployment... removed from the uncertainties of the economy. They are endowed with a lifetime of massive power and above average income. This near total and complete authority is not balanced with a similar level of responsibility because almost no one looks over their shoulders. They are practically immune from public condemnation for their acts."

---

party in that state. For the most part, the individual who is recommended to the president gets the appointment.

One of our recent successful candidates for the federal judiciary is lawyer Daniel Manion of Indiana, a confederate of Senator Quayle. He was nominated for the Seventh Circuit Court of Appeals in 1987. He has never been lead counsel in a federal case. His list of 10 most important cases includes a deceptive trade practice suit over an improper car repair and some minor real estate transactions. His supporters say he's a nice guy, and mediocrity needs to be represented. Although he had very little experience as a federal trial lawyer, he had even less experience as a judge: Absolutely NONE![7]

An individual under consideration for the federal bench usually must have a minimal approval rating of the American Bar Association. Legally, this is not a requirement. However, few judges are selected that do not have the backing of the American Bar Association. The American Bar Association (ABA) is a voluntary labor union which has more lawyers in it than any other organization in the world. In fact, there are more lawyers in this one club than in any single country outside of the U.S.A. The United States has more lawyers than any other country in the world, and ABA membership is open to any lawyer who is in good standing with his/her local bar association.

The purpose of the ABA is to promote the interests of the American lawyers as a labor union, just as the American Medical Association promotes the interests of American doctors. Membership in the ABA is not a license and it is not a requirement to practice law anywhere. It is, however, a political requirement if you want to become a federal judge.

I am not a member of this organization. I get form solicitations in the mail a couple of times a year and other lawyers ask me why I'm not a member. My answer is that I'm not running for judge.

Once a federal judge is selected and confirmed, he participates in a ceremony which vests him with vast power for life, or until he quits.

A federal judge's decisions are subject to review by the circuit court of appeals in his region. Each circuit court panel consists of between nine and 12 justices. Circuit court decisions in turn can be appealed to the nine Supreme Court justices. Out of approximately 20,000 circuit court opinions a year, only about 200 are heard by the U.S. Supreme Court. There-

"You'll get hit by lightning twice before you'll win a Supreme Court reversal."

fore, the federal appellate courts are, in reality, the highest court in the nation for most litigants since the odds of reaching the Supreme Court are negligible.

The Supreme Court refuses to hear most cases because of time limitations. However, when a case is reviewed by the Supreme Court, the circuit decision is changed about half the time. You'll get hit by lightning twice before you'll win a Supreme Court reversal.

Federal judges do not handle the large number of trials that the state judges handle. Perhaps because they have more time to reflect, a greater number of these judges have attained an insight which appears to be wisdom. Many judges do obtain, through listening to trial after trial, a certain amount of wisdom. However, some judges don't obtain any of it. Just as there are some stupid carpenters, some stupid plumbers, and some stupid lawyers, there are some judges that are stupid.

What happens when we get a stupid judge on the federal bench? Nothing. He remains on the bench for the balance of his or her life. Our system has no recall for stupid federal judges. What happens when we get a judge who is arrogant, mean and nasty? Occasionally, people will say mean and nasty things about that judge in the hallways. But that's usually the end of it.

While most Americans don't ever expect to be litigants in federal court, nevertheless, they need to be students of the federal judiciary since the character of the individuals who make up the federal judiciary has an impact on our lives. Decisions made by the federal judiciary collectively will tend to preserve our cherished freedoms, or lead us down the road to totalitarianism.

Once selected and approved, each federal judge has the option to stop being a politician. He's in for life.

E. STATE JUDICIARY

State court judges are purely political animals. In some states they are appointed as are federal judges, and in other instances are elected directly by the voters. This is often tantamount to either a lifetime of unchallenged service (using the word loosely) or a lottery election since most voters

---

"Once a federal judge is selected and confirmed, he participates in a ceremony which vests him with vast power for life, or until he quits."

---

don't even know who their judges are. Most voters take no interest in the judicial elections at all. In some areas, judges are routinely swept in and tossed out with the political party that sweeps the national elections. In most cases, a judge can politick his way to a lifetime on the gravy train. However, during the 1980s a trend is emerging that shows more elected judges being defeated at the ballot boxes than in the previous 200 years of our history.

The judges obtain their political support and money—when needed— from the lawyers who practice in their court systems. Not long ago, for example, California Supreme Court Chief Justice Rose Bird was tossed out by a recall vote.[8] Her constituents were apparently disgruntled at her opposition to capital punishment. She had narrowly won her last election. While there is still a great deal of judicial stability nationwide, gradually the voters are becoming more aggressive toward removing unsatisfactory judges. Most judicial office-holders speak out against this trend. I think it's very healthy. It tends to make judges less powerful.

F. CAMPAIGN CONTRIBUTIONS: THE BEST JUDGES MONEY CAN BUY

In Texas we elect our judges. A Democrat runs against a Republican. For the last 100 years, generally, there were no Republican judges elected; (my grandfather use to say Republican judges were illegal in Texas) consequently, Democrats were appointed by the governor to fulfill the balance of a resigned judge's bench. That appointed judge usually ran unopposed for re-election, and was re-elected over and over again.

Despite the strong possibility of an easy victory when running unopposed, judges often accumulated large amounts of campaign contributions—it was almost a scandal when a judge would not accept campaign contributions.

The judge has virtually unlimited authority to use his campaign funds for anything that even remotely might have to do with running for re-election. For example, there is nothing to stop a Texas judge from putting his wife or her husband in a full-time paying position to help him or her run for re-election. The judge, of course, must do a certain amount of traveling to campaign, and it is not unusual for a judge to buy cars for his campaign committee—which he, his wife and children may utilize. Of course the judge, in order to run for re-election, must remain properly educated. There's nothing wrong with his campaign fund sending him and his wife to London for an ABA Convention. Thus, he maintains his level of excellence. During the ABA's 1985 convention in London, many courthouses across the country practically closed down.

In the well-known, well-publicized case of Pennzoil vs. Texaco, the trial judge, Anthony Farris, received and accepted a $10,000 campaign contribution after the start of the trial from one of the litigant's attorneys. He said he did this because the campaign contribution had been promised prior to the trial, and it was simply being paid at that time by coincidence. Texaco asked that he get off the case; he refused, and he remained on the case. During the middle of the case, he resigned because of health problems, and a new judge who was also a personal friend of the Pennzoil attorney took over.

Judge Farris later died. I can remember Judge Farris fining a client of mine $500 because he did not show up at a deposition while I was arguing an Eighth Circuit Court of Appeals case in Omaha, Nebraska. He chastised me for going off on a federal excursion. My opponent in the case was a big law firm that was a heavy campaign contributor. Fortunately for my clients, the big law firms are not allowed to make campaign contributions to the members of the jury.

Judges are supposed to avoid even the mere appearance of an impropriety. Well, they don't! They don't seek out the appearance of impropriety, but when it raises its ugly head all too often, they don't flinch from it. They look impropriety in the eye and accept it. This does not mean a judge will hand you a medal for pointing an impropriety out to him. When Judge Gregory was presiding over a well publicized probate case in Harris County, Texas, he was charged with an impropriety of which he was completely innocent. The lawyers repeatedly accused him to the point where he withdrew from the case because he stated that the lawyers had accused him so often that he felt he was prejudiced against them and could not give them a fair trial. This is a judge to be greatly admired for his honest approach. Unfortunately, he is the exception and not the rule. I've tried a case before Gregory before, and I think he was mistaken. I think he would have been fair even though he disliked the lawyers who had slandered him.

Most of the time when a judge is accused of an impropriety or favoritism and is asked to remove (recuse) himself from that case, he refuses. Another judge is then brought in to hold a hearing and decide if the original judge can stay on the case. This neutral judge is usually a political set-up who always votes for the presiding judge and against the efforts to oust him. Only once in a blue moon is a judge recused.

The party who files the recusal motion is universally condemned as a trouble-maker. The neutral visiting judge can usually be counted on to issue a few disparaging remarks against those in favor of recusal. In ten years, I've filed four motions to recuse, always in very blatant cases of prejudice. I've lost all four. On one occasion, the judge offered to voluntarily recuse himself.

There are some exceptions to the general rules. I recall one family law judge who refused to take campaign contributions after he was put into office. The rumors and gossip engendered by this attitude multiplied to scandalous proportions. Imagine a judge who would not take campaign contributions! Unfortunately, he died in an automobile accident: a great loss to the county. Houston, Texas J.P. Court Judge Pacetti,—when he learned he had no opponent—refunded all campaign contributions; another man of integrity on the bench. It's too bad they are so few and far between.

I was dismayed, but not surprised to find the following comments in a Houston newspaper in April, 1986: "The Houston Bar Association voted on which candidates in the various judicial races it would give its endorsement to. It voted 100 percent to endorse 100 percent all of the incumbents."[9]

What does this mean? Does it mean that the incumbents are good and the people running against them are all bad or less good? To say that all incumbents are good in any political arena is to make a false statement. That's absurd; that's ridiculous. Perhaps even a large portion of the incumbents are good, but no intelligent person honestly can state that all incumbents are good.

Reading between the lines, what the article says is that the members of the Houston Bar Association, a voluntary association of local lawyers, made a political decision through which they hope to influence voters. Most, if not all, of the incumbent judges are members of that organization, and frequently attend luncheons where members of the bar and the judiciary cement their friendships. An attorney is at a disadvantage if he is not a participant in the social circuit of incumbent judges and powerful law firms. Obviously, a lawyer who devotes his/her practice to helping the downtrodden can't afford to attend many of these functions.

"Imagine a judge who would not take campaign contributions!"

This system of socializing in the political, legal or business field used to be derogatorily known as the "Old Boy Network" because it excluded minorities and females and the less economically privileged. Now, although the socialization process still excludes many and still favors the privileged few, it has now been updated and the process is referred to as "networking" and the practice is considered a professional must.

Should we have judges? Should we have appellate review? Unquestionably, yes. However, enlarging the power of the jury and restricting that of the judiciary on both trial and appellate levels would greatly diminish the potential for political abuse.

Should we ever have trials before the judge, alone? Certainly. Two parties in a case should both have the right to waive their right to jury trial. They would do this when both trusted the judge and respected the judge's personal opinion. The decision would, of course, be optional. Having judges try cases saves money, saves time and saves headaches. It should always be optional though. Individual parties can determine whether the judge is politically oriented, and if so, whether that is an acceptable standard for the judicial, decision-making process in their particular case.

There is a necessary role for honest, intelligent, caring judges to play in our justice system.

In Texas, there is a judicial grievance committee that takes complaints about unethical conduct and improprieties that the judges may be accused of. There has never been a judge in Texas history thrown off the bench as a result of complaints levied against him by the judicial grievance complaint committee. Even one judge, Yarbourgh, convicted of criminal conduct while sitting on the Texas Supreme Court, was not removed by this committee. He voluntarily vacated his seat. Perhaps the prevailing permissive policy toward judicial improprieties will change some day.

The Missouri Plan of selecting judges is supposedly a compromise between unlimited tenure of judges appointed for life, and the political arena, as it exists in Texas and some other states. The governor selects judges from a list. Of course, the governor can "suggest" names that should appear on the list, is politics rearing its ugly head again? Once appointed, the judge remains on the job, unless he is voted out by the citizens, who have regular opportunities to do so. No one runs against him. Citizens just vote no confidence and he's out. No judge has ever been voted out in the history of the Missouri Plan. Perhaps each governor has the talent of selecting only great judges.

G. THE FACTS AND THE LAW; THE JURY & THE JUDGE

In most cases in the United States, two trials are conducted simultaneously, one on facts and one on law. The fact finder can be a judge, an administrative official, or a jury. The law finder is nearly always a judge. In Switzerland in serious criminal offenses the jury decides both facts and law.

Sounds terribly complicated. It's not. Sounds like some very important power goes to the judge. It does. Without repeating the entire history section: The Anglo-American jury system was evolved in England from a hybrid of the Athenian forum and the German jury trial. In both cases the jury made all decisions. Unfortunately, the Athenian system was destroyed by war, and the last vestiges of the German system eliminated by Hitler.

FACTS are: Specific events, names, times, dates, actions, documents, damages etcetera relating to the case under consideration.

LAWS are: Statutes and case law precedents defining the elements of acts or offenses such as homicide, fraud, excessive speed etc.

For example, suppose that Jim was charged with driving 90 miles per hour. That's an alleged fact. However, it's not that simple. Is the allegation true? Jim says he was going 40; the cop says he was going 90. The jury decides the fact: the truth. Perhaps the jury decides he was going 65. Now what?

If the judge decides the law, he may tell them anything over 55 is excessive speed. If you find the defendant was going over 55, you must find him guilty. Of course, the jury can find he was going over 55 and still find Jim innocent by ignoring the judge's instructions. That's called jury nullification.

In a civil matter, suppose that John is accused of cheating Sam through fraudulent misrepresentations. The jury is asked to answer these questions:

1) *Did John tell Sam that the product was good quality?*
2) *Was that statement a lie?*
3) *Did John know that his statement was a lie?*
4) *Did Sam rely on John's representation?*
5) *Did Sam suffer losses as a result of his reliance?*

If you answer yes to all of these questions, answer question 6.

6) What sum of money should Sam get to compensate him? Fill in a dollar amount on the line below.

_____.

This simplification of the elements of fraud shows five questions all of which must be answered "yes" to find fraud in many jurisdictions. The judge decides what questions to ask—what questions equal fraud; what the law is. The judge decides if the jury received enough information (evidence) to make their decisions, and what evidence they will be allowed to hear, and then the judge signs an order.

Some jurors will try to guess the judge's opinion, and rule as they think the judge wants them to. Other jurors will ignore the judge and try to be fair. A smart juror can figure out what's going on with question number 6. However, if the jury answers "no" to any one of the first four questions, Sam doesn't get compensated, even if the jury writes in a sum of money in the last blank. Of course, if the judge leaves off, "If you answer yes to all of these questions..." the jurors won't suspect the result of their verdict.

In some small claims courts, the jurors are told law as argued by both sides and hear the evidence of the facts and without instruction from the judge. The jury says guilty or not guilty, and, if guilty, the jury sets a fine from $1 to $200. This jury is ruling on facts and law.

H. THE SELECTION OF JUDGES; SOME MODEST PROPOSALS

What if we selected judges at random? What if we selected judges from among lawyers at random, but held them accountable to the persons they were judging? What if the losing parties in a case had to make a determination as to whether or not the judge would remain on the bench?

Strange as it may seem, when a judge is nonpartisan and ethical, the parties on both sides usually respect him. Of course, large numbers of people will have a sour grapes attitude and would vote against an excellent judge simply because he did not rule the way they wanted him to rule. Fine. Set up an arbitrary figure. Make the judge obtain the approval of the losing parties in at least 30% of the cases which he or she hears. Put the judge on trial also. Put the judge's fairness and sense of "justice" on trial.

If the judge had less power and had to answer more frequently to the individuals whose cases he adjudicates, would justice more often prevail? Does this proposal sound shocking or somehow blasphemous? If you believe that judges are better than we are, if you believe that judges are more moral than we are, if you believe that there is something in the system which elevates them to more god-like behavior, then I'm arguing to deaf ears. If we have a faith-like obedience to these individuals who have been politically selected, then a change towards a more impartial, equitable system will never occur.

However, if you share my belief that judges are no different from anybody else; that when they don their judicial robes they insert one arm at a time; then you would support a movement to curtail their vast, unreasonable power.

As a society, we Americans love polls. A poll is a survey of a specific number of human beings randomly selected which purports to indicate opinions of the general population. A perennial favorite survey question asks the American people, "Who do you trust the most and who do you trust the least?"

After reviewing some of the polls, we can come to a few conclusions: Included in nearly every list of professionals that we do not trust are lawyers. Almost always, without fail, there are two other professions that we trust even less than we trust lawyers. Politicians are generally ranked below lawyers in trustworthiness. If you had to place a bundle of cash into someone else's hands for safekeeping in an emergency, you would probably sooner place this trust in a clergyman or doctor, rather than a lawyer.

Q: Do you believe in capital punishment?
A: "Of course I believe in Capital Punishment. I believe that everyone in the Capitol should be punished."
—Ajay Lowery—

However, if you had to choose between a lawyer or a politician, for moral wholesomeness, you would probably choose the lawyer.

Fortunately for lawyers and politicians, there is another profession that ranks below both of them: Used car dealers. It seems that used car dealers invariably end up at the bottom of every "trustworthiness" list that they are on. Without them, the politicians and lawyers could be facing the same dire straits and conditions that lawyers and politicians faced during the reign of terror in France under Robespierre.

During the French Reign of Terror, all identified lawyers suffered decapitation. I am reminded of the statement made by *The Justice Times* publisher Ajay Lowery during his campaign for president. A newspaper reporter asked him if he was in favor of capital punishment, and he responded, "Yes, I feel everyone in the capitol should be punished." Ajay lost the election.

What happens when we put these two mistrusted professions together, the politician and the lawyer, and merge these individuals into one? Is the resulting hybrid an individual who is even less trusted and less respected? No. That individual soars to the top of the trustworthiness list. The individual who is a combination of politician and lawyer becomes a judge. Our best lawyers usually do not become judges because they are making a good living in private practice. Our best politicians usually do not become judges because they aspire to be congressmen, senators and presidents. A politician's ego generally goads him to seek frequent media attention and have his name become "a household by-word." Most judges' exposure to the media is more limited than that of more highly visible politicians. There are, of course, exceptions to these rules. I have met judges who are outstanding lawyers, outstanding politicians, and also, outstanding judges. Unfortunately, those characteristics are not often found in the same person.

In the selection of our judiciary, the old adage, "two wrongs don't make a right," could be altered to say that two wrongs frequently make a judge. In any event, we've made some mistakes over the last 200 years in selecting our judges, by assuming that when characteristics of two of society's least trusted professionals (lawyer and politician) are merged in the same individual, that he becomes highly trustworthy. I have a modest proposal: Let's go all the way. In addition to being a lawyer and a politician, let's require from any person who would be a judicial candidate a signed affidavit certifying that he has sold at least one used car.

Another alternative might be to to limit the judge's power!

Another modest proposal for the selection of judges: utilize their financial compensation more efficiently. Rather than pay salaries from $100,000 per judge, let's fill each existing bench with four janitors at salaries of $25,000 each. Each of the four janitors will be less than one-fourth as expensive to maintain, and they will have acquired humility through their years of service—a requirement would specify that they had been janitors for at least 10 years and that they had not put on airs and called themselves sanitation engineers. We will be guaranteed a larger number of people with humility.

We would have four times the number of judges sharing courtroom space—without the regal pomp required by our current judges, courtrooms can be smaller. Perhaps dockets would move more quickly. They would not demand the prevailing judicial majesty. Would they have the wisdom of our current judges? Only God can answer that question. Wisdom is not necessarily required in or acquired through law school. It is not necessarily required in or acquired through the practice of law. Many human beings acquired their wisdom while toiling in the cotton fields. There is no reason to suspect that under the janitorial judiciary, there would be fewer wise judges than currently.

Education: The jurors will have to fill in the void for many of the janitors who do not have any formal education. This will help the Judge maintain humility. Of course many janitors will be self-educated and will not need assistance. This will allow the juries to maintain strength and grow in power again.

Limitation on the time: After sitting on the bench for five years or so having people bow and scrape to him, the most humble janitor might lose his modesty. So it should be five years on the bench, then back to the broom closet. Obviously, we would lose some good judges that way. But, for the most part, we would have an improvement in the system.

I originally made this proposal while speaking before a group of about 400 conservative, patriotic Americans. I intended it as a joke, but the more I thought about it, the more reasonable it sounded.

I. THE PURPOSE OF THE JUDICIARY

The purpose of the judiciary was, and still should be, fourfold:

A. *To protect individuals from the government; and,*
B. *To protect individuals from the masses.*

C. *To enforce reasonable criminal laws.*

D. *To enforce reasonable civil laws and mediate civil arguments.*

Democracy can be as totalitarian and unfair as monarchy. Alexis de Tocqueville, the French historian who wrote *Democracy in America*[10] could foresee the specter of a totalitarian America due to democracy, run rampant.

The constitutional rights our forefathers gave us should be absolute. The jury should have unlimited power to protect human freedom and property. However, our judicial and appellate checks and balances were, and should again be, a protection against jury excesses or jury violations of constitutional rights. Judicial appellate review is a valuable protection. Judicial control and total veto power over a jury's right to hear the evidence and rule all the facts of a case, is *tyranny.*

"Unless the judge supports jurors, or strong, independent jurors are selected with uncommon perception, the government often uses the jury system as a rubber stamp, because the jurors are only allowed to hear what the government wants them to hear."

CHAPTER IV

LICENSED LAWYERS

"There is an old saying that an attorney straight out of law school does $500 worth of work for $5, and an attorney after a lifetime of practice does $5 worth of work for $500."

A. TO LIE OR NOT TO LIE, THAT IS THE QUESTION

"Whether it is nobler to win the case or collect the fee?" I am going to give you what may or may not be an opportunity to better understand lawyers. My opinions about lawyers are part of the public domain; since my comments have been published in various newspapers and magazines.[1]

I would like to share some of my personal experiences gained while I was outside of the system and compare them to what I learned inside the system.

Jonathan Swift, through his character Lemuel Gulliver, describes English lawyers to the natives of a kingdom inhabited by reasonable, intellectual, honest horses (the Hounyhyms) and half-savage, ungovernable humanoids (the Yahoos) in *Gulliver's Travels*[2] and sets the stage:

"I [Gulliver] said there was a society of men among us, bred up from their youth in the art of proving, by words multiplied for the purpose, that white is black, and black is white; according as they are paid. To this society all the rest of the people are slaves. For example, if my neighbor has a mind to my cow, he has a lawyer to prove that he ought to have my cow from me. I must then hire another to defend my right, it being against all rules of law that any man should be allowed to speak for himself. Now, in this case, I, who am the right owner, am under two great disadvantages: first, my lawyer, being practiced almost from the cradle in defending falsehood, is quite out of his element when he would be an advocate for justice, which is an unnatural office he always attempts with great awkwardness, if not with ill-will. The second disadvantage is, that my lawyer must proceed with great caution, or else he will be reprimanded by the judges, and abhorred by his brethren, as one that would lessen the practice of the law."

It is a maxim among these lawyers that whatever has been done before may legally be done again; and therefore they take special care to record all the decisions formerly made against common justice and the general reason of man-kind. These, under the name of precedents, they produce as authorities to justify the most iniquitous opinions; and the judges never fail of directing accordingly.

In pleading they studiously avoid entering into the merits of the cause, but are loud, violent, and tedious in dwelling upon all circumstances which are not the purpose; after which they consult precedents, adjourn the cause from time to time, and in 10, 20, or 30 years come to an issue.

It is likewise to be observed that this society has a peculiar cant and jargon of their own that no other mortal can understand, and wherein all their laws are written, which they take special care to multiply; whereby they have wholly con-founded the very essence of truth and falsehood, of right and wrong, so that it will take thirty years to decide whether the field left me by my ancestors for six genera-tions belongs to me, or to a stranger three hundred miles off."

B. EARLY EXPERIENCES WITH THE LEGAL SYSTEM

I graduated from college in 1973, took my new bride—who would shortly thereafter give birth to our first child—and left Washington University in St. Louis with my degree in English in hand, prepared to conquer the world, and go to school at night and become a lawyer. Applying to law school and saving up a little money took an entire year.

It wasn't that easy. My scholastic achievements and my degree in English were not worth anything on the job market. I was promoted from a three-month minimum wage position as a clerk at Sears Roebuck & Co. to two months of a better paid position, stocking shoes. The change meant I was no longer a respected clerk wearing a cheap tie. I was a mere peon, stocking shoes. I switched because as a shoe stocker, my pay was raised 40 cents an hour. In addition, I was able to do all my work quickly and then, unseen, was able to study in the shoe closet. I was able to accomplish this because my predecessor had never done any work, and my work was rated exceptionally high when contrasted with his. In a few hours on Monday I was able to do more work than my predecessor had done all week. Shortly thereafter, I began attending real estate school at night because I quickly realized that my wife, child, and law school could not all be supported on a shoe clerk's salary.

The interesting thing about that experience which continues to haunt me is that the American dream, for the most part, did not exist in the department store clerk's world. Most of my co-workers, whenever I confided my ambition to enter law school, let me know that people don't go from stocking shoes to becoming lawyers. I did not fall within the parameters of whatever their mental conception of a lawyer was. People expected doctors and lawyers to come from wealthy families. Why? It's expensive to become a doctor or a lawyer.

Since it was my responsibility to feed my family, and since it was my vision to save money to go to law school, I looked for a higher paying job. Although everyone cries about teachers' inadequate wages, I still earnestly looked for a teaching position because: A) it was one of the things that I always wanted to do, and B) while you don't generally get rich teaching, it pays better than stocking shoes at Sears.

I pored over the help-wanted ads and found that there were numerous openings for collection agents.

They hired practically anyone. I decided to give it a try. The agency I applied to offered me commission in addition to a salary that was larger than I had earned at Sears, although still much smaller than I would be able to make as a teacher. Being a collection agent turned out to be an awful experience!

Even though I was hurting for money, I was only able to stomach collection work for one month. I handed in my resignation and gave them one week's notice at the end of three weeks.

I found it distasteful to coerce money out of the people who, for the most part, through one misfortune or other were unable to pay bills. I embarked on a program of asking people to send in whatever they could. Strangely enough, during my last week of employment there, I collected more money than I had in the first three weeks and collected the third largest amount among 15 collection agents. The people who had the first and second largest amounts had the easiest accounts to collect. If the collection agency business changed significantly and a soft sell were put into effect, they would collect more money. It took me approximately two more weeks to get employment elsewhere.

This time I lied about my educational background. I had been rejected by many companies who did not want to hire someone they considered "overqualified" and who, in their opinion, should be teaching. For that reason and because I looked younger than my advanced 22 years of age, I simply lied, and told them I did not have a college degree. I got the highest paying job of my career to that date. I was a sewage ditch digger working ten hours a day from 8:00 in the morning to 6:30 in the evening.

A young black man was hired the same day I was. He received only $3 an hour to do exactly the same work that I was paid $3.50 an hour to do!

We both worked in the ditch, side by side for a month, and then shared salary information. My co-worker and friend became an ex-friend because I was making more money doing the same job he was doing. My boss raised hell with me. He told me in no uncertain terms that I shouldn't share salary information because the company could end up in a discrimination suit.

I had been a civil rights activist in college. I had marched for equal rights. I had collected food and blankets for individuals who had been discriminated against. Now I was suddenly forced to be a racist through my silence.

Digging sewage ditches is backbreaking work. You get into much better physical condition digging sewage ditches than you do working out in a health club. Your body turns rock hard. You go home every night starving. You stuff yourself, and then you ignore the physical affections of your wife because you fall into exhausted sleep immediately. To deaden the monotonous misery of this sort of life, half the people digging the sewage ditches were constantly drunk or on drugs. The operator of the crane overlooking the sewage ditch and all the supervisors, except one, were white men. Everybody in the ditch was black, except me. There was one black supervisor who had worked his way out of the ditch, after 20 years of service for the company.

I recall one day when the alcoholic, white, crane driver in a state of complete and total intoxication dropped two tons of dirt back into the ditch that had just been scooped up. Unfortunately, he also buried three human beings.

The day before, I had been promoted to being an on-top-of-the-ditch-supervisor. Quite frankly, it was risky, and I was not qualified to do the job. The black man with 20 years of experience making $4.50 an hour was ordered back into the ditch. Taking his place I had received a raise to $5 an hour—a good salary in 1973 for a non-labor-union job. The television reporters arrived on the scene of the accident. The chief in charge at the sewage site at the time of the accident was the alcoholic who had caused the accident. He didn't want to be interviewed. Everyone else was nervous and appeared unwilling to be interviewed. I was interviewed, and that night got to see my dirty face on local television. I'm sure I felt a little guilty over my promotion. I also wouldn't cover for the drunk. I told the newsman that if the black man in the ditch was handling the truck, none of this would have happened. I must have made a better impression as a teenager—when I'd had television exposure as a Golden Gloves champion—than I did as an adult, because the following day I was fired.

While working in the sewer ditches, I discovered some things about law that many lawyers never learn. I learned that poor people have more dealings with the law than middle class people. Rich people use the law; while poor people are ground into mincemeat by it. I learned that people who have terrible, depressing jobs with no chance of promotion or advancement, frequently take drugs, frequently violate the criminal laws, and frequently end up in jail, a victim of circumstances, not free will.

I recall one worker who couldn't get an inspection sticker on his car because he was working every day of the week, ten hours a day. A police officer stopped him and gave him several tickets. This seriously depressed him. He talked about it at work. He was unable to attend the hearings, because missing work would have jeopardized his job. A warrant for his arrest was issued. He received the warrant for his arrest in the mail, and in despair, proceeded to get drunk. He drove home drunk.

The same officer who had previously ticketed him, picked him up and charged him with driving while intoxicated. He was again taken to jail. He couldn't raise the necessary money to pay his fines. He couldn't raise any money for a private lawyer; so he was given a court-appointed attorney. The court appointed lawyer pled guilty for him and got him a probated sentence. He borrowed money from relatives, and arranged a payout scheme where a portion of his salary went to repay his relatives the money they had laid out for his fines.

He was under tremendous stress and seemed to be losing money, getting further behind, despite putting in six days of hard labor a week, sometimes seven. I recall that this gentleman's physical appearance deteriorated, and he seemed to age 10 or 20 years right before my eyes. In addition to his legal and financial problems, he feared that his wife, who was staying home with his child, was having an affair with a next door neighbor.

Although the next door neighbor's family was on welfare, they seemed to be getting by a little better than my co-worker. The man of the house was unemployed. He had reported to the welfare authorities that he had deserted his family. Whenever the welfare authorities checked on his household, this man made sure that he was not home. Another fellow worker in the ditch began to taunt our troubled colleague about his wife's

---

"While working in the sewer ditches, I discovered some things about law that many lawyers never learn."

supposed infidelity. This other worker was drugged every day of the week and was frequently so under the influence that he didn't even know his name, but he knew enough to get under my friend's skin.

The day came when my friend couldn't take the sexual insults any more, and the two fought. When the police arrived on the scene, they arrested my friend, who already had a criminal record because of the traffic violations. He was booked for assault and his probation was revoked.

I went to court to testify to my co-worker's good character. My pay was docked for the entire day, and I was told to stay away from this troublemaker or face termination. As it worked out, I was fired shortly thereafter anyway because of my television appearance. The judge seemed to be unfeeling and uncaring. Most of the time, the court-appointed attorney seemed to be sleeping. At one point, I recall the court-appointed attorney talking extensively to the bailiff while my friend was being questioned by the prosecuting attorney.

Looking back, now, with my legal experience, I believe that he was probably either making arrangements to receive his check for representing the gentleman or getting other appointments. The attorney never talked to my friend about the case, and was completely unprepared. My friend was sentenced to jail for six months. I never saw him again.

I had recently completed enough credits to get my real estate license. A sweet, little-old-lady, who sat next to me in one of my classes asked me about my future aspirations. Upon hearing my reply, she giggled, "Hee, hee, if you become a lawyer, that means you'll be a crook. All lawyers are crooks."

I remember doing something that I would in later years regard as very foolish. I attempted to defend "all lawyers." How could I have done this? At that point I was still idealistic or naive enough to believe that the law and lawyers were generally legitimate.

On two occasions, I took time off from my ditch digging to visit the Texas Employment Commission in an effort to find a better job. Finally I found one. I took the written examination to be a social worker and scored the second highest score on the test. My score was a 96 out of a possible 100. The gentleman who beat me scored a 92 and had been awarded 10 extra points for being a veteran, giving him a 102. He got first shot at the next available government job; I got the second job that came up.

I chose the highest paying job available, which was Welfare Service Technician Two. I still don't know what that designation meant. My pay was $715 a month, the highest regular salary I had ever made in my life—

although, at 14 I had made more money selling snow cones, and the fringe benefits were fantastic. My function was to determine if applicants for Aid to Families with Dependent Children (A.F.D.C.) were qualified for benefits under the guidelines of the program. To receive aid, the household had to consist of at least one child under 18 (preferably under six) and one parent with low or no income. With two parents in the home, it was practically impossible to qualify unless one was totally disabled. All of the families in my caseload were comprised of single mothers with children. I did not have one case of a father physically living with his dependent children.

Families that qualified for this government assistance also received food stamps. It was my job to see that the correct amount of funds and food stamps were distributed. At that time, the formulas for eligibility were extremely flexible and open to an enormous amount of subjective interpretation. In fact, I figured out that anybody could qualify for food stamps by manipulating their personal and professional assets. It was possible for a multimillionaire to legally get food stamps. However, through ignorance of proper procedures, it was also possible to be starving to death and not be able to get food stamps. I had stumbled into yet another inequity in the law.

In the culture of A.F.D.C. recipients, it was important to have children, especially illegitimate children, if an individual wanted to stay on welfare instead of being forced to go to work. Our law was teaching people not to work. Our law was also teaching people to have illegitimate children because they were profitable, although the financial allotment per child was minimal. These children were brought into a world where they would live in poverty, in all probability receive a second-rate education, and probably perpetuate the welfare cycle.

I had strong feelings that the food stamp program wasn't working and wasn't equitable. The A.F.D.C. and food stamp programs penalized intact families with legitimate needs, and, thus encouraged families breaking up. These programs gave no incentive to the recipients who wished to better themselves economically, to stand on their own feet financially, and to fully support their families because any increase in their income caused

"Our law was teaching people not to work. Our law was also teaching people to have illegitimate children because they were profitable, although the financial allotment per child was minimal."

them to lose the necessary benefits that would help them get out of the hole economically. Many of the people who really needed these programs didn't get them either, because they could not figure out how the system worked or they had too much pride. On the other hand, there were people with absolutely no need who received benefits.

This complex web of regulations whereby the government took money away from some people (through taxes) and gave it to other people (through welfare) simply wasn't working! None of my fellow workers came to the same conclusions with the same fact situations. My strong feelings on the subject prompted me to write my second book. My first book had been a religious satire, written while I was in college. It was never published. My book on food stamps was published. I received royalties from it. Circumstances surrounding my attempt to publish this second book brought me additional experience with the legal system, which I will discuss shortly.

Being on the government payroll financially enabled me to attend law school. However, I found this job to be the least moral I had ever held. The standards for appraising my work were ridiculous. I wasn't required to produce anything. Intelligence in this job was a distinct disadvantage. Going up the ladder to a supervisory position was generally achieved by longevity or filling out the forms correctly. Filling out forms correctly had nothing to do with justice, fairness or common sense. I soon learned that all of my required duties for the week could be completed in three or four hours on Monday. I also discovered that when I turned in my paperwork on Monday and reported that I had finished my tasks for the week, I got demerits from my supervisor. Therefore, I elected to do the work Monday morning, study for law school the rest of the week, and on Friday turn in my work.

During my term with the Department for Human Resources, a new government was elected in the State of Texas and new supplies were to be issued. Our supervisors told us in no uncertain terms to use up all the supplies that we had, or we could get into trouble. What did "use" mean? It meant consuming huge stores of legal pads, pens, letter openers, staplers, paper clips and related items. I tried to utilize my supplies but was

"This complex web of regulations whereby the government took money away from some people (through taxes) and gave it to other people (through welfare) simply wasn't working!"

nevertheless censured for not utilizing enough.

Everybody in the department was using more supplies than I. It wasn't fair. I was doing my job, using all the supplies I could, even wasting as many supplies as I could, and my supervisor was still angry with me. I made what, at that time, I regarded as a hasty decision. I took my VW Beetle, put down the back seat, and filled it top to bottom with all sorts of bounty. I crammed in a year's worth of legal pads for law school. I stuffed in staplers, date stampers, letter openers and paper clips, filling the back of my VW. I took my supplies home, unloaded them, and returned.

Shortly thereafter my supervisor again condemned me. She told me, "I've been instructed to empty that supply cabinet, and you're the only one in my department who is not doing his share." I was never able, because of the small size of my car, to do my share, but I was able to completely fill the VW Beetle up with supplies three times, enabling me to get through my three years of law school and the first three months of law practice without purchasing office supplies. Still, I had taken less than my allotment, and I remained on my supervisor's hostility list.

The new government took office, new supplies were bought, and the supply room was filled. I noticed that although we were no longer being required to take large amounts of supplies home, my fellow workers still felt compelled to do so.

During my social work career, I wrote the book *"How to Apply For and Receive Food Stamps Regardless of Your Financial Position."* Through publication of this work, I hoped to obtain enough money to finish putting myself through law school and support my family in a lifestyle above that to which they had become accustomed. By that time, I had two children and a wife, and every dollar counted. I gave a handwritten copy of my book to a woman who advertised herself as a publisher.

The woman had the book typed. She then proceeded to tell me that it needed a great deal of work, and that I was going to have to come up with some money to market the book. This had not been our original deal. She was supposed to handle my book purely on a percentage basis. I was angry, and I told her so. I demanded my book back, but she refused to give it to me. I tried to figure out how to file a lawsuit against her in order to get my book back. I could not even afford the filing fees, which, at that time, were about $50.

I approached sheriffs, policemen, constables, and judges with my problem. Everyone let me know that the system had no interest whatsoever in me or my case. Through my research, I discovered that the woman was using an assumed name. Under Texas law using an assumed name required the individual to pay up to $200 a day fine if the assumed name was not filed with proper records.

I sued her in a justice of the peace court for violating a criminal law. I also demanded the return of my book. Filing fees in this small claims court were approximately $10. Legally, I was not entitled to sue her under a criminal statute. In addition, the court's maximum fine for that offense was $200. The court had no authority to order her to return my book. However, I pursued it there because it was the only place I could afford to go and no one stopped me!

Judge Pacetti made the following ruling: The woman who had taken my book had to give it back. If she didn't give it back, he threatened to fine her a lot of money. He also ordered her to either destroy the typewritten copy of my book or give the typewritten copy of my book back to me. He told me that as a compromise for accepting this judgment, if she followed these rules, she would not have to pay any fine and she would not have to pay my court cost of $10. It sounded fair, I agreed. Over the years I have learned the wisdom of this very wise judge: He works very hard to suggest a fair, neutral meeting point both parties can accept. He generally follows the law very closely but often can be counted on to bend it a little to avoid an injustice.

My opponent in this important judicial hearing was represented by counsel—a large man, appearing to be in his mid-40s. Prior to the hearing, the attorney paternalistically tried to persuade me not to pursue my case and to sit out in the hallway with him and chat. I categorically refused. I told him that nothing could be resolved unless they handed me my book and the typed version of the book prior to the hearing. The defendant refused. She said she wouldn't give me my copy back or the typed copy unless I paid her a sum of money which vastly exceeded my resources—and probably exceeded the value of the book. By this time she had wrongfully withheld my book on food stamps for about eight months, and the book's limited value had become even more diminished because there had been two changes in the law.

Following the verdict, the attorney and I left the court room and went to my opponent's office. The lawyer tried without success to get the judge to vacate his opinion. The attorney handed me a release form which he'd typed out. The release stated that I gave up all rights to sue, that I agreed I had received the book, and that the defendant could keep her typewritten version of my book. I refused to sign. The attorney then told me I would not get my book back. After more verbiage from me, he drafted another release form which was considerably more reasonable but still unacceptable to me. The release stated that I had received the book, and that I agreed to allow the defendant to keep the typewritten copy. Again I refused, telling him that that was not what the judge had ordered. He told me that he would go back to the judge and convince the judge that I was being unreasonable. I don't believe that the attorney would have been able to influence this judge, who was a fair and decent man. Nevertheless, I was getting frustrated. I had wasted an entire day in these proceedings. I decided to use "self help." The book, in handwritten form, was simply sitting on the desk.

I just picked it up. The attorney told me that this act would have grave consequences. He claimed that he would personally press charges, that I could end up in jail, and that I was a brash and difficult young man. I invited him out into the hallway and went into the hall myself. When he didn't follow me, I left. I did not ever receive the typewritten version of my manuscript, however, I don't think that the defendant ever derived any advantage from stealing it. The attorney never took any action against me. I decided not to go back into court because of the expense of taking a day off.

That particular attorney now sits on the bench of the Supreme Court of the State of Texas. The manuscript was later published, and I received somewhere in the neighborhood of $10 in royalties.

This summary of my pre-law school experiences with lawyers, courts and government bureaucracy reveals the seeds of some of the concepts which later blossomed forth in *The Underground Lawyer*. Our personalities are molded by our experiences and our environments. As a result of these experiences and those of my next decade, I learned that there are some excellent judges and there are some bad judges. There are some honest attorneys and there are some dishonest attorneys. I also learned that life teaches valuable lessons omitted from the law school curriculum.

C. LAWYERS ON THE SCALE OF JUSTICE

The various bar systems in the United States are not set up for the

"...life teaches valuable lessons omitted from the law school curriculum."

public's benefit. They are merely labor unions organized for the benefit of attorney members. Each of the 50 states has its own state bar association. Each association has slightly different rules. There are various national organizations for lawyers, of which the American Bar Association, is the largest and most conservative. I am not a member of the ABA, by choice. It is similar in nature to the American Medical Association (AMA) which is a national voluntary association of doctors. The purpose of both of these organizations is to: A) protect and promote the interests of its members, who are generally the most conservative members of the various state unions, and B) to present and promulgate propaganda nationwide that is favorable to the interests of those members and to increase their prestige and income.

Fortunately for the First Amendment, the AMA and the ABA often fight each other, thus cutting down on some of the incredible powers that they would have if these giants cooperated. However, on many issues these two unions agree, and when that's the case, public interest be damned! The two, combined, all-powerful unions prevail. These two, mighty unions favor government regulation and intervention in their spheres of influence; however, they want to be the executors of the regulations. They want to expand government regulation over the medical and legal fields, but they want it to be done under the auspices of the unions themselves. They do not want non-doctors or non-lawyers to be wielding government machinery to control their professions. Rather, they want the government to be a tool in their hands, to limit numbers in the profession, and to protect the union's rigid control over their professions. Both organizations strive to make entry into the various state unions as difficult as possible in order to keep down the numbers. Since the members of both unions make substantially more than the average income of people who are not members, most professionals want in.

Many non-union members of various nationwide groups, such as Help Abolish Legal Tyranny (HALT) or Ralph Nader's consumer organization try to educate individuals as consumers of legal services, and attempt to strip away the mystery that enshrouds legal processes. Of course, these groups have come under attack by various state bar associations as encouraging the unauthorized practice of law.

What is a lawyer? He or she is a human being who puts his pants (or

"The various bar systems in the United States are not set up for the public's benefit."

her pantyhose) on the same as you do, one leg at a time. The individual has a college degree, and as a general rule has been to law school and obtained a law degree. Most newly licensed lawyers initially do not have as much practical knowledge of working law as you will have when you've finished this book. Although that person is permitted to go out and practice as a member in the monopoly union of law without some type of apprenticeship, he is a babe in the woods.

Because power corrupts, and absolute power corrupts absolutely, lawyers and doctors tend to become more arrogant and more dishonest than the public as a whole. There are dishonest plumbers, dishonest fast-food cooks, and dishonest mechanics. There are dishonest auto salesmen, used car dealers and presidents. There are dishonest lawyers, too. Because lawyers are exposed to more power than most people, and because lawyers are exposed to more politics than most people, lawyers as a group tend to be less honest than most people.

Since judges generally do not punish lawyers who lie, lawyers lie in court all the time. Since lawyers watch individuals on the stand lie under oath, and since they do not tell on their clients, lawyers become accustomed to living with lies, dealing in lies, and lying.

The legal profession consists of a large number of human beings who come into it generally seeking truth. Later on, when they find portions of the truth, they run. Why? Because the nature of power is to corrupt and the nature of corruption is injustice. As our system becomes increasingly corrupt, justice becomes increasingly harder to find.

I know some lawyers who will not lie. I would estimate that those lawyers constitute fewer than half of the lawyers I deal with on a daily basis. Most lawyers, honest or dishonest, would agree there is a high level of dishonesty in the legal profession. I believe that the incidence of honesty in the general population is considerably higher than this. For that reason, I have learned that the wise words of the elderly lady who poked fun at me with her joke about my chosen profession's dishonesty were, for the most part, true. There are a lot of crooked lawyers.

Against them, I have used what I regard as a surprise weapon which has enabled me to win most of my cases. I thoroughly prepare for trial, whereas many lawyers go to trial not even knowing their client's name or

---

"Most newly licensed lawyers initially do not have as much practical knowledge of working law as you will have when you've finished this book."

---

any of the facts about the client's case. I instruct all of my clients to tell the truth, both the good and bad things about their case. As a general rule, this will often convince the jury, because the other side will often lie. The amazing thing about the jury system is that even with all the strange and unfair rules for selecting them, if you program in the proper facts, the jury will often act like a computer and will come up with a commendable conclusion. The jury will, for the most part, listen to the evidence. The jury will also examine your feet, your shoes, your hair, your eyes, the color of your skin, whether or not your tie contrasts with your suit, and whether or not you are sweating. The jurors will discuss all this. After considering both the relevant and the irrelevant, the jurors will enter all these variables into their collective mental computer and often come up with information that lawyers on both sides, clients on both sides, and the judge were not aware of.

Sometimes the jurors will make ridiculous decisions. I have won some cases that I had absolutely no right to win because I was prepared and because my clients testified truthfully. There were times when the story that came out was not an honest version of the facts because I used the truth in half measures to reflect a changed version to the jurors. As I have advanced in my career, refined my skills and faced better competition, I have attempted to only represent human beings whose position I believe in and whom I care about. I honestly hope to win these cases, because our cause is just. For this reason, it has become increasingly important for me to try to get the whole truth before the jury. As a young lawyer starting out and having difficulty feeding my family, I sometimes took cases which compromised my principles. As a slightly older lawyer with experience and a dollar or two in my pocket, I can afford to live with most of my principles intact.

A lawyer is a lot like an insurance man, a store clerk, an auto mechanic, or you. The lawyer's first general goal is to make a living. There are some very, very good lawyers who win almost all their cases, but are not very good at making a living. Some lawyers are very, very good at making a living, but their professional skills are deplorable. One lawyer who has been practicing several years longer than I have holds himself out as a trial specialist. In nearly 15 years of law practice, he has never won a single jury trial! He never prepares properly, always expects to win, and charges $300

"Many lawyers go to trial not even knowing their client's name or any of the facts about the client's case."

an hour (average rates vary from anywhere from $75 an hour to $200 an hour). This lawyer does not do a lot of repeat business with the same clients.

However, the majority of his cases settle because most lawyers are not willing to go to court under any circumstances. They are afraid to go to court because they are afraid to look foolish. Most of them went to court one or two times, were humiliated and choose not to go through the experience again. They were humiliated, because they were unprepared. They went up against someone else who was somewhat more prepared, or they went up against a government attorney who had an enormous advantage over them regardless of whether he or she was prepared, and they suffered a humiliating defeat.

Less than one percent of the those licensed to practice law try cases on a regular basis. Most people who hold themselves out as trial specialists try anywhere from two to five cases a year. It is very unusual for an attorney to try more than five cases per year although there are exceptions. There are lawyers (mostly handling small criminal cases) who cram in 20 to 30 trials in a year. These constitute less than one-tenth of one percent of the licensed attorneys, and few of them continue at that pace for very long.

Because the lawyer I mentioned previously settles many cases favorably to his clients, his opponents are scared of him. Unlike most lawyers, he will try cases. Unlike most lawyers, he still believes he is going to win the next case. Like most lawyers, he doesn't do much pretrial preparation and generally expects to win because he believes he has an enormous amount of personal charisma.

I do not expect him to maintain his track record of losing all his jury trials for another decade and a half, neither do I expect him to start winning most of his cases. As his reputation increases and his fees go up, the quality of his competition increases and the odds of his winning each individual case continues to decrease. However, his ability continues to increase. If you lose 100 races, statistically sooner or later you're going to win one, especially if your speed does not decrease. The greatest lawyer in the world has a chance of losing a jury trial to the worst lawyer in the world. There are no foolproof methods of predicting jury decisions.

Of course, even the very best lawyer in the world will not do his very best work if he is starving to death. I have seen excellent lawyers lose because they did not have the financial ability to properly prepare the case, and their concentration was distracted because they were worried about paying office rent and their utility bills. Given an equal fact situation and equally credible witnesses on both sides, a good lawyer will beat a bad or incompetent lawyer nine times out of ten. Given an unfair situation against him, a good lawyer will still probably beat the bad lawyer, the majority of the time.

An attorney I know has coined the phrase "Lose your way to riches." I have tried cases with this man, and I regard him as one of the most competent attorneys I've ever met. After winning a long string of cases, he stumbled upon the following formula which made him a multimillionaire: A) Take highly publicized cases, regardless of their financial benefit. B) Charge the largest up-front fee that you can get, forcing the client to pay you everything the client has or can borrow, and if the client is rich, double the fee. C) Do an enormous amount of pretrial research because you can bill out the research at any rate since the client is not privy to the amount of time necessary to do research, and take a lot of the same type of cases over and over again, so that you can bill the same full amount to the next person for the work done. D) Don't do any other pretrial work. If you spend your time with the witnesses, or if you spend your time preparing for the case factually, you will be spending time that you could be using collecting fees and actually trying cases. E) Get the case to trial as quickly as possible because once the trial is over, you're finished with the client, and you have obtained the maximum benefit that you can receive from the client: the client's money. Collect the money, get the case to trial, and finish.

Because of the attorney's incredible amount of personal ability, he wins more cases than he should with his minimal amount of preparation. I recall one mixed victory which this gentleman and I achieved. He brought me in as co-counsel because he wanted to win the case, and he knew that I would prepare diligently for it. There were many difficulties with this case, including the fact that our client had waived his rights more than a dozen times—in writing.

Our client had been offered a $15,000 settlement, which probably cheated the client, but since the client had signed his rights away annually for nearly 12 years, I felt that we had very little chance of winning the case. We were paid in advance. We hoped for a victory in the $1 million range, and we received a jury verdict of approximately $35,000. The jury

> *"Given an unfair situation against him, a good lawyer will still probably beat the bad lawyer, a great majority of the time."*

awarded $1500 in damages and $33,500 in legal fees! Since the client had paid us in advance in full, the entire sum went to the client. I considered it a loss. The client, who received about the same $15,000 he would have received without going to trial, had mixed emotions about the outcome. But my attorney friend considered it a major victory.

This was the first victory in my career that I had ever had in which the client did not receive at least three times the maximum amount of the settlement offered prior to trial. The $35,000 judgment did, however, trigger the downfall of the opposing party's company. Nevertheless, I was quite disappointed. My friend put his arm around my shoulders and walked off with me and asked me, "Why are you so depressed?" "Because," I responded, "we lost." My friend looked at me incredulously. "We didn't lose," he said, "the client lost. We won."

I'm appalled at the nonchalant attitude of some attorneys after a loss. They calmly bid their clients "Adieu" as these "losers" are marched off to jail or slink away into bankruptcy; then they go out and have a beer with the opposing counsel. Sometimes I can do this. But as a general rule I am so accustomed to winning that on those occasions when I suffer a loss, I am a poor loser. I consider a case a loss if the client is unhappy when it's over. I was a poor loser when I lost a boxing match, and I am a poor loser when I lose a legal match, especially if I am convinced, I represented good over evil.

One example comes to mind. Joe Izen (also known as the Great Izen, see chapter V. Part A.) brought me into a case because the opposing counsel was a bully. He had a bad habit of poking his finger into your chest and pushing on you in order to make his point in conversation. I did not know that I was being brought in because of my amateur boxing career; I thought I was needed for my legal expertise.

Our client was suing two large companies and claiming that because both of them had worked together on a project, they should both be jointly liable for his injury which had occurred in the course of his work. One company was covered by worker's compensation, which meant that our client could not receive full value for the company's negligence. The other company was not under worker's compensation and faced greater liability if negligence was proven. However, that company claimed that it had merely hired the other company as an independent contractor, and that it had no responsibility for our client's injury. The dispute boiled down to the question of whether one company simply purchased the services of the other, or whether they were partners, working together toward a mutual common goal. It was our position that they were partners. It was our opponent's position that they were not.

While my co-counsel was handling a portion of the trial, I had stepped outside of the courtroom into the hall to interview the next witness. The man with whom I was attempting to speak was an employee of the company which had been covered by the workers' compensation. His company's attorney had no objection to my questioning him.

Attorney Bruce Littig, who was representing the other company in the dispute, stood in my way when I tried to talk to the witness. In spite of my attempts at politeness, the bullying lawyer began poking me in the chest. I tried to move around him, and he grabbed my shirt with his hands. It had been a decade since I had been involved in any type of fisticuffs. I was still trying to be diplomatic. I asked Littig one final time to get his hands off me. He ignored my request. Instead, he started shaking me. I popped him with a right cross. He dropped like a rock, and all of my animal instincts rushed to the surface. I fell on top of him and began banging his head on the floor.

My client, a powerful labor union man, came over and pulled me off him. I was a little bit shaken up. While my adversary was on the floor taking a short nap, I went over to my client's chief witness and asked him what he saw. My labor union witness replied, "Mr. Minns, what did you see?" I told him I was defending myself. He said, "That's what I saw, Mr. Minns." I then walked over to the other witness I had been attempting to talk to. "Sir, I'm sorry that you had to witness this display of violence." The man was built like a tank. He was about six feet tall, weighed about 250 pounds, had rock-like, muscular arms, and a big earthy grin on his face revealing several missing teeth. His whole body shook, and he laughed as he answered, "Mr. Minns, this sort of thing happens out on the docks all the time. I wouldn't worry about it."

I pondered my next question. This man worked for a company that was opposing my client in litigation, even though he was supposed to be a neutral witness. With some degree of concern I asked, "What did you see?" He gave me a soliloquy: "Mr. Minns. I'm down here to back my company, and I'm gonna have to do that. I know you understand that. I don't personally like Mr. Littig. I'll tell you, I'm gonna do what I came here to do, but, I'm not gonna help that blank, blank, I didn't see nothin', Mr. Minns."

My opponent got up off the ground, blood streaming down his head, and rushed into the courtroom. My co-counsel Joe Izen was conducting cross-examination at the time. I completed my interview of the witness shortly after Littig had left the scene. I expected that Littig was now before the judge, causing me problems, but I was not going to enter the courtroom unprepared. I entered the courtroom with the witness and approached the bench. The judge spoke to me, "Mr. Minns, the rule has been invoked; are you bringing a witness in?" I didn't understand. Apparently nothing had happened as a result of the physical dispute. "Excuse me, your honor," I apologized, and I instructed the "witness" to go wait out in the hall. The trial proceeded for the remainder of the day, and nobody said anything, although I frequently looked over at our opponent and could see the dried blood congealed on his face.

The following day, I got together with my co-counsel to find out what had happened. I learned that my opponent had walked back into the courtroom and yelled out loud, "He hit me!" Everyone looked at him for a few seconds, stunned, as the blood rushed down his face. Izen looked at him sternly and said: "Mr. Littig, please be quiet, I'm conducting cross examination." Littig sat down quietly. Shortly after that, I made my entrance into the courtroom. Nothing else was ever said for the balance of the trial. No other inquiry was made.

At the end of the day, my co-counsel went into the judge's chambers. The judge, prior to discussing the point of law he had on the agenda, asked him, "Mr. Izen, the court's not stupid. What happened between Mr. Minns and Mr. Littig?"

"Well," Izen explained, "It's like two bulls in rutting season, scratching their paws at the ground, and going to charge at each other. One of the bulls finds out he doesn't have any horns, but it's too late." The judge laughed. To this day, the judge never has discussed this incident with me.

D. LOI NGO AND MR. CHO

At one point in my career, I had the privilege of working at the international law firm of William Y. Sim. I was exposed to many worlds I had never seen before.

Bill Sim is a remarkable man who had immigrated from Hong Kong to the United States. Here, he put himself through college and pharmacy school as a bartender. After graduating he moonlighted. By day he sold prescription drugs to support his family; by night, he studied law. After law school graduation, he started his law practice on the side. In a year his firm had grown to the point where he could afford to quit the pharmacy, and he became a full-time lawyer.

When I met him, he was specializing in immigration law. He had five Chinese secretaries who all spoke at least two, usually four, languages fluently. Although he faced competition from 100-man law firms, Sim's office pulled in the largest number of immigration clients in the southwestern United States. Aside from getting rich, Sim was acknowledged as the expert on immigration law. He was always a gracious host to the international clientele he serviced. His competitors were trying, unsuccessfully, to make a dent in his practice by offering other legal services as well as immigration. Sim decided to hire one lawyer who could handle all these other legal services his clients might need.

At this point in my career—after a difficult divorce, the break-up of my law partnership, and a year of part-time work while being a single parent raising a three-and four-year-old—the prospect of joining Bill Sim's firm was attractive to me. Bill is one of the finest lawyer-businessmen I've ever met. He had all the tools: he worked hard, had good judgment, and had a good organization. His clients came in from over the world, although a majority of them came from Hong Kong and Taiwan.

The firm hired a secretary for me, but it was my job to turn her into a legal secretary. Within 30 days we established a fully functioning law office subsidiary to handle non-immigration matters.

Appointments were set up McDonald's style. Each hour I saw new clients. Different secretaries had to be called in to interpret, depending on the client's language. Although I complained about the lack of preparation time, during two years of general practice and trial work we won every single case we tried.

One day in early 1981, I arrived in my office at 8 a.m. to find a nine-member Chinese-Vietnamese army—the Ngo family—waiting at my door for their 11 a.m. appointment. The English pronunciation of their name was "No". I changed it to "New" to avoid the negative connotations of the word "no" before a jury. The first order of the morning was to try to find a common language and then wait until the appropriate secretary came in. The Ngo's spoke Mandarin which is Mainland China's chief language, Cantonese which is the language of Hong Kong and Taiwan, plus Vietnamese and French. Before we got started, a tenth family member arrived: Loi Ngo's daughter, Kiet. She was about five-feet tall, with dark, exotic eyes; long, black hair; remarkably doll-like features; and wore no make-up. She was polite and very charming.

Kiet, a former English teacher, spoke proper English better than I.

Proper English is a language very similar to American so we were able to communicate.

The Ngos' ancestors had migrated more than a 100 years ago to Vietnam. Their ancestors had been wealthy in China, but the government had stolen everything so they fled to Vietnam where they built another family fortune which, in the course of time, was stolen from them by the communists. Escaping with the clothes on their back and their lives barely intact, they trekked through Cambodia and finally ended up in the ocean on a small boat.

Although thousands of people in similar situations died at the hands of soldiers in Vietnam, or in Cambodian slave camps, or had drowned in the ocean, the Ngos managed to reach their new home: a filthy, low rent, high-crime American apartment. For two years, Ngo, his family, and their extended family of in-laws (two daughters and two sons had now married) saved money to buy a home. In two years, the labor of 20 people amassed $16,000 and Ngo went house hunting.

Unfortunately, Ngo met Ronald Cho. Cho was also Chinese-Vietnamese, but he had come by way of Hong Kong after escaping from Red China. He had left his family in China. In America, Cho obtained a master's degree from the University of Houston. Cho's wife became an optometrist and Cho became a builder.

While Ngo spoke no English, his compadre knew everything about America—especially home building. Cho agreed to build the Ngo residence. He first separated Ngo from the $16,000 cash, pocketed the money obtained a loan commitment to buy a lot and build on it.

The house went up, but it wasn't finished on schedule. Cho told Ngo he'd finish it later. The Ngos were dismayed to discover that the house fell far short of the quality custom built home Cho had promised them.

Cho's advertisement called for custom doors, but the doors on the house were cheap and were not sanded down or painted. The contract also provided for a garage and a garage door opener—but the door opener was missing. Cho refused to make the necessary corrections. Ngo asked for his $16,000 back. Cho said "No. Buy now or lose your money."

Ngo was furious but also frightened. He knew nothing of American law and spoke no English. At the time, the interest rate was 12.75 percent—up a full percent since Ngo started negotiating with Cho. The Ngo's entire family savings were at risk. Worse, the bank told him the rate would soon go to 13 percent and then Ngo could not qualify for the loan. Interest rates were skyrocketing at this time, and the bank was an old ally of Cho's and helped him extort and cajole Ngo.

Cho demanded and got a major concession. They agreed that Ngo would write Cho a postdated check, and Cho would fix the house. The deal was made. The sale was consummated, but Cho did no repair work.

In fact, once Ngo's family moved in, even more defects became apparent, the foundation was cracked, the floors were uneven and cracking, the roof was improperly installed and the attic insulation was installed upside down. During the first rain, the house flooded. Cho had not supervised the individuals who built the various sections of the house, and he had used the cheapest materials available—contrary to his advertisement that he used only the finest.

The Ngo family was distressed about the house, but their primary concern was hiring a lawyer to defend Papa on the criminal charges that Cho had brought against him: writing a hot check.

When it had become apparent that Cho had no intentions of repairing the defects in the house, Ngo took steps to prevent Cho from obtaining the funds from the postdated check. Not knowing how to stop payment on the check, Ngo simply withdrew all his money from the account. When the check was presented to the bank, it was returned for insufficient funds and Cho threatened Ngo with criminal conviction, jail, and deportation back to Vietnam for execution.

Ngo believed this powerful argument but was prepared to risk it all until Cho used his trump card—he threatened to prevent Ngo's family from getting their American citizenship. The family turned to Bill Sim for help. Sim allowed me to take the case at a loss.

There are thousands of cases like this in America every day. Most attorneys never handle any of them. The few who do can only handle a select number or go out of business. My personal way of dealing with such situations is to attempt to bring about a fast, semi-fair, mutually agreed on remedy. If that approach fails, I have to decide if I can afford to take the case. I have to weigh a number of factors: How serious is the situation? How much work must be done? Is there any potential for profit? And last, but not least, is there a person involved whose actions cry out for him to be sued?

I called Cho on the phone and let him decide. He could keep his dishonest profit and just leave the Ngo family alone, or he could go through with his action in criminal court. If he did, he had to be prepared to bet his entire company on winning a conviction because if he lost, it would be war. He chose to fight. He told me he'd see me in court.

Although Cho's threats about the seriousness of a conviction were exaggerated distortions, a conviction would give Ngo a criminal record and would have complicated the family's immigration situation. A conviction could also be used against him in a civil suit which Cho threatened to file.

Prior to trial, I pleaded with the district attorney to drop the charges. He kept asking me questions. I finally realized he was only trying to learn as much as he could about our defense, and I gave up. He made a few special deal settlement offers which I rejected, and we picked our jury.

Cho's testimony was bad. There were too many lies, too many holes, and he got angry on the stand.

My defense: Papa Ngo was a good man. Cho was a bad man.

I also had a witness rarer than a unicorn—an honest banker. Papa's banker, without compensation, testified to Ngo's honesty, integrity and genuine intent. Our translator was Ngo's beautiful daughter Kiet, who dramatically and effectively conveyed Papa's story. Our six-person, all male jury practically rose out of its box to absorb her every word and motion. In closing arguments, over the prosecutor's objections and judicial threats, I told the story of the Ngo's. I expected tears. There were none. The jury was filled with anger and hatred. I wondered, had I done something wrong?

The jurors marched off to the jury room leaving the evidence behind. The bailiff gathered it up and proceeded to the jury room. But before he could open the door, a juror called out: we're ready. They had not deliberated a full 60 seconds, which is an unusual situation to say the least. Usually, the longer the jury takes in a criminal case—meaning there is doubt about the charges—the greater chance for a not guilty verdict.

The verdict: Not Guilty! Again, another jury doing justice and not fitting into a stereotype. The jurors wanted to lynch Cho. They had no interest in the judge's instructions or the laws on hot checks. They knew Ngo was a good man and deserved to be found not guilty.

Cho had bluffed, and we called him on it. We sued him for damages for his incompetent construction work, for his deceptive advertising and for abusing the legal process by filing false charges against Ngo. Cho filed a counterclaim for his bad check. We went through hearings and depositions and traded insults for five years. Cho ran through three lawyers before trial, and eventually had a fourth. All four were promised large sums which never materialized. We were set for trial before Judge Shearn

"A witness rarer than a unicorn—an honest banker."

Smith, a man I personally liked but whom my ex-partner had sued and taken to the U.S. Supreme Court in a civil rights case. I had been the unlucky lawyer who handled the only federal hearing against this judge, when Izen set the hearing but was unavailable for the proceedings. He was not my first choice for a judge.

We offered to settle for $15,000 cash, which was about half of what I expected to win if we had a fair trial. Both Ngo and I were broke and wanted to avoid the uncertainty of trial. I was now on my own, without the money and subsidy of my former employer and friend, Bill Sim. Cho refused the offer.

The trial lasted a week. Judge Smith gave me hell most of the week before he started seeing the justice of Ngo's cause and slowly changed his attitude.

The jury found Cho guilty of using deceptive trade practices and awarded us $50,000 in damages. We had only asked for $40,000. In Texas, a finding of deceptive trade practices gives rise to triple damages, so the $50,000 in damages became $150,000. Interest for five years and court costs were also added in, bringing the total judgment very near $160,000! Cho was awarded no money for his claim regarding the bounced check. The Ngos were thrilled and Cho was furious.

A fifth lawyer handled his unsuccessful appeal. A sixth lawyer was brought in to handle Cho's bankruptcy. Cho had played "Bet the Company" and had lost—his company closed down.

The moral is: Sometimes justice prevails and sometimes it pays. Occasionally, it does both.

Cho had run through enough lawyers to start his own law firm. He had two complete trials: the first paid for by the taxpayers, the second not paid for at all. A bevy of civil lawyers, an appellate lawyer and a bankruptcy lawyer all worked on his behalf. The district attorney from the criminal trial appeared and testified at the civil trial. When the last lawyer filed Cho's bankruptcy, I noticed the names of all his past lawyers whose bills were being wiped out. Some of them were mean, some stupid and some were first rate. All worked for free. If they had prevailed, an injustice would have been done.

The lesson is: if you have a good line, you may be able to sell your suit to a lawyer for a free ride.

E. SPECIALIZATION AND NETWORKING

Texas, California and several other states have a program called certification and specialization. The State Bar of Texas requires that when uncertified lawyers advertise, their advertisements must clearly state "Not certified by the Board of Legal Specialization."

Attorneys must meet certain qualifications to be board certified, including: obtaining recommendations from judges and other attorneys, taking certain courses, trying a certain number of cases as lead counsel, and passing a six-hour examination. The fields in which specialty certification is offered include civil litigation, bankruptcy, family law, tax law, personal injury, criminal law and several others.

Does being board certified in a given area mean that an attorney is extremely competent? Not necessarily. Does being certified as a civil trial law specialist guarantee that the attorney has ever won a single civil trial? No! Winning cases is not a criteria. As a matter of fact, an attorney can lose every case he's ever tried in his legal career for 20 years and qualify for certification. Being certified only indicates that an attorney has tried between five and seven cases in the area of certification depending on the state and the area of certification—even though he might have lost all of them.

The label "board certified" could be misleading to the consumer of legal services. While it is a guarantee of a certain amount of knowledge and experience, it does not guarantee expertise. Anyone who hires an attorney, certified or not, should ask the attorney if he has ever done any trial work. Even if you're merely having a will drawn up, or a real estate document drafted, it doesn't hurt to find out if the attorney has ever won a jury trial.

If your prospective attorney has never been to trial, he may be less qualified to answer your questions as to what might happen if a dispute arises than a retired plumber who sits in a courtroom and watches jury trials day in and day out. Even a probate expert with 30 years of experience who has only handled uncontested wills, can suffer humiliating defeat at the hands of a zealous young lawyer who is vigorous in trial advocacy.

Every lawyer, no matter what his practice speciality is, needs to have

"Anyone who hires an attorney, certified or not, should ask the attorney if he has ever done any trial work."

some experience in the other related areas of the law, otherwise he is operating in a vacuum. In the real world, you do not have a pure specialization of law with out any other areas of law intervening.

Although a lawyer might choose to be a generalist, he can still have access to extensive specialized help if he isn't too proud to seek the assistance of specialists in other fields. Most highly sophisticated real estate investors know more about real estate law than the average attorney who does very little real estate work. If attorneys are not too proud to use this resource, they can obtain valuable assistance from non-lawyers who have developed expertise in a particular specialized area.

Most professional criminals know more about criminal law than the average general practice lawyer knows. Everybody knows that the Fifth Amendment gives you the right to not testify against yourself, but most people who are not involved in the current criminal law system don't know that you should keep your mouth shut when questioned by FBI agents, police or other law enforcement officers because they are often trying to put together a case against you.

Court reporters, clerks, law enforcement officials and even insurance adjusters have expertise that a wise lawyer can use. The lawyer who disdains resource people outside the legal profession ignores a treasure chest of knowledge that's available to him.

I think the ideal for a lawyer who has opted for a general practice is to have two or three capable, highly trained legal assistants. They must all be able to write coherently, and their particular personal talents may run the gamut of other skills that benefit a law office, including individuals who love research, those with technological skills for operating videotape equipment and those who are good at negotiating to bring clients and their opposing parties to reasonable settlements.

It is also helpful for an experienced attorney to have in his office or available to help him one or two younger, less experienced attorneys who can fill in for him on hearings or depositions or for signing motions when he is out of town—tasks that must be performed by a union member with a bar card.

No attorney should be without several peers in the profession who provide support systems. They can toss around legal theories and experiences and bounce ideas off each other.

"Most professional criminals know more about criminal law than the average general practice lawyer knows."

To round out the network, a general practice attorney should have some relationships with colleagues who have become specialists in particular legal fields.

In my practice, I have become acquainted with many specialists whom I hold in high esteem. If I have a specific question, I don't hesitate to call them. Sometimes, it is more efficient to ask a trusted colleague for an answer than to re-invent the wheel and spend hours researching the matter yourself.

F. FEES: THE BOTTOM LINE

The lawyer sometimes forgets that the client is in his office because he came in there for help. The lawyer may think the client came only to pay fees. The client sometimes forgets the lawyer didn't cause the problem that induced the client to come in and that a zeal to pursue justice is not his only motivation—he wants to make a buck. When client and lawyer have these respective views, and neither is honest about it, there will be an unhappy relationship. Some of the worst lawyers sincerely promise each client the world cheap or for free for the sake of justice. These guys seldom have the bucks to push a case properly and often don't stay open in private practice. Lawyers charge differently for their services, depending on the nature of the case. One method is called the flat fee. If the cost of a job can be calculated down almost to the penny, such as setting up a corporation or handling an uncontested divorce, this is a great way for a client to proceed. The lawyer and the client both know exactly what they are getting into, and the matter proceeds to a prompt resolution. The flat fee allows the client to know he will get the work done for a fixed amount, and allows the lawyer to know exactly how much profit he'll derive for the time he has to put into the assignment.

For most other types of work, charging flat fees can be dangerous. In criminal law, a flat fee may work to the detriment of the client. A lawyer, logically, will try to get the most that he can for the case. The client will want the lowest fee possible for the case. If the client pays the lawyer too low a fee, even if the lawyer is an excellent attorney , he might not be able to put in enough time to win the case.

However, flat fees seems to prevail in a lot of criminal work, and there's a good reason for it. Human life and freedom is not as important in our legal system as property. For that reason, criminal cases proceed to trial much more quickly than cases involving property rights or money damages, and they can be finished much more quickly. The attorney doesn't have to wait for years and years for the case to come to trial, and for the fee to be paid. For that reason, flat fees in criminal cases make a lot of sense and are frequently used. I have seen flat fees as small as $50 for a traffic ticket and as large as $1 million for a capital offense.

When an attorney accepts a flat fee encompassing the entire service to be rendered, i.e. $1,500 for a bankruptcy or $15,000 for a defense against a failure to file tax returns charge, even if the case turns out to be more complex or time consuming than the attorney had originally expected, he should not request additional fees. If the client is going to pay this flat fee sum over a period of time, a contract between the attorney and client should specify the dates on which the payments are to be made. Most

"Flat fees seem to prevail in a lot of criminal work, and there's a good reason for it. Human life and freedom is not as important in our legal system as property."

lawyers, on flat fee criminal cases, demand as much up front as they can get because fees on criminal cases are much more difficult to collect after the case is over.

Another payment method involves paying an hourly fee for the actual time the attorneys spends on the case. In such cases, a substantial retainer is usually paid in advance, and as the attorney works on the case, the retainer fee is gradually used up. Once the retainer is consumed, either another lump sum is paid in advance, or the law firm sends out monthly bills to the client, who then keeps current by paying the amount due. Some retainers are refundable, most are not. Very few lawyers ever return any of the retainer no matter how little work is done.

Bills sent to clients should be correctly and clearly itemized. Frequently they are not. If a legal assistant is involved, her time is also itemized. I have seen $50,000 bills marked "For professional services rendered." It's not very professional. I have seen bills merely stating dates and vague descriptions of work performed, without indicating how much time was spent on each date.

I recently completed a case where my client, an attorney himself, was sued for an unpaid debt for legal services allegedly rendered by another law firm. The bills which the plaintiff's law firm sent my client showed a huge debt for a relatively short number of hours over less than two months. The bills did not make sense.

When my client filed a counterclaim, the plaintiff's law firm settled for no fee payment and only $250 to the attorney who handled the case for them. The case would still have settled if we had not paid the $250.

Attorneys' bills should indicate the work performed, the date it was performed, the amount of time spent on each task, and the amount billed per task. If an attorney's office uses computerized billing in which computer codes are assigned to common legal services, then photocopies of the time slips should be made available to the clients if they so desire.

A sample time slip is included in the addendum.[3] It is basically a written notation created on or about the time work is done to record the work done for billing purposes. On the upper left-hand side, the date is filled in. Next comes the initials of the lawyer or legal assistant who has done the work. The beginning time can also be indicated. Next: client's name and

---

"Attorneys' bills should indicate the work performed, the date it was performed, the amount of time spent on each task, and the amount billed per task."

---

file such as Mary Smith; Smith vs. Jones. Next is the code. This is the short-hand method for telling the client what you did. The code letter is put in, and then the statement is put on the bill: for example, R for research. Next, indicate the time you stopped. Subtract the start time. Indicate the number of hours or fractions of hours you have worked.

I charge by the tenth of the hour. That means my minimum time slip, at $200 per hour, would show $20. I have instructed my legal assistant to bill by the quarter of the hour. That way, her minimum time slip is, at $50 per hour, $12.50. It would not be profitable for our office manager to handle a time slip showing only $5. The time slip contains a place for remarks. I prefer to give as detailed description of billing as possible, so the client will know as much as possible about the work actually done. The more information put on the time slip, the more the client understands the process included in the amount of work accomplished.

The client is entitled to all of the information in the file, and he should know what he is being billed for. Our office manager receives the time slips. The information is collated, typed and sent out in the form of a total bill on a regular monthly basis.

Are all billings perfect in a good law office? Absolutely not. It's hard to keep good records, but there's a big difference between an acceptable accounting and no accounting at all. Every office makes billing errors, and it is up to the client to supervise these.

It is a wise decision, when retaining an attorney, to get a maximum price guarantee. In return, an attorney retained on an hourly basis, will often want a guarantee of a minimum fee. I like to do business in this manner because it gives me an extra incentive. If I am able to quickly settle or resolve the case, I receive a bonus having earned the fee in a much shorter than expected time. The client benefits by having his case over and his fees kept to a certain amount.

There is an excellent publication, which is anti-lawyer, put out by HALT[4] on "How to Hire an Attorney." It has some very good suggestions about discussing fees with your prospective attorney. Most of the people who would use those suggestions would probably not be able to retain me. I am a capitalist and want to make a certain amount of money in any

---

"It is a wise decision when retaining an attorney, to get a maximum price guarantee. In return, an attorney retained on an hourly basis will often want a guarantee of a minimum fee."

---

case, so I am not interested in negotiating fees with individual clients. However, for a case that I want very badly, or that has huge monetary possibilities, even this author will negotiate.

As an attorney's case load grows so grows the demand on his time. He's less willing to negotiate fees. This does not mean that the busiest attorney is the best attorney. Sometimes, and for some cases, an attorney straight out of law school may be the best attorney. There is an old saying: An attorney straight out of law school does $500 worth of work for $5; and an attorney after a lifetime of practice does $5 worth of work for $500. There is some merit to this claim.

While there are probably more trusting clients cheated by unscrupulous attorneys than there are hard working attorneys cheated by unscrupulous clients, the latter situation has been known to occur. Therefore, it is in both the client's and the attorney's best interests to clearly establish the fee arrangements between them at the beginning of their relationship.

In Chapter XV. part E., I fully discuss the mechanics of the contingency fee method: both my normal 50 percent of net contract and the somewhat deceptive "sliding scale of percentage of gross" which is most often used by personal injury attorneys.

Since the attorney who takes on a contingency fee case is paid only in the event of successfully settling or winning a judgment, the attorney is taking a risk in regard to payment for his time and out-of-pocket expenses. Depending on the case, the risk may be slight, or it may be considerable. Occasionally, the attorney will not see any profit on the case for years after his initial meeting with the client, and of course sometimes he loses. I became so confident of winning personal injury suits that I began to budget based on winning them. I was in practice over ten years before I lost one. It was a slip and fall accident. I spent a week in court with my associate attorney and a legal   assistant. A week in preparation, and $15,000 for depositions and expert   witnesses. When it was over, I was out about $30,000 with nothing to show for it.

On Mom's case, even though it was won twice, I spent about $50,000 and still have seen no return. When a lawyer takes a contingency case, it's often a big risk. It is reasonable, therefore, that the rewards, when they come, should be proportionately higher than on an hourly case. Sometimes, when the outlay of out-of-pocket expenses would be unduly burdensome, a client may pay a certain sum as an advance toward covering these costs. When the final settlement is reached, the advance paid by the client is deducted from the out-of-pocket expenses on a pure contingency fee case. As always, the final fee is contingent on results.

Most people don't negotiate percentages with their personal injury attorney. They get hurt. They hire an attorney they found through Aunt Harriet, a friend at work, or through a television commercial. They talk a little, and they sign what appears to be a non-modifiable form with blanks to fill in.

Here's how I negotiate and why. A normal injury case with clear damages and clear liability, which I value from $10,000 to $50,000, comes in. The client seems fairly easy to work with. I ask for 50 percent of the net and explain the contract. If the client asks if he can negotiate, I say yes.

If the liability is cloudy and the damages are on the low end, I won't drop. It's not worth it. If the liability is clear and the damages are on the higher end towards $50,000, I will consider dropping my percentage from five to ten percent. The factors include such things as: how easy going the client is to work with, do I really want to represent him, how interesting is the case; how much work and the amount of risk that is involved; and how much out-of- pocket expenses are involved and whether the client is willing to pay those expenses.

The $50,000 to $1,000,000 cases are usually too important, economically, to pass up. I would consider dropping my percentage fee from 50 percent to 40 percent, and if the case has a high damage and liability factor, I might consider going even lower. Often my 40 percent is lower than a competitor's 33 percent because of the way the fee is calculated. There are a million other lawyers begging for cases of this type. I have to be competitive.

The tough percentage case: I can take only about one in 10 that come in the door. Sometimes the client will offer me 80 percent. I regard civil rights cases and many wrongful termination cases/discriminatory hiring practices cases in this category. These cases often have a value of $3,000 to $5,000, and I can't afford to take them even if I was offered 100 percent. There are tough cases that need to be filed for the sake of justice. No one else will take them.

"Most attorneys in the large law firms are promoted on the basis of either their ability to generate clients or their ability to charge large fees and justify lots of hours in a case. It seems their records of winning or losing are not as significant criteria as their billing skills."

When I do take one of these tough cases, I usually lose money on it. I want a client with a mutual rapport and a client who understands what it costs me to take the case and won't call five times a day. If I took 20 percent of these cases, my office would close down in 30 days. It's that simple.

G. A LONG LOOK AT LARGE LAW FIRMS

I have come to dislike large law firms, as institutions. Frequently they have an inordinate amount of political power. More often than not, they sell more political power than they actually have through hinting and implying that they can accomplish miracles they can't do. These insinuations help them sell time. Most attorneys in the large law firms are promoted on the basis of either their ability to generate clients or their ability to charge large fees and justify lots of hours in a case. It seems their records of winning or losing are not as much of a significant criteria as their billing skills.

Large law firms take on young lawyers and have them grind out as many hours as they can. After approximately five years, the firms frequently proceed to make life uncomfortable for them because they don't want to pay them substantial increases or make them partners. The young lawyers then leave, making way for a fresh crop of recent graduates. [5]

After leaving the large law firm "nest," they either start their own firms, or more often, go to work as a lackey in a smaller law firm which promises them the opportunity for a partnership some day. These people are trained over a period of years to be very establishment-oriented and to charge large legal fees. As a general rule, they earn more money than the average solo or small firm practitioner—until they are tossed out. Then they may starve if they are unable to land a job with a second string firm. Through this sort of short-term "apprenticeship" system, the attitude and business practices of the large firms have trickled down and are perpetuated in some smaller firms.

The large, unwieldy law firms will some day be as extinct as the dinosaurs. Both automation and the gradually increasing role of legal assistants tend to cut down on the amounts of tasks needed to be done by the army of law clerks and young associate lawyers who are the drones of the large law firms' hives. Large law firms have tremendous overhead costs

"The large law firm's enemy is the impartial judge and the educated jury."

and are required to generate huge amounts of income to pay for their furniture, phone system and bloated payroll. Their greatest marketable asset is their political clout. Sometimes they sell clout they don't really have.

The large law firm's enemy is the impartial judge and the educated jury. Like ponderous battleships that are outmaneuvered by smaller, more efficient cruisers, the large law firms are doomed to sink into oblivion while the solo practitioner or small partnership law firm with full automation and a small well-trained staff of legal assistants and secretaries, sails on ahead. Some will survive by growing even larger. The large law firms of today will be replaced by many smaller firms and a few mega-firms, merging law firms that become as large as cities trimming unwary companies of their profits like locusts over the midwest playing "Bet the Company" with skill.

Unless you are in need of political clout and are certain the firm can deliver, stay away. These dinosaurs can step on you. Since every dinosaur has some great lawyers working for it, you might go to large law firm for that individual. It's possible once you've handed your money over, you'll never see the giant. Most dinosaurs also have what they call "rainmakers." These are the guys who bring in clients. A rainmaker could be an ex-president, the governor or a pretty face. They cost a lot of money. They sometimes have political clout. They seldom do quality legal work because the firm needs them out there promoting, not working—because working in the practice of law isn't profitable enough for them.

The growing Hyatt Legal Clinics and others like them, are another story. They are the K-Marts of the legal industry. No rainmakers, no charisma and few top-flight trial lawyers. However, they will grow. Mass production legal services and expensive advertising campaigns will prevail over the pseudo elegance of the past.

H. A ROGUE'S GALLERY:
"CHARACTER" SKETCHES OF SOME ATTORNEY TYPES

In the section that follows, descriptive names have been coined for the attorneys described. One reason for not using their correct names is to avoid singling out individuals for ridicule, when these people are repre-

"Mass production legal services and expensive advertising campaigns will prevail over the pseudo elegance of the past."

sentative of larger groups of similar characters. Another reason, is because I would prefer not to be sued! All of the characters, however, are based on actual human beings whom I have met in the practice of law.

MR. I. S. FREELEY

Q: Mr. Freely, I haven't been paid in months.
A: What are you complaining about? Look at all those people without jobs.

Let me introduce Mr. I. S. Freely. (The I. S. stands for "I Spend Freely.") He graduated at the very bottom of his class; meaning that everybody who had a lower score than his flunked out of law school. Mr. Freely has the proper image of a lawyer as depicted in the media. He exemplifies the typical sterotype who looks like a lawyer. Many banks would be glad to hire Mr. Freely whereas insurance companies usually pass him by. Banks hire and fire based on looks. Bank attorneys don't usually go to trial; they usually bluff until right before a final court date and then settle. Insurance

---

"Early in his practice, Mr. Freely figured out that although you can only work ten hours in a real 24-hour day, you can bill for 50 or 60 hours in a 24-hour day."

---

companies hire and fire based on actual trial performance because their attorneys are required to be in trial frequently.

Straight out of law school, Mr. Freely follows the well-trodden path which gets many lawyers into unpaid penthouse suites, behind the wheels of an unpaid Mercedes Benz, and luxuriating on unpaid trips abroad. With his platinum American Express card, he orders custom tailored, three-piece suits and plush office furniture.

Mr. Freely is a fairly generous man. He hires a large staff and offers them handsome salaries. Fringe benefits? No problem. Automation? Mr. Freely automates and re-automates every few months. His office has the most advanced technology available. The fact that identical clones of IBM equipment can be purchased from Taiwan at 50 percent less than the original is of no interest to Mr. Freely. He wants the IBM name on his equipment and he is willing to pay for it.

Unfortunately, being willing to pay for it and being able to pay for it is not necessarily the same thing. Therefore, Mr. Freely has to get clients who are willing to pay huge fees. Mr. Freely has to do lots and lots of billing, although not necessarily a lot of work. Early in his practice, Mr. Freely figured out that although you can only work ten hours in a real 24-hour day, you can bill for 50 or 60 hours in a 24-hour day. (Of course, you don't want to bill any one client for more than 24 hours in any single day.) Mr. Freely does one thing and does it very well. His magnetic charm and image draw a host of clients, and he bills them heavily. Mr. Freely practiced law for 15 years and maintained a perfect record: he lost every case he tried! He doesn't do much repeat business, but every client who comes into his office commits everything he owns in the world and future resources also, in order to pay the legal fees. Mr. Freely, isn't cheap. And he isn't any good, either.

I've run into Mr. Freely frequently because I have a substantial multistate practice, and I tend to cross paths with a few other attorneys who also practice in different states around the country. Mr. Freely is frequently on circuit and just as frequently not paying his tips because he only has a wad of $100 bills, and no one has the right change. Once, when Mr. Freely wasn't looking, I grabbed his wad of $100 bills and discovered, to my surprise, that the roll contained only two $100 bills: one on the outside and one on the inside. Sandwiched between were $1 bills! If Mr. Freely's courtroom performance were the equal of his image-making tactics, I have no doubt that he would win a case or two. Why are people so impressed that Mr. Freely has been on the losing end of so many important cases? Beats me.

MR. BET THE COMPANY

Mr. Freely has a lot in common the Mr. Bet The Company, except that Mr. Bet The Company really is rich. Mr. Bet The Company, representing giant industrial corporations, insurance companies and other notables, usually has a bottomless pit of funds. I have seen companies of major standing go under due to Mr. Bet The Company's advice. The companies who rely on Mr. Bet The Company are lulled into complacency by these attorneys who tell them, "No problem. We'll squash the opposition like a bug." They risk their company's assets on a turn of the "Wheel of Litigation." In the event they come up a loser, the recipients of a judgment against them which exceeds the assets of the company, does Mr. Bet The Company shed a tear? Hardly. He's busy counting his legal fees as he slinks off into the sunset. Mr. Bet The Company is often a very good lawyer. In fact, he wins over half his cases. But when he loses, the loss is usually too high.

MR. I. A. WIN

Meet Mr. I. A. Win ("A" as in "Always"). I've read some of Mr. Win's books. I've seen Mr. Win in court. I've had depositions with him and talked with him over the phone. Mr. Win is a liar because nobody always wins. We hold Rocky Marciano in high esteem because he won his boxing matches, but in the realm of law there are no exceptions to the "You can't win 'em all" rule. Why? No matter how good you are, no matter how famous you are, there are cases that can't be won and somebody is going to want to pay you a humongous amount of money to take a helpless, hopeless case. If you keep winning helpless, hopeless cases, you're going to keep getting more of them, and, sooner or later, you're going to lose a helpless, hopeless case. Everyone does.

MR. SHUCKS

After practicing for seven years with only one loss, I suffered my second loss against a gentleman who I regard as dangerous: a good ole' country boy who appeared to be honest, and straightforward. We'll call him "Shucks, I Usually Win."

We were on a first name basis because I developed a bit of rapport with Mr. Shucks. You see, whether Mr. Shucks is bluffing or not, I believe him because I relate to him, and I know that he's being a lot more honest than Mr. Win. Mr. Shucks is a pretty smart lawyer. He is usually an underground lawyer, although not always. There is a Mr. Shucks who represents himself in California (without a law license), who, I understand, has won over 50 cases. Mr. Shucks is the only one of the attorneys that we've described so far in this chapter whom we can distinguish just by looking at him. You can distinguish Mr. Shucks because he frequently doesn't look like an attorney. Sometimes he just looks like a good old country boy.

Often, he is underground so you really don't know exactly what he's doing because he doesn't conform to the existing labor union rules. However, on occasion, you might see Mr. Shucks at a bar convention, sitting at the dinner table with Mr. Freely and Mr. Win, telling them how good they are, and how next time they'll probably beat him. Many lawyers hate Mr. Shucks and feed their egos by feeling superior to him. In fact, Mr. Shucks doesn't usually do real well with judges either except when he deals with good old country judges. He would probably be drummed out of the legal profession if he weren't winning almost all of his jury trials.

MS. INSURANCE PERSON

This lady is tough on paperwork. She hates people who are injured, and recommends that a quadriplegic take two aspirins and go home. She hates paying out any of the insurance company's beloved money to anyone but herself. While insurance companies love to bandy about published stastics proving that victims and their lawyers are getting rich, the facts prove differently.

Most people don't know anyone personally who has ever collected on a $1 million judgment. Most lawyers don't know lawyers who have collected on a $1 million judgment. The common get-rich-quick story is the lawyer who got a big case and referred it to a trial lawyer for a big referral fee. A good half of my practice is referrals from lawyers. It is not a common, ordinary thing. The million-dollar judgments that are awarded are sometimes easier to win than a $20,000 or $30,000 judgment because these are the rare situations where somebody has been mutilated, killed or severely injured. These cases are usually publicized, but they are publicized because they are rare.

The truth of the matter is that insurance company attorneys make money as long as the case doesn't settle. They get paid by the hour from a rich client. They don't like to settle before they run up a big bill. The companies don't like to pay out under the theory that by fighting to the end, they stop people from filing law suits. This isn't true. In fact, the delays often make people less reasonable. After waiting for several painful years to get their medical bills paid, some clients just don't care any more. Sometimes they wear out and settle for a small percentage of what they originally wanted, and sometimes they take the case straight to court. More of them would go to court if they could talk their lawyer into it.

Ms. Insurance Person storms the opposition with a blizzard of legal paperwork. She has a mean looking curved nose which arrogantly bends into contortions as she tells you how ridiculous you and your client are to believe that her client did anything wrong when he drove his 18-wheeler into a freefall skydive from the freeway ramp and landed on your client's head. Delay and unnecessary work is her game, and she plays it with righteous indignation.

Her ally is a specially trained medical doctor who works as a whore for the insurance industry and will testify that an amputee is faking his injury.

CHASE'EM AND CATCH'EM

The dishonest insurance company attorneys are not without their counterparts in the plaintiff's bar. The firm of Chase'Em and Catch'Em,

We chase 'em; We catch 'em. We get the bucks.

Attorneys-out-law, specializes in ambulance chasing and paper shuffling. They handle higher volume, low return, small damages cases. Their clients are people who won't hesitate to fall down in front of a parked car and yell "Whiplash!"

While most attorneys who have a general practice including personal injury cases do a lot of repeat business from satisfied clients—the injury victim will later come in to have a will drawn up, get a divorce, or set up a corporation—Chase'Em and Catch'Em rely on semi-professional, personal-injury plaintiffs as repeat customers for multiple re-runs of the same type of case. In fact, a search of the law firm's file reveals that one of their clients has been in a car wreck, has slipped on ice outside a major department store, and had a tree limb fall on him while walking by a millionaire's mansion, all in the same week. All of these matters are being "litigated"—which in Chase'Em and Catch'Em's office means a demand letter has been sent to the insurance company and litigation is either threatened or suit has actually been filed—although the lawsuit is only filed as a bluff because the matter will eventually be settled. That's because Chase'Em's cases never go to court. Catch'Em tried a case once about eight years ago and lost it.

A typical Chase'Em and Catch'Em client suffers an accident, comes into their office, tells his tale of woe, and receives a small financial advance on his case. He signs away everything, and the case is negotiated without ever talking to the client again. The client will call from time to time and ask if his money has come in. Chase'Em and Catch'Em will often find, and direct their clients to, doctors who run similar types of medical practices.

Chase'Em, sometimes a very seedy looking attorney or sometimes wearing a Brooks Brother's suit, is usually fast on his feet. However, his partner Catch'Em grabs most of the business by sitting behind his desk and adding to his overextended waistline while directing various "runners" in the city who solicit business from truck drivers, ambulance attendants, nurses, doctors, hospitals, chiropractors and funeral homes.

Chase'Em and Catch'Em's advantage over an ethical law firm handling plaintiffs' work is that they don't really care whether the client has been actually injured. They're so greedy, they'll sign on any injury case which slithers up to their door. If you have no actual injury at all, but just feel like ripping some bucks off an insurance company's money tree, as a result of your little fender bender, you'll do fine with Chase'Em & Catch'Em because they will chase you, they will catch your claims, and they will get the bucks.

The unfortunate side effect is that Chase'Em & Catch'Em have a problem telling the difference between a phony claim and a real claim. If you have a real claim and a legitimate cause of action, avoid Chase'Em and Catch'Em like the plague. If you get in their clutches, you'll get paper shuffled along in the same careless, uninterested manner as all the non-legitimate injuries, and you'll receive a small amount of money for your claim compared to what it is really worth. Some very good claims come into Chase'Em and Catch'Em which they settle for next-to-nothing. Many very bad claims come in which they settle for next-to-nothing. All of these next-to-nothing cases add up to a very tidy sum.

Many insurance adjusters get along great with Chase'Em & Catch'Em. They may have lunch with them on a frequent basis. They don't have arguments, fights, and shouting matches such as those which sometimes occur when they're dealing with other members of the plaintiff's bar. In fact, they get along quite nicely for the most part. A Chase'Em and Catch'Em's file can be evaluated at the same rate as a legitimate file and settled for a very small amount, making the insurance adjuster a hero. Meanwhile, the same insurance company's adjusters and attorneys drag a legitimate case out for years, cause severe misery, and loudly publicize outrageous verdicts for quadriplegics while totally ignoring the $1 million profit that Chase'Em and Catch'Em accrued last year from their volume of $2,000 sore neck cases.

In 1985, one of the nation's best plaintiff's lawyers, Melvin Belli, sent a staff member to Texas allegedly to solicit business from the families of victims of an airplane crash. A Texas newspaper accused him of chasing ambulances. The famous trial lawyer replied, "I've never chased an ambulance in my life, I always beat them there."

Belli's retort provides the insurance industry with ammunition to hurl at plaintiff's attorneys in general. While it is very likely that people who signed up with Belli's firm will be well represented and were saved from falling into the hands of some unscrupulous Chase 'Em and Catch 'Em type firm, such bold boasts certainly don't do anything to enhance the image of plaintiff's personal injury attorneys.

Similar allegations were made about American lawyers who rushed to India to sign up clients after the disastrous Union Carbide chemical leak in 1984. The unsavory image of plaintiffs' attorneys created by the press may have honestly reflected some of the facts, but the total impression was misleading. Why? The press only wrote about one side of the issue.

The media failed to report the efforts of insurance companies, whose agents seem to materialize on disaster scenes, with releases in hand, to quickly and quietly settle serious cases for very small amounts of money. I recall a serious truck accident which landed a large number of innocent drivers in the hospital. The truck company insurance adjusters swarmed into the hospital and signed up most of the wounded and some of the dead for less than medical and funeral costs. The ambulance chasers were outrun. The victims were cheated.

MR. COMPATIBILITY

Mr. Compatibility is a nice guy. He wants you to like him, and I usually do. He tends to be somewhat lazy, doesn't do much work for his client. Usually, however, he does a lot better job than Mr. Win, or Mr. Freely because he settles almost all of his cases.

This guy really doesn't belong in a Rogues Gallery at all. The only way he gets into this assemblage is by using his bar card. His parents were white, upper middle class; not rich, but had a heavily padded savings account. His dad spent 50 years working 9-to-5 for Exxon and retired. Mom and dad put him through law school, without the assistance of scholarship money. Mr. Compatibility made mostly A's. He is of above average intelligence. He specializes in bankruptcy law or banking law and works for a medium to large law firm.

He's a junior partner now, and he writes out time slips everyday, making twice what his successful dad made. He has a happy wife, a comfortable house, two cars, and 2.1 healthy children. His healthy children make A's and say no to drugs. Mr. Compatibility never talked back to his parents, never got in a fight at school, never voted for a liberal or a Democrat but enjoyed their company and listened politely and agreeably to their speeches when he was in college. There are two sides to every argument and Mr.Compatibility enjoys analyzing them both. He never raises his voice. He likes to pick up the check but never fights over it. He believes in truth, justice and the American way. His legal analysis is superb. His friends, opponents, parents and secretary like him. Mr.Compatibility is expensive, but he never pads his bills.

Sometimes he takes his client's side, sometimes he takes your client's side, and sometimes he settles because his wife is on the phone and wants him to come home for dinner. In any event, he's not a hard guy to deal with. Although he's not much of a fighter, and a tough attorney can cut him to pieces. He also never loses the company. He never takes risks. He never fights. If something nasty comes up, he refers it to one of his firm's trial lawyers.

MR. IVY LEAGUE

Mr. Ivy League graduated from Harvard or Yale, and at first glance he's hard to distinguish from Mr. Bet The Company or Mr. Freely—they have some similar characteristics.

Mr. Ivy League has every button buttoned, every hair in place, and always just the correctly-colored, coordinated tie. Mr. Ivy League usually has inherited wealth. He's a man of leisure. His father owns one of the major oil companies or a bank or two. In order to keep daddy's business, large law firms are very happy to have Mr. Ivy League in their firm. Mr. Ivy League and Mr. I.S. Freely are frequently close friends, since Mr. Ivy League isn't super discerning beyond physical appearances and since Mr. Freely looks a lot like him; they drive similar cars and go to the same country clubs.

Actually, Mr. Freely always wanted to be Mr. Ivy League anyway. Mr. Ivy League likes to do tax work or real estate mergers, non-taxable swaps or securities and exchange work. He does all of these things using form books and extremely competent secretaries.

You can tell the difference between Mr. Ivy League and Mr. Freely in this way: Mr. Ivy League's fees are very high, but he doesn't charge them; someone else in the firm does. His fees are not nearly as high, however, as Mr. Freely's fees. Mr. Ivy League's secretaries are well and timely paid and do excellent work, although they are very conservative. Their top blouse button is always buttoned, and the blouse is always starched.

Another distinguishing characteristic between Mr. Ivy League and Mr. Freely are their spouses: Mr. Ivy League's wife is beautiful. She's dressed well, and has a day maid, a night maid, and a governess. Mr. Freely's wife works. She's a truck driver who picked up Mr. Freely up at a bar one night and landed him like a helpless fish while he was drunk. She thought she'd retire. She was wrong.

MS. TOUGH GUY AND MR. GUTS

Ms. Tough Guy and Mr. Guts have a law firm with between 25 and 100 people in it. Strangely enough, Ms. Guy and Mr. Guts aren't usually in the giant 200-plus firms—they prefer people like Mr. Ivy League and Mr. Bet The Company. Mr. Guts is rude all the time. His style is intimidation, and he's read, *"Winning Through Intimidation"*[3] six times, the last time backwards. He does superficial legal work, and quite frankly, nobody likes him—not even his mother. He's mean and rough around the edges.

Almost everybody backs down from him. And that's the problem. If you have the courage to stand up to him, you can learn whether or not he really has the guts to go the distance or if he is just a bully who tries to dish it out but can't take it. When the firm of Guy and Guts tells you that they always win, they expect you to back down. If someone offers them an honest no holds barred fight, they're flabbergasted. When that happens, Mr. Guts and Ms. Tough Guy usually turn tail and run or try to show the Dr. Jekyll side of these Mr. and Ms. Hydes. Once they've had the hyde ripped off them, they're vulnerable. Deep down inside they don't want the actual fight.

Most trial lawyers actually go to court for a trial between five (5) and ten (10) times a year. They spend more time getting ready for trial and then settling than they do actually trying cases. One of the most time consuming parts about getting ready for trial is discovery—using the system to learn things about the other side. The most valuable discovery tool is the oral deposition. The lawyer calls on someone to testify under oath before a court reporter who types everything down. The lawyer's questions and the witness' answers are later transcribed into book form.

The lawyer for the witness may or may not let the witness answer a question. For example:

"Why did you kill your neighbor's dog?"

"Objection, my client didn't kill the dog. You are assuming a fact not in evidence," or,

"Objection, fifth amendment. The answer might lead to incriminating evidence," or,

"Objection, irrelevant. The death of the dog has nothing to do with a suit to recover medical expenses for your client's wife for a heart transplant."

When an argument like this comes up, it is usually either negotiated or taken back to the Judge to decide whether or not the question must be answered.

Mr. Guts, however, won't take no for an answer. He may ask the question over again a dozen more times. If you ask him politely to stop harassing your client, he jumps up and down and screams. He makes vicious nasty faces at everyone in the room and threatens you and the witness with torture and great economic loss. Once upon a time Mr. Guts got so mad he smashed his foot into the floor and it fell through. His real name was not Rumpelstiltskin.

MR. I KNOW IT ALL

The Rogues' Gallery would not be complete without "Mr. I Know It All" (IKIA). He was one of the progenitors of the tactic of advertising legal services in the television guides. Mr. IKIA doesn't look like Mr. Freely or Mr. Ivy League. He can't represent banks. Bankers won't sit next to him. He looks greasy. His jet black hair is covered with Vaseline or some sort of oily grooming product, and he has dandruff all over his cheap, black, pinstripe suit.

When I met him, he wore brown cowboy boots which made him a couple of inches taller so that he could look me in the eyes. Over the phone, Mr. I Know It All gave me vociferous hell about a $1,500 case. He

*"Advertising does not mean a lawyer is good or bad.
It just means he advertises."*

told me he was going to bury me, destroy me, and make my client miserable.

At this point in my career I'd just laugh, but then I had only been practicing for a couple of weeks. So I called my client and told him, "Mr. Tank, we can't take this! Let's go for it!" Mr. Tank (assumed name) replied that he'd prefer to pay the $1,500 and get the guy off his back rather than fool with him. Mr. Tank was a very wise man. In my anger and hostility I said, "No." I offered to work the case for free and pay any losses out of my own pocket. I didn't expect to have any losses and perhaps was being overly bold, but I felt certain that I could win the case. Tank agreed.

I prepared several witnesses for this small claims court case, and we went into the courtroom. There was Mr. I Know It All staring at me eyeball-to-eyeball, wearing his speckled white shirt and his ugly circus clown tie. "Mr. Minns," he said, "my client has agreed to drop this action." I told him that we were going to trial, refused his compromise and had a counterclaim against him and his client. He was shattered. He was visibly shaking, his knees were trembling and tears were coming into his eyes as his usual smirk vanished, and his normally sallow face flushed with color. It was a decided improvement.

His voice started squeaking and quaking and he asked if I could give him a few minutes to get some help. I told him that there was no way he was going to get any help. He was going to get poured out on the carpet. I was ready to fight.

When the judge said, "Is the plaintiff ready?" Mr. I Know It All said "No." The judge asked "Why?" Mr. IKIA said, "I need a little help, your honor." I approached the bench and said, "Your honor, we're ready for trial, I've brought six witnesses in here and have done two days of complete and full preparation. We need to go to trial now." The judge said, "Well, if he's not ready, I don't know if I can make him go to trial."

I reminded the judge that we had previously asked for a delay because we hadn't wanted to go to trial at that time. The court had denied our request and had set the case for this trial at Mr. IKIA's request. Now we were there, and we were prepared. If Mr. IKIA had been politically powerful, he probably would have gotten his unreasonable motion granted, but since he wasn't, his motion was denied.

The judge set the case, however, for 1:00 that afternoon, which gave Mr. IKIA several hours.

Mr. IKIA rushed out, and, at his own expense, hired Mr. Tough Guy, who, although obviously unprepared, was raring to go. He told me he was gonna mop the floor with me. He asked my witnesses questions. They had all been instructed not to talk to him. He asked me what kind of case I was going to put on, and I told him, "a winning case." He asked me what the facts were, and I told him to ask Mr. IKIA. He then approached the bench and told the court that I was unreasonable and unfair, and that he was totally and completely unprepared. In this regard, he was telling the truth. He threw himself on the mercy of the court. I told the court that we had expended over $1,500 worth of time, that it was a $1,500 case, and that their motion for continuance had already been denied. Then, Mr. Tough Guy relented, metamorphosed into Mr. Compatibility and offered to settle for $1,500. I reluctantly accepted, and my client gave me half the money as my fee. At minimum wage, I had spent about $2,000 worth of time on the case. My further "reward" was a handful of junker cases from the same client.

If you found this trip through the Rogues' Gallery of attorney archetypes interesting, I suggest several visits to your local courthouse. Observe some trials and hearings. Then try to decide which portrait in the gallery best fits the attorneys you watched—or depict some new "rogues" on your own—you'll find the task worthy of your artistic talents.

I. LAW—PROFESSION OR BUSINESS?

Former U.S. Supreme Court Justice Warren Burger once said that he'd rather dig ditches than advertise if he were an attorney in private practice. I don't know whether he has ever dug ditches, but since I have, I can unequivocally say that if my choice were dig or advertise, my ad would appear tomorrow. After a few days digging ditches, the former chief justice might concur that advertising is the better of the two options and would place his ad for legal services alongside mine.

I find most attorney's advertising copy professionally sleazy and offensive. I don't feel a sense of rapport with most attorneys who advertise, nor do I have any degree of confidence in the quality of their services. The ads—especially those seeking personal injury clients—generally appeal to the greed of potential clients.

However, some of the advertisements for flat-fee services such as bankruptcies, divorces, adoptions, etc., are in good taste. They substantially benefit the community by allowing lawyers to sell these services in volume, get rich, and at the same time, keep the price down. Isn't that what the free market is all about? Some of the divorce and bankruptcy attorneys who advertise are very competent. Advertising does not mean a lawyer is good or bad. It just means he advertises.

We, as law students and practitioners, are repeatedly told by our instructors and by judges who are on a lifetime federal payroll that the law is a profession, not a business. Most of those who advocate the professional theory do little to help the general public successfully handle their legal matters.

Many of the "legal-aid" services aimed at helping indigents probably do more harm than good through their ineptitude. At various times in my career, I have devoted from 10 to 50 percent of my practice to helping people on a percentage basis or on a no-fee basis because I felt like their cause was important or someone simply needed to be sued. The contingency fee system, on many occasions, has made me a handsome sum of money, helping someone who didn't have any resources. Many of these people couldn't find an attorney to represent them and had looked for long periods of time.

The problem, however, in calling law a profession—something loftier than a mere business—is that the nomenclature is misleading, and in our Twentieth Century world, absurd. For centuries in England, the law was practiced by people who handed down their profession from generation to generation. These families were wealthy. They didn't need the money for living expenses. During the Renaissance, the term *"noblesse oblige"* was coined, which roughly meant the obligation of the nobility to bestow favors on the bourgeoisie and peasants because of their own great wealth.

The law practices of these blue-blooded gentlemen were conducted in a professional, leisurely manner. It's rare to see that atmosphere in the practice of law today.

For the average attorney today, the practice of law is the way he puts bread and butter on his family's table. He usually makes more than the average nine to fiver, but if fees aren't collected, the office doesn't stay open. It sounds very grand to speak in lofty terms of the noble barrister who is far above mere monetary concerns, but realistically, being a lawyer in today's America is both a profession and a means of earning a living—a business.

The moral is: Sometimes justice prevails and sometimes it pays. Occasionally, it does both."

CHAPTER V

PRACTITIONERS ON THE FRONTIER

"There is a growing gray area around the fringes of the licensed practice of law, with the role of the non-licensed legal expert coming increasingly into prominence."

A. NON-LICENSED LEGAL EXPERTS

What is the unauthorized practice of law? State bars usually define the unauthorized practice of law as the attempt by an unlicensed person to give legal advice or to represent another individual in a court. Judges have wide discretions to decide who may practice law in their courts. When licensed attorneys need to practice in jurisdictions other than their own, courts routinely allow them to do so.[1]

In Texas, only attorneys can draft deeds. In Colorado, real estate brokers are permitted to perform this function. In Florida, legal assistants under the supervision of an attorney may take depositions, although this is not permitted throughout most of the country. My legal assistant, could very competently take depositions and perform superbly; her discovery would be better than many attorneys I've observed. If Texas law would allow me to delegate that task, I could lower my client's costs, and the law firm would make larger profits.

In California you are not required to have a law school degree. You are required to pass the bar exam and to have studied under the guidance of a licensed attorney or judge for four years. California, supposedly, has one of the toughest bar exams in the country. Should the mere passing of the bar exam be enough? If an individual can pass the bar exam, should he be required to go to law school? Does the bar exam test a person's ability to practice law? Have we screened out all the bad lawyers with our various bar exams? Are we getting better, more honest and more competent lawyers with our modern criteria? Were lawyers like Lincoln and Marshall really so incompetent? Can incompetence be foreseen and prevented with tough screening procedures?

"Does the bar exam test a person's ability to practice law?"

Very few licensed lawyers win a criminal tax case. Should Montana paralegal Peggy Christensen (who has assisted in several such wins) be made a bar member? There are no easy answers to those questions. The very fact that they are asked is disconcerting to staunch legal labor union members.

If the bar exam doesn't test someone's ability to practice law, then it is unnecessary, and we are allowing people to practice law who don't have the skills. If the bar exam does demonstrate someone's ability to practice law, then a legal education shouldn't be required. It could be an additional credential to put up on the wall and use in perhaps selling clients on the use of the attorney's services.

There is a growing gray area around the fringes of the licensed practice of law with the role of the non-licensed legal expert coming increasingly into prominence. What characteristics must this evolving professional possess, and where does his path of enlightenment begin? Quite often, he starts out as a client of a licensed member of the bar. Sometimes, this practitioner on the fringe is a para-professional, either self-taught or with some law office experience.

Skilled trial lawyers usually have the ability to be discerning listeners, able to evaluate, sift, and distill the essence from a client's statements about his case. Ideally, the attorneys' staff will also possess this talent. However, even with the ability to listen and empathize, it is impossible for an attorney to care as much about an individual's case as that individual cares himself! The old adage that the person who represents himself has a fool for a client is not always true. However, the client who takes no interest in his own case is always a fool.

A client is absorbed in only his or her own litigation, whereas the law firm must be concerned about 50 to 100 cases or more, all demanding equal attention. It's impossible for even the most dedicated attorney or legal assistant to memorize all of the fact situations in all of the active cases in one office and be current on all of them. Therefore, it is imperative that a client be actively involved in his or her case. The most efficient lawyer can sometimes be forced to trial unprepared because of unreasonable judges, conflicts in schedule or political favors. The client must be prepared. He should have no conflicts. If he can't control his own conflicts, his case will

---

"If the bar exam doesn't test someone's ability to practice law, then it is unnecessary and we are allowing people to practice law who don't have the skills."

be in jeopardy.

Clients often perform an invaluable service when they send newspaper clippings and magazine articles on issues relevant to their cases. Occasionally, clients do some of the investigative or information gathering work on their own cases—such as obtaining accident reports and staying in touch with witnesses.

My law firm treats its clients as informed, responsible participants in their litigation. When law firms don't keep their clients informed of the status of their case, or have the attitude that the client could not understand the law, then both the law firm and its clients suffer. When a client actively involves himself in his case, he learns something about the law.

I know that every time I go through a complete personal injury trial with a client, that client becomes at least semi-knowledgeable about personal injury law. Why? The more law my client knows, the more the client will be able to help me build his or her case. It is not uncommon for clients to go through a jury trial and come out a two-fold winner: they won the jury verdict and learned more about the way juries work and about the law in that specific case than the average attorney does. How can this happen?

Less than ten percent of the people licensed to practice law try five cases in their entire careers; thus, our office turns many clients into Underground Lawyers who at least have a compass in hand when they go exploring in the forest of jurisprudence.

In our society, too much homage is paid to the title professional when the assistant or para-professional often does a lion's share of the nitty, gritty, unglamorous day-to-day work.

I vividly recall my experience in the hospital waiting for my ex-wife to give birth, January 13, 1975. I was about to become a new dad. I had not received the courses now in vogue and was scared. While we were anxiously awaiting the doctor's arrival, I asked the nurse what would happen in case of an emergency? What would we do if the baby decided to come before the doctor got there? She informed us that she would deliver the baby. "How could you presume to do that?" I asked, alarmed. In a very straightforward, matter of fact way, she admitted that in more than 20 years of nursing, she had delivered dozens of babies when there were no doctors present. She had learned by watching hundreds of different

"Skilled trial lawyers usually have the ability to be discerning listeners..."

doctors perform deliveries. She had coached several new doctors over the years. In much the same way, I have used L.R., my legal assistant, to help train novice lawyers.

Unlike the head nurse in a maternity ward, most doctors don't watch hundreds of babies being delivered by their competitors who might use different techniques. Medics and licensed practitioners watch a few, but the head nurse in a delivery section of the hospital may have a larger quantity of diverse experiences than the baby doctor.

A professional drug smuggler will, as an occupational necessity, learn a great deal about the Fifth Amendment. Such an individual might study constitutional law to a much greater extent than an attorney who specializes in probate law or real estate. The smuggler may never read a scholarly article about it, but he will share war stories in jail and thus enhance his experience.

The individual who gets a master's degree in political science or American history will probably have read and studied the Constitution more than most people graduating from law schools. I have found that in training legal researchers, English and history majors seem to be the most qualified. It is slightly easier to train them in the use of legal research tools than it is to train someone straight out of law school because someone with a degree in such fields already has spent more time using research techniques than the fledgling lawyer. If you are adept in the use of an encyclopedia, you have mastered some of the initial skills necessary to begin legal research.

My earliest pair of clients were a father and son who became multi-millionaires through construction and the buying and selling of real estate. Although I had a broker's license, had taught real estate, had bought and sold property, had been trained by my grandfather, and knew more about real estate law on my first day of practice than the majority of practicing lawyers, those clients' knowledge and ability exceeded mine.

Jim Howze, former president of the Texas branch of Jones Real Estate College, is a scholar on real estate law, who knows far more real estate law than 90 percent of the licensed attorneys in Texas. Howze, who gets embarrassed when I sing his praises, pays lip service to licensed attorneys in spite of his own expertise because he is required to stress in his real estate classes that real estate law can only be interpreted by lawyers. He studies

"The more law my client knows, the more the client will be able to help me build his or her case."

statutes and cases religiously and has taught contracts and real estate history for longer than I have practiced law. He also actively participated in the market itself. Legally, however, he is not permitted to give legal advice on real estate.

My close friend, Mickey Brown, through his work in the law enforcement field, has learned more about some areas of criminal law than many lawyers. He's an expert on arson, search warrants and Miranda rights. Legally, he must sit and listen when an oil and gas lawyer gives inaccurate advice on criminal law.

In the past, lawyers learned through on-the-job experience. The late Garland Walker, former dean of the South Texas College of Law and my daughter Rain's godfather, broadened his students' exposure by inviting practicing attorneys and judges to teach courses. He initiated an internship program which allowed students to train in law offices while continuing their education. Unfortunately, most law school professors are not visionaries like Dean Walker. While the trend Dean Walker pioneered will not die out completely, it is not being adopted to any great extent in our nation's law schools.

Former U.S. Supreme Court Chief Justice Burger blatantly attacked this country's lawyers, stating that 50 percent of them are incompetent. He also noted that there are too many lawyers. In a lecture attended by perhaps 10,000 attorneys, Justice Burger drew an imaginary line in the middle of the crowd and told all the attorneys on one side of his line that they should quit being lawyers, while attorneys on the other side of the line could continue being lawyers. In his estimation, this would begin to solve the problem of there being too many lawyers. There was a great deal of nervous laughter in response to Burger's observation.

It's not the sort of thing you'd hear from your judge back home, running for election and expecting the attorney in his constituency to back his return to power. It's the sort of thing you expect to hear from a man who isn't too concerned with what the audience thinks and who has the arrogance of unlimited power. Of course, he may be right. There may be too many lawyers. However, if you're a capitalist who believes in supply and

"I have found that in training legal researchers, that English and history majors seem to be the most qualified...someone with a degree in such fields already has spent more time using research techniques than the fledgling lawyer."

demand, too many lawyers would tend to lower the legal fees. This is, of course, true, unless prices are kept artificially high through the labor union's techniques.

There should be fewer lawyers. They should be better trained. However, this should be accomplished by the market, not by artificial constraints. To take up the slack, there should be a corps of well-trained paralegal professionals with experience in various diverse fields. This should be accomplished, however, by the dynamics of the marketplace, not the government or legal labor unions.

While often denigrating the skills of non-attorneys, some attorneys, nevertheless, rely on the assistance of non-union members. I recall a young, eager assistant U.S. Attorney prosecuting a failure to file income tax case who heavily relied on the assistance and legal advice of a non-lawyer IRS agent who,after decades of experience, jailing hapless folks that fell into his clutches,declared that he loved his job. I am certain his knowledge of tax law far exceeded that of the young prosecutor.

Smart attorneys appreciate the value of non-legal experts and utilize their skills to the fullest extent allowed by law.

B. THE UNAUTHORIZED PRACTICE OF LAW COMMITTEE VS. JOE A. IZEN, JR.

One of my most interesting cases and a great personal victory for me, my client, and legal assistants everywhere was: The Unauthorized Practice of Law Committee vs. Joe A. Izen, Jr.

Izen had opened a divorce clinic in Fort Worth, Texas, and was advertising divorces for $50 and up. The average price of a divorce through the clinic was less than $200, including the services of a lawyer. For $50, the prospective ex-spouses would come in, agree to all the terms, and tell a legal assistant what they wanted done. The legal assistant would take down all the facts. The facts would be entered into a computer and printed out on a very simple divorce form which is used in Texas and in many other states.

"In our society, too much homage is paid to the title professional when the assistant or para-professional often does a lion's share of the nitty, gritty, unglamorous day-to-day work."

The divorce package was briefly reviewed and approved by an attorney in the clinic who worked for Izen. Since the forms were correct and had been used over and over again, the attorney did not need to spend a great deal of time reviewing the final product. Since the most expensive part of preparing a divorce is the attorney's time, this system allowed Izen to make a profit even at the $50 rate. At the time, in Fort Worth, the cost of an uncontested divorce ranged from $500 to $2,000, depending on which law office the client wandered into.

Mr. Izen, the Unauthorized Practice of Law Committee has psychic evidence that you have non-lawyers typing legal papers.

At one time, Izen's clinic reputedly garnered almost 50 percent of Fort Worth's divorce business. Since he did little advertising, most of that business was the result of referrals from satisfied customers—which is a rarity in the divorce game—from social agencies, and even from a certain judge.

If a client did not feel comfortable proceeding on his own, for an extra $100 an attorney would accompany him in court to obtain the divorce. The clients were informed in writing that it was not legally necessary to have an attorney in an uncontested divorce where all matters had been previously agreed upon. The clients who intended to go to court on their own were prepared by viewing a videotaped presentation of an uncontested divorce proceeding being conducted. In Texas, when both sides agree, answering a few, fast, magic questions gets you your divorce quickly.

Those simple questions include such matters as residency, children and whether or not a property settlement has been reached. These questions on the record are designed to show that the Court has made an inquiry into the relevant issues.[3]

One local judge constantly objected to the clinic's methods because he didn't like people coming into his court without a lawyer. He disliked hearing statements such as "But judge I did it just like the other people," or, "But judge, don't I have a right to represent myself?" He would allow lawyers to conduct the same magic ceremony expeditiously but would set obstacles in the way of those who came in without lawyers.

As a result of his clinic, Izen was charged with the unauthorized practice of law for his use of legal assistants to help the divorcing clients. There were really no substantial issues in the Unauthorized Practice of Law Committee vs. Joe Izen. The bar alleged he was helping non-lawyers practice law. Their surface motive was the noble desire to keep the lofty legal profession in well-trained hands. The real reasons for the assault was that Izen's clinic was taking business away from other attorneys, and his reasonable rates were driving down the market price of divorce attorneys fees in Ft. Worth. It was a simple issue of union members vs. non-union labor.

If a litigant can show that the law is on his side and that there are no facts in dispute, a judge is supposed to grant what is called a summary judgment—an order in the prevailing party's favor, ending the case. This case was a deserving candidate for summary judgment. Most likely it would have been speedily granted had it not been for the political factors involved.

The labor union may allow legally sanctioned perjury, dishonesty, conflicts of interest, and other assorted misconduct without batting an eye,

---

"The labor union may allow legally sanctioned perjury, dishonesty, conflicts of interest, and other assorted misconduct without batting an eye, but its hierarchy will not tolerate unmitigated arrogance."

---

but its hierarchy will not tolerate unmitigated arrogance. My former partner Izen, who is an outstanding attorney with a brilliant mind, suffers from a few problems. He's madder than a March hare, would rather have a good time than win, and arrogantly looks down his nose at his intellectual inferiors.

One vivid example of how outspoken Izen is occurred when a judge ruled in a case over which he had no rightful jurisdiction. I told the court, "Your honor, I would appreciate it if you would review the case and reconsider your ruling." The court replied, "All right. Does anyone have anything to add?" Izen did. "Your honor, that's the stupidest ruling I've heard in a long time. Perhaps the court just doesn't understand the case. I'd be happy to explain it. I used to teach Real Estate law to people without college educations." After that, I gave him the name "The Great Izen" for accomplishing great things just on guts. It was meant affectionately with some seriousness and a little tongue-in-cheek.

Izen never had any qualms about insulting his professional peers, whom he did not consider his intellectual peer, particularly when he saw a fellow lawyer do something stupid. Izen easily made enemies. Couple this with several great appellate victories in California, Oregon, and Florida, and add to it the fact that he had become quite rich through his law practice, and you need only one more element to make Izen hated by every mediocre resident in the legal sewers. Izen decided to sell cheap divorces, and, shades of low class, he advertised the fact!

When the charges were brought against him, I was hired to fight for Izen's Texas license. The stakes were very high: If I lost, he would become America's highest paid legal assistant. If I won, he would have much more fodder with which to insult his detractors.

In order to defend Izen, I needed to know what the charges were. Who was going to testify that Izen had helped non-lawyers practice law? How had they practiced law? Who were these people? The bar could not include the people who had represented themselves with the help of Izen's clinic because all citizens have an absolute right to represent themselves in court.

One of Ft. Worth's leading civil trial attorneys, John Camp, had been persuaded to file suit and seek a temporary injunction against half a dozen people involved in the divorce clinic. He succeeded. This forced the clinic to close. Camp then stepped down from the case and left it to a cast of successors.

After the clinic had closed down, Izen met with some of the former employees and existing clients, and decided to run a new clinic, using many of these former employees and taking an active role in controlling and directing them.

Included on the bar boy's team were attorneys Richard Elliot, B.W. Cruce, Jr., Harry Post and, apparently against his will, Judge Robert L. Wright. Elliot amended the suit, adding Izen as a defendant based on an attached affidavit swearing that Izen had helped non-lawyers practice law.

I was Izen's team.

Elliot claimed his evidence of Izen's misconduct came from Judge Wright. I took the judge's deposition to seek his evidence, and then took Camp's deposition to determine why he had not named Izen in the original petition if Izen had been involved in any wrong doing. Both had no knowledge of unauthorized conduct by Izen. Finally, I took Elliot's deposition because he was the only member of this cast of attorneys willing to say under oath, Izen had violated any laws.

In Elliot's deposition, an inquiry was made into the basis for his signature on an affidavit swearing Izen had broken the law. Elliot gave some fascinating testimony into his own legal practices and integrity. The following excerpted statements are from the sworn mouth of Elliot and are included in the official court records, along with the winning motion for summary judgment.

In this instance, Elliot was being questioned about why he had attached an affidavit to the complaint against Izen, and his answers never told the reasons:

Q. This instrument. What was the reason for it?

A. Well, I believe that a Petition for Injunction has to have some notary on it under the...Here again, I didn't bring my Rules of Civil Procedure with me. But it is normally, I suppose, good practice to have a pleading sworn to.

Q. For what reason?

A. I guess to add some credibility to the allegations. I am not sure in the particular instance.

Q. So, you are not sure why you had that notarized?

A. Well, I believe as I just explained to you, that it was prepared in a form that would be verified or acknowledged because I believe that the Rules don't call for it, it is perhaps good practice in some cases. It's a matter of pleading. I don't think, you know. It is like anything else, a failure to plead is always subject to waiver.

(Continuing the Elliot deposition):

Q. So, you are telling me that it is good practice to have somebody swear to the truth of the matters of the Petition in front of a notary?

A. In some cases, I think that is correct, yes sir.

Mr. Elliot went on to attempt to show that he may not have been responsible for these sworn allegations.

A. The matters and facts set forth in the foregoing Petition are true and correct.

Q. What does that mean, Mr. Elliot?

A. That means they are true and correct of his own information and belief.

Q. Where does it say information and belief, Mr. Elliot?

A. Well, it doesn't.

Elliot indicated in his deposition that he would leave if he was accused of being a perjurer. Elliot had already been accused of perjury in petitions in open court. Nevertheless, his answer to these questions directed at determining his reason for having sworn to the petition, continued to be, "I believe it to be true."

Q. Tell me why you believe it to be true.

A. Based upon what I have read and what I have heard.

The only answer ever given by Mr. Elliot was: "Well, I know Mr. Izen has employed these people." and "I have read their depositions."

Mr. Elliot then went on...

Q. "Are you unaware of the fact that Joe A. Izen had never even met these two people at that time?"

A. "That could be. I don't know."

Q. "If that could be, then how could you swear under oath that he was authorizing this card?" The card implied an association.

The witness then stated that his complaint was based on what he "believed":

A. "I believe it is based on to my knowledge, it's based on what the Tarrant County Grievance Committee, I guess, determined. What the Tarrant County..."

Q. "What was that?"

A. "What question?"

Q. "What did they determine?"

A. "I don't know that these fellows were practicing law."

Q. "You're telling me that as...that you received confidential information that Tarrant County Grievance Committee and that is the basis of your complaint against Joe A. Izen, Jr.?"

A. "No. I am a member of the Unauthorized Practice of Law Committee.

Q. "All right."

A. "And as an attorney, I filed this suit based upon a request of an investigation done by the Committee."

Elliot went on to claim that paralegal Kermit Jackson had been illegally practicing law prior to the time that Izen was made a party to this lawsuit.

Elliot finally confessed that what he had done was not proper.

A. Do you want me to refer to my petition again?

Q. Whatever you are accusing.

A. Since that is what got me into trouble.

Over and over again, Elliot attempted to show that various people had committed the unauthorized practice of law. Over and over again none of these hearsay examples even related to Izen.
Here is another example:
Q. About my client, sir, what did they tell you?

A. Well, your client wasn't at it initially so at that point in time it was not Joe Izen. I had never heard of Joe Izen.

Q. Fine. What had they told you about Joe Izen?

A. We filed it against Littig and Pyles and Kermit Jackson."

Q. I don't represent them, sir. I am asking you what they told you about my client, Joe A. Izen, Jr., if anything.

A. The answer is nothing.

Q. "So you have never personally observed him doing any unauthorized practice of law before, correct?"

A. I have never seen the gentleman before a few minutes ago. That's correct. I don't believe...

Elliot promised, under oath, to supply me with the names and addresses of everyone who had personal knowledge of the allegations in this suit.
Elliot did not supply these.

Elliot then came up with a novel approach to the pleadings and sworn affidavits to the pleadings.

Q. Is it not unethical for you to file an affidavit petition based on nothing but allegations with nothing, without any facts to back it up?

A. No, it is not unethical.

Again, I questioned Elliot in regard to his sources:

Q. "Is there anything from John Camp that you have that proves this?"

A. "What do you mean by have?"

Q. "Anything."

A. "You mean information, verbal?"

Q. "You mean information, verbal, written, psychic, anything!"

A. **"I have some psychic information from him, I think."**

Further questioning of Elliot's psychic information revealed that despite his paranormal or occult powers, the information was neither admissible nor relevant! It became evident that Dan White was the sole source of Elliot's information. He did not reveal the nature of this information. Then he lapsed into an effort to read my notes.

Q. Are you trying to look at my notes? If you are, I will turn them around for you.

A. I can not even read them. They are upside-down.

A. I can't recall what White told me, what Dan White told me.

Q. Why did you tell me under oath that he gave you the information that led you to file this suit against Joe A. Izen, Jr.?

A. Well, it was an impression.

Q. Is this another psychic impression?

A. No...I have realized that once we have started re-going over these names for the second time that he may not have given me any information that led me to...In fact, I am sure of it that led me to...

The first hearing for summary judgment was set by Elliot in Fort Worth. The bar lost by not showing up. They asked for a new hearing and it was granted. I flew to Ft. Worth from Houston again. The bar alleged I had not given them notice of the first hearing.

The trial judge asked me if it was true that I had not told the bar about the prior date. I confessed, "Yes, your honor, that's true." The judge asked, "Then can you give me a reason why I should not grant the bar's motions?"

"Yes, your Honor, they set the hearing." I showed him Elliot's letter to Post—we had been sent a copy. Elliot had set the hearing and given me written notice of the date and time, now he was complaining that he didn't know the date or time. It was not my responsibility to notify him of the date and time he had set the hearing for. It was his job to notify me.

Elliot is still practicing law. The bar did nothing to him for the use of his psychic gifts. Judge Wright was ordered to turn over public records he had allegedly instructed his clerk not to turn over.

We tried to get bar attorney Post to sign the order. His office refused saying in part, "Some unidentified person delivered papers here. We don't even know if she was an attorney." Absurd, as it may seem, it appears that some attorneys feel that only licensed attorneys should be used to deliver legal papers.

The other bar attorney, Cruce, has his own interesting story. A jury found him guilty of defrauding the county and several others. The trial judge reversed the jury. The appellate court reinstated it. Is he still practicing law? You bet.

After several years of pre-trial work, a judgment in Izen's favor was entered against the bar, including court costs of more than $500.

I was not reimbursed for my plane fare or awarded any attorney's fee. The costs have not yet been paid. We abstracted the judgment and filed a lien in Austin on the state bar's building. When time permits, we may foreclose.

Another action, containing substantially the same allegations, was filed illegally against Izen in Houston, less than a year after the Fort Worth bar defeat. This case, after depositions in Austin, was dropped in February of 1988. This time, we are refusing to accept judgment which does not provide for the payment of my legal fee, within the order itself. Of course we may have no choice. The case is in Judge Blanton's court.

C. A LEGAL ASSISTANT TAKES THE STAND

After working eight months in my office, my legal assistant L.R. was served with a subpoena to appear at a temporary injunction hearing to answer questions on her role in obtaining a writ of execution on a final default judgment. Being a bold, outspoken person, she grabbed the subpoena from the process server and firmly signed her name, declaring, "I'll be glad to testify." She was so eager to be heard, she would gladly have foregone the attached dollar which was there as a matter of law in Texas. The server began to leave with the dollar attached to his copy, not her copy. I intervened, grabbing the federal reserve note and handing it to L.R. She and I were accused of allowing a non-lawyer to think.

L.R. took the stand and admitted that she had requested a writ of execution and an abstract of judgment in the case. She testified that all her communications, both verbal and written, with court personnel in this matter were the result of specific instructions from me. She testified that at no time did she ever claim to be an attorney. Three of L.R.'s signed documents were brought into evidence by opposing counsel. Two were handwritten requests prepared by her at the clerk's office, simply asking for the items I had instructed her to obtain. The third item in evidence was a letter prepared at our law office, on our letterhead, which, beneath her signature contained the words "Legal Assistant." L.R. testified that all her actions were within the normal scope of her duties as a legal assistant. No further questions were propounded to her. She was then excused, and was free to leave, but chose to spend the rest of the day observing the rest of the temporary injunction hearing. The losing party argued, unsuccessfully that only lawyers should be able to order certified copies of official court records.

Afterwards, the local rules of Harris County, Texas, included in their next update the sentence:

"Abstracts of Judgment and Writs of Execution must be properly re-

---

"The scope of duties that a legal assistant is permitted to perform has been increasing as the career gains respect and recognition. It is now one of the fastest growing professions in the United States."

---

quested."

What is meant by the use of the word properly is open to debate. Perhaps it implies that the request be made on a law firm's stationery, in the form of a letter bearing an attorney's signature.

The incident shows that legal assistants still have a long way to go before their function is fully respected by attorneys and court personnel. It also serves as evidence of the ridiculous lengths some lawyers will go to in protecting union control over the law.

D. THE GROWING ROLE OF LEGAL ASSISTANTS

A legal assistant is a trained paraprofessional who assists an attorney in many ways to reduce his workload by handling routine tasks which are necessary for moving cases forward. The attorney is then free to work on those matters which only he can legally perform. Some legal assistants or paralegals, as they are often called have completed a course before beginning work. Others are trained on the job. The scope of duties that a legal assistant is permitted to perform has been increasing as the career gains respect and recognition. It is now one of the fastest growing professions in the United States.

The Texas State Bar has created a legal assistant's division, complete with a code of ethics. The bar requires either the successful completion of a National Paralegal Examination or any bachelor's degree plus one year of experience as a legal assistant under an attorney's supervision. When L.R. achieved the milestone of completing one year of service, she filled out the required application and enclosed the following as a list of her duties:

1. Interviewing prospective clients and summarizing their cases for attorney's consideration.

2. Interviewing clients to get detailed descriptions of their personal and professional backgrounds.

3. Proofreading and editing rough drafts of pleadings and briefs for attorney's consideration.

4. Researching legal subjects both in our office library and the County law library.

5. Researching civil suit records, criminal records and property records.

6. Obtaining certified copies, filing documents and performing other administrative type tasks at the District Clerk's office.

7. Obtaining such information as accident and driving record reports, certified weather reports, medical bills, etc. as evidence in trials.

8. Keeping in contact with clients while a legal action is in progress. Keeping advised of their changes of address, medical status, etc. Reminding them of Court dates, etc.

9. Scanning daily newspapers and law-related publications for necessary items relating to any of our firm's cases.

10. Researching through our files and including inactive and closed files for specific names, dates and numbers to complete documents drafted by the attorney.

11. Preparing some routine correspondence dealing with daily business matters of the office.

12. Maintaining time slips to account for the use of time.

13. Drafting law suits and answers to law suits, motions and responses, under the supervision of an attorney.

All of these tasks need to be done by someone in the law office. If the attorney's time is devoted to tasks which call for his specialized skills or union membership, and if the secretary's main role is to produce professional quality written documents and correspondence and to ensure smooth orderly functioning of the office; then there is an obvious need for a law firm to have one or more individuals to fill the diverse role of information-gatherer, liaison person and tyer-up of loose ends.

The general purposes for a legal assistant are:

1. To save the attorney's time;

2. To perform functions which a licensed attorney is not required to perform and thereby enable the law office to make a higher margin of profit and enable the client to obtain the same services for less money;

3. To provide feedback, enabling the attorney to:

    a. Catch certain errors and omissions;

    b. Improve the actual work product by parlaying it with the Legal Assistant.

My personal preference in a legal assistant is a college graduate who majored in English Literature. This person is often skilled in reading, research, grammar and writing. Those are the skills most needed in most phases of law, excluding trial work. There are a lot of good trial lawyers with poor reading and writing skills. Most English majors obtain invaluable skills that many lawyers have not acquired. It is amazing how many lawyers, once they are removed from form books and are required to write a brief—a document written to convince someone of a position based on the law and the facts—have such poor grammatical skills that they cannot effectively communicate.

In 1985, we handled a libel and slander case involving two well known figures in the Houston/Galveston area: one, a millionaire scion of a prominent family and the other a former Texas state senator. Our client, the millionaire, was the Defendant in four separate libel and slander suits filed by the same individual, all of which accused our client of damaging the ex-Senator's reputation and ruining his political career. Our client had filed bankruptcy, so all of these state cases were consolidated as adversary matters in federal bankruptcy court. Our client was covered by libel insurance for the three most recent cases, and was competently represented by defense attorneys secured by his insurance carriers. The earliest suit was not covered by insurance, so the millionaire and his co-defendant had to retain private counsel, namely myself and my colleague L. T. (Butch) Bradt. Depositions, which lasted approximately three days, only dealt with the other three suits.

The plaintiff refused to be deposed by my co-counsel on the remaining cause of action. A motion to compel needed to be filed, calling for the court to order the ex-senator to provide relevant discovery. I had completed a cursory reading of the deposition and dictated 50 pages of notes referencing the 900-page deposition. A large portion of what the ex-politician was saying was so non-responsive to the questions that it resembled a filibuster on the senate floor.

One of the first assignments of my then newly hired legal assistant, L. R., was to fill in all of the blanks in the motion to compel and its accompanying brief, referencing specific citations and quotations from the deposition and plugging them into the appropriate places. This task required the legal assistant to: A) Understand my thought processes; B) Perform a careful, more extensive review of the transcript of the ex- senator's deposition; and, C) Have a basic understanding of the law on libel and slander.

L. R. first did extensive background information research on libel and slander as it related to the specific points pled in the plaintiff's lawsuit. The cost of her time was approximately 20 percent of my time. The law firm was able to bill for a healthy profit on the time she spent, and the client was able to benefit from this important portion of preparation being performed at a lower cost. L.R. then presented her report to me; I reviewed it, made comments, and requested additional work. She followed through, pulling specific cases from the law library.

Once the research was completed and we both had a thorough knowledge of the case law supporting the view point expressed in the brief I had previously dictated, and L.R. had filled in the blanks I had left with the specific references to portions of the deposition and cases, the main questions of the 50-page argument accompanied with a 20-page brief were:

"Did the defendant have a right to continue deposing the witness?" and, "Did the defendant have the right to question the witness on economic loss?" There was, of course, a question of law and a question of fact. Cases had to be found relevant to the instant case which allowed the discovery and which fit in with the fact situation. The plaintiff also had the right to be free from harassment. "Were three days of depositions sufficient? Were all the issues covered? Was additional discovery necessary?" The answer was determined, not only by all of the extensive legal research and review of the deposition but by the revelation of a glaring defect in the plaintiff's logic which was discovered by my legal assistant after two full days of work on the file.

The related causes of action, which were consolidated into ours and to which the deposition referred, all took place after 1980. Bradt and I were defending our clients against allegations of libel which took place in 1979! There was no possibility that any discovery had been given on our matter since no questions had been asked on any actions prior to the filing of the second lawsuit in 1980. In addition, the plaintiff had been claiming that his income tax returns for the years in question should be privileged, but he had asked for the defendant's tax returns produced when the defendant's deposition was taken. My new legal assistant discovered these facts that had previously been overlooked by nearly 10 attorneys who had worked on the case. This is merely one example of how my practice and clients have benefited substantially from her contributions.

E. SMALL CLAIMS COURT

All over the United States there are institutions known as small claims courts, or justice of the peace courts. In these forums, individuals appearing *pro se*—which means they represent themselves rather than using an attorney—can exercise greater authority than in higher courts. For this reason and because of the fact that small claims court judges are frequently not required to have a law degree, I have included this court system in this chapter.

In California, attorneys are not supposed to be present in small claims courts. I am not certain that such a prohibition isn't a violation of the Sixth Amendment right to counsel. Texas attorneys can go into any state court room if they wish and represent anyone. These small claims courts with jurisdictions ranging from $25 to $3,000 depending on the state are set up especially for non-lawyers.

Lawyers sometimes use these courts because they are fast. They generally have smaller juries. They frequently have judge trials. In Texas, you have the option of a jury trial for the payment of a $25 fee. These same courts, handle a great deal of the less serious crimes that are punished with small fines and generally no possible jail time.

There are two types of small claims courts in some states. One is typically a traffic court for less serious criminal matters, and one is typically for small, civil matters. Sometimes the same court handles both criminal and civil matters.

Non-lawyers are usually capable of handling matters in small claims courts. The judges in these courts are supposed to assist individuals in their claims. I have on numerous occasions, for a small fee, drawn up instructions on a specific type of case, prepared the original petition and sent clients on their way to represent themselves in a small claims court.

It is my opinion that if legal assistants were allowed to assist people in small claims courts, a large number of small complaints, which cannot be handled by attorneys because of the expense involved, could be handled efficiently and effectively by a legal assistant. Unfortunately, this cannot be done in Texas. The state bar regards this as the unauthorized practice of law. However, many pioneer-spirited legal assistants may seek to push back the edges of this frontier.

The justice of the peace courts in Texas and elsewhere are still run, to this day, very much like the ancient Magna Carta courts. The jury decides what the law is and what the facts are. The jury is considered to be the equal or superior of the judge, but the judge is there to assist, help referee and to give them advice. For this reason, these court judges tend not to be as arbitrary and unfair as many of the higher court judges.

I also see an enormous amount of folk wisdom in these judges. They tend to deal with a much larger group of humanity than higher court judges. The justice of the peace court is a working court where the docket moves relatively quickly. Although most people do not know it, in Texas, anybody who disagrees with the judge's or the jury's decision has an automatic right to a new trial at the county court level.

The splendid Nineteenth Century observer of American institutions, Alexis de Tocqueville, noted the following about justice of the peace courts:

"It has always been remarked that judicial habits do not render men especially fitted for the exercise of administrative authority. The Americans have borrowed from their fathers, the English, the idea of an institution that is unknown on the continent of Europe: I allude to that of justices of the peace.

"The justice of the peace is a sort of middle term between the magistrate and the man of the world, between the civil officer and the judge. A justice of the peace is a well-informed citizen, though he is not necessarily learned in the law. His office simply obliges him to execute the police regulations of society, a task in which good sense and integrity are of more avail than legal science. The justice introduces into the administration, when he takes part in it, a certain taste for established forms and publicity, which renders him a most unserviceable instrument for despotism; and, on the other hand, he is not a slave of those legal superstitions which render judges unfit members of a government. The Americans have adopted the English system of justices of the peace, depriving it of the aristocratic character that distinguishes it in the mother country..."[4]

F. DECORUM, PROFESSIONALISM

This portion of the chapter is specifically geared toward people who work or who are interested in working in a law office for a union member, attorney-at-law.

What is the image that a legal assistant should demonstrate, and how is the level of professionalism defined? First, let me share with you my belief that image is often merely a plastic cover hiding incompetent work. My skeptical nature rebels against it, but I know it makes a difference and in order to function in the real world, I adapt to it as much as possible when it does not seriously interfere with productivity. I'm an iconoclast and habitually wear jeans and tennis shoes in the office. I don't allow smoking in my office, even if this prohibition causes a scene. My wife and my office manager have both chastised me for my casual dress, but: A) I'm comfortable. B) I hate getting suits cleaned. I require that my staff members ignore my bad example in these two areas, and maintain a professional image in their dress. Our office is tastefully decorated and geared to an image of professionalism. There are sufficient bastions of traditional "image" in the office to form a buffer around me, shielding me against possible negative consequences from my unconventional wardrobe. Of course, for court appearances and certain depositions, I don the requisite attorney's uniform of a suit, tie and dress shoes. To do otherwise might be to sacrifice my clients' best interests for the sake of my personal comfort.

Some cases may have been settled because of the 20 framed certificates on my wall or the expensive art print in my conference room. In fact, when I see evidence of achievement in a lawyer's office, I consider him as more worthy than many others and may be more reasonable in negotiating a settlement. On the other hand, when my adversary's office is dripping with works of original art, ultra-plush carpet, sexy non-working receptionists and gold inlays in the conference table, I know that I'm in the presence of a lawyer who charges a lot for his time, and the party on the other side may not last financially all the way to trial.

I pride myself in thinking that my success is based on substance, not image. However, even underground lawyers must live in the real world where people's eyes frequently work better than their brains; I would be foolish if I said that having the "right image" is unnecessary. The legal assistant should look as much like a lawyer as possible. It commands the most attention. If he looks like a lawyer, he'll be treated like one.

A legal assistant is bound by the same constitutional responsibilities for confidentiality and attorney-client privilege as the attorney himself. This privilege extends to the office manager, secretary, file clerk and even an investigator or accountant if operating under the auspices of the law office.

The attorney-client privilege is a right established and protected by a combination of two constitutional amendments. The Fifth Amendment gives the accused in a criminal trial the right to remain silent. The Sixth Amendment gives a person the right to choice of counsel and effective counsel. Combining these two amendments and the court-mandated interpretation of them, in order to have the constitutionally protected right to effective counsel, the client must be able to talk freely with his counsel. In order to do this, the client must know for certain that the information cannot be used against him in any way. The attorney-client privilege is

---

"The attorney-client privilege is a right established and protected by a combination of two constitutional amendments."

---

meaningless unless the client can feel free to discuss every aspect of his case with the attorney, without fear of any repercussions. The combined weight of the two amendments forces an attorney to remain mute when given his client's confidences.

The right to confidentiality between client and attorney exists on civil matters as well as criminal. The same reasons are valid. It would be difficult for a client to discuss the purchase of an office building with you, if you were free to sell that information to his competitor and potentially raise his acquisition price. Your client's desire to patent a new invention can't be shared with the world before you file a patent for him.

The information that comes to the attorney is privileged, meaning that it is the privilege of the person giving the information to keep it secret or reveal it. The information is that person's private commodity which he may, if he chooses, share with his attorney. It is unethical for the attorney, absent the permission of the client, to divulge it. This privilege extends to everybody who works for the attorney. The privilege terminates when the client agrees to it, when a court orders it, or when the information has been made public in trial or by depositions. If someone not associated with the law firm hears the information, the privilege disappears in a cloud of legal smoke.

An understanding of this obligation of confidentiality and the ability to maintain it is the *sine qua non* of professionalism for legal assistants. The key to total and complete interpretation of this responsibility is: unless you are certain that you have permission to divulge information, shut up. The essence of professionalism in a legal assistant is to give out no information unless you have been specifically instructed to give it out.

Once the legal assistant has mastered that basic premise of professionalism, there are three other major directives to bear in mind: A) Make the attorney and the office you come from look good; B) Use time wisely to maximize profit for the firm, and, C) Do competent work and meet all deadlines.

1) **Making the Law firm Look Good.** The first category is probably essential to any type of business which deals with the public. The business and boss should be made to look good. Why? Because that is how he obtains clients, settlements, and jury victories.

Demonstrate that you and the office care. After more than a decade in the practice of law, I have come to conclude that most attorneys do not care. This is unfortunate, but it is not so much a reflection of the legal profession as it is a reflection of society as a whole. Skilled craftsmen, laborers, artisans and service personnel don't care as much as they did in the past.

There are exceptions to that general rule; there are professionals and tradesmen who care a great deal. A legal assistant can demonstrate her law firm's dedication by specifically letting the client know she cares, and by actually caring enough to get the work done. Some law offices seem to specialize in keeping their clients at bay with a stream of delays and excuses.

Uneducated consumers of legal services generally continue with the same attorney even if he has demonstrated a lack of interest in the client or outright incompetence because they are not well enough informed to be able to judge the quality of what they are paying for. Since they know very little about what the lawyer or legal assistant is supposed to do, they often presume he knows what he is doing and is doing what he's supposed to do. That's dangerous. The most insensitive lawyers may do nothing but take fees. Sometimes, even the most competent ones lose files and if no one checks up on the case's progress, no one knows the file is missing. A conscientious law firm provides its client with copies of all of the work that has been done on their behalf. The legal assistant can explain why each step was taken, and what value the work has to the client's case.

2) **Time is Money.** It is the responsibility of the law office legal assistant to make money. Many offices all over the United States use a three-to-one formula. A legal assistant should generate three times the revenue that the legal assistant costs in basic salary. The cost of a legal assistant is roughly twice the legal assistant's salary. This can be determined by calculating the cost of fringe benefits, bookkeeping, telephone, furniture, office space, support staff, vacations, bonuses, sick leave and all other costs of maintaining the staff member. Above that there is the margin of profit which should be approximately one third. Of course, the larger the profit, the happier the firm, the more valuable the legal assistant.

In order to make money on a legal assistant's time, bills must be sent out. A legal assistant should keep time slips in the same way attorneys do, as discussed in Chapter IV.

Some legal assistants and some attorneys do not keep records of their time. Later on they make rough estimates of the amount of work they have done. The client is often dissatisfied, does not know what amount of work has been done, and does not appreciate a general description of all of the work done. The billing doesn't make sense because the attorney or the legal assistant probably can't recall exactly what he did anyway. It's also potentially dishonest. Sometimes work is charged for what wasn't completed.

However, most of the time the attorney or legal assistant has done more work than he or she can remember and charges less than actual value of the amount of work done. Time slips are a type of time control system which is essential to a profitable law firm, if the firm is honest, and does work by the hour. Without the efficient use of this system, the legal assistant probably cannot justify his or her employment. I have also seen bills that say: "For Professional Services Rendered" and a price: no itemization. This is unprofessional. Strangely enough, thousands of clients accept these types of unexplained billings. An educated client won't.

On occasion, a client will question a bill. My office manager will pull it, pull the time slip and come up with an explanation. If we have failed to find a suitable explanation, the bill is reduced. However, if a client turns out to be a constant nitpicker, we may reduce our clientele by a client.

3) **Competent, Timely Work.** Do competent, timely work. Perhaps the greatest single problem in law offices is the failure to do the work on time. My client Ed Udey, accused of harboring a fugitive, remained out of jail pending his appeal to the Eighth Circuit and his further appeal to the Supreme Court because his motions and briefs were competently and timely filed. Another co-defendant in that case did not get his brief filed timely, and he went to jail pending appeal. His brief was well done, but not timely. Our legal system sets great store by the timely filing of papers.

In the Ngo vs. Cho case, which was discussed in Chapter IV, the defendant, Ronald Cho, was found guilty, in the state court, of knowingly profiting from his false representations to my client. Through a succession of motions filed by his attorneys in state court and bankruptcy court, he avoided payment of any funds for well over a year. On the other hand, the bank where Cho had an account didn't get its response timely filed on a garnishment action arising from that case. Even though none of Cho's money was on deposit there, a judgment was entered against the bank for $166,000. That is a high price to pay for not filing a paper on time.

Getting papers filed on time is essential. It is frequently an unforgivable omission. The most competent attorney in the world has committed grave malpractice which equals or surpasses the least competent practitioner if he misses a timed deadline. One of the main functions of a legal assistant is to make certain that the attorney keeps his deadlines.

Of course, for every one extension of time denied, there are probably 20 extensions of time granted, but even a motion for extension of time must be filed within strict time parameters. Competent work is done by being very thorough. Check the work, re-check it, and check it one more time. Pull out as many grammatical errors as you possibly can. Make your sentence structure run smoothly. Correct typing errors. Correct spelling errors. Every law office typically mails out written products containing some errors. The fewer of them there are, the better the law office looks. Too many of them indicate sloppiness and incompetence. High quality, attractive work helps win the cases.

G. INFORMATION AS A COMMODITY

One of the most important functions in a law office—whether the task at hand is drawing up wills, agreements and bankruptcy petitions, setting up corporations or preparing for trial—is the accumulation of information. A great deal of information can be accumulated just by having the client fill out certain forms.

However, since each case is unique, each client deserves some personal attention which is why it is important for a legal assistant to gather information and to spend some time with each client going over the facts. This is a function enhanced by experience. The more you work in a particular area of law, the more you learn what questions to ask.

Since that is one of the primary functions of a legal assistant, it stands to reason that in the evolution of legal assistants duties, sooner or later they'll be allowed to take depositions. At this time, in Texas, the bar is jealously guarding its monopoly over that area. With legal assistants taking depositions, the cost of litigation would be substantially reduced. Since attorneys tend to grate on each other's egos when they are confronting each other, freedom from the task of taking depositions would reduce tensions and make the practice of law itself more pleasant.

Most of the gathering of information outside the scope of trial is not done through formal discovery methods but by telephone conversations, interviews and perusing documents. Even in preparation for trial, the accumulation of information on your side gained from your witnesses is usually done informally.

The less formally the information is obtained, the less expensive it is. Of course, the information has no value at trial if it is not in an admissible form. Legal interviewing is a skill which requires discernment as to which information is necessary and which is irrelevant, which helps the clients case and which is harmful. When the legal assistant obtains all the information necessary in the preparation of a case and reduces this information to a brief typewritten report, the attorney has been provided with a useful tool for handling the case.

Undertaking the task of information acquisition, one encounters three types of people. Type One consists of those who enjoy sharing and trading information. Type Two includes those persons who prefer stealing your information and giving you nothing back for it, and who try very hard to prevent you from obtaining any of their information. Type Three is reserved for those persons who are restricted from giving out information because the information doesn't belong to them, but to another.

Attorney-client privileged information falls into the third category. Most attorneys obtain a written "power of attorney" from their client at the time of their original contract for legal services, allowing the attorney to have the authority to negotiate and act on behalf of the client. Often this involves the discrete use of privileged information for the client's benefit. There are times when the release of certain information is necessary. For example, when filing the Original Petition, you must include at least certain elements of the fact situation. In criminal cases, information is often given or implied in order to reach a plea bargain position.

Suppose that you are an attorney who has just won a case in the U.S. Supreme Court and another attorney asks for a photocopy of your brief. You may feel free to give that photocopy of the brief. Once it has been accepted by the Supreme Court of the United States, it is now public domain and can be reproduced easily by any number of different computer services. None of the information is privileged. If you determine that you would be glad to help the person who has asked for the assistance and you further choose to explain to this individual the research techniques that you used and the theories you developed, it is your free, professional choice.

Suppose then, the other attorney asked you some personal, private questions about the client which did not come out during the trial and that were revealed to no one other than yourself, these facts are privileged and should be withheld. Even if these facts may be enlightening and may actually help the other attorney's case, the information must be withheld. This information does not belong to you, your client has entrusted it into your keeping and you are not free to release this type of information.

Of course, every successful attorney, legal assistant or ditch digger occasionally meets a Type Two person who only wants to pick his brain and learn the secrets of his success while giving nothing of value in return. Fortunately, when you encounter that type of person, he is recognizable after the first one-sided information trade. You will not give him information again, since he has not reciprocated. So at least, he can only take advantage of a smart, professional colleague once. Sooner or later, the Type Two person's sources of free, professional information will dry up.

The following maxim is a guide to growth: No one knows everything. A sub-category to that maxim could be: No one knows almost everything. Another sub-category is: Almost everyone knows only a small portion of a few things. Each area of expertise has a body of general knowledge. A doctor straight out of medical school will be able to tell you the names of bones and distinguish between the pulmonary system and the skeletal system. Any lawyer straight out of law school will be able to tell you the difference between a tort and a contract or criminal law and civil law. Any boxer, after his first 30 days in the ring, will be able to tell you the difference between the left jab, right cross and a left hook. There are certain essential elements specific to a particular field which are learned quickly by competent people and incompetent people alike, within that field. It is difficult for a lay person, dazzled by the use of professional buzz words, to tell the level of competency of the user.

The law is continually growing and changing. No one has a grasp on everything. In order to stay moderately competent, it is essential to read frequently updated material such as newsletters, law reviews and supplements. Law changes far more frequently than medicine does, because medicine changes only the basis of new empirical knowledge, not preponderance of opinion. A new microbe may be discovered, but there is no medical equivalent of the Supreme Court decision which could find that it is unconstitutional for the thigh bone to be connected to the hip bone. Legal decisions are not always rational.

There are literally hundreds of thousands of new and non-litigated fact situations which come up every day in every county in the United States. The practice of medicine is still more rational than the practice of law. At least in theory, medicine has one goal: The curing or preventing of disease. The law is not headed in any specific direction at all. The law moves toward the creation of civil rights, then permits the destruction of those civil rights a decade later. The vigorous enforcement of constitutional rights may be followed by a period of erosion of those rights, followed in term by a re-interpretation of those constitutional rights.

The point? In the many-faceted practice of law, you need all the help you can get. You have to go to various sources constantly. You have to update your information, you have to improve your research skills and you have to improve your interpersonal skills so that other human beings are also resources: other attorneys, insurance adjusters, real estate brokers, police officers, sheriffs, FBI agents, clerks and legal assistants. Anyone competent in a field which is relevant to any case in your law office is a valuable source worth cultivating. One of the chief functions of a legal assistant is to find information and bring it back to the office.

There are two ways to handle a situation in which you need some information: A) pretend that you have the information, or that you don't need it; B) ask for it or find it. Unfortunately many members of the legal profession do a great deal of blustering and bullying to cover up their lack of knowledge or their lack of humility to ask.

This brings us back to those first two types of people who have information; those who share it, and those who don't. If you have imparted a piece of information to another person, and he knows something you would like to know, he should be willing to share information with you. Some information can be given away freely with the hope of future rewards in return for the information. It is valuable to open up as many sources of trading information as possible. How do you handle the individual who refuses to give out any information at all or, even worse: lies to you and agrees to exchange information? This person teaches you one thing: He is a leech, so don't deal with him again!

There are economic considerations that must not be overlooked. The law office, which sells its time on an hourly basis, sells nothing but information. For that reason, information must be strictly doled out for money unless it is being given to a source which is expected to return the information in kind; otherwise, it is a charity. If too much information is freely given out by a law firm that relies on hourly work for its business, bills can't go out, and salaries won't get paid. Free information will not pay the rent.

"Our office turns many clients into underground lawyers who at least have a compass in hand when they go exploring in the forest of jurisprudence."

CHAPTER VI
CRIMINAL OR CIVIL:

WHAT'S THE DIFFERENCE?

"In order to be a criminal, you must be found guilty of violating one of the criminal statutes."
"Civil Law is the other side of the legal spectrum.
Civil cases usually involve a money dispute."

A. CRIMINAL

1. **Definition** What is the distinction between criminal law and civil law? A criminal statute is a law prohibiting—or in some rare cases—forcing a particular type of conduct. There are many different types of statutes governing criminal conduct, far more extensive than the popular notion that criminal statutes only prohibit killing, raping or stealing. In order to be a criminal, you must be found guilty of violating one of the criminal statutes. Webster defines criminal as:

"...relating to, involving or being a crime; relating to crime or to the prosecution of suspects in a crime; guilty of crime; or disgraceful; also, one who has committed a crime; or a person who has been convicted of a crime."

The definition of crime according to Webster is "an act or the commission of an act that is forbidden or the omission of a duty that is commanded by a public law and that makes the offender liable to punishment by that law; a grave offense against morality; criminal activity; something reprehensible, foolish or disgraceful."

That definition is interesting: It does not distinguish between the person who has committed a crime and the person who has been convicted of a crime. Under the law in this country, the fact that you have committed a crime does not make you a criminal. You only become a criminal after you have been *convicted* of a crime. Almost everybody who watches television understands that you are innocent until proven guilty. This concept is derived from the constitutional requirement that any American is presumed to be innocent until proven guilty. "Proven guilty" means that a judge or jury has listened to the facts and has found the suspect guilty; or an individual has pled guilty and as a result of that admission, has been found guilty by the judge.

That is the law in the United States: you are not a criminal until you are convicted of a crime. Some people believe that if you have committed a criminal offense you are a criminal. A lawyer or any informed citizen who is familiar with the Constitution should say that a person is not guilty unless that person has been convicted.

There are many different levels of government, and each jurisdiction generally creates laws, ordinances or statutes—a violation of which is called a crime. Counties have laws and state governments have laws. Cities or municipal governments generally have lots of traffic laws which are criminal offenses usually punishable by fines ranging from as little as $1 to as high as $1,000.

Murder is a violation of the law in all 50 states. It is defined differently in all 50 states, but basically it is the intentional taking of a human life without legal permission. There are various terms for lesser degrees of offenses which result in human death depending on the state in which you are located. Negligent homicide is a type of killing that is rated as less vicious than murder—killing someone by mistake through negligence. Driving while intoxicated is a frequent factor in this offense. A drunk driver runs into someone and kills him. It's a mistake that could have been avoided. It was careless but unintentional. Capital murder (a murder for which the death penalty may be levied) is generally the most serious crime that can be committed.

2. **Felony or Misdemeanor** Crimes are generally broken down into two categories: felonies, which are serious crimes; and misdemeanors, which are less serious offenses. A felony in one state may be a misdemeanor in another state. Texas has class A, B, and C misdemeanors; first, second, and third degree felonies.

The penalties are as follows:

Class C Misdemeanor up to a $200 fine - No Time.
Class B Misdemeanor up to a $1,000 fine - 6 months.
Class A Misdemeanor up to a $2,000 fine - 1 year.

3rd Degree Felony up to a $5,000 fine - 10 years.
2nd Degree Felony up to a $10,000 fine - at least
2 years max. 20 years
1st Degree Felony - At least 5 years max. 99 years.

Of course, a defendant could get probation and not even go to jail, even if he was convicted and sentenced to do jail time. A sentence on a class B misdemeanor of six months usually means a maximum of two or three months of real time in jail. A sentence of 99 years, probated for five years, means that you don't have to go to jail as long as you obey the conditions of your probation—which could include such terms as being employed, paying restitution, being drug-free, and avoiding the friendship of certain companions. Also, if put on probation, you probably will have to report to a probation officer occasionally—but you don't have to go to jail.

If you are convicted of violating a criminal statute, lose all of your appeals, and your conviction becomes final, you officially become a criminal. Convictions from district court may be appealed in the various courts of appeal. The Texas Court of Criminal Appeals is the court of last resort for criminal matters in Texas.

The practice of criminal law basically consists of prosecuting or defending persons accused of violating criminal statutes. The style (name) of the case might be: The City of New York vs. John Doe, the County of Harris vs. Sally Smith, the State of Alaska vs. Bill Black or, if it is a federal crime, the United States of America vs. Benedict Arnold.

Federal crimes are also classified as felonies or misdemeanors. Some types of murder can end up being a federal crime because you could also be accused of violating the dead person's civil rights—which is a federal crime—by murdering that person. You have also committed the state crime of murder. Although the double jeopardy clause of the Constitution was put in there to prevent you from being tried twice for the same crime, the U.S. Supreme Court has ruled that you can be tried for the crime in a federal court and a state court because the two jurisdictions are separate.

Many people fail to understand the legal niceties of the double jeopardy clause as interpreted by today's Supreme Court. This situation did not arise during the lifetimes of the framers of the Constitution, because the categories of federal crime and state crime did not overlap. It is very unusual to be tried in both federal court and state court for a crime arising out of the same act because everyone really knows it's not fair. When it happens, assume there are political motivating forces in play.

In a criminal case, the government is the plaintiff proceeding against an individual. Two individuals are never opponents in a criminal action. If Sally Smith is beaten by John Doe, she does not become the plaintiff in a criminal suit seeking to put John Doe in jail. She must convince the government prosecutor to file a criminal complaint against Doe based on her testimony. If the charges are filed, the style of the case would be, for example, the State of Texas vs. John Doe. The state would be the plaintiff; Doe would be the defendant; and Sally Smith would undoubtedly be a very important witness.

In criminal law, the government sues an individual for the purpose of taking away his money or his freedom. If the government wins and a fine is assessed, the government collects the money, provided the fine is paid—lots of criminals don't pay their fines. However, if payment is a condition of probation, it's easier for the government to get its money since the defendant has the choice of paying the fine or going to jail.

When a defendant is sentenced to do jail time, the government gets to keep him instead of his money. When a person is sentenced to serve five years in jail, that time has little meaning compared to the time the person will actually spend in jail when we consider how extensively the sentence is usually reduced by credits given for good behavior and other inducements for the convicted person to behave while in jail. For most crimes—not including tax cases a criminal usually serves about one-third of the time he is sentenced to serve, however, this general rule also varies from one jurisdiction to another.

A criminal defendant may be charged in two different ways. The first way—generally reserved for less serious crimes—is by way of an information or a ticket. An information is simply a statement by a government prosecutor, usually based on a sworn complaint filed by a citizen, charging a person with violating a criminal statute. An information can also be based on a sworn statement by a law enforcement officer or government agent that he has witnessed or has conducted an investigation and determined that a criminal violation took place.

The other way a person is charged with a crime is with an indictment returned by a grand jury. A grand jury indictment means that a group of citizens has determined that they have heard sufficient evidence to accuse someone of having committed a crime. In a criminal trial, evidence must be established by standard of proof called "beyond a reasonable doubt." But all a grand jury must do is hear evidence, usually only from the government's side, and determine if the jurors believe the accused person committed a crime.

"...evidence must be established by standard of proof called 'beyond a reasonable doubt.'"

B. CIVIL

Good question, Mr. Foreman. The Defendant hasn't told you his side
because he doesn't have a side. He's guilty. The law doesn't allow
the Defendant's attorney in here because he's guilty too.

Civil law is the other side of the legal spectrum. Civil cases usually involve a money dispute. However, you can still end up in jail in civil
court—although it's rare, by making a judge mad and getting charged
with contempt of court. You can end up in jail without ever facing a jury.
This might occur if you refuse to obey a judge's orders or were obnoxious
beyond the limits of the law. A group of citizens in east Texas gained a
modicum of fame as the "Sitting Seven" in 1985 when they were sentenced to 30 days in jail on contempt of court for their refusal, based on
religious grounds, to rise when a county court judge entered to preside
over his courtroom. They believed it was similar to bowing to an idol.
They served 15 days and were released after the Texas Court of Criminal
Appeals agreed to hear their case. The appeals court upheld the judge's
ruling, and the U.S. Supreme Court has refused to review the case.

This conduct was considered criminal contempt. However, there is also
a charge called civil contempt which can land you in jail. Pastor Everett
Sileven of Louisville, Nebraska, was jailed for 12 days on a civil contempt
charge for refusing to apply for a license for his church school.[1] And, al-

though debtors' prisons are illegal in this country, fathers are put in jail every day for not paying child support. In the majority of jurisdictions, failure to pay child support is a civil offense, although some localities consider it a criminal matter.

A civil court can grant injunctions, which is an order not to do something, against an individual or entity. If you disobey the order you can be held in contempt of court and sent to jail. This is an extreme type of remedy which is rarely granted, but it does exist and is sometimes exercised.

As a general rule, a civil lawsuit consists of one party suing another party for money. In the judicial arena, a party can be a human being, a corporation, a trust or a partnership.

Sometimes a suit demands specific performance, in which the plaintiff is asking the court to order the defendant to do something. Specific performance demands, under some circumstances, may be a violation of the Thirteenth Amendment of the U.S. Constitution prohibiting slavery. Example: Actress Gloria Glamour agrees to act in a role. She later changes her mind. She violates her written contract. She cannot be forced to act in the movie. This would be slavery. She can, however, be ordered to financially compensate the studio who owned her acting contract. The sum of money in question is called damages. Damages are the amount of money necessary to soothe the feelings or to repair the harm done by the bad guy to the good guy.

There are two main categories of civil litigation (if we preclude family law). One arises from contracts. The other is based on torts.

1. **Contracts** A contract is a binding agreement to do something. Our Constitution specifically protects contractual rights, although they have been extensively modified during the last 100 years. If you do not perform according to your contract, you may be sued. In order to be enforceable, the contract has to fit certain rules. A mere agreement is not enforceable unless it fulfills the requirement of a contract. Generally, a contract must have five elements:

A) *Consideration*—this means that someone had to agree to give up something in exchange for something else. If I give you $100 that's not a consideration, but if I give it to you in exchange for your promise to work for me a week, then it's a consideration.

B) *Specificity*—a contract must state clearly what the consideration is and what it's being exchanged for.

C) *An agreement* by two or more parties.

D) *Be in writing* and signed by both of the parties—however there are some jurisdictions and situations that allow oral, non-written contracts to be enforced. In some jurisdictions, the contract must be in writing and be signed as evidence that both parties were committed to fulfill the contract

E) *Legality—A contract must be legal.* As a general rule, a minor cannot enter into a contract. Therefore, any such contract signed by a minor would not be enforceable. In most states, prostitution is illegal. Therefore, a contract for prostitution services would be illegal.

2. **Torts** A tort is an act performed which damages another individual or entity which gives rise to a cause of action. The English legal system, which most states have adopted, held that it was illegal to do certain things because the court said so. An example of this would be battery. Battery is a rude or offensive touching of one human being by another human being. If you hit someone in the face, even though there was no statute forbidding it, you would be liable for damages that occurred to the person you struck. If you merely approach and menacingly threatened to hit someone in the face, you have committed the tort of assault. Often, assault is followed by battery as night follows day. The victim could sue you for assault and for battery. A jury would decide if damages should be awarded to the victim for suffering this indignity.

There are many different types of tort actions: personal injury claims arising from negligence (such as carelessly striking someone else's car with your vehicle), intentional infliction of mental distress (unsolicited, obscene phone calls), interference with right to contract, slander and libel (telling or writing damaging lies about someone). Some torts have been incorporated into statutes. The trend is to put all torts into statutes to control them by legislation.

In Texas and in the federal court system, there is the Deceptive Trade Practice Act. This allows consumers who have been deceived by retailers or service industries to file a lawsuit for damages arising from the alleged deception. Prior to the Deceptive Trade Practice Act, you had to prove that the people knowingly and intentionally deceived you. That was the tort called misrepresentation or fraud. The plaintiff in a deceptive trade practices suit alleges that the defendant knowingly represented his goods or services to be of a different quality than they were; that the plaintiff was induced to rely on these representations; that the plaintiff actually relied on them and was damaged thereby. A successful deceptive trade practice suit can result in triple damages being awarded to the plaintiff. Unfortunately, in the few years since the DTPA was passed, it has been legislatively diluted through successive changes.

A tort created by common law becomes more political as the political body codifies it and redefines it.

Automobile accidents are torts if caused by someone's negligence. As a general rule, any legal action in which someone has been personally injured or damaged due to someone else's carelessness or from a faulty product is a tort, providing it did not arise as a result of a contract dispute. Sometimes elements of tort and contractual disputes are mixed in a single cause of action.

C. ADMINISTRATIVE LAW

There are now entire fields of law virtually non-existent at the time of adoption of the Constitution. Welfare, social security and other regulatory agencies have spawned their own quasi-judicial systems. As the various government bureaucracies have mushroomed, both in numbers and power, their independence from the judiciary branch has increased. Many areas of law are handled primarily by executive branch employees and not the judiciary.

If, for example you are denied relief from the Social Security Administration, you appeal to that administration. Not happy? Appeal to its own appeal board. Still dissatisfied? Go to a Social Security judge. If you don't like his decision you may take it to the agency's appeals council. Beyond that, there is recourse to the federal courts, but the recourse is severely limited.

The hearings at administrative tribunals are relatively informal. Rules of evidence are interpreted loosely. The downside is that the litigant never gets to go before a jury. Worker's Compensation matters on the state level begin with administrative hearings, but may be appealed to state district court in some states. Decisions on immigration and Freedom of Information Act complaints may be appealed from the administrative to the federal judicial arena.

"There are now entire fields of law virtually non-existent at the time of adoption of the Constitution."

CHAPTER VII
ANATOMY OF A CIVIL LAWSUIT

"The single greatest reason for defeat is the failure to get evidence before the jury in a clear, persuasive, admissible form."

This chapter puts you in the shoes of a legal assistant or attorney meeting a new potential client, analyzing the client's situation, and taking appropriate action. Real examples are used.

A. INFORMATION GATHERING PETITION AND FILING

When a potential client comes into the office, the first task of the attorney or legal assistant is to gather pertinent information. This information is utilized to determine whether or not a lawsuit should be filed, and, if so, what type of lawsuit. The matter should be categorized into a general area of the law such as civil or criminal, and then whether it's a tort or a contract dispute; and finally into its specific niche, such as personal injury, wrongful discharge, breach of lease etc. Obviously, if the matter is criminal it doesn't belong in this chapter, although some civil litigation often has criminal overtones.

Sometimes there are actions that must be taken before a lawsuit is filed. For example, under the Texas Deceptive Trade Practice Act, 30 days written notice must be given of a claim before you can file the lawsuit, unless you are filing a counterclaim.

Often more information must be gathered before a case can be properly evaluated. Before filing a personal injury suit arising from an automobile wreck, it is advisable to obtain the police report of the accident.

Before filing a suit for breach of contract, you must review the disputed contract, to ensure that your prospective client's interpretation of the matter is correct.

If one of the prospective defendants is a corporation, you must contact the secretary of state's office and determine the name and address of the corporation's registered agent, who must be served with the petition.

Once the necessary information is accumulated and the prerequisite work is done, the original petition or complaint is drafted. It identifies the parties and states the grounds for jurisdiction—why this suit should be filed in the court where it is being filed. It also includes an address where the defendant can be served. It states the cause of action (why the plaintiff has a right to file this lawsuit, and why the defendant should be sued, and it states the amount of damages, or other forms of relief, being sought by the plaintiff.)

A useful example to illustrate the process involved in determining the type of suit to file is a personal injury case we handled, which had a rather complex fact situation. This example also clearly illustrates the filtering progress that's necessary, after obtaining the facts of the case, to determine the specific damages and type of action to be filed.

Our client, an Old West style Texas boy (originally born in Tahiti) Dick, was driving down Katy Freeway in his truck when an old rust trap vehicle came hurling past him and scrapped the side of his truck causing him a whiplash as he skidded off to the side of the road.

Dick is no weeping willow. He collected his thoughts, pulled back onto the freeway, pushed the gas to the floor in pursuit of the hit-and-run death trap. His souped-up truck quickly caught the escaping vehicle, and he forced it to the side of the road, and got out of his truck and approached the vehicle.

Pouring out of the rust bucket were three dirty, long-haired individuals who approached Dick brandishing tire irons. Dick, who was a clean-cut, lean 200 pounds of Texas beef, must have appeared to be easy prey for the terrible trio—they had him alone on the side of the feeder road, apparently unarmed. The three skinny cave men creeped up on the buffalo. But under his coat, Dick had an iron of his own: a .45 automatic pistol, which he pulled out and directed to the attention of the malnourished cavemen.

The cavemen would have quickly attacked an unarmed man, but Dirty Dick was apparently too much for them, and they started to retract, but Dirty Dick said no. One shot in the air and a verbal order was all it took to get the cavemen's attention and have them lined up against the side of their rust bucket for a citizens arrest.

Now an officer pulls up, and from behind his car he asks Dirty Dick to please give him the gun. Dick says okay, so the officer cautiously approaches and takes Dick's weapon.

The cavemen—a natural enemy to the cowboy and not quite comfortable in the presence of the cop—ask if they can split. The cop wants to arrest Dick, who is now exhibiting some of the symptoms of whiplash, loss of orientation, headaches, dizziness and nausea, for being crazy and dangerous, when an independent concerned citizen pulls up.

This citizen confesses that he had sat, with headlights off, and watched the whole thing from a safe 30-foot distance. Dick was not crazy and dangerous, the observer said, he was really Dirty Dick and the cavemen were really the criminals.

The officer's subsequent search of the three individuals revealed empty hypodermic needles which could have been used for drugs. He determined that he did not have sufficient evidence to arrest those individuals for suspected drug use.

Our client sustained back injuries and wanted to sue the driver as a result. The police report was obtained. We had to weed out the extraneous matters. The possible criminal drug use of the suspects was relevant to a personal injury suit. Good stuff for a jury. Had our client committed an assault against the side-swipers by holding them at gun point? No criminal charges were filed since these individuals chose not to do so.

The significant remaining issue was the negligence aspect of the side-swiping. Negligence means failing to use that standard of care that a normal and prudent person under the same or similar circumstance would use. Gross negligence would be an extreme failure to use the proper standard of care.

This was a personal injury: a tort. A lawsuit could be filed against the only person in the vehicle personally liable or responsible for the mishap, the driver. If the owner of the car was not the same individual as the driver, it is possible that some liability could attach to the owner. It's not a good policy to let drug addicts drive your car. While the evidence was insufficient to make criminal charges on drugs stick, there was sufficient evidence to file criminal hit-and-run charges and sufficient evidence to get the drug issue to a jury.

We decided to file a lawsuit against the driver of the vehicle. We had to include the driver's full name and address so a process server could serve him with the petition. The petition must cite facts to prove plaintiff's right to receive money from the defendant to recompense him for his injuries. The suit must include a statement of: A) What did the defendant do? B) What did he do that was wrong? C) Was this improper conduct of the defendant the actual cause of an accident? D) If it was, did this accident cause the plaintiff to be damaged or injured?

After all of these elements had been dealt with, the next question was: What were the plaintiff's (Dick's) damages? This portion of the lawsuit will generally be a little bit vague at this stage. Often, a plaintiff does not even know his full damages until after the lawsuit is over. In a personal injury case, the law entitles a plaintiff to recover his past and estimated future medical expenses; lost time from work, future lost earnings, and a monetary award to compensate for his pain and suffering. All of these elements need to be included in the petition. If the full extent of the amounts of these various categories of damages are unknown at the filing stage, a phrase such as "in excess of $50,000" may be employed. A typical personal injury suit petition is included in the Addendum.[1]

The suit is then filed at the county clerk's office, after payment of a filing fee. One copy of the lawsuit is kept in the law office. A copy should be sent to the client. The clerk stamps the date on the petition. The suit is assigned a case number which appears at the top of all documents connected with the suit. If there is more than one court in the particular jurisdiction, the suit will be assigned to a court at this time. Often a lottery system is used to determine which court gets a particular case. Sometimes it's politically decided.

B. SERVICE

After the suit is filed, it then must be served on the defendant, at his residence. It might be served in that same county or jurisdiction where the lawsuit was filed, or it might have to be served in another state or even out of the country. The original signed petition stays in the court's file for review by the judge and the public at all times.

A copy of the lawsuit, plus a citation, is then delivered to the process server—who now has the responsibility of serving the defendant. The purpose of the citation is to inform the defendant that he has been sued and is obligated to answer within the prescribed period of time. The process server has the responsibility of finding the defendant and then handing the citation and petition to the named individual, or registered agent of a corporation. When service is executed, a copy of the citation is signed and dated by the process server and returned to the court.

If the defendant lives within the jurisdiction of the court, most of the procedures described above generally are handled by the county clerk who channels the suit to the proper law enforcement official or process server to effect service. The plaintiff's attorney should follow up with phone calls several days after filing to ensure that the suit did not get "lost" in a filing cabinet or on someone's desk at the courthouse. Until the citation has been returned, indicating the suit has been properly served, the plaintiff should keep in contact with the clerk and/or process server to determine if any problems arise and what can be done to resolve those problems.

It is important to track the officials down and make certain the petition is served. It is also important to make certain that it gets done on time. An overwhelming majority of all causes of action must be filed within a certain time frame governed by statutes of limitation. In Texas, for example, a lawsuit based on an automobile collision generally must be filed within two years from the date of the collision. Also, the plaintiff must diligently try to serve it. If it is not served on time, you could lose the entire cause of action.

The citation must make its way back to the court file as proof that the suit was properly served. The purpose of service is to give the defendant notice of the lawsuit and afford him the opportunity to respond to the complaint. It is unconstitutional to sue somebody and try to get a judgment against him without giving him notice of the claim against him. How could he defend himself?

The type of service just described is called personal service. It is the fairest system available. There are many other types of service depending on the jurisdiction. Any less fair service should be avoided whenever possible because the process may be challenged later. Sometimes, however, the plaintiff has no choice if the defendant can't be found because he has moved or he is deliberately avoiding service. Different methods of service may be approved by the court after a showing of good cause. The court may permit service upon an adult family member who resides with the defendant or even the receptionist at the defendant's place of business. Another form of alternative service which may be utilized only with the court's permission is called "service by publication," in which a brief summary of the suit is published in a local newspaper in the defendant's community. The defendant is obligated to answer the suit, as if he had been served personally.

C. ANSWER

After being served, the defendant is required to answer the complaint

"It is unconstitutional to sue somebody and try to get a judgment against him without giving him notice of the claim against him."

within a specified time frame. Generally the answer comes in the form of a written statement. The requirements for the written statement vary in different jurisdictions. In Texas, the most common type of answer to a petition consists of a general denial. Pursuant to Texas Rules of Civil Procedure Rule 92, the defendant denies everything, and forces the plaintiff to prove his allegations.

This statement, written down with the cause number and style of the case, is legally sufficient in many cases. However, there are many causes of action which cannot be answered with merely a general denial. For example, if a sworn account suit over a delinquent debt if filed—in which the plaintiff attaches an affidavit swearing that the debt is legitimate, due, and unpaid—then the denial also must be sworn and fit certain prerequisites. The answer must be filed timely.

The papers attached to the suit should pronounce an answer date, usually depending on jurisdiction, 10 to 30 days. If the document is not answered on time, the plaintiff may request a default judgment, which means judgment may be rendered against the defendant without the defendant answering or refuting the charges made in the complaint.

Often the plaintiff still must prove his damages to the court's satisfaction. The default judgment can, under the proper circumstances, end the lawsuit. Once the default judgment is signed by the court under the existing rules of Texas Rules of Civil Procedure and notice is given by the court to the defendant at his last known address, the defendant has 30 days to figure out what has happened and ask for a new trial. The defendant will usually get the new trial but may be required to pay the legal fees for his failure to timely respond to the original suit.

After the summary judgment is entered, or if the motion for a new trial is denied, the judgment is final—at least on paper. The suit is not necessarily over, however, because there are still appeal options which exist. And you should remember that just winning a judgment does not automatically put money in anyone's pocket.

D. DISCOVERY

After the defendant has answered the lawsuit, both sides have the right to gather information from each other. This process of requesting and furnishing information is known as discovery.

A litigant must be prepared to take discovery and to respond to discovery requests. Discovery is exactly what the word implies, a search for information. During discovery, each party attempts to find out exactly what happened, and to pin down the testimony of all of the potential witnesses.

The four major types of discovery are briefly discussed in this chapter.

1. **Deposition.** A deposition involves requiring a person, who is either a party to the litigation or a witness, to appear at an agreed location to answer questions under oath. The person to be deposed is known as the witness or the deponent. A written notice of intention to take deposition must be served on the person who is to be deposed. The notice may be accompanied by a subpoena *duces tecum* requiring the witness to bring certain documents to the deposition with him. If the party being deposed objects to the notice or the subpoena *duces tecum*, he may file a motion to quash or a motion for protection, both of which would be asking the court to intervene to either prevent or postpone the deposition or to excuse the witness from the requirement of bringing some of the items demanded.

At the deposition a court reporter, or maybe a photographer with videotape equipment, will take down every word that the witness and attorneys say. In some respects, a deposition is like a trial. The attorney on one side asks the witness questions, while the opposing counsel is there to protect his client's interest.

What facts and information must be obtained from the other side? First of all, there are usually introductory questions which request the witness' full name, address, social security number, driver's license number, date of birth, work history, educational history, and a sketch of family background. This information gives the attorney a general idea of the type of person the witness is. Asking these preparatory questions enables the attorney to more effectively elicit information relevant to the case because he knows what sort of person he is dealing with.

Preparation prior to the deposition frequently determines how effective a deposition will be. It is important to map out all of the important and relevant questions. It may be difficult to get a second deposition from the same person. The goal is to tie down the witness' testimony so there will be no surprises at trial, or to make the testimony available for trial without bothering the witness again.

When the testimony of doctors is necessary, the doctors are often deposed in advance because: A) Sometimes they don't show up at trial. B) Sometimes they might have to wait a whole day in court to testify and doctors charge a lot of money to sit and wait—and might get mad and switch sides. C) Most doctors hate court. If you don't require them go to court, they may be more cooperative. D) Many doctors hate lawyers. Anything you can do to make them happy could help keep their bills and tempers down.

In some instances, testimony obtained in a deposition is used to ultimately impeach the witness at trial. "Impeach" used in this context, means to contradict or show dishonesty. If certain facts are known before the deposition, the attorney might be able to get a witness to lie during the deposition, and use the lie against him at trial. Sometimes a brief yes or no answer can later be explained away. Sometimes it can't. Liars tend to lie, and juries know this. The trick is in catching them.

A list of every potentially relevant question should be drafted prior to the deposition. It is good practice for the attorney to confer with his client prior to the deposition of the opposing party or an adverse witness to allow the client to assist in preparing the questions to be asked. As a general rule, the client will know a great deal more about the fact situation than anyone in the law office.

Preparation is also essential before your own client is deposed by opposing counsel. The attorney or the legal assistant should sit down with the client and review his answers to interrogatories, so he will not say anything contradictory in his deposition. The client should be instructed to dress for the deposition, just as he would for his trial—especially if a videotape is made.

Also, it's important to know that sometimes jurors make up their minds frequently based on the appearance of the parties. When a person looks and dresses with integrity, the jury frequently assumes integrity even when it doesn't exist. If a person is extremely sloppy or disorderly, the jury may value that person less highly, and even tend to doubt the veracity of his testimony.

The client must be thoroughly prepared for cross-examination by the opposing attorney prior to giving his or her deposition. If the client has been cross-examined by his own attorney in a role-playing situation prior to the deposition, he will be prepared for the real thing. In far too many cases adequate preparation is not done because of cost in time and money, when in reality most of the preparatory work could have been handled

"It's important to know that sometimes jurors make up their minds frequently based on the appearance of the parties."

efficiently by a legal assistant.

2. Requests for Production of Documents or other Tangible Items. A written request for production of documents or other tangible items, such as photographs, drawings or product samples, may be served on a party once the defendant has answered. The request might ask that those items be brought to the opposing attorney's office, or the request might be for the items to be made available for photographing, or examination by an expert witness for the opposing party. As with the notice for taking depositions, if a party does not feel it should produce the requested documents or other items, they may file a motion for protection, explaining to the court why the request should be voided. The motion should be filed timely.

Possibly half of the pre-trial hearings in civil cases involve discovery requests concerning motions to compel or protective orders. One side wants to have the judge compel the other to produce documents, witnesses or information, and the other side does not want to do so. Today in both federal and state courts, there are increasing requests for sanctions for impeding the discovery process. The requests for sanctions are increasing in number and severity. If there is flagrant abuse of discovery, such as repeated failure to attend depositions and answer interrogatories, the ultimate sanction could be granted: striking the offender's pleadings, which is canceling one side of the suit and thereby making the other side the winner without a trial.

3. Interrogatories. Interrogatories are written questions served on the opposing party in litigation. Interrogatories must be answered in writing, under oath and usually within 30 days, depending on the jurisdiction. Some jurisdictions have little regulation of the interrogatory process, but in other states it's tightly controlled. In Texas, only two sets of interrogatories may be served on a party without the court's permission, and each set can contain no more than 30 questions—a requirement which is often circumvented by asking multi-part questions.

Interrogatories are a much cheaper form of discovery than depositions since the expense of a court reporter is avoided. Usually, interrogatories on a party are served and the answers received and reviewed before that party's depositions are set. Knowing some of the answers in advance can save considerable time in depositions. A legal assistant can draft all of the questions, submit them for the attorney's approval, and, once approved, send them out. The questions can be very comprehensive, and the answers extremely helpful.

Our office has a standard of interrogatories on automobile accidents that is included in the Addendum[2]. They are modified annually and also adjusted for case distinctions. These questions have been carefully prepared to elicit the important facts about the way the accident happened; the identities of witnesses to the accident, expert witnesses who may be called in to testify; and the name of the defendant's insurance company and the policy limits!

The disadvantage of written interrogatories is that the party's answers are not spontaneous. Frequently, the attorney for the other side will answer for his client and then merely have his client sign them.

When one of our clients is served with interrogatories, usually by sending them to our office, we immediately send him a photocopy of the questions, for him to answer to the best of his ability. When the client has completed this task, he sets up an appointment to come into the office, to confer with the legal assistant or attorney, and develop the final answers to interrogatories. An attorney should advise his client to answer the interrogatories simply and briefly so that any honest discrepancies between the answers and later testimony cannot be used against him at deposition or trial. Honest people, especially under the stress of unfamiliar, intimidating situations, often have variances in their stories. Shrewd opposing attorneys love to confront them with these discrepancies.

4. Requests for Admissions. Requests for admissions are very similar to written interrogatories. By means of a written instrument, a party is asked to admit or deny something, such as: Admit that on March 4, 1986, at 7 p.m. you were on Interstate Highway 45 going north. The respondent is required to admit or deny this. The respondent might also object to the request or might say that he has insufficient information to either admit or deny. Sometimes requests for admissions and interrogatories are combined in the same document such as:

Request for Admission #5

John Smith was a customer in good standing at Piggy Savings and Loan.

Admit _____ or Deny _____

Interrogatory #5

If Request for Admission #5 is denied, state the reason for such denial.

If the requests for admissions are not answered timely, all of the facts may be deemed admitted. Attorneys are sometimes able to make use of this discovery tool to wrest damaging admissions from their opponents, simply by their opponents' failure to respond timely.

When an opposing party has answered interrogatories and requests for production, has produced documents, and has been deposed, the attorney should have enough information to set the case for trial.

E. MOTIONS

A motion is a written request that the court take some action. Depending on the particular court and jurisdiction involved, a motion can be made orally or in writing. Most higher courts require that motions be made initially in writing if time permits. When an oral motion is made, it must be made on the record which means there must be a court reporter present making a record of everything that's said. Off the record means no one is taking it down—officially. Sometimes they do, and sometimes they don't. The integrity of the recorder is the real key.

Motions are usually accompanied by a proposed order for the judge to sign. The person filing the motion is generally referred to as the movant. The person required to answer is referred to as the respondent. Either the plaintiff or the defendant may be a movant or a respondent on any motion, and may, at the same time, be a movant on one motion and a respondent on another.

There are numerous motions that may be filed. As previously stated, the most common types of motions deal with discovery: either motions to compel discovery; motions for sanctions for failure to comply with discovery rules; or motions for protection from the opposing party's discovery efforts is a motion.

The most significant motion is for Summary Judgment, which, if granted, short circuits the civil process and brings a case to an end without a trial. A motion for summary judgment is filed by a litigant who feels that no trial should take place because there are no important facts in dispute and the law is on the movant's side. A party filing a motion for summary judgment asserts that the law indicates that his side would win regardless of whether or not a jury is impaneled or what conclusions it reached. Such a motion should be supported with a brief addressing all of the issues and citing case law to support the motion. The motion for summary judgment should be accompanied by properly sworn affidavits of witness.

It is not easy to win a summary judgment. Depriving a party of trial is a serious step. Judges are loath to grant such a motion if even a relatively small fact question is in dispute. Rulings on motions for summary judgment lean toward the party trying to defeat the motion.

In a summary judgment proceeding, the evidence is reduced to writing. A response opposing a motion to summary judgment has more chance of success when it is well fortified with affidavits and a memorandum of law. In Texas, the response to a motion for summary judgment must be filed at least seven days before the hearing date. The court rules on the written evidence and considers the oral arguments of counsel if an oral hearing has been requested and granted. It is good not to waste time trying frivolous cases. However, the danger is that many judges abuse their power and unreasonably deprive a litigant of a jury trial. The litigant's only remedy is to appeal.

A motion for continuance asks that a trial or hearing be postponed to a later date. This type of motion is second in quantity only to discovery related motions. In order for a continuance to be granted, some good cause has to be shown—illness on the part of a litigant or counsel; the necessity of counsel being present at a previously set trial, hearing or deposition; extremely heavy caseload of counsel or the coming of the Messiah. The motion should also state that it is not being filed for the purpose of delay, but that justice can be done. The motion must be supported by an affidavit.

Similarly, a motion for extension of time can be filed if a party requires extra time to file a brief, produce some documents or comply in some other fashion with a request or order. In this too, good cause must be shown. When the government asks for extra time, it is usually granted. In fact, in my practice, civil and criminal trial or appeal, the government's various extension motions have been granted by the courts in every instance submitted.

If an attorney finds it necessary to remove himself from a particular case, he must file a motion to withdraw. If another attorney is taking the previous one's place, a motion for substitution of counsel must be filed.

If a judge has ruled unfavorably to a party, a motion for rehearing or motion for reconsideration may be filed by that party.

If a settlement has been arrived at, or a verdict rendered at trial, a motion to enter judgment is filed, accompanying a proposed final judgment itself. This final judgment is a prerequisite to enforce a jury or judge verdict. Within 30 days after a final judgment, a motion for new trial can be filed.

Motions should be accompanied by a proposed order which the movant would like the judge to sign. A typical motion to compel and order is included in the addendum.[3]

Motions must either be set by submission, meaning that they will be presented to the judge on a certain date without the need for an oral hearing unless the respondent demands it, or they may be set for an oral hearing by the movant. The clerk of the court where the motion is to be filed informs the attorney's office of the next available date for submissions and hearings. Not all judges grant oral hearings just because parties request them. Many require that good cause be shown for a hearing. One federal judge in Delaware let me handle pre-trial hearings by phone, while another federal judge in New York handled most of the hearings by mail. U.S. District Court Judge Fong in Hawaii made me fly there to handle every motion in person.

A copy of all proposed motions must be served on the opposing party or party's counsel in the time frame established by each particular judicial district. In Texas, if a motion is set for submission and the respondent wants an oral hearing, the response and request for oral hearing must be filed at least five days before the date the motion is set for submission.

F. SETTING FOR TRAIL

Every jurisdiction has different procedures for scheduling a case for trial. Basically, either a party asks the judge to set a case for trial or the judge just does it. Sometimes, neither happens and the case just sits for years. Trial settings are generally granted after all of the parties concede that discovery is finished, and they are ready for trial. The trial may be before a judge or a jury.

Most federal courts set up a table for all events leading up to a trial date. Some don't. In the Norma Ginter case in Arkansas, Judge G. Thomas Eisele waited a couple of years. When I asked for a trial, he set it. On the day of the trial, he dismissed the case. It's now on appeal.

In federal courts the judge unilaterally sets the case for trial, often without consulting either side. Obviously this can cause a problem if you are already set for trial in another state or speaking at a conference in Switzerland that week. A motion for continuance must be filed, sometimes argued, and then ruled on. A lot of time is wasted and legal fees go up.

At trial, the judge or jury determines what the facts actually are. Did the defendant cause the accident by his own negligence? Was it negligence for the defendant to allow his three-year-old child to drive the vehicle blindfolded while the defendant was sitting in the back seat giving him directions? If so, was this also gross negligence? By evaluating the evidence presented, the judge or jury answers all of the questions which were deemed relevant. The judge applies the law to those fact situations. The jury reaches a verdict or the judge makes a finding, and the trial is over.

G. EVIDENCE

One of the major jobs that has to be done in the preparation of trial is to gather evidence in admissible form. The evidence is that tangible thing that is put in front of the judge or jury to prove the facts you want to establish. Every relevant fact which is disputed must be proven by evidence.

Evidence can be presented in many different ways. Most evidence is presented through testimony. Testimony involves a human being getting on the witness stand and making statements under oath. The judge or jury, whichever one is the trier of the facts in each case, is the one who determines which party's version is true. In a jury trial, the jury is the trier of fact. In a judge trial, the judge is the trier of fact. The finder of law is always the judge, although this was not the case under Magna Carta nor the U.S. Constitution 200 years ago.

Let us examine the method of preparing evidence in the personal injury auto case described in Chapter II: A pickup truck with two passengers stopped for a traffic light. A car carrying a female passenger and her husband, who was the driver, stopped immediately behind them. A third vehicle, driven by an intoxicated person, smashed into the second car forcing it into the truck. The third individual then fled the scene of the accident. A fourth party observed the complete episode.

Our client was the female passenger in the second car. Without evidence, none of these facts could have been proven. How was this case proven up at trial?

To begin with, an investigation of the facts was made, starting with our client's version of the accident. In this particular case, the client was a professional bartender and recognized the defendant driver's symptoms of intoxication. Another major witness was the client's husband who was driving the car. He raced out of the car, saw the license plates of the fleeing individual and called the police. The police tracked the miscreant down, and found out that he had previously been arrested for driving while intoxicated. The owner of the car turned out to be the boyfriend of the driver.

We now knew the names and addresses of the defendants from the police reports and other evidence, and suit was filed, served, and answered. The accumulation of evidence continued. We served interrogatories on both defendants. We obtained a certified copy of the results of the driver's previous arrest for drunk driving. During his deposition, we confronted him with our knowledge; we probed until we learned of another such conviction. We anticipated opposing counsel's possible objections to this admission so research was done to find case law showing us that this information was relevant and could be brought before the jury.

During his deposition, the defendant indicated that the road was wet. We obtained the appropriate weather report from a Houston paper showing it was a dry day. To make the newspaper report admissible evidence for use in court—so we could refute his claim that the road was wet—we had the report certified as a true and accurate copy (sworn to before a notary).

Facts in evidence are those which the jurors have in front of them to use in making up their minds on a verdict. In this instance, the individual had been drinking just before the accident occurred. He admitted this in the pre-trial deposition we had taken. We chose to bring his past record before the jury to show that his drinking and driving was a continuing course of action, and that he was frequently intoxicated. We sued the owner of the car for knowingly allowing his unfit friend to drive his car. The owner either knew, or should have known based on their close personal relationship, that this driver would be likely to drink on the day in question. The depositions of both defendants were taken.

Depositions can be used in trial in lieu of live testimony. Someone takes the stand and reads from the paper. Obviously, depositions are not as convincing as live testimony or videotaped depositions. The jury cannot see the witness. If you have a bad witness you don't want the jury to see in person, it is a good idea to tie down his testimony in a written deposition

"Facts in evidence are those which the jurors have in front of them to use in making up their minds on a verdict."

so you don't have to have him appear live at trial.

In the accident case we've been examining, I planned to put the defendants on the stand because the jury would hate them. I also wanted their depositions for the possible purpose of catching them in a lie and discrediting their testimony, and also to tie down their story.

To prepare for trial, we had to track down all our fact witnesses. In this mobile society, characterized by frequent job and residence changes, often people don't stay put for the two or three years it takes to get a case to trial. Sometimes, even though the law firm seeking them uses private investigators or skip tracers, some witnesses simply cannot be found. One reason for taking depositions is to preserve testimony in the event that witnesses cannot be located at time of trial—or if they change their mind and refuse to cooperate.

Honest, truthful people will tell stories a dozen different ways, depending on what information they have before them, and how well their memory has been refreshed. With thorough preparation before trial, I help the witnesses structure their truthful story. Obviously, their story must be true. However, a truthful person who has forgotten certain details and who is not prepared, may give erroneous testimony in a deposition or at trial, and may not reflect the actual situation. The witness must be prepared so the truth can be properly presented to a jury. Truth is, of course, in the eye of the beholder and varies from person to person. Two very honest advocates will give two entirely different descriptions of the truth. For that reason, it is valuable to assist your witness in structuring his testimony so the truth can be packaged in the most favorable light.

In preparation for the personal injury trial we've been discussing, we were fortunate enough to be able to contact the driver and passenger of the pick-up truck which had been in front of our client's vehicle. The husband was a retired deputy sheriff and the wife had been an insurance adjuster. Their testimony was extremely valuable.

We were unable to locate one of the witnesses who had observed the accident. He had given our client's husband his business card, but by the time the case came to trial, he was no longer working at the same place. We hired a private investigator who found that the witness had once worked for the same flower shop as the defendant driver. Supplemental written interrogatories were directed to the driver asking him if he was acquainted with this person or knew his whereabouts. We had to file a special motion to compel to get these answers. The answers—which may or may not have been truthful—were negative.

Written records may also be in evidence at trial. There are certain rules and regulations in every jurisdiction for the proper verification of the records so that they are admissible.

As a general rule, hearsay is not permitted. Hearsay occurs when a witness repeats a statement allegedly made by a third party who is not in court, in order to prove a fact. There are many, many exceptions to the hearsay rule, and in most jurisdictions, hearsay is presented more often than not through one of the loopholes.

What is hearsay, and what is the most common exception to the hearsay rule? Let us imagine Jane Doe is testifying. Jane might say, "John Jones said that it was a clear, moonlit night." That is hearsay if it is intended to prove the weather conditions. We want to hear from Jane what she knows, not what John said. It is not fair because John isn't there to speak, and you have a right to get the information from the horse's own mouth. The Sixth Amendment to the U.S. Constitution guarantees you the right to cross-examine the accusers against you. But, what if John is dead? What if we need his truthful honest weather words? That's how exceptions to the rule of keeping hearsay out got started. The most common exception to the hearsay rule is the use of a hearsay statement for the purpose of impeachment alone. Impeachment means to contradict or show weaknesses in the statements of other persons. Suppose Suzy Silly has testified that it was raining that night. Jane's testimony is not proving the weather. It is casting doubt on the veracity of Suzy's testimony.

You do not want to develop any of your evidence on the basis of hearsay if you can help it, because the judge may keep it from the jury. You want all of the evidence, if possible, to be presented through direct evidence in testimony. You also want it to be presented in the most convincing light. Hearsay is not as believable as direct testimony.

The burden of moving forward in a civil lawsuit is in a plaintiff's hands. This is an enormous burden. It means if you have no evidence, you lose. The party complaining must have evidence with which to convince the jury.

The witnesses should be prepared to tell their portion of the story in an orderly fashion. If possible, duplicate witnesses should be available to reinforce each portion of the story so that it can be more persuasively presented to the jury. It's a question of trial strategy whether or not to use duplicative testimony. It may be more believable or it may bore and thus lose the jury. The eliciting of testimony from your witness on the stand is called direct questions. You may not lead them to the answer. In other words, you cannot suggest the answer within the context of your question.

Questioning the opposing party is known as cross-examination. In cross-examination, leading questions are permissible. An example of a direct question would be: Where were you on the night of July 12, 1984? An example of a leading question would be: At 10 p.m. on July 12, 1984, were you at the International House of Pancakes on Westheimer Road?

What role does a legal assistant play in the production of evidence? The legal assistant is instrumental in keeping in touch with the parties and witnesses and in gathering certain records and other written evidence. The legal assistant can prepare direct questions before trial. Many cross-examination questions can be prepared in advance; however, others will occur to the attorney at the time of trial based on the opposing witnesses' testimony.

Time limitations frequently prevent an attorney from being fully prepared for trial. That is one of the values of having a legal assistant: there's another pair of hands—and another brain—working on trial preparation.

The general public may have the attitude that right generally prevails in our courts. Nothing can be further from the truth. Right or wrong frequently has nothing to do with trial. The only thing that is relevant to the outcome of a trial is the evidence that is put before the jury. A substantial number of attorneys do not understand this. Throughout most of their career, they have suffered defeat while representing just causes. They assume that the system itself is unjust. This is not true. There may be unjust judges or even some unjust jurors, but the system itself is not unjust. The single greatest reason for defeat is the failure to get evidence before the jury in a clear, persuasive, admissible form.

H. JUDGMENT AND APPEAL

When the trial is over, the plaintiff has gained nothing and the defendant has suffered no loss until an order is actually signed directing money to be transferred to the plaintiff or specifically ordering certain actions to be taken. The order has to be drawn up. In a civil action, the order is usually drawn up by the victorious attorney. The judgment itself is the court's

"The only thing that is relevant to the outcome of a trial is the evidence that is put before the jury."

YOU ARE INSTRUCTED TO DISREGARD THE WITNESS'S STATEMENT

order. Some judges sign judgments very quickly, and others take a great deal of time to sign them. Justice is not served when it takes a long time for the judgment to be signed. Depending on the jurisdiction, within 30 days after the judgment is signed, either side can ask for a new trial which comes before the appeal process. In some jurisdictions, a motion for new trial is a prerequisite for appeal, and in some jurisdictions it is not. If a new trial is denied, the case is then handled on appeal.

A notice of appeal must be timely filed and usually an appeal bond to cover the cost of the appeal must be posted. The party taking the appeal requests the court reporter to prepare the statement of facts (a type-written version of all testimony at trial) and a transcript and agrees to be responsible for the cost involved. The cost of the official court reporter is very high. Court reporters usually have the right to negotiate terms. In the Udey case in Arkansas, the court reporter sold me a copy of the three-week trial for $700 on terms. In the Brownlee trial in Delaware, the original transcript in a three-week trial cost me $1,500 on terms. Both were fair and reasonable: Both occurred in federal court.

Court reporters have official prices, but these prices are negotiable. In the Ginter case, we were charged $1,500 cash up front for one-half day of pre-trial testimony. It was highway robbery! We paid it anyway; we had to have the testimony to beat the murder charges.

The transcript and statement of facts together constitute the record or appeal. The timely filing of the record is the burden of the appellant. If the record cannot be filed on time, the appellant must submit a motion for extension of time, accompanied by the affidavit of the court reporter.

In Texas state courts, the appellant's brief must be filed within 30 days of the filing of the record on appeal. But the time requirements will vary according to jurisdiction. The brief includes a summary of the facts of the case from the appellant's standpoint. It discusses each one of the ways in which the appellant feels the trial court committed errors or overstepped its discretion. Each matter becomes a separate issue on appeal.

Relevant statutes and previous court decisions are analyzed and included under the appropriate issues to bolster the appellant's position. Either party can request oral arguments on appeal. Depending on the jurisdiction, within 10 to 30 days after receipt of the appellant's brief, the appellee must file his brief.

Once the briefs have been filed, the court of appeals will reach a decision based on the briefs. Either side may appeal the appellate court decision to an even higher court. Normally, for cases which have arisen in state court, the highest state court is the final arbiter. Matters don't cross from the state courts to the federal system unless constitutional questions are raised.

I. THE BOTTOM LINE

Law, contrary to textbook interpretation, is a business. No one ever does everything that can be done to prepare. A working day must be divided among many tasks. The importance of discovery and pre-trial preparation must be weighed against the loss of doing it in terms of labor and out of pocket expense. Two weeks of work (100 hours at $150 per hour or $15,000) might be required to prepare a specific case properly, but perhaps only $5,000 is at stake. Compromises must be made. One common compromise is simply to avoid cases with little monetary amounts contested.

"The general public may have the attitude that right generally prevails in our courts. Nothing can be further from the truth. Right or wrong frequently has nothing to do with trial."

CHAPTER VIII
LAWSUIT BLUES

"The single most difficult time of any fight is not the training for the fight, but the waiting for the fight to proceed."

When I was a young man preparing for a fight during one of the Golden Gloves tournaments, walking around the outside of the ring preparing to enter for combat, I bumped into the ugliest, meanest looking monster I had ever seen in my life. He appeared to be deformed. He was obviously the recipient of many knife wounds, head buttings, scars and other ogre-like manifestations of war all over his face and body. Frankenstein and the Hunchback of Notre Dame would have been afraid to meet this ruffian in a dark alley or even a lighted one. As a matter of fact, it would have been kinder to meet him a dark alley rather than a well-lit boxing ring because in the dark alley you can only be beaten to death.

It was at this point that I questioned the wisdom of following in my father's and grandfather's footsteps by taking up boxing. I suspected that although I could both take and deliver a pretty good punch, those abilities alone were not sufficient to enable me to be a boxer. I suspected that I was, at this point, deficient in that element which we call "courage."

Courage, my father once taught me, was the conquest of your fears. A man of courage was a man who could put these fears to one side and do what he had to do anyway. The absence of fear is not courage. The absence of fear is insanity. All sane men fear.

It was not too long after I had been taught this simple but valuable lesson that I found myself standing in the corner opposite this monster. I can remember the words of my coach, Mickey Brown: "Mike, what are you so scared of?" he asked. My answer: "Mickey, that's the meanest looking ___ ___ ___ I've ever seen in my whole life."

Mickey, offering his own homespun wisdom in a fashion similar to what my father would have done, asked me: "Mike, why do you think his face is so messed up?" I didn't have an answer, but Mickey responded: "His face is so messed up because he can't fight." Looking at that face, his advice sounded good and I wanted to believe it, but as is usual with most fights, the fear doesn't dissipate until the fight begins.

The fight was over in the first round. My opponent couldn't defend himself and couldn't land any punches. He was like a punching bag, absorbing blows on his scarred face. The fight ended on a technical knock-out.

What's my point? The single most difficult time of any fight is not the training for the fight, but the waiting for the fight to proceed. It is not the fight itself but the fear of the unknown prior to getting into the ring.

As an attorney representing other human beings, I know that when we step into the courtroom ring I am dragging a non-fighter into the courtroom with me, my client. If the person has any fighting experience, boxing, wrestling, karate, street fighting, chess, spit-ball throwing in school, I know that that person will feel more comfortable in the courtroom than someone who is a total innocent in the art of combat.

In the courtroom, not only do you have to look for blows being tossed at you, but you have to look at blows being tossed at your client and all the other people involved.

With that in mind, I want to share with you the Judy Jones case. In this case I am utilizing fictitious names to protect the identities of any guilty parties. Every name in this chapter is completely fictitious and hopefully cannot be traced to the real people involved. The case is real; the people are real—but the names are changed, so you can't trace them, and I won't expose allies.

Judy and her child were driving on the freeway when they swerved off and hit a tow truck driver's vehicle. After the impact, they pulled over to the side of the road, and another car smashed into them. Judy's car then caught on fire. The tow truck driver risked his life, jumped into Judy's car, pulled her and her small child out of the car and flung them a distance. The car then exploded, slightly injuring the tow truck driver, but neither Judy nor her child sustained so much as a scratch.

Judy hired an attorney who filed suit against the tow truck driver, the tow-truck company, the person whose car was being towed by the tow truck driver, and the person who inadvertently struck her car while it was protruding into traffic off the side of the road.

I would not have gotten involved in this case had it come into my office through the front door. Judy may or may not have been able to find other counsel in the areas which surround the City of Houston, where nearly 20,000 attorneys reside and practice law in that area.

An attorney, who had himself been injured in a car accident, convinced

"Courage, my father once taught me, was the conquest of your fears."

me to take about 40 cases that he had pending as a personal favor, and Judy's case was one of those 40 that I inherited. The attorney also had been the victim of a $250,000 theft by his office manager, which depleted his cash flow for handling contingency fee cases. And as a result of his inability to attend to his caseload due to these two circumstances, the State bar was attacking his license. To help a friend in his hour of need—and to protect all the unknown clients from having their claims dismissed or running into a statute of limitations problem—I agreed to take on these cases without meeting the clients or knowing anything about the cases.

This action created an unhappy mess in my own practice. It took me two years and a great deal of personal financial expense to resolve the problems. No work had been done on any of the files. None of the clients had had any of their calls returned for six months to a year. In some of the cases no suit had been filed at all, and the statute of limitations was getting near. None of the cases had been properly developed. None of the cases were ready for trial. All of them had suffered from the lapse of time. All of the clients were extremely angry and were threatening lawsuits and grievances. I spent approximately a month meeting with all the clients. I gave each one of them my word that I would either keep their case, or send it to another attorney—or give the client a sound reason why I couldn't.

Also, I gave each and every one of them an opportunity to take their files away without cost, without any charge from me or from the attorney who had previously handled their file, and here I use the term "handled" very loosely.

Of the approximately 40 files, only three of them elected to leave my office after an initial conference. Of those three, two asked to come back, and I refused to take the cases back.

One of the cases went through five or six attorneys before the client returned and asked me to take the case back, but I refused. As a general rule, the more lawyers a person has run through, the harder they are to deal with.

I referred 20 of the cases to other attorneys. Of the remaining 17 cases, I settled 12 and tried five. All five of the cases that I tried resulted in a judgment in favor of my client.

When I heard the facts of Judy Jones' lawsuit against the tow truck driver, I was horrified. I explained to her that it was extremely difficult for me to justify a suit against the man who had saved her life. I had some real, moral problems with such a case. Since I had promised her that it would be handled, I would do my best to get another attorney to handle the case.

Another attorney had an office in the same building that I worked in at the time. Since he is a friend of mine, I will not mention him by his real name, but I'll refer to him by the name "Dilly." Dilly had just started his practice of law and was eager for case referrals. As a solo practitioner, it is a benefit to have other attorneys to whom you can turn from time to time for mutual assistance.

These people are also sources of additional business and can take cases like Judy's off of full hands. I referred Judy's case to Dilly. There were a half-dozen defendants, all represented by large firms with insurance companies as their real clients. Apparently, all half-dozen had decided that this would be the case for the year that they'd win. They would not settle it under any circumstances. They would fight to the end. This is exactly the type of case that Dilly needed to enable him to get his feet wet in trial techniques—A guaranteed trial; a guaranteed head-to-head confrontation with a large number of opposing insurance attorneys. If Dilly got out of this alive, he would know more about personal injury litigation than most practitioners find out after 10 years of experience. It's also the type of case many people call frivolous, and that most competent attorneys won't touch with a 10-foot pole.

I put Judy's case (and Dilly) out of my mind and went on with my practice of law. Several months later, I received a call from Dilly at the court house.

"Michael, we're in big trouble."
"What do you mean, Dilly, we're in big trouble?"

"Well," Dilly responded, "Remember Judy Jones' case?"
"Vaguely", I replied, anticipating with dread another series of questions.

"Well, it's set for trial today, and I don't know what to do."
"Well, Dilly, try to win the darn thing," I instructed.

"Hey, Minns," he stated, a little angry at this point, "You got me into this mess, and you're gonna get me out of it."

"Dilly," I answered, "you're on the case. You're the attorney of record. You're licensed in the State of Texas. It's your case. I want nothing to do with it."

"Well," he responded, "If you don't get down here to the court house,

I'm leaving, and Judy can try her own case."

I went down to the court house. Judy wasn't there. Her attorney hadn't contacted her and told her about the trial date. Apparently she had not been in contact with her new attorney for long periods of time; what a mess! Had we gone to trial at that time and date, I feel relatively confident that we would have been poured out. The fact that Dilly was completely and totally unprepared, the fact that all the insurance attorneys were hanging over him like vultures, the fact that the judge wanted to move the docket—all would contribute to the ultimate defeat of Dilly's clients: Judy and her child.

We had a case with lots of potential damages but no one at fault except perhaps the client. The child could, of course, sue the mother, but I have consistently refused to take intra-family suits. I didn't like the taste of the case to begin with. I didn't think that a precedent should be started which would suggest that a person has a cause of action against someone who has saved her life.

These weird cases are the exception rather than the rule in lawsuits. No lawyer wants to try an almost sure loser. However, it's the type of lawsuit that receives front page publicity from a severely slanted point of view. As a general rule, if the jury is told all the facts and situations, the jury will not reward a person for filing this kind of lawsuit.

We needed to settle the suit for harassment value. Even though I don't file suits for harassment, I had been conned into this one, and I was stuck with it. In order to accomplish even this, we still had to establish that Judy and her child had been harmed. It seemed obvious that anyone who had come close to witnessing her own death and the death of a loved one would undoubtedly suffer some type of emotional trauma. How much trauma? No one but a shrink could tell us with the necessary authoritative intonations to satisfy a jury. I suggested to the insurance company attorneys that our client had suffered severe emotional trauma; that we did not have a report available (all of which was true), but, that if they would like—since not one of these brilliant defense attorneys had asked for the names of our expert witnesses—we would be willing to grant a continuance for that purpose. At this point, the insurance attorneys were quite perturbed since their failure to inquire about our experts was nothing short of malpractice, and this could have serious consequences if they lost.

Faced no longer with a cringing, unprepared Dilly but with a potential challenge to their malpractice policies, the attorneys for the defendants graciously agreed to give us an additional two months in exchange for an opinion from a shrink.

I suggested that the group of them get together and try to come up with some sort of reasonable sum, and I believed we would have settled for something reasonable right there on the spot if Dilly had not cringed so much. Cringing is a sign of cowardice. Insurance vultures react to it by getting meaner. I am fond of the old saying, "a coward dies a thousand times; a hero only once." Actually a coward and a hero both suffer substantially, but the hero gets the fight over with win, lose, or draw; the coward never gets the fight over with and so continues to suffer.

Dilly was destined to die a thousand times with this case. It wasn't doing me any good either.

I explained to Dilly that he needed a shrink's report. Dilly had some connections with shrinks and referred his client accordingly.

The shrink's report was excellent on the issue of damages. Clearly, mom and daughter had suffered tremendous trauma over the past few years since the accident. They were both upset. Mother couldn't eat properly and was losing weight. Daughter exhibited symptoms of anxiety. Both of them had dread feelings of some unknown disaster which was about to befall them. That's not uncommon after a serious brush with death. Both of them felt alienated. Classic trauma! The shrink was willing to testify that the trauma was severe.

As I read the report, I got a little bit excited. Perhaps I had been overly pessimistic about the value of the case. When I finished the entire report; I sighed, "Dilly, there is no proximate cause relationship in this report." Dilly asked, "What's a proximate cause?"

"Dilly, proximate cause means fault." Actually, it means there must be a direct link between the event which caused the harm and the harm done. I was over-simplifying it and some of my non-lawyer friends would have been upset at the insult, but with Dilly I had to break it down to its lowest common denominator and leave out some of the legal niceties.

"What do you mean by that?" Dilly inquired.

"Dilly, just tell the shrink we need to know the proximate cause of the trauma. Tell the shrink to put it in writing. That should explain it to your satisfaction." An experienced trial shrink knows many legal terms just as a

---

"Actually a coward and a hero both suffer substantially, but the hero gets the fight over with win, lose, or draw; the coward never gets the fight over with and so continues to suffer."

---

good personal injury lawyer knows a couple of medical terms.

A report was sent to opposing attorneys without proximate cause and the opposing attorneys started to murmur. A settlement offer came in at a ridiculously low figure of $2,500. There was, of course, the chance that the tow truck driver was at fault for being on the side of the road in the place and position which Judy had hit him. Quite frankly, I was unconvinced of this, and still felt that morally the tow truck driver should have been rewarded for risking his life, instead of being sued.

The shrink's supplemented report returned. Judy's trauma and the trauma of her child was proximately caused by her lawyers! She was never able to get them to call her back. She had no idea about the status of her case. The only lawyer she had any rapport with or respect for (me) had sent her to another lawyer who seemed to lack any knowledge about what was going on. This increased her trauma by lowering her self-esteem. The constant dickering with her own attorneys had caused her trauma which the shrink stated would last through the rest of her life.

The child's trauma, thankfully, was minimal. The shrink predicted that when the suit was over, it would diminish, and eventually go away over a period of several months, perhaps a year.

Dilly was horrified. "How do we keep this away from our client?"

"Dilly," I responded, "we don't. First of all, it's your client, not our client, and second, the client has the right to see everything in the file. I also strongly suspect that the client knows this because her shrink figured this out after talking to the client."

The client refused to settle. She didn't like Dilly and demanded that I call her. I had to call the client and convince her to settle the case. I do not like to push clients into settlements, especially low ones, but in this case I did. The client finally settled. The $2,500 and certain costs were agreed upon, and the matter was returned to Dilly. The insurance company and the lawyers delayed paying the claim for a year. A normal delay ranges anywhere from a day to two weeks; anything past two weeks is inexcusable.

Dilly, unfortunately, got nothing in writing and did not push them to wrap the case up. The insurance vultures left the meat on the table to

---

"...over and over again lawyers representing clients seem totally oblivious to the fact that their clients are undergoing severe trama because of the continuation of the litigation.."

---

gather maggots and interest. It is hoped that Judy's psychological trauma has now abated.

With several years experience under his belt, Dilly now has become a top flight family and criminal lawyer. He stays away from injury cases.

Litigation is tough on everyone. Sometimes the price of being involved in a lawsuit is worse than the results of the actual lawsuit, good or bad. Even people who have been involved in dozens of lawsuits still experience a certain amount of trauma when a constable serves them with a new petition.

Sometimes individuals suffering from physical ailments which induce psychological trauma, undergo a substantial amount of healing immediately after the settlement. Why? Does that mean they were con-artists merely malingering until the insurance company paid them a ridiculous amount of money? Absolutely not. It means that the insurance company's refusal to make a fair, reasonable, timely settlement resulted in inflicting additional trauma on a human being faced with the uncertainty of litigation.

Litigation is usually an unknown factor, and it is frightening. I am amazed that over and over again lawyers representing clients seem totally oblivious to the fact that their clients are undergoing severe trauma because of the continuation of the litigation. Large numbers of lawyers seem to become immune to this over a period of time. It is perhaps one of the greatest shortcomings in our adversary system of litigation. On the other hand, no amount of coddling and attention is enough to calm the fears and concerns of some clients. If possible, these cases need to be settled out of court.

It is wryly humorous to note that on those occasions when one of these attorneys is sued, he undergoes pretty much the same type of trauma that his clients had been undergoing for years. These same attorneys who never return a phone calls to their clients expect and demand constant attention from their attorney. Lawyers are among the most difficult clients to represent. I know because I have had the opportunity, or sometimes misfortune, to represent a lot of attorneys in my practice.

"Sometimes the price of being involved in a law suit is worse than the results of the actual law suit, good or bad."

CHAPTER IX

THE CRIMINAL LAW GAME

"Through a combination of the erosion of some constitutional guarantees and the public's ignorance about their rights, the American criminal justice system is not functioning in the way our forefathers intended."

A. FROM CRIME TO INDICTMENT

The authors of our Constitution preferred to free 100 guilty persons rather than convict one innocent person. The Fourth, Fifth, Sixth and Seventh Amendments all protect the rights of the accused; the Eighth protects both the rights of the convicted and the accused. The accused is to be bonded out of jail until trial, and the convicted are not to suffer cruel and unusual punishments. The Constitution, however, is less concerned with the rights of convicted criminals than with the rights of those presumed to be innocent.

Through a combination of the erosion of some constitutional guarantees and the public's ignorance about their rights, the American criminal justice system is not functioning in the way our forefathers intended. All too often, it is only professional criminals who are aware of their rights. Everyone has seen movies and television shows where criminals are taken into police custody whining or snarling, "You can't do this to me! I know my rights! I want my lawyer!" Yet the ordinary, generally law abiding citizen who finds himself enmeshed in the criminal justice system is very likely to be in an emotional "state of shock" when the "Miranda"[1] rights are read to him and is so easily bullied by law enforcement and court personnel that he doesn't exercise his constitutional rights.

A wise, constitutionally minded Supreme Court panel gave us the Miranda warnings, a gift to free, honest American people to help them obtain access to their constitutional rights when they needed it most but were under duress incapable of making important decisions which require clarity of thought.

It is a deplorable condition when only professional criminals care whether law enforcement officials intrude into their homes, or question them without the presence of counsel on matters relating to the commission of a crime. It is unfortunate that a professional criminal who is pulled over to the side of the road knows not to divulge information to a police officer, while the average citizen, conditioned since elementary school that "Officer Friendly" is on his side, freely makes statements which are later used against him.

Our grand jury system, reduced to being a rubber stamp for the prosecutor, presumes the guilt rather than innocence of the individuals brought into its jurisdiction.

The Fifth Amendment right to refuse to testify against yourself was included in the Constitution in protest against the European penchant for torturing suspects into confessions.[2] Our forefathers did not want our justice system to be sullied with such techniques. They provided the right to remain silent in the face of government officials' questioning and interrogation. Yet, former Attorney General Ed Meese indicates that only guilty people use the Fifth Amendment. His position appeared to be only guilty people are accused of crimes. Perhaps this was a premature comment on the accusations which he ultimately faced.

Harvard Law Professor Alan Dershowitz teaches that while law enforcement officials do not want to convict innocent people, most of these officers tend to believe that the people they accuse are guilty. For that reason, he concludes, most law enforcement officials will lie if they believe their lie helps to convict someone they believe is guilty. Most judges know this.[3]

The oath to God in front of the jury has been trivialized to the extent that it would be laughable were it not so tragic. Some lawyers refer to the courthouse as Perjury Palace. A prominent Houston attorney is fond of telling the following story regarding the space in the dome of our old Courthouse building. He points upward saying:

"Do you see that bare spot? There used to be a statue of the goddess of justice up there. One day she took off her blindfold and looked down into the courtrooms and saw what was going on in there. She just spread her wings and took off and was never heard from since."

Many commentators look at the jury decisions and use their human

---

"All too often, it is only professional criminals who are aware of their rights."

"OF COURSE, ONLY GUILTY PEOPLE REFUSE
TO TALK TO THE POLICE."
— ATTORNEY GENERAL EDWIN MEESE —

foibles as an indictment against the jury system. They ask: How can intelligent people do this? How can they allow this vicious criminal to go free? Rarely do they say, how could the jury have convicted this poor person? Why did the jury believe the sensational press versions and ignore the evidence? Occasionally there is a public outcry about someone convicted without any evidence against him, and the accusatory finger again cites a flawed jury system. These criticisms of the jury system are seldom warranted. When juries make mistakes, the overwhelming cause is that they were not permitted to examine all the facts. This happens for a number of reasons:

"It is a deplorable condition when only professional criminals care whether law enforcement officials intrude into their homes, or question them without the presence of counsel, on matters relating to the commission of a crime."

1. The defense attorney is stupid;

2. The defense attorney lacks courage and creativity;

3. The defense attorney cares about nothing except collecting his fee, whether hired and paid privately or court-appointed;

4. The defense attorney has been convinced by the prosecutor his client is guilty and he expects to lose, so he does;

5. The defendant's attorney is lazy or too busy to prepare his case for trial. It isn't important enough for him to try real hard to win. He wants to please the judge and doesn't fight too hard;

6. The prosecutor deliberately withholds evidence which would tend to prove the defendant innocent, but he doesn't care. He needs the conviction to run for office;

7. The judge hates the defendant, the defendant's attorney or all defendants and deliberately tries to let the jury know he thinks the defendant is guilty. The best lawyer in the world fights a tough uphill battle when he has to fight the judge.

Everyone can do everything right, competently and morally and a mistake is still possible—our system is human because it relies on human beings. This is why all possible doubts should be resolved in favor of the defendant.

Under early common law, soon after Magna Carta, it was extremely difficult to convict people and turn them into criminals. There was the presumption that the accused person was innocent unless convicted by members of his own community. At the dawn of our own republic, Thomas Jefferson reaffirmed the doctrine that no man should be found guilty of a crime unless his own friends and neighbors agreed that he was guilty.

The brilliant eighteenth century author, Thomas Paine, stated "a society can be determined to have a good government only when the prisons are empty and taxes are not oppressive."[4]

"When juries make mistakes, the overwhelming cause is that they were not permitted to examine all the facts."

Let us examine our criminal justice process. Before a criminal justice matter may be initiated, there must have been the commission of a crime, or at least the representation of a complaining citizen or a law enforcement official that a crime has been committed.

The next step is that an individual must be accused of having committed the crime. While the accusation process differs widely all over the United States, there are some general procedures which are usually followed.

The constitutional protections of the Fifth and Sixth amendments are (or should be) available in all jurisdictions. Unfortunately, the Bill of Rights has been held to generally give protection against federal authority, but not as strongly from potential local government abuses. Whether or not a particular constitutional right exists in a particular case varies from one jurisdiction to another. However, the Fifth and Sixth amendments are usually binding on the state authorities as well as federal.

The Fifth Amendment provides for a grand jury investigation when there is an accusation of a "capital or otherwise infamous crime." The Sixth Amendment guarantees a speedy, public trial, an impartial jury, the right to confront witnesses against you, the right to a compulsory process for summoning the witnesses in the accused's favor, and the right to assistance of counsel. Frequently, prior to a grand jury indictment, there is a preliminary hearing before a judge or magistrate to determine whether there is sufficient evidence to turn the case over to a grand jury. Usually the judge or magistrate finds that there is sufficient evidence to do so. At these preliminary hearings the accused has the right to cross examination if the judge will allow it. Frequently the judge does not allow it, and as a general rule this does not constitute reversible error.   In the case of serious crime, a grand jury must decide whether or not there is sufficient cause to accuse an individual.

In a less serious crime, some jurisdictions have the grand jury option available. Sometimes the constitutional provision for a grand jury indictment for incidents of major crimes is blatantly ignored, as I mentioned in the charge of capital murder against Norma Ginter in Arkansas where there never was sufficient evidence to convince anyone of the charges and no effort was made to get a grand jury indictment.

An individual may be accused by a law enforcement official by means of a document called an information, which states that a crime was committed. The crime could have come to the attention of that official by means of a complaint from a complaining witness, a party who was victimized, or by the testimony of another law enforcement official.

If a grand jury returns an indictment, it means that the jurors found sufficient evidence to hold the accused over for a trial. However, the accused is still legally presumed not guilty since he has not had the opportunity to confront his accusers or present his side of the question.

The person now stands accused of either a misdemeanor or a felony. At some point in time, this individual is arrested or booked formally. But he is still cloaked, under American law, with the presumption of innocence. However, it is an invisible cloak unless it is effectively depicted for the jurors. People tend to believe that where there is smoke there is fire; and that where the smoke is an indictment, the fire is criminal guilt. The indictment itself is no longer a constitutional protection as our forefathers conceived it. It has become a tool used by prosecutors to overcome the trial jury's presumption of innocence.

I represented a woman who, along with her spouse, was indicted on several counts of failure to file a personal income tax return. During the trial the prosecutor kept harping on the grand jury indictment. He used the words "grand jury" about 70 times, apparently in an effort to convince the jurors that if the grand jury saw fit to indict, who were they, the members of the petit jury, to dispute that decision? They should find her guilty. The prosecutor acted as if the trial jury's purpose was to review and to affirm the grand jury decision. What a shameful perversion of a process intended to preserve the rights of the accused!

The Sixth Amendment rights to be informed of the nature and cause of the accusation against you and to confront the witnesses against are often fundamentally violated. On all levels of the criminal justice system there are a plethora of confusing statutes open to contradictory interpretation which even lawyers and judges do not clearly understand. Some jurisdictions permit defense attorneys to file such documents as motion for clarification of the charges or a request for a bill of particulars to obtain a full description and enunciation of the crime the accused is facing.

An individual can be charged with a crime and not even be told what statute he allegedly violated. The individual, at the time of his indictment, may not know whether he has been indicted for a misdemeanor punish-

"The Fifth Amendment protection of a grand jury indictment has now been turned into a Fifth Amendment hammer with which to beat people over the head in front of the trial jury."

able by a $200 fine or a felony punishable by 10 years in jail. To be in accord with the Constitution the indictment should clearly define what conduct the accused is being charged with and the degree of jeopardy he faces. Unfortunately, as the law is currently interpreted in the United States, clear, unequivocal charges are not required. Accusations should be more in keeping with common sense; such as "On March 1, 1986 John Doe stole Sam Smith's television. Article XYZ, Statute 123; a misdemeanor punishable by one year in prison or a $1,000 fine."

On the opposite side of the spectrum and equally unjust is the situation in which a valid indictment leading to a well deserved conviction is thrown out by an appellate court due to silly legal technicalities. The Texas Court of Criminal Appeals once reversed the conviction of an individual who had committed many robberies because the indictment did not say that the property was wrongfully taken from someone who had a greater right to possession of the property, but merely stated that it was wrongfully taken.

Thus our flawed criminal justice system on one hand lets guilty people go free if indictments vary a hair's breadth from their bureaucratic requirements and don't reiterate word-for-word the weird things that our law would have them say; on the other hand, we put innocent people in jail because indictments do not clearly and succinctly inform them of the charge against them so they can prepare an adequate defense. Furthermore, the Fifth Amendment protection of a grand jury indictment has now been turned into a Fifth Amendment hammer with which to beat people over the head in front of the trial jury.

B. A TRIP TO THE CAN

The United States of America, the individual states, and even tiny municipalities all have it within their power to lock people up in jail for periods ranging from an hour or two—to life.

A bit of folk wisdom from a professional criminal bears repeating; "You can beat the rap, but you can't beat the ride." If you are accused of a crime, you will, in all probability, be arrested, taken to a jail, booked— meaning fingerprints, strip search and assorted other public humiliations—and warehoused for a while with a lot of other human cargo. A large percentage of your companions will know the ride well. Some might be professional criminals. Others are just unlucky people with very little money, or with an attitude problems: i.e., they have attitudes that those in

authority disagree with. Some might have unwittingly committed a crime they did not know existed. The group might include a young woman who spurned a pass made by an officer, a teen-age boy who was too close to the

"The U.S. Supreme Court has now ruled that you can be jailed without bond at all, prior to trial. It's theoretically possible to serve your sentence before trial, or at least to be punished before you've even had plea and arraignment and a trial."

scene of a crime he did not commit, a middle-aged housewife whose bank had mistakenly dishonored her check or even an elderly woman whose driver's license was mistakenly shown as revoked in the state's computer. If you know there is a criminal charge against you, it is wise to retain counsel, who might be able to manage an easy booking without the ride.

Being arrested is humiliating and bad for your reputation. Almost everyone who sees an arrest in progress believes the suspect has done something wrong. The arrest of a suspect takes a lot of police labor, jail space and bureaucratic time. The process is expensive, and, in most cases, totally unnecessary!

For tax crimes, traffic offenses, check problems and a wide range of other non-violent misdeeds, a number of other options could have been used: a phone call or letter from the government authority to the suspect, the filling out of some forms regarding the suspect's address, phone number, and persons to contact, and the scheduling of a trial date works well, when utilized.

Unfortunately, our system likes to process people without warning and often without even telling the person what he is accused of. Many honest citizens waive every right the sharp cop can trick them into waiving after their rights have been read to them. Professional criminals know their rights, they know to keep their mouths shut and wait for legal help! The Miranda decision attempts to balance the scales for the nice guy caught in the criminal justice system unaware. For that hapless individual, confusion reigns: What did I do? Where am I going? Does anyone know where I am? Where am I? How do I get out of here?

The Eighth Amendment gives everyone the right to post bond and leave jail. If he does not appear at the designated time, he loses his money. In most jurisdictions, there are professional bondsmen who supply this money—but their services do not come cheaply. The cost of the bond can run from about 7 to 50 percent, and the fee is NOT REFUNDABLE!

If a suspect is charged with attempted murder, the court may set bail at $5,000. The bondsmen may charge $750 in cash, and require that family members of the accused come up with pledges of cars, televisions, sports equipment and other items as collateral. If the suspect does not show up in court, the bond is forfeited, and the bondsman loses the full $5,000 he guaranteed. However, in many jurisdictions, he may keep his money if he is able to return the suspect to the can.

A good bondsman has connections and can move things faster to find you and secure your release. Bondsmen's rates vary widely, but tend to be competitive within a given jurisdiction. Often attorneys are able to secure bonds for their clients at a reduced rate, because the bondsmen look upon attorneys as a source of repeat referral business. If you've got a lot of bucks, a good attorney and a good bondsman can get you out of the can faster than any other combination, except a political connection to a judge. If a judge says "Out now!" you're sprung immediately, since the judge could jail any jailer who refused to release you.

Norma Ginter, a capital murder suspect in Lawrence County, Arkansas, spent seven months in jail before being bonded out. An individual suspected of attempted murder spent a mere three hours. A man accused of slashing his brother-in-law's car tires—in retaliation for the beating of the suspect's sister—was in the tank for 24 hours before his release. A young woman charged with writing a bad check spent from noon to 3 a.m. in a local Texas jail.

Sometimes an accused is denied bond because the court believes he or she is too dangerous to let loose, or that the suspect is likely to flee. This determination can be fought by filing a writ of habeas corpus. The U.S. Supreme Court has now ruled that you can be jailed without bond at all prior to trial. It's theoretically possible to serve your sentence before trial, or at least to be punished before you've even had plea and arraignment and a trial.

A small businessman in a rural area had been wrongfully convicted of arson when his insurance company—reluctant to pay a claim for an accidental fire which had destroyed a saw mill on his west Texas property—brought criminal charges against him. His former attorney advised him to waive a jury trial and bring his case before a judge who was known as a hanging judge. He was convicted and given a 10-year probated sentence.

When I first heard about him, he was facing revocation of his probation because he was accused of assaulting a police officer who had come on his property on a flimsy pretext, without a warrant. The 55-year-old man had received serious injuries as a result of that officer and three comrades beating on him. When he hired me as his attorney, he had already spent 45 days in a county jail. After a five-hour hearing, I obtained the subject's release on a $5,000 bond. He was ultimately exonerated of the assault charges, but his probation was revoked by the judge without a hearing and he had to do time on the arson charge.

It would take several volumes to cover a comprehensive overview of all the possible scenarios of going to jail in America. I would like to present an example, in this case a composite character of real life people, of a 22-

year-old mother whom I will ask you, the reader, to imagine is your younger sister, whom we'll call Mary Doe I. She'll go to jail for you and give you a brief tour of the facilities there.

It's 5:30 p.m., and your sister has just left work. She is driving to the day-care center to pick up your three-year-old niece to take her home and prepare the family's dinner. She stops for a red light.

Unknown to your sister, there is another young woman in a neighboring state, who, by an unfortunate coincidence, bears the same name, same date of birth, same petite, blonde physical appearance and a CRIMINAL RECORD! Mary Doe II had deliberately written a hot check, fully intending to keep the merchandise she acquired by means of this deceit. Mary Doe II was caught, tried, convicted and sentenced to 90 days in jail. She was allowed to remain free on bond, pending appeal. She panicked and fled the state. She hasn't been seen or heard from since. By fleeing, Mary Doe II not only lost her appeal, but incurred a charge of failure to report to jail. She also committed the federal offense of being a fugitive who crossed state lines. The FBI and state authorities are looking for her. She has a rap sheet showing three separate crimes, even though they all stem from the original bad check incident. Instead of 90 days in jail—which probably would have realistically been about 30 days—Mary II now faces a five to 10-year prison sentence.

At the red light, a patrolman pulls up alongside Mary I's car and notices that she is quite beautiful. He flashes his light on her and she jumps like a startled deer. The officer asks her, "May I see your driver's license?" She responds "What have I done?" The officer; "Just doing my job, ma'am; can I see your driver's license, please?" Your sister is nervous. She has never been late to pick up her child, and she knows the nursery closes promptly at 6pm; traffic is heavy, and she is worn out from a hard day at work. She hands the officer her license.

He glances at it nonchalantly and keeps the conversation running, "Pretty cloudy day, huh?"

She says dully, "Yes, officer. Is there anything wrong?" "Well, just doing my job", the officer replies, but now he is getting impatient. Hoping that she would flirt with him, he looks at her ring finger and notices that she has a wedding band. "So, you're married?" he asks.

"Yes," she responds.

Your sister is the type who really doesn't like it when people ask that question with an obvious touch of lust in their voice.

The officer doesn't like her brusque "Yes."

Retaliation! The officer decides to check her ownership papers, her insurance papers, her tags, and see if her back lights work properly. They do.

Your sister, feeling harried, asks, "What's going on?" The officer, disappointed and frustrated, wants an excuse to harass her. The officer is your basic overweight, not real bright, unpleasant bully. He has been separated from his wife for three months and is being divorced.

The officer tells your sister that he is going to run a check on her, and he does. BINGO! A live one! Apparently your sister has quite a rap sheet! Cautiously, he comes back up to the car, opens the door, and tells her to get out.

She is startled. She is upset. She asks, "Why?"

That is all it takes for the bully to spring into action. He yanks her out of her seat, throws her up against the car, pulls her hands behind her, and cuffs her in a ceremony that takes less than 60 seconds.

Then, he begins to frisk her. "What are you doing," she screams anxiously.

"Lady," he responds, "you gotta rap sheet on you a mile long. I have to do this for my own protection." For the officer's own protection, your handcuffed, 95-pound sister gets a very thorough frisking.

The officer is agitated. In his imagination, he had envisioned the possibility of overcoming the young lady's resistance, and perhaps sharing hard luck stories of his divorce with her, all in a quiet and secluded area. Now, he realizes he has a criminal on his hands and he must take all necessary precautions. He tosses her into the back seat of his car, locks the rear doors and radios instructions for her vehicle to be impounded.

"What's going on, what are you doing to me?" she pleads. The officer responds, "Lady, I don't need to tell you nuthin'. I'm taking you in."

The officer drives over to the police station, fills out some forms, turns her over to the custody of a female officer who gives her an extremely thorough search, and seats her on a bench to which she is now handcuffed.

By now it's 7pm and your sister's husband is on his way home with his daughter after being called and angrily chastised by the staff of the day care center because his wife had not picked up the child on time. By now, of course, he is worried and frightened, and your niece is crying, wanting to know where her mommy is.

Brother-in-law has called you now and you're alarmed. His parents arrived to take care of the child and are telling him in no uncertain terms that they knew all along that Mary was not a woman of great character, and they have always suspected that she has been fooling around on him.

Hubby is not in complete control of his sensibilities. He is bewildered, scared to death, and unable to take charge of the situation. So you must.

You have a Ph.D. in chemical engineering and you've worked for a major oil company for 10 years—but you've never been involved in anything like this. When things came up, you handled them in a precise, mathematical way. You know that now, the rational thing to do is call the police. You start with the city police, then call the sheriff's office and state law enforcement officials. All the police agencies tell you that you have to wait at least 24 hours before you can file a missing persons report. Then you call the local hospitals. You call all your relatives and her friends. You call Mary's boss and co-workers. No one knows where she is. No one has any ideas. No one can even imagine what's wrong with her.

Meanwhile, your sister is frantic. What happened to her child? Can she get to a phone? Can she tell her husband what's going on? How could this nightmare have happened?

Several male officers are talking about her in lewd, offensive terms. All of them presume that your sister is guilty. All of them think she has done something pretty serious. None of them believe the mistaken identity stuff. They all let her know that, too. She still hasn't been told what she is accused of having done. Mary wonders, was it the late utility payment, or did we made a mistake on our tax return?

Now, it's time for the paddywagon to relocate prisoners from the city jail area to more permanent arrangements at the county jail. She now is thrown into the back seat of another police car and moved to the larger facility. There she meets some new female acquaintances. One of them is a hooker; another is a drug dealer; a third woman is a street woman that would have trouble being a hooker and isn't quite certain which planet she is on; and a fourth is a rather mean, semi-toothless wretch with needle marks all up and down her arms, sporting scars on her face and tattoos on her arms. She ogles your sister admiringly and wants to get to know her.

There is one toilet in the middle of the room—and it's filthy. Your sister wants to get something to drink. She can drink from the sink sitting right over the toilet. It's obvious that the toilet hasn't been cleaned in a while,

"Prisoners, for the most part, are treated equally: all are treated with a notable lack of compassion, with no respect and no concern for their dignity as a human being."

and that on occasion some inmates have used the cleaner areas of the floor.

Your sister doesn't smoke, doesn't even like a smoky room, but most of the other prisoners chain smoke—making the room so thick with smoke you could cut it with a knife.

The hooker somehow managed to sneak a knife into the jail and has let Mary know that she might use it just to make a point.

Now, it's 10:15pm and your sister can't use the phone, doesn't know where she is—and you don't either.

Although it's getting late, she and her fellow prisoners are being shuffled around the jail facilities for the official booking procedures: everybody gets their pictures taken, fingers printed, and then stripped nude, given jail uniforms and thrown into regular cells. Once this process has been completed, the prisoner's name, location and offense are entered into the computer—and they can easily be located.

In many police departments this procedure could be quicker with pen and paper because the expensive computer terminals are often not efficiently utilized by operators only vaguely familiar with them. This whole booking, identifying, and record entering process can take any-where from 30 minutes to three hours.

Next, a judge must, at least perfunctorily, review the charge and set bond. Even if a bondsman has already been contacted, and all the paper-work completed, the bond itself cannot be prepared until the judge sets the amount.

Meanwhile, your sister waits—stripped of all her clothes and posses-sions that have been routinely put in a large manila envelope.

Prisoners, for the most part, are treated equally: all are treated with a notable lack of compassion, with no respect and no concern for their dig-nity as a human being. However, a prisoner with a relative or other con-tact with local government can usually get some preferential treatment—which might be an isolated cell, the privilege of not being too thoroughly frisked, being able to remain in street clothes, or of receiving decent food other than stale peanut butter sandwiches.

In your frantic search for your sister you called a corporate attorney friend who handles only oil and gas matters. He gives you the name a general practitioner attorney who offers you redundant advice; call the police agencies, the hospitals and any personal friends who might have heard from Mary. He also asks if there is any chance she has committed a crime or would have run off?

You ask the attorney to see what he can do to help at this point, even though you don't know just how he can help. In a smaller town, you might know the name of the right attorney to contact for help. In a big city, there might be 1,000 lawyers who are the right ones to handle your case and do a good job for you, but unfortunately there are probably 10 times that number of wrong lawyers available to help.

An excellent criminal attorney, which you don't suspect you need, or even a general practitioner with some criminal law experience would most likely have some ties to a bonding company.

Your best team is the right lawyer and bondsman for expediting the release process. But first, you have to know that Mary is in the clutches of the criminal justice system. You must learn where she is being held, what crime she has been accused of, what bond has been set, and who the right lawyer and bondsman are.

It is now 2:30am, and the attorney you called calls you back to tell you that he's located your sister in the county jail. He has already contacted a bondsman friend who's on his way to the jail to see what needs to be done.

Since this bondsman obtains about 10 clients a year through this particular attorney, he's willing to give him extra special service—making the personal trip to the jail. The bondsman goes down to the jail and flirts with the head computer operator in an effort to expedite getting all the information he needs.

It's possible that you could have gotten this information on your own. It's more likely that it would take you about six extra hours. You probably would have waited in a long line of other teeming, unhappy, worried human beings and when you got to the front of the line, you might have been told that your sister's name wasn't in the computer.

With the bondsman's help, Mary's name is located and the computer screen shows: "Fugitive—$50,000 bond."

Murderers and rapists are getting out on $5,000 bonds but your sister has been accused of one of the most heinous of all crimes in the United States of America—not doing what she was told to do! She didn't turn herself in and she didn't fill out all the papers they wanted completed. It makes little difference that the alleged crime took place in a state which your sister has never even visited.

The bondsman is concerned because he simply doesn't like to write bonds for fugitives. He is afraid he could lose his money. Not only that, this case has been assigned to a mean judge who hates criminals, and if they don't show up on time, the judge requires the bondsman to forfeit the bond immediately. Before the bondsman writes a $50,000 fugitive bond he might demand that the lawyer he's working with guarantee the bond.

The legal fees on an arrest for bad check charges can run from nothing (out of friendship) to $5,000. If a lawyer is retained to handle a case which is complicated by serious charges involving an out-of-state fugitive and extradition proceedings, even a $25,000 fee would not be out of the question.

A hearing will be held in federal court to extradite your sister back to the state which is accusing her of having escaped. The federal court decides whether she goes back, and then that state decides what to do with her. Quite possibly, if she allows them to ship her back to the other state, the feds might even drop the fugitive charges against her.

Because of the ridiculously high bond, and because of the bondsman's concern over the fugitive risk involved, so much time has elapsed that it is now 7am. You and your brother-in-law are waiting at the jail. Law enforcement officials work their way through a dozen forms and reports that have to be made and your bondsman completes his pledge that's based on everything you own. And although you love your sister, you almost have to start wondering if there is any truth to these charges levied against her. You really have to wonder if she's there at the jail, because for hours you still haven't seen her, heard her or talked to her.

Only the lawyer got in. He talked to her for the first time about 6am Then, at last, she knew that someone knew where she was and hoped someone was trying to get her out. Mary told the lawyer that she was innocent, but he tells you that they all say that. You just can't be sure.

Your sister is finally released at 10am. Her husband is glad to see her. He knows for certain that she hasn't done anything wrong. He doesn't believe any of the charges and he never believed the foolish rumors about infidelity. She still doesn't understand what happened to her. She has learned that it has something to do with bad checks and she's scared to death that she made some error in balancing her checkbook. It's been explained to her many times how unlikely it is that the computers made a mistake.

She is out of the can. She is ordered to report to a federal judge on the fugitive proceeding in 24 hours. She does. She pleads not guilty, and because of the attorney's forceful discussion, bond is not increased. A date is set for her extradition hearing to the neighboring state.

"You can beat the rap, but you can't beat the ride."

The outcome of a situation like this would actually vary greatly depending on the judges, the jailers and police officers. I have had the privilege of knowing a number of decent, honest police officers who know this sort of thing goes on every day, and do not approve it.

A million other things could occur following Mary's release. She could plead guilty and get probation in her own home state. She can fight it. She can fight the extradition and win if she proves she wasn't the person who committed the crime and was convicted. She could lose at her extradition hearing and actually be removed to the other state. She may or may not be allowed to stay out of jail pending appeal. If she loses the extradition hearing, she has to go to the neighboring state, and be tried in that state. There, she would again try to prove she is not the person who had committed the offense. Ultimately, with competent help, it is highly unlikely that she would ever serve real time, although it is not impossible. It is also possible she might plead guilty to get the whole thing over with and accept probation. The more money and the more good luck she has the better off she is.

Although you're pleased with the way you've handled the family crisis, you're now financially strapped. You lent $10,000 to your sister, and you are concerned about getting all the paperwork finished. You don't want this to happen again by accident—but more unusual things have happened. You also want to make sure you get everything you own decollateralized from the bondsman when the ordeal is over.

The bondsman, when he paid the bond and got your sister out, told the clerk laughingly, "This one is innocent. All my clients are innocent. Heh heh". The sheriff responsible for the jail conditions is re-elected in the next election. The police officer is never disciplined.

You only hope that you, your sister, or any of your loved ones never have to take another trip to the can.

C. LET'S MAKE A DEAL

Most cases, both civil and criminal, are not brought before judges or juries—they are compromised. Criminal cases are usually compromised by the following general rules of thumb:

"...most prosecutors do not care. His chief interest is whether or not he can secure a conviction. He would rather secure a conviction against an innocent human being than lose a case against a guilty human being."

---

1. The prosecutor's office is familiar with the customary sentence meted out for the particular offense of which the defendant stands accused, and can hazard a fairly accurate guess as to what sentence the judge or jury would decide upon after conviction.

2. The prosecutor knows whether or not that type of crime, with the kind of evidence the government has, will probably result in a successful conviction.

3. The prosecutor wants to get a confession and an agreement to serve the maximum amount of time with the minimum amount of effort, so that the prosecutor can get promoted or brag to his boss and get an ego boost from feeling that he's done his job efficiently—prosecuting and convicting human beings.

4. The prosecutor does not want to look foolish; he does not want to lose, and he does not try cases unless he believes he can win.

5. However, the prosecutor tries most cases if they cannot be settled by plea bargaining.

6. If the prosecutor thinks he cannot win the case and the defense attorney has not ruled out the option of trial, the prosecutor will tend toward generosity in a plea bargain. A few prosecutors may actually go out of their way to dismiss cases against innocent people.

However, most prosecutors do not care. If a prosecutor feels he will be made to look foolish, he may drop the case or transfer it to another prosecutor. His chief interest is whether or not he can secure a conviction. He would rather secure a conviction against an innocent human being than lose a case against a guilty human being.

Most prosecutors want to believe they prosecute only guilty people and will go to great lengths to delude themselves. There are also some prosecutors who will sacrifice their own career objectives rather than put an innocent person in jail. These guys are not in great abundance.

7. Most prosecutors negotiate for an agreement of plead-out where the defendant accepts a harsher sentence (with or without probation) than the prosecutor feels the jury or judge would actually assess. Such a deal might

still look good to the defendant because he is in terror of being given the maximum sentence for his offense. The maximum sentence is very rarely applied.

8. Most prosecutors have a standard deal for a standard crime, which they will try to get you to accept. Some judges will not accept these pre-packaged deals and will not allow them to be entered. Prosecutors vary their terms accordingly.

9. This standard deal which the prosecutor determines after receiving the file is highly negotiable. Many defendants and some lawyers don't know this. Like a lion stalking its prey, the prosecutor won't educate his quarry or the quarry's "protector" if he can help it.

10. One factor the prosecutor uses to his advantage is that he usually knows the judge far better than the defense attorney does; prosecutors are generally assigned to a particular court where they try cases over and over again. A defense attorney, although he may have tried several cases in a particular court, would not normally live in one courtroom.

11. The prosecutor is frequently a legal specialist in certain designations of crime and has more experience in that area than even the most experienced general criminal practice defense attorneys. Of course, every day, in some court, there are prosecutors who are trying their first case. These people always suffer a disadvantage against experienced defense counsel.

12. Generally the prosecutor will offer a *pro se* or *pro per* a less advantageous deal than he would offer a defendant represented by an attorney. Reasons: (a) the attorney is a member of the union, and future co-operation may be necessary; b) the prosecutor knows that he can take advantage of the individual representing him or herself.

13. The prosecutor negotiates on plea bargaining terms with the defense counselor in the prison market place for pieces of the human being's life and/or money from the human being and/or other confessions from the human being and/or evidence which could hurt other people and/or anything else which the prosecutor believes that he needs.

"A jury trial is a toss of the dice."

The game is "Let's make a deal."

Innocence or guilt is frequently irrelevant and often ignored throughout the negotiations. If it is considered at all, it is just one of many variables. The possibility or probability of conviction or non-conviction and the possibility or probability of length of sentence are likely to be the primary topics on the conversational agenda between prosecutor and defense attorney. I have, on several occasions, approached prosecutors with the novel concept that my client was innocent. Generally the prosecutor responds with rudeness and occasionally questions my sanity. What could be more irrelevant in the nitty-gritty of criminal prosecution than the accused's guilt or innocence?

D. COURTROOM SCENES

To experience the emotional and physical atmosphere of a criminal courtroom, you are invited to view through my eyes the following scenes, observations of courtroom impressions from 1982, 1977 and 1986 respectively. The first segment was written four years before the rest of this book and represents a stage of this underground lawyer's development.

American Justice—State v TON 10/6/82 A parade of nonconvicted suspects shuffles in, they're connected by a long chain of handcuffs. Each allegedly innocent suspect follows, pulled by his handcuff, linked in the chain, dressed in dirty white prison smocks. One clean-cut, young suspect is in a sports coat. Why?

The constable informs me that the gentleman in the sports coat is set for trial today. Subjects going to trial are allowed to dress like suspects as opposed to dressing like convicted criminals. Is he guilty? God only knows for sure. The officer says he is. His lawyer and the prosecutor probably don't care. They care about winning and what type of production they will put on.

A jury trial is a toss of the dice. Some jurors will release a man who shot the president, and some will convict an 80-year-old grandmother who never had a parking ticket or uttered an obscenity. All competent lawyers know that it is a crap shoot. Some lawyers win more often than others because of their rapport with the jury or other skills, but no one over the span of a long career, always wins the crap shoot. Some guilty will go free, d some innocent will be jailed. The innocent may plead guilty to avoid rap shoot. His lawyer may encourage him to do so to push the cash or out of fear.

My client, Mr. Ton was falsely accused of severely beating another man with whom he had been doing business. The indictment did not clearly designate the charge. It only said he was accused of a crime. After investigating the facts, we learned his crime was a class A misdemeanor punishable by a $1,000 fine and one year in jail. My client could not speak much English at the time. Now, several years later, he is fluent.

My client was innocent. The prosecutor did not care. The judge instructed me to plead out—make a deal admitting guilt—which theoretically protects my client from himself, and that I should assume he was lying to me and therefore guilty.

We refused and demanded a speedy, jury trial. We were reset twice. Both times we had prepared for trial. Both times the boastful, arrogant prosecutor begged for more time. On the third trip for trial, the prosecutor had begged off the case. The new prosecutor had little or no experience, no preparation and no witnesses present, except her non-English speaking client, the alleged victim. The prosecutor zealously put her non-case on and lost. Later, a couple of clients read the dark, back pages of the newspaper and informed me that we had made print—congratulations! Great work! Actually, I felt the victory was rather hollow, and that I hardly deserved any congratulations for getting an innocent man off when the opposition couldn't prove he was guilty, anyway—the opposition was incompetent and unprepared.

1977: Another incident of courtroom drama that unfolded years before and left a lasting impression on me. While sitting in a courtroom waiting for my client's hearing to take place, I heard a judge sentence an old man to 20 years in prison. The judge's insensitivity made this pronouncement more abhorrent than the sentence itself. I had been practicing about six months and I still thought judges were superior, enlightened beings.

The old man trembled and started to cry. He left his place in front of the bench and tried desperately to go behind the bench. A startled bailiff stopped him. "Please your honor," he whimpered, "I can't possibly do that much time." The man was guilty. He had pleaded guilty and made no effort to deny it. His crime was burglary; no weapon involved. His granddaughter was in the hospital. He had no insurance and needed the money to keep her there. Two other grandchildren lived with him. His wife of 40 years had died a few weeks earlier, and the funeral costs had wiped him out. Three banks had turned his loan requests down. He had one prior arrest; a conviction for unlawfully carrying a weapon. He had pled guilty that time too. All this he poured out to the judge, pleading for mercy. His court-appointed lawyer stood mutely aside and appeared uncomfortable either because he had not made an impassioned plea or even a listless plea for mercy; or more likely because his client, overwhelmed with his lawyer's ineffectiveness, decided to take matters into his own hands. The lawyer was embarrassed but not enough to make a scene or do some actual work.

The judge really seemed concerned. He listened patiently. Finally, like a benevolent father—although the defendant was a good 20 years older than the judge—the judge gestured paternally for this aged figure to come up close to the bench. The old man, his posture exhibiting defeat and pain, hobbled up to the judge. His Honor spoke: "The court understands. Just do the best you can."

The old man was turned over to the custody of the deputy and the court recessed. The lawyers in the courtroom, defense and prosecutors, snickered or laughed. No one wanted to be on the outs with the judge. Only one, young, idealistic lawyer refused to laugh. To punish human conduct for the benefit of society is one thing; to ridicule a human being we disapprove of is unforgivable—intentional cruelty. It took years to beat some of the idealism out of this green, well meaning observer.

1986: The final segment of this trilogy is included to convey the feel of a federal courtroom. The very structure is designed to strike terror into the hearts of litigants, attorneys, jurors and observers.

The courtroom of the presiding judge of the Southern District of Texas measures 36' x 36', about the size of the average American home. The judge sits at an elevated, throne-like desk—fully 20 feet across—and is protected by another desk of the same magnitude about five feet in front of his where the court reporter sits. Behind the judge, permanently affixed to the custom-paneled, courtroom wall, are 18, 2 1/2-foot wide by 3-foot long, marble blocks all placed together to form one giant Roman temple-like backdrop. From floor to ceiling, the marble edifice stands about 15 feet high. In the dead center of the marble backdrop is the majestic, intricate gold symbol of office.

The judge sits behind his "desk" in front of the gold symbol and marble

---

"The doctrine of harmless error has seriously undermined our legal system. Prosecutors all over the country deliberately create error for the purposes of getting convictions."

backdrop in a large, green leather, executive chair, a microphone at his disposal in front of him, a large mounted American flag to his right. The effect is powerful and intimidating. The judge sitting on the bench is the Honorable John Singleton, chief judge of the Southern District of Texas.

The courtroom is so large that communications must be accomplished by microphone. Along each wall which joins the front and back of this palatial room are large pictures of past judges who presided over the Southern District of Texas.

All walls are decked with strong, brown, wood panels. The spectators' benches are all dark brown wood, slightly lighter than the walls which causes the benches to cower slightly to the power of the towering, dark brown walls. All chairs in the courtroom are dark green, out of the same material as the judge's bench but much smaller.

The courtroom is not a friendly place to be. If I were to coin a name for the architectural style, I'd call it Roman Gothic. If the architectural and decorum of the courtroom was designed with intimidation in mind, my compliments to the designers, they have succeeded.

E. THE APPELLATE PROCESS

Most criminal appeals are filed because of allegations of reversible error. Reversible error means a mistake committed by the judge and the error was so harmful to the rights of the accused that the accused did not get a fair trial and is legally entitled to a new trial. The defendant, who has been found guilty, attempts to get the appellate court to say: A) there was not enough evidence to find the individual guilty, and, therefore, the verdict should be reversed to not guilty; or B) there was enough evidence to find the individual guilty, but it should be reversed and sent back to the lower count for a new trial because prejudicial evidence was also entered or impermissible conduct occurred which prevented the defendant from getting a fair trial.

The issues on appeal include any factor which may have prejudiced the accused's right to a fair trial, such as: the defense attorney was not permitted to properly examine prospective jurors or to fully cross-examine witnesses; the judge abused his discretion by instructing the jury that the defendant was a liar.

Under early, English, common law and even today, under English jurisprudence, if there was error—meaning the rights of the defendant in trial were not completely upheld—the defendant was entitled to a brand new trial. In the United States and England today, appellate courts have decided that an error can be harmless, i.e., it doesn't affect the outcome of the case; therefore, a new trial is not necessary.

The doctrine of harmless error has seriously undermined our legal system. Prosecutors all over the country deliberately create error for the purposes of getting convictions. They rely on the hope that the appellate courts will find the error harmless and that the conviction will stand. Most convictions will stand.

It is not a requirement under the Fourteenth Amendment due process clause that the states have an appellate procedure. The Supreme Court has held that

"...while a statutory review is important, it must not be exercised without discrimination. Such a review is not a requirement of due process"[5]

Although most states have the appellate process machinery in place, the Supreme Court ruled that a state is not obligated to provide appeal for criminal defendants.[6] Without an opportunity for a state appeal, the trial court is rendered the court of final jurisdiction unless a federal question can be raised to warrant seeking a federal review of the case. How many innocent Americans have been unjustly branded criminals after having been ground up in the gears of this monstrosity we call our criminal justice system? The only one who knows is the Greatest Judge of all, who will mete out justice for all eternity.

"You have the right to remain silent. Anything you say can and will be used against you in a court of law. You have the right to talk to a lawyer and have him present with you while you are being questioned. If you cannot afford to hire a lawyer, one will be appointed to represent you before any questioning, if you wish. You can decide at any time to exercise these rights and not answer any questions or make any statements."

CHAPTER X
HABEAS CORPUS

*"...the American writ of **habeas corpus**...*
This proceeding is the prisoner's single
most effective final legal weapon."

Habeas Corpus—A Get out of Jail Free Card.

A. DEFINITION

"Habeas Corpus Ad Subjuciendom" is a writ directed to the person detaining another (jailer of some sort) and commanding him to produce the body of the prisoner and obey the further orders of judge who issued the writ.[1]

Habeas Corpus is a Latin term meaning: "You have the body." It derives from the Latin Verb *"Habe"* meaning "have," and the Latin noun meaning "body." A writ is an order from an authority, the king, the government, or a judge directed to a constable, a sheriff, a policemen, or a jailer to do something. Writs are customarily issued by judges to carry out or enforce their orders.

Sir William Blackstone referred to Habeas Corpus as **"The most celebrated writ in English Law, and the great and efficacious writ in all manner of illegal confinement"**.[2]

For all practical purposes the American writ of *habeas corpus* is filed as an application for a writ of *habeas corpus* for the purpose of securing control over the body for release of the body. The application can be filed in any state or federal court, trial or appellate level, before or after conviction, whenever an individual's liberty has been taken away, without due process. This proceeding is the prisoner's single most effective final legal weapon. The trick is, of course, to file the papers correctly.

Let's examine the history of this procedure, and then we'll offer some basic guidelines that should be followed. This overview of *habeas corpus* will not create scholars—only serve as an important backdrop to the concept.

B. HISTORY

Basically, the writ challenges the authority of the individual or entity who deprives another of his liberty, and is designed to give a person whose liberty is restrained an **immediate** hearing to inquire into and determine the legality of the detention.[3]

The origins of this hallowed common law writ are lost in antiquity and have no absolutely known source, although some speculation traces its roots to Roman law.

After Magna Carta, the writ became commonly utilized in England, even against the King. The writ crossed the Atlantic with the English colonists, and was incorporated into the U.S. Constitution as an absolute right. In each jurisdiction, statutes have been passed to tell you how it can be used. You must conform to the statutes. However, a statute that effectively denies *habeas corpus* relief is unconstitutional. State courts are not required to provide *habeas corpus* relief, although most do. The federal court in each state is constitutionally bound to hear a citizen's *habeas corpus*. Some states recognize both a statutory *habeas corpus*, and a common law *habeas corpus*. The remedy varies significantly from state to state. Obviously a common law *habeas corpus* is easier for a non-lawyer to file. He would not have to locate the applicable statute and not be bound by all of the complex rules.

Habeas Corpus can be suspended only in case of rebellion, invasion, or to ensure public safety.[4] The state laws may be more liberal than the federal laws. If you are incarcerated under state authority, you will want to file under state law first, and if unsuccessful, then file under federal law. If you are a federal prisoner you have no state remedy.

One of the worst recent legislative developments is the creation of so-called "other remedies" which a prisoner may be required to pursue before he may file for *habeas corpus* relief. Some jurisdictions require that a motion to vacate or correct a sentence or a writ of *corum nobis*—a writ of error directed to another branch of the same court—be filed first. The failure to pursue these other remedies first can be used by a court as an excuse to deny *habeas corpus*.

These are remedies that a prisoner, representing himself, may not even know about.

C. BASIC GUIDELINES

Habeas corpus prevents illegal imprisonment by providing for an immediate hearing on the issue of whether a prisoner's basic rights to due process are being violated.

Courts enforce a duty on attorneys not to overuse the writ. There are situations when an attorney is not as effective in asserting habeas corpus for a client as the individual himself might be because some attorneys hesitate to file a *habeas corpus* for fear they will be sanctioned if it is deemed without merit. The man in jail is not so concerned about judicial sanctions.

A writ of *habeas corpus* will generally not be granted when there is another adequate remedy which the applicant has failed to pursue. A petitioner should do the most thorough research that he can in order to uncover any other motions that he may have been required to file before he applies for the *habeas corpus*. The application should include the statement that no other proper remedy is available.

Applications for a writ of *habeas corpus* are to be filed as separate documents, not merely as subsections of other pleadings filed in the criminal matter in which the petitioner is enmeshed.

---

*"One of the most important uses for **habeas corpus** is to free a person from illegal detention when there is no indictment or information or charge against an individual."*

Claims for *habeas corpus* relief may arise from any sort of restraint of liberty: under custody of municipal, county, state, or federal authorities and in some jurisdictions, may even arise from the potential loss of liberty when an individual is free on bond, probation or parole. The courts are divided on the question of whether *habeas corpus* may be sought in those latter situations, and some have found the seeking of that relief to be appropriate only if the conditions of freedom are unnecessarily restricted.

A petitioner for a writ of *habeas corpus* must show good cause in his application. The issue involved is the legality of his detention and not his guilt or innocence. One of the most important uses for *habeas corpus* is to free a person from illegal detention when there is no indictment or information or charge against an individual.

After a prisoner has been charged by indictment or information, it is harder to get *habeas corpus* granted. Now there legally exists some authority for detainment. It is tough to get a federal court to test the sufficiency of a state court indictment.

Unreasonable delay in state court proceedings may be a grounds for *habeas corpus* relief—but the delay needs to be dealt with by means of motions on the state level first.

Suppression of evidence by law enforcement officials may be sufficient grounds for granting *habeas corpus* after conviction, but the evidence must be credible and favorable to petitioner's defense.

Habeas corpus is considered a civil proceeding brought by the petitioner. While a prisoner may not be prevented from access to the courts for filing *habeas corpus,* an indigent petitioner is not guaranteed the right to court appointed counsel for this proceeding.[5] Of course, a petitioner may represent himself.

The petition for a writ of *habeas corpus* may be filed by the prisoner or by anyone who has an interest in his freedom; i.e., a husband, wife, father, mother, grandparent, guardian, brother, child or other relative. The person who files the petition must show that he has some standing to act in the interests of the prisoner. Some jurisdictions allow a non-family member to file a writ on behalf of a prisoner, whereas others do not.

The petition should require the respondent, the jailer, to show cause why

---

"Habeas corpus prevents illegal imprisonment by providing for an immediate hearing on the issue of whether a prisoner's basic rights to due process are being violated."

---

the writ should not be granted. The burden of proof is on the respondent, but courts tend to look favorably on the respondent. There is no right of a jury trial in a *habeas corpus* proceeding, although some jurisdictions allow for an advisory jury. There is a presumption in favor of the validity of any prior proceedings or judgments.

The petitioner needs findings of fact and conclusions of law from the court whose ruling he is challenging. Vigorous demands must be made by the petitioner, or the court may tend to forget or delay the compiling of these essential documents.

The more evidence, supported by affidavits, attached to your application for writ of *habeas corpus*, the more likely it is to be heard. The court doesn't have to hear the application unless it shows sufficient grounds for relief.

D. THE SAGA OF A. J. YOUNG

Early in our law practice, the Great Izen and I handled a *habeas corpus* situation which encompassed both federal and state courts: the case of A. J. Young.

We were helping a woman to regain legal custody of her children from her ex-husband who was living in another state. The children resided with her already. Ultimately we succeeded in this endeavor. We were receiving a $30 weekly check for the custody case. My client was living with her second husband, A.J. Young, who was providing for her, her four children, and our law office.

At 3am one morning, I received a phone call from my client explaining that the provider for her family, and our fledgling law office, was in jail. At 2am the FBI had raided their home. They announced with loudspeakers that our provider should come out with his hands up. He did so and was arrested. The large posse—consisting of several FBI agents, deputy sheriffs, and at least one Texas Ranger—succeeded in capturing the unarmed man and taking him to jail.

Although the Sixth Amendment of our Constitution states that you have the right "...to be informed of the nature and cause of the accusation..." in the real criminal world, people are seldom told what crime they are accused of committing. Officers take it for granted that the suspect knows. One of the first tasks of the suspect's attorney is to figure out what offense his client

"One of the first tasks of the suspect's attorney is to figure out what offense his client has been charged with."

has been charged with.

If the attorney has done a lot of work in that county and is familiar with the local abbreviations he can usually figure it out pretty quickly. However, sometimes the attorney will be wrong. The next thing the attorney has to do is to find his client. In a small town there are usually only one or two jails. In a metropolis there can be a mixture of federal, state, county and city officials involved in the arrest, your client can be in anybody's jail, anywhere.

My new client, A.J.—the new husband of my old client, Carol—could not readily be located at 3am. They had just carted him away.

My first problem was to try and figure out what he had been charged with. His wife had no idea. After talking with her about an hour and a half over the phone, we figured out what we suspected was the only crime he'd ever committed. He had come to the United States from Germany. He had never been naturalized in the United States and had not obtained legal residency. He had also changed his name.

We concluded he had probably been arrested for this immigration violation. It would explain the intervention of massive federal forces. In light of the unfortunate fact that we live in a racist society, and that the Houston area has always had more than enough illegal aliens from many various Hispanic and Oriental countries to keep the Immigration and Naturalization Service busy, it seemed strange that this vendetta would be waged against a white, Anglo-Saxon, Protestant. However, Carol's new husband had come from New York, so we theorized that the investigation must have started there and traced the "suspect" to Houston.

By nightfall, we were unable to find out what jail he was in, but we did learn that he was scheduled for an arraignment hearing in federal court at 10 o'clock the next morning. The federal court appearance seemed to confirm our conjecture that our client was accused of an immigration violation, which is a federal offense. Subsequently, we learned that A. J. Young was being held for extradition to New York, where he had allegedly been convicted of some yet undisclosed crime.

A.J. had been held in the rehabilitation center—a place populated by dangerous criminals: mobsters, drug addicts, and assorted bankers, lawyers, and accountants who just happened to be in federal custody. The federal agents normally drop federal fugitive charges on extradition once the suspect is apprehended and turned over to state authorities.

When he was arrested, A.J. was put in leg irons, hand irons and shoulder irons—so much iron that he easily could have been mistaken for a robot. He had been escorted by FBI agents, sheriffs and Texas Rangers into the Harris County jail. At the same time this great and dangerous criminal was brought into the county jail, a gentleman suspected of being the Montrose Area rapist, perpetrator of a series of rapes near downtown Houston, also was brought in.

Because of all the attention created by my client's arrest, the non-handcuffed, unbound, unchained, accused rapist simply walked out of the jailhouse and disappeared until he was found a year later—after committing several more rapes in Florida. I doubt that the victims of this offender in Florida would agree with the judgment of the Texas law enforcement officials who considered it less vital to restrain the rapist than to secure my client.

At this time, neither Joe Izen or I had ever appeared in federal court before—and neither had a license to practice there. Nevertheless, having tracked our client from the state courts into the federal court, we weren't about to lose him again. We entered the courtroom.

I approached the court clerk and asked for a cause number and crime. The bailiff instructed me to sit. He said I couldn't ask the clerk for information, but he proceeded to tell me where I could go, what I could do, and a long list of other things. In this situation, I unconsciously donned what the Great Izen calls my fighting gear. I told the bailiff that if he wanted to arrest me for doing my job, to do it; but I suggested he allow the court to make the rulings. I reminded the bailiff that his authority came from the court; that he had no personal authority, and that I bet the court hadn't ordered him to keep me from looking at the public records. The bailiff scratched his head, looked at me as though I was crazy, threw his hands up in the air, and allowed me to look at the public records. He should have recognized me because I was, of course, dressed in my attorney uniform: coat, tie and briefcase. Even though I did not have a federal court license no one questioned my legitimacy.

The federal court judge appeared and called our cause number among many others. The suspects were encouraged to waive extradition and be sent back to the state asking for them. My client was not about to give up his rights so easily. He told me that his ex-father-in-law had brought the charges against him, and that if he went back to New York he'd never see the light of day. He had no qualms about stating the fact that he didn't want to waive any of his rights. He did not want to be extradited to New York! He wanted to fight this thing tooth and nail. Quite frankly, it did not seem like a wise thing to do.

The judge told our client, "You have no way of winning this. Nobody ever wins these extradition cases. If you don't waive extradition, you will sit here in a Texas prison for several months until finally you waive extradition or have an extradition trial, and then you'll be sent back to New York. You probably won't be given any credit for the time that you serve up here. You will just be throwing your time away."

Then he peered at Joe and me and said: "These young men really aren't capable of properly instructing and guiding you. I suggest that you agree to the waiver and return to New York. Do I hear a motion?" I approached the bench, "Your honor, I'd like to speak with my client for a minute." The judge smiled benignly, expecting me to convince my client to waive his right to an extradition trial in Texas.

I told A.J.: "Well, A.J., I'm not going to push you into doing anything. I don't know anything about extraditions, don't know anything about what you've been accused of, and have no idea whether or not the judge is completely right. Nevertheless, I'm here to represent you, I think you ought to listen to the judge but you tell me what you want to do." A.J. looked me dead in the eye and told me to fight.

He'd already paid my law office several hundred dollars and he figured we owed him a fight. He'd take his chances. I approached the judge and said: "Your Honor, my client refuses to waive extradition." The judge practically leaped off his bench, scowled down at me, and indicated that I was crazy, that my client was crazy, and that justice would ultimately lead to severe punishment. He let us know that he thought we were playing a foolish game and that he suspected we were doing it purely for the legal fees. He also implied that if we proceeded in this fashion, we would be jeopardizing our license to practice in his court. I noticed my co-counsel, the some-day-to-be Great Izen, starting to rumble and get angry. Knowing him the way I did, I suspected that he was about to shout at the judge: "You can't take away our licenses because we don't have them!" In any event, I pulled Izen away, and told our client that we would speak with him shortly.

A.J. had been convicted in New York of behavior that was a misdemeanor in Texas. He had been renting his apartment furniture with an option-to-buy. By mutual agreement, the parties decided that the lease would be broken and A.J. would get a certain portion of the furniture he had been paying for on the lease plan. A.J. moved out, taking his few pieces of furniture with him.

The landlord then filed criminal charges against him alleging theft of a few secondhand furniture items. The charges lingered on for years before any action was taken. A.J. was dragged into court on numerous different occasions and finally ran out of money and couldn't afford legal counsel. Finally, he received appointed counsel and proceeded to trial.

The landlord told the jury that A.J. had stolen $1,500 worth of furniture, and that he had found the stolen furniture in A.J.'s living quarters and had reclaimed it. The landlord said nothing about the lease; he said nothing about receiving any money from A.J.

A.J.'s lawyer advised him to plead the Fifth Amendment, and he did not take the stand. Having heard the testimony of only this one witness, the jury rendered a verdict of guilty as charged, leaving the court to sentence him at a later date.

A.J. was thunderstruck. He did not consider himself a criminal and did not consider this a satisfactory resolution of his dilemma. He skipped the state. He was never sentenced.

A warrant was issued for his arrest as a fugitive, as a bond jumper, and for the original criminal verdict. A.J. believed that his ex-father-in-law and his ex-landlord, who hated him, had concocted this scheme. Years passed. A.J. simply forgot about the unpleasant event.

He was vividly reminded of it at 2 in the morning when the law enforcement "army" surrounded his home and started yelling at him with bull horns. A.J.'s bond was set at $50,000. No bonding company would post it. Bonding companies like to set up bonds for doctors and lawyers on drunk driving charges and the children of doctors and lawyers on drug charges. They like to take stereos, diamonds or cars as collateral.

They don't like to bond fugitives because fugitives have been accused of fleeing from justice—just what the bond is supposed to deter. No one would post A.J.'s bond. Even if a bondsman had been willing to post the bond, A.J.'s family couldn't come up with the necessary ten percent to pay for the bond.

The constitutional purpose for bond is to ensure that the defendant returns to trial. Bond has to be a sufficient amount to ensure that, but it should not be so high that the defendant cannot raise bond. The Eighth Amendment states that, "Excessive bail shall not be required." Most states have similar statutes.

We filed a petition for a writ of *habeas corpus* in the justice of the peace court which had originally set the bond. The assistant district attorney told

---

"The constitutional purpose for bond is to ensure that the defendant returns to trial."

---

us that no government agent had ever lost an extradition case in Texas; that we would lose; that our client would be extradited; that we would be made to look foolish—and possibly be punished by the State Bar of Texas. This threat, of course, held more water than the federal judge's threat since Izen and I were both licensed in Texas, the only license either of us had at the time.

Judge Pacetti lowered the bond from $50,000 to $25,000. Of course, our client couldn't raise the $25,000 either. In this situation there is a conflict as to what motion should be filed. Should a motion for bond reduction be filed or a petition for a writ of *habeas corpus* be filed? Most states require you to seek the bond reduction first. The theory is: even if you are being held illegally, you are being held in lieu of posting bond, therefore an attempt to get the bond reduced must be made before seeking a writ of *habeas corpus*. Was A.J. being held illegally? It was a complex question.

It boiled down to this: If New York wanted him but Texas wanted him more, New York would still be entitled to get him under the full faith and credit clause in the U.S. Constitution in Article IV, Section 1 and Section 2, Part 2. However, the extradition order would have to be signed by the Texas governor or a similar official with authority or by a judge.

There is almost no due process right or requirements to prevent extradition from one state to another.

In any event, we decided to challenge every portion of the warrant including the stated identity and charges. The warrant was improperly drawn. You could not identify our client from the warrant; you could not tell what crime he was accused of from the warrant. All the paper work was incompetently done.

We then proceeded to file a petition for writ of *habeas corpus* and motion for bond reduction in the district court. We were assigned to Judge Routt's court.

A.J. had now been in prison for a month. No hearing had been set for his extradition, but requests for the governor's signature on the extradition papers had been sent from New York.

During the combined *habeas corpus* and bond reduction hearing, the prosecutor was completely and totally unprepared—officials did not even bring our client into the court room. The prosecutor asked if the hearing could be reset. I told the judge that they had custody of my client, that they had violated the spirit of *habeas corpus* and had lied to the court on the bond hearings. They had indicated that he was single, the truth of course was that he was married and provided the sole support for his wife's four children and for his general contracting company which employed several people.

The judge was upset that state officials had not brought A.J. into the courtroom and ordered them to do so. That afternoon he was brought into the courtroom, and the judge lowered his bond from $25,000 to $2,000. The prosecutor had a fit. He told the judge that A.J. would skip, that ultimately the extradition papers would be signed, and that the judge would be making a fool of himself. Judge Routt told him that it was his responsibility as a judge to lower the bond when it had been proven that the prisoner could not raise it, and that he would reset the *habeas corpus* hearing for 60 days at which time he would consider dismissing the state's action altogether.

It took an entire day to get the $2,000 bond together and to get all the paperwork properly prepared—but A.J. was ultimately released. The arresting officers were furious. Prisoners were surprised. In fact, a small riot took place in the Harris County prison when A.J. got out. We had been told by a deputy sheriff that there was no way our client would be getting out. Officers had told A.J. we were nuts and he should hire one of their friends. We had upset the apple cart a bit.

Our next step was the state capital in Austin. We drew up a 20-page legal document indicating that the governor was not required, as a matter of law, to sign extradition papers. Governor Dolph Briscoe just happened to be running for re-election that year. By this time, we had enlisted the aid of the leaders in A.J.'s church in circulating petitions, and had gathered the signatures of more than 200 potential voters who supported our position against the extradition!

In addition to presenting the legal arguments and the petition by concerned citizens asking that Texas not turn over its now-native son, we also indicated that we were prepared to bus these 200 people to Austin to personally address their government for the purpose of protecting the prisoner. The angry prosecutor sent nasty letters but did not attend the session.

The governor refused to sign the extradition papers.

At the *habeas corpus* hearing, A.J. was present along with many of his friends, his employees, and, of course, his wife and stepchildren.

The proceeding lasted about 10 minutes. I reiterated what had been said at previous hearings. The court remembered our case, and I let the court know that the governor had supported the court's earlier decision in reducing bail. The prosecutor could not state why he was not prepared to proceed on the extradition hearing and could not state why the proper extradition papers had not been received from New York. The *habeas corpus* relief was granted, and the defendant was discharged. The $2,000 bond was refunded.

Judge Routt still sits on the bench and hopefully, is still doing a fine job in administering justice.

The purpose of the writ of *habeas corpus* had been served. The state had not effectively demonstrated why the prisoner should be held or that they had a right to continue holding the prisoner. He was therefore ordered released. An enormous amount of work was done in order to get the prisoner completely freed after a total of 60 days—30 of which he spent inside a jail. However, had the judge refused to issue the writ, an appeal could have been made. Had this appeal been unsuccessful, then a petition for the writ could have been filed in federal court. If we had been set before the same federal judge who had originally considered the extradition, I suspect that we would have lost and been forced to appeal to the Fifth Circuit and from there to the U.S. Supreme Court.

Given many alternative situations, I cannot predict what could or would have happened. If A.J. ever returns to New York, his freedom could still be in jeopardy. I don't know what happened to the Montrose Area rapist, but I hope he served at least as much time as A. J. did.

"Although the Sixth Amendment of our Constitution states that you have the right '...to be informed of the nature and cause of the accusation;...' in the real criminal world people are seldom told what crime they are accused of committing."

CHAPTER XI
CIVIL RIGHTS

*"A civil rights attorney is a Don Quixote tilting against
the windmills of government attorneys with large
bankrolls and against defendants cloaked with
various types of immunity."*

A. AN OVERVIEW

The United States Civil Rights Act was originally passed in 1864 primarily for the benefit of the freed slaves. At one time, it was called the Ku Klux Klan Act for obvious reasons.

The Thirteenth Amendment freed the slaves. The Fourteenth Amendment extended the Fifth Amendment due process rights, which protects citizens from the federal government, to include protection of citizens against state governments.

All over the South, although the institution of slavery was defunct once the former Confederate states re-joined the Union, conspiracies and plots rose up to prevent the ex-slaves from becoming truly free men. They were denied their civil rights, including the right to vote, the right to hold political office, and the exercise of many other constitutional rights.

A series of civil rights laws were enacted, known as 42 USC 1982, 42 USC 1983, and so on, through 42 USC 1988. This legislation was passed, directly attacking the actions of organized government officials on the state level when they interfered with the free exercise of constitutional rights. Jefferson and de Toqueville would have loved it.

Traditionally, governments possessed substantial degrees of immunity from suit or prosecution. Even the Magna Carta did not give citizens the right to go on the offensive against the king. All the Magna Carta and the jury system provided was a degree of defensive protection against the government. Those concerned that putting too much power in the hands of a jury would threaten government had nothing to fear. Although the legitimate purpose in the separation of powers is for the judiciary to protect individuals, the judiciary has assumed the role, in recent years, of protecting the government. Nevertheless, the Civil Rights Act constituted a new step in breaking down the shield of government immunity.

While individuals' rights are still being violated for racial reasons, that is not the main thrust of this chapter. However, no American should forget the words of Martin Neimueller, commenting on Nazi Germany,

"In Germany they came first for the Communists, and I didn't speak up because I wasn't a Communist. Then they came for the Jews, and I didn't speak up because I wasn't a Jew. Then they came for the trade unionists, and I didn't speak up because I wasn't a trade unionist. Then they came for the Catholics, and I didn't speak up because I was a Protestant. Then they came for me, by that time, nobody was left to speak up."

The civil rights of the American Indian in Colorado, the Vietnamese fisherman in Galveston, Texas, the black tenant farmer in Mississippi, and the Rumanian refugee in New York City are your civil rights too!

The civil rights legislation passed by Congress shortly after the Civil War gathered dust on law library shelves for a century. Then the statutes were dusted off and again utilized for protecting ethnic minorities and others who had been denied their constitutional rights.

Beginning in the early 1960s, sit-ins, picketing, demonstrations, and other confrontations led to a revitalizing of the old civil rights causes of action. This era saw the initiation of numerous civil lawsuits based on 42 USC 1983, calling for judicial intervention when individual constitutional rights were violated under color of state law.

Since the idea of civil rights lawsuits against government officials has been opened up again, the public hasn't been too willing to close the book and allow more dust to settle on it. The civil rights statutes that were designed to protect the rights of racial minorities evolved into causes of action available to anyone whose constitutional rights were being taken away from them.

If a police officer beats someone to death because that individual is black, the police officer is violating that individual's civil rights. If a police officer beats a white man to death because that individual has an ugly face or is exercising his First Amendment right to freedom of speech, the white man is no less dead and has been no less deprived of his or her civil rights

---

"The civil rights of the American Indian in Colorado, the Vietnamese fisherman in Galveston, Texas, the black tenant farmer in Mississippi, and the Rumanian refugee in New York City are your civil rights too!"

---

than the black. Should civil rights be limited to ethnic minorities? The answer, of course, is absolutely "No." To limit to minorities access to the courts for redress of civil rights would be as fundamentally evil as the racism which plagues these minorities.

The basic purpose of the Civil Rights Act was to protect constitutional rights for citizens in the United States. There are portions of the various statutes specifically set up for the protection of minorities. However, the majority of the civil rights enactments do not purport to be legislated only for minorities protection.

It is illegal to deprive any citizen of the United States of his or her constitutional rights. The individual, as a general rule, is required, however, to exhaust state remedies before filing an action.

Most state governments grant themselves a certain amount of immunity from prosecution. All that is necessary is for the state government officials to declare that they cannot be sued. However, since the U.S. Constitution is supreme, a state government cannot give its law enforcement officials the right to violate a citizen's federally guaranteed rights.

Civil rights litigation is tough. When you sue government officials, they get free, government attorneys who spare no expense on the defense. When you sue an official of the federal government, his lawyers are from the U.S. Attorney's office—which is actually the largest, best funded, law firm in the world. Many judges view all actions against government officials with skepticism at best, and horror and hatred at worst.

Civil rights cases against police officers and government officials are fraught with difficulties and are always an uphill battle. Suits against prosecutors and judges are much worse! Substantial case law backs up the position that both judges and prosecutors, because of the nature of the authority vested in them, are completely and totally immune from suit under the Civil Rights Act if they are acting within their jurisdiction. Is there any chink at all in the armor of immunity? Yes! Where is the out? If a prosecutor exercises authority where he has absolutely no argument of jurisdiction or if a judge sitting on the bench exercises authority where he has no arguable jurisdiction, then either of them may be held accountable

"The civil rights legislation passed by congress shortly after the Civil War gathered dust on law library shelves for a century. Then the statutes were dusted off, and again utilized for protecting ethnic minorities and others who had been denied their constitutional rights."

under the Civil Rights Acts. An example: the prosecutor takes a case before the grand jury. The grand jury no-bills the accused—this means that the grand jury found that there is no probable cause to hold the accused. Then, the prosecutor goes out and arrests the individual and brings him to trial on the same charge. This might constitute a serious enough abuse of the prosecutor's office to give rise to a cause of action for civil damages.

If a judge leaves his bench, walks across the street and gets into an argument with somebody in a bar, pulls a gun on that person and directs his bailiff to arrest the individual, the judge is clearly exercising jurisdiction that he does not have. The bailiff and the judge can only exercise jurisdiction over a subject who is properly before the court.

In my own practice, a situation occurred when a judge ordered my client, attorney Joe Izen, to come before the court and show cause why he should not be held in contempt of court. This was before Izen had made an appearance in front of the judge, and the judge had no jurisdiction over him.

What the judge wanted to do was punish Izen for teaching people how to handle their own divorces without a lawyer. I took the deposition of that particular judge. The judge backed down on his charges against Izen. My client decided to wait to determine whether or not he would file a civil rights action against the judge. It might have been an extremely interesting case. Does a judge have judicial immunity for his actions if he acted without any authority? However, since I successfully defended my client in a related case against him filed by the State Bar of Texas, filing the civil rights suit seemed unnecessary. There are only so many battles you can fight.

Another Civil Rights Act requires government officials, if possible, to prevent other government officials from violating individuals' civil rights. An example of this would be a situation in which one police officer stands by and makes no effort to stop another police officer from killing a suspect.

Traditionally, police officers have cooperated with each other in a sort of Mafioso brotherhood: one police officer would watch a police officer plant a gun on a dead suspect! The honest cop, although not approving of the action, would, nevertheless, either remain silent or back up the story of

"The basic purpose of the Civil Rights Act was to protect constitutional rights for citizens in the United States."

the dishonest cop. Under 42 USC 1986, the honest cop has an obligation to do his best to prevent the violation of civil rights. If he does not, he also can be held liable in a civil rights action.

What are your constitutional civil rights? Read the Constitution! Read the amendments to the Constitution! Does anyone stop you from voting? Has anyone stopped you from speaking in a group? Has anyone stopped you from printing information? Has anybody stopped you from publicly addressing your government? Has anybody beaten you half to death for exercising any of your constitutional rights?

The bottom line on the Civil Rights Acts is that they were passed for the purpose of ensuring that local governments and government agents do not prevent you from exercising your constitutional muscles.

At times, our rights are referred to as "constitutional privileges." A privilege is something that is given to an individual who has earned it or proven himself deserving. A right is something that you are born with. The distinction between a right and privilege is an important one. Every right guaranteed us in the Constitution and its amendments is something we have been given freely and do not have to earn. We may have to protect the right; we may have to litigate or fight to keep the right; but it is ours absolutely. We are not required to take any tests before we are permitted to exercise our constitutional rights. We are not required to prove our worthiness to use them. Even prisoners have them. They cannot be ignored or taken away without due process, and most of them are inalienable rights which cannot be legally taken away through any process!

The majority of attorneys in private practice won't take civil rights cases. A civil rights attorney is a Don Quixote tilting against the windmills of government attorneys with large bankrolls and against defendants cloaked with various types of immunity.

A good reason why an attorney would not get involved is shown in the example illustrated in the case of *Bell vs. City of Milwaukee*.[1] The Seventh Circuit Court of Appeals decision, rendered September 4, 1984, concerning an action that started in 1958, is 70 pages long!

The case involved the February 2, 1958, death of Daniel Bell at the hands of two Milwaukee police officers. The police officers were going out on patrol to check some vacant homes and arrest some "niggers." Daniel Bell was stopped because his vehicle was missing a tail light. He apparently panicked and fled, and was shot to death by the officers.

Bell's persistent family and attorney endured 21 years of cover-up, a conspiracy of silence by members of the police department and the district attorney's office, and uncooperative judiciary members. They could not get their case before a jury. No judge would allow it. In 1978, one of the police officers finally admitted that he had lied about the Bell shooting.

At the trial in 1979, one of the police officers pleaded guilty to reckless homicide and perjury. He was sentenced to seven years in prison and got out after three. The City of Milwaukee decided not to use its option to appeal to the U.S. Supreme Court after the Seventh Circuit ruled in favor of the plaintiffs. The trial court awarded $1.5 million in damages to Bell's family. The court of appeals reduced the award to approximately $1 million.

Since my office filed the Norma Ginter case in 1985, our office had to use $50,000 worth of unbilled legal time just to get to first base—it took more than 18 months of litigation before the first depositions were taken. That figure gives the reader some idea of what Bell's attorney must have spent. How much work does it take during a 21-year period to prepare a case for trial? What does it cost to have an attorney away from his law office for a trial that lasts several months? Even then, approximately one-third of the judgment was taken away by the appeals court.

Both a book and a television movie have been based on the Bell case. The Bell case—which was handled by a courageous attorney, and litigated by decent, desperate steadfast relatives of the deceased—is not the success story that it looks like. It is a significant victory of course, for the litigants, the trial attorney, and for the country, legally. Unfortunately, Bell's father died without knowing the outcome.

A similar case occurred in Houston, Texas, in 1978, when police officers shot and killed an unarmed, white Louisiana teenager, Randall Webster, who had been joy riding in a stolen vehicle. A throw-down gun was planted on the youth to back up the officers' story that they were returning fire. Justice finally triumphed after the boy's father had died.

As Ex-Chief Justice Pope of the Texas Supreme Court claimed: "Justice delayed is justice denied." If we have to wait 21 years for justice in civil rights cases, we are reduced to the situation described in the case of Jarndyce and Jarndyce in Charles Dickens' Bleak House.[2] When the Jarndyce case was finished, the family estate was totally depleted by costs of court and attorneys' fees. Youngsters, who had been bequeathed rocking horses in the estate, were grown up, graduated from college and had bought their own horses and ridden off into the sunset. Our system often defeats the purpose of litigation even when the litigation is successful. To paraphrase a medical cliche, "The lawsuit was a success, but the client died."

Many people who have been exposed to the current American system could not distinguish the following excerpts from Charles Dicken's *Bleak House* from an account of Twentieth-Century American jurisprudence.

Read it to victims of the legal system and see if they can tell you the country, century or author:

"...which has its ruined suitor, with his slipshod heels and threadbare dress, borrowing and begging through the round of every man's acquaintance;..." (Destroyed the people who came there for justice.)

"... which gives to monied might the means abundantly of wearying out the right; which so exhausts finances, patience, courage, hope; so overthrows the brain and breaks the heart; that there is not an honorable man among its practitioners who would not give—who does not often give—the warning..." (If you have the money to delay trial, you will win over someone who does not.)...

Dicken's expression of "monied might" buying justice could certainly have come straight from Spooner or Bastiat. However, it comes straight from Dicken's own life. He wrote *Bleak House* after emerging from a decade trial on his own copyright infringement suit. Dickens warns about the courthouse:

"...'Suffer any wrong that can be done you rather than come here!'"

Any explanation would be redundant.

"Standing on a seat at the side of the hall, the better to peer into the curtained sanctuary, is a little mad old woman in a squeezed bonnet, who is always in court, from its sitting to its rising, and always expecting some incomprehensible judgment to be given in her favor. Some say she really is, or was, a party to a suit; but no one knows for certain, because no one cares." [2]

How many linger at our courthouses today?

"It took a little more than four months to write the U.S. Constitution. In less than an additional year, the states had ratified it, and within another year the government machinery described in the Constitution was substantially in place and functioning."

. *"A sallow prisoner has come up, in custody, for the half- dozenth time, to make a personal application to purge himself of his contempt; which, being a solitary surviving executor who has fallen into a state of conglomeration about accounts of which it is not pretended that he had ever any knowledge, he is not at all likely ever to do. In the meantime his prospects in life are ended."* (A protester of probate taxes doomed by his inheritance.)

"This scarecrow of a suit has, in course of time, become so complicated, that no man alive knows what it means. The parties to it understand it least;..." (This comment exposes the foolishness of the great fallacy-ignorance of the law is no excuse.)

It took a little more than four months to write the U.S. Constitution. In less than an additional year, the states had ratified it, and within another year the government machinery described in the Constitution was substantially in place and functioning.

Keeping all of the above in mind, how ludicrous it seems that a simple automobile wreck case can take three to five years to get into court. A civil rights suit, may take an entire lifetime. Are today's legal authorities so enlightened and so important that on every slight, automobile vehicle injury they have five years worth of things to tell us that are worth listening to or reading? Is it possible that their works are less worthy of our attention and admiration than those of the framers of the Constitution? The fact that the document which established the foundation of our legal system was framed in less than half a year, condemns our current system by its very example, ridiculing the vast, unending myriad of incomprehensible and unfair legal delays and paper mountains which is today's standard operating procedure.

The second half of this chapter deals with the criminal and civil aspects of my most important civil rights case, that of Norma Ginter, a simple housewife who was charged with capital murder in the blood bath of the attempted apprehension of an individual identified as the federal fugitive,

"The fact that the document which established the foundation of our legal system, was framed in less than half a year, condemns our current system by its very example, ridiculing the vast, unending myriad of incomprehensible and unfair legal delays and paper mountains which is today's standard operating procedure."

245

Gordon Wendell Kahl, on June 3, 1983.

B. THE GINTER CASE

The Ginter case illustrates the difficulty and complexity of a civil rights case. The criminal and civil aspects of the Norma Ginter case, which began in 1983, and now, guaranteed to run most of 1988, possibly into 1989 and even potentially into the 1990s, is moving, for the third time, into the Eighth Circuit Court of Appeals arena.

I represented Norma Ginter in her defense against capital murder charges. I worked on the Ginter/Russell/Udey federal harboring trial and represented Irene and Ed Udey. I did not represent Norma Ginter in that case. In 1985, I filed Norma Ginter's civil rights suit. In Arkansas, the federal rule requires that a case be brought to trial within six months after it's filed. But during three years, we only once got close to having a trial.

The Ginter case involved a state capital murder case in Lawrence County, Arkansas, a federal trial in the Western District of Arkansas for harboring a fugitive, an appeal to the Eighth Circuit Court of Appeals, an appeal to the U.S. Supreme Court, a civil rights suit in the Eastern District, a premature appeal to the Eight Circuit, proceedings which led to the eve of trial in the civil rights case—only to end in a final judgment dismissing all defendants. Now the entire case is before the Eighth Circuit set for oral argument on September 22, 1988. It will be 1989 before an opinion comes out. The loser will undoubtly appeal to the United States Supreme Court. In order to prepare for trials and briefs, research had to be done both in Arkansas state law and federal law.

1.**The Facts** Gordon Wendell Kahl, a vocal opponent of the IRS, was convicted in Texas, in 1977 of two misdemeanor offenses—willful failure to file income tax returns for the years 1973 and 1974. He was sentenced to one year of imprisonment on the first count, (he ended up serving six months in the Federal Pentitentiary in Leavenworth, Kansas). His sentence for the second count was five years of probation, which included filing income tax returns and abstaining from any "tax protestor" type meetings. After Kahl's release from prison, he moved back to his former home in North Dakota. He attracted unwanted attention from law enforcement officials because he attended, and spoke at, patriot meeetings.

During an apparent attempt in February, 1983, to arrest Kahl for a misdemeanor probation violation, law enforcement officers started shooting, and Kahl's son, Yorie, was critically wounded by one or more of the local and federal law enforcement officers who had set up the roadblock on an isolated stretch of road near Medina, North Dakota..

During the shooting, two federal marshals were killed. Kahl was alleged to have been responsible for these deaths by returning fire after his son was shot. It is my personal opinion that, in fact, he did return fire and he did kill one of the federal marshals. It is my personal opinion that the other federal marshal was probably shot by his own men due to their incompetence. Kahl put his wounded son into an abandoned police car—since after Kahl started returning fire, most officers ran away, abandoning their cars—and drove his son to a hospital.

Kahl had the paranoid delusion, according to government sources, that the law enforcement officials were out to kill him. He felt he had no chance other than to flee. In letters written by Kahl during his flight—which were subsequently published for nationwide circulation—he said that he thought he was about to be killed, and had premonitions of what was to come.

A nationwide manhunt was set up by the U.S. Marshals Service to apprehend Kahl. "Wanted" posters were circulated. A $25,000 reward was offered for information leading to his capture.

James Blasingame, the head of the FBI in Arkansas, stated under oath that while Kahl was not on the FBI's 10 most wanted list, he would have been on the 15 most wanted list, if there was such a list. Such an extensive manhunt was obviously the result of the two U.S. marshals being killed in the February shoot-out with Kahl.

Should the two marshals have been killed? Did Kahl shoot in self defense? Was any of the fighting necessary? Was it caused by over-eager and incompetent law enforcement officials acting in an incompetent way? I wasn't there. I don't have all the facts. A book was written recently, *There Was a Man—Kahl* by Capstan Turner and Ajay Lowery[3] that reports on the entire Kahl saga from the tax case beginning in Texas to the roadblock shoot-out in North Dakota as well as the fiery aftermath on June 3, 1983 in Arkansas.

In response to the nationwide manhunt and the wanted posters, a woman named Karen Russell Robertson informed the FBI—in exchange for the $25,000 blood money—that her father, Art Russell, and two couples, all residents of northeastern Arkansas, were apparently involved with Kahl.

Karen and her two daughters were living in her father's home. He cooked and cleaned and paid the bills. According to Karen, Kahl stayed with them several months. In the evenings, her father, his visitors and sometimes others would study the Bible. Arthur Russell subsequently was charged with the federal offense of harboring a fugitive for allegedly hiding and protecting the man identified as Kahl. Two couples were charged with the crime also: Ed and Irene Udey and Leonard and Norma Ginter.

On June 3, 1983, after a 24-hour aerial surveillance of the the Ginters' home in rural Lawrence County, a horde of law enforcement officers converged on the house in northeastern Arkansas. This army of more than three dozen law enforcement officers from the U.S. Marshals Service, FBI, Arkansas State Police and county and city officers—including Sheriff Gene Matthews, State Police investigator Ed Fitzpatrick and Ravenden Town Marshal Tom Lee, U.S. Marshal Jim Hall, and James Blasingame, the head of the FBI in Arkansas.

Leonard Ginter said that about 5:30pm. that day he left the house for some early evening fishing, leaving his wife and near-deaf house guest watching the evening news on television. The guest was sitting with his back to the front door. A few moments later, Norma—believing she had heard a noise outside over the blare of the television—stepped out to see if Leonard had changed his mind about his fishing trip. The Ginters' home was constructed to be energy efficient, built into the side of a hill with only the front of the house exposed, making it difficult to hear from inside the house.

However, Leonard had only gotten to the end of his driveway before a train of unmarked cars topped the hill that his house was built into, blocked the road and forced him to stop. Leonard's fishing pole lay in the back seat of his car beside an unloaded .22 rifle. On the front seat with him was the .22 revolver he brought to protect himself from poisonous snakes at his fishing hole. Leonard was forced out of his car, taken back to the house by several officers, and ordered to call his wife out of the house.

After hearing a noise, Norma came out of the house and she and Leonard were quickly handcuffed and thrown face down into the dirt about 10 yards from the entrance of their home. No megaphone was used, no one was asked to come out of the house.

From this moment on, the versions of what happened vary widely. Law enforcement officials say Norma told them that no one else was in the house. Norma's affidavit says she was too terrified to answer questions and just looked at her husband.

Within minutes, Fitzpatrick, Matthews, and Hall entered the premises and one of the officers shot the Ginters' guest in the back of the head. The Arkansas medical examiner said the man died instantly from the gunshot. No one else has been allowed to examine the body.

After two quick shots were fired inside the house, Fitzpatrick ran outside the house and unloaded the four rounds in his shotgun through a window, hitting Matthews with some of the buckshot.

Law enforcement officials told reporters that the man they identified as Kahl and Sheriff Matthews exchanged fire inside the house, with both shooting each other. Their version claims that Kahl was lurking behind the refrigerator and fired on Matthews. At the same instant, Matthews had to be shooting Kahl in the back of his head. Doesn't that seem to be a bit farfetched? The fact is, the refrigerator was so snug up against a wall that a cockroach would have had trouble getting behind it!

Since the law enforcement officers' version of the deaths of Kahl and Matthews is patently absurd, one is left to wonder what really did happen. Based on various accounts I have heard, and the money I spent on investigators, I believe the gentleman identified as Kahl was sitting at the kitchen table watching television when someone simply walked up behind him, shot him, and killed him instantly. There was no exchange of fire.

As law enforcement officers who attacked Kahl in North Dakota discovered, Kahl was a marksman. His attackers were not. If there had been a mutual exchange of fire, the three law enforcement officials would have been dead—and the fugitive, if he was Kahl, might still be alive today. A trained marksman who can kill with one shot has an advantage over others with only average skills with a gun.

Perhaps fearing that they had murdered the wrong person—since the dead man closely resembled a neighbor and friend of the Ginters who was well known to Sheriff Matthews—Kahl's killers proceeded to destroy any way of identifying the corpse. They chopped off the hands and feet, and piled mattresses and other flammable materials over the mutilated body. Is it fair to blame those three? Maybe not, but, the hands and feet were removed, the body was burnt and no one has come forward with a plausible excuse or explanation.

Fitzpatrick testified under oath that he believed Kahl and Matthews had each fired one shot. But Hall was a bit more cautious, saying he hadn't seen most of it.

Who killed Kahl? We may never know. Of one fact we can be certain: It was not Norma or Leonard Ginter because they were already in police custody but were about to be charged with capital murder.

Later that evening (the farce lasted almost three hours) an FBI agent ordered local town marshal Tom Lee to pour kerosene taken from a nearby farm into the Ginters' house through an air vent on the roof. After the fuel was poured into the house, and no fire started, law enforcement officers fired hundreds of rounds of bullets and tear gas into the house until it burst into flames, destroying everything that Norma and Leonard Ginter owned in this world—while firemen and a fire truck waited nearby.

Tom Lee admitted to his role, but he also admitted that he didn't think it was a good law enforcement practice.

Interestingly enough, the deed was actually described *as arson* by FBI Agent Dero Downing under oath[4]. Arson is, of course, a criminal offense. Arson is defined as "the wrongful destruction of property through fire."

FBI Agent James Blasingame, who was in charge of the assault on the Ginters' residence, admitted that the scene was one of pandemonium, uncontrolled and unmitigated violence.

After the fire burned out, the remains of the body said to be Kahl's was pulled out through the house's front window with a pitchfork—it was decapitated, de-footed, and de-armed. State Medical Examiner Fahamy Malak said he believed the fire just melted the feet and hands off.

Ridiculous! The killing of Sheriff Matthews, the burning of the evidence and the Ginter home, and the pinning of false charges of capital murder on the two Ginters was all part of a disgusting cover-up supported by more than a dozen law enforcement agents and the judiciary.

Following the June 3, 1983 massacre, Arthur Russell, Leonard and Norma Ginter, and Ed and Irene Udey were charged in federal court with harboring the federal fugitive Gordon Wendell Kahl.

In the harboring trial, I represented Ed and Irene Udey. The Great Izen represented Arthur Russell. Federal Judge Franklin Waters, in the Western District of Arkansas, found the Ginters were indigent and appointed Charles Karr of Fort Smith, Arkansas to assist them on the federal harboring charge. Charles Karr was not about to lie down for anybody. He fought vigorously on behalf of Norma and Leonard. He did not, however, put any personal financial resources into the case although Izen and I personally incurred thousands of dollars worth of expenses for which our clients could not reimburse us.

In the harboring trial, the government was represented by long-time

Assistant U.S. Attorney Larry McCord, and political appointee Asa Hutchinson. McCord was honest, hardworking and tough. He knew the rules of evidence like the lines on the back of his hand. A top flight pro. If the defense team could choose its competition, we'd rather have someone less competent; but the taxpayers get their money's worth from this guy and we couldn't complain.

As the politically appointed U.S. Attorney, Hutchinson was the headliner who talked to the press. He was mean and shallow, and I wouldn't trust him with a wooden nickel. When McCord beat us, Hutchinson took credit. Later, apparently trying to take advantage of the publicity he got for himself during the trial, he ran for the U.S. Senate, and thank God, got beat soundly.

Judge Waters was pro-prosecution from the start. Nevertheless, I have a high regard for his integrity. He is an intelligent and compassionate man, but at the time of the trial he had only been on the bench a short time and was severely limited because he had very little experience with criminal law as either a judge or as a private attorney. I believe he took the judicial bench because he wants to serve, not because of a lust for power.

Unfortunately, at the time of the Ginter/Udey/Russell trial he was blinded by a law-and-order attitude and wanted to get the case over quickly. I hope that our trial in his early judicial career helped him to become more skeptical of the government authority he respected so much at the time. He has the potential to be a great judge; but in the 1983 criminal trial he was too naive, and allowed the government to manipulate the evidence.

Judge Waters and the prosecutor pushed the case to trial rapidly. The facts were only partially known to us at the time. None of the attorneys really knew what happened and our motions for extra time were denied. Discovery was limited to almost nothing.

Although I believed there was some evidence showing that the burned-up body pulled out of the Ginters' home was Kahl, I also believe that much of this evidence had been fabricated. Medical examiner Malak testified that he examined 32 teeth found at the scene and identified them as Kahl's teeth. But Kahl's daughter testified that he had lost several teeth in World War II and didn't have 32 teeth. She said Kahl's teeth were rotten and decayed, not bright and clean like some of those Malak produced.

"The jury should decide what is relevant and what is not relevant."

In my opinion, false testimony was put into the record to prove what law enforcement officials thought to be true but couldn't honestly prove—that the man killed and burned in the Ginters' residence was Kahl. However, the jury was not allowed to make that fact decision, and this element was also appealed.

In order to prevent identification of the body, it appears that the deceased man's killers had cut off his hands and feet, tossed them away and covered the remaining body with easily combustible mattresses. Weeks later, a *New York Times* reporter found one of the severed feet while looking through the charred debris at the Ginter house.[5]

The jury was not allowed to know about the fire which destroyed the Ginters' home. Since no Arkansas law enforcement officials would investigate the fire, we hired Texas arson investigator Roy Paul who found evidence that flammable accelerants had been used inside of the Ginter house. Chemist Floyd McDonald analyzed those samples and confirmed the presence of accelerants.

The evidence clearly indicated arson—yet to this day no federal or Arkansas authority has investigated the possibility. Also, when Medical Examiner Malak testified, he said he found no evidence of accelerants on the dead man's body or clothing. Ha!

The court ruled that the intentional burning of the Ginter house was irrelevant. Again, this is one of my basic disputes with the direction our legal system has taken. The jury should decide what is relevant and what is not relevant.

Izen wanted to ask the jury to consider Arthur Russell's defense of "necessity." The gist of that defense was that, even though Russell might have violated a federal law, he did so to prevent the commission of a more serious crime—the murder of Gordon Kahl by law enforcement officials. That is, he committed harboring in order to prevent murder.

This legal theory could have won the case. This legal theory could have convinced a jury to release the defendants. Although the evidence was overwhelming that the officers intended to kill Kahl, we were not allowed to use it.

The three attorneys representing the five defendants cooperated with each other fully out of our sincere belief that our clients—if they had actually harbored a fugitive, had done so in an attempt to save a man's life.

"Sometimes the difference between a great victory and a great defeat can be very slight."

Russell was convicted of harboring a fugitive, sentenced to six months in jail and actually served four.

Leonard Ginter was sentenced to two five-year terms but ordered to serve them concurrently. The practical effect of this is that the two five-year sentences become one five-year sentence, and instead of a possible ten years, Leonard Ginter actually served about three and a half years of the five-year sentence before being released.

Norma Ginter was convicted and sentenced to the time that she had already served in jail, which at that time had been six months.

However, she would still serve one more month in jail before being released on bond on the pending state charge of capital murder. As soon as she was released from federal custody, we pulled out all the stops and got her out of state custody.

My client, Irene Udey, was found not guilty.

Ed Udey, who in my professional opinion was technically not guilty under the law, was found guilty and appealed his case and lost a two-to-one decision at the Eighth Circuit. He was allowed to stay out of jail pending appeal to the entire panel. He then lost a five-to-four decision when the entire Eighth Circuit panel voted not to review his case. That's a tough way to go. One vote different on either one of two decisions and Ed Udey would have never gone to jail. He didn't go to jail, however, until we appealed his case to the U.S. Supreme Court, and lost there. He served about two years and is now free. Sometimes the difference between a great victory and a great defeat can be very slight.

For his own personal religious reasons, Ed Udey—who is not Jewish—does not eat non-Kosher foods. While he was serving his two years in jail he was force-fed intravenously because he refused to eat the prison food. While in prison, he won a Fifth Circuit decision allowing him to practice his religious diet.

Waters was under lots of pressure to give everyone heavy sentences, but he ignored the pressure when he sentenced Arthur Russell and Norma Ginter. His sentencing was fair and it was clear he didn't relish this part of his job.

Since the harboring trial is worthy of a whole book in itself, and that's not our purpose here, I'll just briefly touch on some highlights.

Before the harboring trial began in Harrison, Arkansas, the town had been whipped up into a frenzy of emotion. There were enough law enforcement officers brought into town to make many an endangered dictator feel secure.

There were daily threats on our lives. An anti-Semitic group in the audience stuck a note under the door of the room Joe Izen and I shared at one of the local establishments. The note read, "One of you is a Jew and our artists are creating caricatures to determine which one it is. The Jew will be bombed." I am quite proud of my heritage. As I previously explained, three of my four grandparents were Jewish, although my last name comes from my British, Episcopalian grandfather.

My friend and co-litigator Izen has a name that sounds deceptively Jewish, but he is Lebanese and somewhat anti-Semitic.

Once the trial got started, an artist's rendition of Izen was slipped underneath our door, stating that they have proven beyond any doubt which of the two of us was Jewish—and it was clearly Izen. I told Izen I'd prefer for him to get a different room, even though it would increase our expenses of trying the case, because I didn't want to get bombed. He didn't appreciate my humor.

During the trial the local newspaper carried a front page article saying: "Posse Comitatus to Bomb Court House Tomorrow." I took this to Judge Waters immediately and asked for a mistrial. I argued that if a mistrial were declared, the trial could start over another time when excitement died down a little. Then, our clients might have had a fair trial.

There was a climate of hysteria running through the town during the federal harboring trial. The courtroom was packed, standing room only every day. The jurors were so frightened by this time that they would have distrusted an angel in the courtroom. I argued that although the jurors had been instructed not to read any newspapers, it was likely that at least some of the the jurors and alternates had heard from their families or friends that the courthouse was going to be bombed tomorrow.

The court asked the jurors if any of them had been reading the papers or discussing the case in violation of his orders. The jurors made no movement whatsoever. The judge instructed the jurors if they had violated his order to "raise your hand right now." Nobody raised a hand.

With that, we continued. But I thought that was reversible error because there was such little likelihood that none of the jurors had heard—directly or indirectly—of the bomb threats. The threats, I believe, contributed to the conviction of my client.

The local media—*The Arkansas Democrat*, the *Memphis Commercial Ap-*

"Even though it is untrue, the press likes to print it—
sensationalism sells papers!"

---

peal, and the *Harrison Times*—started out apparently favoring the prosecution, but truth won out in the end and the coverage became more sympathetic to the defendants.

In another incident, one of Arthur Russell's daughters—not the one who betrayed him—charged into the courthouse and took photographs of jurors. I have no idea how she got past the electronic surveillances and searches. It seems as if all these searches do is delay the people who are supposed to be there and cause log jams in the lobbies—the fruitcake usually gets through anyway.

One of the jurors screamed, "It's the posse, they're after us," and marshals immediately rushed in and saved the juror's life by confiscating and destroying the camera. Why did Arthur Russell's daughter do that? I can only speculate that she may have been trying to record for posterity what was happening to her father. She is not a member of the posse comitatus or any other organization.

However, the incident added fuel to the doubts in everyone's mind that none of the jurors had heard any rumors or read the newspaper articles in which the posse had supposedly threatened to bomb the courthouse.

The term *"posse comitatus"* actually refers to a group of private citizens deputized by local sheriff's to enforce the law. Many states have provisions for them in their laws, charters or constitutions; Arkansas does. It is also the name adopted by a small group of people alleged to be militantly opposed to the IRS. Since I have never met any of these people, I am skeptical as to whether or not they exist. None of the patriots I have met are involved with them and none of those people accused of harboring Gordon Kahl were.

Nevertheless, the FBI and the IRS disseminate dishonest information to the press, labeling innocent people like Norma Ginter as militant and dangerous. Even though it is untrue, the press likes to print it—sensationalism sells papers! The problem is, after someone is unfairly labeled as a member of this possibly non-existent group, accidents often happen—their homes get burned down or they get shot. I addressed a letter to *Newsweek* on the subject of inaccuracies in their printed story on radical right wing groups.[6] This does not mean there are not dangerous radical groups in America. There are.

In addition to the federal "harboring" charge, Norma Ginter had been charged with capital murder. Throughout the nerve-wracking months, she was first offered the right to plead guilty and do life rather than get the death penalty. Negotiations continued, but the deals offered were absurd.

Finally the prosecution was willing to have Norma plead guilty to the equivalent of a parking ticket, but she emphatically said: "No."

She wanted to go all the way to trial. She would not sell out and plead guilty. When I first met her, Norma Ginter was in a hell-hole prison; she was in shock, trembling and afraid. By the time of the last hearing on the murder charge, she had become a tower of strength—which must have been a gift from God.

That was a difficult time for me as an attorney. After having gone seven straight years without a loss as a trial lawyer, the setback in Ed Udey's harboring trial was emotionally devastating. I advised Norma Ginter that if she went to trial, she would win. However, I was so disillusioned by what had happened to Ed Udey that I no longer felt certain that just because someone was innocent that justice would prevail. Norma's courage inspired me. Together, we perservered until we got the charges dropped and her name vindicated!

We demanded a trial. Continuances were granted to assist the government, which was not ready for the case. We demanded trial again. Further continuances were granted. Norma spent a month in prison until being released from prison on bond and we still pressed for trial.

Murder charges had been filed against Norma by Lawrence Country Prosecutor James Stallcup, who was at the scene and who saw Norma and Leonard arrested before the shooting started. Stallcup accused Norma of conspiring with Kahl to murder Sheriff Matthews—which is capital murder and punishable by death. Stallcup claimed that this elderly woman was so dangerous that she had to be held in jail without bond until trial.

Norma insisted she was innocent of the murder charge, and after a bitter, protracted seven-month war, Stallcup dropped all charges against her. However, he said he still believed that she was guilty, but that she had suffered enough. We are not talking a mere accusation of negligent homicide or second degree murder, she had been accused the intentional, cold blooded killing of a sheriff acting in the line of duty.

Winning over James Stallcup and forcing him to back down wasn't the accomplishment of a clever lawyer using strange, indecipherable legal technicalities to free the guilty as some people have described it. It was a labor of hard work and love for an honest, God fearing mother and grandmother to get enough of the truth to surface.

2. **The Litigation** Preparing our brief to the Eighth Circuit on the Ginter/Udey/Russell federal harboring case was a mammoth undertaking.

First we pulled the harboring statutes from the United States Code and then we examined all of the cases cited under the harboring statutes. Then we shepardized (used a source which tells when a case has been quoted in another case) the cases up to the most recent date. This helped us enormously because we were now aware of what had happened in the history of convictions under the harboring statute. Then we looked up individual words in *Corpus Juris Secundum* and American Jurisprudence: (both legal encyclopedias) such as "conspiracy" and "harboring." We followed up on these words and tracked them through their history in litigation. We updated. We then took all the cases that seemed important or relevant and ran them through Westlaw's "Shepard's" computer program. For more information on research techniques, see Chapter XIII.

At times we were referred to cases that were not available in libraries and in which the full text had to be taken from the computer. It's cheaper to pull the book out and photocopy the case than it is to use the computer time and have it printed. However, you use the computer option if you have no other access to the case. By these methods, we found all of the cases. When we had our final cases, we shepardized those final cases to see every time they had been quoted anywhere and brought them up to date. We then went through the transcript of the trial itself several times, pulling out significant sections, favorable or unfavorable to our position, for use in the brief.

The worst single miscarriage of justice that happened during the harboring trial was the conviction of Norma Ginter. In my opinion there was even less reason to find her guilty than there was to convict Irene Udey, who was found not guilty. Norma Ginter had given a voluntary statement, saying that the man in her home was Kahl, and that she didn't want him in her home but that her husband was the boss and there was nothing she could do about it. The judge refused to allow this portion to be read to the jury.

Charles Karr, who represented the Ginters in the harboring trial, worked with Izen and me on the appeals. My brief was the first one out, so both the other lawyers were free to utilize it in the preparation of their briefs. I believed this issue of the incomplete statement was the strongest issue for Norma Ginter's appeal.

If the judges want to render a ridiculous decision but they don't want it to affect the future of law enforcement, they simply put on their opinion, "Do not publish." It is not published and it is not law. If the judges want to make a statement on the law by publishing their opinion, but the fact situations don't support what they want to do, they simply alter the transcript to make the fact situations to suit them. It reminds me of the statement of the great jurist, Clarence Darrow, who said: "There is no justice in the courts or out of the courts." Darrow was one of the most exceptional attorneys of all time and he died in poverty. He was attacked and brutalized by the authorities, by government, by bar committees, by grand jury investigations, and was even put on trial with his freedom imperiled. Darrow was unquestionably an underground lawyer. There have always been and always will be attempts to bury underground lawyers. They cause trouble. They rock the boats.

Research for the capital murder case involved looking up the Arkansas capital murder statutes and cases based on the statute. Our intention was to distinguish the facts of Norma Ginter's situation from any of the sets of conditions under which a charge of capital murder could be correctly brought, under Arkansas law.

When the harboring case and the capital murder case were over, all that was left was the decision whether or not to follow up with civil suits.

One of Gordon Kahl's daughters originally indicated that she wanted to sue. Since I was already planning on handling Norma Ginter's suit, I did not think I could represent her also. I do not know whether she has filed suit. Arthur Russell's home had been robbed by the agents when they searched it. His life savings in silver had been taken out and confiscated. His suit against the despoilers is pending in Arkansas.

On May 17, 1985, Norma Ginter filed suit against all the officials who had participated in the act of burning her home and charging her with capital murder. The case was originally styled as Norma Ginter vs. James Stallcup, James Blasingame, Jack Knox, Tom Lee, City of Ravenden, Roy Norvell, Boone County.

We knew we had to be in federal court to get fair treatment. We found several federal civil rights violations and began to research them based on the fact situation. We found violations of Arkansas state laws against arson and causing a catastrophe. We sued under both. We filed under the civil rights statute 42 USC 1983, and Arkansas state statutes.

The case was assigned to Chief Judge G. Thomas Eisele of the Eastern District Court of Arkansas. Virtually all the law enforcement officers named in the lawsuit asked the court to grant them special privileges not given to regular citizens—and in most cases Eisele granted those special privileges.

This is definitely a situation in which the court has too much power.

Reading between the lines of Judge Eisele's scholarly opinions, I suspect that even the judge himself feels the U.S. Supreme Court has vested too much power in the government with the immunity doctrine:

"The Court is somewhat uncomfortable in not permitting the plaintiff to conduct discovery in this case with respect to her claims against the movants, Mr. Blasingame and Mr. Knox. However, the Court is convinced that it would not be vindicating the policy of the Supreme Court...if it permitted discovery to go forward under the facts and circumstances of this case."
—page 24, Judge Eisele's Order, February 24, 1986

Unlike many of the judges that I've practiced before, Judge Eisele has a reputation for general excellence. It is apparent to anyone who reads his orders that he is a legal scholar. However, his orders in the Ginter civil rights case also demonstrate a predilection to favoring government officials. Though I have never met the judge in person, I have a profound respect for his scholarship.

Nevertheless, Judge Eisele, relying on Supreme Court decisions and his own personal opinions, butchered large portions of Norma Ginter's civil rights case and guaranteed that —without appeal —major portions of the lawsuit would never be brought before a jury, and worse without more discovery the truth would never come out.

Eisele ruled that FBI chief James Blasingame had absolute immunity from the charge of burning of the Ginter home. Eisele ruled that there was no absolute finding that burning someone's home down during an alleged attempt to apprehend a dangerous fugitive was constitutionally forbidden. Hopefully, this judgment will be overturned by the Eighth Circuit Court of Appeals.

Eisele also ruled that using fire is a legitimate part of the government's arsenal when apprehending a fugitive. If this usage is not constitutionally forbidden, there should certainly be some guidelines which must be followed prior to implementing fire. Judge Eisele's opinion indicated that government should not be forced to wait before taking the incendiary option. Thus, Blasingame was released from the law suit.

The individual who actually poured the fuel down the roof of the Ginter home was released the day before trial. I flew into Arkansas for the trial not knowing it had been canceled.

Did Prosecutor James Stallcup have the right to charge Norma Ginter with capital murder when there was no evidence against her, whatsoever?

Judge Eisele made the finding that Stallcup was shielded by prosecutorial immunity for any liability arising from his filing capital murder charges against the Ginters:

"even if he did so with malice coupled with...evil and sinister motive, ...and...knew the charge to be baseless in law and fact."
— *page 27, Judge Eisele's Order, March 7, 1986*

There is some reason to give limited immunity to prosecutors. If prosecutors can be sued by disgruntled former criminal defendants every time they file a case, they might be hesitant to file cases.

In this case, Eisele went too far. Norma Ginter was not brought before a grand jury. The Fifth Amendment, that guarantees individuals the right to a grand jury indictment for capital or serious offenses, meant nothing. Grand juries, to some extent, protect accused individuals against overly zealous prosecutors. Stallcup did not seek an indictment: he merely signed a paper known as an information accusing her of capital murder.

The judicial and prosecutorial immunity doctrine has created a privileged class of people with superior rights to American citizens: federal and high ranked enforcement officials. It is shockingly similar to the ancient type of government where the king ruled absolutely, secure in the knowledge that he could not be sued or punished. There are cases giving immunity to government officials for heinous acts.

Stallcup filed a motion for summary judgment which was granted, in part. His deposition, and that of Tom Lee, were taken in November, 1986. The deposition of Perry Webb — a Lawrence County deputy sheriff who had been on the scene of the shoot-out — was taken in August, 1987.

In both cases, at the last moment, Judge Eisele granted the motions for protection of the federal witnesses, so that we were never able to get the depositions of the custodians of the records of the FBI and the U.S. Marshals Service. By this time, Blasingame had disappeared so completely, that we couldn't even find him to serve with a subpoena. The Georgia address we had for him turned out to be that of his son.

After more pleadings were filed on both sides, Judge Eisele granted Stallcup's motion for summary judgment. Later, he granted the City of Ravenden's motion to dismiss. Finally, the only defendants remaining were Lawrence County, Arkansas and Tom Lee.

I wrote a strongly worded letter to Judge Eisele, in which I urged him to simply dismiss the whole case, so that I would have a final, appealable judgment on which I could proceed to the Eighth Circuit, rather than going through a whole trial, when the heart of the case had already been cut out.

Instead, Eisele set the case for trial on November 30, 1987. We gathered our witnesses, and I arranged for another attorney to cover a personal injury trial set for the same day in Houston. After waiting two and a half years to try this case, I was not about to ask for continuance of the trial date. I had to leave most of the final trial preparation in the hands of my staff since I was in a two-week trial on a willful failure to file case in Honolulu, Hawaii, and did not get back to the office until November 23, 1987, three days before Thanksgiving and only a week before trial.

In the meantime, after taking no action in this case for over two years, the attorneys for Lee and Lawrence County filed motions for summary judgment, one of which we did not even receive until the day before Thanksgiving, the last business day before the trial. Of course there was no way to adequately respond to these eleventh-hour pleadings and prepare both for this trial and the personal injury trial in Houston.

A pleading was filed to make the court aware of the impossible burden we were under, and to inform the court that the motions for summary judgment were untimely—since Judge Eisele had ruled that no more motions could be filed. However, Eisele chose to ignore his own ruling and ordered me to respond.

Norma Ginter, our witnesses, and I were in the federal courthouse in Little Rock, Arkansas, on November 30, 1987, only to find ourselves locked out from the court, literally and figuratively. The courtroom was locked! A clerk questioned our presence there and informed us that Judge Eisele was in another city that day. Unbeknownst to us, Judge Eisele had granted motions for summary judgment of the last two remaining defendants. Almost a month later, he signed a final judgment, disposing of the whole case.

Now we are again before the Eighth Circuit appealing the dismissals of all of the defendants! If the appeal is unsuccessful, the case will be over in late 1988 or 1989. If we succeed on appeal, the case could last well into the 1990's without money and possibly beyond the life of Norma Ginter.

"The bottom line on the Civil Rights Acts is that they were passed for the purpose of insuring that local government and government agents do not prevent you from exercising your constitutional muscles."

CHAPTER XII

FREEDOM OF INFORMATION ACT

& PRIVACY ACT

"The Freedom of Information Act and the Privacy Act are two golden keys, unlocking the government storehouse of information to the average citizen."

The Freedom of Information Act (generally referred to as FOIA) is one of the most important legacies of the Lyndon Johnson administration. Originally passed in 1966, the FOIA has been expanded and re-energized by succeeding administrations and is now even stronger and healthier.

It is one of those statutes that might have been included in the original Constitution or Bill of Rights, and if the need for it could have been anticipated, it probably would have been included. Why couldn't it? We didn't live in a world of paper in 1791. Documents were much briefer and the reservoir of information on individuals was much more limited.

Today, our government maintains more information on its individual citizens, through the executive branch, than any company, organization or other country in the world on its members or citizens. This massive store of information continues to be a source of growing concern to freedom-loving individuals who want to preserve their privacy and shield themselves against the type of government that is described in George Orwell's "1984."

Our government collects massive amounts of information on us throughout our lives. Although the social security number was not legally intended to be used as a national identification number, it is now used for that purpose. All of us have read numerous front page newspaper stories about the IRS's problems with their massive computer files. The government maintains a "Big Brother" file on each and every one of us, and the sheer magnitude of material is guaranteed to surprise everyone.

"The purpose of this brief chapter is to acquaint the reader with the Freedom of Information Act (FOIA) and let the reader know the power this act places in citizens' hands."

The purpose of this brief chapter is to acquaint the reader with the Freedom of Information Act (FOIA) and let the reader know the power this act places in citizens' hands.

What is the government doing? What does it want to know about you? How is it investigating you? Who else is investigating? How is it spending your money? The purpose of the FOIA is to enable citizens to obtain information from the government.

What does the FOIA do? It sets up guidelines and procedures for obtaining from the government the information it is keeping. Under FOIA, any person has a right to access information from everything in any executive branch agency records, except certain areas that are specifically exempted by statute.

Any discussion of the Freedom of Information Act must include the Privacy Act, which was passed in 1974. While the FOIA was passed for the purpose of allowing people to obtain the secrets that the government held, under the theory that the government was custodian of records for us and not for itself or its employees, the Privacy Act is more personal.

The Privacy Act was developed primarily for individuals to obtain personal information on themselves. Former Chief Justice Earl Warren brought the need for the Privacy Act and the FOIA Act into clearer perspective with his observation that secrecy in government is the incubator for corruption.

The method for triggering the FOIA is simply mailing a letter to the federal agency from which you are seeking information. Due to the high probability of your letter getting lost in the bureaucratic maze, send it by certified mail so that you will have proof that you sent the request to the government agency to which it was addressed. The letter should be directed, if possible, to the specific individual who has control of the information you are seeking. Also, an identical request should be sent certified mail to the head of the particular agency. Names of the individuals and agencies can often be obtained through the Federal Register, sometimes through the public library or through information services in your local federal courthouse.

Your letter should identify itself as a request for information pursuant

---

"The FOIA was passed for the purpose of allowing people to obtain the secrets that the government held, under the theory that the government was custodian of records for us and not for itself or its employees."

to the Freedom of Information Act and, if the information is personal to you, the Privacy Act. The desired information should be described as specifically as possible—for example, the military service record of Peter Paul Pott, United States Navy, rank, serial number, date of birth, social security number, dates of service etc.

Many people dislike using their social security numbers as identification, and some have gone so far as to file documents rescinding their social security numbers. If you are one of those persons and have not used your assigned social security number in years—and you are seeking information from a federal agency that keeps information by social security numbers—distasteful though it may be for you, it makes sense to include your former social security number in your request letter. Otherwise, your information may not be retrievable.

Once your letter has been received, the agency has 10 days to either give you the information and bill you for reasonable and necessary copying charges; give you an excuse for not giving you the information; or ask for an additional 10 days in which to locate the information and provide it to you.

If you obtain the desired information, there is no need to go any further.

The agency may ask for a 10-day extension to which they are entitled. It's highly possible that they will take an additional month. You may or may not wish to wait a month or six months before taking the next step.

The government agency officials might refuse to give you the information on certain legal grounds, or they may never get back to you at all. They are required to spell out their reasons for refusal. You are not required to accept their explanations. If you do not agree with their grounds for refusal to give you the information, or if you've gotten some response such as, "Your request is too vague to comply with," you can send another request making it more specific, or you can appeal through the administrative procedure. You cannot go into court without exhausting all of your administrative remedies. The administrative appeal procedure is simply another request addressed to the head of the agency or the appropriate appellate authority within the agency or to whom it may concern. If you don't know who the appropriate appellate authority is, address it to

"Former Chief Justice Earl Warren brought the need for the Privacy Act and the FOIA Act into clearer perspective with his observation that secrecy in government is the incubator for corruption."

"Appropriate Appellate Authority." Send three separate appeals to all three separate individuals. Your appeal may be very formal or very informal. The appeal can be a letter stating that you disagree with the findings and wish to appeal the findings, or it could be in the form that you might use for law suit.

Rather than examining the Freedom of Information Act from a standpoint of what you can get from it, it is more time effective to examine it from the standpoint of what you cannot get from it, and then determine whether or not information has been wrongfully withheld from you.

If your request is in the public interest, the agency has the option of not charging you for copying or reproducing the information. Normally, the agency may bill you only for photocopying and incidental expenses collecting the information. Since you are a member of the public, it is quite possible that your request is in the general public interest. Let your own discretion and conscience be your guide. In my opinion, it is difficult to conceive of a situation in which the release of government information is not in the public's interest.   There are certain statutory exemptions to the requirement that federal agencies release information pursuant to FOIA. We will examine each exempt category.

1. **National security.** You are not entitled to know that the president has ordered a surprise attack on Libya prior to the attack taking place.

2. **Related Solely to the Internal Personnel Rules and Practices of an Agency.** If it has nothing to do with the public, then you are not entitled to the information. This is a tricky area, and an area involving a great deal of litigation. Is the IRS Special Agents Handbook an internal manual? The answer: No. It is not. However, it has been withheld under some circumstances under this guise. Do you have a right to know about the work records of a public servant? No. There may be reasons why you are entitled to this through litigation, but not under the Freedom of Information Act.

3. **Miscellaneous Exceptions** which say you can't get the information, including:

a) records that would interfere with criminal proceedings still pending,

"Under FOIA, any person has a right to access information from everything in any executive branch agency records, except certain areas that are specifically exempted by statute."

b) records that would prevent someone from having a fair trial,

c) invasion of another individual's privacy,

d) disclosure of identity of a confidential source,

e) disclosure of investigative techniques and procedures, or

f) endangering the life or physical safety of law enforcement personnel.

It is important to understand that there is a FOIA requirement that if the information is not given to you, you be told specifically why. The reasons should be in one of the exemption categories should specifically list the exemption, and should give you some reason why. If nothing has been properly given to you, then the agency has violated their requirements under FOIA.

4. Trade Secrets. The government has access to private enterprise trade secrets which they don't have to reveal. You are not entitled to receive the secret formula for Coca-Cola.

5. Inter-Agency Memos. Unfortunately, if you are not involved in litigation, there is not a good reason for the agency divulging its inter-agency correspondence. You are not entitled to know that John Jones of the CIA has sent Sam Smith of the FBI a love note. This information is an inter-agency memo. It may or may not relate to information on work within the agency itself, and this also may be a violation of an exemption under number 6.

6. Personal Privacy. Do we need an explanation? Suppose the two above fictitious agents were caught and that nothing was done to either of them other than a little note placed in each of their files. These personal work files, even though they work for the CIA and FBI, will probably not endanger national security, but would only serve to embarrass the two agents.

7. Law Enforcement. You are not entitled to information which you could not otherwise receive about a pending criminal case. This is a very sticky legal issue. What if you could have gotten the information through other channels? Different jurisdictions have interpreted this question in many different ways. Obviously, you are not entitled to the government's entire strategy when they're planning a drug bust, but if the bust is over, are you entitled to the entire case? Under some circumstances yes; under other circumstances no.

8. Regulations or Supervision of Financial Institutions. This is an unfortunate exemption. It keeps information about banks and other lending institutions from being publicly disseminated. You will have to rely on other sources of information when you are deciding whether or not you want to put your money into a specific bank or savings institution. Is this good? No. The government however, regards it as essential because there are so many banks which are on the verge of failure. There are also bank secrecy acts which are to protect depositors. Frequently the banks ignore those anyway.

9. **Geological and Geophysical Information Data.** Including maps and wells. Unless you are in the oil industry or related industry this is of no concern to you. In any event, there does not seem to be a great deal of litigation on FOIA requests in this area in any event. Probably the people that want this information have other means of getting it. To summarize, the FOIA process works as follows:

The Freedom of Information Act lawsuit must be based on the failure of the government to provide the necessary information and the right of the individual to obtain the requested information. You can file the petition almost anywhere. The plaintiff may file in the federal district court in the District of Columbia, Washington D.C. Or a plaintiff may file in the federal district court where the desired records are kept, or where the plaintiff resides or where his chief business is located. However, the court may decide to transfer the case from the venue where you filed it to another location.

Once the FOIA suit is served on the government agency's head, the agency is required to answer as in any other civil lawsuit. If the government claims that the information is too sensitive or you are not entitled to it for any of the reasons previously stated or any other reasons, you have the right to ask the judge for an in-camera inspection. In an in-camera inspection, the judge can privately look at the records in his chambers and listen to the government's arguments. The judge will decide whether or not the government has a right to withhold the information. While a citizen could hardly expect to receive reports of covert military operations under the FOIA, he should have a right to receive purely personal information—even if it is potentially sensitive.

For example, suppose the IRS investigated every juror on the panel that found you not guilty of willful failure to file and charged one of them with a crime. Disclosure of these facts does not violate national security. However, unfortunately, many judges won't even require the government to show them the entire portfolio. You'll have to appeal, but most appellate panels won't even make the federal agencies obey the law.

The court, pursuant to the Freedom of Information Act, has the authority to order the government agency to turn over the disputed information. The government is subject to fines and to being assessed for court costs. The court is not required to order the government to pay attorney's fees.

If you want information concerning general activities of the executive branch of the government, you should make a request under the Freedom of Information Act. If, however, you want information about yourself, you should make your request under the Privacy Act. You may make your request under both the Freedom of Information Act and the Privacy Act (a proposed form is contained in the addendum.[2])

The original 1966 Freedom of Information Act proved to be too weak. In 1974, along with the new Privacy Act, Congress passed the amendments to the Freedom of Information Act. President Ford vetoed them, but Congress overrode his veto and passed the legislation which put some teeth into FOIA. Wise decision. The amendments which hastened the process of obtaining government files became effective in February, 1975. Comprehensive indexes had to be established to facilitate administrative processing of FOIA requests and shorten the time in which the government could respond.

The Freedom of Information Act and the Privacy Act are two golden keys, unlocking the government storehouse of information to the average citizen. This disclosure is definitely necessary if America is to continue to be the land of the free.

"If you want information concerning general activities of the executive branch of the government, you should make a request under the Freedom of Information Act. If, however, you want information about yourself, you should make your request under the Privacy Act."

CHAPTER XIII

RESEARCH

"The purpose of legal research is to answer questions. A skilled legal researcher goes to the next step which is to discover new, unasked questions and find the answers."

A. THE BASIC TOOLS

Think words. Think encyclopedia. Think laws. Now stop thinking for a moment. If you did these exercises properly, you are halfway to basic legal research.

If the prospect of legal research seems intimidating, don't despair. Thousands of lawyers never do any research at all—they fake it. If you find that legal research isn't your strong point, you won't be a very good legal assistant because they must know how to do research. Again, don't despair, you could still be a lawyer—as long as you can get into one or more of the unions. If you can read, you can do basic research. Read the first six words of this chapter again, now proceed.

Good legal researchers think like a shopper in a library selecting the appropriate words and phrases and books, like a builder in a supply store selecting the proper materials for his project or like the homemaker in a supermarket selecting the ingredients for her family's dinner. Legal research is a matter of words. Becoming familiar with the key words is important. Law books are filled with indices in alphabetical order. These are the tools to unlock the treasure chest of legal research. A law library is a legal supermarket with legal information. Just as a grocery shopper needs to know in what aisle to find the frozen peas or the instant mashed potatoes, the consumer in a law library needs to know where to find exactly what he is looking for.

A legal research project will usually begin with either a question that needs to be answered or a position that needs to be supported. Looking up the major topics in "Words and Phrases" type books or indices may lead you to certain statutes or cases. There are sets of law books actually called "Words and Phrases." In legal research, the shortest distance between two points is rarely a straight line—rather it's a circle. If exploring the various aspects of your question or issue leads you back to the same cases, you're probably doing something right; and those cases you keep returning to are likely to be the ones most relevant to the issue you're researching.

What is the purpose of legal research? The purpose of legal research is to answer questions. A skilled legal researcher goes to the next step which is to discover new, unasked questions and find the answers. A detailed explanation of this process follows.

Every aspect of the law can be reduced to questions and answers. The question that you start out with may be an extremely broad, general question and have several extremely broad, general answers. The broad, general answers need to be broken down to specific questions and specific answers. Many times you cannot get the specific answers to the questions that you want, but you can come very close. You come very close by finding similar answers and then assuming that these similar answers answer the question in your particular case.

For example, suppose that a client of yours has been charged in federal court with willful failure to file income tax returns. Like most lawyers, you've never handled a failure to file case. What to do? First, you must know as much as you can about the charges themselves by first reading the federal statutes. In this case, you already know from the indictment served on your client that he is charged with two counts of 26 USC 7203. Sometimes the indictment does not tell you what specific statute has been violated, and you have to figure it out. (This is fundamentally unfair. Some judges agree and will dismiss the indictment, others won't. Then you have to figure it out. This happens more often in state indictments than Federal Indictments.) That means that he is charged with violating Section 7203 of Title 26 of the United States Code which are the federal statutes passed by Congress put into an organized code form.

Law libraries have annotated versions of most statutes which contain the citations of cases on that specific section of the statutes that have been ruled on previously by higher, appeal courts. In this case, under the annotated statutes, numerous cases will be cited under Section 7203 telling how various federal appeal courts have ruled on certain aspects of that section. Write those cases down because you will need to review most of them. In many cases, the annotated citations will also refer to reference materials such as research papers or law school reviews on particular topics which are wonderful background material for starters. Often the

"In legal research, the shortest distance between two points is rarely a straight line—rather it's a circle."

citations are so numerous that a researcher must initially confine the research to specific topics to make the research project manageable.

Suppose in this case, your client had insisted on his innocence, and you're preparing for trial. One of the questions that must be answered is whether your client actually did, willfully, fail to file his income tax returns. Most of the time if an individual is charged with willful failure to file, it's because he did not file a return *or* the return he did file was deemed inadequate by the I.R.S. You will also need to determine whether or not your client had sufficient income to have been required to file. The only remaining issue is intent ...willfullness. Cases cited in the statutes would give the researcher an idea of how the courts had ruled on the issue of willfulness, but you can also read legal definitions of the word in the book *Words and Phrases* and it will also give you federal cases which have defined the word. The definitions in the cases vary widely from a pro-conviction definition like, knowingly violating the law to a more defense oriented one like evil motive. Your goal is to present the best definition to the jurors and put on evidence to show that your client fits that definition.

This example proves the circular theory of research even though the project is just begun. Most likely, you will find some of the same case citations in the statutes under willful failure to file and in the definition of "willfulness" in *Words and Phrases*.

If you are in a municipal or justice of the peace court on a traffic case, the same process would be used. The traffic citation most likely will refer you to a city or state statute that covers the violation you're charged with. Before a lawyer or citizen can start to defend himself on a charge, he must know specifically what he's charged with and what the prosecutor must prove. And again, a set of annotated city or state statutes will refer you to cases that have already been decided on the charges you're researching.

Of course, the particular question that needs to be answered will determine where you start your research. Taking the first example further, suppose that your client already has been found guilty of failure to file his income tax returns. He is unhappy with the verdict, and you want to get him a new trial. You are doing research for an appeal to a higher court. Your broad, general question:

"How can the client obtain a new trial?"

First, you must find legal errors committed by the prosecutor or the court which are so harmful or prejudicial that a new trial must be given. One way, would be to start with the federal court rules. In this instance, federal rules describe how and in what instances a person can seek and obtain a ruling on a motion for a new trial. Particularly in the case of the federal courts, an attorney or pro se handling his own case should not take the first step without first obtaining a copy of the rules for the particular court in which he is operating.

This could easily be compared to trying to locate an office building in a large city without an address or without a city map. You might possibly drive around town for days and accidentally find the place, but if you want a fair chance of locating it you should obtain an address and then get a city map so you'll know where to find that address. In this case, the federal or state statutes could be described as the building's address, and the federal or state rule book would be the city map.

If you research specific questions, you get specific answers if they are available. New cases are published every day because in theory they answer new questions. If you ask general, umbrella questions, you get general, umbrella answers. In order to ask the umbrella questions, only a slight amount of legal experience is necessary.

Frequently, someone with no legal training can ask important, broad general questions. However, you would be surprised how often many intelligent and educated people are unable to come up with this first question, and in fact, start out with an even broader question. Let's get back to the appeal on the failure to file conviction and start our research with the general question: "What can I do?"

First, you should carefully review the indictment or information and all motions made to and ruled on by the court before and during the case. Then you should read the testimony taken during the trial and the statement of facts—then the researcher will have some specific questions.

For example, Question: "Does the record show that the defense attorney was not allowed to properly cross-examine the witnesses on all relevant points?" Answer: "Yes, No, Maybe."

Question: "What specific restrictions did the court place on the defense counsel during cross-examination? Were these limitations legal?" The answers to any of these questions can lead to many different line of questions to research.

One of the most important skills a legal researcher can develop is asking the correct questions. Without the questions, the answers cannot usu-

"Unfortunately, the skill of discerning which specific questions to ask is acquired by relatively few legal assistants and even fewer attorneys."

ally be found. Unfortunately, the skill of discerning which specific questions to ask is acquired by relatively few legal assistants and even fewer attorneys. Legal research is done to answer the case's specific questions. Almost always, while doing legal research and evaluating the information obtained by the research process, additional information will surface which can be utilized in answering these questions and making them more and more specific. New important questions will pop up. Sometimes you find the answer to the original question. At other times, you find the answer to a similar question which may, in turn, give rise to a more specific question whose answer will be more relevant and/or helpful to your specific case.

Most of the available answers to the questions in law are ultimately found in the following sources:

1) *Statutes, which are the laws passed by local governments, state legislatures or Congress;*

2) *Case law, which are the rulings of the appropriate appeal courts and are usually published, indexed and available in law libraries;*

3) *Government regulations and opinions, which do not necessarily have the force of law and are less significant than statutes and cases, however, they can be extremely important when determining how government officials should conduct themselves;*

4) *Opinions by legal experts, which come in many different forms such as books, papers presented at seminars, or law journal articles. These articles have no force of law, but are usually very helpful in developing a history and background of a particular question being researched.*

Utilizing past cases to determine present law is based on the process called "*stare decisis,*" a Latin term meaning "it stands decided." This is the pillar of our legal system in England and the United States. It means that once a court has made a decision involving certain fact situations, that decision will be used in future decisions based on the same or similar fact situations. Ultimately, law is not a science like medicine but an art, like philosophy. Words are not subject to an exacting empirical measurement

> *"Utilizing past cases to determine present law is based on the process called "stare decisis," a Latin term meaning "it stands decided." This is the pillar of our legal system in England and the United States."*

to the extent that temperature may be measured by a thermometer. The 11 circuit courts spread out over the United States having power over the hundreds of Federal trial courts often interpret the same words and statutes differently. The Great Izen's victory in the Dahlstrom case was on an interpretation of the first ammendment in the 9th circuit (California) by a 2 to 1 victory decision. It changed the tax laws of the United States. My appellate loss in U.S. v. Udey in the 8th circuit in Omaha, Nebraska was a 2 to 1 loss with Chief Justice Lay voting for reversal on rehearsing en banc,[9] before a nine-judge panel. Again one person's opinion was the deciding factor between defeat and victory. We lost a 5 to 4 decision. The lottery system which determines the judge who presides over a trial on the panel which hears an appeal leaves a great deal to chance. The identity, personality and preconceived opinions of these judges significantly influences the final outcome.

The early English system had courts of law which rendered decisions based on the common law—the law that was commonly followed through custom usage and word of mouth as opposed to law created by written statutes. Common law is the ancestor of case law. Originally, cases were not written down. The practice of writing them down and utilizing them for future instruction gave birth to the concept of stare decisis.

For example, "libel" is the use of printed words to damage someone's reputation. The words must be untrue, must be circulated in written form to others, and must injure the person's reputation being spoken about. If you are sued for libel, can you determine if the person suing you has suffered economically? Yes, you can. Therefore, can you demand to review the past income tax records and bank statements from the person claiming he has been harmed to determine if he lost money?

You will be looking for an appellate court ruling that says a defendant in a libel case has the right to obtain these tax returns to prepare his defense. However, you may find a case that says they do not have the right to obtain these tax returns. In that situation, you want to distinguish that case from your own by showing the differences between that case and yours.

B. FINDING CASES IN THE APPELLATE REPORTER SYSTEMS

There are basically three types of appellate courts: state, federal, and administrative. State and federal appellate systems will be discussed in this chapter. Administrative courts are briefly described at Chapter VI C and are described further in the chapter on Social Security.

An appeal is the process by which a decision in a trial court is challenged in a higher court. The higher court then makes a ruling, discussing the case and the reasons for its rulings. After the appeals court rules on the case, it determines whether or not the case adds significantly to the development of the body of the law in the particular areas discussed. If the court decides an important new point of law has been made, it may order the case to be published. All U.S. Supreme Court decisions are published and most state supreme court's opinions are published. If a case is published, it will be printed in law books that will be circulated to law libraries all over the United States, and it will become stare decisis.

Think of a stack of books piled on top of each other from the floor to the ceiling. The first book has cases from 1880. The book on the top of the stack has cases from 1990. If you've found a case in some book in the stack which seems to say "You win!", your task is now to check all the way up to the top: to see if there are higher court cases since then that support or attack your position. The 1990 book may not be on the stack yet, so you have to find it.

If you can find a more current higher court case supporting your position, you're probably okay. If not, you peel books off going back for the last time the highest court ruled. Unless you are doing historical research you may not be interested or have the time to go to the floor looking for 1880 cases. In real life, the books aren't horizontal, they are vertical on a library shelf. A computer tracing specific words can do this search very quickly. You want to find the highest, most recent appellate decision upholding your position.

1. THE STATE APPELLATE REPORTER SYSTEM

A. BACKGROUND INFORMATION

In Texas, there are two appellate jurisdictions—one for criminal and one for civil and they function in the following manner:

All criminal and civil cases start out in the appropriate trial court. A judge or jury makes a finding of facts. The judge applies the law to those finding of facts, and a written decision is issued, called an order. In a civil lawsuit, the person who files the suit is the plaintiff, and the person who is being sued is the defendant. The style of the case would be plaintiff versus defendant, i.e., Sam Smith vs. Bill Brown. In this illustration, Smith is suing Brown, and either party may appeal from a trial court decision. In a criminal case, the style would be Texas versus the defendant, i.e., Texas vs. John Jones. In criminal cases the defendant may appeal all guilty verdicts, but the government cannot appeal a final not guilty verdict.

There are three levels of trial courts in Texas: the justice of the peace (J.P.) courts, county courts and then to district courts. Cases are appealed to the appellate court with proper jurisdiction over that specific trial court which heard the case. J.P. court decisions are appealable to the county court, where a new trial is granted. County court and district court decisions may be appealed in one of the 14 courts of appeals.

Texas is divided into 14 court of appeal districts, called the First Supreme Judicial District Court of Appeals, Second Supreme Judicial District Court of Appeals and so on up to the Fourteenth.

The court of appeals makes the decision whether or not it wants to reverse or sustain the order of the trial court by answering the questions raised by the person making the appeal. The appellant urges the appeal court to reverse or modify the order because of certain errors made by the trial court. The appellee wants the appeals court to sustain the opinion of the trial court.

If the opinion is printed, it becomes stare decisis. In Texas, the published opinions of the state courts are printed in a set of volumes called *Southwest Second*. This reporter includes all the cases published in southwestern states, including Arkansas, Oklahoma, Texas. These volumes are published by West Publishing Company, the largest publishing company for case law in the United States. The original set of *Southwest Reporters* are numbered Volumes 1 to 300 and are abbreviated as S.W. At that time, West Publishing Company considered the system was becoming too cumbersome, and started with Volume I of *Southwest Second*, referred to as S.W.2d. The cases are published in chronological order. The trick is to find the cases that you want.

Once you have the name of the case, it is very simple to find it. There are index systems (Tables of Cases) which list the names of cases and direct you to the various case reporters in which the case can be found. The name of the case is generally similar to the following: Texas vs. Jones, if it's a criminal case, or Doe vs. Smith, if it's a civil case. In any event, the specific location of that case is called a citation. A citation includes the volume number, the name of the set of books and the page number where the case begins.

There frequently are several citations to the same case because a particular case might be published by several law book companies. West Publishing Company publishes sets of "reporters" called the Pacific Reporter, Atlantic Reporter, Northeast, Southeast, and others which are geographically titled. There are other reporters that are limited to specific topics such as bankruptcy cases or tax cases.

There are literally hundreds of law book publishing companies. Some of the major publishers are: West Publishing Company, Bancroft Whitney, Matthew Bender, Butterworth, Shepards, and Kluer Law Book Publishers. Reporters simply report the cases word for word as they are given by the respective court. However, each reporter also has its own style breaking down the case into various questions and answers and summaries.

In certain specific areas of law, some of the smaller companies produce books to be easier to read. Kluer and Butterworth are both very easy to understand. Knowles Law Book Publishing Co. has produced some excellent basic books. Clark Boardman Publishing Company produces some well researched, easy to follow books.

Of course, the authors of the books are a very important factor. Each publishing company hires or contracts with authors to write the books.

Since the law is an ever-changing field, book supplements and updates are needed annually. I prefer working with hardbound books which have newsprint pocket parts added into a slot on the back cover, as yearly supplements, as opposed to the loose-page, hole-punched concept, where the front cover lifts off, and certain pages are substituted for obsolete ones each year.

Some of the most basic books published come from the various state bar for the continuing education and professional development of licensed lawyers. Under some circumstances, these books can be purchased by legal assistants and non-lawyers.

B. CITATIONS

Let's assume that the case of Sally Doe vs. Sam Smith—which generally will be abbreviated as Doe vs. Smith—was sent to the West Publishing Company while Volume 90 in Southwestern Second was being compiled. The case would be included, in chronological order. The volume's pages are numbered one through approximately 1000. Suppose the first page of the case was printed on page 392 because the last reported case had ended on page 391. The citation would read Doe vs. Smith 90 S.W. 2d. 392.

To find the case you know that you would go to the Southwestern Sec-

Example I

ond series, pull volume 90, and turn to page 392. On page 392, you'll find the beginning of that case. Sometimes specific quotations are taken from the cases and then you are referenced to a specific page that contains the quotation rather than the beginning: such as, a reference to a comment on 90 S.W.2d 395. At the top of page 395, you'll find in small print saying: "Cite as 90 S.W. 2d 392." If you turn to page 392, you will find the beginning of the case. Please refer to Example I.

Texas is unique—in that the state has a dual court system, with civil cases going one appeal route and criminal cases taking a different route. Most states have only one highest appellate court which is usually that state's supreme court. In most state appeal systems and in the federal system, the supreme court rules on both criminal and civil cases. When an appeal is taken to one of the supreme courts, it is asking the court to review a lower appellate court's decision. Most of the time the supreme court will decline to review it. In these cases, when you are doing research, a citation will note in the case reporters: "Writ Refused." It is important for researchers to note that a certain appellate court decision was appealed to the higher court and not reviewed. If the U.S. Supreme Court does not review a particular case, the final decision on the case is made in the lower court.

When an appeals court reviews a case, it will either reverse, sustain or remand the case back down to the trial court, with specific instructions for correcting mistakes made previously. In most cases, the state supreme court is the end of the appeal process. However, all state courts are bound by the supreme law of the land, the U.S. Constitution, and if a state court ruling violates the Constitution, the decision may be appealed to the U.S. Supreme Court

In certain criminal matters—such as habeas corpus petitions—state cases may be removed into federal court for additional review. In a civil case, where a party seeks the protection of the federal bankruptcy court, that case can be removed to federal court for further consideration. There are several other circumstances under which cases can be moved into federal court, but the federal courts prefer to stay out of the state jurisdictions.

2. THE FEDERAL APPELLATE REPORTER SYSTEM

The federal appellate system is similar in many respects to the state system. Federal district court is the only trial level court where live testimony is put on. Appellate decisions are made by reviewing trial court orders that are challenged. Written appeal briefs refer to errors made by the trial court, then prove those errors were made with evidence from the transcript and pleadings filed with the lower court. The appellate briefs cite relevant law, and argue the issues. Appellate courts may allow attorneys to make oral arguments to assist the court in its decision.

Appellate procedures are fairly uniform throughout the nation, but each circuit and each court has its own peculiar rules. The United States is divided up into 12 regional circuits and one national circuit for specific types of cases. The 12 regional circuits are called the U.S. Court of Appeals for the First Circuit, the U.S. Court of Appeals for the Second Circuit, through the U.S. Court of Appeals for the Eleventh Circuit plus the U.S. Court of Appeals for the District of Columbia. Please refer to Example II, a map showing the states covered by each federal circuit. Each circuit has jurisdiction over the federal trial courts in the states included with that circuit.

Every state has at least one United States District Court, a federal trial court. Larger states are divided up into districts geographically, such as

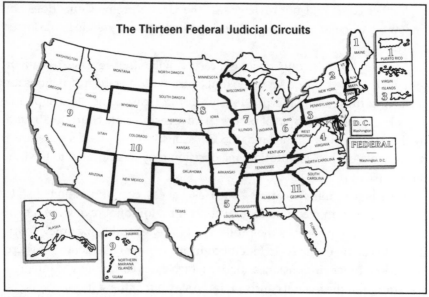

The Thirteen Federal Judicial Circuits

Example 11

the northern, southern, eastern and western districts. Each district will have at least one and possibly several different trial courts. A district may be further broken down into divisions. Federal trial court decisions are sometimes published, and would be found in a set of volumes known as Federal Supplement, abbreviated FSupp.

The thirteenth federal appellate court—which is equal to the other 12 circuits—is the U.S. Court of Appeals for the District of Columbia in Washington, D.C. This court has jurisdiction over the national federal courts. These are courts set up to handle specific issues, such as the U.S. Tax Court, the U.S. Court of International Trade, the U.S. Court of Claims, and the U.S. Court of Military Appeals. These courts have jurisdiction over specific types of cases throughout the entire country.

All circuit appeal courts—and all trial courts under them—are expected to give consideration to the rulings of other circuit courts. Conflicts between circuits are either ignored or resolved in the Supreme Court,

"The only court of appeals over all the federal circuits is the U.S. Supreme Court. Approximately 20,000 cases are appealed to the U.S. Supreme Court each year, but the court only agrees to hear about one percent of those cases, only 200."

which has constitutional jurisdiction over all the courts.

The most important cases are the ones reported in the circuit courts and the supreme court. An appeal can be made from any of the federal district courts to the circuit court covering that district. Texas, for example, is part of the U.S. Court of Appeals for the Fifth Circuit which includes Texas, Louisiana, Mississippi and The Canal Zone. Cases appealed from any of the federal district courts in any of these states must go to the Fifth Circuit court, which normally sits in New Orleans, but can sit anywhere in the circuit the judges choose.

Significant federal appellate decisions are published in volumes known as Federal Reporter and Federal Reporter Second, which are abbreviated F and F2d respectively, and have the same chronological relationship as S.W. and S.W.2 mentioned earlier. For example, the Eighth Circuit's decision on United States vs. Udey case, in which I was one of the three attorneys representing the appellants, was rendered when the 748th volume of Federal Reporter Second was in preparation. (Please refer to Example I, Finding a Citation.) The next available page was 1231. Therefore, the citation of U.S. vs. Udey is 748 F.2d 1231.[1] A few pages of this case are included in the Addendum.

Supreme Court decisions are published in the Supreme Court Reporter, abbreviated Sup. Ct. or S.Ct., and also in the U.S. Reporter and several others. The Supreme Court Reporter and U.S. Reporter cross-index each other.

Decisions involving interpretations of federal court rules are published in a set of volumes called Federal Rules Decisions, and such citations are abbreviated FRD. Obviously the interpretation of court rules can also end up in other volumes if the case reaches the Supreme Court.

The federal appeal courts make decisions in much the same way as the state appeals courts do, based on the questions which are presented to them by the party appealing the case. If the opinion is published, it will be included in the current volume of published federal cases; usually, Federal Second (F2d).

The only court of appeals over all the federal circuits is the U.S. Supreme Court. Approximately 20,000 cases are appealed to the U.S. Supreme Court each year, but the court only agrees to hear about one percent of those cases, only 200.

All U.S. Supreme Court decisions are published, but they still only make up a very small proportion of the total number of published cases because so few are heard compared to the number of federal appeal court decisions. For most practical purposes, the federal appeal courts are the courts of the last jurisdiction. Nevertheless, the opinions of the Supreme Court of the United States are binding on all circuits. Decisions reached by one circuit might influence another circuit, but one circuit is not bound to follow another's rulings.

C. ENCYCLOPEDIAS—GETTING INTO THE QUESTION

There are numerous sets of legal encyclopedias. Two sets of national, legal encyclopedias are American Jurisprudence and Corpus Juris Secundum, abbreviated C.J.S. which is the second set of "Corpus Juris," whose title is the Latin term meaning "body of the law."

Both of them work on the same principle. You start with either a fact situation or a legal question and try to find that word or phrase in the index. You might start with tax offense, cross-examination, contracts, etc. Of course, all of these terms are generally too broad, and you want to get the specific words involved in your case. However, reading the broad general descriptions helps to give you a feel for the subject just as in other encyclopedias.

The words lead you to specific page citations in the volume itself. Once you find the relevant section, review the caption summary of the law as it exists in the 50 states and under federal jurisdiction. Footnotes at the bottom of the page tell how each of the states has interpreted various aspects of the law. At that point you will be directed to citations for specific cases defining that principle of law. Pull the cases from the appropriate reporter, and your research is underway.

American Jurisprudence, abbreviated Am.Jur., is easier to read because it offers a more general overview of certain questions; but on the other hand C.J.S. cites more actual cases and is more detailed than Am.Jur. When I had to choose between the two systems, I chose C.J.S for two reasons: 1) Since it is published by West Publishing, it ties into the West system better than Am.Jur., and more important, 2) When I was trying to decide between the two, I found a set that had been donated to the University of Houston Law School that I could practically steal for $200 cash. I couldn't turn it down. It was two years old. To update it cost me $500.

However, the cost of the sets aren't the only consideration. These companies make lots of money by selling books, but the real profit is on the updates. At West alone, I spend nearly $1,000 each year just for the pocket parts and replacement volumes. Once you bite on their book hook, you pay every year or your set becomes outdated.

In the back of each volume of most legal encyclopedias is an annual insert which updates each volume. There you will find the latest cases on that particular issue.

Other research volumes like Matthew Bender come in three-ring binder type books that allow changes to be inserted inside the actual volume by substituting new pages for the old. Both of the two major competing encyclopedias C.J.S. and Am.Jur 2d use the pocket part method. Occasionally an entire new volume is printed and substituted for an old one.

D. DIGESTS

There are also books called digests that contain short summaries of cases listed under certain categories. Detailed breakdowns are not provided, but usually a number of case citations are given in the case indexes. You find specific words in the word indexes; the words lead you to cases that deal with those topics. Once you find the category that you are looking for, again you have found cases. These cases are the beginning of your research. Finding the first case, which is relevant to your particular fact situation is extremely helpful and an important step because this case will lead you to other cases.

E. TREATISES / LAW BOOKS, ARTICLES, LAW JOURNALS, HORN BOOKS

For the researcher who will take the time to really get involved in an issue, there are numerous books written on specific aspects of the law. There are also numerous articles, usually in law journals, that offer a good history and assessment of the current law on specific subjects. Most law schools and bar associations publish their own law journals that each month contain many articles written by legal scholars, judges, and outstanding students. Law libraries usually receive the monthly journals, and at year end a compiled set of the journals that are indexed for reference. If the article is particularly noteworthy, it might be cited in an annotated statute or rule book.

These scholarly articles are usually filled with citations and offer the reader both a complete history of that area of the law and an assessment of how the courts are currently ruling. Generally the author is either an authority in that area, a student in law school studying that area, or a judge. This is often an excellent place to begin research.

Law books called "Hornbooks" deal with specific areas of the law. They are also helpful in getting into an area of the law. A hornbook is a book prepared by a legal scholar generally for use by law school students. However, these books are very general in scope and not geared specifically toward the practice of law in the real world. While they often quote "real" cases, they nevertheless are a very poor second cousin to the law books published by practicing attorneys who specialize in the field they are writing about. Hornbooks are probably the single best way to learn a new area of law.

There are hundreds of publishing companies in this country that print specialty manuals on everything from aircraft to copyrights, and from delinquency and divorce to taxes and international trade. Every lawyer in the country is on a mailing list for these books. They are generally expensive—averaging $50 to $100 or more a book. Many of these books are not found in many law libraries.

Most state bar associations will often not sell to non- lawyers because of Union Rules, but the multitude of free enterprise companies will sell to anyone with the money. All of the major law book publishing companies who sell sets of books use commissioned sales people who generally are not lawyers. While they obviously view lawyers as their most likely prospective customers, they will also gladly jump on non-lawyer clients at the mere mention of a possible commission sale.

F. STATUTES

Your case may involve a particular law created by the legislature. For example: willfully failing to file your income tax return by April 15th is a violation of 26 USC 7203. There are numerous services that publish state and federal statutes, such as Vernons Annotated Texas Statutes or United States Codes Annotated.

Every law school has local and federal case reporters, U.S. statutes, and state statutes. Depending on its size and sophistication, it may or may not have statutes and case law of other states and some of the more specialized case reporters. Some public libraries, and most courthouses have at least a small law library which will include the state and federal statutes and a few case reporters. Public law libraries funded by county money are usually completely unrestricted as to who may use them. Some schools restrict access to students or alumnae only.

Some courthouse law libraries restrict access to lawyers only, but the rule is not generally enforced and may be illegal since public funds keep these places open. Some of the librarians are worth their weight in gold. Even the best researcher in the world needs to be pointed in the direction where the books he needs are shelved in a particular law library.

Most of the rest of us also ask for and obtain valid research assistance from the librarians. Of course, a few librarians are bureaucratic and rude. They seem to think their function is to keep the books dusted rather than share the information. Fortunately you will find most law librarians to be courteous and helpful—especially to lawyers, so if you are not a lawyer, wear a suit to the library and you'll probably be treated like one. Never claim to be one if you are not. The suit will proclaim you a professional. You may, in most states, be a paralegal just by saying you are. Generally there is no license. Paralegals get to go many places where lawyers go. I recommend wearing a suit and tie in order to obtain maximum assistance.

G. ANNOTATIONS

Many of these case reference books and statute books are "annotated." A volume of annotated statutes means that the complete text of each statute is followed by a section of notes describing the legislative history of the statute; opinions from experts; and citations of cases which construed that particular statute. It is an excellent source of answers if there is a statute covering the area of law you are researching. The annotated statute volumes will refer you straight to specific cases.

H. CASE TO CASE REFERRALS

Once you have gotten inside some relevant cases, it is important to find the most current cases that exist on that topic. You need to determine whether or not a particular case you're relying on has ever been overruled, and you need to find out when that case has been quoted in similar cases. You need to find the cases which might hurt you by going against your desired position—so you won't be surprised later—and you may find other cases that are more specific and more helpful to you.

Each case leads to other cases in several different ways. First, examine the published case itself. There will be head notes in the case talking about specific types of law. You can refer again to the portion of the U.S. vs.

Udey case in the Addendum for an example of what the headnotes are like. You can check under those head notes in various digests or encyclopedias published by the same publisher to find other cases which are relevant.

The key numbers grace the opening of each case, and each question of law addressed is broken down and briefly discussed by number before you get into the case itself. West volumes discuss cases by these key numbers in all their publications attempting to group areas of the law together as an aid rather than indexing.

It is dangerous to avoid indexing and rely totally on the key number system. The more varied your approach the more valuable your final product. What if you are trying to find cases never related to your subject before? The safest method, however, is to pull all of those other cases with the same key number. After pulling those cases, you will determine a great deal about the history of your case law. You analyze those cases to determine whether or not they are relevant, and then those which you feel are relevant should also be shepardized. Each time you shepardize, you will find fewer and fewer cases, because the closer you get to the current year, the less often it has the possibility of being published.

Any published case will be based on prior existing cases and opinions and will discuss these cases and other opinions. If they appear to be particularly relevant, pull those cases. Of course, many areas of law can be discussed in one case. Many cases cited in a case you have found may not pertain to your specific question and are not important to you. For example: You are looking for a case because you were bitten by your neighbor's dog, and you suffered from a non-infected, non-diseased mouth impression in your leg. You did not seek medical attention. You find a case in which a rabid police dog chewed a suspect in half and the hospital staff sewed him up improperly and ignored their duty to test for rabies. Because this case has something to do with dog bites, you'll probably read it. You may also photocopy the whole case for future reference, but other potential issues—medical malpractice, police brutality, unnecessary force, etc. which appear in the published case have nothing to do with your case.

Nevertheless, a broad, general reading of the entire case is essential to make certain that it stands for the proposition that was indicated in the encyclopedia or other journal that sent you to the published case in the first place. Mistakes are not infrequent in these small capsule summaries which purport to describe cases.

I. SHEPARDIZING

Shepard's Publishing Company has published a set of volumes which is so widely used that the process of utilizing them to find all references to the case is called "sheparizing." Other publishing companies allow you to accomplish this same function, but Shepard's is the most frequently used and will be discussed here. Shepards Citations are a set of books which list every single citation of a particular case which is quoted in another published case. This leads you to more recent cases, since a case can't be quoted before it is published. It also will let you know if the case has ever been reversed, or if a decision is still pending on it. It will also lead you to any of the other cases on the same point which have cited the case you're researching. If the case you're looking up has never been quoted, you might suspect that the point of law you are researching or the case you have found is not very significant.

If the case is not in your jurisdiction i.e., a Ninth Circuit case when you live in the Fifth Circuit, the decision is only useful in an advisory capacity as opposed to being mandatory. A mandatory opinion is one that has direct jurisdiction over your case and must legally be followed.

Shephard's Citations contains far more numbers than words, since it only lists cases by their citations, not their styles. The Addendum includes a sample page of Shepard's Citations with the reference to the U.S. vs. Udey case circled.[2]

There are sets of Shephard's that are companions to accompany Federal Reporters and state or regional reporters. They may cover anywhere from a one week to a 10-year period, depending on what editions your law library has. For example, if you want to see if the particular case with the citation 748 F2 1231 was ever referred to, you would get the volume of Shepard's that would include Federal Reporter's Second Volume 748— possibly a volume labeled Shepard's Federal Citations, Federal Reporter Second, Volumes 500 to 800. You would get to the page where 748 F2 is listed. Underneath, you would look for the listing of page 1231. If the case was ever cited, you would then find other citations of cases and sometimes a note as to whether the case was affirmed or reversed. Care must be

"Shepards Publishing Company has published a set of volumes which is so widely used that the process of utilizing them to find all references to the case is called 'sheparizing.'"

taken in looking up the numbers and copying down the correct numbers since no styles are used. There is a computerized version of Shephard's Citations which saves human labor, but it is quite costly. By its very nature, Shepardizing is a legal research task eminently suited to automation.

The Shepard's citations also tell which areas of the law reviewed in a case are discussed. This helps limit your work. Why pull the case if it discusses points of law in your case which are not relevant to your questions—such as medical malpractice and police brutality in the dog bite case which clearly involved no doctor or police? A complete and thorough research job will pull all of these cases even though they are not likely to be relevant.

J. LEGAL RESEARCH IN THE FUTURE: THE END OF THE CURRENT LEGAL SYSTEM: MY PREDICTIONS AND REASONS—MARCH 1989

In this regard I am one of the many oracles who time alone will prove right or wrong; so far my educated guesses have been proven reliable.

In 1977, Minns, Izen, Bradt & Associates paid $17,000 for a program and some disks for a C.P.T. word processor. On the dissolution of Minns, Izen, Bradt in 1980, I traded to Izen and Bradt my one-third interest in the $12,000 equity for 100 percent interest in a paid-off IBM typewriter that cost $1,200 new. In 1982 the 1977 C.P.T. was no longer in use at all! I gave the IBM to my mother who still uses it.

In 1977 we were the toast of Harris County. Our computer image helped us grow fast. No one was making paper products as pretty as ours. Perfect margins were a legal publishing miracle. At about $300 a month for the C.P.T., one secretary could do the work of three. Anyone behind on the technology—and that was 95 percent of the profession—was simply outclassed.

In late 1986 I purchased a used, 10-megabyte hard disk imitation IBM from a bootleg Korean company for $850. Rather than a mere word processor, which was just a fancy typewriter, this machine is a full functioning computer and can out-perform the first Minns-Izen-Bradt machine like the Concorde out performs the Wright Brothers' first set of wings. It's faster, quieter, smaller, prettier and holds a thousand times the information of the now extinct dinosaur word processor. Also, the machine can talk to other machines by phone all over the world and transfer information instantaneously.

For about $200 a month it can access all of the printed cases in most law libraries. To keep 10 percent of these cases in bound volumes it costs about $300 a month. Right now the bound volumes are nearly obsolete. I put my book money into other things, statutes, digests and especially specific books and treatises.

The $200 per month doesn't make sense yet, because we can still photocopy cases in the law library downtown cheaper and it's expensive to put a case on the screen and then print it.

However, if we need a reference in a hurry, we call a research service such as United Law Search in Tulsa Oklahoma,[3] which can access the desired information on its computers and send it to me by phone or through the mail; that service, through its reasonable billing, saves me money. They also shepardize instantly on their computers. Eventually the main companies will force the major suppliers to be more accessible to small law offices by lowering prices, or they will lose their market share.

Science already will allow us to put every single reported case in the United States on one real thick hard disk. It just hasn't been done yet. Why? None of the law book companies want these disks available to be instantly copied for less than $100—remember that the book companies are selling the same cases in book form for $50,000 to $100,000.

Why couldn't a computer hacker copy only the public record part—no head notes or intellectual property owned by any of the various book companies—and sell the program for $500 each? First it's a lot of work. Second the companies might try to sue him...if they could catch him.

Now that it is possible to enter material into computers with ease comparable to photocopying, I predict that soon thousand of pages will be produced this way. The public cases are available to the public, therefore, sooner or later law libraries will be available on disks. As the prices drop new markets will be sought in non-lawyer circles.

As the speed for finding and indexing information on disks increases, computer hackers will have at their fingertips information superior to that of any 1988 lawyer.

The law will be categorized and re-categorized with improved indexing, and ultimately available to everyone. Of course we already have talking computers, they are just too expensive and too primitive. However, with improving technology they will become easily available, inexpensive

"The aura of mystique surrounding lawyers is based primarily on their monopoly over legal information."

and fast.

Why go to a lawyer for your will if you can ask a computer to form one based on your questions and based on the most recent cases giving you logical likely outcomes and suggestions? You won't. Legal labor unions will fight against this just like railroad workers' unions kept coal shovelers on diesel powered trains for years, but sooner or later the inevitable technological tide will turn and wash away most of what we call "lawyers" today.

Oral advocacy, and fingerprint-based machines for notarization with standardized forms and standardized easily understood law will be the wave of the future. It won't be easy, the wave will have to erode some powerful legal rocks, but the wave will be persistent and finally succeed.

In 20 years the current concept of what attorneys do will no longer exist at all! However, a major revolution in most law offices will occur again over the next 10 years.

It has already occurred in the last 10 years! It was just slower. The next decade will be faster and more dramatic. For $500, I have a high-speed, high resolution "Fax" machine that can send messages instantenously (8 seconds a page) to clients in Switzerland for a couple of dollars. Meanwhile 3/4 of the small firms in Texas spend $20 or more to send copies by messenger across town in an hour. In 1988 less than 5% of small businesses use these type of facilities. In 1990 over half will. In the mid 1990s, they will be required standard home fixtures. New rules will be needed for faxing letters of credit, contracts and checks. Today no one is impressed by wordprocessing.

Virtually all competent business offices today are computerized for typing and billing. In 10 years, every single function will require the computer. The lawyers who do not adapt—and at least one-third of them will not —will be reduced to bankruptcy or to rendering political favors or to eking out a minimum wage living.

In the last 10 years, free market competition has been started among lawyers with advertising. In the next 10 years... legal assistants, Underground Lawyers, and computers will enter the competition.

For the past 50 years, large, centrally located law firms dominated the industry. In the next 10 years medium-sized firms, small networking firms sharing information by computer, and mega-large impersonal corporate firms with computer access will totally dominate the market. The 50 to 100 year old prestige firms will either change, revert primarily to bestowing political favors, or go belly up.

Today, rather than bite the dust many of these firms are already changing by merging with more lean business-oriented firms or spreading out with acquisitions and opening smaller satellite offices. Why have an entire staff in an expensive downtown office when a branch office can fax information faster than a secretary can carry it across the floor from one room to another?

The sharing of laws across state lines and research into many different areas will begin a supermarket access to all law and gradually make the laws of each state more homogenous.

There are still millions of New York residents who don't know that in Texas there is no state income tax, and that in Alaska, during the oil boom, the government actually paid its citizens money. In the past, shopping for state laws was the privilege only of the big corporation. In the future, every interested person will be able to know the law everywhere.

Europe is gradually becoming one legal community in the common market. In the next decade or two most of Europe will have one set of laws. All European states will become more homogenized.

The "United" States will become homogenized—most states will adopt or create similar rules to the federal court—and these two great legal "states" will begin to share legal information and compete. Legal conditions will become priorities in business decisions. This competition and sharing will lead to a homogenization of international laws and the computer hacker in California will try to convince the judge's computer to consider a legal concept created in Italy as a modern hybrid of an ancient Roman law discovered by a French archaeologist.

The international legal community will begin to compete with American lawyers. Japan will join in because it will not want to forsake its current path to world superiority in banking. Hong Kong and Taiwan will merge with western powers to consolidate their laws, unless they merge totally with Mainland China which is highly likely. Law itself will become an international product to a greater extent than it is today. Hong Kong's merger with Mainland China would lead Mainland China into capitalism. The spreading of legal information on small inexpensive portable computers can not be stopped.

The Soviet Union will be in jeopardy of facing revolutions as the flow of information spreads. The result could be an international community or a

"Every aspect of the law can be reduced to questions and answers."

last ditch war.

The skills used today to do non-trial work—which is 99 percent of the work done by lawyers today—will be antiquated and studied by historians not practicing lawyers. The law will be more readily available to everyone. Pleadings and petitions will be filed instantaneously by computer. They will no longer be mailed.

The aura of mystique surrounding lawyers is based primarily on their monopoly over legal information. This will end. Even the trial advocate as we know him today will vanish. All things being equal information-wise, why is a lawyer more competent to handle a trial than a speech major, drama coach, director, or even a mere unlicensed politician—he isn't!

The automation of legal information will totally change the law field in 20 years. However, the battle for control will be hard fought. Actual utilization will not keep up with technology available until the unions are busted.

The busting of the unions will speed up when a booming new area of litigations arises—law suits against lawyers for criminal and civil misconduct. Three of the biggest areas will be against divorce lawyers, probate lawyers and insurance lawyers. When underground lawyers begin accepting the cases of these angry people, the flood gates will burst open and the unions will begin to make major concessions.

"The automation of legal information will totally change the law field in 20 years."

CHAPTER XIV

THE INTERNAL REVENUE SERVICE:

OUR AMERICAN GESTAPO

"...they can levy against a middle-class citizen or individual who might not even owe any taxes, take their property, and never return it because most people don't have the knowledge, ability, or endurance to do anything about it."

A. THE IRS SPECIAL AGENT

As a civic duty, I allowed my bride to drag me off to a cocktail party a couple of years ago. Not being much of a party person it was a major sacrifice, but I vowed to make the most of it and endeavored to play one of my favorite games: "People Watching." The kids love it, and it's excellent training for trial work. You look at people, try to figure out what they are like, and then find out if you're right.

One curious person was in a corner all by himself, looking shy, a little nervous—and in his cheap black suit, with his dull striped tie pulled right up to his neck—even a little sinister. Now I had a Coke with something in it and a mystery. Was he a criminal? Was he an undertaker? Surely he wasn't a salesman of any type. The party was semi-formal (not semi- as in suits instead of tuxes, but semi- as in jeans not okay but slacks will cut it). The suit was his choice so I surmised he didn't have a nice suit but wanted to wear the one he had on to show professionalism of some type.

I found myself intrigued and wishing the kids were there. This could turn out to be a Twilight Zone-type intelligence builder for the kids. As a child, I learned a lot about life with my father and grandfather playing "people watching." Why had he been invited? Well, that didn't help. I didn't even know why I had been invited. Someone knew someone who thought my name would be good to add to the list, and my wife felt it would be good to be there.

Was he a kindred soul? A rebel of sorts? I didn't think so—rebels don't usually wear vampire black suits. A CPA: hungry, yet not starving? Closer. The look fit, but CPAs are out there hustling business unless they are on a salary or don't need it.

This character was taking up my time when there were other people to watch. I just couldn't pin him down. I silently gave in and approached him. I'd solve the riddle directly and move on.

"Hi. My name is..."

He shook hands gratefully and then after exposing me to a fast smile, his expression turned into a near sneer, and he rocked up on his toes back and forth swaying as if to tell me he was looking down at me.
"What do you do for a living?" he asked.
"Why?" I asked, doing what my wife calls being anti-social.

"I'd like to know," he pressed, now actually leering at me, head pointed in my direction.
"I sue people," I answered.

"Oh, I see," he commented as though he were solving an ancient mystery. You make a living suing people. Lots of auto accidents?"
Cutting him off, I asked what he did for a living.

"You first, my friend." he demanded with a tone of authority.
"No sir," I firmly responded. "Tell me first or I'll leave you alone again, and you can continue your conversation with the wall."

He told me. He didn't want to. It was obviously the reason why he had been abandoned in the first place. I knew whoever invited me to the party would not see me on her guest list again.
He was an IRS agent!
An IRS agent can empty a party room faster than a great white shark can empty a swimming pool.
From those wonderful folks who brought you the voluntary income tax system and made certain it wasn't voluntary, comes—courtesy of the Freedom of Information Act—the unauthorized, confidential "Handbook for Special Agents."
We will start this chapter by examining this "treasure."
The IRS operates through a series of agents. An extremely informative publication which sheds considerable light on their pernicious policies

"An IRS agent can empty a party room faster than a great white shark can empty a swimming pool."

and procedures is the Handbook for Special Agents. Through the Freedom of Information Act, it is available to the citizens who paid for it to be printed.

The field soldier and the ground agitator of the IRS is the collection agent. Like a free enterprise collection agent, he wants to collect your money to gain points on his way up the collection ladder, and doesn't particularly care what he has to say or do to collect the money. Unlike the private collector, who is usually a liar and a bluff with very little authority and lots of potential liability, this collection agent has incredible power, limited liability, and only one fear—looking weak, foolish or ignorant. Most IRS agents were picked on in grade school or beaten by their parents and are in their position because an individual without a lot of leadership potential can swiftly rise through the ranks to incredible, intimidating power. No Peeping Tom ever got to enjoy the personal, private-life history of all his acquaintances as the IRS collection agent can avail himself of, with a mere touch of a computer button.

IRS agents have powers that no other government agents have. They can levy on your wages and your property without a court order. For all practical purposes, they can levy against a middle-class citizen or individual who might not even owe any taxes, take their property, and never return it because most people don't have the knowledge, ability or endurance to do anything about it.

IRS agents can garnish wages—even in states like Texas and California where it's not legal—without an evidenciary hearing. They can file unsworn liens on real property and usually no one stands up to them.

Although the U.S. Constitution guarantees you the right to a jury trial in matters concerning more than $20, our courts do not enforce this constitutional right when the IRS is one of the litigants. The indigent taxpayer who does not have any money to pay the disputed tax and then file a lawsuit against the government and seek the ruling of a jury, can only go to a U.S. Tax Court judge who is often—you guessed it—a retired IRS agent. The cards are stacked against the taxpayer from the beginning.

The few congressional enemies of the IRS don't last long. Congressman Ron Paul, a capitalist gynecologist with great devotion to the Constitution, couldn't do anything significant in the House to thwart the

---

"IRS agents have powers that no other government agents have. They can levy on your wages and your property without a court order."

IRS, so he ran for the Senate without sufficient capital for a campaign and lost in the primary. He remains, however, a significant political figure, particularly since his 1988 Libertarian party presidential candidacy.

Former Idaho Congressman George Hansen, who publicly exposed many of their IRS' atrocities, was indicted and convicted of irregularities in his filing of financial disclosure statements when he was only doing what was a common practice among politicians. Both he and 1984 Democratic Party candidate for vice-president, Geraldine Ferraro were questioned on a similar alleged offense: Only Hansen was charged and convicted. Mrs. Ferraro was in no danger since she did not criticize the IRS. (At least federally. Locally her family has obviously undergone selective targeting by political opportunists. Right or wrong the local war against her never started until it had political value.) Hansen was allowed to remain free pending appeal. After he made public plans to speak before a Congressional committee investigating abuses by the IRS, his freedom was mysteriously revoked and he was sent to prison.

Only the formidable innocent warrior Senator David Pryor from Arkansas seems to have survived as a fighter for the taxpayer who never gives in. Is he a man of colossal courage? Is he a man so clean the IRS can find no skeletons? Is he an Underground Lawyer? Is he crazy? I have no answer, but he's my hero. If I lived in Arkansas, I'd vote for him.

Nearly every president in recent memory has been elected at least in part criticizing the IRS: Nixon, Carter and Reagan all promised reform. All promised protection from the abusive IRS. All were elected with that promise. McGovern and Mondale who failed to make the promise suffered historically prominent defeats at the voting booths.

In Chapter 300 311(B) of the *Special Agent's Handbook*, the IRS states its goal:

"The highest priority of the Criminal Investigation Division is to create maximum positive impact on the compliance attitudes and practices of taxpayers through an effective General Enforcement Program."

Commissioner Mortimer Caplin, (now retired) on the cover of the

---

"IRS agents can garnish wages—even in states like Texas and California where it's not legal—without an evidenciary hearing. They can file unsworn liens on real property and usually no one stands up to them."

---

handbook, states: "Agents...our tax system is based on individual self assessment and voluntary compliance...the material contained in this handbook is confidential in character. It must not under any circumstance be made available to persons outside the service."

By virtue of *your* power as a sovereign citizen of the United States and the Freedom of Information Act, here are a few excerpts from the handbook. The newer versions have less volatile information. Much is now provided in pure agency policy booklets to escape public scrutiny under F.O.I.A.

332.25 PAYMENTS TO INFORMANTS

(1) "Instructions concerning rewards for information submitted to the IRS are contained in IRM 9371. Instructions concerning confidential expenditures and courtesy expenditures which involve payments to or on behalf of informants are contained in IRM 9372 and IRM 9373.3."

(2) If inquiry is made as to the amount which may be received, the inquirer should be furnished with a copy of Publication 733, Rewards for Information Given to the Internal Revenue Service, pertaining to rewards for information about violations of the internal revenue laws."

Nice guys. Fortunately, very few people seek these rewards. The handbook directs agents to consider embittered spouses, in the throes of divorce, as potential informants. Usually the informant's reward is tied up in red tape for years and if delivered at all reduced significantly. Many informants find the IRS is less than honest with them-and they wind up cheated out of their expected "reward" which allegedly ranges up to 10% of the total collected because of their tip, with a maximum of $100,000.00.

334. (12) 4 MAIL COVER

(a) "'Mail Cover' is the process by which a record is made of any data appearing on the outside of any class of mail matter, including checking the contents of

---

"Although the U.S. Constitution guarantees you the right to a jury trial in matters concerning more than $20, our courts do not enforce this constitutional right when the IRS is one of the litigants."

---

any second, third, or fourth class mail matter as now sanctioned by law, in order to obtain information in the interest of protecting national security, locating a fugitive, or obtaining evidence of commission or attempted commission of a crime."

Did Congress originally intend this act to aid the IRS? Hardly. Do we want this group of bloodsuckers to have this type of surveillance power without even the predicate of suspecting a crime? The IRS can go on pure personal fishing expeditions. Does it violate the spirit of the Fourth Amendment? You decide.

338.1 BANKS

(3) "...The cashier ordinarily is the business manager of the bank and is the one to whom requests for information are usually made...The special agent should make every attempt to establish a good working relationship with such employees;"

The booklet discusses obtaining information from Western Union, AMEX, Diners Club, Carte Blanche, FBI, CIA and a hundred other sources. Many banks institute a special officer to cooperate with IRS agents.

341.337

"Recording the proceedings of a public meeting is a permissible means of surveillance."

When a case leaves the collection agent and goes to the special agent, it is in the hands of an official higher up the ladder whose primary job is no longer to take your money but to put you in jail. If an IRS agent wants to, he can pretend to be a lawyer, priest, rabbi, doctor, or even a compassionate, caring human being, and the courts have backed this charade.

If the special agent interrogates you, he must read you your rights, but the collection agent who gets points for taking your money or stealing your car doesn't have to since he's not a police officer. However, anything

---

"Nearly every president in recent memory has been elected at least in part criticizing the IRS: Nixon, Carter and Reagan all promised reform."

---

you say to him can and will be used against you by the special agent if it gets to him.

If you do voluntarily testify to him without being advised of your rights, you can expect your conversation to be read back to you when the agent testifies in federal court. Most of the failure to file convictions start out with innocent discussions with collection agents.

As long as the IRS has not instituted a criminal case, the collection agent can—without due process, prior to a recommendation for criminal prosecution—use his civil summons power without judicial intervention.

367.572 RIGHT TO STAY COMPLIANCE

Formerly, if you told your bank or employer, in writing, within 14 days, not to comply with an IRS summons, they were not supposed to. Afterwards a judge would decide. The IRS had to request a hearing and then win before obtaining the records. The law was recently modified shifting the burden. Now, the taxpayer must ask for the hearing and win, or else, he loses.

36(L0).1 IF YOU DON'T SHOW UP FOR A SUMMONS:

(1) *"...The witness or the witness' representative should also be informed that in the event of refusal or failure to comply with the summons, consideration will be given to resorting to the judicial remedies provided by law."* The special agent is *not* instructed to give further details.

(2) *"If a taxpayer or witness appears in response to a summons and claims either the self-incrimination privilege of the Fifth Amendment or other privilege, the special agent should continue with the examination even though it is clear that the questions will not be answered."*

When a person uses the words "self incrimination" this term generally signifies to the IRS agent that the person has committed a crime. This conclusion is not supported by the Founding Fathers' reasons for including in the Fifth Amendment that portion which prevents government from

---

"If an IRS agent wants to, he can pretend to be a lawyer, priest, rabbi, doctor or even a compassionate, caring human being, and the courts have backed this charade."

---

compelling a person to be a witness against himself.

Remaining completely silent is a lot better than incriminating yourself in the eyes of the agent by claiming the right against self incrimination. Many citizens regret having said too much—but hindsight is always 20/20.

If you find yourself on the other side of a desk from an IRS special agent who is asking you pointed questions, you should consider: A) Politely tell the agent he is scaring you to death. B) Ask him to wait while you get a tape recorder so you can play everything back to your spouse, banker, lawyer, accountant, or confidant. C) Ask him to please carefully explain all of your rights and all of your jeopardies. Ask him to advise you whether or not you should speak to him and whether or not he will help protect your constitutional rights. D) Ask him to put his questions in writing so you can seek help. E) Ask him to put everything in writing so you can tender it to your legal advisor for help. F) Instruct him to call your attorney.

If you ignore an IRS summons, a proceeding may be filed against you in federal court, which is officially classified as neither criminal nor civil, but "miscellaneous"—a petition to enforce IRS summons. Typically, you would be ordered to appear in court and show cause why you should not produce the documents and give the testimony which the IRS is seeking.

The next typical step in the process is for the judge to order you to comply, and threaten you—if you fail to obey his orders—with contempt of court. If you disobey a court order you can be held in criminal contempt and jailed. However, it is easier to hold you in civil contempt, and jail you because civil contempt does not create a criminal record and you have fewer constitutional protections.

Big deal, you say. Jail is jail, you say. For shame. You ignore these interesting legal distinctions. Some lawyers may view a civil contempt sentence of six months as a major victory over a criminal contempt of one month. Most clients only see the amount of time in jail as significant.

The IRS special agent is also a trained witness. This booklet and other training courses teach him how to testify. In a criminal trial of an individual he has investigated, the special agent gets to listen to the entire trial. Usually the defendant's witnesses don't get this opportunity.

The special agent is represented by tax counsel in Washington, the U.S.

"Most of the failure to file convictions start out with innocent discussions with collection agents."

Attorney, and many others. He is authorized to carry weapons and he's the kind of guy you don't want your daughter to bring home.

You want surveillance, you've got it.

381. SURVEILLANCE.

(1) "Surveillance is an investigative technique where an individual or group of individuals are physically observed by special agents in order to obtain information, leads, and evidence that have tax significance and would not normally be available through other investigative techniques. Special agents...may need to conceal their identity during the surveillance by assuming a temporary identity..., and

(7) Surveillance activities. "Surveillance activities at tax protest meetings will be limited to attendance at those meetings for the purpose of obtaining information concerning new techniques being advocated in the so-called tax protest movement..."

382 UNDERCOVER WORK.

(1) "A penetration-type undercover operation is an investigative technique where an authorized IRS employee assumes an identity or a job or profession other than his/her own for the purpose of legally securing information...In this role, the undercover agent actively attempts to gain the acceptance and the confidence of known or suspected tax law violators and/or their associates."

(6) "The selection, training, and cover documents for all agents who will be involved in penetrating-type undercover activities will be provided by the National Office Criminal-Investigation Division." (Another source of support and training for the special agent).

(11) "...while acting in an undercover capacity, agents are not required to advise a subject of his/her Constitutional rights as contained in IRM 9384.2:(2)(b)."

"The special agent is represented by tax counsel in Washington, the U.S. Attorney, and many others. He is authorized to carry weapons and he's the kind of guy you don't want your daughter to bring home."

445.7 PROCEDURES IN TAX PROTESTER-TYPE CASES.

(1) "Each protest return received from the Chief, CID will be immediately assigned for evaluation. This evaluation will be completed within 15 working days...

(3) "Cases selected for investigation will be designated as priority cases and investigated as expeditiously as possible..."

737.72 SPECIAL AGENT.

(1) "Testifying in court is one of the most important duties that a special agent may be called upon to perform. The agent's testimony concerning admissions of the taxpayer may be vital in establishing willfulness..."

Attention: If you are a "tax protester" or even a normal Joe or Jane, when a special agent calls on you, your name may have been put in a nasty black book, and there may soon be a criminal information or indictment form with your name on it. The special agent is your adversary in all respects. He prepares the case against you, directs the legion of government attorneys against you, and even takes the stand as a trained expert to tell the jury what he believes you are thinking. Give him half a chance, and he'll put you in jail. Give him a whole chance, and he'll put mommy and daddy in jail, leaving the children to cope on their own. If you don't like jail, you don't like the special agent. His only job is to put you there.

Obviously, if you go into a automobile show room and don't know that everything is negotiable and offer the list price for the car you want, the car dealer is going to sell it to you at that price; just like a politician will sell his words; just like a lawyer will sell his. "Let's make a deal" is very much a principle of IRS negotiations, also. Those whose principles will not permit them to negotiate with the enemy are often, unfortunately, grist for the evil IRS mill.

The most common offense of so called tax-protesters is willful failure to file.

"The most common offense of so called tax-protesters is willful failure to file. When the IRS charges a citizen with this offense, the conviction rate—thanks in some small part to prosecutors and judges and sometimes jurors who also voluntarily pay taxes—is a steady 95 percent."

When the IRS charges a citizen with this offense, the conviction rate—thanks in some small part to prosecutors and judges and sometimes jurors who also voluntarily pay taxes—is a steady 95 percent.

Since "willfulness" is an element of the offense, a person is guilty only if he has an evil, malicious or willful motive. However, a recent review of court opinions throughout the federal districts shows that the definition is now changing. The court no longer has to define it as evil motive in many jurisdictions. Now the courts are beginning to only require the government to show that the reluctant citizen was required to file an income tax return, knew he was required to file, and he made a conscious decision not to do so.

Alas, the judge will tell the jury, "The tax protester is wrong." But did he know he was wrong? Most so-called protesters honestly believe they are in the right, and therefore they are not legally criminals and should be found not guilty. Most are indicted and convicted based on the judge's instructions coupled with the special agent's expert opinion that the defendant is an insincere liar. Special agents interview suspects who are not trained to remain silent to be protected by the fifth amendment. The suspect often frankly and honestly explains his position to this "agent" actually looking for legitimate answers, while the agent takes self-serving notes which he will later type up and then use as evidence to secure an indictment. No self-respecting drug dealer would fall for this, but then he *knows* he's a criminal. The tax protestor who believes he's following the law is an easy target.

More people go to jail because of innocent conversations with these special agents than for violating any other federal offense.

The special agent should not be confused with IRS computer jockey clerks, or collection agents. He is, indeed, as he claims "special" in the same way that tooth decay, vampires, and diseased hookers are special—they do their best to start looking sweet, but in reality you're better off without them. The odds of justice prevailing for you decreases from 90 percent in your favor to 5 percent in your favor once they get their teeth into your neck and start sucking your blood.

The special agent may be likened to the evil vampire, Count Dracula. Rather than holding up a cross—this agent is trained to ignore morality

---

"More people go to jail because of innocent conversations with these special agents than for violating any other federal offense."

---

symbols—the victim should use the Bill of Rights. A recitation of the Fifth Amendment has been known, on occasion, to make this evil beast flee.

B. IRS—CIVIL PROCEDURE

No one understands the Internal Revenue Code. Anyone who says he does is either mistaken or lying. Many people through experience and reading can give you some good ideas of how some of it works, or doesn't work. Some basic information is briefly summarized here.

Before the IRS can take any civil action against you, a debt must be established. The debt is established by assessing you. You can be assessed in two ways: voluntary, self-assessment or government-assessment.

The voluntary self-assessment is what most Americans do each year, begrudgingly during the second week of April—they file an annual tax return commonly called form 1040 or 1040A or 1040EZ. If you are required to fill out this "voluntary" form by having a minimum amount of gross income and you intentionally fail to do so, you can be charged with 26 USC 7203, failure to file, which is a criminal offense. Many people are charged with this offense even if they accidentally fail to file or believe they are not required to file although this is contrary to the statute.

After you assess yourself, if you do not pay the assessment, the IRS can seize anything you own to pay the assessment. They also add severe financial penalties and interest for non-payment. Sure, you're supposed to have the right to due process before the government takes something that's yours—but try telling that to the IRS! Some people get lost in the system or move and are never found, but most of these people are followed by revenue agents and computer-generated forms.

Seizure is seldom the IRS' first step. They would prefer to collect through letters and phone calls. The schedule for the payment of the debt is usually very negotiable, but some agents are very difficult or impossible to deal with. Wages can be seized, even in states where this is illegal. An IRS notice of levy or lien can be filed in your local real estate or court records and many former friends and associates will avoid you like the plague.

"The voluntary self-assessment is is what most Americans do each year, begrudgingly during the second week of April—they file an annual tax return commonly called form 1040 or 1040A or 1040EZ."

You cannot appeal the debt you have acknowledged you owe. It has the same force and effect as a court judgment.

The other form of assessment is government-assessment. If you do not make a self-assessment, and the IRS believes you have a tax obligation, they may simply assess you based on their own "estimates." Many people wait their entire lives and are never assessed. Many are never found. As the massive IRS-government computer grows, we will all be plugged in, observed more closely and checked on more often. This will happen very soon.

Even if you did make a self-assessment, the IRS may take your tax form and change the amount due. This could come as a result of an audit in their office, an error picked up by this giant computer—which we'll call Big John after the pseudonym given to people who frequent prostitutes—or through a tip from a paid informant. Although the IRS advertises a ten percent bounty for informants, very few Americans are willing to turn their friends and relatives and business acquaintances in for money; and those who do are often disappointed when the money comes in slowly, or not at all, and then it's taxed.

You have to ask yourself why the IRS added to your self-assessment. Why would this happen? The taxpayer added incorrectly on his 1040? The taxpayer left off his attachments? The taxpayer deducted as a business expense the medical bills for his mistress' breast enlargement operation?

The taxpayer's home interest deduction is over $50,000 while his income is only $51,000 and Big John kicked it out for special evaluation? The taxpayer is audited and $5,000 of his deductions are disallowed creating a liability instead of a refund.

If you haven't self-assessed, an assessment often is made without any tax return based on a secret audit, a collection agent's figures, a W4 form—without credit for most deductions—or an IRS error. This is called a substitute return.

Big John gets hungry or angry and mails out a computer form assessment which may or may not be owed and may not make any sense at all. Big John doesn't always make sense. He only always makes paper. You are assessed.

Big John picks up your income from a W4 form, from a 1041 form

---

"You cannot appeal the debt you have acknowledged you owe. It has the same force and effect as a court judgment."

I thought I added up the figures correctly.

(trust), from a K1 form (trust or partnership distribution), or from one of many other possible forms being fed Big John—under the 1986 tax act all real estate transactions will be sent to Big John. Someone simply uses this information, sometimes with your permission, sometimes without it, and writes up a return for you and assesses you.

When the government assesses you, Big John will send you a letter saying you owe him money and should send it in. You do not have to pay it right away—maybe not at all. You do have to oppose it in writing within 30 days or it can become final administratively. The response date is not within 30 days of receipt, it's within 30 days of the date of assessment. Phone numbers and names of persons to contact which are mentioned on the written assessment generally are not helpful and often impossible to read. You must object, timely, in writing. If you call the service and they give you advice or instructions, you cannot legally rely on the advice, and your 30 days is ticking away. You lose. When you lose, you get the 90-day letter.

After you protest, the service must evaluate your protest and consider it. If they rule against you (you can ask for an administrative hearing). If you lose at that level, you'll get a 90-day letter. This means you then have 90 days to file a suit against the IRS in U.S. Tax Court.

You say you want a jury before you pay? Tough. You must now pay for a jury by paying the disputed debt and then filing for a refund in the federal court (here you can get a jury trial) or in the U.S. Court of Claims (no jury trial here). If you don't have the money to pay, you have no option, you either lose or sue in tax court. The tax court consists of a judge, no jury. The judge is often a former IRS agent! His decisions are appealable to the circuit court. If you lose, the assessment becomes a collectible judgment just like the self assessment. The process can last years. If you don't file a suit in the tax court or pay within 90 days of the date on the letter, you lose and get a final assessment without a trial.

Unless an agent has reason to believe you are trying to sell everything and skip the country or join the massive underground economy, the agent is not legally allowed to seize your property without a final assessment. A seizure means that the IRS could haul off all your vehicles, completely wipe out your checking and savings accounts, or take practically all your wages from your employer. Nevertheless, illegal seizures happen. On occasion, a citizen who does everything by the rules is wiped out by such an illegal seizure or just a misunderstanding. Big John can be very mean, very unreasonable, and very arbitrary.

The bottom of the totem pole is the revenue agent. His job is to collect money. The audit agent actually is required to think and make calculations. It is also his job to collect money. He reviews returns thoroughly.

Both agents have the job of collecting information. Your return and the various agents' data are all fed to Big John.

Big John is the largest computer in the world. His main body sits in West Virginia and his tentacles stretch to regional offices. He was built at a cost of over $100 million for hardware—and that was just for the home office. Since software/hardware ratios are about 85 to 15 we can estimate total costs in the neighborhood of a billion dollars. Special access codes are needed to get inside Big John. However, hundreds of people have easy access to the special access codes. Big John holds more information on U.S.

"Big John holds more information on U.S. citizens than Russia, Poland, Nazi Germany, and certain totalitarian, Latin American countries had or have today on all their citizens combined."

citizens than Russia, Poland, Nazi Germany, and certain totalitarian, Latin American countries had or have today on all their citizens combined. Under the new tax law this information will be radically increased.

Most of the small revenue agents can get access to some of this information. During a trial the government can and often does pull this information on all the jurors. Most of these rules and methods have added to the power of the I.R.S. over the years. *None* of the recent (last 20 years) statutes have diminished their power. Only Senator Pryor's "Taxpayer's Bill of Rights" currently holds any major modification promises and efforts are underway to cut some of its teeth out.

C. BIG JOHN AND JOE OLIVER

In West Virginia lurks the largest most powerful government computer in the world. No Soviet computer or Iranian spy shop has as much information as the computer I have dubbed Big John. The purpose of Big John is to accumulate public, but private, information on all American citizens and aliens who have a social security number.

The 1040's are broken down into categories and the information is programmed in, other data the federal agents have collected on individuals is added, and only a select few people are given access to the computer. The complete computer file is called National Computer Center Transcript—Complete, or the the Master File Complete. The information is in secret code. The codes are explained in the "not for public" code book called the Automatic Data Processing "ADP" code book. Not all agents have access to it.

One of the most insidious codes is the TC 148, which tells IRS agents that this particular individual is an illegal tax protester and may be harassed and denied all administrative rights. The very name "illegal protester" is an insult to the First Amendment to the Constitution. Non-violent protest is never illegal. The code is a form of censorship.

The "tax protester" label is placed on individuals for a multitude of reasons. A citizen may protest the IRS, may be a member of one of the many legitimate church groups the IRS has singled out for persecution, may be a former winner in tax court, or may have been inadvertently

"The purpose of Big John is to accumulate public, but private, information on all American citizens and aliens who have a social security number."

picked up by a routine privacy- invading IRS mail cover as a subscriber to a magazine on the IRS hit list.

The TC-148 designation may be branded on a man, woman, or child because they didn't demonstrate the degree of homage or fear required by an IRS agent's ego when he audited a victim or met one at a party. John Wayne the actor and Howard Jarvis the champion of California's Proposition 13 referendum on state property taxes each made the list.

The use of the code TC-148 is a throw-back to illegal, immoral government oppression like the incarceration of honest Japanese citizens during World War II, like the tragic McCarthy interrogations which ruined lives and destroyed careers for political reasons, and like the murders of blacks and civil rights workers during the sixties. It is evil incarnate. This stamp is nothing but trouble, and it can hit someone like the flu, without warning and it can stay for life. It can end up on a citizen's transcript by error. It is

> *"The use of the code TC-148 is a throw-back to illegal, immoral government oppression like the incarceration of honest Japanese citizens during World War II, like the tragic McCarthy interrogations which ruined lives and destroyed careers for political reasons, and like the murders of blacks and civil rights workers during the sixties."*

almost never removed.

George Joseph Oliver had it on his file and all he knew was he had problems. I met Joe Oliver and his sweetheart Charlie (a charming lady christened "Charlie" after her daddy) a mere ten days before Joe's trial on tax charges was scheduled in Fort Worth, Texas. This delightful pair were in love with each other and they were in love with love. Although they reminded me of high school sweethearts, they weren't in high school and they weren't teenagers. They were both in their late 50s. They were so perfect for each other they seemed to have shared their entire life together but they hadn't. They had found each other after Joe's bitter divorce, and each discovered a fresh, new love that was more than they had ever known before. But a dark shadow loomed over their happiness.

I took Charlie and Joe to dinner with another client of mine from New York, who was also battling the IRS. Joe was looking at the wrong end of a two-year possible sentence for two counts of willful failure to file an income tax return for the years 1980 and 1981. Joe and Charlie were worried. They had traveled from Fort Worth to Houston to hire me but I had a New York client and one from Hong Kong in the office the same day so I could only see them in between shuffles.

My office manager, Linda, was on vacation. L.R. had just gotten back from her vacation and was facing a pile of work on her desk. Assistant office manager Tracie was assuming new tasks in order to step up. Linda was leaving in December to have a baby, after five years with me. Every summer I take a month of low-level work to spend quality time with my kids. This year I had taken off three weeks. All of these events were combined with two U.S. Supreme Court appeals, one Fifth Circuit appeal, one Texas appeal, one Texas Supreme Court appeal, three summer trials—and of course my normal practice. We were up to our limit and couldn't handle more work. Not counting hearings, we had scheduled two more August trials and three September trials plus one in Hawaii, one in New York, and one in Maine, representing the pastor of a church.

Nevertheless, here is Joe Oliver, he needs help, and L.R. wanted us to take the case. To make a sad plea harder to ignore, Peggy Christensen called and asked me to take the case as a personal favor—and I owed her one for help she gave me on another case that was pending before the U.S. Supreme Court. Obviously we took the case anyway or I wouldn't be

"Willful failure to file—the government's most effective weapon against its citizens criminally."

writing about it, but the client couldn't put up the full fee. I had to advance the money for a lot of my out-of-pocket expenses and look to his integrity for future payments. I have not been disappointed.

Oliver had been designated "TC-148 Hold IS P" for years. In 1972 he received his first audit and he got a new one every year for seven straight years, and each year they went back a year for a double audit. In 1973 and 1974 Joe went to tax court and won.

In 1977 he was assessed an additional $8,500 he didn't owe. He filed in tax court. The IRS offered to settle for $4,000. NO, said Oliver. How about $2,000? NO! Well, how about settling for $1,000? NO, again said a stubborn Oliver. Finally they agreed to take $4, that's right, four dollars—but Oliver still said NO and he quit filing his 1040's under advice of a new accountant. Instead he filed the W4—exempt. In 1987 he was charged with willful failure to file—the government's most effective criminal weapon against its citizens who dare to challenge the I.R.S.

The government's standard argument is the accused isn't paying his fair share. The burden is on the government to prove beyond a reasonable doubt that the defendant did not file and knew he was supposed to file.

On Monday, August 17, 1987 my father's birthday and Charlie's birthday, we picked a jury. From Tuesday to Thursday that week we tried the case.

The IRS special agent testified under oath he knew Oliver was intentionally violating the law, yet his own report showed he believed Oliver was relying on the advice of a California Legal Advice/Legal Insurance Group.

Agents, friends, employers, former tenants—Joe had formerly owned six rent houses and over the years had many tenants—were brought in from all over the country to show Oliver made big bucks and didn't report them. The revenue agent then testified Oliver owed a lot of money; but did he?

Deductions for state paid taxes of $200 to $400 were estimated by the revenue agent at only $39.85. Repair bills on rental property had been either disallowed or spread out for depreciation over 15 years rather than three.

With the testimony of former 20-year veteran IRS agent, now turned

---

"The burden is on the government to prove beyond a reasonable doubt that the defendant did not file and knew he was supposed to file."

---

whistleblower, Paul DesFosses, we showed Oliver might not owe any money at all. The government attempted to impeach DesFosses because he had clients all over the United States and gave free advice to many churches. Rather than hurting his credibility, this attack impressed the jury with DesFosses' integrity and hard-earned reputation.

The government's research had ruined Oliver's former marriage, alienated him from his children, interfered in his relationship with his church, eliminated his bank credit and rendered him unemployed for the first time in years. The TC-148 had hit him like an incurable, undetectable disease and plagued him for over a decade. This man who refused to pay the IRS $4 he didn't owe—as a matter of principle—wore this designation not as a shameful scarlet letter but as a badge of honor: worn defiantly in the face of misguided government power.

The special agent showed Oliver had filed in the past so he clearly knew he was obligated to file. The stuffings were knocked out of this argument however, when the judge allowed us to read from the special agent's report, his findings that Oliver was in fact sincere—he actually believed he was not required to file for 1980 and 1981. Without this information the jury decision might well have been different. The agent testified that we were misinterpreting his report.

Government attorney Jimmy Tallent was a very skilled veteran of 23 years, with eight and half years doing tax work. Tallent said he'd never seen one of the IRS computer transcripts before—that's how secret it is! He argued the usual party line in criminal tax cases: Oliver had failed to pay, he knew he had to pay, so he was a bad man. He argued well, but it was a hollow argument in light of the evidence.

I spoke on behalf of Oliver for justice, the jury delivered TWO NOT GUILTY verdicts. Oliver and Charlie were free. A lot of prayers were answered.

D. THE EVOLUTION OF THE INCOME TAX

Until 1913, there were no income taxes in the United States—although one had been imposed as an emergency to raise revenues for the Civil War. Some individual states from time to time proposed a progressive tax, but as a general rule, they were ruled unconstitutional. An 1894

"With the passage of the the Sixteenth Amendment, income taxation became possible."

---

income tax bill was ruled unconstitutional by the U.S. Supreme Court.[2]

With the passage of the the Sixteenth Amendment, income taxation became possible. There are a large number of people today who do not believe that this amendment was properly passed. The theory is well documented and makes a great deal of sense; however, the courts have ruled time and time again that this argument is irrelevant and may not be used to avoid the payment of income taxes. To hold the belief that because there were not enough votes to make income taxation legal, income taxation is, therefore, not legal, is to hold a belief that you will probably not see supported in the courts during your lifetime. I respect and will defend the right of anybody who holds this principle to speak it publicly.

I thank God, as well as the makers of the Bill of Rights, Constitution, and Declaration of Independence for the freedom to trade these ideas and hear them. Unfortunately, our society has become so indoctrinated with the Sixteenth Amendment and has accepted it to such an extent that it can only be eliminated through the passage of another amendment, a change of heart by the Supreme Court or effectively abolishing all laws which implement the amendment—and none of these measures are likely to occur.

For that reason, I advise clients not to use this defense or rely on it. It is a losing battle. Might does not make right, but might often does win out over right. Your chances of winning are better following the government's rules.

If the judges in our courts would honestly tell jurors that they had the right to disregard the law as it is told to them by the judge and make a determination themselves as the Magna Carta jury was allowed to do, jurors en masse would put holes in the laws that apply to the Sixteenth Amendment. They would not accept income taxation if they knew that it was within their power to abolish it.

On the other hand, jurors are told by the judge they have no such power, and they are told by the prosecutors, with the judge's blessings, that income taxes are an evil necessity that we all must endure. The jurors

> *"If the judges in our courts would honestly tell jurors that they had the right to disregard the law as it is told to them by the judge and make a determination themselves as the Magna Carta jury was allowed to do, jurors en masse would put holes in the laws that apply to the Sixteenth Amendment."*

are also being told that they are being forced to pay the defendant's fair share—which is a blatant lie. First, two-thirds of government revenue is raised without personal income taxation (through such sources as corporate taxes, sales and excise taxes), and second, no one's share can be called fair because of the arbitrary and capricious methods of collecting and assessing taxes. However, convictions will surpass vindications and jurors will remain impotent and non-essential.

Sixteen years after the income tax wrapped its ugly tentacles around this nation's throat, we were plunged into the great depression. It is interesting to note that throughout this sixteen year period (1913-1929), the rate of taxation steadily increased. It is also interesting to note that when President Reagan lowered income taxes in 1981, the economy was instantly stimulated and started to improve.

I think the explanation is a lot simpler than people have been led to believe. This country was started with a rebellion against the payment of taxes that we endured under English rule.

Of course there are all kinds of taxes. Even people who do not file a 1040, who do not send money to the government on or about April 15th of each year still pay taxes.

How? The government prints more money than it makes and lowers the value of the money that is currently in circulation, which is called inflation. Inflation taxes everybody and taxes everybody in proportion to the existing dollar amount. If there are two dollars in existence and one apple to buy, you may pay the two dollars for the apple. If two more dollars are printed and the number of apples stays the same, the apple costs four dollars.

Even after 1929, income taxes were relatively innocuous. When the government sought extra funds to fight World War II, the temporary "victory tax" was conceived, and has now mushroomed into the present evil colossus that we now call the income tax.

Somehow, once the politicians discovered the tax wagon and realized all of the potential benefits—including giving them a means of buying future votes with free lunches, and patronizing companies with thousand dollar screws, they just couldn't give it all up when the war ended. Congress still hasn't.

When we tax things, we reduce the incentive and increase the cost of the object. It makes good sense to tax vices in order to raise money. Gov-

"The power to tax is the power to destroy."

ernments need to raise money. When governments end up raising more money than they need, they start spending more in order to find ways to justify their conduct. Under President Andrew Jackson, the U.S. Treasury actually had a surplus, and we had *no income tax.*

How? Obviously we were raising more capital than was being distributed by the government. Yet there were no income taxes. There is truth in the maxim, "The power to tax is the power to destroy."

The income tax, as it now exists, is the most awesome, powerful system of collecting revenues ever created in the history of mankind. Our so-called voluntary system of paying taxes was enforced and is enforced today through fear tactics. We pay because we are afraid not to. We also pay because we, as decent human beings, want to pay our fair share, but who decides what our fair share is?

The old lie that ignorance of the law is no excuse, is nowhere more cruel and malicious than when related to the collection of income taxes. No one honestly understands the Internal Revenue Code. Judge Neely described it in a nutshell when he volunteered his experience:

"In 1978 I attended a seminar on federal estate and gift tax sponsored by the American Law Institute, where the Internal Revenue Service lawyers responsible for this area frankly confessed that they did not understand the Tax Reform Act of 1976. They were, indeed, so confused that there was hardly one question asked by the audience which they satisfactorily answered. Not only did they allow that they did not understand the law, they opined that the Congress which wrote it did not understand it and that the courts would seem to understand it only because the courts would make it up as they went along and pretend to understand it." [3]

In a free society, the amount of voluntary contributions should be up to the free will of individuals. Long before the government got involved in the collection and distribution of wealth, churches and civic organizations raised large amounts of money, goods and free services. For the most part, these benefits were distributed efficiently to deserving recipients. Food stuffs and other goods and services were distributed on a local basis, without waste. This efficiency was possible because the human beings who voluntarily gave their money over to a local entity were around to watch

---

"The old lie that ignorance of the law is no excuse, is nowhere more cruel and malicious than when related to the collection of income taxes."

---

and make certain that their dollars were judiciously utilized. The beneficiaries of this bounty often saw the generous hands that fed them and felt morally obligated not to bite these hands by eating too much, and they felt obligated to repay these hands by pulling themselves up by their boot straps and becoming a helping hand to others.

Now, their symbolic descendants receive random amounts of government dollars from sources whom they never see and don't understand. Human beings are forced to contribute under threat of a jail sentence. This is the moral equivalent of robbery at gun point.

The taxpayers have no control over what is being done with their money and thereby receive none of the good feeling that is the reward of charitable persons so they see little of the benefits of their sacrifice. It's a form of slavery.

Government officials owe promises and favors to people who help get them elected. Politicians have decided to sell us out. Why? Because, as has been said over and over again, power corrupts. It is easier to get rich selling a $640 toilet seat or a $2,000 monkey wrench to someone who is being offered this bargain at gun point and who has no way of defending himself, than it is to work for the money.[4] Any laugh we can derive from seeing evidence of the government's waste of our hard earned money is a wry one. It's a cruel joke, and the joke is on us.

The notion that our government should be able to take wealth away from human beings who created it by means of their labor and then redistribute that income to whomever the government sees fit is not only ridiculous, it is un-American. The jury system, if effectively brought back, would protect us against this pernicious practice which is sapping the vitality of our nation.

Prior to 1913, we took better care of the needy than we do in 1988. We did it because we cared and we had control over our own personal money. The concept that government knows more and better how to spend our money than we do is a hollow, dishonest concept. The implication is that our politicians are wiser and more generous than we are. Perhaps it's true. Those persons with an unscrupulous nature are apt to be generous with other people's monies.

"The IRS today runs checks on all of us and has accumulated a dossier on each of us filed under our government given identification number —the social security number."

If money has to be raised, it can be raised in many ways other than this public intrusion into our private lives. The IRS today runs checks on all of us and has accumulated a dossier on each of us filed under our government given identification number—the social security number. Of course, there are people who have dropped out of this system, sometimes at great personal cost—such as being fired for not disclosing a social security number.

The government knows our professions, incomes, family members, religious preferences, who we vote for, and a great deal of other unnecessary personal information. It requires us, as slaves, to work approximately the first three months out of every year for the benefit of people we have never met and possibly would not like. It is this form of economic slavery and government intrusion into our personal lives that would have given George Orwell, author of 1984 (Big Brother is watching you) even greater cause for alarm.

We can learn a lesson from our forefathers who understood that taxing is a depressant. If you tax something, you hurt it. If you tax alcohol, you lower alcohol consumption; and if you tax cigarettes, then people smoke fewer cigarettes.

However, we have also learned that vices are going to be bought and sold regardless of the tax, so taxing vices is a valuable source of continuing revenue. It also helps to control the vice. If we were to allow heroin and cocaine to be freely distributed at pharmacies, through doctors' prescriptions, we could control their use. We could tax these substances and lower the costs. I have no doubt that there are some cigarette smokers who would kill for a cigarette if they couldn't obtain it at a reasonable price. Obviously, heroin is much more addictive and much more dangerous than nicotine, but there are some people who can control their heroin intake better than others control their nicotine intake. Heroin, and other dangerous drugs, contribute so much to crime because its distribution is controlled by lawless people. If these substances were to be distributed freely, under government control, with offenses subject to trial by juries, you might find a reduction in crime.

"We can learn a lesson from our forefathers who understood that taxing is a depressant. If you tax something, you hurt it. If you tax alcohol, you lower alcohol consumption; and if you tax cigarettes, then people smoke fewer cigarettes.

Taxation is the power to control. The taxation of prostitution would allow the government to license it, tax it, control it and clean it up. Prostitution does not diminish when legislation is enacted against it. Rather, the control of it is left in the hands of those persons who are not law abiding, and the revenues go into the underground economy. Legalized and taxed, it would be a steady source of revenue and the great evils of forced slavery, and teen-age prostitution might be eliminated or at least severely reduced.

One of the greatest freedoms this country once offered was the freedom to pursue work untaxed. For the first 150 years, this country was prosperous and growing. The one thing that we did not ever tax, because we encouraged it and people flocked to these shores because of it, was work.

An article printed in major national newspapers indicated that the Federal Reserve Board could account for only about $18 billion of the $153 billion worth of currency that records show should be circulating in the United States. No one is sure where the rest of the money has gone, but some suspicions are: overseas accounts, drug dealers, prostitution, gambling syndicates, organized crime, people's private hoarding of money, or the underground economy, of which the writer, Paul Magnusson, says:

"The government has always been aware of an underground economy whose medium of exchange is cash and barter and whose purpose is to escape police and the tax collector's attention. The nation's nearly $4 billion gross national product is understated by an estimated 5 to 32 percent because the underground economy is not part of the measure."[5]

Could it be that oppressive taxation has driven some of the most enterprising entrepreneurs underground?

When an individual works and produces, the individual creates additional jobs. Small business owners who open up a hamburger restaurant, auto repair shop, or even a small law office soon add employees to the firm and create a marketable inventory by means of their individual ef-

---

"One of the greatest freedoms this country used to offer was the freedom to pursue work untaxed. For the first 150 years, this country was prosperous and growing. The one thing that we did not ever tax, because we encouraged it and people flocked to these shores because of it, was work."

---

forts. This thing called work made our country wealthy. Now we call work a four letter word. A person who works hard, long hours is not praised for his industriousness but is labeled a workaholic. Work is considered a disease, and someone who works too hard is considered to have psychological problems.

Remember the old fable of the ant and the grasshopper. The ant worked hard and accumulated a hoard of food in his bomb shelter built underground with painstaking labor and good craftsmanship. The grasshopper laughed, ate, danced and jumped and played. Why worry about a cold tomorrow that may never come? When winter snows came the industrious ant went into his warm home and did quite well. The grasshopper froze to death.

If there was a modern American version of the ant and the grasshopper fable, the industrious ant would be consigned to a psychiatrist's couch. The government would take one-fourth of his food and tax his home, while the grasshopper would use food stamps to acquire most of the ant's hard-earned winter supplies.

When you tax wages, you tax work. When work is taxed, people are discouraged from working. The more you tax work, the less people are willing to work, the less work is performed, the fewer goods and services are produced. It's really that simple. The framers of the Constitution agreed that two portions of the new document were not to be changed prior to 1808 under any circumstances. These sections singled out for special preservation were Article I, Section 9, Clause 1, relating to free immigration and Article I, Section 9, Clause 4: "No *capitation or other direct tax shall be laid*, unless in proportion to the census or enumeration herein before directed to be taken." Simply stated that means no income tax.

Our forefathers were tax protesters. The Boston Tea Party was the climactic explosion which followed many, many tax protester meetings. The First Amendment includes this sacred right to peaceably assemble and

"Benson a retired Revenue Agent and Beckman traveled to all the states, reviewed all the original documents, and summarized the facts on each state's alleged ratification. Their theory is that there were irregularities in the ratification process of 34 of the 38 of the states, which allegedly approved the Sixteenth Amendment. Authors conclude that amendment has not been constitutionally ratified."

petition against the government. Our forefathers guaranteed that there wouldn't even be a debate about income tax until after 1808. In order to pass an amendment, two thirds of both the houses of Congress must propose it, and then it must be validated by three-fourths of the states—either by their legislatures or by constitutional conventions.

In the preface to their book *The Law That Never Was*,[6] authors Bill Benson and Red Beckman state that:

"...the same enemy that destroyed the Roman Empire has now invaded and conquered the minds of millions who are now addicted to the drug called 'government money.'"

Benson, a retired Revenue Agent and Beckman traveled to all the states, reviewed all the original documents and summarized the facts on each state's alleged ratification. Their writing demonstrates a shrewd, careful, legal analysis.

Their theory is that there were irregularities in the ratification process of 34 of the 38 of the states, which allegedly approved the Sixteenth Amendment. Therefore, the authors conclude that amendment has not been constitutionally ratified. The theory is currently being litigated all over the United States. For political reasons, it will be defeated. Every court that has reviewed it so far has rejected it.

Their argument is historically accurate, it is morally right—but it is legally wrong because judges determine what is legally right, and they will continue to vote against this and any other theory changing the mandatory filing of tax returns and payment of income taxes. With this warning let's examine the Sixteenth Amendment more closely.

At the time of the ratification of the Sixteenth Amendment to the Constitution, there were 42 states. Simple arithmetic tells you that three fourths of 42 is 31.5 states, meaning that it would take at least 32 states for ratification.

In U.S. Solicitor General Reuben Clark's 16-page legal memorandum, dated February 15, 1913 written to Secretary of State Philander Knox, who must certify the results, Clark indicated that 38 states had ratified the Sixteenth Amendment to the U.S. Constitution. Apparently this memorandum entitled "Ratification of the Sixteenth Amendment to the Constitution of the United States" was deemed necessary because of arguments concerning certain irregularities in the states' ratification process.

The Solicitor admitted that there were many typographical errors and slight discrepancies in the amendments. Only four states returned "absolutely perfect" copies of the resolution. Also, he noted, 22 states' resolutions had errors in capitalization or punctuation and 11 states' resolutions had errors in wording. But, Clark stated that:

"It should, moreover, be observed that it seems clearly to have been the intention of the legislature in each and every case, to accept and ratify the 16th Amendment as proposed by Congress...the errors appear in most cases to have been mere typographical and incident to an attempt to make an accurate quotation."

Of course, back in 1913, clerks and office personnel did not have the advantage of our modern word processors and photocopying machines, but the correct rendition of 30 words is not such a formidable task. A fifth grade student would most likely be able to accomplish it with ease. In contrast, in the Bill of Rights all ratifying states in all ten amendments got every word, every comma and every period right.

Clark was well aware that "under the provisions of the Constitution, the legislature was not authorized to alter in any way the amendment proposed by Congress, the function of the legislature consisting merely in the right to approve or disapprove the proposed amendment.

"It is recommended, therefore, that the Secretary issue his declaration announcing the adoption of the 16th Amendment to the Constitution." Philander Knox did so on February 25, 1913.

The solicitor argued in his 16-page memorandum that the numerous errors were unimportant. The solicitor declared there were errors in ratification resolutions of both the Thirteenth and Fourteenth amendments, although he declined to share with us in his letter what these errors were. He argued that the Fourteenth Amendment "has been repeatedly before the courts, and has been by them enforced." His effort was to establish a precedent for overlooking "errors." He did not cite a single specific case.

The Solicitor's opinion, in and of itself, did not have the power of a decision of the court. He ignored the historical fact that both the Thirteenth and Fourteenth amendments were adopted by large margins and

---

"Viewing into the context the great importance our forefathers seemed to give to the freedom from an income tax by making it one of only two portions of the Constitution that could not be changed for 21 years—even by amendment!"

---

that in the Thirteenth Amendment there was no ambiguity in the meaning. It clearly abolished slavery. However, the Sixteenth Amendment, short as it was, lent itself to ambiguous interpretations which are still debated three-quarters of a century later. There was a clear discrepancy in meaning between some of the officially adopted texts in various states of the Sixteenth Amendment.

There was no excuse for the procedural differences in the various typed copies and sloppiness in the so-called adoption of the tax amendment. Since all of the 42 states had identical copies of the Sixteenth Amendment provided by Secretary of State Philander Knox, the legislatures should have been able to return exact copies.

The Sixteenth Amendment is one of the shortest amendments to the Constitution. Many other long, verbose amendments were ratified perfectly. It is not advisable to overlook such carelessness, especially when viewing into the context the great importance our forefathers seemed to give to the freedom from an income tax by making it one of only two portions of the Constitution that could not be changed for 21 years—even by amendment!

In *The Law that Never Was*, Benson advocates throwing out some states' ratification because a word was not capitalized or a comma was left out. The federal courts have not supported this position.

Nevertheless, a reader can go through Benson's book state by state and determine for himself the extent which he disagrees with Benson. This particular reader was convinced beyond a reasonable doubt of illegalities in the ratification process in more than six of the 34 states where discrepancies were found. If Benson and Beckman are right on seven of the 34 states, then the three-fourths ratification requirement clearly was not met.

Were I advising a judge who was reviewing Benson and Beckman's evidence, I would recommend a vote in their favor to rule that the Sixteenth Amendment was not ratified properly. However, because of the long passage of time and because of the plethora of court decisions and legislation which have grown up around the Sixteenth Amendment, when circuit judges review the cases based on this theory, they are afraid to reverse, to find the Sixteenth Amendment was properly ratified or to ignore the issue. The Supreme Court is not very likely to review the ratifi-

"Through the Freedom of Information Act, some frightening, internal government publications have become available to Americans."

cation process of the Sixteenth Amendment.

However, if there were a large groundswell of public opinion strongly opposed to the Sixteenth Amendment and of the opinion that the amendment was not properly ratified, and if the justices of the Supreme Court held to the principle that the Constitution should be literally interpreted, there is a remote possibility that the Supreme Court would find that the Sixteenth Amendment had not been properly ratified. Therefore, all case law supporting it would be void.

Since this position is not politically acceptable and since the media for the last 50 years has basically supported confiscatory taxation, no immediate change is likely to occur. Reliance on the illegitimacy of the Sixteenth Amendment as a reason for not filing or paying income taxes is a serious mistake, likely to cost you money or jail time. Like many areas of law, political realities mean more than truth.

E. THE ILLEGAL TAX PROTESTER

Through the Freedom of Information Act, some frightening, internal government publications have become available to Americans. IRS training manuals are available. They are not sold in bookstores, but they are generally sold through various groups who have ordered them through the Freedom of Information Act and have had them publish them at nominal costs. Some, once they become public, are available at government book stores for inflated prices.

Isn't this a little harsh for not filing my tax papers by April 15th?

One frightening publication is The Illegal Tax Protester Training Reference Guide put out by the Department of the Treasury. The book basically states that there is such an individual called an illegal tax protester (ITP), and that this individual is evil and dangerous. The sad and frightening thing about the book is the nomenclature. Tax protesters are carrying on the tradition of President Ronald Reagan, President George Washington, founding father Roger Sherman, author of *Caveat Against Injustice*[7], and individual persons in between who protested unjust taxes. It is inconceivable that protesting taxes could ever become an illegal act in and of itself. The title of the manual, however, clearly suggests that protesting taxes is illegal behavior. A truer interpretation of the situation is that these individuals are *protesters of illegal taxes as they perceive them.*

The 1985 manual refers to, on page one, a current illegal tax protester movement. The manual tells IRS agents who these illegal tax protesters

"Probation and Fine!"

Isn't this a little harsh for an accidental rape and homicide?

are, where they are, how to find them and how to identify them. Some of the people in the manual would be surprised to find their names there.

On page 1 and 2 it is states that:

"much of the rapid growth in the current ITP movement may be attributed to a number of key persons who are making speeches and conducting seminars in all parts of the country. During these presentations, gross misrepresentations and false information about the tax laws are presented to the public as fact."

While I uphold the individual author's right to exercise free speech and free press, it is upsetting that publication has been printed by our government at our expense. The implication is that the seminars are dishonest. The inference in the Illegal Tax Protester Manual is that the tax protest movement which includes many clergymen is filled with dishonest people. The publication implies that there is something sinister about people who are familiar with the Constitution, who gather to discuss their own personal opinions regarding the Constitution, and who dare to question government authority are somehow dangerous. The truth is that many nationally prominent C.P.A.'s, attorneys, ministers and constitutional scholars and political candidates, congressmen and senators speak at these meetings. Of course to be fair, there are *also* a lot of con-artists selling silver bullets as well as an assortment of certifiable fruitcakes...just as you find at any large gathering of people.

And if we are being *really* fair and investigate *some* of the fruitcakes on closer examination are very rational and have stories that should be told.

As previously stated, individuals like Howard Jarvis, the author of Proposition 13 in California and John Wayne have been labeled tax protesters. Even Ronald Reagan has claimed that distinction! On the other hand, there are a lot of nuts out there selling snake oil and magic charms to ward off IRS agents.

Some of them sell courses that promise freedom and a tax-free existence for thousands of dollars. Often when the purchasers are a trial away from jail they call me, broke, and ask for credit. The medicine men are usually not around once their students have bought all their goods and

"I have met religious leaders whose interpretations of Scriptures honestly believed they are precluded from participating in the IRS taxation system as it now exists."

are facing jail. To prepare someone like this for trial takes twice as much effort. They first have to be de-programmed to understand reality. For every rational well written book like Bill Benson's there are ten that make no sense and have no foundation at all.

Students are taught to speak Latin invocations and utter strange jurisdictional arguments and the judge will vanish in a puff of smoke. The only one who vanishes is the magician with student's money.

The manual also suggests that illegal tax protest groups encourage members not only to submit false and invalid W-4 forms, but also to persuade their colleagues to engage in this type of protest activity. There is the implication that tax protesters network through different organizations, all of which are suspect and some of which are dangerous and violent.

The manual basically breaks tax protest movements into several different concepts: 1) gold-silver standard, 2) trusts, 3) ministries and churches, and 4) constitutional argument. Actually, proponents of the gold-silver standard and those who find the income tax unconstitutional should probably be in the same category, since the gold-silver monetary standard is set forth in the Constitution.

The government manual contends that people who file tax returns asserting their Fifth Amendment right against self- incrimination—instead of furnishing some of the information sought on the 1040 form—have violated the law and cites *United States vs. Sullivan*[8], to bolster its position.

The Supreme Court ruled in Sullivan that you could not legally fill out a Fifth Amendment return in which you gave no information at all and claimed your Fifth Amendment right as to the entire form. There is not a definitive ruling by the Supreme Court determining that you can not file specific Fifth Amendment objections to specific items on the return. In fact, the opposite is true.

For example: If you obtained your income through illegal gambling and you reported the money but refused to reveal its source, under Fifth Amendment protection you would not be guilty of violating IRS regulations. One tax attorney, on cross examination in a case I tried, suggested the best approach was not to plead Fifth Amendment honestly—as is your constitutional right—but to fudge and simply be vague about your occupation. It's advice to a drug dealer was to put down retailer. This implies that if the numbers seem to work, drug dealing is fine. No one in government cares—they don't check the profession—they just want the money out of a crime. The individual is the only one who can tell whether or not some admission might tend to incriminate him.

Our forefathers and the original Supreme Court would not have found a 1040 form completely filled with Fifth Amendment objections to be illegal. They would, on the other hand, have found the entire structure of the Sixteenth Amendment income tax and the evil empire of the IRS to be un-American and unconstitutional.

The IRS Illegal Protester Manual is very misleading. The fact that you can't file a blanket Fifth Amendment return does not mean that certain portions of the return can not be filled in with the Fifth Amendment refusal to testify.

The IRS separately categorizes "the illegal church ministry protester." In my speaking engagements at numerous seminars throughout the country and in my nationwide trial practice, I have met religious leaders whose interpretations of Scriptures honestly believed they are precluded from participating in the IRS taxation system as it now exists. They seem to be concerned with the separation of church and state, the absolute sovereignty of God; and the preservation of the Constitution, particularly the First Amendment—freedom of religion. They have, for the most part, legitimate ministries.

The message in the IRS Tax Protester Manual suggests that the majority of these ministers are not legitimate. This is unfortunate. Many of them have vocally disputed various state governments and the federal government's right to force them to obtain licenses—permission from the government to exist. The IRS is the champion and patron saint of all regulations.

In the area of trusts, I have seen some non-legitimate activities. Some promoters sell "kits" of trust documents, certificates, contracts, etc. for anywhere from a hundred to several thousand dollars which are practically worthless. However, the Illegal Tax Protesters Manual does not distinguish between a few promoters who are selling worthless photocopies of strange instruments and the majority who are advising their customers to use legal alternatives to the current tax structure.

"The Illegal Tax Protester Manual also implies that people who attend public patriot meetings, or who gather in organized assemblies to redress grievances to the government are doing something wrong; in spite of the fact the First Amendment gives us the right to peaceably assemble and to petition our government with complaints."

Trusts are a long-time facet of the American financial scene. One of their major purposes for establishing a trust is to legally avoid taxes by using the government's guidelines. American taxpayers are entitled to arrange their financial affairs so that they are required to pay the least taxes possible. This is the American way.

The overwhelming majority of trusts are owned by aristocrats like the Rockefellers, Fords, Carnegies and others. They were started in England for the purpose of avoiding inheritance taxes. There is no reason why the average American citizen should not take advantage of legitimate trusts, set up at reasonable cost, to eliminate substantial portions of their income tax burden. The implication in the Illegal Tax Protester Manual is that everyone who has a trust, whose name is not Rockefeller, is a crook.

Izen and I represented Traves and Faye Brownlee in Delaware on a tax case. A large portion of the case was concerned with an overseas trust which IRS Special Agent Lafferty had determined for himself was illegal. The trust was determined to be legitimate. Small wonder! The presiding Judge owned a trust himself. It is possible that the prosecuting attorney owned a trust. Aside from members of the jury, I was one of the few people in the courtroom who did not own a trust. Unless you have some type of valuable property to put into the trust, it is not a very important or necessary vehicle. At that point, having come through the impoverishing process of a divorce and through financial losses that I sustained by winning freedom for Norma Ginter in her capital murder case, I was not in the market for a trust. The postage to mail copies of it would have set me back.

Robert Chappell's book *Secrets of Offshore Tax Havens* quotes excerpts from the Brownlee trial, including my objection to witness IRS Special Agent Lafferty deceiving an individual by leading him to believe a legitimate trust was a sham:

"Let me give my reason for objecting to the ruling. The credibility of the witness is at stake. This witness lied. This witness said that it was a sham when in fact, he knew it was a legitimate trust..."[9]

There were officers in the trust company who were convicted of crimes. Of course, the same can be said for Merrill Lynch and most other large

"I believe firmly and strongly that when you don't question authority, you are taking a tried and proven path to losing your freedoms."

companies. Does this make the company illegitimate? Even if it were, would this void the written trust? Of course not.

The IRS lumps the good in with the bad, the innocent with the guilty, and in fact, ends up convicting innocent people through its guilt by association tactics.

In the Brownlee case, several people confessed to violating tax code criminal statutes and agreed to testify against my client and her husband. Chappell quotes my trial objection in which I accused an IRS agent of dishonesty:

"I believe he lied to Mr. Betleum in order to get him to confess to a crime he wasn't guilty of. That is at issue. The Internal Revenue agent lied, I believe... I believe that the agent was dishonest, and I believe his credibility is at stake, and I believe originally Mr. Carpenter was misled...I believe Mr. Lafferty mislead Mr. Carpenter in that area."[10] *[Carpenter was the U.S. Attorney]*

The Illegal Tax Protester Manual also implies that people who attend public patriot meetings, or who gather in organized assemblies to redress grievances to the government are doing something wrong; in spite of the fact the First Amendment gives us the right to peaceably assemble and to petition our government with complaints.

One cannot assume, as the IRS apparently does, that because people are in the same room, attending the same patriotic meeting, that they share identical views. Perhaps, in a crowd of several hundred people in the Soviet Union or Cuba, an overwhelming majority might tend to agree on most major political and economic topics, but such a situation is hardly likely among a group of people who encourage the free interchange of ideas.

Most people I have met who attend patriot meetings do share a strong support for the Constitution and the Bill of Rights, but beyond that they are characterized by a strong spirit of American individuality. The patriots are not a monolithic, ideologically rubber stamped group. The members of the audience are generally well read. Most of them have attended several trials; thereby, helping to keep our system of public justice a little bit public. People in the audience pick and choose ideas that they wish to

---

"A federal judge in the Southern District of Texas was reported to have thundered at a 'failure to file' defendant, 'The Constitution is irrelevant in this courtroom!'"

---

adopt and reject those which they are not comfortable with.

About the only consistency that I have seen between meetings is that there is a high incidence of religious activity and patriotic fervor. It would be unusual to find an atheist attending these meetings. It would be unusual to find a communist in the crowd—unless he was a spy, or an undercover IRS agent. There is a strong sense of genuine inquiry and truth-seeking at these meetings.

By implying that all people who attend these patriotic meetings are doing something that is illegal, the Illegal Tax Protesters Manual is doing something that is un-American.

One of the strongest parts of this frightening training manual is in Section 4-3, where the IRS agent is cautioned:

> "If any of the following occurs during your contacts with the public, you may be dealing with an illegal tax   protester: You are questioned extensively about your authority and qualifications for conducting your work. This can be coupled with an attempt to engage you in a debate over the merits of the protest."

This tyrannical assumption is appalling. Individual freedom should be cherished. The First Amendment rights of freedom of assembly, freedom of speech and freedom of the press, and the American penchant for a good argument are precious. I believe firmly and strongly that when you don't question authority, you are taking a tried and proven path to losing your freedoms. When an official government publication implies that there is something wrong with questioning government authorities, our liberty has been alarmingly eroded.

Another characteristic the manual attributes to so-called tax protesters is:

> "insisting on being accompanied by numerous witnesses during meetings with service personnel. This serves to intimidate you and disrupt the office."

How sad! How naive! The IRS must fear its agents are quite weak, to be intimidated by a citizen they have summoned, just because he has brought along witnesses. That citizen may be facing civil or criminal prosecution based on statements which may be attributed to him, which may or may not be true. The witnesses are there solely for the citizen's protection. What does the IRS have to fear, especially in light of the admission in Section 4-4 that "most ITPs do not advocate violence." It makes one wonder whether IRS agents sleep with a night light on or check under their beds for mythical Posse Comitatus members. The tactic of individual interrogation has proven effective in many totalitarian countries. A man severed from his friends and neighbors becomes weaker.

Section 5-3 warns the IRS agent about "conversation about the constitutional dogma":

"Do not engage in any conversation regarding these subjects." The IRS agent is instructed not to discuss the Constitution of the United States.

A federal judge in the Southern District of Texas was reported to have thundered at a "failure to file" defendant, "The Constitution is irrelevant in this courtroom!"

When a failure to file case comes before a jury, and the defendant has relied on the unratified Sixteenth Amendment defense, judges routinely instruct the jurors that the amendment was properly ratified. On the other hand, many judges rule it can't even be discussed. This generally should constitute reversible error since the defendant is thus deprived of an opportunity to testify on issues relevant to his state of mind.

If an individual truly, honestly and legitimately believes that he is not required to file income tax returns because the Sixteenth Amendment is null and void, then under the spirit of the law the individual is technically innocent of the charges of willfully not filing a tax return. Unfortunately, this is no guarantee that he will be found not guilty. Failure to assert this defense will, however, practically guarantee a conviction. However, the individual could still be forced to pay all taxes and penalties for a civil judgment which does not require willfulness or an intentional violation of the law. The majority of the juries who have heard this defense—with the limitation of the instructions placed on them by the judges who strongly favor conviction—have found in favor of conviction.

Former Congressman George Hansen produced and distributed a video tape demonstrating some of the excesses of the IRS. His tape shows how the IRS has held children for ransom, broken into people's cars and homes, used massive displays of force in order to intimidate individuals, and arrested people who—even under the most flexible IRS guidelines— did not owe the alleged delinquent sums. According to ex-IRS agent, and founder of the IRS Whistleblowers' organization, Paul DesFosses, Hansen was set-up for an unfair conviction by IRS agents.

One blatant abuse of power took place when the IRS moved into a day care center and took all of the children hostage in order to collect tax money the day care center allegedly owed. When the parents came to pick up their children, they were forced to write out checks to the IRS for money they allegedly owed to the day care center, before they were allowed to claim their children.[10] Imagine the panic of the children! Imagine the fear of their parents as they submitted to this extortion.

American citizens must wake up to the grave threat to their liberty which the IRS represents.

It's sadly ironic that the President of the of the same government which issued the Illegal Tax Protester Manual spoke the following stirring words to a crowd in Oshkosh, WIsconsin, on May 30, 1985:

"America was born in the midst of a great revolution, sparked by oppressive taxation. There was something about the American character - open, hardworking and honest —that rebelled at the very thought of taxes that were not only heavy, but unfair.

Today the proud American character remains unchanged. But slowly and subtly, surrendering first to this political pressure and then to that, our system of taxation has turned into something completely foreign to our nature—something complicated, unfair, and in a fundamental sense, un- American." [11]

If Ronald Reagan had been an ordinary citizen, he might well have been branded with the TC148 code.

F. LAW AND PLUNDER

In an environment where law is worshipped and love of government is praised as a virtue, unscrupulous persons who wish to enrich themselves at the expense of those who create wealth through work may see government as a vehicle to achieve their personal goals.

In a democracy—where the tyranny of the majority is unchecked by strong, independent juries—the logical progression is for these parasites to buy votes. The funds to buy these votes are often obtained through the maintenance of a political machine which exists because of its ability to rob the working people.

"Under the pretense of organization, regulation, protection or encouragement, the law takes property from one person and gives it to another; the law takes the

wealth of all and gives it to a few—whether farmers, manufacturers, ship owners, artists or comedians. Under these circumstances, then certainly every class will aspire to grasp the law, and logically so."[12]

"As long as it is admitted that the law might be diverted from its true purpose—that it may violate property instead of protecting it—then everyone will want to participate in making the law, either to protect himself against plunder or to use it for plunder."[13]

Money, unfortunately, is not the only tool for the purchasing votes. Every evil mankind possesses—loving a free ride, racism, paganism—has enough supporters to form its own political group which can trade votes for favors. Such a trade labeled the escaped slave Dredd Scott as property and a non-person. It was appropriate and valuable to pay off racist policies with a political conviction. It could be done only without a free, impartial jury system.

In 1848, twelve years before the Civil War, Frederic Bastiat examined the American jurisprudence system, the American free enterprise system, and the American legal system and came to the conclusion that:

"...even in the United States, there are two issues—and only two—that have always endangered the public peace...What are these two issues? They are slavery and tariffs (taxes). These are the only two issues where, contrary to the general spirit of the Republic of the United States, law has assumed the character of a plunderer...Slavery is a violation, by law, of liberty. The protective tariff is a violation, by law, of property."[14]

The violation of these two human rights—and the attempted enforcement of an immoral law—would ultimately lead to the near destruction (by means of the Civil War) and in a more modern sense, the future disintegration of the American Republic (by means of income taxation). The Civil War was waged with one of its principal concerns being the immoral bondage of human beings in the service of other human beings without any form of compensation...slavery! The other form of involuntary servitude, a type of taxation which was evolving and which in Bastiat's time was still in the embryonic stage, was not re-spawned until 1913: the income tax!

Bastiat was prophetic when he indicated that the taxation process in the United States was going in the wrong direction. In 1895, less than 50 years after Bastiat wrote, the United States would pass the first income tax law—but at this time, the Supreme Court would throw it out. It would not become the law of the land—assuming you believe it ever became the law of the land—until 1913.

Bastiat examined two types of legal plunder, and a third, preferable alternative: one, the few plunder the many; two, everyone plunders everybody; three, nobody plunders anybody.

"(1) Limited legal plunder: this system prevailed when the right to vote was restricted. One would turn back to this system to prevent the invasion of socialism.

(2) Universal legal plunder: We have been threatened with this system since the franchise was made universal. The newly enfranchised majority has decided to formulate law on the same principle of legal plunder that was used by their predecessors when the vote was limited.

(3) No legal plunder: This is the principle of justice, peace, order, stability, harmony and logic". [15]

Bastiat cautioned us, we must remember that law is force:

"When law and force keep a person within the bounds of justice, they impose nothing but a mere negation. They oblige him only to abstain from harming others...You say, there are persons who have no money ,and you turn to the law. But the law is not a breast that fills itself with milk...Nothing can enter the public treasury for the benefit of one citizen or one class unless other citizens and other classes have been forced to send it in...The law can be an instrument of equalization only as it takes from some persons and gives to other persons. When the law does this, it is an instrument of plunder." [16]

Bastiat believed that legislators—who desired to redistribute income from those who earned it to certain supposedly deserving individuals—secretly despised the general run of humanity and felt vastly superior to the average citizen.

"According to Socialist writers, it is indeed fortunate that Heaven has be-

---

"The 9-to-5 worker is a virtual part-time slave working a third of the year to pay federal income taxes, and much of the rest of the year paying property, sales, gasoline, and other hidden taxes. "

---

stowed upon certain men—governors and legislators—the exact opposite inclinations, not only for their own sake but also for the sake of the rest of the world! While mankind tends toward evil, the legislators yearn for good; while mankind advances toward darkness, the legislators aspire for enlightenment; while mankind is drawn toward vice, the legislators are attracted toward virtue. Since they have decided that this is the true state of affairs, they then demand the use of force in order to substitute their own inclinations for those of the human race...What is liberty? In short, is not liberty the freedom of every person to make full use of his faculties, so long as he does not harm other persons while doing so?... I do not dispute their right to invent social combinations, to advertise them, to advocate them, and to try them upon themselves, at their own expense and risk. But I do **dispute their right to impose these plans upon us by law—by force— and to compel us to pay for them with our taxes."[17]**

Bastiat decried the tendency of citizens to press for financial boons from public funds administered by the legislature. He attempted to portray the absurdity of such actions:

"Have the people ever been known to rise against the court of appeals or mob a justice of the peace, in order to get higher wages, free credit, tools of production, favorable tariffs, or government—created jobs? Everyone knows perfectly well that such matters are not within the jurisdiction of the court of appeals or a justice of the peace. If government were limited to its proper functions, everyone would soon learn that these matters are not within the jurisdictions of the law itself." [18]

The country began its economic tax decline in 1913. Congress passed the first statutes legalizing lawful national plunder against individuals on a communal basis: the income tax. It began as a two percent tax and accelerated past the wildest dreams of its authors until it reached a climax around 1928.

In 1929 the country reached other heights in the diminishment of human freedoms as it traveled towards a socialist economy—rewarding the nonproductive, taxing the productive.

The economy got worse. Our government needed a legal cure. The legislators created magic money and started pumping it into the economy at a large rate. The great wealth of this nation deteriorated from the time of Andrew Jackson—who had a surplus in the treasury—to a deficit budget under Roosevelt.

Roosevelt's New Deal philosophy was, "If you need something, the government will give it to you." Since the government didn't make anything, didn't build anything, didn't create anything, the only way it could give it to you was by taking it away from you and other people.

The very rich and very powerful refused to participate in this system of plunder unless they too could be plunderers. They operated huge, large scale munitions plants and other factories and began selling products to the government.

The poor, the least fortunate, and the least capable saw the New Deal as a remarkable opportunity to band together in democracy and dispossess the wealthy of their goods.

Unfortunately for them, the extremely powerful and wealthy controlled their own politicians. Large groups of poorer people locked together in democratic institutions and created power blocs in order to plunder. Who did they plunder? Since the overwhelming majority of the masses and the workers were in the middle classes and were not organized, they were plundered.

A newly formed two-headed monster, a grotesque hybrid of the interests of the poor and the extremely wealthy, had been spawned to plunder the middle class and working class, turning them into slaves.

Our society has evolved into a comical-tragic situation. While the federal reserve system manipulates the value of currency and manipulates the lives of the 9-to-5 workers, the workers give thanks that they are able to accumulate enough funds to pay another monthly mortgage. The 9-to-5 worker is a virtual part-time slave, working a third of the year to pay federal income taxes and much of the rest of the year paying property, sales, gasoline and other hidden taxes.

Taxes are used in a two-fold plundering process: A) The politically powerful or wealthy—who control government and politicians through their purse strings—receive their share of the plunder, and B) those at the other end of the scale receive their share of the plunder through welfare-type schemes. The middle class gets squeezed dry in the process.

It is harder and harder for someone from the middle class to rise into the elite class. The harder it gets to climb the socio-economic ladder, the more members of the middle class realize that they need to align them-

"The majority of the taxpayers believe that as long as they play by the rules, hire a competent accountant, and file properly, they are safe. Nothing could be further from the truth."

selves with one of the two dominant groups, thus polarizing the fabric of society. For the most part, they realize that they are not capable of aligning with the upper class—since only a small portion of them, through luck or extreme industry, are able to join that elite class.

Thus, a great portion of the middle class tends to join the lower classes in order to become part of plundering operations.

The Republican and Democratic parties have legislated smaller political parties out of existence. Each of the national parties receives a portion of tax moneys for its treasuries. Each of the national parties possesses enormous control over tax revenues. Ajay Lowery, former presidential candidate, and publisher of *The Justice Times* has coined a creature called an "Eledonkephant" to symbolize his concept of our two major parties as one mammoth beast which produces large amounts of manure: the national deficit.

Both parties appeal to their various constituencies. The Republican Party appeals primarily to the upper classes through its traditional aristocratic image. The Democratic Party traditionally marshals the support of the lower classes and ethnic minorities. Both parties are in a constant see-saw struggle to plunder the middle class. Obviously the Republican Party does not mind plundering the lower classes. The lower classes, through the Democratic Party, eagerly plunder the upper classes. Since the middle class has no protector at all, it's easier to align against them.

What is the ultimate effect? The unfortunate effect is that fewer and fewer people are willing—or able—to be part of the middle class which is the backbone of this country.

On October 3, 1913, Congress passed the first income tax regulations based on the Sixteenth Amendment. The floor meetings and arguments are quite interesting. Some Senators feared that the tax rate, which varied between one percent and six percent in 1913, would be increased once the camel had gotten his nose under the tent with the passage of the law.

Other Senators, including William F. Borah of Idaho, were offended by these fears. "Who," he asked, "could impose such socialistic confiscatory

---

"The average American, struggling just to stay even, pays one third or more of his income in taxes while some of the richest individuals and largest and most profitable corporations in the country pay no tax at all. The average American will work 121 days this year just to pay his taxes."

---

rates?" Looking back over the last 75 years, we could tell him, and tell him, and tell him.

Congress, acting on its new power—assuming the Sixteenth Amendment was constitutional—created a one percent income tax on October 3, 1913. It was a graduated income tax, ranging from one percent to a maximum of up to six percent up to the first $500,000 in income. After that there was no additional taxation.

Today, we have the Social Security tax which calls for a direct seven percent paid by each employee. The employer pays an additional seven percent that creates the fiction that the employee is only paying half of the costs of Social Security.

As a matter of fact, the entire amount ultimately comes out of the employee's pocket. If the employer did not have to pay anything to social security, he could have increased the employee's salary by that amount.

Thus, we have a 14 percent minimum tax for poverty level workers, and the tables at the bottom of the income tax 1040 supplement schedules (1986 figures) quickly show us that the overwhelming majority of Americans—even at poverty level—pay more than this 20 percent tax which had been so dreaded by an earlier generation of legislators.

Today, the American taxpayer complies and pays because he's simply afraid. The majority of the taxpayers believe that as long as they play by the rules, hire a competent accountant, and file properly, they are safe. Nothing could be further from the truth.

When the little guy is hit by the IRS, he is hit hard. The little guy does not know how to defend himself against this Colossus. His cars are stolen; his home is seized; he is doomed to financial ruin and sometimes even prison. Astonishingly, a large number of major, anti-tax authors have been imprisoned: Tupper Saussy, Irwin Schiff, George Hansen and Robert Chappell, have all been indicted and convicted.

The facts of life often hit home when a taxpayer has his first encounter with the IRS. The auditor may question every number on his tax return, demand the backup paper work for every minute item, and let the taxpayer know that his honesty and respect for the law are being seriously questioned.

"Inheritance taxes make a mockery of the lives of successful people who pay off a home to leave it to their children or run a small or large business in order to leave it to their children."

The reaction of Mr. Naive Taxpayer is usually the same: "How can this be happening to me? I'm a nice, law abiding guy. Can't the tax man see that. How can this sort of thing be happening in America?"

The average American, struggling just to stay even, pays one third or more of his income in taxes while some of the richest individuals and largest and most profitable corporations in the country pay no tax at all. The average American will work 121 days this year just to pay his taxes.

On a daily basis, the typical worker must put in two hours and 40 minutes of an eight-hour day to pay all of his taxes. In 1929, the average person worked just 40 days a year to pay his total yearly tax levies.

On the other hand, former Vice President Nelson Rockefeller, a multimillionaire, paid no federal income tax for several years running. John D. Rockefeller, III, pays ten percent federal tax as a matter of personal principle. Apparently, he can manipulate his tax exemptions to produce whatever return he feels is appropriate. Texas oil billionaire Bunker Hunt managed to live in luxury for many years without paying any income taxes at all.

An often unfortunate irony is that the cooperative taxpayer fares much worse than the individual who relies on his constitutional rights. Cooperation is dangerous.

If the government, for whatever reason, wants to bankrupt an individual or a company, it will find a way to accomplish its goal. Chappell points out:

"The Government of the United States can act only through its agents. Many of its agents are young attorneys who would kill their grandmothers or put someone out of business in order to get their names in the newspaper."[19]

Of course, the federal probate taxes operate under the theory that wealth after death should be confiscated and not left to your children. Crusading lawyer Milton Friedman, in his televised reports, "Free to Choose: A Personal Statement," asked some very important questions. There are those who think it is not fair for some children to start out with

"The greatest amount of our taxation budget does not go to welfare. It goes to buy $3,000 nuts which we can pick up in the hardware store for a few pennies. It goes to buy $700 toilet seats. It goes to build giant, billion-dollar ships which have already been proven to be obsolete."

large amounts of wealth and other children to start out with nothing, "but is there any distinction between the inheritance of property and the inheritance of what at first sight looks very different: inherited talent?"

Some youngsters have inherited wealth not in the form of bonds or stocks, but in the form of talent...Yet many people resent the one, but not the other. If you want to give your child a special chance, there are different ways to do it. Buy him or her an education, buy him or her a business, buy him or her property. "Is there any ethical difference between these ways...of using your property? Or, again, if the state leaves you any money to spend over and above taxes, should you be permitted to spend it on riotous living, but not permitted to leave it to your children?"[20]

As a human species, perhaps the most important and desirable thing about us is our love of family and our family unity. One of the prime motivations to strive for progress, found new businesses, invent new products or increase agricultural output is the desire to make a better life for our children. Progressive, high inheritance taxes can thwart that ambition. Most people assume that a fair share of their estate will be inherited by their children. Inheritance taxes make a mockery of the lives of successful people who pay off a home to leave it to their children or run a small or large business in order to leave it to their children.

G. DEVALUED CURRENCY; DEVALUED WORK; HIDDEN TAXES

We followed the path of England, Spain, and the Roman Empire when we took ourselves off of a sound currency system—which was mandated by the U.S. Constitution. Removing the country from a sound currency system is, in itself, one of the most insidious taxes that exists. It punishes thrift and rewards living in luxury from future revenues.

Franklin would now have to say a penny saved is no longer a penny earned but a foolish outdated concept. A penny saved is a penny soon diminished.

If the government can say what currency is, if the government can ig-

"Occasionally the press or some whistleblower within the bureaucracy issues a report showing that contractors are stealing money wholesale by charging ridiculous and outlandish prices for common hardware items or by being allowed to have cost overruns on their contracts. Still, nothing is done."

nore Article 3, Section 5, then the government is free to print as much money as it wants. We were unconstitutionally taken off the gold standard; then we were taken off the silver standard. When we left the silver standard, no standard was put in its place. There is now no backing for the United States dollar except in our imaginations.

Abraham Lincoln foresaw an even greater danger to the country than the Civil War. He stated that the greatest danger to the Union was the lure of government money for government jobs for people without working. Lincoln's fears have been realized.

However, even Lincoln could not have anticipated that government outlays would exceed assets. Lincoln was afraid that the growing number of recipients of comfortable government appointments would wreck the Union by taking all of its money. Lincoln could not have predicted that a quarter of a century later the friends of paper money would merge to form a powerful block and ultimately, over 100 years later, would sell out the future of the country by mortgaging it with paper debt.

We tend to look up to our senators and our congressmen as successful human beings. These people have not become successful by the sweat of their brow or through creating inventions or by raising the standard of living for individuals. What do senators and congressmen do? They pass laws. That's all they do—other than trying to stay in office and collecting revenues so that they can campaign for re-election.

What do the laws do? Laws, basically, do the following things:

A) *They restrict our freedoms;*
B) *At times, they tend to restore freedoms that they previously restricted;*
C) *They take our money;*
D) *They spend our money;*
E) *They provide for the general welfare;*
F) *They provide for the common defense.*

There isn't anything else that they can do. Under the guise of providing for the general welfare, our laws have provided for the general welfare of a select few. They have provided for the general welfare of some people who will not work. They have provided for the general welfare of people

---

"Originally bid contract prices have no meaning whatsoever because our kind government will allow them to charge, double charge, and recharge."

---

who will steal.

The greatest amount of our taxation budget does not go to welfare. It goes to buy $3,000 nuts which we can pick up in the hardware store for a few pennies. It goes to buy $700 toilet seats. It goes to build giant, billion-dollar ships which have already been proven to be obsolete.

How does this happen? Pure and simple: human greed.

If we have no fixed standard for the creation of wealth, other than how much money the government can print, there is every reason to assume that people who have put themselves into office for their own personal gain will continue to print up, wholesale, vast amounts of this currency and line their own—and their friends'—pockets with a considerable portion. Why not? Nobody cares. Nobody watches over them.

Occasionally the press or some whistleblower within the bureaucracy issues a report showing that contractors are stealing money wholesale by charging ridiculous and outlandish prices for common hardware items or by being allowed to have cost overruns on their contracts. Still, nothing is done.

Originally bid contract prices have no meaning whatsoever because our kind government will allow them to charge, double charge, and re-charge. If you want to bid on a government contract which allows you cost overruns, you can guarantee, if you're dishonest, that you will be the lowest bidder. Simply bid half of the cost for actually producing the work. You will succeed in underbidding and undercutting all the honest bidders who will charge the actual cost plus 10 to 15 percent profit. Then, after you get the job, quadruple the cost with cost overruns which you could not have originally anticipated.

After all, who would have ever suspected that you intentionally and knowingly made a bid which was less than your actual cost for producing the product? Why do the costs always overrun? The answer is obvious: because it's profitable and because it's built into the contracts. If the congressmen or senators cared anything about the value of work or the economic soundness of our country, they wouldn't allow these cost overrun contracts to exist.

Economist John Kenneth Galbraith, who subsequently admitted that he was mistaken, stated,

"It doesn't matter how high the national debt becomes. We only owe it to ourselves. The American people are not intelligent enough to spend their own money; therefore, the Government should take it away from people (through taxes) and

spend it for them."[21]

Most IRS personnel and government employees awarding contracts still operate under the theory Galbraith repudiated.

For years, I considered myself a civil rights lawyer. An uninformed friend of mine who apparently is unaware that civil rights violations still exist, remarked that I was a civil rights lawyer in the 80s with no place to go—so I started defending people against the IRS. I do defend people against the IRS, but civil rights violations still occur daily. Age discrimination is perhaps the most heinous, but sexual harassment of women at work, and discrimination against blacks, Hispanics, orientals and Jews, while diminished, still looms powerful in places and still subtly lowers the quality of life for everyone.

The single greatest threat to our freedom, the Constitution, and the American way of life is not the Soviet Union or Red China—it is the IRS and the tax code.

Nothing is sacred to them. They have cut the heart out of our Bill of Rights. People are put on the dreaded TC-148 list for exercising their freedom of speech against government excesses, as set forth in the First Amendment: "Congress shall make no law...abridging freedom of speech or of the press; or the right of people to assemble, and to petition the government for the redress of grievances."

Citizens are required to divulge private facts about their houses and effects when they have not even been accused of a crime. Yet, the Fourth Amendment says: "The right of the people to be secure in their persons, houses, papers, and effects, against unreasonable searches and seizures shall not be violated." This amendment was included by a people familiar with the tyranny of government and British soldiers who felt free to enter anyone's home for any reason. Our forefathers demanded protection from these intrusions.

People are brought to trial without being indicted and are compelled to sign the 1040's under penalty of perjury—thus testifying against themselves. Their property is confiscated by the IRS often before trial. Yet, the Fifth Amendment says: "No person shall be held to answer for...infamous

"The single greatest threat to our freedom, the Constitution, and the American way of life is not the Soviet Union or Red China —it is the IRS and the tax code."

crime, unless on...indictment of a grand jury,...nor shall be compelled in any criminal matter to testify against himself, nor be deprived ...of...property, without due process of law..."

Trial by jury on civil tax matters is gone (unless you pay the bounty in advance), and you face a tax court judge who was previously approved by the IRS. Yet the Seventh Amendment says: "In suits at common law, where the value in controversy shall exceed twenty dollars, the right of trial by jury shall be preserved,..."

Article I, Section 9 states in relevant part "No bill of attainder or ex post facto law shall be passed." An ex post facto law is a law passed made retroactive. Yet every tax act passed in the last eight years has had some retroactive provisions—and by interpreting the acts after they are passed, years later, the IRS changes them. Many Americans take a deduction only to learn a year later, it is being retroactively removed.

Article I, Section 9 also states, "No tax or duty shall be laid on articles exported from any state."

Of all of the violations against human freedoms this one is the most hidden, but the most destructive of our national ability to compete internationally and thus make a living.

The violations of basic freedoms sanctioned by the judiciary with regard to the Bill of Rights is clear, ongoing, and by and large ignored by the public. Drug dealers, rapists, and murderers are not subjected to the vicious denial of due process of those put on the TC-148 list.

The only real tax that exists is a consumption tax. If Farmer Brown withheld 15 percent—half from laborer Felix, half from himself for social security and then and 20 percent for income taxes—this 35 percent is part of the cost of doing business. Since Farmer Brown must make a profit, he adds it to his basic costs.

If Felix gets $1,000 per month in salary, he gets $1,000 minus $75 deducted for Social Security, and minus another $200 for income tax, and he ends up with $725. That's Felix's real income. All Felix has to live on is $725. But even though Felix only gets $725, Farmer Brown's real cost is $1,075, which is Felix's original $1,000 plus another $75 for his portion of Felix's Social Security tax. That's what Farmer Brown must pay.

Assume that Farmer Brown's total costs, including labor—both his own and his employee's—for X amount of grain is $2,150.00. Of that amount, $550 is for taxes. The pre-tax cost is $1,600. In real life of course, the equations are more complicated and the taxes are higher.

In most European Commonwealth countries, there is a flat consumption tax called the value-added tax. It's like a sales tax. Labor may appear to cost less, but that's untaxed labor. American labor without income taxes is actually less expensive than most commonwealth countries.

Farmer Schultz's German customers pay the value-added tax. If it cost Schultz $1,600 to make X grain his local customers pay an extra $550 value added tax.

When Farmer Brown sells his goods at cost to Farmer Schultz's customers, he must charge $2,150. However, when Farmer Schultz sells his goods to Farmer Brown's customers, his government refunds the value added tax giving Farmer Schultz an economic market advantage from $1,600 to $2,150.

Actually, it costs Schultz more than Brown; he's not as efficient and the real price is about $1,800 to $2,150 or 16 percent less. Adding all the other income tax costs, Schultz's product is approximately a 20% bargain compared to Brown's. Many governments actually pay their producers to sell abroad giving them another five to 10 percent advantage.

Can you guess why Farmer Brown is going belly up? Why are American cars having trouble competing? Instead of a subsidy like other governments give, we pay a huge tax penalty—because of all the income taxes on all forms of labor that go into producing any American product.

Do we help the poor by not having a sales tax on food? Absolutely not. Farmer Brown has already stuck his tax bill into your loaf of bread and the rich, poor and middle class all pay when they buy.

As it is now, consumption is actually taxed. It is just done in a dishonest, round-about way that no one really understands. Yet, to protest this insanity sounds unpatriotic.

Can you guess why the nation's founders did not want to tax exports? Is Congress and the IRS tricking us, themselves or everyone else? You can bet your tax refund no one is fooling the rest of the world. They buy the best deal. The label "Made In America" used to mean high quality. Now it means high prices with hidden export taxes and even Americans are buying electronics, cars, hardware and computers from every other nation that undersells us.

"Lowering the corporation tax will encourage foreign investment and hopefully an international competition to lower taxes."

H. THE NEWEST NEW TAX CODE: ANCIENT HISTORY BEFORE IT WAS SIGNED

I hesitate to write this portion of the chapter because it will become obsolete by 1990 and this book first published in late 1989 is not intended to be outdated in two short years. Nevertheless I will in this brief section join the thousands who will interpret for profit the 1986 brand new, better-than-brand- X, improved income tax code.

In December of 1986, Congress passed with President Reagan's blessings the 1986 Tax Code. It provided that most of the 1,000- plus pages of changes will be phased in over three years, with some taking effect over a much longer span. This legislation was the most sweeping overhaul since the 1954 Tax Act.

The Revenue Act of 1987, passed December 22, 1987, made changes in the 1986 act, just as Congress had been making changes in the 1954 act for over three decades. However, to make things even more exciting, the Revenue Act of 1954 was not totally replaced. Parts of it remained. What is the law? First, read and interpret the new law. Then, figure out the new regulations relating to it. Then, see if part of the old law, unreplaced, overlaps, and if the old regulations apply. Then wait, because much of the new law hasn't been interpreted yet, and you can only guess what it means. Then, thank your Congressman. He outdid himself in 1986.

Every president elected in recent history has campaigned in part on promises of a fairer tax structure, which every individual citizen takes to mean "lower for him, higher for someone else and less confusing for everyone."

When Mondale promised higher taxes, we believed him. He failed to carry even his home state. No one who pays taxes considers higher taxes to be fair, unless he is a politician.

The administration was concerned about the current rebellion which was allowing a growing amount of untaxed wealth to change hands in the so called underground economy—which is not related to The Underground Lawyer. Disenchanted taxpayers felt cheated because the system was too complicated and unfair. President Reagan's call for a second American revolution to overhaul the tax system was enthusiastically

"Children over the age of five are now required to obtain Social Security numbers and submit social security identification."

received by all who were naive enough to believe that reform was really possible without dismantling the IRS system and starting from scratch.

It's possible that no one read the full text of the 1986 Tax Act before it was signed. Who among our illustrious politicians had the time and the requisite background to understand it? Not any of the experts, that's for sure.

Lawyers, CPAs and financial planners will reap fortunes helping people decipher the new, simple tax code.

As bad as the 1954 tax code was, appeals were faster, bureaucrats were fewer, and regulations fewer. With the backlog of appeals, the million-plus bureaucrats and the certified public accountants and lawyers, this time it will be more confusing.

The good news is that if there are no changes in 1988, there will be only two tax brackets compared to 14 in 1985. However, they must be phased in; 1987 actually has more varied tax brackets than 1985. The other good news is that taxes appear to be lower. Americans are typically so industrious that the mere suggestion we might be able to keep more of what we earn is an incentive to start working harder. Because taxes appear to be lower, we will produce more. More loopholes were taken out than put in. You decide if that's a blessing or a curse.

Lowering the corporation tax will encourage foreign investment and hopefully an international competition to lower taxes.

The rest is mostly bad news. New loopholes are being lobbied in Congress right now! There are fewer safeguards to protect against IRS abuses. Penalties and fines are stricter and harsher. Children over the age of five are now required to obtain Social Security numbers and submit social security identification.

All real estate transactions must now be reported. Millions more will be spent to pay for the paper. Entertaining business clients will be only 80 percent deductible. Restaurants will have trouble with this, and quite possibly a black market will flourish to create higher food bills. The food industry will spend millions to change this law.

While taxes appear to be lowered, they are actually about the same. Corporations pick up the slack and pass the increases back to us in the form of higher prices. The increasing deficit will cause more printing press money to be created. The temporary lull in inflation will give rise to a new dramatic fall in the dollar. Temporarily, American goods will be easier to sell. We'll witness a short term better trade balance. New tax loopholes will be created, this time only by extremely powerful lobbies. The price of being a politician will go up.

To this date, there's no way of telling how many special exemptions have been written into the new tax code for those favored by our politicians. If newspaper accounts that I have seen are any indication, there could be thousands, or the two I've seen could be all—but that's not likely. It is likely that those are only two of the many that have been brought to the public's attention throughout the country.

These are excellent examples of how the tax code was revised in 1986 to the advantage of the politically powerful, and to the disadvantage of the average taxpayer.

First, newspaper articles out of Little Rock, Arkansas reveal what's called a chicken war between two major, national companies that market chicken products. Tyson Foods of Springdale, Arkansas—owned by Democrat Don Tyson, and sister- in-law Barbara Tyson—is a $1.7 billion business with 25,000 employees and is probably the largest chicken producer and processor in the country. Don's friends in Washington put a special exemption in the tax bill that allows Tyson to compute its taxes as if it was a "family farm." This means that Don, who's worth $400 million and Barbara, who's worth $325 million, are allowed to defer indefinitely the payment of $135 million in taxes.

Tyson's biggest competitor, Charles M. Harper of Omaha who's runs the $1 billion ConAgra chicken company doesn't have Don's friends in Washington. Harper didn't get the special exemption and had to pay his taxes.

Harper, a Republican, was not too chicken to take his beef to Congress. The tax writers agreed to end Tyson's exemption, but it has cost taxpayers an estimated $700 million already.[22]

In another case, a 75-year-old widow of a prominent Fort Worth businessman, who has a personal friend in Congress, had her own private designer loophole customized for her. Geraldine Ballard lives in a exclusive Forth Worth residential district in a house valued at $600,000. It is part of an estate left by her late husband worth an estimated $12.5 million. Pending before Congress in 1988—while it was revising the loophole-filled 1986 tax code—is an exemption tailored specifically for Mrs. Ballard that allows her husband's estate to avoid an estimated $4 million in fed-

"CPAs and accountants administer our tax system. Without them, we'd face the likelihood that government servants would be calculating our taxes."

eral income taxes. The following legislation has been proposed to amend the new act:

"For purposes of Section 2656 (b) (8) of the Internal Revenue Code of 1986, an individual who received an interest in a charitable remainder unitrust shall be deemed to be the only non-charitable beneficiary of such trust if the interest in the trust passed to the individual under the will of a decedent who resided in Tarrant County, Texas and died on October 28, 1983 at the age of seventy-five (75), with a gross estate not exceeding TWELVE MILLION FIVE HUNDRED THOUSAND AND NO/100 DOLLARS ($12,500,000.00), and the individual is the decedent's surviving spouse."

Re-read the preceding section again, ignoring the gobbledygook and the fiction that this loophole is written in general terms for anyone to whom the facts would happen to apply.. How many people died on October 28, 1983, age seventy- five (75) with $12.5 million and a complex trust? Guess? None other than Joseph Ballard, Geraldine Ballard's dear departed spouse! Her savings stand to be in the neighborhood of $4,000,000.00![23]

The newspaper article describing the pending exemption, described it as "one of scores of similar special-interest deals awaiting congressional action." There are over 650 of these exemptions now known. The Joneses down the street don't get them. The names are concealed to protect the lucky. It takes political stroke to be so lucky. It's an example, one of many, of the dishonesty of our tax system, reformed or unreformed, which begs for a sales tax, the only way to avoid rampant theft and political distribution of money, benefits and privileges.

The alleged goals were no more loop holes, the end to shelters, slower depreciation, tougher loss provisions. Were these goals achieved? Let's look at another example.

Congress decided to give $1 billion to native Alaskans plus a whole lot of land to help them out. Alaskans have no state income tax so they clearly need federal help. The money was put into 12 corporations and many Alaskans received stock simply because they were Alaskans. In a transaction jeered at in 1867 as "Seward's folly," the United States purchased

---

"The CPA's credentials make him the most respected tax preparer. If he has a business degree or advanced degree in accounting, finance or economics, that's an additional plus. His job is to prepare accounting work."

Alaska from the Russians. Now, more than 120 years later, under the new tax code, we are buying Alaska again.

This deal beats out the Panama Canal give-back for sheer folly. Most of the shareholders of these native corporations lost everything to con artists that came to Alaska like a windstorm sweeping over the vast icy regions to grab free federal bucks. They bought cancer cures and Florida swamp land and oil and gas rights on the moon.

In 1983 Chugach Alaska Corporation received coal deposits and timber from the federal government which were appraised high and sold low in 1987. This allowed them to report a huge paper loss even though all of the actual sold land was profit because it had been a tax free gift.

The 1986 tax reform act allowed native Alaska corporations to *sell* their losses. Chugach sold its losses for $48 million. Estimates are—the exact figures are kept secret—that the losses were $125 million.[25]

Congress helped out these struggling companies and also allowed big companies to buy big tax write-offs. Manipulation over? Ridiculous. With this transaction Congress rewarded mega- business and mega-incompetence and will charge the American middle who is generally unrepresented.

In 1990 the new improved tax code will be modified. By 2000 the so-called historical change will be largely unremembered history—soon to be totally forgotten by most.

The new code became effective in 1987, meaning that April 15, 1988 was the first time that the average citizen had to come to grips with it. Considering extensions that are often granted, some personal returns under the 1986 law were not due until October, 1988.

However, before the ink was dried, the 1987 Tax Act was passed changing laws before they became effective. Immediately, bureaucrats began rewriting the IRS regulations interpreting the new law. Anyone who tells you he understands it is lying. In fact, many of the federal judges who will ultimately tell us what it means have not been appointed yet. IRS personnel will give conflicting advice to taxpayers. Disputes will arise which the courts will interpret. Why have a tax code so complicated and ambiguous that it needs constant interpretation—like it was written in a foreign language? No one, not even the drafters, knows its meaning.

"Perfect accounting cannot guarantee you'll never be audited. Perfect lawyering cannot guarantee you won't get sued and have to go to court."

We all know its purposes; simplicity, and less manipulation. A fifth grader can tell you how simple it is. What about manipulation? The last overhaul created more confusion and inequities than ever before. The political pay-backs and give- aways were increased. Spending increased.

The new tax reform act signals a new age of more and faster new tax laws.

I. CPAs: WHO NEEDS THEM?

Certified Public Accountants (CPAs) are accountants who have fulfilled certain state regulations, testing, education, and in most states some type of continuing education and received the "approval" of the state. Their unions are not as powerful as the bar association or medical association, so: A) they do not control competition as well, and B) they often make less money.

CPAs and lawyers have been known to fight like doctors and lawyers, real estate brokers and lawyers, lawyers and lawyers, and cats and dogs. Why? First, lawyers fight with everyone. Second, lawyers and CPAs often compete in the gray areas not under total lawyer control and in some not-so-gray-areas.

CPAs and accountants administer our tax system. Without them, we'd face the likelihood that government servants would be calculating our taxes. Without accountants, the so-called voluntary system would break down in a week. CPAs collect money for the government.

CPAs compete with mere accountants like lawyers compete with mere legal assistants. CPAs sometimes compete with lawyers. They give advice: economic, numerical and legal. Some states permit CPAs to set up corporations. Since both CPAs and lawyers charge fees for these services, they sometimes attack each other.

Knowing all this, do you deal with CPAs or stay away from them? If you are in the system, you deal with them.

The CPA's credentials make him the most respected tax preparer. If he has a business degree or advanced degree in accounting, finance or economics, that's an additional plus. His job is to prepare accounting work. His signature and his designation carry some weight. A lawyer—even

---

"If you can afford long term tax planning, consult privately with a lawyer, then with a CPA. Use their expertise to manage your affairs effectively."

---

with tax certification or extra degrees is usually not trained specifically in filling out the forms with the numbers. There are thousands of inexpensive CPAs who use computers efficiently and who will fill out your returns and later back you up.

If you end up in litigation, the person who filled out the form would be your witness. Thus, even if he were an attorney, he would not represent you in a criminal or civil trial. If you have the resources, I recommend hiring a CPA.

What qualifications should you look for in a CPA? For a criminal trial, your CPA must work through your lawyer if you have one. The best are people with private and public accounting experience and a decade of work inside the IRS. To be an expert witness in a criminal tax trial, the CPA must be knowledgeable on the inner workings of the IRS and able to fill out the forms. In a civil trial, your CPA should be familiar with the forms, have at least ten years of experience preparing forms, and have handled at least 20 contested hearings or audits. IRS experience is not necessary. Your CPA needs to be a good, confident-sounding witness.

For day-to-day, year-to-year work, I prefer CPAs who have not worked for the IRS. Although I've met, trusted implicitly and worked with many CPAs who are former IRS employees. Unless I know them personally, I would be concerned about their long-term loyalty and perspective.

You should look for CPAs who will not back down from a position they believe in. They should keep up with all new deductions and subscribe to several services. They should be competitively priced and give annual maximum estimates. Your CPA should be on your side. If you want clean records, you need a clean CPA.

There are a lot of con-artists out there. If your CPA grins at you like the Cheshire cat and tells you you'll never get caught doing things like deducting your girl friend's bikinis as a necessary medical expense, writing off his bill for advice, or hiding the matter from your wife as a necessary legal expense—you may be dealing with a con-artist. If you have no current girlfriend or wife, you may be dealing with an incompetent con-artist.

If he answers the question, "Can you guarantee I'll never be audited?" affirmatively, then you *are* dealing with a liar. Perfect accounting cannot guarantee you'll never be audited. Perfect lawyering cannot guarantee you won't get sued and have to go to court.

"According to recent government statistics, 34 percent of government revenues come from income taxes."

A trial is a fight, and so is an audit or civil review. The better your help, the better your odds of winning. With a CPA's signature on the return and assistance at audit, your odds of winning are greater no matter how good or bad your papers are filed. If there is a substantial likelihood of civil or criminal litigation, you should have a lawyer available at all times.

If you can afford long-term tax planning, consult privately with a lawyer, then with a CPA. Use their combined expertise to manage your affairs effectively. One or two hours of each, separately could be worth a lot. You might even play them off against each other. If they are both good and if your business justifies it, get them together. Each may carry malpractice insurance. If they do, it's your policy also at no extra charge.

Don't pay a lawyer to calculate your returns. Don't even use the best CPA in the firm to do that! Pay the highest hourly rates for the brains; let the staff personnel paid at the lowest rate calculate on the computer.

If your CPA is cautious about the IRS and has some contacts there, that's healthy. If he's afraid of the IRS or has too close personal ties with the agency's employees, that's bad. If your protector is a coward, you're not very safe.

Most audits are short and routine and can be handled by your CPA or lawyer alone. You don't need to be there. All you can do is open up doors. However, if your CPA or lawyer is not on your side, you could be negotiated away.

The worst CPAs or lawyers are *not* the ones who trade your life away because they are selling you out for favors or a reward—that's very rare— the worst ones flush you down the drain because they can be easily convinced you are wrong, or they are scared, or worse, they don't even know what your goals are because they were too stupid to figure them out.

A lot of the rules on CPAs are like doctors or lawyers or any other professional. Some are good, some are bad, some are very bad.

For a *small fee*, even a simple return can use the added protection of a CPA's signature. For any type of potential tax litigation, anything less than a CPA for potential testimony is foolish. Paying legal fees, for basic accounting work is money down the toilet.

The big firm? The medium firm? The small firm?

"The ridiculous part about the graduated income tax is that the extremely wealthy and extremely clever have never paid it."

My vote is almost always the small firm. You can know your CPA on a first name basis, and he can know your files. I recently saw a brief, one-page corporate franchise return which involves no federal tax expertise. My legal assistant filled it out, and I proof read it. I had asked the client *not* to bring it to me. My office does not fill out tax forms, but the client insisted. The client was a source of a lot of money to me, so I agreed. The client paid $200 for about 15 minutes work.

The next year the client returned with the same easy-to-prepare form for the same inactive corporation. I told him about the minimal amount of work it involved, and that I would charge him $400. He said, "Go ahead." To make my point more emphatically, I filled the form out while he waited, copying the previous year's form. I handed it to him five minutes later. "Did I make my point?" I asked? "No," he replied. "My CPA charged me $2,500 two years ago. I'll be back next year."

I referred him to a new CPA.

Many of the larger CPA firms are billing factories just like the larger law firms. You pay for prestige and possibly connections. If you need this kind of power, go for it. If not, save your money. Get better service and go for the smaller CPA firm.

A CPA should pitch you for your business by showing you how much time, tax money, and anxiety he can save you. If on top of that, this professional can offer some additional sound advice on other aspects of your business and personal finances instead of just on taxes. That's a bonus. Look for it.

J. HIGHLIGHTS OF THE OMNIBUS TAXPAYER

The grand designs implied by the name of the "historic tax bill" called the "Omnibus Taxpayer Bill of Rights" is misleading. The act lacks the teeth originally promised when it was fighting through Congress to the President's desk. It has a title full of sound and fury implying far-reaching changes pretending to be on a par with our original Bill of Rights; but the body of the Bill signifies far less than its name promises. Paraphrasing Texas Senator Lloyd Bentson who told Vice-Presidential candidate Dan Quayle in their famous campaign debate, "Senator, you're no Jack

---

"As an alternative to the present system, we can abolish the income tax and replace it with the European system of a value-added tax."

Kennedy" we could say to this new act "Bill, you're no Bill of Rights." Nevertheless, the Bill adds some very significant safeguards. The taxpayer is now better off since January 1, 1989 the effective date of the Bill. Each section of the act has its own effective date, some sections starting as early as December 31, 1988 and others as late as 180 days after January 1, 1989.

The Bill began when two congressional champions of fair taxation, George Hansen, Congressman from Idaho and David Pryor, Senator from Arkansas decided to put an end to some of the IRS tyranny. Ultimately, in hearings before Congress evidence surfaced of the incidents like the nursery school takeover where IRS agents held children for ransom (as parents came to pick up their kids they were required to pay debts for the nursery school directly to IRS agents who had levied on the school). As other atrocities were revealed, it appeared that passage of a major relief bill was imminent. In the interim, Hansen was indicted and convicted for not putting everything on his financial disclosure form (the same alleged abuse of former Vice-Presidential candidate Geraldine Ferraro, who served in the same Congress with Hansen) and the bill slowed down. Pryor never gave up, and although the Bill kept getting watered down (especially in the House with its former leader evicted), it came to fruition October 21, 1988. Ronald Reagan signed it on Saturday, November 21, 1988 along with a potpourri of other legislation. Today, it can be read in the Congressional Record H-10978 through H-11065 (with a few other Bills mixed in). It is now codified and available in easy to read print in law libraries everywhere.

HIGHLIGHTS

Recording. In the past, IRS agents often argued that the taxpayer could not record meetings. Most taxpayers sheepishly obeyed. The few who didn't often had a very short interview. The new law specifically allows tape recording by the taxpayer, and, if notice is given, the IRS agent can also record the meeting. The taxpayer may purchase a copy of the IRS recording, if any. If you are called for an audit or other meeting and do not have an attorney or C.P.A. present, this "new" right is essential to exercise. It's risky to rely on the Government's tape. They may lose it or force you to file a suit to get a copy. A tape recorder often effectively cuts down on bullying tactics and can be used later when the taxpayer's version of a meeting varies substantially from the Service's version. I was able to use a recording a client of mine took of an agent in Philadelphia to keep the client out of jail. The agent had given him inaccurate tax advice. If you are going to an audit and don't have effective counsel with you, don't leave home without your recorder. (Effective April, 1989)

Right to Counsel. If you ask, all meetings (except criminal investigations) must stop to give the taxpayer time to hire counsel with a power of attorney. This counsel may be: an attorney, a C.P.A., or an enrolled agent. The IRS must deal through your agent. However, if the Service feels your agent is causing unnecessary delay or hindrance, they may tell you directly. Often meetings directly with the taxpayer turn out to be fishing expeditions, to which the Government is not entitled. Going fishing, when you are the bait, can be harmful to your economic health. In criminal cases, which are not addressed in this act, the taxpayer can still exercise his Fifth Amendment right by refusing to testify. (Effective April, 1989)

Written Advice. If you rely on IRS written advice (not over the phone, oral advice) directed specifically to you, and it's bad advice, you can't be made to pay penalties or additional tax due to the erroneous written advice. Unfortunately, most of the Service's advice is oral.

The advice must be based on full disclosure by the taxpayer. The taxpayer can't give a false set of facts or incomplete narrative and then rely on written advice based on the faulty foundation. In the past, if you relied on IRS personnel's erroneous advice you were stuck. You still are, but if the "advice" is in writing, and if you told the whole truth, you can escape penalties. Remember, the presumptions are **against** the taxpayer. In civil litigation, the taxpayer is still presumed guilty (unlike the presumption in criminal cases still covered by the real Bill of Rights). (Effective January 1, 1989 but regulations will not be ready until July 1, 1989)

Office of Ombudsman. An old office with some new teeth. Now the ombudsman can issue Taypayer Assistance Orders.

The word ombudsman comes from ancient Norwegian. In Norway, the ombudsman was a government official who examined government agents for abusive actions against citizens.

This may be the best part of the new act. If the taxpayer's property is improperly levied or attached, he can write the ombudsman for relief (on a form to be prepared by the Secretary of the Treasury). If the ombudsman believes the request for relief is justified he can terminate the levy or attachment and release the property.

The price you pay for the ombudsman's assistance, is that the ticking away of time under any statute of limitations stops while his Assistance Order is in effect. This could extend the time of your liability for a debt to the IRS. The ombudsman can only act if the taxpayer is suffering or is about to suffer a significant harm. Like his Norwegian predecessor, he can also go out looking for abuses on his own. Unlike the more powerful Norwegian Ombudsman, the American tax ombudsman's efforts can be vetoed by high ranking members of the agency being checked. A district director or a regional director of appeals (or their superiors) can cancel the Taxpayer Assistance Order of the ombudsman. A separation of this power from IRS officials would give it more teeth. (Effective January 1, 1989.)

Evaluation of Employees. IRS employees will not receive raises or promotions based on the dollar amount of delinquent taxes they collect. Results, such as seizing a widow's pension or putting someone in jail shall not be the criteria for advancement. While the Service has denied that this was ever the criteria, former employees of the Service testified to the contrary before Congress. Effective Janaury 1, 1989 it will be illegal.

Tax Liability Installment Payments. Written agreements made by the taxpayer and the IRS are now binding. The IRS can't make one and then ignore it if: a) You follow it timely; b) You give adequate and updated financial information and unhappily; c) The Service doesn't feel its money is in jeopardy.

The "Service" has a proven track record of preferring to collect money rather than miss an opportunity to do so. Under the new Bill, it will be as it has been for the last forty years—easy for the IRS to "feel insecure." If the Service wants to violate the agreement, it must give 30 days notice.

This portion of the act is helpful but very weak. Do penalties stop accruing? Apparently only if it is agreed to. There is no guarantee that an agreement will be entered into and no requirement that the Service negotiate in good faith. (Effective January 1, 1989)

Assistant Commissioner for Taxpayer Services. A new office that was established known as "Office for Taxpayer Services" with a new commissioner whose job is to help taxpayers. Unfortunately, the new Commissioner reports directly to the Assistant Commissioner of the Internal Revenue Service. This is another case of the fox guarding the chicken coop.

The office gives advice (usually oral, therefore not binding), makes forms (supposedly that the taxpayer can read), and along with the ombudsman, reports yearly to Congress. (Effective July 1, 1989)

Levy and Lien Charges. IRS must now give 30 days notice instead of ten before it takes (levies) a taxpayer's trailer or bank account. The time means nothing if the IRS feels the tax is in jeopardy. Wage exemptions are raised to the amount of allowable deductions divided by 52. (A four-member household with head of house blind could keep about $800 per month as opposed to about $300 now. It wasn't enough to live on before. Now, if you don't have a house payment, car payment or utility payment you might squeeze through.

The exemption for personal property of $1,500 was raised to $1,550 in 1989 and $1,650 in 1990.

These changes won't mean much. However, some levy changes will. The IRS can't levy property and sell for a loss. Pure vindictive sales are not illegal. One common occurrence was the seizure of a car that was worth little more (and sometimes less) than the debt owed against it. The tax-payer who was behind on taxes was often behind on other bills also and lost his credit. He couldn't easily replace the car and without it, couldn't go to work. The IRS didn't make any money since the car with the bank lien had no value. Now banks aren't suppose to turn over money immediately. You've got 21 days to fight back after the notice of levy. Does the time start from the moment you actually receive the notice or from the day the IRS says they mailed it? This is an important unanswered question because the Bill doesn't say and currently most federal courts say from the day the Service says they mailed it — even if the taxpayer says he never got the notice.

The notice provisions are still woefully inadequate.

If the levy is creating an economic hardship or destroying a business it is possible to set it aside, unless releasing it would jeopardize the IRS' creditor status. (Effective January 7, 1989)

What is reasonable? The courts and the treasury department will have to decide.

A lot of businesses are closed each year due to seizures by the IRS which collect few if any tax dollars and stop the flow of future tax dollars and create unemployment. This very valuable portion of the new Bill is too vague. The tendency will be to continue closing small businesses until the Ombudsman office effectively intervenes, and to allow medium size and large companies to stay open if they hire competent counsel. The IRS will no longer be able to seize property while the taxpayer is obeying determinations derived from an audit.

One Houstonian is currently serving time in a federal penetentiary because, after his hearing, he saw his car slapped with a stamp that said "Attached By IRS." Already frightened by an intimidating hearing, not knowing his rights, he jumped in the car and drove away. He was charged with a federal felony, stealing property in the possession of the Government. At trial, he fired his court appointed counsel (who had no tax experience and who had advised him to plead guilty) and represented himself.

Cost and Legal Fees. Legal fees can be recovered by a prevailing taxpayer in a dispute where the IRS has acted unreasonably; if the taxpayer exhausts all of his administrative remedies within the IRS, and the winning taxpayer has not protracted the proceedings.

This is a nice addition to the rules, but a close look takes a lot of wind out of its sails. Absent special circumstances, the maximum award is $75 per hour. Most tax lawyers charge $200 per hour and up. The little guy's cases (being handled pro bono, for free, or at a reduced rate) have to be put on low priority by the few tax lawyers who will even take them. Will this conduct constitute "protracting litigation" by those who are most in need of having their legal fees paid? It won't be easy to collect fees. However, cases like Sammy Lott's, (a client of mine whose wages, home and possibly his wheelchair were subject to an IRS levy) which resulted in a judgment against the IRS will no longer be rarer than unicorns. Sammy's judgment was secured because the IRS set several hearings and did not attend them. The IRS was sanctioned for doing this. (You will find the entire Sammy Lott story in Chapter XXVII., Section I.) Merely winning the case would not have been sufficient to secure a judgment. All parties, civil or criminal, can be sanctioned for improper conduct. Many judges however are reluctant to hold the IRS up to the same standard as other parties to litigation. (Effective December 31, 1988 on levies and actions **after** that date.)

Civil Cause of Action for Damages. If an employee of the IRS recklessly or intentionally violates someone's rights in a collection action which is not properly authorized, the United States may be sued for as much as $100,000. All administrative remedies must first be exhausted, the Service must deny all claims, the taxpayer must have taken all steps to mitigate his damages, and then the taxpayer must win in court. There is a two year statute of limitations, **and** a frivolous claim is punishable by up to $10,000.

This will be an area of substantial litigation and appeals.

It will effectively reduce abuses, but it stops short of what is needed. If the agent were also personally liable for reckless and intentional violations of the law, in much the same way as police officers are, the agent on the street would be much less vindictive. The character of the IRS would change overnight. Prior to the act, when the IRS said a taxpayer's business, say Sam Jones, Inc., owed taxes, it could close the business down and liquidate it, or seize checking accounts letting outside checks already written bounce. Even when a case was being litigated in tax court, the Service often illegally collected money.

Later, when it turned out that Sam Jones, Inc. didn't owe any money but was due a refund, the company was still ruined. Now the company, if it wins in trial, can recover up to $100,000. Still not a lot of help if the business was worth $2,000,000 and if six families lost jobs. An Agent X who improperly levied the account because the secretary of the corporation wouldn't date him, can't be sued personally. (Effective January 1, 1989)

Tax Court Jurisdiction. The biggest change in jurisdiction is that before if you had a case in tax court and the IRS pretended they had already won, you had to file in district court to stop them from illegally levying against you. Now you can file for relief in the tax court.

What does this mean?

If the IRS assesses you and you don't believe you owe the assessment and you don't want to pay in advance, you file suit in tax court. The tax court then decides whether you owe the debt or not. No debt can legally be collected **until** you lose but the IRS computers regularly ignore that and take your money anyway. Your only remedy as to file in the federal district court for an injunction stopping them until the tax court ruled.

An even better remedy would be to notify the IRS agent responsible that he had illegally levied against someone and needed to release the levy. If he refused without court action, he would be personally liable for damages and legal fees. Illegal levies would drop dramatically. This is **not** however the new law.

In effect, the taxpayer had to file two suits. Now he can file one. (Effective on new suits, January 1, 1989.)

Conference Locations. Before you went where you were told to go. A Houston resident could end up in Chicago. This occured when a taxpayer moved after the audit year but before the actual audit, or because of an IRS computer or personnel foul-up. As a rule, the IRS would usually change locations when asked. Now the Service must go to the office nearest you, unless they give a good reason why not. This won't change much for most taxpayers, but will make a big difference for a few. One of my clients, a engineering consultant whose assignments required frequent moves, was summoned to an audit in Texas while he has living in Connecticut. He requested that the audit be held in Connecticut. By the time the creaking bureaucratic machinery had relocated the audit to Connecticut, my client was already living and working in Kansas. After a dozen years of unsuccessful civil harassment of my client, the IRS filed criminal charges against him for willful failure to file tax returns. I was hired ten days before his trial. A wise, compassionate jury acquitted him on both counts. This Bill might have saved my client a lot of aggravation and expense.

Written Rights. Everytime a taxpayer has a hearing, the IRS is now required to give him written notice of all of his rights including appellate rights relating to the hearing. (Effective Janaury 1, 1989, **but** they have 180 days to draw up the list of rights.) This is not required in criminal investigations. The accused is still, however, under the Miranda interpretation of the Bill of Rights (Fifth and Sixth Amendments) to be read his rights when he is arrested. Training manuals for IRS Special Agents (who investigate and prosecute criminal tax violations) instruct the agent to read a criminal suspect his rights during any interview whether he is under arrest or not. Sometimes Special Agents violate this instruction.

Tax Preparers. Tax preparers are not permitted to give your personal information to others. There are already laws against this. The Bill added some more. The old one year in prison possibility still has plenty of teeth. The addition is not helpful. (Effective December 31, 1988)

Homestead Exemption. The IRS can't take your home without a very good reason. Before the Bill, your home was just another piece of meat if you had an assesssment against you. To proceed against your home, the IRS must believe the assessment is in jeopardy. This could be a source of significant litigation if the Service does not seriously curtail its home shopping activity. The same taxpayer who simply can't afford to fight a $1,000 tax dispute even though he doesn't owe the tax, will sometimes fight to the death for his home, metaphorically and actually, even if he does owe the tax.

CONCLUSION

The new taxpayer Bill of Rights is not a real Bill of Rights. It faces many of the major problems with the Service head on, but backs off on most of them. Nevertheless, significant changes have been made, and while the taxpayer is still not on an equal footing with the Revenuers when he's dragged to his knees, he may fall on knee pads.

K. SOLUTIONS

According to recent government statistics, 34 percent of government revenues come from income taxes. The income tax could be eliminated completely, and it would still be possible to generate enough income for the government's legitimate functions if the present course of irresponsible spending were abated.

The ridiculous part about the graduated income tax is that the extremely wealthy and extremely clever have never paid it. With all the loopholes, appeals and opportunities for deductions, the very wealthiest in our society have paid little or no taxes. In theory, the graduated income tax may sound fine to its supporters. In fact, it is easily exploitable.

Those persons who are the smartest and strongest escape a great deal of taxation by figuring out the rules and playing by them. Those people who are the most dishonest escape it by cheating—if you consider devising plans to keep your assets "cheating."

Those people who are the least productive in society also pay no taxes. The burden of an income tax inevitably, and in all situations, has always fallen on the working class, the lower middle class and upper middle class.

Politicians on the right and politicians on the left scream out "Let's be fair." The only thing all the politicians have always admitted is that it has never been fair. It never will be. One of the effects of the graduated income tax with graduated loopholes is to keep successful middle class workers out of the upper classes.

You need money to establish trusts, to hire CPAs, to keep lawyers on retainers in advance of earning significant income—or you won't be able to protect that income and keep it. Many people who receive one-time, large sums and who would normally be catapulted into the aristocracy, do not have the time or money to pre-plan, so most of their assets are taken away.

Revenues can be obtained simply by creating more inflation. I am personally opposed to this. A better solution would be for the government to exercise better management over the revenues it has. We can stop paying $700 for a military toilet seat or $250 for a military hardware screw which can be purchased for seven to eight cents in the hardware store. We can make the theft of public money a criminal offense. We can prosecute and put the parasites in jail. The congressmen and bureaucrats who profit from the theft of so-called public funds should be treated as the common criminals that they are.

A fair and honest jury system would permit informed citizens to return guilty verdicts that would eliminate this sort of practice.

We have never had a jury trial in which the maker of a $700 toilet seat had to explain why he charged that amount when his contract said he would provide the toilet seat for $20. We've never had a jury trial in which the government bureaucrat who authorized the $700 payment was required to justify his behavior.

As an alternative to the present system, we can abolish the income tax and replace it with the European system of a value-added tax.

The value-added tax concept is quite simple; at each stage of manufacturing as value is added onto a product, it is taxed. A flat percent tax could be attached to every item purchased in the United States. Once the new bookkeeping methods were in place, the amount of accounting required under this system would be significantly less than under the present system.

Merchants in most states are already accustomed to dealing with sales taxes for state revenue purposes. A five percent across-the-board tax would not in and of itself be good for the economy—because taxes of any sort are always bad for the economy—but the tax would raise more revenue than the government currently gets.

The value-added tax system would eliminate the need for 90 percent of the IRS personnel—which would itself save taxpayers billions of dollars annually. Only a small staff would be needed to audit the collection of the sales taxes. An enormous amount of litigation would also be eliminated. The amount of record keeping necessary for businesses would probably be cut in half. All of this freed-up labor potential could be devoted to increasing the gross national product.

How do we eliminate the income tax amendment? Of course, the most effective way would be to pass a constitutional amendment eliminating the Sixteenth Amendment. Prohibition was legalized with the Eighteenth Amendment and we abolished it by passing the Twenty-First Amendment. However, it's very difficult to get amendments passed.

A second method would be for the U.S. Supreme Court to review the Sixteenth Amendment and rule that it had not been properly ratified. This would be a tough one—because in all probability, it would take five new justices on the Supreme Court which itself could easily take 40 or 50 years to accomplish. In the alternative, one or two very strong-minded, strong-willed Supreme Court justices might convince their fellow justices to carefully re-examine the Sixteenth Amendment. I regard this as even less likely than the passage of an amendment eliminating income taxation.

The third and easiest way is simply to pass a law voiding the laws passed after the Sixteenth Amendment, which set up the machinery for the collection of such taxes. When the Sixteenth Amendment was adopted, laws had to be made and passed in order to put it into effect.

Those laws implementing the Sixteenth Amendment could be repealed in one fell swoop by a majority vote of the Senate and House. The real problem is that nobody seems to be pushing in this direction.

Men who have the integrity of former Congressman Ron Paul almost never run for political office. And when they do, their political ideology and integrity prevents them from making deals and getting much accomplished.

When Paul ran for the U.S. Senate, he couldn't raise substantial money for the campaign because he was ethically unwilling to trade promises of future favors for current campaign contributions. Paul quit politics and became a full time capitalist—printing newsletters and giving speeches, as well as maintaining his medical practice as a gynecologist. I welcome his 1988 candidacy. I hope its not his last bout in the political arena.

The fireball speaker, former Congressman George Hansen, made IRS reform a key plank in his agenda, and he didn't just use words—he became their public enemy Number One. Hansen produced and distributed—for television stations that were bold enough to air them, stark, realistic dramatizations of how IRS agents actually collect revenues. What happened? He was convicted of violating an obscure financial disclosure law and sent to a federal prison to prevent him from testifying further before a Congressional committee looking into IRS abuse.

If this value-added concept was adopted, most CPAs, accountants and tax lawyers would be out of work. For this reason alone, our respective unions will fight to the death for income taxation in some form. The only real solution would be to allow jurors to judge the law on a case-by-case basis.

"As the massive IRS-government-computer grows, we will be plugged in, observed more closely and checked more often."

CHAPTER XV

THE INSURANCE CON

*"The insurance company makes its big money
on the use of your money."*

A. INTRODUCTION

A jewelry merchant or a shoe manufacturer charges the highest markup on his goods that he can so he can make the most profit. Members of all labor unions want the largest amount of hourly income that they can get. The industrial plants and factories that employ these workers want to pay the smallest amount of income and benefits they can pay.

It is the nature of man to want to make a large profit. There is not just a thin line, however, but a thick line between honesty and dishonesty. If the jeweler tells his customers that he has the lowest prices in town and in fact he has the highest prices in town, the jeweler is a liar. He is dishonest. If he simply bargains for the best deal he can get and the customer bargains for the best deal that the customer can get, that's honest negotiations.

In a communist or totalitarian society, people still try to get as much as they can get. The difference is, they lie about it. A free capitalistic society is characterized by the honest negotiators, looking at each other eyeball-to-eyeball, admitting that they are trying to make a good deal for themselves. There is absolutely nothing wrong with this.

With that in mind, I want to discuss the insurance con artist game so popular today.

Insurance companies and the attorneys who work for them routinely delay justice but report to newspapers and radio that the problems are caused by too much personal injury litigation. Then they take refuge behind the media smokescreen they created. Through a multimillion-dollar international scheme, the insurance industry has convinced most people that it is suffering. The industry's propaganda has convinced most people because they had no interest or economic motivation to study the facts.

Wall Street's values for insurance company stocks have never been higher than they are today. These poor insurance companies are—for some reason—still able to pay massive dividends to their shareholders over and above what they were paying in their big years. The demand for insurance company stocks is pushing their value through the roof. They're going up, not down. Why? If the insurance companies are losing their shirts, why are people buying insurance stocks as though there were a shortage? Figure it out. The insurance company is pulling off one giant hoax.[1]

B. THE SECRET REVEALED

The insurance industry does not lose money unless they plan poorly. A determination by the insurance companies and the various regulatory boards is made as to how much will be lost in a given year for a given type of policy and premiums are set accordingly. Example: In one company, 1,000 home owners will pay $500 a year for their policies totaling $500,000. This figure is based on the assumption that paying claims due to fires, thefts and other casualties and also paying legal fees and other expenses of doing business, will cost the company considerably less than $500,000 and will enable them to make a profit.

During the late 70s and early 80s, when interest rates soared through the roof, insurance companies wanted to sell extra insurance policies at any price. Why? Well, of course, they always want to sell insurance policies for their customary profit but what people don't understand is that the insurance company doesn't make its big money on the policy.

The insurance company makes its big money on the use of your money. The hypothetical $500,000 does not sit inactively in the insurance company's coffers. The money is loaned out to banks, governments or businesses often to buy real estate or to make investments. When interest rates are high, the insurance companies want more money so that they can loan it out at very profitable rates.

For that reason the insurance industry lowered its fees and became very competitive for a brief period of time in order to grab those precious insurance dollars. Now that interest rates have plummeted, the insurance companies are paying the price for their greed.

The public is currently bombarded with television shows, newspaper

---

"Wall Street's values for insurance company stocks have never been higher than they are today. These poor insurance companies are—for some reason—still able to pay massive dividends to their shareholders over and above what they were paying in their big years."

---

and magazine articles deploring the litigation explosion or insurance crisis in which they claim dishonest plaintiffs' attorneys deliberately encourage the filing of baseless personal injury lawsuits and demand and win exorbitant damages. The attorneys filing these suits are depicted as parasites, seeking all the money they can get and serving their own self-interest rather than the collective good of society.

These statements are partially misleading because they fail to distinguish between lawyers who work for victims and lawyers who work for insurance companies. They fail to distinguish between the majority of legitimate personal injury suits and a few dishonest ones. The lawyer who works for the victim customarily works for a percentage of what he wins. Since most wins come from settlement—only 5 to 12 percent of the cases go to trial, and the remainder are settled[2]—it makes sense that the victim's lawyer *never* profits from delay. Since the insurance company lawyer is paid by the hour, he is motivated to delay.

C. JUSTICE DELAYED IS JUSTICE DENIED

Let us consider a typical case of an automobile accident victim who is willing to settle promptly for a fair amount. I represented a father and teen-age son who both suffered minor whiplash injuries when their car was rear-ended in 1981. Soon after the accident, they would gladly have accepted $5,000 to compensate them for their injuries.

Did the erring driver's insurance company cough up the money? No! Its tactic was to delay for five years. The company's train of thought was: "The interest we will make on that $5,000 is worth it, and maybe five years from now the poor victims won't say, 'We need more money because we had to wait so long.' The poor victims will be worn out and will probably take $2,500. Maybe we'll get lucky, and they'll forget about the accident!"

The insurance industry may have to pay out more in legal fees for the delays, but that's fine. They just go to the legislature and show them how much they're paying in legal fees and demand that the premiums be increased.

Low fees gets the business in the door; fees get raised again to cover the costs. Since higher costs mean higher fees, profits (which are based primarily on interest on accrued fees not yet paid out) are higher.

"The insurance company makes its big money on the use of your money."

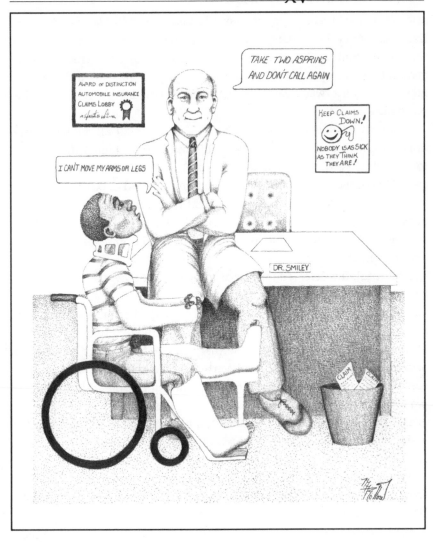

My clients, the Joneses, came to me from another attorney, a non-trial lawyer. He was a smart negotiator who threw in the towel and decided to give up. The insurance company had turned down his offer to settle for $5,000. It was turned over to me for trial. In a phone conversation with opposing counsel, I offered to settle for $10,000. The insurance attorney

"The money is loaned out to banks, governments, or businesses often to buy real estate or to make investments."

said, "Not until I take some discovery." I told him, "No." Discovery takes time and money; besides, I felt we had a claim that was legitimately worth the $50,000 policy. The insured knew he had hit our client from the rear end and our chiropractor bills showed an injury for this amount of settlement discovery was wasteful. No satisfactory settlement could be reached.

A couple of days prior to the May 1986, trial—after all the work was done—the insurance company lawyer offered $10,000. I refused. We went to trial. The verdict, after a two-day trial, was $12,500. We were also awarded court costs of $800 to cover the filing fees and deposition costs. A great victory? No. A victory? Yes. A great defeat for the insurance company? Yes. They spent a fortune on trial. They brought a chiropractor in from Kansas City to complain about our local chiropractor's diagnosis and treatment.

After trial, the defeated insurance company attorney told the judge he had been willing to pay more than the $12,500 but that I was too greedy. Isn't it funny that he never told me that? Perhaps he was turning a loss into a win by changing the facts. It wouldn't be the first time I'd run into that tactic—not even the first time that year. A fair verdict could have ranged from $10,000 to $50,000. Nevertheless, the refusal to settle prior to completely preparing for trial served no one but but the insurance company and its attorney.

Did the insurance company spend an extra $7,000 on a $12,000 judgment they could have bought for $5,000 plus enormous legal fees? They certainly did. Figure in at least another $5,000 for legal fees.

They played the odds. Because for every case that goes to trial, there are 10 that settle for a $1,000 without a lawyer, 10 more that settle for less than $5000, and 10 more that later accept the $10,000 before trial.

How can the insurance companies then say they lose money when they really make money? Presto-chango-magic! On their balance sheets, when they are sued for the $10,000 that they justly owe, they take $10,000 and show it as a loss. However, they don't show the interest and they don't show the fact that even if they have to pay that $10,000, eventually, they won't do it for five years. It will be held in a magic, interest bearing, on paper only, account called loss reserves.

"The loss reserves system is a pyramid scheme to con state legislatures into allowing high premiums and to avoid paying federal income taxes."

Jim Mattox, attorney general of Texas, and the authorities of New York, California, Massachusetts, West Virginia, Alabama, Minnesota and Wisconsin did not call it "magic." They called it "consumer fraud" and "conspiracy." On March 23, 1988, anti-trust suits were filed against major insurance companies in those eight states, citing such conduct as conspiracy to artifically constrict the insurance market and victimizing policy holders. [3]

Why do they allow a human being to suffer when the only legitimate reason for an insurance company's existence is to pay off suffering people? Why do they allow their own insured customers—who in good faith bought their insurance policy for the purpose of paying off legitimate claims against them—to suffer through depositions and endless litigation? Why? Because the insurance industry won't be blamed, the lawyers will be blamed. Which lawyers? The ones who file the lawsuits, of course! The insurance company lawyers will be the heroes. After all, they are just defending the poor insurance company.

The loss reserves system is a pyramid scheme to con state legislatures into allowing high premiums and to avoid paying federal income taxes.

Look at this example: The automobile of policy holder John Smith hits victim Sam Doe and creates $10,000 in legitimate damages. A lawsuit against Smith is filed for $25,000 to allow negotiating room. The insurance adjuster evaluates the claim at $20,000 so that even if he settles it for $12,000 he'll look good. Smith's policy is canceled. Smith is scared to death. His policy is for $20,000 and he has been sued for $25,000. His insurance company appointed lawyer won't tell him what's going on and will not even return his calls.

The insurance company offers a $1,500 settlement and spends $1,500 a year for five years on legal fees because Doe's lawyer won't take this ridiculous offer but also is afraid to go to court.

In year one, the insurance company, on paper only, puts $20,000 in its loss reserve account. It makes 10 percent profit per year on this account, and in year one, gets to pretend for tax purposes and for purposes of increasing its policy premiums that it actually lost the $20,000 plus the $1,500 in legal fees. A pretty cute magic trick! In real life, the stock went up and the shareholders got dividends. In paper fairyland the company lost

---

"If you want to find a good insurance human being the best place to locate him or her is in the rank and file of the sales force."

money.

Five years down the road—during which time Smith never knows what's going on—Doe breaks down and says, "I'll take anything." Doe settles for $3,500. He actually gets 60 percent or $2,100, and must pay $850 for expenses—leaving him $1,350. His lawyer gets 40 percent or $1,400, of which $850 has already been spent for out-of-pocket expenses for a portion of five years. The insurance lawyer at $1,500 per year clears $7,500.

The insurance company must now reclaim $16,500 of its magic paper loss. The pyramid will cover it. They have replaced this case with three more $20,000 magic paper losses, so they never pay a cost. When the pyramid can no longer do this, the company goes out of business and doesn't pay its taxes. The owners start a new insurance company. Someday when the biggest giants get to the top of the pyramid they'll need major legislation to protect them. With our money and their promotional experts, they'll buy it.

D. THE GOOD INSURANCE MAN (OR WOMAN)

Everyone associated with what has become a very evil industry is not evil, just as all lawyers are not crooks.

There are, if you can believe it, some insurance adjusters who want to be fair to their customers and who want to help the deserving victims.Although they usually don't keep their jobs for long. If you want to find a good insurance human being, the best place to locate him or her is in the rank and file of the sales force. I believe the proportion of good insurance people is roughly proportional to that of good doctors, lawyers and psychologists.

The insurance industry started in England. Shipping was a risky business. If you got to the East Indies and back you were rich; but if your ship sank, got waylaid by pirates, or suffered any other of a myriad of possible misfortunes, you could be wiped out. Why take the chance? A lot of ship owners got together and each pitched in enough to cover the loss of a ship or two—thereby protecting themselves from a catastrophic loss by spreading the risk among a large number. The owner who lost his ship stayed in business because the group covered his loss.

"You can legally cushion the risk for theft, fire, death and personal errors with insurance just as the early ship owners did."

If your home burns to the ground, the loss of family pictures or items of sentimental value is not replaceable. However, insurance can cover the cost of replacing clothes, furniture and the home itself. If you hurt someone through careless driving, it isn't fair for them to have to bear the expense of their medical attention—or for you to suffer anxiety over the costs and legal problems—when the matter is covered by insurance which you purchased for just such an occasion. You can legally cushion the risk for theft, fire, death and personal errors with insurance just as the early ship owners did.

It's possible you'll have to sue your insurance company to make them honor their agreement—unfortunately this is always a very real possibility, but at least you'll have someone to sue. A few companies now sell legal insurance to cover some of this expense of being sued.

The good insurance agent can be a best friend. He is often an independent, but may work for only one company. Some insurance companies have good track records for integrity regarding settlements and some have bad ones. Consumer Reports and other organizations review them on occasion and rate them.

The good insurance agent will care about you. He'll try to find you the best deal and intelligently discuss your specific needs. He'll often help you process your claims and he may be a great source of information about the insurance industry. The good agent is sympathetic when a claim must be processed and he's scrupulously honest. He returns his phone calls even though his business is so large he's had to double his space twice in 10 years. Does he work on a commission? You bet he does!

When someone tells me he's only interested in helping me rather than making a profit, I take a walk. If he's telling the truth, he isn't going to be in business for long. And if he's lying, well, he's just lying. You'll run into enough liars in life without looking for them. You'll never run out of them, so it's unnecessary to save any of them for later use.

The best way to find this good agent is to get a referral from someone you trust, or through trial and error over the years. Even a bad insurance sales agent will usually not be your worst enemy. If the company he sells for exists and is state licensed it will probably be around in case of an accident.

What most bad insurance sales people often do is: A) Not sell you what you really need; B) Sell you a lot that you don't need; C) Not be around when things go wrong; D) Deal with weak or borderline companies; E) Deal with companies who often do not pay legitimate claims; F) Not maintain a working knowledge of their industry; G) Not maintain errors and omissions insurance to cover their own mistakes—everyone makes mistakes.

If your ship comes in, you probably didn't need the insurance, except for peace of mind, but you did help that poor guy whose ship was hijacked by the ruler of a terrorist nation. If your ship does not come in, and you're not covered. You're sunk. You may never sail again.

E. CONTINGENCY FEES: BANE OR BLESSING?

The insurance industry has launched a massive publicity campaign against plaintiff's lawyers who work purely on a percentage. They handle their clients' personal injury or damages claim on a contingency basis, which means for a percentage of the amount achieved through settlement or judgment of the matter. If their clients lose, they lose.

These attorneys eat off the same plates as their clients. If their client doesn't eat, the attorneys don't eat. There is, however, a legitimate argument against plaintiff's attorneys who take contingency fee cases. It's in the best interests of the attorneys to charge the largest percentage of the entire case that they can get; whereas, theoretically, it's in the clients' best interest to pay the smallest percentage to this attorney.

It's the situation of a merchant and a customer bargaining over a price in a capitalistic market place. It may seem that the plaintiff's attorney is an uncontrolled capitalist whose interests is opposed to those of his or her constituency.

However, if, the attorney's superior skill obtains a settlement or judgment more than three times what the client could have gotten on his own with the other party's insurance company, the client has certainly benefited.

You can argue that the attorney isn't needed. In fact, you can argue that real estate brokers, mortgage bankers, wholesalers and all other middlemen aren't needed—and, in fact, sometimes they aren't. If you can get a fair settlement, you don't need an attorney on a personal injury case.

Even in the 90 percent plus of personal injury cases that don't go to trial, insurance companies usually offer fair and substantial settlements

"Often, an unrepresented personal injury victim's most effective, rapid settlement argument is: 'I am about to turn this matter over to my attorney.'"

only when there is a viable threat of being forced to go to trial against a competent attorney—and even then there are no guarantees.

Often, an unrepresented personal injury victim's most effective, rapid settlement argument is: "I am about to turn this matter over to my attorney." If you choose not to hire an attorney and to attempt settlement yourself this could be your strongest line. If your bluff is called, you are a fool if you don't hire an attorney.

Up to this point, an insurance adjuster is handling the case. The insurance company has the adjuster on a salary or on a-case-by-case basis. The insurance company's cost goes up once suit is filed because they must retain an attorney to defend the insured against the suit. Some insurance companies now have in-house counsel—a permanent attorney on a salary. These companies don't need to worry about saving legal fees. However the best defense attorneys usually won't work for a salary (preferring, instead, to rack up high hourly fees), so on a really tough or important case, expect a competent adversary, usually an attorney maintaining his own office and billing the insurance company at an hourly rate. The greater the plaintiff's attorney's reputation, the larger the potential settlement offer might be.

To prepare an average $10,000 personal injury case—including discovery and the usual frivolous pre-trial motions normally filed by the insurance attorney so that he can charge his client the extra fees—normally takes from 50 to 100 hours. The average attorney's hourly rate ranges anywhere from $50 to $500 per hour. For this example, we'll consider the rate of $100 an hour. This means that between $5,000 and $10,000 worth of billable time is utilized for the preparation and trial of a personal injury suit.

A large number of offices in the country use the following typical scale of attorneys' fees on contingency, personal injury cases. The attorney gets 33 percent of the gross revenues if the case is settled before suit is filed, or 40 percent of the gross revenues after suit is filed—whether it is settled or tried.

A competent lawyer will usually file suit because most insurance companies generally don't start to negotiate seriously until suit has been filed. There are many exceptions of course. The client may be unwilling to settle. The client may have a weak case and discovery would only serve to make it weaker. When out-of-pocket expenses in a personal injury litigation are considered—the percentages split between the attorney and the client can be misleading. Most clients think they are paying 33 percent when they are actually paying 40 percent—unless they are clear on whether the percentage comes from the gross proceeds before expenses, or the net proceeds after expenses are deducted.

Of course, sometimes you can explain it many times and still someone not used to contracts or figures will not understand. The actual fee split roughly runs about 50 percent of the net profit. This is fairly stable across the country but will vary from one attorney's office to another and of course from case to case. Some very profitable cases cost very little to develop and some very small cases cost a lot to develop.

One personal injury case I had involved a client who had spent a month in a hospital under the care of a surgeon. The accident was caused by a drunk driver who struck my client's car from the rear. The only major expense in developing the case was paying the fees of the one doctor for the time spent in preparation of his testimony.

Another personal injury case involved a referral. The client had moved and had three separate doctors in two states. Travel expenses, doctors' fees for depositions and both out of state and local court reporters had to be paid. The cause of the accident was hard to prove and an accident reconstruction expert had to be hired. The client had to be flown in for trial and put up in a hotel. Had I not needed the good will of the referring attorney, I would have turned the case down. A flat fee of the 50 percent of the net profit guarantees that the attorney won't make more than the client. I like to be up front about it and let my clients know exactly how my fee arrangement works. It eliminates a lot of possible misunderstandings later on.

It still sounds greedy doesn't it? From the insurance company's propaganda, it certainly does. From a dollars and cents point of view, it isn't. To win the $10,000 judgment the attorney risks $1,000 in out-of-pocket expenses for two to five years. If the case goes to trial, the attorney probably puts in $10,000 worth of time. Even if it doesn't, the attorney could exert $5,000 worth of effort on the case. On a 50-50 split after expenses, the attorney makes on this example $4,500.

The insurance attorney, however, makes more than the plaintiff's attor-

> *"There are an endless number of plaintiff's attorneys who never go into the courtroom. The insurance companies and their attorneys know this and they delay until the very last minute and then pay the plaintiff's attorney and the victim next to nothing."*

ney. While the plaintiff's attorney puts up his time and his money for out-of-pocket expenses for a period of years, the insurance attorney is guaranteed a meal ticket. The plaintiff's attorney is guaranteed nothing but the privilege of eating his meal off the same plate as his client. Are there a lot of plaintiff's attorneys who give bargains? Yes.

There are an endless number of plaintiff's attorneys who never go into the courtroom. The insurance companies and their attorneys know this and they delay until the very last minute and then pay the plaintiff's attorney and the victim next to nothing. The trial-shy attorney can make more money through a volume practice than some trial-oriented plaintiff's attorneys, because he doesn't put any time, effort, or labor into the cases.

F. CONCLUSIONS

Is there a solution? The doctors and insurance companies propose that we limit plaintiffs' attorneys' fees while failing to curtail the hourly fees for the defense lawyers. Throughout most of the world, individuals can't afford to hire a lawyer on a personal injury suit because the individual is required to pay cash up front. Lawyers in many countries are not allowed to share, as American lawyers are, in a capitalist system on a percentage basis.

In our system, the lawyer who handles personal injury cases does not usually get paid by the hour. He or she gets paid on a percentage of the profit or gross proceeds according to the agreement. The lawyer has to gamble the value of his time, risking the possibility of no payment at all, sometimes for five, six, seven years, and in the case of a civil rights cases, for a decade or even two decades.

The risk is substantial: The higher the risk, the greater chance of getting nothing; the higher the fee should be. In the United States, if you have a good case against a solvent defendant, you can afford a good lawyer. A solvent defendant may just be someone with insurance. In fact most solvent defendants are either rich defendants who had insurance to protect their wealth or people who had insurance to protect their peace of mind, honor a contract, obey a statute or just through prudence or luck. For that reason, aside from divorce and contract suits, most civil litigation involves insurance companies one way or another. It's as simple as that. On a per-

> *"On a personal injury case, you don't have to be rich to hire an attorney."*

sonal injury case, you don't have to be rich to hire an attorney. This is one part of the American jurisprudence system that makes good sense.

One possible method of compensating accident victims, which springs up perennially, like a dandelion, whenever this subject is discussed, is the elimination of the practice of personal injury law by having the government protect and compensate the injured. You won't see the insurance crisis criers offering this solution, because this solution would write them out of the game. You won't see plaintiffs' or defendants' lawyers advocate this plan either—we'd both lose. You might see some large companies who'd like public protection push it some day after they have spent the premiums they made.

National accident medical and work relief has been instituted in New Zealand and it appears to work. It could work here—with a few modifications: A) Free medical care. B) Unemployment compensation for victims who can't work, educational benefits, and where applicable rehabilitation money. C) You cause an accident, you lose your license. D) You fake an accident and get caught and you go to jail. E) No Insurance. No courts. No Lawyers. All drivers pay an accident tax equal to their current insurance premiums.

This system won't be utilized anytime soon. No one wants it. Insurance companies don't want the government to control them—they only want the government to control their enemies and of course, that's the same with all the other players.

Is there a medical malpractice crisis? Yes, there is. The crisis is that the same doctors who are sued and ordered to pay $1 million in damages are sued and ordered to pay $1 million over and over again. These doctors keep killing, maiming and diminishing the quality of human lives. They are protected.

Is there a problem with sky-rocketing automobile insurance rates? The obvious solution is to allow juries to take away the drivers' licenses of repeat drunk-driving offenders—and to allow punitive damages to be assessed when the jury feels that the evidence justifies the imposition of such measures.

Anyone knowledgeable about the injury part of the legal industry will tell you these self-evident, truthful facts:

My proposed solution is to unleash the power of a fully informed jury. Lately, jury verdicts have been getting smaller in terms of real dollars. How can this be? Don't we read daily the large verdicts? Why? The public is being brainwashed into believing that the insurance companies are losing their shirts and need help. The citizens are hearing only one side of this issue.

The solution to this problem would be an honest jury system. Let the jurors hear everything, including the fact that the defendant has insurance; the arguments of the insurance company; and the arguments of the plaintiff's counsel. No money need be spent in advertising to brainwash the prospective pool of jurors in advance because the actual jurors would hear all the information. It would all be done in the courtroom. The insurance crisis would vanish overnight. Unfortunately, in our present system, jurors are exposed to lies outside the courtroom and are not told the truth inside the courtroom.

"The solution to this problem would be an honest jury system. Let the jurors hear everything, including the fact that the defendant has insurance; the arguments of the insurance company; and the arguments of the plaintiff's counsel."

CHAPTER XVI
THE BANKING SCAM

"The game: Banks use our money for free booty,
then charge us a handsome fee."

A. LEGAL SLAVERY

Will Rogers is the author of the slogan, "I never met a man I didn't like."

Will Rogers never met the officers of First City National Bank, Texas Commerce Bank, Commonwealth Mortgage Co., Houston Southwest Bank, Katy Savings and Loan or Meridian Savings and Loan, all of whom I have had to sue. Christian scriptures show the only action of violence by the normally gentle founder of their faith as an attack on the money changers who degraded the Temple with their thievery![1] Thomas Jefferson said, "Banking establishments are more dangerous than standing armies."[2]

Do we need the banking industry? No. We need access to and transfer of money, but it does not have to be from banks. Is the banking industry in trouble? Yes. It is a refuge of the incompetent and the unfeeling. I have witnessed a lot of incompetent judges who seem to lack the capacity to feel compassion or mercy. However, I have observed more hardness of heart and conscious indifference on the banker's part than from any other group with the exception of IRS agents. The bankers, however, do not have the degree of government protection enjoyed by IRS agents or power of a judge, and, with competent legal counsel, a citizen can often successfully thwart bank official's efforts at petty despotism.

Competition challenges the banking industry. Insurance companies that have more money at their disposal than banks have launched a large-scale competition, offering customers some of the same financial services previously only offered by banks

Whenever I refer to "banks" in this chapter, I mean both commercial banks and savings and loan associations.

If the trend toward de-regulating the insurance industry continues, I believe that this ruthless industry will force all but the very smallest, most conservative banks and the very largest, most powerful banks to consoli-

Banking establishments are more dangerous than standing armies.
—Thomas Jefferson—

date or close down. Twenty years from now, we may still have creatures called banks but these animals will bear little or no resemblance to what exists today. International banking will no longer be an exotic thought but every middle-class worker will be at home with the concepts of money exchange.

Government guarantees and subsidies could become part of the stan-

> *"The top business graduates are heading for the future—the financial services industry— leaving the dregs to the banks."*

dard loan practices. Most banks today cannot stay in business with their under-educated, under-productive, sexist machinery, if they have to be held accountable for their theft and malpractice. The top business graduates are heading for the future—the financial services industry—leaving the dregs to the banks. The banks must follow them or obtain massive welfare from the government, or close down. There are no other options.

Stock brokerage houses are also beginning to compete with banks. The money market funds and non-banking controlled organizations such as Sears & Roebuck are encroaching into the territory that money lending institutions used to dominate as their unchallenged monopoly. Employees' credit unions are competing on a massive scale. Quite frankly, the banking industry is not faring well against the competition.

Banks borrow their money from various federal depositories and lend it back to us, the taxpayers, at higher rates. As much as government control is undesirable, it would be better to borrow the money directly from the government than pay the rates the banks demand in order to borrow it from them.

Our American banks, in order to show good profit and loss statements and in order to have big loans as opposed to small loans—which are less profitable to them—allow large-scale debts to be incurred by crooked real estate entrepreneurs, crooked foreign governments, and con-artists with big paper financial statements. These people are first in line to get the money and they get it at a lower interest rate than the rest of America. When they are late in paying, they get an easy extension and a smile.

The middle class, small business owner who has never been a penny short or a minute late on any payment, frequently has to stand in a long line behind irresponsible and lazy friends of the banking industry. If the little guy ever pays late, he gets a nasty letter, a penalty and a credit rating demerit.

We are witnessing a wholesale destruction of the banking industry by its own collective greed.

In theory, the Thirteenth Amendment of the Constitution eliminated slavery, but the banking industry and the IRS are doing their best to protect a type of slave industry. The average American, in the course of his or

---

"In theory, the Thirteenth Amendment of the Constitution eliminated slavery, but the banking industry and the IRS are doing their best to protect a type of slave industry."

---

her working life between his or her 20th birthday and 70th birthday will spend 30 years paying on a home loan. This represents between a 25 percent and 50 percent of his or her earnings. This same person will pay another 25 to 30 percent of his or her earnings to the IRS, and another 15 to 20 percent of earnings will vanish, due to government printed money which fuels the inflation and confiscates our wealth.

It's amazing that this country has been productive enough to survive when all of these forces are stealing work product from us.

Lending institutions steal from people daily. The largest single financial transaction the average American consummates is the purchase of a home, which involves paying interest to a lending institution for almost half a lifetime.

B. ESCROW AND INTEREST STEALING

When we put our earnings in saving accounts, the lending institutions are actually borrowing it from us at low interest rates. They also borrow from the government at low interest rates. Then they turn around and lend it to homeowners, auto purchasers and developers of small businesses—all at a tidy profit. Lending institutions also, with their near monopoly over the money for our homes and cars, escrow—set aside— our money during the year to make tax and insurance payments at the end of the year.

The use of escrow money is another clever method of income theft. They overcharge you each month, making you pay one-twelfth of their estimate of what it will cost at the end of the year for taxes and insurance on your house. They claim to put this money in a non-interest bearing account, but loan it out to others at high interest rates. And if you've overpaid, they just leave the money in the account for another year without you earning the interest on it.

With their three-piece suits and impressive desks, our bankers maintain a false image of competency, integrity and good judgment. In reality, bankers have the dubious distinction of engaging in theft on a scale topped only by the IRS.

While the escrow account theft is one of the most insidious of the mort-

---

"When we put our earnings in saving accounts, the lending institutions are actually borrowing it from us at low interest rates."

---

gage company's and bank's interest-stealing cons, another is simply the fact that you are not told how principal and interest works when you borrow to buy your home. How is it done? Most home owners who pay a mortgage pay money into what is called an escrow account each month.

Example: You signed a $50,000 note to buy your home. The note is amortized over 30 years, at 10 percent interest. This means that during the 30-year period, you must repay the $50,000 note while at the same time paying the interest due on the unpaid portion of the loan. When the entire amount, principal and interest, is added together over the entire 30-year period and divided by 360 months, it comes to $438.79 per month or a total of $157,964. This information is easy to look up in a small book of tables published by most title companies and many banks titled *Amortization Book* or *Amortization Tables*.

The same loan amortized over 15 years has a monthly payment of $537.31 or a total of $96,715. Why so much difference? Why does $100 more per month cut the number of payments in half? It is because you are borrowing the bank's money for a shorter period of time. Remember, the interest is *most* of the debt, in fact, two-thirds or more of it.

When you make a monthly mortgage payment, you pay interest first. And most of the payment initially goes to interest. Month number one you pay $438.79, and of that amount $417 is interest. A mere $22 was applied toward the purchase of your home. Now, you only owe $49,978. Now, recompute your principal and interest payments based on the $49,978 and you'll learn that for your second month's payment, $416 will be interest and $23 will be applied to principal.

At this rate, it takes a long time to significantly reduce the principal. At the end of five years—if any service charges have been applied—you might not have reduced the principal at all. Most people incorrectly assume that they are significantly reducing the amount they owe on their home each year they make payments. Despite complaints, bankers seldom tell these customers what to expect five years down the road.

This is not theft. This is mere deception. The theft arises out of the escrow funds and improper posting. Property taxes and insurance costs vary from one place to another, but for the purpose of our example, let's assume the taxes are $600 a year and the insurance premium is another $600. These costs would add another $100 to the total monthly payment.

Besides the $438.79 for principal and interest, the homeowner must also pay $100 for the taxes and insurance for a total monthly payment of $538.79. When that first monthly payment is made, the additional $100 is placed in a non-interest bearing account—but it is actually being used by the bank—until the taxes and insurance are due a year later.

You pay top dollar to borrow the bank's money. The bank borrows yours for nothing.

Besides the schemes already mentioned, unfortunately, there are dozens of other schemes, such as late fees. Mortgage companies normally charge a five percent penalty for payments that are paid late—usually after the 15th day of the month if the payments are due on the first. In our example home purchase, the late fee amounts to an additional $21. That means that if our hypothetical home buyer paid late one month, instead of $22 being applied to reduce principal, only $1 would have gone for that purpose, after the bank received its late fee.

What if the bank received your payment on time, but didn't process it quickly enough to your account. Oops. Most people might never know anything was wrong until they received their year-end statement, and even then might assume it was their fault or the mail system's. When in fact the bank is pulling a double scam by cashing your check on the first of the month, crediting it to your account on the 16th—giving the bank 16 days of interest-free use of your money—and making you pay an undeserved penalty.

In another example, suppose the bank pays your taxes late—so they can get maximum use of your money—and you are assessed a penalty. No problem. The penalty is paid from your escrow account and the bank increases the amount of money you are required to put into the interest-free account.

In another case, the bank sets your escrow fee too high. No problem. After the excess accumulation is discovered when you get your year-end statement, the bank will A) Keep doing it; B) After fighting with you, pleasantly lower payments; C) Mess around a while, then pleasantly refund your excess payment without penalty or interest—maybe even lowering your payment.

Never expect a bank to pay you interest on excess funds that have been kept in an escrow account without a court order!

Another bank scam is sitting on checks. As of September 1, 1988 the Federal Reserve Board set limits on this behavior.[3] Although we can send a package by Federal Express almost anywhere in the world in about 24 hours, can pick up a phone and talk instantly anywhere in the world, the Nineteenth Century pony express was faster than transferring a check from one bank to another—even though they are just across the street from each another. I waited eight weeks for Benjamin Franklin Savings & Loan to clear a check from the Bahamas, and then they *charged* me for the privilege of doing business with them.

I waited 10 weeks for a check from Cayman to Benjamin Franklin Savings to reach Houston. It's a two-hour plane flight. The check went from Cayman to New York, a 10-hour flight, and then to another intermediary in one hour. Every bank that touched it took some piece out of it, and no one paid interest. It took a week for the check to get from the local branch office of Ben Franklin to its downtown sister bank. Ben Franklin would probably sue if he knew how his name was being used. After this, and other episodes, I quit doing business with that bank.

The game: Banks use our money for free booty, then charge us a handsome fee.

The solution: Take them before juries.

C. RARER THAN UNICORNS: THE HONEST BANKER

On one occasion, I dealt with an honest, decent, caring man who, for reasons I can't explain, ended up being a bank president.

At the time, I was representing Mr. Ngo, a non-English speaking, Vietnamese gentleman who had been cheated by a con-artist posing as a building contractor. Their story is more fully told in Chapter IV D. Ngo had written a check that inaccurately had been labeled "insufficient funds." The president of that bank came to testify at the criminal trial when my client was charged with writing a hot check. Without the banker's testimony, my client probably would have been found guilty.

The bank president took time off from work to testify, and refused a fee to compensate him for his lost time. He also took time from his office to talk to me. He returned my calls regarding the case. His motive? As difficult as it may be to understand and accept in a banker, it was purely to see that justice was done. He was pleased to do his part to help justice and was always friendly and courteous. He always refused any monetary compensation.

He testified truthfully and honestly. He was the epitome of what bankers hold themselves out to be—but in most cases are not. He was an intelligent, articulate, caring, honest man. He was genuinely interested in helping his customers.

When Ngo's civil trial took place more than three years later, I called the bank where this banker had worked, I was told that he no longer worked there, and they wouldn't tell me where he was working. Why? Apparently large numbers of people had asked for him and were transferring their business to his new bank. His former employer didn't want to lose the customers. So we had to hire a private investigator to find the banker.

Although I had developed a great deal of respect for this banker, I was afraid that since Ngo was no longer a customer of his and had not been for over three years, the banker might not be as willing to serve justice. He still was.

At the second trial, he testified again, and again without compensation. And, he testified truthfully and honestly. The man was a great witness. The very best witnesses are those who have a strong professional image—and who can't be bought. When witnesses testify truthfully and maintain good eye contact with jurors, the jurors respect them whether they are ditch diggers, auto mechanics or bank presidents. This man was a rare gem and an exception in his profession.

While this gentleman is clearly an exception, what bankers are as a rule is clearly illustrated by the following stories.

D. THE CONDO/CONTRACT CON

My client, whom we'll call Mrs. E, applied to assume a loan on a condominium in which she was the tenant. She signed a contract with the owner and filled out all of the bank's papers. She had worked all of her life and had paid all of her bills on time.

Two things happened: A) The person who signed the sales contract with her refused to go through with the sale. He decided that he hadn't made a good deal and he wanted to break his agreement and not sell the unit. Shame on him! B) The lending institution found out that my client was married and refused to allow her to buy the unit in her name. The bank wanted her husband's name on the deed and the contract. The implication was that my client, as a woman, was not capable of buying the property in her own name.

Two separate lawsuits were filed and had to be juggled simultaneously. The first was a specific performance lawsuit against the owner in state court, and the second was a sex discrimination lawsuit against the bank in federal court. I drafted and filed both the lawsuits, settled one and arranged for an associate to finalize the other. In both cases, the opposing attorneys were incompetent and were mowed to the ground.

In the first lawsuit, the owner had no case whatsoever. He simply didn't want to close the deal. What did we do? Mrs. E was living in the condominium and stopped paying him rent. We filed suit for specific performance—demanding that he perform specifically and sell the unit as he had agreed to do. The owner wasn't as smart as he was greedy and his attorney was his peer. No action to throw her out for non-payment of rent was filed, and no counter-claim was filed.

Texas law strongly favors the landlord on the issue of non-payment of rent. In this case, the landlord was now living in Louisiana. He was hit in the pocketbook. No monthly payments were being made pending the lawsuit, but the owner still had to make payments to his lending institution. Mrs. E, if she lost the property would at least have benefited from a few months of free rent.

We sued the lending institution in federal court for sex discrimination. We didn't want to settle with the lending institution before we had either beaten or settled with the owner, and we didn't want the two of them to get together. Fortunately—since both defendants were incompetently represented—they didn't file the necessary discovery motions, and never found out about each other. If they had found out about each other, they could have united and caused us more problems.

After about a year, the owner realized that it was not to his benefit to make mortgage payments and not receive rental payments. However, if the lending institution foreclosed, my client would have to move out and would not be able to buy the condo from him.

At the end of one year, my client settled with the owner. He agreed to honor the original contract, selling the unit at the originally agreed price. My client agreed to resume rent payments until the loan was cleared. My client benefited because the unit had gone up in value during that year and my client had not spent any of her money. All of the documents were signed and the final judgment entered giving a local attorney the power to sell the unit.

At this point, one of the lawsuits was settled.

My associate L.T. "Butch" Bradt—who later became a banking expert—took over the lawsuit against the mortgage company and performed brilliantly. Butch had researched the case thoroughly and had determined that the mortgage company's position—insisting that my client's husband join her in the contract—was untenable. After hearing both sides, the federal judge instructed the mortgage company lawyers to allow the transfer of title immediately or the judge would see that it was done on very unpleasant terms.

The mortgage company conceded, and were forced to pay their own legal fees, my client's legal fees, and several thousand dollars damages. Our client became the new owner of the condominium unit by assuming the loan without her husband, and using the mortgage company's money from the damages awarded in the state lawsuit, was able to assume the loan.

Ridiculous? Absolutely. Two foolish and incompetent clients with foolish and incompetent attorneys had taken a mole hill and turned it into a mountain. Butch and I walked away with handsome fees, and our client walked away with the condo, a year's free rent and money in her pocket. Was it essentially fair? Quite frankly, our client received significantly more than was due her.

E. WHO'S ACCOUNTABLE FOR THE ACCOUNT

In another case involving a bank, I represented a client who was involved in a business partnership dispute. My client filed suit against her partner, and filed a separate action against the bank. The action against the partner was settled the day before trial, and at the other party's request the settlement was sealed. That means no one gets to read any of it or see any depositions, and it means that the case won't be discussed in this, or any other book.

My client's partner had a large amount of money deposited in the bank. Based on her partner's advice, my client had opened an account in the same bank. Only my client and her mother had the authority to sign on that account. The ex-partner went to the bank and argued that since there was a dispute between that partner and my client, the bank should prevent withdrawal of the funds in my client's and her mother's account.

In violation of the contractual agreement between the bank and the account holders—which provides that only those persons whose signatures are on file for that account can withdraw from it—the bank official decided that ex-partner should also have access to that account. Remember, only my client and her mother were authorized to control the account. Nevertheless, the bank official took all of the money out of the account, and wrote out a check to my client and her ex-partner.

"Any lawyer who is capable of trying cases and is also capable of settling cases is a valuable commodity."

The effect of the bank's action was to place my client's personal funds into a non-interest bearing check that required the ex-partner's signature. The bank took the money out of the account without telling my client or her mother—the only two people authorized to sign on the account.

Unaware that they no longer had an active checking account, both women continued to write checks—and several checks bounced. Sound like fun? Well, it wasn't for my client and her mother. Had they been damaged? You bet.

The total amount of money involved was $3,300, but damages resulting from the bank's violation of banking principles and the infringement on customers' rights were far in excess of that sum. Most of the time a bank can win a case like this for the simple reason that no one files suit. People are afraid of banks and don't want to sue them. I've never figured out why because banks are usually not competently represented. And, it's not usually profitable to sue over an amount of money as small as $3,300, but once sued the banks are in a pickle. No one likes bad bankers, and some people don't even like good bankers.

In this case, the bank was represented by an extremely competent trial attorney. He is similar in nature to the honest bank president I described earlier. Under the right circumstances, he can be lethal because: A) People tend to like him. Quite frankly, I liked the guy and so did the judge; and B) He was capable of trying and winning cases on his own.

Any lawyer who is capable of trying cases and is also capable of settling cases is a valuable commodity. This lawyer didn't try to con me. He admitted that the bank's position was difficult, but he was not willing to concede the amount of damages that I was seeking for my client. He offered a quick and reasonable settlement—but we had different ideas about what was reasonable. I wanted to close the bank down; he wanted to keep it open.

We settled fairly quickly for $10,000 plus court costs. Did he do the bank a good service? Unquestionably, yes. It would have been impossible to find a jury that would not have ordered the bank to return all my client's money. That amount up to $2,000 would have automatically been tripled if the jury found the bank's actions deceptive. That gets us up to $6,000. And, if we could prove the remaining $1,300 was wrongfully confiscated, that amount also would have been tripled.

Also, the jury probably would have awarded actual damages for the bounced checks and the credit problem that resulted—which could be a virtually unlimited sum. And we were entitled to attorney's fees.

Attorney's fees for trial would have exceeded $10,000.

The bank's attorney knew that if we had won a jury verdict, it would have likely been $20,000 or more. Settlement was a smart move for both parties. We had achieved a fair sum through settlement—three times the amount stolen.

Let's examine the deposition I took of the individual who had authorized taking money out of my client's account. The deposition of the banker is what induced the bank to settle. I know of no better way to dispel the fiction concerning the integrity and intelligence of bank officials than to let one such official speak out.

First, I wanted to narrow down the bank's policy. Was it the bank's policy to let unauthorized people draw money out of an account? The bank's official gave an excellent example of how careful a bank had to be with its customers funds. I asked her to describe their policies, using for example, an unrelated, fictional account. In this excerpt, the answers are from the clerk and the questions are mine.

A—Okay. Suppose that you went to the bank and opened an account and your name is Michael Louis Minns and that's how you signed your signature card, Michael Louis Minns.

Q—Yes, ma'am.

A—Suppose you went to the grocery store and you signed M. L. Minns.

Q—Okay.

A—When the check got to the bank, the signature would not be like the one that is on file.

Q—Okay. And, so, the bank would not honor the check for that reason?

A—The bank would have an option in the matter. It might choose to call the customer and say, "We have a check in. It's signed differently. Was this your check? May we pay it?"

Q—Okay. Now, what if there was an entirely different name on the check? Would the bank honor the check? Let's say that the account said Clara May Clerk and the check came in signed Johnny Smith. Would the bank honor that check?

A—If Johnny Smith had been a signer on the signature card.

Q—And that's the only way that anybody can write a check on an account is to be a signer on the signature card?

A—Generally you wouldn't sign a check unless it was your account.

Next, I wanted to establish what had happened to my client's money. This wasn't easy. Observe the dialogue: I ask questions, and the witness attempts to ignore answering them about our specific case.

Q—Okay. Now, Exhibit 2 consists of two pages; and this is a letter which I sent the bank addressed to a bank officer. What is this letter about? What's the content of the letter?
A—This letter has to do with the $3,388.02 that this lawsuit has to do with.

Q—And this money was withdrawn from the account?
A—That is correct.

Q—Okay. On whose authority was the money taken out of the account?

(Witness - asks for assistance from her attorney)
Opposing counsel - You have to answer the question, if you can.
Do you understand what he is asking?
The Witness - Do you mind rephrasing you question?

Q—Yes, ma'am. I'd be happy to rephrase the question.

$3,388.02 was taken out of the account of number 025-000. On whose authority was this done?

Opposing Counsel—You need to listen to the question in the way it was phrased.
The Witness—Well, I have listened. And I still don't understand what he wants to know.

Q—Let me try again.
A—Okay.

Q—Who are the two signatories on that account?
A—The two signatories on the account are M and H.

Q—Okay. And these are the only two signatories on the account, correct?
A—That is correct.

Q—All right. Did one of them give you permission for your bank to take the $3,388.02 out of the account?

A—No, they did not.
Q—Okay. But the money was taken out of the account?

A—Yes, it was.
Q—Okay. On whose authority was this money taken out of the account?

Opposing Counsel—By that do you mean—I think he's concerned about who removed it. You're not asking that—are you asking why it was removed?
Mr. Minns—Who authorized it to be removed?
Opposing Counsel —Okay. Do you understand?
The Witness—I'm sorry. I really don't.

Q—Okay. Well, when I talked to you earlier I asked you how people could sign on checks and take money out of the account; and you told me that only signatories to the account could take money out of the account.

Now, we've just established that the signatories to this account did not take the money out. So, I'm trying to determine who took the money out and how they had the right to do that.

A—Well, I'm sorry. I don't know quite know what to tell you.
Q—Well, who took the money out?

A—The bank withdrew the money from the account.
Q—The bank you work for withdrew the money from the account?

A—Yes. That's correct.

Q—Who gave the bank permission to take the money out of the account?
A—No one gave the bank permission to take the money from the account.

Q—Why did the bank do this?

A—*The bank felt that it was in the best interest of both parties to withdraw the money from this account.*

Q—*Being the best interest of M and H to take the money out of their account?*
A—*Those two parties; and the other party to the lawsuit, C*

Q—*(Ex-partner) is not a party to this lawsuit. (Ex- partner) is not mentioned in the letter as a party to the lawsuit.*
Are you saying that (Ex-partner) told you to take this money out of the account?
A—*(Ex-partner) made demand on the bank for the moneys in the account.*

Q—*And based on her demand, you took the money out of the account?*
A—*Not based entirely just on her demand.*

Q—*Well, what else?*
A—*(Ex-partner) presented assumed name certificates to us showing that she and M owned this company.*

Q—*This is a company account, now?*
A—*Yes. This is a business account.*

Q—*And she showed you assumed name certificates showing that she owned the company?*
A—*No. That's not correct. She presented assumed name certificates to us showing that she and M owned this company. And I did know —*

Q—*Do you have that in the file? That assumed name certificate?*

Opposing Counsel—That's one of the exhibits in there.
The Witness—Yes. You will find that in there.

Q—*Okay. We will get to that. What else? Go ahead.*

A—*And I did know that these two ladies had been in business together, had had several companies together. And frankly, I thought that it looked like they were having one of those little disputes that, you know, people will work out for themselves.*
Q—*Is there any other reason why you took that money out of the account?*

A—It seemed to protect the interest of both parties.

Q—Do you know whether or not any check has ever been bounced on this account since you withdrew the money from the account?

Opposing Counsel—I'm going to object to the clarification of the question, basically. If we're going to get in an argument on semantics, we need to clear it up right now on whether or not the money was withdrawn from the account.

Mr. Minns—Okay. Your client has testified that the money was withdrawn from the account.

Q—Do you want to change your testimony now that you have had your attorney's instructions, or is that truthful testimony that the money was withdrawn from the account?

A—The money was withdrawn from the account.

Q—All right. Now, after the money was withdrawn from the account, did any checks bounce on that account?

Opposing Counsel—If you have personal knowledge. I'll object. And the question is asking her to come to a conclusion unless she has personal knowledge of those facts.

The Witness—All that I can say is that I personally overdrew that account, paid it into the overdraft. As far as whether any checks were returned after that, I do not know.

Q—So, on your own authority, then, you decided that what would be best is to withdraw these moneys from this account. Is that correct?

A—It seemed in the best interest of the bank and in the best interest of the two parties concerned.

Q—Well, there are three parties that you've told me about. Which two parties are you talking about?

A—I'm referring specifically to C and to M.

Q—Okay. How did it help M for you to take the money out of her bank without her permission?

A—(Ex-partner) was making demand for the funds and presented certain evi-

dence that indicated that there might be reason to think that the money was hers. She presented, as we have said, the assumed name certificates and indicated that the source of the funds in the account was from her account.

Q—How did that benefit M? What you did—you said you did it for her protection. How did you protect her?

A—It didn't give (ex-partner) an advantage over M in that the check was made payable to (ex-partner) and M.

Q—In effect, you were forcing her to negotiate with (ex- partner) in order to use the money out of her own bank account?

Opposing Counsel—I'm going to object. That's not a question. And it asks for a conclusion. I instruct you not to answer it.

We had to reconvene the deposition to get the bank records showing the bounced checks and transfer order. When we met for the second time, we discovered the evidence that many of my client's checks had in fact bounced. The banker who was deposed finally admitted that she had tampered with my client's account, on her own authority, with no legal right whatsoever. She had been dealing with the ex-partner of my client for eight years and had tended to take ex-partner's word about the facts and had arbitrarily sacrificed my client's interest to her ex-partner's.

My opposing counsel didn't particularly like wasting time in a second deposition. He was a no-nonsense, business sort of guy who liked to get things done quickly and effectively on behalf of his client. You don't see a lot of these kind of guys practicing law for banks. The bank clerk was being as evasive as she could be to avoid admitting that my client and her mother's checks had bounced because the bank had closed their account without notfication. A lot of lawyers on an hourly fee basis will file pounds of unnecessary paperwork and fight to the bitter end because it is profitable. This lawyer was interested in finding out what the facts were and then if justified settling. He's the kind of lawyer I recommend hiring and in fact I have on occasion recommended him.

F. THE LATE FEE FRAUD

I've done my share of suing banks professionally and in my personal capacity. In the case of Minns vs. Commonwealth Mortgage Company,[4] my friend and experienced bank warrior, L.T. (Butch) Bradt, represented me—but because I was so angry, I took the deposition of a senior vice president of the bank and others myself.

Commonwealth had a mortgage lien on my house for $75,000 with escalating interest rates, starting at 12 1/2 percent the first year and reaching 15 1/2 percent the fourth year. Was it outrageous? Yes. But in 1982 all the rates were outrageous. We expected to refinance when rates went down.

Commonwealth started charging me penalties for allegedly late payments and arbitrarily started changing the amount of the monthly payments. On two occasions during the same month, Commonwealth told me that I owed three different amounts for my monthly payment. Quite frankly, I didn't know how much I was suppose to send them.

On another occasion, the bank mailed the coupon and the check back saying it was the wrong amount. I sent it back by certified mail, since the coupon I enclosed was the most recent one I had received. Commonwealth Mortgage then charged me a late payment penalty.

This was upsetting because I had been paying on time. I usually put the check in the mail during the first week of the month. I was concerned that it wasn't reaching the company on time since they frequently charged a penalty for late payment. In order to protect myself from harassment, I started sending the payments in by certified mail. I also began examining the back of my checks to ascertain when the checks cleared.

I discovered that they were charging me late payments for checks that had been paid and had cleared on time. Our contract allowed me 15 days from the first of the month before a penalty could be assessed. They were counting my check as much as 30 days late; in some cases, 30 days after they had cashed it!

Commonwealth officials sent a collection agent to our home who interrogated our 10-year-old son. They sent us letters indicating that the note could be accelerated and we might lose the house if we didn't cooperate. When my wife or I attempted to talk with representatives of Commonwealth, we were shuffled around and referred to various people who frequently did not answer questions or letters.

I sued Commonwealth Mortgage—but the collection calls continued. In an outrage, I decided to take the deposition of the officer responsible for such unconscionable conduct. Robert Bell was sent over to my office to be Commonwealth's scapegoat.

I will share with you excerpts from the actual deposition:

Q—What is your position with Commonwealth?
A—I'm Senior Vice-President in charge of Escrow Administration. That's in the Loan Servicing Division.

Q—What is your function?
A—What do you mean what is my function?

Q—What does that mean?
A—Escrow Administration includes the payment of insurance, the maintaining of our insurance records on our mortgages, the maintaining of our real estate tax records on our mortgages and the analysis of the escrow requirements on the mortgage.

Q—Mr. Bell, did you bring my file today?
A—Yes.

Q—Mr. Bell, would you hand me the file, please?

Robert Bell and his attorney did not produce the documents I had asked for. The papers he handed me were incomplete. Defendant's counsel, Mr. McNaught, claimed the majority of the file was privileged work product done in response to the litigation. Bell had brought along a microfiche of my file rather than a print out. A machine to read this type of data is not standard equipment in most law offices.

Mr. Bell then offered a handwritten summary of the bank's record of my loan. I wanted the real records. He offered me a "version" of the real records. Even as he was tendering it, he called attention to three errors it contained.

Q—Okay. Other than those three errors, is this in perfect reconciliation with the other records?

A—Yes.

Q—Mr. Bell, let's look at the first page of Bell Exhibit 2. Now on the column marked "Payment Due Date," with a 1 over that, at the top of that it has, "M.L. Minns—Loan No. 782520." Whose handwriting is this by the way?

A—That's mine.

Q—So you personally prepared this sheet?
A—Yes, sir.

Q—And you prepared it by looking at the original records?
A—Yes, sir.

Q—I'll ask you one final time, you're certain this is correct, these figures are correct?
A—To the best ability and knowledge and interpretation of the original records, these are correct.

Q—There seems to be a little hesitancy in your asking my family to pay money based on these figures, so, again, is there any possibility that there will be any more mistakes other than the ones you've already pointed out?

Mr. McNaught—I don't think that's a fair question. It's kind of a compound question.

Q—Is there any possibility that there are any other errors on this?
A—Not to my best knowledge.

Q—Would it help to give you some more time to look at them and check them?
A—Can I state that the figures that were developed on this sheet was what I interpreted off of the ledger which I think I said earlier—to my best knowledge, I interpreted the figures from the ledger to this schedule properly.

Q—Well, penalties have been charged, foreclosure notices have been sent out and I want you to tell me under oath if those were based on the figures on Bell Exhibit 2.
A—Okay. Bell Exhibit 2 in regard to penalties assessed was an interpretation based on when the payment was due as to when we reflected the mortgage payment paid or posted on our records.

Q—Mr. Bell, I don't like the use of the word interpretation. Artists and scientists interpret. Archaeologists interpret. Accountants and engineers figure up exact figures.

Mr. McNaught—It may be easier to say what you mean when you say interpretation.

The Witness—What I mean when I say interpretation is I took the ledger records, the detailed records and transferred those records onto this schedule and, based on the due date of the mortgage and when those records indicated that we applied the payment received from the mortgagor that there was either late penalties due or not due, based on those two dates.

Q —Are they correct dates?
A—They are correct dates based on the postings off of our records.

Q—When you get a check, is it posted the same day you get the check?
A—Under normal circumstances, if the payment is tendered in the correct amount based on the records that we reflect it is posted within a 24-hour period.

If it is not tendered in the exact amount of the payment indicated on our records, then there could possibly be a delay in the posting of that payment because it has to be reviewed.

Q—In other words, when is the due date on this particular loan?
A—The due date is the first day of the month.

Q—When is the delinquency date?
A—It's 15 days after the due date, so it would be on the 17th of the month.

Q—On the 17th of the month?
A—Yes.

Q—If it's due on the first and if there's 15 days, then it is not delinquent until the 17th?
A—Until the 17th of the month, right.

Q—So if it comes in on the 17th at 5:00 o'clock p.m., then it should not be posted?

A—No. It is delinquent on that day.

Q—If it comes in on the 16th day of the month, there should be no penalty?

A—Yes, sir.

Q—If it comes in on the 16th day of the month and because of your 24-hour posting you don't post it until the 17th, would it then be posted delinquent?
A—It's received prior to the closing of the cash on the 16th of the month, it would be recorded as posted that day. Can I explain?

Q—Yes. Explain in detail.
A—We use what is called a lock box to accept and process our payments. that's with Texas Commerce Bank.

The payments, if they are tendered as we instruct our mortgagors to our lock box bank and they are in the amount of the mortgage payment, then they are processed the day they're received in the majority of the cases.

If they are not in the amount of the mortgage payment, then they are sent to our office for a proper review and application.

The next issue we dealt with was the multiple coupon books calling for the payment of various different amounts due for the same month.

Q—How does the customer ordinarily determine what amount he's supposed to send Commonwealth each month?
A—Normally by his coupons.

Q—Do you ever have a situation where you send in a one- year period four different coupons to the customer with four different amounts?
A—That's possible.

Q—In that situation, which one of the four amounts should the customer send in?
A—Well, he should send in the appropriate one for the payment that's due.

Q—Well, let me ask you—let me rephrase the question.
Have you ever sent four separate amounts for the same monthly payment on coupon books?
A—I'd have to say yes.

Q—Which one of those four, assuming there were four separate coupons for say April 1, 1982, which one of the four should the customer send in?

A—I don't know.

Q—Assuming the customer didn't guess the right one of the four, since you don't know which one to send in, and it was the wrong one of the four, assuming it was too much or too little, would you then send it to the other office and it would be marked late?

A—Well, it would only be marked—are we again talking on the 16th of the month? Because if it was received on the first of the month and it was sent out, it wouldn't be marked late.

Q—Let's say it was received on the 10th of the month and it wasn't—the customer, taking these four slips, picked the wrong one—I guess the odds would be against the customer picking the right one—the customer picked the wrong one and mailed the wrong one in.

That means the wrong amount would be moved out of your normal circle.

It wouldn't be posted at the time on the 10th, correct?

A—Okay. Let me go back to redefine the way the payments are processed to help clarify that point.

Q—Please do.

A—The instructions our bank has—our lock box bank is that if a payment comes in with a coupon—okay—let me back up one minute.

We place with the bank on a daily basis what we call a stop deck.

A stop deck indicated these are the loans we do not want them to take payments on for whatever reason. All right?

Q—What's that word?

A—Stop deck.

Q—All right. You don't want them to accept the payment?

A—Right.

Q—All right. Go ahead.

A—Assuming there is no—that a loan is not on the stop deck, then if the payment amount equals the coupon amount, they will process it through their computer and accept the checks.

Q—You're saying that the payment amount might not be the same thing as the coupon amount?

A—No. What I said was—is that the payment amount, meaning the check tendered—

Q —Right.
A —equals the coupon amount tendered with the check.

Q—Right
A—If those two equal each other —

Q—Yes.
A —the bank will deposit the check and notify us of the amount of the payment that was posted.

Q—100 percent of the time?
A—100 percent of the time.

Q—Now —
A—Assuming there's no stop deck or there's not stop on it. Okay?

I asked about the records showing when coupon books were sent and got an amazing answer:

Q—And so you have no coupon cards and no way of telling me the amount of those coupon cards?
A—Those records are not available now.

Q—Where are they?
A—They're destroyed. They're gone.

Q—The bank has destroyed the records of the coupon cards?
A—Let's put it this way: they were not maintained. They were not kept.

Q—That's incredible. You're telling me that no one in that bank can tell how many coupon cards they sent out for the same monthly period?
A—Not at this time, no.

Q—And they can't tell the amount that they told me that I was supposed to pay?
A—No. I can —

Q—Is this a common thing for Commonwealth to send out four sets of coupon cards for the same month in the same year on its accounts?

A—No.

Q—How many times has this happened?

A—I don't know.

Q—Okay. But you do know that it has happened numerous times?

A—I know that there is—let me clarify.

First of all, there are situations where we would provide coupons on certain types of loans that would overlap each other.

If, for instance—and I'll give you just a for instance here to help define this—if we sent out a set of coupons—which normally they cover a year's period, because we analyze our accounts one time a year—and the customer called in and said, "I lost my coupons, would you please send me another book," well, that second book is still going to cover basically the same period the first book covered or if a customer called in and said, "I received a set of coupons. They appear to be in the wrong amount. Would you please send me a correct set of coupons," then the book we would send out at that time would also cover the same period.

Q—Okay. Let's speak about this specific case, because in this case the customer never lost any of the coupons.

Tell me why in this specific case numerous different coupon books are sent out?

A—I don't know.

The deposition continued along these lines. Next, I questioned the officer on the bank's policy in regard to posting checks.

Q—Is it possible that the bank cashed them before they posted them?

A—I don't know.

Q—Is it possible that the bank did not go through its standard policy of posting these things within 24 hours and, in fact, posted them sometimes 48 hours late?

A—I don't know.

Q—Is it possible that sometimes they posted them six weeks late?

A—I don't know.

The bank officer admitted, in the record, that an apology was in order.

Q—If you received my check on February 1, 1985 and you reflect on your records that you did not receive it until February 26, 1985, would the bank owe me an apology? Yes or no?

A—If we received our check prior to December the 15th and didn't post it—I mean not December—February —

Q—We're on February 1, 1985 on column 1. Do you see that?

A—Yes.

Q—Circle it, please. I want to make sure you see it. Put an X by it to make sure that you see it in that little column right by it. Okay.

A—Yes, sir.

Q—Let me walk over and make sure that you see it so that my copy reflects the same X as your copy. Okay. That February 1, 1985 on the second page of Bell Exhibit 2, it shows that you posted it February 26, 1985; is that correct?

A—We posted the February installment, yes.

Q—If you received it before February 15, 1985, do you owe me an apology?

A—I know what you're saying.

Q—Circle the one you say—February 26, 1985. Circle that, please. All right. We're looking at the same figure. I can see by your circle, correct?

A—Uh-huh.

Q—If that came into the bank on February 15th or earlier, do you owe me an apology?

A—Yes.

Q—If that came in on February 15, 1985, is this exhibit deceptive?

A—I can't say. I don't know when it came in.

Q—I know. If it did, is the exhibit deceptive?

A—No. I wouldn't say it was deceptive because—

Q—Is the exhibit lying to us if it says—

A—No. The exhibit only illustrates when the payment was actually applied.

Q—All right. It doesn't illustrate when you received it, when it was received?
A—Right.

Q —But it does illustrate that you charged me a penalty, doesn't it?
A—It indicates that we would have assessed a penalty for that installment.

Q—No, sir. It indicates that you did assess me a penalty, correct?
A—That's what I just said, that we did assess you a penalty.

Q—I misunderstood you. I thought you said that it indicated that you would have assessed a penalty.
A—I said "would"?

Q—Yes.

The Witness—Right. Correct.

Mr. Minns—The record should reflect that Mr. Bell has done a lot of scribbling and notes on Bell Exhibit 17 on the side parameter.

The Witness—Which I apologize for.

Robert Bell admitted that collections representatives had continued to call me after I requested that Commonwealth only deal with me through my attorney. He further admitted that one of their representatives reported speaking to a youngster.

I could not elicit from him a firm figure as to what their late payment penalty was, or even what my next monthly payment should be.

Q—For the purposes of the record, then, Bell Exhibit 18 is wrong; that being the handwritten entry, correct?
A—To my best knowledge.

Q—And the computer record, Bell Exhibit 17, is wrong?
A—Appears to be so, yes.

Q—And Bell Exhibit 2 in column 6 alone would appear to be correct?
A—To my best knowledge, yes.

Q—Although it's possible that Bell Exhibit 2 is wrong and the computer is right?
A—I don't know.

Q—Okay. And it's also possible that all three are wrong?
A—I can't say. Anything's possible.

Q—And it's possible that the bank doesn't even know how much I owe them?
A—I don't know.

Q—And it's possible that you don't even know how much I should pay next month?
A—Presently I don't know what your current payment is, right.

In addition to Mr. Bell's deposition, I also took the deposition of Wanda Jackson, another Commonwealth Mortgage Company employee who admitted to similar confusion.

I answered interrogatories and submitted them to the court. I had tape-recorded telephone conversations with Commonwealth employees. In all cases, I told the people that they were being tape recorded. Nevertheless, they talked on.

In May 1986, I had to give my deposition. The deposition lasted from 2:30 in the afternoon until 6:30 in the evening—four more hours of attorney's time for McNaught's client and four more hours of court reporter's time billed to the shareholders of the bank.

In my deposition, I was asked why I felt that the bank had operated with malice. I told Mr. McNaught that I considered it to be malice to question my 10-year-old child; I considered it to be malice to continue to make collection calls when I was current; I considered it to be malice to continue to do so even after they had been sued; I considered it to be malice to harass me at work and to harass my wife and child at home.

Mr. McNaught indicated that he didn't believe that I had tried hard enough to work things out with the bank.

I kept my promise and sued Commonwealth. Did they like it? No. In fact, the bank employees seemed surprised that I had sued them. The case dragged on for three years without the bank making any settlement offer. Legal fees for the bank mounted up in a case in which there was absolutely no chance that Commonwealth could win.

Finally, while my attorney, Butch Bradt, was in trial on the Health Club case, which is described in Chapter III C., I settled Commonwealth case myself. Commonwealth agreed to lower the balance on my note from $73,495.56 to $59,000. This is a considerable drop, when you consider that after five and a half years of ownership and 72 faithful monthly payments, the balance had decreased less than $1,600 from the original $75,000.

Under the terms of the settlement, I was allowed to pay my taxes and insurance directly, instead of paying it into a Commonwealth escrow account—literally allowing them to borrow the money interest free for a year. They also allowed me to stop paying the one-half percent Private Mortgage Insurance. This coverage does the homeowner no good. It only protects the mortgage company. If the homeowner defaults after having made at least 60 consecutive payments on time, the insurance company pays the lending institution the balance. If Commonwealth wants such coverage on my account, they will now pay for the premiums themselves.

Taking into consideration a contractual interest reduction which went into effect last year, my monthly payment dropped from a high of $1,200 to a low of $500. My schedule of total remaining payments dropped from 30 years to 18 years. I still don't know how much I was cheated out of with late payments and I don't think the bank does either. With the settlement completed and the payments lowered, it doesn't matter.

G. MORE SCAMS AND SUITS

I have handled another dozen cases against banks for clients, past and present, which won't be reported here because the space won't permit the rendering of them all. However, I will briefly comment on two other cases that were settled shortly before this book was published.

An individual had a Gold American Express Account with Texas Commerce Bank—Lakeside Branch. The bank had declined to renew this customer's line of credit because he refused to provide them with an updated financial statement. For that reason, he wanted to talk to the bank officials prior to paying off the line of credit. A great deal of difficulty ensued, and the customer did not make the payments on the account for several months.

The bank and the customer made an agreement. In return for the removal of any negative reports entered by Texas Commerce against the customer's credit record, he would convert the line of credit which he was obligated to pay to the bank at 14 percent into a 17.99 percent promissory note by borrowing the entire amount of his debt plus interest.

"The most damaging entry on a credit report is the statement that a debt has been written off as non-collectible."

At that point, he didn't check to see if he really owed the entire amount or not. He just wanted to get Texas Commerce off his back and not suffer a credit loss, so he agreed to those terms. He executed the note and paid the bank off in full. What did the bank do? They filed a report with the credit bureau saying that he hadn't paid them. In fact, Texas Commerce alleged that they had written off the account as a bad debt. This action hurt the gentleman's credit. The most damaging entry on a credit report is the statement that a debt has been written off as non-collectible.

Since the bank told the customer, in writing, that they hadn't submitted any damaging credit report, he had taken their word for it. He made all the payments on the promissory note on time. Did Texas Commerce report each payment as it was made? I leave that for you to guess.

When the customer learned what Texas Commerce had done, he asked the bank to correct the report with the credit bureau. The bank filed a new report—a year later—that said the customer had been frequently paying late but had finally eliminated the debt.

Bottom line: The customer sued the bank for the damage done to his credit rating. After a large file full of discovery documents changed hands, the suit ended up being settled for a satisfactory clearing up of the customer's credit, and attorney's fees paid by Texas Commerce.

In another case, a man and his wife had a VISA account with First City National Bank. Their credit card was lost or stolen, they didn't know which. Under the Federal Debt Collection Act regulating credit cards, the customer asked the lending institution, to send him copies of all of the statements showing that either he or his wife had signed for the charges—which added up to the $1,600 that First City claimed. Since the credit card was missing, the customer needed to be certain that some unauthorized person had not been running up the charges. Is this unreasonable?

Apparently First City thought so. They never sent their customer the statements. Was this couple trying to cheat First City out of its money? Absolutely not. The customer told the banker in clear and unambiguous terms that every single slip which bore his or his wife's signature would be paid under the terms of contract with the bank. The bank never sent the papers. They just sent bills. The customer filed suit.

Through the discovery process, it became known that the bank didn't

> *"In a computer wire service age,*
> *they clear checks slower*
> *than the pony express."*

keep the original records with the customer's original signatures. Only microfilm records were maintained, photocopies of which were very difficult to read. Many of these photocopied charge slips were not identifiable. Neither spouse could recognize the signatures at all.

After voluminous discovery and an enervating period of waiting, this suit settled, with First City dropping its claim against the man and his wife and paying costs of court.

H. THE FUTURE FOR THE CURRENT OLD TIME BANKING INDUSTRY

There is none! Our banks have become nickel and dime and dollar and percentage robbing machines. They rob from the middle-class with exorbitant credit card and auto loan interest rates and and give multimillion dollar unsecured loans to professional con-artists and dictatorships. They are subsidized by the government. In a computer wire service age, they clear checks slower than the pony express.

Until the late '70s, all national and international non- cash money transferences were set up to use banks. In 1988 we still rely on them but they are already obsolete. By the year 2000 they will no longer exist in the form they inhabit today.

As the consumer obtains access to communications services and new age banks, they will leave the old age banks in droves. More banks will close their doors, be taken over in mergers, or reorganized in the next 10 years than in the last 300 years. The reorganizations will strap government insurance so much that interest due will often be frozen and many banking with old age banks will receive long-term payouts after reorganization rather than cash.

New modes of electronic payment and checking will eliminate check clearing delay scheme. Competition will be available at your door step by computer. You will shop for credit cards and money the way you shop for groceries, and opening new accounts will be done at home by instantaneous computer entry. If banks try to stop this or prevent it through politics and scams they will only delay the inevitable. The tide of technology will again wash over the scams of the old banks. The new bank may be a friend with a Swiss account who programs her number into a user's channel for borrowers and offers it on terms that coincide with yours.

The current banking system simply does not make sense. It's not competitive and it relies on outdated, non-competitive government protection and subsides. The laws are changing, consumers are becoming more educated, and technology is demanding to be a part of the selection process.

I. CONCLUSIONS

In the course of my dealings with banks as a customer, and as an attorney, I have found that while the public believes that banks keep accurate records to the penny, the truth is that their records are often not even accurate to the hundred-dollar mark. A few words of caution when dealing with banks:

A) Don't trust the bank.

B) If you have to deal with a bank, try to find an honest banker. I've found a couple; I'm sure there are at least another dozen out there somewhere.

C) Check the figures. The contracts and payment schedules are terribly complicated, and it may be wise to have a professional's assistance.

D) Banks and the credit card companies that deal through banks cheat people with great regularity. Investigate them, and, if wrongdoing is apparent, sue them.

"...while the public believes that banks keep accurate records to the penny, the truth is that their records are often not even accurate to the hundred-dollar mark."

CHAPTER XVII

REAL ESTATE

"What is real estate? Real estate is land or dirt and everything that is permanently attached to it."

A. THE EVOLUTION OF TITLES

Real estate instruments often have a certain mystique about them. To a neophyte, they may seem quite foreign and intimidating. As a general rule, these documents are worshipped by our society. Real estate instruments are locked away in safety deposit boxes and pulled out as indications of wealth or ownership of property. Frequently when non-lawyers transfer real estate from one person to another they physically hand over the deed that they received when they took the property. Generally, this type of transfer is only symbolic.

What is real estate? Real estate is land or dirt and everything that is permanently attached to it. If you have a piece of dirt and you put a car on top of it, the car does not become part of your real estate because you can just get in it and drive it off. However, if you build a house on that piece of dirt, one would presume that it's your intent to leave it there—being permanently affixed to the dirt, it has become part of the real estate.

In the beginning, God created the earth—or, if you want to, you can subscribe to theory that the earth got here through a series of coincidences and created itself. Regardless of the theory you subscribe to, sooner or later man arrived. Man began to congregate in groups just like all of the other animals. He decided that he would like to own his own space. If someone got too close to him, he would hit him over the head with a club or shoot him with an arrow.

Technology, of course, would someday allow groups of people to attempt to settle territorial disputes by dropping a bomb on the encroacher and later, claiming the turf. Nuclear technology has changed this basic concept. After a nuclear war, the conquered land may no longer have any

"Real estate instruments are locked away in safety deposit boxes and pulled out as indications of wealth or ownership of property."

value. Perhaps, then, the need to conquer no longer makes any sense either.

Over the ages, people began to acquire large portions of property, far beyond a simple dwelling place and family farm. William the Conqueror claimed most of England as his domain. Large-scale conquests created a new problem. How do you maintain control over all of your land? What do you call this control and what do you do with it? William had several good ideas which, to some extent, are still used today. As the Conqueror, he made himself the king. King William then rewarded his loyal fighters with titles. These titled lords and ladies held large portions of the king's property and paid him certain annual tributes for the right to be seized of the property. This seizing was the right to be on the property, subject to paying tribute to the king from the receipts of the property. William also brought with him the Norman concept of trial by conquest. The winner of a fight gets the spoils, the theory being that divine will selects the proper winner.

As time went on, land and land holding became more complex. Wars continued in the tradition of William the Conqueror. His heirs and friends also wanted to be conquerors. However, their goals of conquest were for new territories. The now-Anglicized Norman trial by conquest would be exported back to the continent of Europe, like the Japanese would some-day export cars back to the Americas. Expenditures went up to finance all the mini-wars, and inflation set in. More revenues were needed.

The feudal system was replete with problems. Frequently noblemen didn't pay their debts to the bourgeois class. If they didn't pay the debts, they might suffer permanent loss of credit, but because they were noble-men they did not face debtor's prison.

In Shakespeare's Merchant of Venice, a rather unworthy nobleman pledges to his Jewish banker, Shylock, a pound of flesh if he does not pay. Portia, the heroine and lover of our dandy, disguises herself as a member of the bar and argues that Shylock may have his pound of flesh so long as he takes no blood—a mere legal technicality. Shylock can't accomplish one without the other; he must suffer the loss of his money.

However, now the mere threat of the loss of blood requires Shylock to pay damages. Shylock is ruined and humiliated, the debt is never paid and England has supplied its answer to the Spanish Inquisition.

The real point is that the nobles went unpunished when they cheated others. The testimony of one nobleman was superior to a hundred money lenders. The nobleman always won.

Up to this time, only the Moslems or Jews were money lenders because of the prevailing Christian ethics against usury. But as times changed, the Christian church gradually realized that charging interest wasn't so bad and about a thousand years ago lifted its ban against collecting interest. Now, noblemen had a way to turn their hard assets—land and castles—into more spendable cash. Many eager Christian noblemen joined in the money-lending game and loaned money at interest to other noblemen. Things were different now, the money had to be paid back or debtor's prison became an unhappy option for noble debtors.

Now, it was lord against lord. When there was a financial dispute between nobility something very similar to what we call due process went into effect. Each side expected and often received a fair trial. The Merchant of Venice logic was now unacceptable.

A lord could send another lord to debtor's prison. Debtor's prison, an institution with deplorable conditions, was where one was permanently consigned unless he could pay his debts. Since he was incarcerated and not able to earn money, he could never pay his debts and often died in prison.

A plan had to be worked out to enable one to raise money quickly. The main thing that a nobleman had was his land, but he didn't own it. He was "seized" of it. He had to be able to transfer his seized position for money in order to stay out of debtor's prison.

An elaborate ceremony resulted. The lords would go out to the land and dance up and down and have a big party. Upon the conclusion of the ceremony, the lord transferring his land for money would reach down to the earth, physically grab a handful of dirt and hand it over to the new owner.

As the number of transactions grew, so did the types of ownership that could be conveyed for currency. It was possible to be seized of the southeast, one-quarter square-inch of the land, or to be seized of the right to collect tributes from the north-half of the estate for a period of ten years.

There were rights to dig a well and obtain water from a certain section of the land, the right to cross over the land or till the land—and all these could be transferred from one buyer to another. In short, many different types of rights could be given or sold away.

As the imaginations of cash-hungry landholders created new distinctions, land rights became increasingly complicated and needed to be reduced to writing. England passed the Statute of Frauds which stated quite simply that all land-conveying transactions had to be reduced to writing, or they were invalid.

The system was devised to replace the ceremony of "seizen." The king no longer owned the land. An individual owned it. This right evolved into what we know as title. Written records were maintained demonstrating the various rights of title. The ability to transfer this newly evolved thing called title grew and grew, and of course, the king taxed the transactions.

By this time, also, it was possible to transfer a property title during an owner's lifetime. After the owner died the property would revert to his heirs. This is the reason for the language at the bottom of most deeds which includes "successors and heirs." The buyer of piece of property today usually does not have to worry about the seller's heirs raising a claim to the land, but it is still in many deeds across the country.

A quick look at America before being invaded by Europeans will show the shortcomings of failing to recognize the value of real estate. Our American history generally teaches that when settlers from Europe arrived, they found a wild, untamed and unpopulated country, and they had to subdue it. In reality, America was already populated—by Native Americans (American Indians).

The Native Americans had absolutely no concept of land ownership in the way Europeans defined it. The Great Spirit had created the land. No one could presume to "own it." To them, "owning land" was as absurd as owning portions of breathable air would be to us (although that, too, may become an ownable, marketable item in the future). The key concept for the Native Americans was the right to "use" the land. Let's consider the deal the white man made in New York, trading a few costume jewelry beads for Manhattan. Without any concept of land ownership, it's easy to see why the Indians believed they were getting the best of the white man. After all, before this transaction, no one had even paid a single bead for the island.

One of my first cases in 1977 had to do with the succession of real property rights. The litigation had been going on for over a decade when I got involved. My client had purchased a piece of undeveloped land which had been the subject of a will made in the early 1800s before written conveyances of property were required in Texas.

The original owner, a rancher, left one of his two children the land and his other child the cattle. My client purchased the land from a descendant of the heir to the land. More than 25 years later, he was sued by a descendant of the other branch of the family—whose ancestor had received the cattle—who felt she should have rights to the land.

After a year on the case, we won a jury trial. A year later the judge signed the order. Two weeks later, he ordered a new trial. A year later the new trial took place, and we won again! My client's partner was represented by a certified trial expert who insisted on drawing up the order, which he did incompetently. The other side appealed and a third trial was ordered.

We won the third trial through a technicality and also took over my client's partner's interest by suing him. My client's ex-partner was a lawyer whose malpractice caused an oversight in the original deed to the two partners 30 years earlier. Real estate litigation can be complicated. Lawyers tend to be conservative with the language of documents. One hesitates to take out the archaic sounding common law language from a deed because no one knows whether or not a court will find a deed to be valid without that portion even though statutes in most states do not require it. In any event, the old legal maxim that, "If you are not certain you don't need it, put it in anyway," keeps thousands and thousands of word processors and copier machines running throughout the country today.

B. THE SUN TZU STORY

The traditional importance of ownership of land is as deeply embedded in the Eastern culture as it is in our Western heritage.

One of my favorite real estate stories is written in the Chinese book *Sun Tzu, the Art of War.* [1] I have taken a few liberties with the story.

China, in its feudal days, was divided into many small monarchies. Our story concerns several of these kingdoms whose territories bordered on each other. Monarch Binh was a bit more powerful than his neighbors, and since they all bordered on each other, he felt somewhat threatened. His neighbors coveted his land—but he also coveted theirs. Land was the one commodity that made you more powerful than your neighbors.

From time to time the monarchs would confer with each other, feeling each other out, in order to determine whether or not they needed to maintain combat-ready troops on the border or whether their neighbor was

"One hesitates to take out the archaic sounding common law language from a deed because no one knows whether or not a court will find a deed to be valid without that portion even though statutes in most states do not require it."

weak and vulnerable to an attack.

Monarch Ao was the greediest in the region. He desired to intrude onto Monarch Binh's domain and he wanted to expand his conquest in the other direction toward Monarch Zen's territory. He particularly watched Zen's territory because that kingdom seemed militarily weaker. The only factor that saved Monarch Zen from Monarch Ao's lust for conquest was that Monarch Ao was afraid that if he attacked Monarch Zen, his other border would be vulnerable to possible invasion by the powerful Monarch Binh. Monarch Ao wanted to test Monarch Binh to see how warlike he really was.

Monarch Binh presided over his small kingdom in relative security, content with this relatively stable balance of powers. One day, Monarch Ao, testing him, asked him if he could ride his great and beautiful horse. Monarch Binh's great and beautiful horse was the pride of his kingdom.

In fact, legend had it that it was the most magnificent horse in any kingdom. Would he allow his competing monarch the thrill of riding on his beautiful creature? He discussed this with his advisors. All but one of his advisors advised him not to allow the monarch to ride the horse. The exception was the Monarch's most valued counselor, Sun Tzu. Sun Tzu advised him that riding the horse was of no consequence; since it was of no consequence but merely a matter of vanity, it should be allowed. The other advisors argued opposing positions strenuously stressing that it would cause the king to lose face and be looked down upon. To the advisors' amazement, the Monarch decided to lend the great horse to Monarch Ao.

Monarch Ao, himself, was quite astonished.

Although he also had many beautiful horses in his stable, if he had such a wonderful horse as this one, he would never have allowed Monarch Binh to use it.

The ride was exhilarating. In fact, Monarch Ao decided he would keep the horse. Did he want to risk war over the acquisition of the horse? No. He decided to test the waters carefully. "I have decided to keep your horse, Monarch Binh" he stated. "But, of course, I must do so only with your approval, and I am willing to pay a reasonable sum for the beast after I have had the opportunity to ride it for a few months. Because my family has become so enchanted with the horse, I would prefer not to return it even though you demand that it be returned. What is your answer?"

Monarch Binh assembled his advisors. There was an uproar. All of his advisors, save one, demanded the king avenge his honor, and command the immediate return of the horse, threatening war should his ultimatum not be honored.

Monarch Ao, in fact, was so concerned over his perhaps hasty decision that he had maneuvered most of his soldiers into a defensive position on the joint border between the two kingdoms. He had already decided in his heart to return the horse if war was threatened.

All of Monarch Binh's advisors, except Sun Tzu, urged war. Sun Tzu's words to the king were quite different than those of his peers, "Your Majesty, the horse is of no concern. You have many other steeds who are almost as fast. Your pride in the horse is pure vanity. The kingdom can do without it."

Monarch Binh, in an astounding gesture, agreed to forfeit the horse. He asked Monarch Ao to kindly give a fair price for the animal, and he would consider the matter closed.

Monarch Ao concluded that Monarch Binh was a coward and he embarked on his battle plans to destroy his kingdom. How could Monarch Binh allow such an insult if, in fact, he had the ability or the courage to stop it? Nevertheless, it would not be wise to attack Monarch Binh without first consolidating the other neighbor's forces under Monarch Ao's complete and full control.

Why take any chance at all? Since Monarch Binh would tolerate any insult, Monarch Ao would first go and subdue Monarch Zen. He began to building up his armaments and preparing for war. Residents of Binh's Kingdom and Zen's Kingdom were afraid. No one knew who would be attacked.

After a time, Monarch Ao was fully armed and prepared to conquer the Kingdom of Zen, but he decided to test the waters further to make certain the former lion was still a lamb—he added a final insult.

Monarch Ao demanded one of Monarch Binh's favorite concubines. In fact, he told Monarch Binh that his demand was so strong that absent Binh's capitulation, Ao might be forced to declare war on Monarch Binh. Monarch Binh alerted his troops and conferred with his advisors. Again his advisors indicated to him that Ao's demand was a slap in Binh's face and an insult, and that he must not give up his concubine. Sun Tzu again had contrary advice, "Your majesty, we are not ready for war. We must begin the preparations for war immediately, but, we should do so quietly."

"Why quietly," inquired the king? "Because," responded Sun Tzu, "war is ultimately inevitable, but it is better to have our enemy either overestimate our strength or underestimate it."

"What about my favorite concubine," the king asked? Sun Tzu replied, "Your majesty, I am certain that you have had many joyous experiences with her, but I am also aware that she is nearing the age when it has been your custom to relegate concubines to a lesser status. If you give this concubine to Monarch Ao, she will receive glorious treatment as the most prized of possessions. If she remains, she will ultimately have less prestige. Keeping her is mere vanity. War for the sake of the concubine risks not only your kingdom but also the concubine herself."

The king shrugged his shoulders wearily and told his advisors, "We must, of course, prepare for war, prepare to defend ourselves, but for now, we must take every means at our disposal to postpone the war and keep negotiations open. I will send a message to Monarch Ao and request peace; and they will take along my beloved concubine."

Monarch Ao received these messengers gleefully. He took note that Monarch Binh was beginning to fortify himself for the inevitable defense against him, but he felt certain once he had conquered Monarch Zen, the united forces would be so intimidating to Monarch Binh that no battle would take place.

Ao's historians began writing about the certain conquest of the Kingdom of Zen, as though it were a mere historical interlude prior to the surrender of Binh's Kingdom, all foregone conclusions. For the entertainment of Monarch Ao, a clown was dressed to resemble Binh and was subjected to various degradations by Ao's court.

Monarch Ao attacked the Kingdom of Zen. He anticipated a very short war. He bid Monarch Binh's diplomats to return home bearing this message: "Our kingdom has grown powerful and mighty. Our people need more land. Fortunately, we are able to satisfy most of these needs by seizing all of the Kingdom of Zen. It will be necessary, however, to obtain a small token of land from your kingdom. As soon as we have conquered the Kingdom of Zen, we will accept a token of our mutual friendship and admiration: a small area of your land bordering our two provinces. This will make war between us unnecessary and our mutual Kingdoms can exist in peace. Please advise."

Monarch Binh's messengers returned with Ao's message; heads bowed. Sun Tzu was standing at the right hand of his majesty. Proud and erect, The King spoke; "Now, my advisors, with this new information, pray tell, what do you advise me to do for my kingdom?"

Almost in unison, the advisors responded, "Your majesty, you have a great deal of land, a small portion of it is inconsequential. We fear that after Monarch Ao has conquered the Kingdom of Zen, we will be at his mercy. We must buy peace at the cost of a token of land."

"And now, my sad, cowardly advisor, Sun Tzu, what do you recommend to your King?"

"Your majesty, you have no choice. There are no options. There never have been any options. You must wage war immediately. You must never give up one particle of our kingdom's soil. You must proceed immediately, with force, to take advantage of Monarch Ao's war with Zen. You must decide who will be your ambassador. Your decision must be clear and unequivocal so that your ambassador can convey a strong message to Monarch Ao."

The king pronounced, "I agree. All is replaceable except the land. The division of the land is the destruction of the kingdom itself. All is vanity except the land. Above all, the land must remain intact!"

"Sun Tzu, you are to lead an invading army, now! I have given instructions to my generals to prepare for war. They are mounted and ready to leave. As a sign of my decisions, you will drag before you the heads of my other advisors on a rope chain. Those who advise the destruction of the kingdom are traitors and must be executed."

Monarch Binh defeated Monarch Ao, seized the Kingdom of Ao, and humiliated the vanquished foe by putting him in a cage and parading him throughout the newly established joint kingdom. Monarch Binh subsequently wrote to Monarch Zen, to liberate him from his obligations to the now powerless Monarch Ao. Monarch Binh, then incorporated these new grateful subjects into his kingdom. This triple sized kingdom prospered under the rule of several generations of Monarch Binh's heirs.

The moral of this story is: Value land above all; ownership of the land is equated with power.

C. THE BUNDLE OF RIGHTS THEORY

This theory has been taught in many real estate schools and law schools across the country. Most authors claim it for themselves, and continuing in that line, this author will also claim it. While the original source is unknown, my use of the illustration is my original interpretation.

"Value land above all; ownership of the land is equated with power."

Picture in your mind a bundle of 50 sticks. Each one of these represents a right to the title of real estate. One of them constitutes 92 percent of the oil under your land. Another represents the right to three percent of the oil under your land. A third stick represents the right to one percent of the oil, plus the right to negotiate on behalf of the other 99 percent, regarding the sale or lease of the ownership of the oil, the executory rights. This is another stick in the bundle of rights. In other words, without that right, even though you own 92 percent of the oil rights, you have nothing to say about the negotiation or distribution and sale of those rights, you can only receive the money after the person who has the right to sell it makes the deal and distributes it to you. These are types of rights which are commonly bought and sold in the United States today.

A surface land title gives you the right to do anything on top of the land but nothing underneath the land. Common sense usually prevails and you are allowed to put in sewage pipes, television cables and other similar utilities underground. You have the right to lease the surface of the land for five years and one day if you chose to do so to someone else, but you cannot lease the sub-surface rights out for a second if you don't own them.

For example, if John Smith owns 100 percent of the surface of a parcel of land, including any improvements such as buildings, he could sell or lease the 100 percent surface rights to Sally Sue, but he cannot sell 25 percent of the underground mineral rights because another individual, Sam Doe owns them.

The rights to the surface, to water or to minerals may be leased, as well as sold. Hopefully you have now grasped that the lease could be for three years and six hours or any other term that is negotiated.

The right to own the land during your entire lifetime, only, is called a life estate. This is what originally was conveyed under ancient English law, since at that time, the law required that the land would revert back to your heirs after you died. The original English possessory rights of seizen did not include title, only a life estate of sorts with the balance to lord's heirs. The right to the land after you die is the reversion interest of the land estate. This is what could not be conveyed until the law changed to permit it. The total number of sticks in the bundle of rights is infinite, limited only by law or imagination.

Throughout the United States where some type of statute of frauds has

---

"A surface land title gives you the right to do anything on top of the land but nothing underneath the land."

---

been passed, title to real estate cannot be conveyed without a written document specifically describing what is being conveyed. There are, of course, numerous exceptions. In Texas, a lease for one year or less can be made orally.

The transfer or conveyance of all of the property rights that you own is generally called fee simple. In Texas, if you draft a deed with the common law language in it, you are conveying 100 percent of the conveyable title. The deed must contain any exception to total conveyance—it must mention any aspect of the property that you do not have the right to sell, or any portion of the property rights that you want to keep.

For example, John Smith owns a piece of property known as Yellow Acres. John Smith bought Yellow Acres from Sam Doe. Sam Doe did not sell him all of Yellow Acres, he retained 25 percent of all of the mineral rights. John Smith is now selling Yellow Acres to Sally Sue. When Sally Sue pays John Smith for the property, the deed he will give her must make note of the fact that he does not own the 25 percent of the mineral rights which still belong to Sam Doe.

In addition, John Smith might create another exception, stating that he is retaining 25 percent of the mineral rights. That means that Sally Sue will own all the surface rights to the land, but only 50 percent of the mineral rights. See Example I.

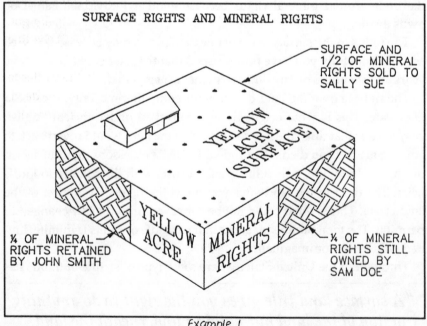

SURFACE RIGHTS AND MINERAL RIGHTS

SURFACE AND 1/2 OF MINERAL RIGHTS SOLD TO SALLY SUE

YELLOW ACRE (SURFACE)

YELLOW ACRE MINERAL RIGHTS

¼ OF MINERAL RIGHTS RETAINED BY JOHN SMITH

¼ OF MINERAL RIGHTS STILL OWNED BY SAM DOE

Example I

Texas law provides that you convey all rights if you do not specifically except them. In most states, the law is just the opposite, requiring that all rights conveyed be specifically mentioned in the deed. Included in the addendum is an example of a Warranty Deed.[2]

An enumeration of what is being conveyed must be committed to writing. It must describe with exact particularity every stick in the bundle of rights which is changing hands. This document is known as a deed. Of course, you can only sell what you own. If you sell more than you own, you can be sued for not transferring everything that you sold. The deed tells the buyer what the buyer is getting. It is like a bill of sale. The deed must name both a grantor, who is the party selling the property, and a grantee, who is the party buying the property.

The deed must sufficiently describe the property with a legal description; and it must provide for some sort of consideration, which is often the phrase "ten dollars and other good and valuable consideration." This means that a valid contract was executed and something of value changed hands. There must be actual delivery of the deed.

The deed should include any restrictions on the simple title such as mineral rights, rights of way, easements, etc. It should also include any restrictions on the property due to any other documents on file—such as promissory notes, other deeds, etc. to which the property is subject. This prevents the grantor from having future legal complications if the grantee later claimed that he thought he was buying more than he actually got. Limitations in the deed protect the signer of the deed, but limit the title rights to the grantee.

Since the deed is an instrument of such major importance, the parties to a land sale and purchase often enter into an agreement prior to the deed, known as an earnest money contract which sets forth a detailed checklist of the items to be conveyed. The earnest money contract is, in effect, a script for the deed and the closing.

The grantee must give something of value to the grantor—which is sometimes money but more frequently a promissory note. This person, if he obligated himself to pay, becomes an obligor, and the person he obligates himself to pay is the obligee. The person may also have become a payor by paying the money and the other person become a payee. If the person does not have the money and it must go to a third source, the per-

*"The rights to the surface, to water or to minerals
may be leased, as well as sold."*

son may mortgage the property thus becomming a mortgagor to a lending institution who becomes a mortgagee.

The person who does something is the *or* person and the person to whom or for whom it is done is the *ee* person. In my entire law career, I have never seen an exception to the *or-ee* rule.

Most deeds conclude with a habendum clause—the part of the deed that says "to have and to hold" and has four or five lines of common law language referring to the heirs. Sometimes the grantee signs the deed in order to accept some of the continuing terms. As a general rule, it is no longer done and not required.

All that's left now is for the grantor to sign the deed, and usually this must be notarized to be legal. In some instances, the grantee is also required to sign the instrument. Once the deed is recorded in the real property records of the proper county, the chain of title is complete.

D. LEGAL DESCRIPTIONS: THE CASE OF THE CENTURY-OLD SAPLING

A legal description is specific written information by which the reader of the document can find, with certainty, the property that is being described. At first guess, this might seem to be very simple. Suppose the property is the third house on Yellow Acre Street, with a mailing address of #3 Yellow Acre Street, Yellow City, Texas, U.S.A. Does that describe the property adequately? For most of the 200-year history of the Texas the answer would be "No." Today, with our relatively efficient postal system and local maps, the answer is probably "Yes."

However, when title companies, banks, and lawyers speak of legal descriptions, they mean a paragraph setting forth the boundaries of the property in great detail. In the above situation, you could locate the property, but you would not necessarily know the exact boundaries of the property. It is also possible that there is more than one street with the same name in that city. It is also possible that it is a very small street and not identified on any real estate records in the county hall of records.

The legal description consists of words that sufficiently and adequately describe the tract itself. The dimensions and the boundaries of the property are defined by what is called metes and bounds or distances and

"The transfer or conveyance of all of the property rights that you own is generally called fee simple."

boundaries. The measurements are generally taken by a surveyor. In most states, you must obtain a license to be a recognized surveyor. A century ago, lawyers and surveyors were frequently the same person. Abraham Lincoln did surveying work.

In order to understand what dimensions are used to describe a piece of property, please look at Example II. We'll start out with a square, which

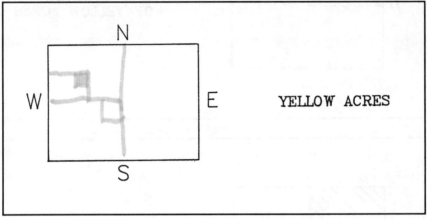

Example II

we'll call Yellow Acres. Yellow Acres has an N at the top of the square, an S at the bottom, an E on the right-hand side, and a W on the left-hand side. In this example, N stands for north, S stands for south, E for east, and W for west.

Now, let's take and shade in the northwest one-quarter of Yellow Acres. A legal description of the shaded portion would read: "the northwest one-quarter of Yellow Acres." It is sometimes abbreviated further to read: "the NW 1/4 of Yellow Acres," see Example III.

Our next example will be a bit trickier. Here, we're going to shade in the southwest one-quarter of of the piece of property described in the previous example. The legal description of this would be called: "the southwest one-quarter of the northwest one-quarter of Yellow Acres, and it could be abbreviated: "the SW 1/4 of the NW 1/4 of Yellow Acres," see Example IV. Going one step futher, we could identify the northeast quarter of the southwest quarter of the northwest quarter of Yellow Acre, see Example V.

You now have the basics of a legal description. Of course Yellow Acres

"The deed tells the buyer what the buyer is getting. It is like a bill of sale."

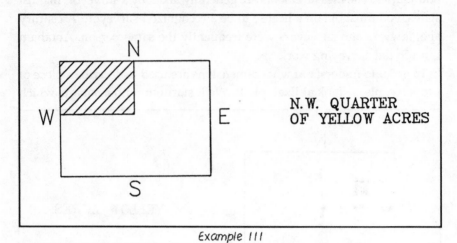

Example III

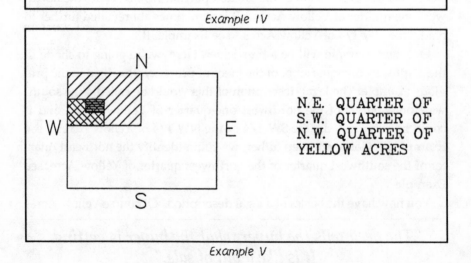

Example IV

Example V

itself must be located through some plat or survey, but once you have determined the dimensions of Yellow Acres, you can divide it and subdivide it in as many sections as you need.

Disputed surveys and inaccurate property descriptions are the basis of a great deal of real estate litigation. One such case made a distinct impression on me at an early age.

Property descriptions have to start somewhere, and in rural areas that haven't been divided into lots by developers, that starting point might be the intersection of two roads, the bend of a river or an oak tree. This is called the point of origin.

As a precocious child curious about the practice of law, blessed with a grandfather who was also curious about that subject, I watched several trials with him. We observed one trial in which the issue was property boundaries. The only question in the trial was, "Where did the property begin and end?" I went up to the front of the courtroom during breaks in the trial and looked over the notes to see what the lawyers were doing and why. Granddad encouraged this approach, even though it seemed that the lawyers preferred not to deal with an inquisitive 10-year-old. I was a serious reader at that age, devouring anything with ink on it—from comic books to law books and from newspapers to graffiti on restroom walls.

The trial lasted about two weeks, and Granddad and I saw most of it. The whole issue boiled down to which of two experts, both surveyors, the jury believed.

Although it's been over a quarter of a century, I would like to review the testimony I heard. One of the experts, who had been doing surveys for a local bank and several lawyers for about 10 years, said he had spent an entire week on the property involved in the lawsuit and had checked and rechecked his calculations. He had used as his point of origin on his first survey an abandoned creek and on a second survey the northwest corner which intersected with two farm roads. He'd placed a metal plaque in both places and made his measurements from there. The expert's testimony was sincere and believable but not nearly as credible as the second expert.

"POINT AND PLACE OF BEGINNING. Those are the key words in a metes and bounds description. No matter how many twists, turns and curves the property line takes, it must get back to "the point and place of beginning,"

The other expert had been a surveyor for two years, but previously he had assisted his father who had been a surveyor for 25 years. Father, son, and grandfather (who had always wanted to be a surveyor), had gone out to this particular property frequently, and surveyed it together because it just happened to be near their house, and they had all aspired to be surveyors.

This second expert followed the example of the original surveyor, more than 100 years ago, and used a pine tree sapling as his point of origin. The results of his survey were totally different from the results of the first party's survey.

The sincere attitude of the second surveyor inspired great confidence. Even the first surveyor, who watched the entire trial, stared in amazement and confusion when he heard the second testimony. He was put back on the stand, and told the jury that the second surveyor sounded so sincere and confident, that he had quite frankly to doubt his own measurements—even though he had checked and double-checked them.

The case went to the jury and the deliberations began. Everybody knew who was going to win the case. What I wanted to do was look at the survey and try to understand it. At first glance it appeared that the second survey was more credible than the other man's survey because it was identical, word-for-word, to the original survey and started from the same point of origin as the one that had been taken 100 years ago.

However, the 10-year veteran's new survey was entirely different from the original. I brought those two documents over to my grandfather, and he compared them and then he started laughing loudly.

The surveys were still in the courtroom because no one—the lawyers, bailiff or the judge—had bothered to give them to the jury even though they were the basic evidence involved in the case. Also, none of the jurors asked for the documents.

While the jury was still deliberating, Granddad said, "Now, I know that it's not true what they say about lawyers. Everybody says lawyers are the most dishonest people that God ever put on this earth, and it's just not true. Surveyors are more dishonest."

The jury came back in, and as everyone expected, rendered a verdict in favor of the second surveyor's client. Granddad and the lawyer sat and talked for a minute, and Granddad went to the bench to enlighten the judge about a point over which the lawyer was still confused. Back in those days, the courtrooms were a little less formal and no one objected to Granddad's intervention.

SUBDIVISION PLAT

YELLOW ACRES SUBDIVISION

N

BLOCK 1		BLOCK 2	
LOT1	LOT2	LOT1	LOT2
LOT3	LOT4	LOT3	LOT4
LOT1	LOT2	LOT1	LOT2
LOT3	LOT4	LOT3	LOT4

W

E

DEDICATED ROAD

BLOCK 3   MAIN ROAD   BLOCK 4

S

Example VI

At the lawyer's insistence, Granddad told the judge: "Judge, this must be the oldest pine sapling in the world." Granddad explained that after a pine sapling is about five years old, it ceases to be a sapling and becomes a tree. The court agreed. Either a tree had been cut down and a new sapling was planted on the same location as the original sapling, or somebody had lied. The lawyer requested a new trial, and the request was granted. The new trial resulted in a different verdict.

"In order to prove that you own a particular piece of property you should be able to trace your chain of title back to the original owner's acquisition of the property from the sovereign of the soil."

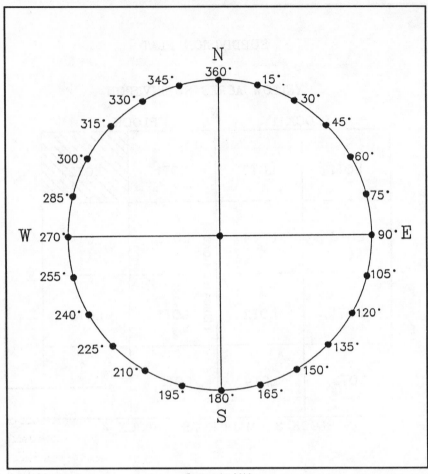

Example VII

Most property in today's cities are described by block and lot numbers. When houses are built in developed communities, most often the entire development has been platted. This means that a developer has taken a certain area of land, and divided it into lots, and has recorded that plat in official county records, so that the plat is a recorded subdivision and the lots are also part of the plat.

The parcel of property in Yellow Acres Subdivision, which is depicted on Example VI, most likely would not be referred to now as the northeast one-quarter of the northeast one-quarter, but rather as "Lot 2, Block 2 of Yellow Acres, a recorded subdivision."

Outside of most residential areas, the land has not been platted for development. In such cases, the land is described through a metes and bounds type of description, using latitude and longitude. Those are lines

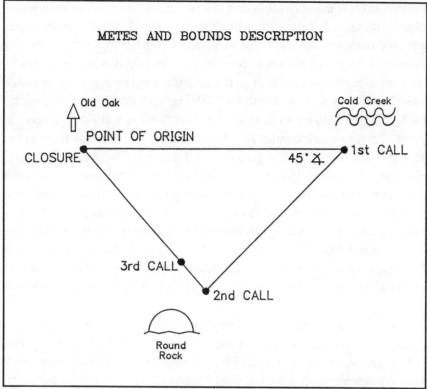

METES AND BOUNDS DESCRIPTION

Example VIII

running north and south around the earth, dividing the circumference of the earth into 360 degrees. When metes and bounds descriptions are used, rarely will that description mean much to anyone but a surveyor. However, along with such metes and bounds descriptions, a more general description is attached similar to this: "...or more commonly known as the old Bailey Farm."

In Example VII, you see a circle labeled with the four directions. A circle consists of 360 equal parts called degrees. Each quarter section contains 90° (1/4 of 360). In order to find a piece of property, you first find a common point to begin your description. This could be a bend in a river, the corner created by the joining of two existing streets, or an extremely old oak tree. Once the original point is agreed upon, that point is called the "point of origin." The point of origin (somewhere along the boundaries of

"The most common causes of title problems are liens— which are documents setting forth a claimed debt against a piece of property."

the property) is the only thing that is arbitrarily chosen rather than scientifically measured. Your survey unit (sextant) is put over the point of origin. The distance and the angle in terms of degrees to the next point is measured. The exact direction from the point of origin is written down as well as the exact distance. If there is a straight line then you have an easier task. If not, you have to break the distance up into different segments. Each change of direction is termed a "call,"and is related to a specific point. Turn now to Example VIII. Assuming that the Old Oak is the point of origin, the boundary line goes east, 900 feet to the bank of Cold Creek, (your second point). This is your first "call." You continue to your next point from the call, measuring south 45 degrees west, to the second call, the round rock. From Round Rock, the distance back to the point of origin must be described, such as running thence northwesterly 900 feet, to the POINT AND PLACE OF BEGINNING. Those are the key words in a metes and bounds description. No matter how many twists, turns and curves the property line takes, it must get back to "the point and place of beginning".

This basic sampling of real estate exceeds the knowledge of the majority of the people practicing law today. There are no survey courses given in law school. Although it is the job of the surveyor to do the actual work and measurements, it is a good idea for the attorney, the legal assistant, and you, the reader, to understand these basic concepts:

1. The points and the calls must close. If they don't come back to the point of origin, you do not have a legal description. **2.** The legal description on your proposed deed should match exactly the legal description that is on the original survey. A single incorrect call on a deed could render the entire deed inaccurate.

E. CHAIN OF TITLE

In order to prove that you own a particular piece of property you should be able to trace your chain of title back to the original owner's acquisition of the property from the sovereign of the soil. The sovereign of the soil in Texas could be the State of Texas; it could have been the Nation of Texas; the Government of Mexico; or the Government of Spain. On some occasions, more than one sovereign gave property rights to the same

"When a grantor signs a warranty deed he is guaranteeing the entire chain of title."

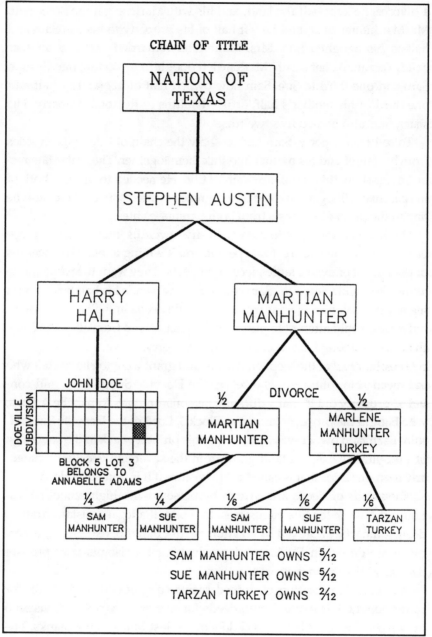

CHAIN OF TITLE

NATION OF TEXAS

STEPHEN AUSTIN

HARRY HALL

MARTIAN MANHUNTER

JOHN DOE

DOEVILLE SUBDIVISION

BLOCK 5 LOT 3
BELONGS TO
ANNABELLE ADAMS

½ DIVORCE ½

MARTIAN MANHUNTER

MARLENE MANHUNTER TURKEY

¼ ¼ ⅙ ⅙ ⅙

| SAM MANHUNTER | SUE MANHUNTER | SAM MANHUNTER | SUE MANHUNTER | TARZAN TURKEY |

SAM MANHUNTER OWNS ⁵⁄₁₂

SUE MANHUNTER OWNS ⁵⁄₁₂

TARZAN TURKEY OWNS ²⁄₁₂

Example IX

piece of property which often causes a title problem.

Consider Example IX, in which Stephen Austin received a large land grant from the sovereign Nation of Texas. He gave a portion of it to Martian Manhunter and a portion of it to Harry Hall. Martian Manhunter got a divorce; he kept half the land, and his wife Marlene got the other half. Mr. Manhunter died, and he left half of his property to his son Sam and half to his daughter Sue. Mrs. Manhunter remarried and had another child, Tarzan. At her death, Marlene left one-third to Tarzan, one-third to Sam and one-third to Sue. Sam now owned half of his father's half and one-third of his mother's half, or five-twelfths of the total property. His sister, Sue, also owned five-twelfths.

To sell his property, Sam had to show the chain of title on both sides from his father and his mother and link them together. The real estate record must show this complete chain of title. He needed to probate both of his parents' wills, get the court to recognize his interest in the land, and he had to file proof of interests from both parents' estates.

He then had the right to convey his five-twelfths interest in the property if that was his desire. Most people aren't willing to buy five-twelfths of a single lot or even a large piece of property. They want the whole piece of property with clear title. Sam could try to persuade his half brother and his sister to sell him their shares and execute deeds in his favor. Another individual could attempt to purchase the tract of land from all of the heirs, thus consolidating his ownership of the property.

The other half of the Stephen Austin land grant went to Harry Hall who conveyed it to John Doe who set up the Doeville Subdivision and conveyed property out to many different persons: one was Annabelle Adams, who bought the property known as Block 5, Lot 3 of the Doeville Subdivision. Each land owner was able to track his property back to the sovereign of the soil. The original land grant from the sovereign is called a patent and each one after that is called a conveyance if it is done by a deed.

Thousands of deeds are written by persons with high school educations who work for title companies. In Texas, if a legal assistant drafts a deed, it must be approved by an attorney. In Colorado, real estate brokers can write deeds. In Florida, independent legal assistants may prepare deeds and their names appear on them.

Although the drafting of a deed seems complicated or difficult, for someone who has worked with deeds for five or six years and has seen hundreds of them, it becomes child's play—just filling in the blanks. The tricky part is incorporating new changes that were not there in the original deed.

Most draftsmen just copy the contents of the existing deed into their own format. Often they want to make the new deed look special so they can charge more for it. Most state bars now produce fairly simple forms with extensive instructions.

On most commercial tracts where large dollars change hands, the deeds along the chain-of-title are usually custom made, expensive and sometimes very long—although not necessarily better than the forms. In most residential transactions where the fees are small, the deeds are rapidly processed almost always the short, simple forms.

On a $1 million deal, a $3,000 fee is practically unnoticable; a $5,000 fee that clears up a major problem is cheap. The more liens, the more conveyances, the more complex the chain of title, the more careful the draftsman must be. The greater the value of the transaction, the greater the need for safety. The legal description is generally the same unless the plot is divided. If the plot is divided, then a surveyor should come in to create a new legal description, which depicts the reduced plots.

In the previous example, if Sam Manhunter wanted to clear up his title, he would have to do it by getting all of the other heirs to sign over their interest to him. There are many other things which keep a title from being clear.

The most common causes of title problems are liens—which are documents setting forth a claimed debt against a piece of property. Liens might be filed by contractors who have built, repaired, improved or remodeled a piece of property. These are known as "mechanics and materialmens liens." Suppose that Mrs. Adams who owns a house and lot in the Doeville Subdivision (which was depicted in Example IX) contracts to have her roof replaced, but is dissatisfied with the quality of the work and refuses to pay the contractor. The roofing contractor might file a document called a "Mechanics and Materialman's Lien" for the the value of his labor and materials, let's say $2,500.

Suppose Mrs. Adams does not pay her federal income taxes. The IRS could file a tax lien on her home for the amount due, let's say for $1,800. Let's also suppose that she borrows $500 from her bank, a dispute arises with the bank over re-payment, and the bank files a lien on the property for that amount. If Mrs. Adams also fails to pay her local school tax assessment, that agency might also file a lien on the property for $150.

Suppose Mrs. Adams is sued by her sister-in-law who claims that she should own the property. The sister-in-law could file a Notice of *Lis Pendens* (meaning litigation pending in which the rightful title to the the prop-

---

"Drafting a deed should be done under the supervision of someone who has done it before."

---

erty is in dispute) which ties up the property. It tells anyone who might purchase the property during the course of the litigation, that if the plaintiff wins her lawsuit, the new owners will lose the property, because they bought it from someone who did not have the right to convey it. In the event that Mrs. Adams loses her suit to her sister-in-law, then the chain-of-title is diverted in a new direction, and the sister-in-law establishes a new chain of title.

Normally, no one buys property when ownership is contested. Items such as liens and Notices of *Lis Pendens* are "clouds on title." Some may be legitimate and some may not be legitimate, but they have to be resolved if Mrs. Adams wants to sell her property. If Mrs. Adams sells the property and doesn't tell anybody about these difficulties by including them in her deed, the buyer is apt to be angry because he may end up paying the I.R.S. lien, the school tax, and the other problems which are associated with the property.

When a lien is paid off, the person or entity who filed the lien must file a release of lien, which cancels the lien, with the property records department. Quite often people pay off liens, but the lien is not removed. When a lien is paid off, removal is not automatic. If no one files a release of lien, the lien simply remains on the record. The release should clearly identify the lien that's being released.

In the event that a release of lien cannot be obtained from the person filing the lien, the only option is litigation or getting someone such as a bond company to guarantee that the lien is not valid. If they are wrong, the bond company pays off the lien. An order of the court may be obtained which eliminates the cloud of title. Such an order can be filed on the real estate records.

One duty of a legal assistant may be to call people who have filed liens on a client's property to find out the basis for the liens and get a release escrowed. In other words, a legal assistant will agree that Mrs. Adams will pay the $150 in school taxes at the time she the conveys the property. A release of lien will be drafted, executed and held in escrow until the money is received. Then the release of lien will be filed.

When Mrs. Adams sells her house, she won't get to keep all the money she receives, since an appropriate portion will be placed in escrow to pay the IRS, the bank, the school district and any of the liens that are legitimate claims against her.

Each of these parties will file a release of lien for the claim they have made against Mrs. Adams' property. Of course, the entire sum does not necessarily have to be paid to release the lien. That can be negotiated. For example, an agreement might be reached for Mrs. Adams to pay $110 instead of $150, and still have the entire school tax lien released.

Delivery of the deed simply means handing the deed over to the party who is suppose to receive the property. If the deed is written and executed but never handed over to the other party it does not transfer title. This practice is reminiscent of the ancient medieval custom of physically handing over the dirt.

We haven't come very far since the original ceremony. The ceremony is now conducted at the office of an attorney, a title company or an experienced real estate developer. The transfer of papers occurs rather than the transfer of soil. Actually, the ceremony is legally unnecessary.

F. DEEDS, CONTRACTS AND CLOSINGS

When a grantor signs a warranty deed he is guaranteeing the entire chain of title. Suppose Stephen Austin gave a general warranty deed guaranteeing full title to Martian and Marlene Manhunter. Sue Manhunter inherited her portion and sold one-half to her boyfriend. Under a general warranty deed, Sue's boyfriend would have the right—if it was later discovered that there was a cloud on his title—to sue Sue, Martian Manhunter, and Stephen Austin. An example of a Warranty Deed is found in the addendum.[2]

Sue is personally liable for the entire chain and any defects to which she did not specifically mention in the written deed. That is why it is extremely important to resolve any problems with the deed.

However, Sue has another alternative. She can issue a special warranty deed—which means something less than a general warranty deed. As a rule, most special warranty deeds include the language "by, through and under me" or similar words, which means that Sue guarantees that no defects in title occurred during her possession of the property; a purchaser could not go beyond her ownership to her father's or to Stephen Austin's ownership or title. Nevertheless, the purchaser would still own the entire chain of title.

With the special warranty deed, if Mr. Boyfriend later discovered a defect in his title, he—not Sue—would be responsible for suing Mr. Manhunter or Stephen Austin for shortcomings in their general warranty deeds.

Ownership can also be conveyed through a quitclaim deed, which means the grantor "quits" having any "claim" he may or may not have had to the title. Suppose Sam Manhunter wants to consolidate title, but neither his sister Sue nor his half brother Tarzan are willing to assume any liability of giving Sam a general warranty deed. Instead, both might sign a quitclaim deed, giving Sam whatever interest they have in the property without representing that they have any claim. Sometimes it's easier to obtain a quitclaim deed because there is no risk of liability as there is with a general warranty deed. An example of a Quitclaim Deed is found in the Addendum.[3]

Ever since the original Statute of Frauds in England—and similar fraud statutes were brought to this country—an agreement to transfer real estate must be made in writing, subject to various limitations. The actual transfer must also be in writing. This agreement to transfer real estate goes by different names. In Texas, it's called an earnest money contract. In other states, it might be called a contract for sale, a contract for deed, or similar names. At this point, the reader may wish to review the portion of Chapter VI. part B describing a contract, since those elements apply to real estate contracts, as well.

The goal of an earnest money contract is to achieve a closing. Today's closing is equivalent to the ancient seizen ceremony in which the nobleman symbolically passed ownership of his estate by handing the buyer a handful of dirt. In the closing ceremony, a deed is generally signed, given over to a title company to be filed at the courthouse. Once it has been registered and photocopied, it is returned to the new owner as his personal evidence of ownership. File marks and numbers are assigned to the deed so anyone could locate the deed in the property records.

In Texas, the state Real Estate Commission has ordered real estate brokers to use commission-approved forms, or those prepared by an attorney. Even with this restriction, the seller of the property—who has the right to be his own attorney—still has the right to prepare his own contract. It appears that many real estate brokers, especially the older ones, draft their own contracts. This is strictly prohibited but commonly done.

At the same time, the earnest money contract is signed, and a sum of money, equivalent to a small percentage of the total purchase price is usually tendered by the buyer to the seller or a third party such as an escrow agent. In theory, the escrow agent is completely neutral. In practice, the escrow agent is usually an attorney or a title company who is generally partial to the party that brings him the most business. The escrow agent is often required to be bonded. He can be held personally liable in the event he breaches his duties under the agreement.

As an example, a sum of $1,000 is paid as earnest money on the purchase of a $100,000 parcel of real estate, leaving a remaining balance of $99,000 to be covered at closing. The $1,000 would be held by the title company in its neutral escrow account. The title company gets the benefit of the money unless there is a written agreement stating that it should be in an interest bearing account and setting forth who should get the interest.

As a general rule, the money is put into a non-interest bearing account. The escrow agent, who is supposed to be neutral, cannot legally use the money, but he can benefit by placing the money in a lending institution that values the escrow agent's business of bringing in non-interest paying money.

There are other costs associated with closings on real property. The title company will often sell a policy guaranteeing that the title is good, and that the seller is actually the current holder of the title. The title policy is in small print and has many different exceptions that severely limit the actual value of the insurance. The most common limitation of those policies is that the boundaries of the land are not insured; however, for a small, extra premium the company also will insure the boundaries of the property. It is a good idea to have this insurance. The question of who pays for this title insurance can be decided by negotiation.

A pro-rata share of property taxes is often paid at closing by the seller. Let's assume that property taxes on the $100,000 parcel of property are $1,000 per year and closing is taking place on July 1. In this case, the seller and the buyer would equally share the taxes since the property is being sold half-way through the year. At closing, the seller would pay buyer $500 as his share of the real estate taxes for the first half of the year, and at the end of the year the buyer would have to pay the entire $1,000.

At closing, the seller's $500 would be put into an escrow account. Also, any other expenses the seller owes (such as deliquent Homeowner's Association maintenance fees) should be put into the escrow fund.

Let us assume that there is also a lien against the property for $2,500. The Earnest Money Contract normally would refer to this lien describing it and providing for its release. These details generally occur simultaneously at the closing. Credit is given for all the interest, and the deal is closed.

The more parties involved, the more complicated a closing becomes. The purpose of this chapter is merely to acquaint the reader with some basic definitions and some information regarding in chain of title and deed draftsmanship. Drafting a deed should be done under the supervision of someone who has done it before. It should not be done by an unsupervised first timer whether that person is an attorney or a legal assistant, or a reader of this book!

If the purchaser is borrowing money to buy the house, the lending institution will want its interest secured by the property itself. In Texas, the security agreement is accomplished through a signed deed of trust and a promissory note. An example of a Promissory Note is contained in the Addendum.[4] This is the purchaser's promise to pay the money on certain terms and conditions.

A deed of trust conveys from the new purchaser a special interest to an individual who is supposed to be a neutral third party. This individual holds very limited authority to sell the property at a public auction under certain specific limited conditions—if the note is not properly paid. An example of a Deed of Trust is contained in the Addendum.[5]

In many states, mortgaged property must be foreclosed on through a court proceeding. However, some states, like Texas, have laws providing for non-judicial foreclosures, in which your signature on the deed of trust waives your right to a trial or legal hearing, and allows the trustee to foreclose and sell.

If no deed of trust is executed, then a judicial foreclosure order is necessary before the sale. The judicial foreclosure is more expensive and time consuming. It is fitting that there are sufficient legal protections before a property owner can be divested of real property through foreclosure, because, as Sun Tzu wisely pointed out, land is everything.

"Ever since the original Statute of Frauds in England— and similar statutes were brought to this country— an agreement to transfer real estate must be made in writing, subject to various limitations."

CHAPTER XVIII
WHAT YOU NEED TO KNOW

ABOUT NOTARIES

"The proper function of a notary in the United States is to assure the authenticity of signatures on real estate and motor vehicle conveyances, consent forms, wills, depositions, contracts, agreements and other important documents."

A. THE ROLE OF A NOTARY

Most Americans have had some occasion to have a document notarized. What does this mean? First, you had to find an individual who was a Notary Public. Perhaps, your search took you to your bank, to a real estate broker, or to your attorney's office. Before you signed the papers, the notary probably asked for some proof of identification such as a driver's license or employee identification card or social security card. The notary recorded the identification data in a record book.

You were then asked to raise your right hand and swear that you were the person you claimed to be, and that the document you were about to sign was for the purpose it stated on its face. For example, that you were signing a motor vehicle title because it was your intention to sell the vehicle, and that you were selling it of your own free will.

Then you signed the document on the appropriate line. The notary dated it, filled in her commission expiration date, signed her portion and affixed her official notary stamp or seal. You may have been asked to sign the notary's book, right beside where the identifying data was recorded. Now, the notarized document was handed back to you. Did you wonder, "Was all that identification and swearing really necessary? What a waste of time!"

The verification of signatures is important, particularly on life changing documents. It can, however, become a somewhat meaningless ritual if a

"The notary is personally liable for any defects in the notarization process, which damage a party to the transaction."

notary does not follow the proper procedures. The notary is personally liable for any defects in the notarization process, which damage a party to the transaction.

Notaries are officers of their particular state. They submit a written application for the position, in which they identify themselves and show that they have never been convicted of a crime. After receiving their state commission, they are authorized to purchase a notary seal and a stamp with their name and the date when their commission expires.

Notaries may charge for their services. Fees vary from state to state, but are generally no more than a few dollars. A court clerk who knows you need help fast for an upcoming hearing may handle your signature on a *gratis* basis or hit you for the maximum. An airport notary, who knows he is your last chance to get your papers properly authenticated, may charge an illegal four or five times the maximum fee and you won't worry about it. Many law offices, medical offices, real estate offices and banks will notarize their customers' signatures at no charge, as a courtesy.

Notaries are required to check the identity of their constituents. They must keep a bound book containing records of all their notarial acts, including when they acknowledged a person's signature, what type of document was signed, and what method of identification was used. The identifying numbers must be written down. Some jurisdictions require that the constituent (signer of the document being notarized) sign the notary's book. There has been some discussion about the possibility of the fingerprints of constituents being required in the notary books, beside the signature.[1] The notary's book is a matter of public record, must be open to inspection, and may be subpoenaed in court. Anything short of diligent maintenance of this book is notary malpractice!

In most states, Notaries must post a performance bond with their state Notary Commission. The amount of the bond, which is $2,500 in Texas, will vary from state to state. This bond protects parties who have been damaged as a result of a notary's negligence in the performance of his duties. A notary has the option of purchasing "errors and omissions" insurance. This protects the notary personally in the event of a lawsuit based

> "In most states, Notaries must post a
> performance bond with their state
> Notary Commission. The amount
> of the bond, which is $2,500 in Texas,
> will vary from state to state."

on shortcomings of performance as a notary.

In most Latin American Countries, a notario has to have more education than most lawyers do in the United States. For that reason, large numbers of people from Latin America become notaries in the United States, and write back to their friends bragging that they have become notaries. To their friends and family that individual has become a huge success in America.

In Texas, a Notary Public is forbidden either to translate the title into the Spanish equivalent, "Notario Publico" or to advertise his services without explaining the difference. There have been abuses in the office of notary by unscrupulous individuals who advertised themselves as "a Notario Publico" and charged Hispanic immigrants large sums of money by using their supposed expertise in straightening out their immigration status.

The proper function of a notary in the United States is to assure the authenticity of signatures on real estate and motor vehicle conveyances, consent forms, wills, depositions, contracts, agreements and other important documents.

Notaries often become careless in exercising their duties. An example of the erosion of the notary's role is the way motor vehicle titles are sometimes handled by both new and used car dealers. The transfer of title document is often signed with most of the spaces blank, then it is handed to somebody else who notarizes it without ever having seen the individual whose signature he notarized. In some states, this abuse of the office of notary is a criminal offense. In all states, such a charade is ridiculous. If the notary is not going to fulfill his function by checking the authenticity of a signature, then there is no need to have a notary.

The following case portrays the human tragedy that can arise out of a fraudulent real estate conveyance, complicated by a woefully inadequate, unauthorized notarial act. It is one of many such stories.

B. JUSTICE FOR JOHNSON

A slick con-artist, Harvey Baum, advertised that his business offered financial services and loans. Lena Johnson, drawn by Baum's ad,

---

"In most Latin American Countries, a notario has to have more education than most lawyers do in the United States."

---

approached his place of business for a loan using her adopted mother's Christmas gift—a microwave oven—as security.

Baum asked the young woman whether she had anything else of value. She replied, "Only my house." (It was actually her adopted mother's house.)

Several days later, this erring young woman returned to Baum's place of business, posing as her adopted mother, Millie Johnson—who was more than 30 years her senior. She was accompanied by another young woman who was posing as Lena Johnson. Lena had borrowed her adopted mother's driver's license and brought along her deceased, adopted father's will allegedly to show that their house and an adjacent lot had been left to Millie Johnson.

Lena believed that she was borrowing money and putting the house and lot up as security. Harvey Baum, instead, had both Lena (posing as Millie) and the friend (posing as Lena) sign a warranty deed giving the house, the lot it was on, and the adjacent vacant lot to Harvey Baum. These confused, misguided, young women signed whatever so-called loan documents the devious Harvey Baum put in front of them.

Harvey Baum's wife, Sandra Kost Baum, had been a notary for six months. A notary should know that it is not proper to notarize a document from which the notary might financially benefit. A wife who is a notary has a disqualifying interest in real estate her husband is acquiring and is barred from notarizing signatures conveying property to him. A notary is obligated to check the identification presented by the signer and verify that the signer is, indeed, the person she purports to be. Sandra Kost Baum failed in her sworn duty to verify the signer's identification. Despite Lena's transparent subterfuge of donning a gray wig and glasses, there is no way that a woman in her mid-twenties could transform her appearance into that of a woman in her early sixties, without the aid of professional, Hollywood type make-up. In fact, Sandra Kost Baum never met Millie Johnson, the woman whose signature she notarized. If Sandra Kost Baum had fulfilled her duty to verify the purpose for signing the document (asking the alleged Millie Johnson whether she was signing this *deed to her house* of her own free will), the ensuing tragedy might have been

---

"Notaries often become careless in exercising their duties. An example of the erosion of the notary's role is the way motor vehicle titles are sometimes handled by both new and used car dealers."

---

averted. She also did not keep a bound book to preserve data about the documents she had notarized, rather she trusted her memory.

Lena did not intend to sell her adopted mother's house. She did not know she had signed a deed. She just wanted some quick cash. Harvey Baum just wanted a quick acquisition of ill-gotten gains. In a deposition taken later, he admitted that he had acquired homes in about 50 similar transactions.[2]

On the next business day, Harvey Baum recorded the fraudulent warranty deed, a fraudulent disclaimer of homestead and several fraudulent affidavits in the Harris County Property Records.

About two weeks later, Millie Johnson—a hardworking, religious woman in her 60s who was working as a housekeeper and who assumed the major responsibility for the care and support of her two granddaughters, Lena's children—was shocked to be served with a forcible detainer lawsuit which Baum had filed in the local justice of the peace court to throw Millie Johnson out of her home.

Millie Johnson had never met Harvey Baum, who now claimed to be the owner of her house. The resulting confusion drove Lena to a suicide attempt, at which time both mother and daughter learned the truth about the loan.

A builder who had been remodeling Mrs. Johnson's home—Frederick Cilurso, who is also a close friend and client of mine—referred her to my law office. Mr. Cilurso may be an easier touch for a sob story than I am. Over the years he has been a constant source of business from people in trouble who can't afford to pay. He has also testified in numerous lawsuits as an expert in construction and remodeling. In my cases his record is three wins, no losses.

Mrs. Johnson received her notice while I was vacationing with my family in a secluded beach spot. If an answer to the forcible detainer was not filed in seven days, Millie Johnson would have been thrown out of her home. My legal assistant handled this matter by drafting a document called a general denial, had another attorney approve and inspect the form answer, and then sign it.

By demanding a jury trial and paying the required fee, we got the forcible detainer trial set back several weeks. When you are injured in a car

---

"A notary is obligated to check the identification presented by the signer and verify that the signer is, indeed, the person she purports to be."

---

wreck, the insurance lawyers often delay trial for years, when a multi-million dollar corporation fails to file an answer on time, it often gets a second and third opportunity; but the system allows people like Baum—in instances like this, to move in with the speed of lightning, and elderly widows who do not file their answers on time are thrown out of their homes all over this country, every day.

Our lightning rod was the jury fee—Millie Johnson's constitutional right, which deflected the trial date and gave us breathing time. We gathered information including some facts about the individuals we were planning to sue.

It seems that Harvey Baum was no virgin to civil or criminal law. He had been handled by the police half a dozen times, and had once been convicted of arson by a jury, but an appellate court had reversed the jury finding on a technicality. During the pendency of our suit, Baum was facing aggravated perjury charges in an unrelated matter.

On the civil side, Baum's computer sheet listing all the suits to which he was a party was several pages long and included what appeared to be a divorce action that both Baum and his wife denied. His wife was the granddaughter of a millionaire who founded a well-known, Houston area furniture company, Finger's Furniture. A bankruptcy filed in 1984 shielded the Baums from most of these civil actions. Their testimony at deposition in November, 1985 notes that they were happily married. They were divorced in the early part of 1986 before our trial on damages, but they were re-married before September, 1986.

We filed an answer in the justice of the peace court to keep possession of the house, filed a notice to take Harvey Baum's and Sandra Kost Baum's depositions, and filed a suit in the district court alleging the forgery to get back title to the house and keep possession of the house while the suit was pending.

We sued Sandra Kost Baum also, for her notarization of her husband's signature on the fraudulent deed and asked for depositions in that case too. We filed a notice of *lis pendens* to tie up the property so Harvey Baum could not sell it. We then asked the justice of the peace court judge to dismiss the forcible detainer action because it dealt with title to property, not

---

"The system allows people like Baum—in instances like this, to move in with the speed of lighting and elderly widows who do not file their answers on time are thrown out of their homes all over this country, every day."

---

mere possession.

Ultimately, justice of the peace court Judge Paul Till reviewed the records and dismissed the forcible detainer. This veteran Justice of many seasons reasoned that the title dispute must be resolved before possession could be alleged.

We called in a handwriting expert who examined photocopies of the forged documents. Millie Johnson had to provide a handwriting sample. In the presence of the expert, she had to repeatedly write her name, other names, and several words, using a variety of writing implements—pencil, pen and felt tip marker. The expert's conclusion supported our contention that Millie Johnson had not signed the deed or the other documents accompanying it.

District Court Judge Geraldine Tenant, a woman with a no-nonsense approach, a good head on her shoulders, and, I believe, a love of the English language, was assigned to hear the case we'd filed. I'm always glad to be assigned to her courtroom, because, as a former English teacher, I prefer literate judges when I can find them.

Mr. and Mrs. Baum were represented by a young woman attorney who filed a motion for protection from the depositions; thus, in effect entering an appearance in the case although no answer had been filed. This young woman would qualify for one of my rogue's gallery portraits—Ms. Tough Guy. She was mean and vindictive. She refused officially to enter an appearance until her client was served, and the record showed that one of the two was avoiding service.

Nevertheless, their attorney actually appeared in court. Appearing is part of the legal game. Before a court can act with any degree of legal authority, a plaintiff must serve a copy of her suit on the accused defendant. The defendant must answer within 20 days or a default judgment against him can be won without trial. However, if the defendants voluntarily appear either by filing a written answer or actually showing up in person or through an attorney in court, the formality of service is no longer a requirement.

We filed a motion to compel the Baums to show up for depositions, and the motion had to be heard by another judge because Judge Tenant was attending a seminar. The substitute judge ruled against us, and said we were moving too aggressively and fined my client $100.

I told the judge that she was indigent and couldn't afford to pay the fine, so he directed me to pay it. I did. I have learned the hard way that fighting small, insulting fines can take all of your time. You end up losing the trees and missing the forest. Also, it's bad economics to spend $1,000 worth of time to fight a $100 fine.

My unworthy opponent threatened me with a suit and humiliation. She demanded I get off the case and allow another, more competent lawyer to fight with her. I declined, telling her I could not give up the opportunity to lose to such a self-proclaimed, distinguished, legal expert. Alas, our fight was never to occur. She quit after one more hearing, this time a hearing in Judge Tenant's court which she lost.

It took five months and five hearings before I finally got the Baums' deposition. Harvey Baum and Sandra Kost Baum gained 40 extra days of delay through Harvey's *pro se* motion for protection from a deposition set by a court approved agreement between me and their first attorney.

Their first attorney filed a motion to withdraw, and it was heard one day before the deposition. She no longer wanted to work for a man who was neither paying her nor communicating with her, according to her pleadings. Harvey Baum appeared in court that day with the motion he or Sandra had typed—he must have learned something from all his frequent dealings with courts. Harvey Baum told the judge that he had no attorney and no money to hire one. She gave him 30 days to find an attorney and another 10 days for the attorney to familiarize himself with the case.

The Baum's must have waited until the eleventh hour of the 39th day to hire a new attorney. He was a specialist in criminal matters, perhaps more suited to Harvey Baum's usual circumstances and had not had any time to prepare for this deposition. Apparently, he never got paid either.

The deposition given by the Baum's had more holes than an old tennis shoe. One of its chief values was its entertainment potential. It was broken up by several 15 or 20 minute intervals; Baum would rummage through his briefcase crammed with papers to search for his driver's license, which he finally produced; or to search for some mythical documents that he knew he hadn't brought with him since they never existed—such as a copy of Millie Johnson's receipt for cash he allegedly gave her.

Harvey Baum brought none of the documents we had subpoenaed: the newspaper advertisement for his financial services company, any authority to prove that he was permitted to be a lender, and most importantly, any receipts or business records showing any sum of money he allegedly paid the woman he claimed was Millie Johnson. He could not recall how much money he claimed to have paid Mrs. Johnson for her home, except to narrow it down to somewhere between $1,000 and $10,000.

During Harvey Baum's deposition, Sandra Kost Baum fidgeted in her chair, nervously stroking the fur coat she held in her lap, and looking with daggers in her eyes at her husband.

During her own deposition Sandra Kost Baum admitted she had been extremely negligent in her duties as a notary. She kept pleading poor memory and lack of skill at estimating age. Isn't it possible to confuse a 25-year-old with a 60-year-old?

The attorney who represented the Baums during their depositions assured us that we'd receive all the requested documents within two or three weeks. Six weeks later we were still waiting!

Unpaid, lawyer #2 also withdrew from the case, leaving the field open for lawyer #3—an aggressive criminal attorney who was also representing Baum on an aggravated perjury charge. On one occasion, Baum's presence was required at hearings in both the criminal matter and our civil proceeding. The prosecutor on Baum's criminal matter went about his work with all the fervor of a dead fish. I offered to assist him in building his case by supplying him with additional evidence of Baum's fraudulent activities but he wasn't interested.

In January 1986, we filed a motion for sanctions against Harvey Baum and Sandra Kost Baum citing their abuse of the discovery process. I relied on the Texas Supreme Court decision in *Downer v. Aquamarine*[3] which affirmed that three flagrant abuses of discovery justify the use of extreme punitive measures. We asked Judge Tenant to strike their pleadings. That means that it would be as if they had never answered the suit, and a default judgment could be taken against the Baums after we proved up Millie Johnson's damages.

Now that the Baum's were in divorce proceedings, they were represented by separate attorneys. They showed their continued insensitivity to the case by not even appearing in person at the hearing on the motion for sanctions. This time, an older, more seasoned personification of Ms. Tough Guy, was hired to represent Mrs. Baum. She was big, tough, mean and fat—but with more skill than the Baum's former attorney. Mr. Baum's new lawyer was a nice guy, just out of law school who went to the mat for free—it was idealism expecting to get paid but wishing for experience over money.

Judge Tenant, the epitome of fairness, attempted to reach the Baums by telephone. Harvey Baum's excuse for his absence was that he was about to be hospitalized due to a fall he had sustained at home. Judge Tenant had a telephone conversation with the attorney Baum had hired to negotiate a settlement—Baum still expected Millie Johnson to pay him something!

Baum's counsel indicated to me that Harvey Baum would be willing to testify against his now soon-to-be-ex-wife if I'd leave him alone. Needless to say, I passed up the offer.

After the hearing on the motion for sanctions, I returned to my office. Before the day had ended, Judge Tenant's clerk called to inform me that both defendant's pleadings had been stricken. A hearing on damages before Judge Tenant was set for Friday, April 4, 1986.

The following journal was written by me as I sat in Judge Tenant's courtroom the day of the hearing on damages, accompanied by Mrs. Johnson, my legal assistant, the builder who had been remodeling Millie Johnson's home, and one of Millie Johnson's employers—the latter two were there to testify as to damages. The later excerpts from May 15, 1986; June 17, 1986; July 1, 1986; and August 18, 1986, were written in my office.

April 4, 1986: It's 11:02 a.m. I am in Judge Tenant's court room. We were the last case on a 24-page, computer generated docket with four cases to a page. The way the docket moves, we could be heard by 11:30 a.m. or never. We are waiting to put on Mrs. Johnson's case.

The Baum's are on their fourth and fifth lawyers in this proceeding alone. Each has a separate lawyer here and separate divorce lawyers in the Family Law Center across the street to the north. Across the street to the east, Harvey Baum is being represented by a different criminal lawyer in the perjury case. Across the street to the west is the county administration building where the fraudulent deed is filed in the property records. About six blocks to the southwest, at the Federal Building, the Baums had filed bankruptcy in 1984.

The Baums have spread their "nectar" all over the courthouses of this city. Harvey Baum expects to win all the cases. He might. He has never served a day in jail except while raising bond. He has never had a conviction stick. He shows no current judgments against him.

I wait. Unpaid. Will we win? Will we get money? Will Millie Johnson keep her home? Will her church, her boss, and her friends win with us? Will she be tossed into the streets, or worse, will she wait and wait for years of delay and appeals? The pressure of waiting is often far worse than a total defeat. Although the Baums' pleadings have been stricken, without a final judgment, they can be reinstated at any time.

"The pressure of waiting is often far worse than a total defeat...The court process is often more painful than punishment. It's slow. It's tedious, and it's uncertain."

The court process is often more painful than punishment. It's slow. It's tedious, and it's uncertain. Are all the papers in order? Will the judge read them? Judge Tenant is a judge who will.

We hope; we sit; we pray; we wait.

I am actually drafting these notes while waiting in the courtroom. A competent woman judge. A sharp, caring, black court coordinator, educated and efficient, by her side. He watches the court room, alert to the people around him, knowing many of them by name.

It's 11:20. The 400 attorneys waiting for the 10:30 docket are down to 300. If it takes an hour per 100 lawyers, and if I am number 399 or 400, I've got three more hours. Will my witnesses leave? Will I go out of business? Will I miss "Twilight Zone" tonight at 7 p.m.? Will my car get towed?

I trusted Judge Tenant. Millie Johnson hadn't slept well for a year due to anxiety over this case. We waived our right to a jury! We needed speed. Judge trials are faster than jury trials. We were dismissed for lunch and reconvened at 2 p.m. All the witnesses testified and the lawyers argued until 4:45 p.m. The judge said she would rule next week.

May 15, 1986: Still no ruling. Mrs. Johnson wants to fix her leaky roof, but it's not possible. With the title defect, she can't get refinancing. Still no answer.

June 17, 1986: Our order is in. It comes in the form of a letter from the judge. We have won!

It comes 73 days after the trial.

Millie Johnson will stay in her house. Title will be cleared in her name with the fraudulent conveyance and all documents filed in support of it, declared void. The judge ordered $1,500 in actual damages, $5,000 in punitive (punishment) damages and $10,000 in attorney's fees. She also instructed an agreed order to be drafted.

Everyone is happy but me. I'm relieved to have Mrs. Johnson safe and to have a happy client and be on the verge of closing a file, but I'm disappointed. I expected more. I have a jury trial in an unrelated case to finish before I can draw up a judgment on this one.

July 1, 1986: I drew up the judgement to conform to Judge Tenant's order. Harvey Baum's attorney approved it. Sandra Baum's attorney won't approve it without a personal phone call. I try. I call four times. I can't get through. I have L.R. try. She won't talk to L.R. any more.

"If lawyers' personalities and egos could be minimized,
I could close many more cases much faster."

This is the second time in this case a woman lawyer refuses to talk with my legal assistant. Both seem to take it as some sort of slight. They are too good to talk with a mere legal assistant. If lawyers' personalities and egos could be minimized, I could close many more cases much faster. Trying to massage those two egos took time. For some reason, women lawyers seem to be more sensitive to this unintended slight than men with regard to routine chores. I'll talk to a sewer digger if it will settle a case (pun intended since I was once a sewer digger.)

I have L.R. draft a letter. There is no response. We file a motion to enter judgment. This will, of course, create more delay, but there is no choice. We could wait months for the attorney to co-operate. Until the judgment is signed, we have nothing. After it is signed, there may be a motion for a new trial hearing and possibly an appeal. The case is now 13 months old, and we are where we are only because of pushing and because of a judge who let us push. In my opinion, a jury would have given us much more, but it would have taken much longer. The judge has been fair and has given money for punishment damages. An important point will be made—if we get the judgment signed, upheld and finalized.

Collecting the $16,500, however, is another ball game. This book will be published before that ball game starts. L.R. has now called a dozen times to check with the clerk and see if he has presented the order to the court for signature. He has, but we must all wait or in the alternative set another hearing date. We wait.

August 18, 1986: On the 31st day of July 1986, we received a note card that the judgment had been signed on the July 29, 1986. L.R. had been on the phone with Judge Tenant's clerk that same day trying to find out if the judgment had been signed—the clerk, a sharp, well organized and polite man said he could not find it, and the computer had no record of it.

Other matters were pressing. We could not call every day. My time and L.R.'s time was at a premium. Almost a year to the date we took Mrs. Johnson's case, another home swindle case came in. I had to turn it down. I cannot have too many of these cases open at the same time or my office will close down. These people will probably not find competent legal help and will probably lose their home. Until the Johnson judgment is final, it still requires work and takes up space on my docket.

We ordered a certified copy of the judgment and an abstract of the judgment. The certified copy is an officially stamped copy of the order. I never close a file until I have one of these in my hand with a copy to our client.

In Texas, the losing defendant has 30 days *after* the judgment is signed to file a motion for a new trial. If it's filed within that time, the court has control over the judgment for another 45 days, and it can be appealed during that time. Until the signed judgment is cold for 30 days, it has no value.

On August 18, 1986 we still did not have a certified copy back. We could be: A) Nowhere; Needing to get the judgment signed; B) Ten days away from a final judgment; or C) One to ten days away from a motion for a new trial if the defendants chose to file one—if they even thought about it.

On this August 18th morning, I am sitting in Judge Marsha Anthony's court waiting for trial. The defendant is allegedly in the hospital. Often, people seem to end up in the hospital on the day of trial. I have contacted the hospital to confirm the defendant's condition. She is in the surgical intensive care unit, allegedly, with a cracked skull. It is unusual for a defendant to crack her skull to get out of a trial. I am inclined to believe her attorney on this one occasion, although he has been lying to me for the full two-and-a-half years this case has been pending.

Judge Anthony is a gracious woman. Intelligent, friendly, and not too pushy. A former teacher. I like her. The local bar has voted her least competent. Her clerk confides that he thinks she's crazy.

Tomorrow, I have another trial setting. I have planned on both cases going to trial, hoping to close at least one of the files. Not counting my general practice, corporations, uncontested matters, etc. I have 48 open, active, trial files. Our staff can handle 40 well. I have ten new ones that are begging to be opened. Should I hire more staff? If I don't, will our work quality drop?

Last week, I settled a personal injury case. It should close this week. Johnson could close next week and become a collection judgment as opposed to one with active trial potential. If this case settles today, and my trial concludes. This week, I will have closed four files. Four clients can begin a new phase of their lives.

If no motion is filed by August 28, 1986 (my 35th birthday), Millie Johnson's case will be over. I am concerned about the title issue. Her daughter forged Millie Johnson's name, then allowed a friend to forge her own name. The will, leaving the house to Millie Johnson was never probated, on the advice of Mrs. Johnson's former attorney who thought the proceeding was unnecessary. In Texas, a will must be probated within four years of the testator's death, or the will becomes void.

Without a will, Millie Johnson owns only half the house; her adopted daughter owns the other half. Does the daughter's forged signature or her friend's validate a conveyance of her half- interest to Harvey Baum? None of Baum's attorneys raised this question. If they did, I would have had to represent the crazy daughter and prove she was mentally ill, in order to throw out her conveyance or show good cause why a will should be probated 20 years late. The law, as it is written, is not perfect for Millie Johnson even though, morally, she is perfectly right in her position. There is nothing to do but wait, and it's impossible not to worry.

Millie Johnson's home, title, and life, remain potentially tied up until the entire affair is over.

August 20, 1986: Today, a certified copy of judgment came to our office for inspection. It was the same one I had drafted, and it was signed on July 29, 1986 as previously indicated. The judgment could be used to clear Millie Johnson's title, *but* the district clerk left off several exhibits necessary to be canceled, namely the forged deed, Harvey Baum's false affidavit, and other absurdities he filed. All the documents must be removed to clear Millie Johnson's chain of title. L.R. made a personal trip to the courthouse to straignten out the clerk's error.

The real concern, of course, was the eight-day wait.

The week passed and Millie Johnson's judgment became final, my best birthday present.

Affidavits and copies of the judgment had to be filed to clear up her chain of title. A writ of execution had to be ordered to collect the judgment from the Baums.

We followed up on the Baums. It appears that Harvey Baum and his ex-wife have re-united and are once again married after a very short divorce. Harvey Baum seems to be doing okay. Both Baums, with an expensive lawyer in the room, tell the constable they are broke.

A series of demand letters went to Western Surety, the insurance company that had written Sandra Baum's notary bond. When the company refused to pay its $2,500 bond, I gave them 30 days to pay, or I would file a law suit. I forwarded a copy of my demand to the Texas Insurance Board. I was so certain that I would have to sue Western Surety that I even drafted the law suit. They surprised me and paid.

The $2,500 just about covered my firm's out-of-pocket expenses on the case, labor not included. Ten more cases like this in one year could close my doors, but we have a happy ending and a $15,000-plus judgment left earning interest—which may never be collected or could become a pleasant surprise—a notary commission which should be revoked, a home saved, and a good story.

Millie Johnson's case, like so many others, still goes on, because there are no easy answers.

We had Harvey and Sandra Baum's former residence posted for a constable's sale to satisfy the judgment. We learned that the property had already been deeded back to the individuals from whom the Baums had been purchasing it. However, the conveyance occured after our abstract of judgment was filed. The title is in a state of confusion. Now, two years after the judgment, no money has been collected, but Harvey can count on us keeping tabs on him and the interest builds up. We could collect it all tomorrow, or die before another penny comes through. Mrs. Johnson's title is clear, she's happily living in the house and her roof is fixed also.

"Verification of signatures is important, particularly on life changing documents."

CHAPTER XIX

CORPORATIONS

"The corporation has all the rights of a human being, with few exceptions."

A. HISTORY AND BACKGROUND

What is a corporation? A corporation is an entity recognized by law by one of the 50 states, the federal government or a foreign government as having an independent existence and a paper life of its own, subject to certain rules.

Black's Law Dictionary defines a corporation as:

"An artificial person or legal entity created by or under the authority of the laws of a state or nation...ordinarily consisting of an association of numerous individuals...which is regarded in law as having a personality and existence distinct from that of its several members...with the capacity of continuous succession..."

Most of this country's corporations were formed by the methods set forth in this chapter.

Corporations are set up under the various state governments. A person or persons intending to set up a corporation must apply to the state government for a corporate charter, which means that the applicant is requesting permission to do business in that format. Generally, a small annual fee is charged.

A corporation is formed when a state or foreign government grants a charter to the persons who have applied for the charter and met the requirements for forming the corporation. The requirements generally are: answer a few questions, make a few decisions and send some money.

There is generally an annual fee charged by the issuing authority, but it is usually quite low. The federal government taxes a corporation on its income, unless it was created as a non-profit organization—meaning the

"Most of this country's corporations were formed by the methods set forth in this chapter."

corporation is set up for some charitable reason rather than making a profit. Most of the state governments also tax corporations on the basis of their income. Some do not. Neither Texas nor Alaska have a personal nor corporate income tax at this time.

After the requirements are met, the choices made and papers completed, permission is granted to be a corporation and the charter is returned to the originators. Now the corporation exists. The corporation has all the rights of a human being, with a few exceptions. The corporation cannot vote. The corporation can commit criminal offenses and be fined. Since a corporation is only a piece of paper, it cannot be put in jail. The corporation can own property. The corporation is different from a human being, however, because a corporation is owned by its shareholders in much the same way as slaves used to be owned by their owners.

The corporate form of enterprise has a long history. The United Kingdom would issue a charter to individuals for the purpose of doing business under certain rules and regulations. The East India Company was established to make a profit for its members—as well as to further the acquisition of new territories for the sovereign who authorized its existence. The charter was subject to the rules and regulations of the government.

The British and Dutch East India companies are the forebears of current major national and international corporations.

These companies existed by virtue of permission by their government. They were owned by individual investors who owned shares of the company. The French, the Spanish, the Dutch and English Companies were the most important. These companies had their own private armies, warships and rules subject only to the nation they paid tribute to. These capitalist investors were one of the leading forces of organized colonization in the world: their motive was profit.

Both the Dutch and the French companies were ultimately terminated by combinations of free enterprise, corporate military war and corporate mergers. What was left of each was purchased by the English East India

---

"A person or persons intending to set up a corporation must apply to the state government for a corporate charter, which means that the applicant is requesting permission to do business in that format."

Company which ultimately took over most of India and probably had more power than Coca Cola®, Shell Oil, Exxon and Nestle's Chocolate combined have today.

The wars between the Dutch and the English corporations lasted 200 years. Between 1602 and 1696 the Dutch company never paid its shareholders less than 12 percent and sometimes paid as high as 63 percent. In 1632 the Dutch killed many of the English agents and became the chief India company for years. In 1724, after a substantial decline, it failed to pay a dividend and was soon taken over by a British attack.

The English company was formed in 1600 by Queen Elizabeth I. It had to fight not only the Dutch—who defeated it for over half a century—but internal competition which was ultimately bought out. In 1854, under the Act for Better Government of India, the crown took over the company's 24,000-man army; and on January 1, 1874 the company was finally taken over by the government. England began its steep and rapid decline.

The English and the Dutch had established through these corporations an international presence they would never lose. Today the Dutch East Indies possession called the Netherland Antilles is the home of Shell Oil, which is still an international power with a larger budget than most nations.

A couple of centuries ago, only a select few groups of persons could have charters. People received charters to set up various types of colonies, settlements, business ventures or a combination. This official permission was hard to come by. It was all high level politics.

Nowadays, the granting of most corporate charters in the free world is not politically motivated. This is not to say that all of the process is free from political machinations. Banks, for example, have special rules and regulations for obtaining charters. The granting of which is extremely political.

The overwhelming majority of corporations set up in the United States are formed quite similarly with only slight differences from state to state. Anyone with the filing fees can buy a corporate charter.

> *"A corporation is formed when a state or foreign government grants a charter to the persons who have applied for the charter and met the requirements for forming the corporation."*

Most of the states, through their secretary of state, provide forms for setting up simple corporations. This simple corporation form requires:

A) Disclosing the number of shares of stock issued;

B) Naming the people who are going to be the directors of the corporation;

C) Including a statement about the minimum purchase price of its stock;

D) Determining what that minimum value of stock will be; and

E) Making decisions about some basic governing rules and regulations for the corporation.

After having worked for an immigration firm for two and a half years during which I set up large numbers of corporations on a rush basis, I created my own form which is included in the addendum.[1] This form is designed to elicit information which is necessary for applying for the corporate charter, and additional information which could be useful to the law firm in its continued representation of the corporation.

Since the law changes frequently and is different in each state, it would be wise to consult with a knowledgeable person before completing forms for a corporation. The form I developed enabled me to take down the client's information quickly, hand the outline to the secretary, and receive from her typed corporation charter papers—without any additional instructions from me.

We ordered corporation kits from one of the many different companies that sell standard stock certificates and embossing materials. These kits basically form the paper body of the corporation with standard by-laws. A legal assistant filled out the various blanks from the information form and contacted the client if any other information was necessary.

B. SHAREHOLDERS' RIGHTS

Generally, corporations pay lower taxes than individuals, although the new 1987 tax rules have changed some corporate prerogatives. The highest corporate tax rate in 1988 is higher than the highest individual rate.

"Generally, corporations pay lower taxes than individuals, although the new 1987 tax rules have changed some corporate prerogatives. The highest corporate tax rate in 1988 is higher than the highest individual rate."

The lowest corporate rate of is still a savings opportunity for high tax bracket payers. Professional corporations, lawyers, and CPAs receive no special corporate lower rate. This law will be contested, and perhaps modified.

Under a corporation, income can be divided up, creating smaller income streams, allowing the individual who controls the corporation to have two relatively small incomes as opposed to one twice as large. For example, if the corporation earns $50,000, $25,000 will be given to the individual and $25,000 can be kept in the corporation. Since we have a graduated income tax, dividing the money up into smaller portions generally broadens the tax base and each pays less taxes. It increases the cost of doing business because the corporation has to file its own tax returns.

With the new tax code, the corporate tax advantage still exists, but is not as important. With only two levels of graduated income tax, savings will be smaller. Fringe benefits will still be important in tax planning. For example: as a corporate expense, medical insurance is 100 percent deductible. As a personal expense, it is not.

There are two other prime reasons for setting up a corporation. First, the corporation shields the stockholders from personal liability for the actions of the corporation. If the stockholders do not personally authorize a specific action or are not personally involved in that action, they usually cannot be held personally responsible. Second, ownership can be divided by the centuries-old method of shares. The corporation's actual and potential assets and liabilities are divided into shares.

The number of shares is totally arbitrary. The incorporator may want to create a million shares for his entity, a thousand shares, or just ten shares. It makes little or no difference how many shares are in the corporation. Let's assume that the corporation has one thousand shares.

To begin functioning, the corporation must have a certain amount of operating money, usually a very small amount. In Texas you need a minimum of $1,000 to start your corporation. Let's assume that the par value of each share is $1, and there are one thousand shares. That means that each share must be purchased for at least $1. If you do not want to have an arbitrary value for the purchase of the stock, most states permit you to have stock with no par value.

"The British and Dutch East India companies are the forebears of the current major national and international corporations."

A public company is one that has its shares bought and sold in the open market place on a large scale. The federal government gets involved if the shares cross state lines. Each state government has its own rules for how many shareholders or how much capital makes the company public.

The largest public companies are traded on what is called the stock market and generally means one of the two large markets in New York, the New York Exchange or the American Exchange, or the smaller volume market in Chicago.

The United States has one of the most restricted and carefully observed stock markets in the world. Theoretically, these controls are to protect the public shareholders. In reality the controls seem to offer very little protection. Small investors get wiped out by fraud or unfair tactics everyday. The government intervention A) raises the cost of selling and buying stock, B) contributes to more companies going under and C) makes it more difficult to compete abroad.

A company with less than 20 shareholders is considered a closely-held corporation, and it is safe from the federal regulations for registering it as a public company. With public companies that have a large number of shareholders, the government wants to know what is going on at all times. For the small corporation, this is not necessary.

Going back to the example referred to earlier, let's assume that the company issued 1,000 shares of stock and that each of the five shareholders purchased 200 shares at $1 per share. With this $1,000 in the corporation coffers, the corporation now issues each of its five*shareholders 200 stock certificates.

Once the corporation is set up, the initial directors resign, and a shareholders meeting is held for the purpose of electing the directors who will

---

*"A company with less than 20 shareholders
is considered a closely-held corporation,
and it is safe from the federal regulations
for registering it as a public company.
With public companies that have
a large number of shareholders,
the government wants to know
what is going on at all times.
For the small corporation,
this is not necessary."*

---

run the corporation for its first year. The directors in turn hire a president, vice-president, secretary and treasurer unless the corporation's by-laws allow the shareholders to elect them.

The shareholders must meet every year to choose new directors. The directors, who represent the owners, can meet more often and they control routine corporate policy decisions too important for the officers to decide but not important enough for the shareholders. The shareholders and directors can be one and the same.

Generally, the directors set policy for the corporation, and the officers run it on a day-to-day basis. Some type of agreement for their compensation needs to be made. Theoretically, the shareholders own the corporation. If there is a profit, it is generally distributed to the shareholders in the form of a dividend on a pro rata basis. For example, if there are 1,000 shares and there is a $1,000 profit, the corporation's directors issue dividends of $1 for each share held.

Think of a corporation as a pie. The shares are the portions of the pie. These shares control votes. If J.P. Tycoon owns five shares, he gets five votes. If there are three other individuals who each own one share, J.P. will be able to out-vote the three every time. He will completely control the company.

Depending upon the rules established when a corporation is established, minorities can be given more influence in the company that the example mentioned above. If we allow for such things as cumulative voting and many directors. If we have four directors and eight shares, but allow each shareholder to vote four times for each share he owns, we will have a total of thirty-two votes. If the three shareholders all vote their cumulative twelve votes for one director, that director will probably be elected. Most corporations do not have cumulative voting.

In smaller corporations, if shareholders don't own at least half the shares issued by the company, they might not be able to win an election or have much influence on the company. However, in larger, public corporations shareholders with only five to 10 percent of the shares might have considerable influence.

If these minority shareholders think they've been cheated, they have the right to file a lawsuit against the majority shareholders. This type of suit is ordinarily called a shareholder's derivative suit. Without this right

---

"Generally, the directors set policy for the corporation, and the officers run it on a day-to-day basis."

---

the minority shareholder can be at the mercy of the majority.

This type of suit might be filed against one majority shareholder who had the company furnish his home, pay his mistress a salary, and cover his child support payments—all this plus his personal salary. The minority shareholders might be unhappy with this arrangement especially if they receive no dividends.

TWO SHAREHOLDER'S DERIVATIVE SUITS:

In the first, Daddy on his deathbed signed a power of attorney to his trusted employee who promptly took over the company by giving himself majority control. Daddy's four kids who still owned 20 percent of the company received no dividends for ten years while the former employee—now majority shareholder—lived on the fat of the company and got rich. Unfortunately one of our clients had, on each anniversary, signed a paper approving all company transactions.

The jury awarded our client $1,500 plus nearly $40,000 in attorney's fees. We split this with the clients and then sued again. The majority shareholder got the message, the company was liquidated and the assets were divided up.

In the second case, Daddy Greenbucks financed a young would-be tycoon in his remodeling business. The entrepreneur used Greenbucks' connections and money to live high on the hog, travel, date and steal from his patron. Greenbucks owned a minority interest in the company, the would- be tycoon owned the rest, and ran the company. The suit was ultimately settled when the remodeler paid back his benefactor some of what he had stolen.

"The overwhelming majority of corporations set up in the United States are formed quite similarly with only slight differences from state to state."

CHAPTER XX
POWER OF ATTORNEY

"A power-of-attorney is a written document giving an individual the right to act in the place of the principal and as the principal's agent for doing certain specific things."

People misinterpret the word "attorney" to mean "lawyer." This is not a correct definition of the word "attorney." According to *Black's Law Dictionary:*

"In the most general sense this term denotes an agent or substitute, or one who is appointed and authorized to act in the place or stead of another. An agent, or one acting on behalf of another."

Attorney means simply an agent and no more. There are different types of agents just as there are different types of attorneys. The words can be used interchangeably. An agent is one who substitutes himself, herself or itself for another person or entity. This other person is called the principal. Sometimes a corporation acts as an agent for an individual or vice/versa.

Since a corporation is in reality nothing but paper, the only way it can do anything is through its agents. At a Texaco, Inc. owned gasoline station, the Texaco company is the principal and the gas station attendant pumping the gasoline is an agent for the Texaco. The person who hired this gasoline attendant is an agent for Texaco with superior authority to the agent who is dispensing the gasoline. The president of Texaco, Inc. is also an agent of Texaco with authority over those who report to him. He has more authority to represent his principal than the gas station attendant.

The law requires certain types of agents to have licenses. An attorney-at-law is an agent who is acting on behalf of somebody in a legal situation.

"An attorney-at-law is an agent who is acting on behalf of somebody in a legal situation. All 50 states and the federal government require certain licensure before an individual can act as an attorney-at-law."

464

All 50 states and the federal government require certain licensure before an individual can act as an attorney-at-law.

The Sixth Amendment to the U.S. Constitution, which gives individuals the right to have counsel at trial, contains no requirements that a person acting as someone's counsel have any type of license. However, the U.S. Supreme Court has interpreted the Sixth Amendment right to require an individual to obtain a license before he can act as a legal counselor for someone else in state courts. Federal courts require their own independent licenses and these requirements vary from federal district to district and circuit to circuit.

An attorney-in-fact or someone with the power-of-attorney is not necessarily a lawyer. The overwhelming majority of people with a power-of-attorney are not lawyers. A power-of-attorney is a written document giving an individual the right to act in the place of the principal and as the principal's agent for doing certain specific things. Most powers-of-attorney are unlimited i.e., they contain no written exceptions to the attorney-in-fact's authority.

One interesting situation which allegedly occurred in the last century in England helps demonstrate how much power can be given to an agent. Before going on a journey, an individual left his best friend an unlimited power-of-attorney.

The friend then proceeded to sell everything the principal owned, and even started divorce proceedings against the absent principal's wife. He subsequently married his best friend's wife in his own name and consummated the marriage. He left his principal—and now potential ex-best friend—divorced and penniless. To put the icing on the top of this sourdough cake, he then married somebody else to his best friend and proceeded to consummate that marriage for his friend.

Suit was filed to set aside all of the transactions. The court ruled that: A) All of the power-of-attorney privileges prior to the divorce were legitimate; B) The divorce itself was sustained since the friend had unlimited, unqualified, power-of-attorney to do anything in his friend's place; C) The second marriage of his principal was sustained since he had the right to do anything in his friend's name; however, D) that marriage was not legally consummated since it would not be legal to hire someone to consummate

---

"Attorney means simply an agent and no more. There are different types of agents just as there are different types of attorneys."

---

a marriage—doing so would be an act of prostitution and contrary to public laws.

The principal was allowed to terminate the second marriage by annulment rather than divorce. There was no jury trial. All these findings of law were made by the court. All of those persons who relied on the legitimacy of the power of attorney were entitled to keep the benefits of their bargains. Did the principal sue his presumably ex-best friend for breach of trust? That's another story.

Most powers-of-attorney are unlimited. They are contracts written up by printing companies and used by bank secretaries or automobile dealers who are transferring title. Generally, they should be notarized. Although this is not, in most jurisdictions, a requirement of law. Frequently notarization is necessary in order to record documents in real property records or for automobile vehicle transfer records. The majority of power of attorney documents do not include time limitations, and, therefore are presumed to continue for an infinite time.

Of course the power of attorney will terminate if the principal dies; if it is renounced by the principal at any time; or if the principal no longer has authority to have an agent for any number of reasons, such as the principal's lack of sound mind. In any event, the overwhelming majority of powers-of-attorney are drafted by people who are not aware of the enormity of the authority they convey when they fill in the blanks.

Many Americans have handed over absolute unlimited authority to many strangers or near strangers. These written instruments of great power are spread out over the country in many different files. For the most part, they are never used. Nevertheless, on rare, strange and sometimes very undesirable occasions, they may be used to the total destruction of the principal who executed the power-of-attorney.

A general, unlimited power-of-attorney in all probability should never be executed. The only time that there may be any value in executing such a document in haste is when it has been drawn up in order to accommodate somebody who is leaving the country, going to war, or going to jail and doing so right now!

Unfortunately, these are also the worst times to make such a hasty decision to leave unlimited power in the hands of another. Sometimes, however, there is no practical alternative if only a printed form is available and

---

"An attorney-in-fact or someone with the power-of-attorney is not necessarily a lawyer."

---

no one present knows how to modify it. The other side of this coin is that you may be the one entrusted with the authority, and you believe you might need the authority under the circumstances.

The power-of-attorney's purpose should be expressly limited. The rights and powers to be conferred should be specifically spelled out. The principal should have this power-of-attorney automatically extinguished at a time certain in the future. If the principal wants to extend it, he can write another power-of- attorney.

In the author's law practice, powers-of-attorney to the law firm are routinely signed by clients, permitting the law firm to act in the client's name in all circumstances relating specifically to the particular matter we are handling for that client.

These powers-of-attorney have natural terminations built into them; they all state, "this power-of-attorney shall remain in force and effect until final judgment or settlement of the above mentioned matter." The author has also prepared powers-of-attorney for clients, authorizing other individuals to act for our clients in strictly limited matters, such as the sale of a house or a car. A sample power-of-attorney is included in the addendum.[1]

Durable Power of Attorney: In some states you can sign a power of attorney which is still good if you lapse into a coma or lose your ability to function. This is a hybrid power between mere power-of-attorney and executor of an estate.

"The overwhelming majority of powers-of-attorney are drafted by people who are not aware of the enormity of the authority the convey when they fill in the blanks."

CHAPTER XXI

TRADEMARKS, COPYRIGHTS, PATENTS:

OWNERSHIP OF NAMES AND IDEAS

"Ownership rights in the name, if any, begin only after use of the name in a particular type of business. There are ways of checking names nationally and in fact recording your use in the stream of natural commerce."

A. TRADEMARKS

If you've never seen the name Coca-Cola® (Coca-Cola® is a registered trademark of the Coca-Cola® Company) then you are not living in 20th century U.S.A. In the 1980s, the name became an "in" in clothing for kids (and some parents). The slogan "The Real Thing" and "Coke is it" were drummed into my generation from the cradle. They were drummed in by spending a mega-fortune on advertising, public relations drives, and then selling it millions and millions of times. You don't have to be a student of the law to realize that a big company owns that name and wouldn't like it, if you opened your own little mom and pop store and called it Coca-Cola®, or started your own "swell tasting" soda pop and named it Coca-Cola®. While I have deliberately avoided giving legal advice in most of this manuscript—I'm going to go out on a limb and risk giving some; "Don't start up your own company and name it Coca-Cola® unless you can get permission from the Coca-Cola® Company."

As an American whose business requires an occasional trip away from the U.S. borders, I am proud of Coke. It's one export of "ours" everyone wants. You see it everywhere. Coke cans labeled in dozens of foreign languages. Sometimes we think it's "ours", but of course, it's not. It's theirs and if you try to steal it, you'll be in more trouble than you can imagine. The name belongs to the Coca-Cola® Company and its licensees (those persons or companies who, generally for lots of money, have received permission to use the name).

Remember the 1984 Los Angeles. Olympics? Remember the huge prices people paid to use the logo (the five interlocking rings in the most commonly used colors of various national flags), and call themselves sponsors?

We've also seen names like Gloria Vanderbilt or Calvin Klein on the seats of jeans.

These symbols, or little characters, or special ways of writing of a name are generally called "logos" and they are used to identify products. They cost time or money or inspiration or luck to envision and process. How do you own or come to own them?

The U.S. has one of the most complicated and least efficient methods in the world. We'll examine it.

First: When you are born you get a name from your parents. You own certain rights to it. Of course, you may not be the only David Drake or Sam Smith alive and therein lies an occasional problem. What if one Sam Smith born and named in 1941 opens Sam Smith Golf Supplies in 1980. Does he stop Sam Smith born in 1951 from using the name Sam Smith in his business? The law is not too clear. The first Sam to use the name in the stream of commerce owns a common law right to continue using it in that manner. Our golfing Sam, if no one else ever tried to use the name to sell golf supplies prior to 1980, probably has the "best" claim to the name for golf usage. It extends to golf products, perhaps golf shirts. What if young Sam tried to bring out a product line of Brook's Brothers type suit? Well, of course, he can't use the name "Brook's Brothers" for a suit, that's taken. He might name his enterprise "Sam Smith Suits." If the 1941 Sam Smith who owns the "Sam Smith Golf Products" name, decides to branch out into dress suits he may find that the 1951 Sam has beaten him to it and probably owns the name. There could very well now be a lawsuit. The suit would be a close call.

Since most companies, most people, and probably most Smiths would prefer to avoid litigation, there are a lot of options in the stream of commerce. One option is that neither Smith gets real big, both sell Smith suits, and both Smiths live and die without ever knowing about the competing Smith. This happens all the time. The case isn't tried because no one knows it exists and no one cares.

Another option is that someone else could claim the name. John Jones could start a corporation which he names Sam Smith Golf Products, Inc. If there are no similar uses of that name as a corporation, John's proposed name will likely be accepted by his State's Secretary of State or similar

---

"These symbols, or little characters, or special ways of writing of a name are generally called 'logos' and they are used to identify products."

official, and he will be (upon payment of the appropriate fees) awarded a corporation with that name. Generally, no one else can successfully apply for that exact name (or one very similar) within that State.

Another option is simply to apply to a parish (Louisiana) or county (most other states) or other appropriate governmental office for a legal "fictitious" or "assumed" name. Once filed, the particular jurisdiction gives him a certificate saying "John Jones" can use the name "Sam Smith." Many states have no other ownership vehicle—some do, similar to the federal trademark process.

However, ownership rights in the name, if any, begin only after use of the name in a particular type of business. There are ways of checking names nationally and, in fact, recording your use in the stream of national commerce.

First use is best use. First use in the particular area you want is good. First use in your area and first in any area combined is better.

You can also check every store, newspaper and Yellow Pages in the country. If no one has ever seen or heard of the name—it might be available. There are private services which work primarily for law firms which make broad general searches and also check the office of U.S. Patents and Trademarks.

You can apply for a trademark in the U.S. by submitting your logo or name and filling out the appropriate forms. This application allows you to claim the trademark, if no one else has claimed it either by using it, by registering it or by implication. If no one fights your claim, in about two years, you will very likely succeed in getting it registered. These terms are shown by "™" or "®" following a name or logo. ™ means you have claimed it, are using it and believe you have the right to it. ® means the government has agreed with you. These little symbols should follow the use of each trademark name or symbol. Until it has been used in commerce, you cannot register the name or symbol.

The big guys will often make a sale of their product at 9:00 a.m. and then file their trademark application at 9:01 a.m. after running intensive marketing tests and surveys and wide-ranging investigations to make sure no one has the name.

If one Smith uses Smith Golf in one city and another Smith subse-

---

"™ means you have claimed it, are using it and believe you have the right to it. ® means the government has agreed with you."

---

quently takes the rest of the planet both may have rights in their own limited territory. The little Smith will often sell out to the big Smith, sometimes for a large sum.

In some states, you can apply for and receive a state trademark. Since the federal trademark is superior, it is always wise to get the federal protection. Consider the additional protection in your particular state. If you can get both do it. International rights are also available.

B. COPYRIGHT

You trademark symbols and names. You copyright works of art, a letter, a book, a story, a film, a poem, an advertisement, a painting. All these types of creations may be copyrighted. To copyright is to claim something as your own which you individually, as a team, or as a buyer, created, directed, wrote, drew or purchased. Law is currently evolving to protect rights of developers of computer software, since "custom written" programs which take great numbers of man-hours to produce, can be copied and "pirated" almost instantaneously.

When a written work is circulated in any way, the writer must demonstrate on its face his intention to preserve his authorship rights by printing or typing "Copyright 1988" or language to that effect. The author can file for formal copyright protection by filling out a two page form, paying a small fee and depositing one copy of an unpublished work or five copies of a published work with the Copyright Office.

Although the process is a lot easier than trademarking, the value and power of a copyright should not be underestimated. Litigation and substantial penalties can arise for copyright infringement. You can never copy and use someone else's trademark but you can under the fair use doctrine copy very small portions of an article or book to discuss it or review it. Under current U.S. law your copyright lasts your lifetime plus 50 years and then it becomes part of the public domain. That means everyone owns it.

"To copyright is to claim something as your own which you individually, as a team, or as a buyer, created, directed, wrote, drew or purchased."

C. PATENTS

Patents constitute the right of exclusive ownership, for a period of time, of an idea for a new invention and/or the actual new invention itself. Again, inthe USA it is tougher than in most free countries to get these and protect your ideas. The entire engineering schematic and "new idea" must be clearly reflected. You run into the designation "patent pending" all the time. It means a patent has been applied for but has not and may not ever be granted. If a patent has been granted, there should be a number for it. No one else can use it legally without your permission. However, more theft goes on in patents than trademarks or copyrights because understanding patents takes both engineering and legal background of some type. Utilizing a patent usually takes capital. Typically, patent thieves have lots of bucks, the victim (the inventor) often does not, and the victim's case is expensive to pursue. When David and Goliath battle in America, Goliath wins 9 times out of 10.

One great patent,"bet the company case" was between Kodak and Polaroid, in which Kodak was sued for infringing on Polaroids's patented instant developing process with Kodak's Instamatic Camera. Polaroid won, and the Kodak Instamatic was pulled off the market.

"More theft goes on in patents than trademarks or copyrights because understanding patents takes both engineering and legal background of some type."

CHAPTER XXII

PUBLIC EDUCATION

*"If you believe in freedom, you believe in
free choice in education."*

"...public school officials worry that some parents use the ruse of home schooling to keep children home for baby sitting or work purposes."[1]

After reading that sentence, in a local newspaper, I was reminded of an event I witnessed three years ago in a courtroom. A baby had burned himself on an iron carelessly left on the floor. Mom did wrong. Moms and dads do wrong everyday. Some are better, some are worse, none are perfect.

The overwhelming majority of parents, however, are far better than the government—and some of us believe God places children with parents, not the government. A young, idealistic but arrogant social worker who had never had children and probably never had to live in a home without an ironing board decided that this Mom was unfit. She seized the child.

Three days later Mama was in court trying to get her baby back. The burn could have been worse. It would probably not leave any scar. The independent hospital examination had found no signs of child abuse, but the social worker was convinced Mama was unfit. In my expert opinion as a daddy, a school teacher, a lawyer, and a fellow human being, I could tell instantly that: A) Mama had made a terrible mistake leaving the iron out; B) Nevertheless, overall she was a good mama; and, C) Mama and baby were both suffering terribly because of a three-day separation.

Right won out. The woman had pawned everything she owned of value in order to hire a smart, caring lawyer—obviously the lawyer cared about his fee also. She was fortunate enough to be before a judge who was concerned and ordered the child returned immediately. Justice was done but at a heavy price. The woman would never fully trust the government again. The social worker was fuming. She'd make a better case next time— and probably win. Mom would have a long, uphill battle to regroup and redeem a few of her possessions.

The real question, which goes beyond the matter of education, is whether or not we want public officials involved in our lives to the extent they are now? After a 100 years of expecting more and more direction and control from the government, many citizens are unhappy with what we received.

Public officials may claim to be worried that some parents might not be fit to educate and raise their children. However, more than a few parents, with far greater cause—declining test scores, rampant drug use, escalating violence in schools, and self-serving teachers' unions—fear that public officials might not be fit to educate their children.

The question is one of freedom of choice, freedom of thought, and to some, it is freedom of religion. Is the government smarter than we are?

Are politicians the best parents? Should politicians tell us how to live? The questions about whether government should regulate church and private schools, or should prosecute parents who choose to home school their children are becoming more explosive.

No one has ever demonstrated that children learn more in public schools than they do in a well run home education program. In fact, children taught at home have an advantage because their teacher has a vital, personal stake in their success. Home schooled children can learn family moral values along with their academic subjects. Instruction can be paced according to their individual needs and can be flexible enough to allow time for them to pursue their natural talents and interests. There is more time for real learning when the teacher isn't burdened with such time-consuming tasks as filling out endless bureaucratic forms, collecting milk money, herding queues of youngsters to the bathroom and water fountains, and breaking up schoolyard brawls.

Home schooled children are less likely to become victims of playground bullies, child molesters, or teen-aged gangs. They are exposed to far fewer infectious diseases. They grow up more individualistic because they are insulated from the peer pressure that has such pervasive influence on most of this nation's youth, ranging from relatively minor choices as taste in music, clothes, and hair styles to more serious matters such as drug or alcohol abuse and promiscuity.

Home schooled children need have no fear of standardized tests. When used, those tests generally show the home school children's performance to be above the national average.

Some parents also feel very strongly that the public schools are being used as indoctrination centers to train America's youth to be loyal, obedient, non-challenging citizens. These same parents believe that citizens should always cast a jaundiced eye on the activities of government. If these home schoolers are raising a bunch of individualistic citizens who will constantly be challenging government to follow the rules, then maybe our current government officials, who don't want their luxury boats rocked, have a reason to be concerned about these children being home schooled!

These are subjective opinions. The fears of public officials are also subjective. However, the failure of the current system is a verifiable statistical fact: Johnny cannot read, think or ask questions. The public schools are not doing a good job.

The patriotic, constitutional, pro-family answer is quite simple: parents should decide the type of education that is best for their children. Some parents believe they have a religious duty to their Creator to raise the children in a certain manner and teach these beliefs to their children.

If a public official wants to allay his fears that certain parents may not be fulfilling their responsibilities to their children, he can take Mama and Papa before a jury. Of course, the jury should know that it has the power to make the final decision, not the judge. If the jury finds that current law to be wrong with respect to individual parents, those parents would be free to continue to educate their children privately. The jury would not be limited by judges' or legislators' instructions.

Most juries would favor the parents, but judges frequently use their influence to sway jurors—or the judges just ignore the jury's decision, and of course in many jurisdictions, a jury trial is not even an option. If the state in the last 75 years has decided it should control education out of the home, why can't it go into the home and tell parents about books kids should be allowed to read and what religions are preferred? "Too extreme" you say? Early Americans, 200 years ago, would have revolted against compulsory public school education of any kind.

Most states currently spend close to $5,000 per child, per year for students in public schools. Most parents can find better systems for their children for less. Smaller systems also encourage more parental involvement and closer family ties[2].

Church schools, whose ministers choose not to submit to government licensing standards, are also subjected to harsh government actions.

Dr. Everett Sileven, educator and pastor, was thrown in jail for four months for refusing to obtain a state license for his school. Pastor Sileven

"The questions about whether government should regulate church and private schools or should prosecute parents who choose to home school their children are becoming more explosive."

describes his conflict:

"... judges throw preachers in jail for passing out tracts, holding home Bible Studies, operating children's homes and schools without state licenses... judges uphold licensing of professionals for the benefit of special interest groups...The worst crime you can commit in America is to defy a judge! I got 120 days in jail for that when my cell mates had from 1 to 60 days for drunken driving, breaking and entering, assault, drug sales, drug possession, arson and cattle rustling..."[3]

Many ex-school teachers, including the author, and many current school teachers, can find more fault than merit in today's public school systems. Many of the best of these educators would gladly move to one-room schools with smaller classes. If you believe in freedom, you believe in free choice in education. If you believe in families, you can't believe in government answers to problems government may have created.

A certain amount of public money is dedicated to each child for the purpose of that child's education. The money comes from, as a general rule, non-federal revenue, real estate taxes, sales taxes and state income taxes. Some of the world's most exclusive and expensive private schools are cheaper.

If the state gave each parent a $5,000 coupon that could be used to send their children to a church or private school, we would see a marked improvement in public education. The public schools would have to compete by showing genuine performance.

Sadly enough, when the home-schooled student or religious school student who attends an unlicensed school agrees to take a standardized test, the government usually objects strenuously.

Pastor Sileven explains that:*"In fact, church schools have a tremendous track record of teaching their children much more than is taught...at the public schools...In fact, our record is so good that most states object to test scores being entered into the court record when they are trying to close down one of these schools."*[4]

Frank Turano, a non-lawyer—and in my opinion an underground lawyer—and his wife, Maureen Turano, fought the public school system before Judge Quinn in Massachusetts. Mrs. Turano was a former public school teacher, and he was a city policeman. They wanted to teach their two girls at home, but the local school officials objected.

After a long hard battle through the state's court system, the Turanos won. Mrs. Turano states, "We are now the primary educational influence (for our kids) instead of the public school system. We chose not to confer that responsibility on the state."[5]

The Turanos won—and their children won, too.

As a parent of a 10, 11 and 12 year old at the time I met Turano in 1986, I was particularly impressed with the well written, thoughtful portion of the foreward to Frank Turano's book which was written by his 11-year-old daughter, Kelli:

"I have been out of school for two years now and have found that learning without pressure, and being able to choose my own interest is much more fun. When I was in school, I worried about who would steal my lunch money and what I would find missing from my desk at the end of the day."[6]

The child's message was particularly cogent to my wife and me. One of our three children likes school. She used to love it. The second is bored but does his work. The third rebels against the syndrome Ralph Waldo Emerson deplored:

"We are students of words: we are shut up in schools, colleges and recitation rooms for 10 to 15 years, and come out at last with a bag of wind, a memory of words, and do not know a thing."[7]

The world mocks our high school students who cannot read and write. Turano's complaints awaken my own unpleasant memories of fourth and fifth grade.

"What has happened to the zest and curiosity they once possessed? It seems that it has been replaced by the idea that one cannot learn without a teacher and a textbook , and that learning is a mandatory chore which must be tolerated if one is to succeed in today's society."[8]

Turano also complains about his children's involuntary servitude and the state's desire to exercise parental control over his children. It reminded me of a personal experience my wife had when our oldest son was 12 years old.

A teacher—who had been experiencing difficulty with his entire class—mistakenly chose to discipline Jourdan as an example to the class.

In this instance, Jourdan had not earned or deserved punishment. A vice-principal informed us that Jourdan had been spanked. She did not call to tell us he was going to be spanked. She called to say he had already been spanked. My wife and I disagree on corporal punishment. I believe almost anything can be talked out. She believes in the rod, and if the rod breaks, it's the child's fault.

With two of the three kids, I'm almost always right. With the third, who has inherited from God knows where, a stubborn streak, sometimes she's right. On those occasions, I leave the room. This ex-boxer and battle-hardened trial attorney can be counted on to cry more than the kids. However, we are in complete accord on one issue: no one outside our home administers physical discipline.

My wife was furious. The vice-principal simply told her it was the school's policy, and there was nothing she or anyone else could do about it. We were supposed to believe that "the school" (the particular individual or individuals were hiding behind the institution rather than accepting personal responsibility)—knew what was best for Jourdan.

The more my wife demanded control over her child, the more intractable the vice principal became: "The policy was set—the policy had to be followed." My wife was expected to accept it meekly, out of faith. I took the phone and asked the vice principal for an explanation. The explanation was simply, "It's our policy." I explained to her that if a parent had a policy of coming to the school and shooting teachers who had a policy of spanking kids, it wouldn't be legal.

Perhaps my point was made. Jourdan hasn't been spanked again in that school. That event occurred in the spring of 1986, and was one of the factors that led us in the spring of 1988 to take him out of the public school system—and at great expense put him in a private school. We were angered over this incident and considered filing a suit. The spanking wasn't the point; the vice principal was telling a child's mother the school could do what it wanted with the child. The parents' opinion was quite unimportant.

More recently, my family doctor, who is also a client and a personal friend, called me in a highly agitated state. He wanted to know what legal action parents could take against a physical education teacher who had paddled their 12-year-old son—to the point of drawing blood—and against other school officials who assisted in concealing the evidence and hiding the incident from the parents.

A letter was on file at the child's junior high school explaining that the child should not take part in football or other contact sports because of a congenital abnormality in certain blood vessels on his upper legs. Both physical education teachers were aware of the boy's condition. Yet, to discipline this child for playfully scuffling with a classmate, the teacher paddled him on the buttocks, which caused a rupturing of the nearby fragile blood vessels of his leg.

The child's parents were not called—only his family doctor. In an effort to conceal the incident, school officials hastily washed the boy's underwear and jeans to remove the bloodstains. The boy's family doctor made light of the incident, saying that no permanent harm had been done.

Nevertheless, on the same doctor's recommendation, the boy was taken to a nearby emergency room, where my family doctor was the physician on duty. Dr. Lynn Gibbs, a family practitioner, is also certified as a surgeon and emergency room specialist. He was the Texas light heavyweight Golden Gloves Champion and also a graduate of my college, Washington University as well as Harvard.

Lynn was indignant when he learned of this unconscionable use of force that could have caused a life-threatening hemorrhage. When the parents got to the emergency room and discovered what had happened, the boy's father itched to do physical violence to the two physical education teachers.

The parents quit using their former family doctor who had not even notified them of the incident and who didn't seem to appreciate the potential seriousness of the injury.

The small, rural school district was nervous about a potential lawsuit. The principal of the elementary school where the injured child's younger brother and sister attended was asking the younger siblings about their brother's condition and whether their parents were angry over the incident.

I met with the parents and the injured child in my office the next day. The boy was so emotionally traumatized that I had to take him to another room and speak to him alone—using all my parental communication skills—in order to extract the story of what happened.

We examined the school's discipline policy, as explained in the student handbook, which the parents had brought along. We looked up statutes and case law which, unfortunately, showed that the school district and the teachers would most likely be found immune from suit—because they were acting in the course of their perceived duty. A possible chink in the armor might have been that the paddling should have been done in the presence of an administrator, but it was done in the presence of the chairman of the physical education department. The school's policy was unclear about whether this chairperson was considered part of the administration team. We wanted to give the parents some time to cool down before embarking on what would have been a costly, fruitless suit. Litigation creates stress. Litigation involving children directly involves even more stress on those who are least able to handle it. The decision to sue a school which a child attends, should not be made in haste.

It was clear; the child did not want to undergo the stress of litigation. It was clear; the Dad was ready to go on campus and challenge the coach. The doctor was so upset, I was concerned he might go after the coach. He was a former light heavy weight state champ. I was a featherweight city champ; if he and the father had a mind to challenge the coach, they'd roll over me like a tank over a willow tree. Of course that was not really my concern. When child abuse is concerned, most decent people get angry and sometimes do things that are counterproductive. In many ways, the entire public education system is abusive to children. I saw my job to put the fires out and then help the family decide whether litigation or compromise was the best alternative for them. The victim's future safety had to be secured in some way or litigation and possible criminal action would no longer be an alternative but a necessity.

We suggested that the parents take two months to make up their minds. The doctor seemed satisfied that there would be no permanent physical damage, although the emotional trauma would certainly remain.

I wrote a strongly worded letter to the principal of the junior high informing him that the parents had consulted me. I informed him of the change in doctors, of the parents' explicit instructions that NO CORPORAL PUNISHMENT was to be administered to this child, and that no teacher, administrator or any school personnel was to talk to the child about the incident.

I wrote similar letters to the principal of the younger siblings' elementary school, and to the principal of the high school where the child's two older brothers attended, and were star athletes. The school officials contacted me and promised no further physical punishment. No suit was filed, and we assume everything is now satisfactory because the family has not contacted us further, and they have subsequently sent me new business. These parents did not have the resources to put their kids in a private school or the education of the Turanos to have school at home.

Even after these experiences, I still do not agree entirely with Turano's legal conclusions, but I do entirely approve what he and his wife have done for their children. I applaud his courageous fight in court, but I give equal credit to Judge Quinn who ruled in Turano's favor.

The Turano victory was achieved with: A) Great personal courage; B) Great love for his kids; C) A clever underground lawyer's mind and; D) A judge of rare integrity and ability.

Turano's interpretation of the law, was honest, clever, and in some instances, brilliant. When I discovered I was speaking at the same seminar with Frank Turano, I took advantage of the opportunity to speak with him and have him autograph my copy of his book. Turano noted:

"We have had almost no inquiries from school officials concerning our methods, progress, principles, and objectives. Their main concern seems to be to protect the portion of money which has been allocated to the school for children's education."[9]

The law supposes that public officials, in this case not even elected officials, have more concern and love for our kids than we do.

I have met many parents who agree with Turano's legal position, which is basically the same position that many so church-sponsored schools throughout the nation have been taking: that the Constitution and early American law was clear that the education of children is a parent's responsibility, and not one that the government can just assume without the parents' specific consent.

However, many parents are finding out that the current legal position of school and other public officials is that the state has a primary responsibility for any child's welfare and education, and that responsibility is higher than the parent's.

In the words of one of Dicken's characters:

"If the law says that, then the law is an ass."[10]

"...the Constitution and early American law was clear that the education of children is a parent's responsibility, and not one that the government can just assume without the parents' specific consent."

Albert Einstein proclaimed:

"It is, in fact, nothing short of a miracle that the modern methods of instruction have not yet strangled the holy curiosity of inquiry; for this delicate little plant, aside from stimulation, stands mainly in need of freedom...It is a very grave mistake to think that the enjoyment of seeing and searching can be promoted by means of coercion and a sense of duty."[11]

As a former teacher of fifth grade, seventh grade, tenth grade, twelfth grade and college level, I found Turano's secret plan—he refused to allow the school district to obtain it since he believed they had no right to even review it, but now shares it with us in his book—to be very stimulating.

The public education system in our country is too rigid, too inflexible, and too expensive. It should be optional, and if huge tax funds must be collected to finance it, parents should have the discretion of directing where the funds should go, for the benefit of their children.

Our private school systems today are isolated and must compete with compulsory financed, inferior public schools whose large salaries to administrators might as well be spent on $700 Pentagon toilet seats for all the good they do our children.

If a child can demonstrate requisite reading, writing and calculating skills, should this be sufficient to free him from 12 years of unfruitful activity? Is the force of law properly compelling our children in the right direction? Public education continues to be a costly thorn in the side of our nation.

If all schools had to compete for children, if parental legal rights over their children's education were restored, academic performance would improve overnight.

The basic premise behind our public education laws, in that government officials know what's best for our kids, condemns the United States to producing an inferior product.

"...parents are finding out that the current legal position of school and other public officials is that the state has a primary responsibility for any child's welfare and education, and that responsibility is higher than the parent's."

CHAPTER XXIII
AMERICAN DIVORCE:

DISORGANIZED CRIME

"The American divorce system is a tragedy causing more hardships to America than heroin or cocaine because it uses children as cannon fodder to enrich our least scrupulous lawyers, and our least ethical psychologists and psychiatrists often under the supervision of our least competent judges."

A. AN OVERVIEW

Due to my own divorce, my ex-wife's need to find herself, and my children's right to have a fulltime parent, I spent a year raising my children—then ages 3 and 4—as a single parent. I still look back on it as one of the best years of my life. I quit my trial practice, worked four hours a day and got into fulltime parenting. I lost interest in the law.

The law just wasn't as important as getting breakfast ready for my son and daughter, having birthday parties, spending quiet time with each child separately in the evenings and listening to the accounts of their day, observing their new ideas and new friends, watching their personalities develop, playing games and trading recipes with other care-taking parents—all mothers at that time except for me.

At the same time, my ex-father-in-law was busy warring against me, using up his life savings and even spying on me through one of our firm's secretaries who had once worked with him. Despite my winning trial record in representing others, I heeded the advice, "He who represents himself has a fool for a client and a jackass for a lawyer." I had been practicing law for less than two years when I filed for divorce in 1979.

In the matter of my divorce, I relied totally on outside counsel. My attorney accepted a $5,000 retainer—a mere pittance compared to the fortune spent by my ex-wife's father—a $25,000 non-refundable retainer *plus* a $25,000 non-refundable bonus which did not include an hour of work and ultimately, with five lawyers not counting mine, or the *ad-litem* lawyers, a total which was somewhere between $150,000 and $250,000, according to the testimony presented at the first major trial. Thousands of

483

dollars worth of fees were incurred before the first trial, $6,000 in fees were charged by *ad litem* attorneys, and additional thousands were squandered for years of extra litigation.

In the beginning, I tried to settle with my ex-wife, offering her half of our approximate $250,000 estate, joint custody, and substantial child support. We spent six hours together discussing and negotiating. We finally agreed on everything. The next day, her attorney, worried that something might be slipping through his fingers, talked her into breaking our deal. Throughout the initial litigation, which lasted a year, lawyers on both sides encouraged war. After the divorce, litigation continued for another five years. Suits were filed against me for such outrages as allegedly allowing the kids to color on a wall in the hallway. The filing fees on the suit exceeded the cost of painting a wall over.

The ensuing litigation lasted five years, in which I spent more than $20,000—even considering large discounts for my union membership. Apparently my ex-father-in-law, who had spent considerably more, concluded that he could not afford to fight anymore. The ex and I, however, have since become reasonably cordial. A separate book could be written about the courtroom experience, but it would not fit here.

My law firm, Minns, Izen, Bradt & Associates, was destroyed. My savings were eliminated. I had to cover thousands of dollars in community debts and checks that bounced when my spouse pulled the money out of the checking account on advice of her attorney. I had to pay the legal fees resulting from the five-year battle. As a result of this experience—and my observations of other victims of divorce both male and female—I have some strong convictions about American divorce and American divorce lawyers.

Professionally, I started over again less than from scratch working for Mr. William Y. Sim, one of the finest immigration attorneys in the United States.

I had the privilege of working for him for two years. The larger law firms were beginning to realize there was a lot of money to be made bringing rich and middle-class people from other countries into the United States and were beginning to dabble in immigration law. To counteract this new source of competition, Mr. Sim wanted to add a division to his law firm to handle trial work, business law, corporate law and general practice law as well as discreet uncontested divorces, like the large firms. I became that division.

Working for Mr. Sim, I got to meet important families from all over the world who were sending their sons to the United States to start businesses. One recurring theme came up when I discussed their sons' futures—whether they were from Hong Kong, Taiwan, Russia, Nigeria, Iran, England or elsewhere. The parents did not want their sons to marry American women! They had heard that the sons risked losing their fortunes, their children, and their freedom in American divorce courts.

The rumors they had heard are somewhat true but alas, the American divorce system can be equally cruel to the women involved and even more cruel to the children.

The American divorce system is a tragedy causing more hardship to America than heroin or cocaine, because it uses children as cannon fodder to enrich our least scrupulous lawyers, and our least ethical psychologists and psychiatrists, often under the supervision of our least competent judges.

The adversary system should be altogether dissolved or radically changed when it comes to family law. Most of the players involved won't do this—it would cost them too much money. There are a number of family law lawyers and judges who agree with this proposition and are setting up some viable alternatives, but they are in a minority. With that predicate, I present to you the American divorce game: disorganized crime!

Unless you are in a small community where one judge does everything, there are probably judges in your area who specialize in what has been renamed from "divorce law" to the more respectable term of "family law." A more appropriate term would be "anti-family law."

In most jurisdictions, there is no jury in family law matters. When the jury does have some power, it is very limited. The lawyers who specialize in family law are often too incompetent to conduct a jury trial properly. The outcome of such a jury trial in a divorce matter is usually determined by random chance, sexual prejudices or even the weather.

The judges on the family law bench are almost always the bottom of the barrel—the least intelligent, the most political, the least knowledgeable on the law. Why? A relatively small group of family law specialists are constantly dealing with the same small group of judges, day in and day out. In this in-bred, stagnant environment, these lawyers must cater to these judges even more than other lawyers who have the option of less emascu-

"The adversary system should be altogether dissolved or radically changed when it comes to family law."

lated juries. Very few successful lawyers who yearn for the rewards of the bench, intellectual stimulus and public service, consider family law a respectable bench. Some practitioners use it as a stepping stone bench to a more legitimate bench.

Some of these judges will actually demand specific campaign contributions from the lawyers who practice before them, cornering them in the hallways or calling them on the phone. One family law judge who was retiring from the bench had a big fundraising campaign before he left the bench. Why raise campaign funds when you are never going to campaign again or when you have no opponent in the upcoming election? Ask the judges.

The family law courtroom used to be a place for losers—lawyers who could not make money in legitimate areas of law. It still is, but now, everyone loses except the lawyers. Many of the lawyers are there because they got laughed out of other courtrooms or found a way to practice law without ever reading it. The judges are there because someone owed them a political favor but just couldn't bear to put them on a real bench that required thinking. But don't be misled. Family law court power is the real thing, just at a less respectable level.

When a man or a woman is going through a divorce, he or she is in the gutter financially and emotionally. The majority of family law lawyers keep them there as long as possible, and rob them in the process. If you have the money and you're going to have a fight, you need a family law lawyer for political clout and a real lawyer to run the case.

The criminal lawyer wants repeat business. Professional criminals use their lawyers over and over again and send them other clients they meet in jail. Most professional criminals spend some time in jail no matter how good their lawyers are.

The corporate lawyer or real estate lawyer must show performance to a sophisticated client. These clients learn to compare lawyers, lawyers' fees and work product, and they often become very discerning in their selection of counsel. Often, they are as knowledgeable as their attorneys in drafting the contracts that are his daily bread.

The insurance defense lawyer—while his tactics are often less than moral as he strives to achieve his main goal of charging a lot—at least has

"In most jurisdictions, there is no jury in family law matters. When the jury does have some power, it is very limited."

The firm of Shyster & Charlatan, Board Certified Family Law Specialists: Buy One Divorce, Get your Next One Free!

to perform. His trial record is carefully monitored by the insurance adjuster and he must be more than a pure bluff. No one can represent insurance companies and not go to trial. The competition for those guaranteed large monthly checks is substantial. The personal injury plaintiff's counsel has to win or not get paid. He works on a percentage of what he gets for his client. For this reason, all of these types of attorneys are accountable to their clients, to have a continuing output of high quality work product.

However, the family law lawyer usually never sees his angry, disgusted client once the divorce is over. It's a one-shot play. A fast settlement or even a quick trial, and the game's over. The money stops. The most financially hazardous situation in law is when two family law lawyers are egging on their respective clients to do battle over the couple's life

"When a man or a woman is going through a divorce, he or she is in the gutter financially and emotionally. The majority of family law lawyers keep them there as long as possible, and rob them in the process."

savings and children. These lawyers encourage fighting, not settlement, although they rarely go to trial. They prefer to use up all your money in their comfortable offices rather than the heated trial pit.

Even worse, while Mom and Dad each have a lawyer, the judge frequently assigns a third attorney to charge Mom and Dad to represent the kids. Whose side is he on? Guess. Neither parent will ever hire him. His biggest client is usually the judge, and he often pays his client with campaign contributions. The theory is that neither parent cares enough or is objective enough to represent their own children, so a stranger with training in the law is selected to fill this void.

Experts? Although there are many fine psychiatrists, psychologists, and counselors who offer marriage counseling, family therapy and children's psychiatric evaluations, there are also a large number of these professionals who make six-figure incomes testifying in family law courts for Mom or Dad in divorce cases. In excess of 90 percent of the time, this expert's opinion will be in favor of the party who hired him or her, because the expert wants more business from lawyers who want to win their cases or at least justify a fight.

A few common tactics: Use a mother's child as a bargaining tool in the hands of a husband who didn't want the child in the first place, leave her emotionally weak, and get her to settle for keeping the child, with no assets and almost no support. Immoral? Of course. But, it's standard operating procedure.

Have Dad, who has raised his son by himself for two years while Mom "found herself," divide his son's college money with Mom, split custody and pay child support, under the threat that most men lose in court. Out of fear of losing his son he'll deal. Smart tactics again. Standard operating procedure.

Pull two children apart by sending them to opposite shrinks who each say the other parent is crazy. Lots of fun! Lots of profit. Lots of jokes about it at cocktail parties.

Threaten to cut off one parent from the kids, or bankrupt a parent. Let each side know the other side is immoral. Let the two attorneys get

---

"The fastest growing poverty class in America consists of single female parents without support systems. A second economically disadvantaged group is made up of re-married middle class men who are told to support two households or go to jail."

---

together and bad mouth both clients to fan the flames of animosity. Keep the prospective ex-spouses apart and enraged until they are broke.

Our system may not be the worst in the free world, but it's a sure contender. The alleged purpose is for the best interests of the child or fair distribution, but the reality is that no one is benefiting but the least moral, least competent group in our legal labor unions.

At William Sim's office, we handled about 50 divorce cases during the year I was there. The terms of all but one of them were agreed to by both parties. We charged $500 plus about $50 in filing fees. The husband and wife got together and made all their decisions peacefully. Occasionally there would be a rift, and we would bring them both in to the office and settle it.

I refuse to do any family law work now. In the last seven years, I made three exceptions for friends or long-term clients to protect them from the union. All were settled on a friendly basis. While listening to over 200 different, prospective divorcing couples in my career, only three could not agree before spending a lot of money with divorce lawyers.

The fastest growing poverty class in America consists of single female parents without support systems. A second economically disadvantaged group is made up of re-married middle class men who are told to support two households or go to jail.

These hard working men, through fear and a false sense of duty, are paying for a system that has turned sleazy, gutter lawyers into millionaires, reduced the standard of living for the middle classes and destroyed the spirit of many good women and men by using their own children and life savings as grist for its evil mill. These men commit suicide at an alarming rate. After that, they support no one.

B. TALES OF WOE

Sue Warfield Munoz's case demonstrates the aftermath of a poorly handled divorce that left an errant husband with all the property and his once devoted wife with two children and the clothes on her back.

Former husband K.D. Warfield had accumulated a vast amount of debt. He had a personal relationship with several employees at Katy Savings and Loan that made it possible for him to borrow large sums of money from them. Shortly after divorce proceedings started, ownership of the lending institution changed hands and Katy Savings & Loan became Meridian Savings and Loan.

THIS COURT FINDS YOU HAVE BEEN AN
EXEMPLARY WIFE AND MOTHER FOR 25
YEARS OF MARRIAGE: ACCORDINGLY
YOU ARE AWARDED THE OPPORTUNITY
TO START OVER AGAIN FROM SCRATCH,
NEW JOB, NEW CREDIT, NEW FRIENDS,
NEW FUTURE, NEW WORLD. GOOD LUCK.
                    CASE DISMISSED.

Basically, to avoid a protracted fight, Sue agreed to accept a $200,000 cash settlement of the divorce, which would come from the sale of their country home and ranch—valued at about $1 million but encumbered with a debt of about $300,000. Husband was to keep all the couple's other assets.

Sue received a promise to pay, guaranteed by the ranch home. This promise to pay is called a promissory note—a piece of paper which pretends to be worth the amount shown on its face, in this case $200,000. Banks, lending institutions and cautious creditors usually want something more substantial than a written promise to pay—they want something substantial pledged, so that if the promisor doesn't keep his promise they can still collect. This is usually called security.

One of the best types of security is valuable real estate. More than one debt may be secured by the same piece of property. For example, the real estate in question was worth $1 million, and it could reasonably be expected to secure both the $300,000 and the $200,000 obligations. However, if additional debts were added, the arrangement would become risky.

If the promises are not kept; the security is often sold quickly at a public or private auction for cash. If you're able to sell a million-dollar property quickly, for cash, the property usually will not bring the full value.

The numerical positions of lienholders on a property which secures several notes is a matter of paramount importance. In most jurisdictions, a lienholder's place in this pecking order determines whether the lien is meaningful or worthless, because it is the order in which the secured parties get paid. In the Warfield case, the bank's $300,000 was a first lien and Mrs. Warfield's $200,000 was a second lien. This means that if the property was sold, the first $300,000 went to the bank and the next $200,000—if any remained—went to Mrs. Warfield for her second lien.

After the divorce, the former Mrs. Warfield married her erstwhile gardener, Manuel Munoz, who helped her raise her children, while their natural father contributed almost nothing to the daily support of the two school-age youngsters.

Ex-husband Warfield and Meridian Savings had a mutual problem. He owed them an additional debt of $500,000. He wanted the debt wiped out and Meridian wanted the real property. Warfield faced the possibility of getting nothing anyway. A foreclosure price of $500,000 would not have been unreasonable or unforseeable. The bank could not put a third lien on the property as long as Warfield lived there—it was his homestead!

How could the bank and Mr. Warfield solve their mutual dilemma—at the expense of Mrs. Munoz if necessary? Warfield agreed to change the first lien from $300,000 to $500,000, with small print at the bottom of the new promise, to add any other debts. The other debts could not be properly secured by Warfield's homestead, so he signed an affidavit that it was not his homestead. However, we discovered later that he had apparently abandoned it in spirit only—his body remained in the house until Meridian encouraged him via court order to leave.

In order to consummate this deal, the bank wanted Mrs. Munoz to agree to subordinate her second lien to the bank's new lien, or the new bank lien would be third in line to be paid when the house was sold. Why would Sue be willing to do this? What could she possibly gain? Answer:

nothing.

Warfield told Munoz the bank would give him extra time to sell the house if she signed the subordination agreement. He said he needed the extra time to get a better price. He assured her that it wouldn't hurt her and it would prevent a foreclosure which would wipe out her second lien. The bank wouldn't discuss anything with her. She signed the subordination agreement. The first lien for $300,000 became a first lien of $500,000 because of Warfield's undisclosed other debt.

Mr. Munoz, who was also my gardener at the time, told me about the case and introduced me to his wife. I agreed to represent her. We sued her former spouse and the bank. The trial court dismissed the bank from the suit by granting summary judgment in their favor, the jury awarded $1.4 million against Mr. Warfield. I've enlisted a local counsel in Hawaii, where Warfield now resides, to attempt to collect the judgment. So far, an indigent ex-wife with two kids remains indigent as far as Mr. Warfield's resources go.

We appealed Judge Kitzman's ruling in favor of the bank. Since our client was indigent, the judge granted her request to proceed as a pauper despite the bank's objection. This court ruling meant that she did not have to pay certain court costs necessary for the preparation and filing of the appeal. Both sides filed briefs. The case was settled about ten days before oral argument on the appeal was scheduled. By agreement, the terms of the settlement agreement may not be divulged.

The following, brief tale of woe—as well as much of the above story of Mrs. Munoz—was written on August 24, 1987, while I was sitting at the counsel table in a family law courtroom, waiting for a temporary injunction hearing.

This client, an emotionally vulnerable young woman, is being sued by her former divorce lawyer for every penny she has. He's already been overpaid. God willing, I won't be called to this area of the law again. I only accepted this case as a result of a promise I made to my Creator. During a night of prayer, I agreed to handle this case if God would help me win the Oliver case. He delivered. I am here, fish out of water again, and hoping to get out.

Our hearing was set for 9:30 a.m. It's 11:35 now and my client, L.R. and I are waiting. Here's another story, whose conclusion will not be reported in this book. The client's entire estate was tied up by the court without notice. Her former lawyer wants $20,000 for his work when there was no trial, only a settlement, he took no depositions, and there were no children.

She had found this lawyer, certified in family law, through an ad he had placed in the television listings section of her local newspaper.

C. ADULTERY, INVESTIGATORS AND ASSORTED BEDLAM

Certified family law expert John Nichols re-entered my life through a back door almost a decade after he cleaned out my ex- father-in-law with a $150,000 divorce fee and after he destroyed a settlement agreement between my ex-wife and myself that left us both broke and me heavily in debt.

Joe Izen, my former partner, and frequent client, had been thrown out of his love nest mansion by his bride of eight years, Martha Izen, affectionately called Marty. She and her shrink had determined Joe was bad for her self concept, and she set his luggage out on the front lawn and changed the locks.

Joe was crushed, but he accepted the reality of the separation, moved into his office building —which fortunately had a shower and bath (he had purchased my 1/3 interest in the building when I, going through my divorce nine years earlier needed the money)—and agreed to pay Marty $6,000 a month to get by while they worked out the details. As the months passed, the agreement began to shape up. The Izens had agreed to evenly split their estate. It was worth somewhere between $500,000 and $1,000,000, including nearly a quarter-million in cash. Marty would get a nice house with a swimming pool, paid off in full. The tie up was on child support. Joe offered $800. Marty wanted $1,200.

Marty had come into the marriage with a beautiful blue-eyed blond baby who had unfortunately been disclaimed by her dentist dad. Joe raised the baby girl as his own and she was soon joined by two healthy boys. They went from a small apartment to a mansion; Joe provided well for his family. Europe and the Bahamas were often on the agenda but Marty—as others have—grew discontent. Thus the separation.

Enter Michael Easton, private investigator. He met Joe at the courthouse one day and got a contract to work for him—including $20,000 up front, a car, a radio, a phone, a platinum American Express card and an office. Unfortunately, Easton was a terror. No control. No loyalty. Easton's behavior included a large helping of criminal activity, which led to one guilty plea on charges of criminal phone harassment against a lawyer, a finding of criminal insurance fraud,(written by the late Judge Ross Sterling), theft charges and a breakup with Izen without a refund.

Easton convinced Marty that A) Joe was sleeping with her friend and Joe's secretary, Karen; and B) Joe had salted away millions of dollars and he could prove it all. Why did Marty believe him? The stress of divorce? Her shrink? Your guess is as good as mine. She paid Easton a $10,000 fee, and cleaned out every account she and Joe had in America and the Bahamas—including a trust account containing money that belonged to his clients, not him.

The day after the last bank withdrawl, Marty entered the office of family law expert John Nichols. Armed with the word of a convicted criminal and a distraught psychiatric patient—and having received and deposited a sizable retainer check—Nasty Nichols outdid himself.

He filed suit against Joe implying child abuse and adultery, and he also sued Joe's secretary, Karen, alleging she was responsible for breaking up the happy home. Karen had been a friend to both Joe and Marty, and had been a babysitter to the three Izen little ones—but now she was the evil homebreaker.

Joe's clients, whose money he had taken and placed in escrow, threatened suit. Easton rifled files in Joe 's office and handed them to Nasty Nichols. Joe's money was all gone. Marty had also emptied their retirement accounts subjecting them to tax penalties. Easton also became active in the state bar's ongoing endeavor against Joe. His cash gone and his office disoriented, Joe had to borrow money to pay his office phone bill. Joe asked me to get involved, and I turned him down cold. No divorce court for me. SORRY. I would give him moral support and possibly a loan but no involvement.

Nichols agreed to let $25,000 go to an attorney for Joe if he could keep his $25,000, and the agreement between Joe's lawyer and Nichols' was struck. Joe's lawyer quickly used up his money, had heart problems and got off the case. Joe hired lawyer number two for $10,000 up front.

Marty paid Nichols another $25,000. Actually in 1988, the $50,000 he got from Marty was a lot less than the $150,000 he got from my father-in-law in 1979 and 1980. Basically, I believe his fee was whatever the market would bear.

Karen called. She was innocent. She was the sole source of support for her daughter. (Her ex had not degraded her with regular monthly payments.) Her life consisted basically of a 12-hour work day and a 12-hour mom day. Work and daughter; No dating; Extremely religious, prim and

*Do you swear to take this man for everything he has or will have,
when divorce do you part?*

proper—She was upset!

What did she want? She wanted the judge to say she was innocent, and she wanted a long-term legal fee payout. I felt the case could be wrapped up fast since she was innocent and there would be no evidence other than Easton's allegations. Joe also called, and asked me to represent Karen.

A quick resolution and I would be helping Joe's office out and would be helping a woman who had been a friend to me, and Joe and Marty. I was also hopeful that I could interject myself as a friend of all three and help resolve the situation. I knew Joe had never run around at all. I knew Karen was innocent. I suspected Marty was ill-advised. I filed a written appearance on Karen's behalf.

Joe dropped his agreed $6,000 monthly payment to $4,000. Marty was angry. Nichols was confident. They went to court and lo and behold, the judge ordered Joe to pay $2,000 a month.

I tried to call Nichols, but he wouldn't take my calls, so I decided to prepare for trial. I set Marty's deposition, giving plenty of notice so there would be time for the opposition to request a re-setting, if necessary. Depositions are usually set for agreed times, but without phone calls it's hard to make agreements.

The afternoon before the deposition was set, I was served with a motion for protection. Marty could not come. The motion was set for 8:30 a.m. in a divorce court 30 miles away. I was upset. Why hadn't I been given a courtesy call? Why the fight so fast? Why was I, without a gun to my head, going to appear in a divorce court again? I was not happy or optimistic.

Family law expert Nichols, and non-family law me, were to appear before family law Judge Thomas Stansbury—whom Nichols knew and I didn't. My dread proved unjustified. When I entered the courtroom at 8:00 a.m. I saw circulars and news articles placed there by the judge for attorneys to read. Some were highly critical of the family law court and system. Gee, it was hard not to like this judge.

Judge Stansbury knew Nichols, but he at least appeared to be neutral. On top of that, he had read every word of the pleadings. Nichols argued against the deposition, I argued for it and demanded attorney's fee. Despite my non-family law status, the judge was fair. No money for my trouble, but no long delay for Nichols. The deposition was re-set for the afternoon of that same day and the papers and tapes I had requested must be produced.

In the afternoon it was a no-show. The judge's order was disobeyed. Both Joe's lawyer and I filed motion for sanctions. The judge listened patiently to each side. I still felt uncomfortable in the court. The judge discussed the law with us, demonstrating a comprehension of the law equal to that of any federal judge I had been before.

I still expected him to extend some favoritism to Nichols, but I was optimistic. I'd get strong discovery orders. He ordered what a good federal judge would. He ordered Nichols' client to pay me $1,050 in sanctions, and $850 to Joe's lawyer. However, still showing good objectivity and fairness, the judge said the money did not have to be paid if the suit against Karen was dropped. Good. At $200 an hour I had already over spent the $1,500 I'd agreed to accept for the case.

I thought the case was over. It wasn't. They paid and showed up, but they didn't bring tapes they claimed were incriminating. Easton had them. They hadn't asked for them. Nichols said they didn't have to. I would later use this statement against his client. We made a deal to receive the tapes and finish the deposition later.

When they showed up again, they had tapes but they had nothing to do with Karen. Marty claimed that was *another* tape, which Easton had never possessed, and she had not brought to the second court ordered production. Now that tape appeared to have been accidentally erased.

She still believed Joe and Karen were an item, but something new came out: Marty had a boyfriend. Joe's lawyer took the boyfriend's deposition while I watched. The boyfriend was angry. "Why am I here?", he asked. "What's this got to do with me? Sure we had sex. So what?" I passed a friendly note to Nichols that I wanted the boyfriend to take an IQ test. He smiled. Marty didn't.

I asked Nichols after that deposition to drop the case, have Marty apologize and we'd all go home. No dice.

The case went on. Nichols set and took two depositions and didn't bother to tell me or invite me. He called it a mistake. I called it an outrage, and I set another motion for sanctions for November 4, 1987.

At the hearing, Nichols argued he was now ready to conditionally drop the case. The judge wanted to know what that meant. All of us wanted to know what Nichols meant.

By the time the hearing was over, and for the next several months, it became very clear what Nichols meant. Nichols, Marty and sidekick Easton never had the evidence that they claimed.

Nichols had entered the arena for a $25,000 fee at a time when most issues had been settled between Joe and Marty Izen. Could he have justified that fee by preparing a few papers to implement the terms already agreed to, or was it necessary for him to create utter havoc and bedlam to justify the expense?

From beginning to end, it was clear that the conflict raised by Easton and Nichols could not be supported with any evidence, and most of the tactics clearly were to stall and delay.

Repeated depositions were set up without success, repeated hearings were held without producing a resolution. Months later, after numerous no-shows and failure-to-responds, the court awarded a series of penalties to me for Nichols' conduct. A final judgment was entered, but even then Nichols continued his stall by requesting a new trial. Each delay cost both parties unnecessary fees and expense. Each delay resulted in more penalties being assessed against Nichols' client.

"Currently, 99 percent of all divorces could be handled like they were in Bill Sim's office: no pre-trial fights, no need to take the cases to court. Why squander resources with a non-trial attorney, who doesn't know how to properly prepare for trial anyway, for a trial that never takes place?"

By March, 1988, a final judgment in favor of Karen was rendered and judgment and penalties had reached more than $5,000. I was happy to beat Nichols, and I felt good knowing there was one such excellent family law judge around.[1] The Final Judgment and Judge Stansbury's *Findings of Fact and Conclusions of Law*[2] are included in the Addendum.

While Karen's name was legally cleared she still regretted the loss of Marty's friendship and emotional turmoil.

At this time, Izen is broke; Marty says she's broke; Nichols has filed personal bankruptcy; the once uncontested divorce is now also a custody suit; and a new suit is pending involving Izen, Marty, Nichols, and Izen's client, Conroe Office Building, Ltd.—which claims its money has been taken from Joe's trust account. Over $120,000 from a Bahama account and some amount between $10 and $80,000 from numerous other accounts are missing and at least partially unaccounted for.

Karen and I are out of the litigation. We placed a lien on all of Marty's community interest for Karen's $5,000. Marty's home was sold before the divorce to pay back payments. After all expenses, a little over $1,000 was left which went to Karen. I honestly wish Joe, Marty, and the kids all good luck. Act One of this family law circus is over, but there could easily be ten more. Act Two was a five week custody trial. Joe was represented by one of Texas' best, Martin Cardin. Marty had another family law expert, Don Royal. On October 20, 1988, the jury gave the couples' two sons to Joe. Joe is becomming a model father, and I am proud of him and his two boys. The suit against Nichols and the Izen property division will be heard later. I'll watch this sad tragic-comedy from a distance. If I could place a bet on it, I'd bet the Honorable Judge Stansbury sheds a tear or two over this. From what I learned about him, he's not in favor of family law blood letting. The only thing I can guarantee is that other than the collection of some large legal fees there will be no winners.

D. SHORT-TERM SOLUTIONS: IF YOU'RE GETTING DIVORCED SOON

What can Americans do now and for the future?

Currently, 99 percent of all divorces could be handled like they were in

---

"Make sure you want to get a divorce. Many people are pushed into divorces they didn't want so a lawyer can make a fee."

Bill Sim's office: no pre-trial fights, no need to take the cases to court. Why squander resources with a non-trial attorney, who doesn't know how to properly prepare for trial anyway, for a trial that never takes place?

Use divorce clinics like the "Great Izen's." The big complaint that I've heard is "they leave a lot of loose ends." That's true. Many do, but so do most of the family law specialists whose work I've had the task of reviewing.

Use one lawyer for both of you—just make sure he's interested in justice.

Use simple, uncomplicated, self-help forms provided in many bookstores.

Caveat (beware!)—some clinics cost more than the small one or two person law office.

Use lawyers who subscribe to arbitration. There are some very good family law lawyers and mental health experts who specialize in non-litigated solutions. If you are in a potentially volatile divorce situation these people can save you and possibly your children years of grief and rebuilding. If you are buying an arbitrator, make sure you're getting honest mediation and not a come-on to get you into a war. Don't end up in a war against a ruthless foe if your ally is an arbitrator who never fights. Good arbitrators should know the players in your city and be able to advise you properly. Arbitrators possess a degree of trust and vulnerability. Unfortunately, because of the unethical nature of the contested divorce game, the nice guy can finish last. This could be changed, when someday children and former clients start suing divorce lawyers for messing their lives up.

Make sure you want to get a divorce. Many people are pushed into divorces they didn't want so a lawyer can make a fee—just as some medical doctors push people into unneeded surgery. If you're going to get a divorce, anyway: try to settle and try to do it quickly. A long, drawn-out case is good for no one but the lawyer.

Terrible problems are caused by judges who are politicians and know little about raising children—particularly when bottom-of-the-barrel lawyers are encouraging the spouses to fight.

If you enjoy soap operas, you will probably enjoy talking to professional divorce attorneys. Otherwise, you might be annoyed by their gossipy inability to protect their client's personal confidences in much the same way that you might be offended by the conduct of a shrink, who in casual social conversation divulges his patients' innermost secrets for the purpose of gaining a chuckle or two.

Divorce lawyers don't need to impress the client to keep the client's business. In fact, they know in advance they're not going to keep the client's business. People usually don't ever want to see their divorce attorneys again.

When the case is over, the attorneys lose. Their fee collecting is over. For this reason they tend to exaggerate and encourage fights between the parties to prolong the conflict. Children are destroyed. Daddies lose their children. Mommies lose their support systems and their children become members of the nation's fastest growing poverty class.

Most states now allow relatively painless divorces with relatively simple procedures. Check them out and watch a few divorces before you get yours.

E. LONG-TERM SOLUTIONS: FOR MAJOR CHANGE.

Don't allow anyone to specialize in family law.

Don't allow lawyers to campaign for or contribute to family law judges they regularly appear before. Records of campaign contributions should be maintained in easy-to-read public records in each courtroom, so that the attorneys can check their opponent's influence.

Encourage settlements by creating simple forms for both parties to fill out in separate rooms before notaries. Let notaries file the divorces.

Make all custody joint-custody unless one spouse can and is willing to prove, in front of a jury, that the other is unfit.

Have non-lawyers as independent referees. Let them sit down with those couples who can't agree on everything. These referees can be priests, rabbis, ministers or counselors.

Every year these referees must please both the majority of husbands and wives or lose their rights to participate. The participants must pay the referees.

The rare individuals who could not settle or be reasonable, go to a jury. The jury would have the authority to make an example of the disagreeable spouse. With the proper safeguards early in the process, very few, couples—less than one percent—would ever get their cases to the jury. Today, five percent of the cases reach the jury.

If only the winning lawyer gets paid, for trial and trial preparation— and he got paid by the losing party—lawyers would be less likely to encourage litigation, because the lawyers would fear an unchained jury and would have less chance of padding their own pockets with needless conflict. It could be a criminal offense for these family law specialists to divide the fees awarded by the jury between themselves under the table.

Require all divorce court judges to have been married and divorced at least once and been the primary caretaker for at least one small child for at least a month.

Would this create a perfect system? No.

Would it create a better one? Yes. No one who intentionally set out to create a bad system could have devised one worse than what we now have. There is virtually nothing in the present system worth saving.

"Our system may not be the worst in the free world, but it's a sure contender. The alleged purpose is for the best interests of the child or fair distribution, but the reality is that no one is benefiting but the least moral, least competent group in our legal labor unions."

CHAPTER XXIV
THE SHRINK IN LAW

"...to find a psychologist or psychiatrist to testify under oath to whatever you want him to say is not difficult."

One thing that every judge and every trial lawyer knows—although only the honest ones will admit it—is that to find a psychologist or psychiatrist to testify under oath to whatever you want him to say is not difficult. The single requirement is that you pay him money.

Unlike IRS agents, some shrinks are popular party guests. They draw a crowd and regale their eager listeners with stories about their latest custody trial testimony or with amusing anecdotes about their patients.

There is one psychiatrist who has a reputation for testifying that a person—any person—is a danger to society and a sociopath. A sociopath is someone without the capability to restrain his impulses in line with society's moral demands. Such a person will continue to be destructive all his or her life—and therefore, should get the death penalty.

This psychiatrist is an expert in what he does and behind his back has been called the "killer shrink." He can go into the jail cell and ask the patient a few questions, and, as a result of this examination, reach a conclusion within minutes.

The "patient's" attorney should advise his client to plead the Fifth Amendment and not talk to any shrink. Most of the time this technique works. Faced with this tactic, the normal shrink cannot get testimony, cannot make the person take a test, and cannot certify that the person is insane. This killer shrink is alleged to be the exception. He testifies that the patient's lack of cooperation, hostility and very demeanor is adequate enough for him to certify that beyond a reasonable doubt the individual is a sociopath.

For the right price, he could just as easily testify that the judge or lawyers are sociopaths. He's very good; and as a professional witness, he usually convinces the jury.

There are few—if any—objective ways to evaluate the success of psychologists or psychiatrists. Some statistics indicate fewer people recover from emotional problems when treated by psychiatrists or psychologists than when they are not!

In the case of the medical doctor working with a seriously physically-ill patient, the patient either recovers—whether by the physician's skill or by the grace of God—or dies. The results are starkly visible.

With a shrink, often no one really knows if he is succeeding or not. As long as the patient is alive, keeps coming back, and paying his fees, the shrink is perceived as doing a good job. Some of these professionals view the world in two categories of people: those with mental aberrations or illnesses and those who get paid to treat them.

There are four professions in particular in which patients or clients get intimately involved on a very close personal level with the mentor: lawyer, medical doctor, psychiatrist or psychologist[1] and clergy. There are some people in all of these professions who take advantage of their clients/patients of the opposite sex—and sometimes the same sex—to gratify their lust while lining their pockets.

The vast majority of lawyers in this country, although they might be unscrupulous enough to steal every penny they can get from their clients, do not take sexual advantage of their clients. The family law practitioners may indulge in that vice more than other members of the bar. Most professional women are offended by any type of pass or innuendo suggested during business. However, during a divorce or separation period, even the most monogamous person is often filled with self-doubt which results in vulnerability to the approaches of others.

The family law lawyer will be offered opportunities on a regular basis. First, because emotions run very close to the surface in all of these cases and people in a divorce need support systems in the worst way. Second, because the victims in divorce often need a hero and that need is coupled frequently with a desire to prove themselves sexually. This combination results in passes being made by the client to the lawyer.

In my 13 years of practicing law on non-domestic cases, not a single female client, and very few female opposing counsels have ever made blatant overtures to me. However, during the first five years when I handled divorce law, I can recall numerous subtle and often direct offers—at times in lieu of fees—from female clients, as well as some implied invitations from female opposing counsels.

While I have always been monogamous, it was not difficult to be pro-

---

"There is one psychiatrist who has a reputation for testifying that a person—any person— is a danger to society and a sociopath."

---

fessional, avoid any liaisons, and still comfort the client. However, during my divorce and separation the temptation was so strong that I stopped doing family law during that time. In recent years—because of my personal distaste for that area of the law and the people involved in it —I have eliminated most divorce law from my practice, except an occasional uncontested divorce for a special friend, long-term client—or to sue a divorce lawyer for malpractice.

When the lawyer goes through the same emotional problems that the client is suffering, expect problems. Within a year or two after the period of intense emotional crisis, this problem usually dissipates, and a normal working relationship can resume.

The patient-shrink relationship is even more personal than the attorney-client and the veil of privacy is equally pierced. The lawyer must know the basic details. "Did you run around on your husband?" The shrink seeks more details. "Did you run around on your husband because of a conflict with your father?"

Relatively few medical doctors will take sexual advantage over the people entrusted to them. Some women in our society worship doctors, just as they do judges, and, like some judges, some doctors also take sexual advantage of nurses or other women who are prey to this type of professional.

The overwhelming majority of clergymen in this country do not take financial or moral advantage of their parishioners. I have seen many families straightened out, many children set on the right path and many individual human beings freed from tangled webs through the counseling of their family priest or minister or rabbi.

There have been a few occasions when I did not agree with the advice given, but I never saw any harm done as a result of their advice. I have seen clergymen raise funds for individuals who are undergoing severe hardships, put roofs over their parishoners' heads and help them into a healing situation. Perhaps all this is possible because most clergymen possess an abiding moral faith, whereas there is no such requirement for some of the other professions discussed in this chapter.

I have never personally known of a case in which a pastor took physical advantage of members of his flock. While I have occasionally read newspaper accounts of such incidents, fortunately they are few and far between.

Part of the problem is this need to diagnose and label normal human conduct under stress as "abnormal." Normal people in litigation experience stress and have difficulty coping, and under such stress they act abnormally normal. For example: bankruptcy is not a good self-image maker nor is the imprisonment of the breadwinner can cause the caretaker parent and child to do strange things they otherwise wouldn't do. Stress makes healthy people sick, physically and emotionally...but that doesn't mean they need lifetime care. A good friend, a detached but understanding doctor, a social worker, a minister, a paramour, even sometimes your cat can be a valuable asset to your normal recovery.

Part of the solution, however, is just the removal of the stressful problem. Completion of trial. Receiving a divorce. Having a neighbor fix the defective roof. I've seen ministers get out to fix the roof, or raise money for a defense fund. I've never seen a shrink do this. On one occasion, I recall a woman whose husband was incarcerated. She was suddenly a single working mother where formerly, she had been a housewife. After two months, she told me she was losing her mind due to the pressures of her child running amok, household chores, and work. I sent a maid over that day and offered to cover three visits to a psychologist which I knew and trusted who had a very good track record for helping people cope with stress. She said thank you, but if it was all the same, she'd like the maid back three times. Sometimes maid therapy is the best therapy money can buy.

I do not want to start mass hysteria against the psychologists and psychiatrists of this country, but stastics reflect, the incidents of their sexual harassment of patients are significantly more frequent than the other professionals mentioned above.[1] The transference phenomenon—wherein patients project their emotions for others in their lives on to the psychiatrist as their love object—is human behavior that shrinks are supposed to be on guard against. The psychiatrists and psychologists have an obligation to be aware of this occupational hazard and to keep this kind of fantasizing in the patient's mind—and off the couch![2]

Mental health practitioners have a high rate of suicides. Large numbers of them may have been attracted to their field because they had emotional problems themselves and were trying to deal with their own inner turmoils. Obviously, it would be an error to categorize the whole profession in that manner.

The Good Shrink: Many normal, emotionally stable people choose to

---

"In legal work, there are times when the testimony of a mental health professional is necessary."

---

practice in the mental health field. Doubtless there are large numbers of patients who owe their sanity and even their lives to dedicated mental health professionals.

In legal work there are times when the testimony of a mental health professional is necessary. Frequently, in a personal injury case where mental anguish is claimed, such testimony is needed to establish that aspect of damages.

In a criminal case where a particular state of mind is an element of the offense—such as willful failure to file a personal income tax—psychiatric testimony theoretically could be used to show that the defendant did not have that required state of mind. The author appealed to the U.S. Supreme Court in this very matter.

At the trial, the judge excluded the testimony of both a psychiatrist who had known and treated the defendant's family in the past and a psychologist who had recently assessed the defendant's state of mind. In what seemed to me to be a ridiculous conclusion, the judge ruled that the testimony of mental health professionals was irrelevant to showing a defendant's state of mind. The Supreme Court agreed.

In one particular case, a trial court judge practically condemned by insult the entire psychiatric profession. The Second Circuit appeal court overruled his decision.[3]

Many problems for children, and their teachers, and their parents, which were once not detectable and not treatable, are now detectable and curable by competent professionals. The divorced man or woman who is properly comforted and counseled by a caring professional often can cut a period of lost years into a period of lost months. A caring professional can help the patient avoid actions which can take years to forget. If someone volunteers that he's feeling suicidal, send him or her to a psychologist not a lawyer. If he wants to kill himself because he is broke, make sure the doctor works for a charitable institution or takes insurance.

A competent doctor with good insight can be instrumental in explaining to a jury a person's motivations and personal conflicts.

Conclusions: Shrinks are like everyone else. They like money. To make money they have to sell their time. Some make their money treating pa-

---

"Many problems for children and their teachers and their parents which were once not detectable and not treatable are now detectable and curable by competent professionals."

---

tients. Some make their money testifying, and some do both.

If a shrink makes half his income from lawyers, then that shrink has learned how to give lawyers what they want. They want testimony, and they want it to support their position. If the lawyer wants Grandpa to be nuts so his client can take over the management of Grandpa's assets, the shrink will probably conclude that Grandpa is nuts.

The best doctors in this profession can often be ferreted out with some easy techniques: Does she explain things? Is he caring without being overly compassionate? Has he or she been highly recommended by someone familiar with his work? Are you told you only need a few sessions or perhaps none at all?

The bad ones often give signs and signals out too. Does the shrink seem to be hiding something? Are your questions answered with strange enigmatic sounding empty phrases? Have you been told during your last 55-minute analysis session at least three times that you must be an 80s person and instantly release all of your pent-up sexual frustrations with the first highly educated, sensitive person you meet—who happens to have a couch available? Are you told you need a lifetime of constant therapy? If you detect these signals from your prospective shrink, do not make a second appointment.

A consumer of mental health care services—just like a consumer of furniture, automobiles, plumbing services or legal services—must be aware of standards and must look for quality performance and value in the professional he chooses. An uncomfortable number of these people associated with the law are nothing more than hired guns skilled in appearing to have wisdom and training in testimony techniques to convey impartiability; while being ever vigilant to pursue and secure their next testimony tribute...a verdict for their side, a dollar for their purse.

"A doctor with good experience can be instrumental in explaining to a jury a person's motivations and personal conflicts."

CHAPTER XXV
PERSONAL INJURY

*"People hurting people...The result, for the victim,
is called a **personal** injury."*

A. CATEGORIES

People hurting people: recklessly driven cars, incompetent doctors, dishonest or incompetent lawyers, slippery floors, unsafe escalators, physical assaults, malicious words, dog bites and asbestos poisoning. These are a few of our people-hurting-people tools.

The result, for the victim, is called a *personal* injury. After criminal matters and divorce, personal injury is the most common category of litigation in America. An injury of this nature against a person is also called a *tort*. The word *tort* actually means a wrong done to another individual.

If the defendant in a personal injury suit is insured, his insurance company hires an attorney to represent him. There are several categories of personal injury lawsuits. By far the most common are lawsuits which arise from motor vehicle collisions.

Another broad category is litigation over slip and fall accidents resulting from such conditions as slippery floors, obstacles, or ice and snow on pathways.

Premises liability suits arise from accidents caused by poorly designed buildings, doors, elevators, escalators, etc.

Defects in consumer products, such as a car that tends to slip into reverse or a toaster that causes an electric shock, form another category of personal injury, often known as products liability.

Medical malpractice suits arise when a person has been damaged by the acts or omissions of a doctor who did not follow standard medical practices while caring for his patient, such as cutting off the wrong leg or performing an operation on the wrong patient.

There is a sub-section of the personal injury field which concerns workers injured on the job or workers who contract an illness from work-related conditions: worker's compensation. Employers carry insurance to protect them in the event an employee is injured in the course of duty.

Unless gross negligence is involved, employers are protected by the worker's compensation policy from suits by their employees which exceed the policy's coverage. Most states have administrative judges or review boards that handle worker's compensation cases. Either party, the injured worker or the insurance carrier, may appeal the board's decision to the state civil courts. In Texas, state law limits attorneys' fees to 25 percent of the total award on worker's compensation cases. However, the burden of proof (and the workload for the lawyer) is smaller. The lawyer does not have to prove fault, only that an injury occurred on the job.

Chapter XV fully discusses the insurance industry's role in personal injury cases, including the concept that insurance agents will not begin to negotiate fairly except when threatened with a lawsuit or until after the lawsuit has been filed. However, there are some personal injury victims who do not want to be involved in litigation, either because of the stress it produces or the time it takes. They make a conscious decision to accept less than the maximum value for their claim, in return for a fast, negotiated settlement. Often, these victims use the services of an attorney to assist them in their negotiations with the insurance company. With the advice of an attorney, the personal injury victim learns what he is entitled to be recompensed for, and is advised not to sign any of his rights away. Even if a lawsuit is not filed, the personal injury victim who is represented by an attorney usually gets a larger settlement than one who is not. The mere presence of a bar-card-carrying union member on the negotiating team at least raises the threat of suit, and pries open the insurance wallet a little wider.

While I prefer to file suit immediately for my personal injury clients, I am sensitive to their wishes, and will, if it is my client's preference, accept a reasonable settlement before suit is filed. Although by means of the contract for legal services, the client has conveyed an interest in his case to me, it is, after all, HIS CASE, and HIS BODY that was injured.

B. LIABILITY

A personal injury file needs to be prepared in the same manner as any

---

" In Texas, state law limits attorneys' fees to 25 percent of the total award on worker's compensation cases. However, the burden of proof (and the workload for the lawyer) is smaller. The lawyer does not have to prove fault, only that an injury occurred on the job."

other law suit, whether you anticipate trial or settlement. If it's not ready for trial, it's not ready for settlement. If you only prepare for settlement and not trial, you're bluffing. When you bluff, you put the client's case at risk.

Perhaps half of all personal injury suits in this country involve automobile collisions in which somebody has been injured. The victim sues the driver or the owner of the vehicle which caused the collision. Evidence must be gathered and presented as in any other civil lawsuit. The first element that must be proven in a personal injury trial is fault. The facts of the accident must be reconstructed through evidence to show the proximate—the legal word for *direct*—cause.

In an automobile accident case, liability is proven by finding the witnesses and getting their statements. This testimony can be preserved by preparing sworn written statements or by making written or videotaped depositions which can be introduced in trial.

Other evidence of liability for the collision could be pictures of the vehicles and accident scene, the police report, the newspaper reports of weather conditions, or the testimony of an accident reconstruction expert, who might use computer analysis of the accident. All of these possibilities should be considered, otherwise you may not have enough evidence to prove fault. Unless you're able to prove fault, you have no cause of action. The injured person can also testify at trial offering evidence of fault. It's usually valuable to any case to have other witnesses and other evidence to bolster the claim.

Medical malpractice is one of the most difficult personal injury fields as far as proof of fault is concerned. It must be proven that the doctor was negligent; that he failed to use the standard of care that an ordinary, prudent, medical practitioner would have used under the same or similar circumstances. It is often impossible to win a medical malpractice case unless you have an iron-clad case or an extremely rude and obnoxious doctor.

In most medical malpractice cases, the defendant doctors are found not at fault. As a general rule, only situations of the most heinous misdeeds will result in verdicts favorable to plaintiffs. Anyone can be sued and

"A personal injury file needs to be prepared in the same manner as any other law suit, whether you anticipate trial or settlement. If it's not ready for trial, it's not ready for settlement."

many very good doctors have been sued by patients who may have had unrealistic expectations.

A review of malpractice cases shows that bad doctors commit the same errors over and over again until someone can prove the mistakes and get them before juries. If the jury had the ability to take the incompetent doctor's license away and to stop repeat offenses, we would soon see malpractice insurance rates drop substantially.

The problem is that our judges prevent jurors from meting out punishment to the doctors who have constantly and continuously punished society—so the damage caused by these miscreants is borne by their victims and other doctors who pay higher insurance premiums. If jurors had more information and more authority, most of these cases would never get into court because the insurance companies would be afraid to face the jury's wrath and would be motivated to settle fairly. The very worst doctors would have to stop practicing because jurors would yank their licenses or because they would not be able to obtain liability insurance.

The following is a true example of a doctor who committed a heinous crime. While intoxicated, he made a forced delivery of an infant who should have been delivered by C-section. In a state of inebriation, against the instructions of the trained nurse, he forcefully delivered the baby, breaking the baby's spine and paralyzing the baby from the neck down for life. That doctor continues to practice medicine!

During the malpractice trial, a settlement was reached, and the insurance company agreed to pay the baby's parents $2 million. That may seem like a large sum of money, and was described by the media as such. However, the $2 million would not even cover the medical expenses the baby would have incurred in the course of his lifespan.

The parents had to sleep in shifts, with one always remaining awake to watch that the baby did not suffocate—since the baby could not even turn over. After the settlement was negotiated, both parents fell asleep, exhausted by the stress of litigation. The baby suffocated and died.

The insurance company withdrew its settlement offer since there would be no lifetime medical expenses or special education necessary. Not a penny was paid!

---

*"The first element that must be proven in a personal injury trial is fault. The facts of the accident must be reconstructed through evidence to show the proximate —the legal word for **direct**—cause."*

The attorney who represented the doctor's insurance company was so appalled that after the case was finished, he quit representing the insurance company permanently and changed to plaintiff's practice—suing people whose negligence harms others.

Judges sometimes abort the value of the jury and use their discretion to prevent the righting of such grievous wrongs. Many of these cases are taken away from the jury by a granting of a summary judgment by the court, finding there is no need for a jury to rule on a particular issue.

There have been a large number of successful verdicts against incompetent obstetricians—doctors who deliver babies. The jury's emotional feelings toward the child and the enormity of lifetime injuries frequently overshadow the jury's tendency to worship doctors. Where a suffering child is involved, jurors are able to overcome this superstitious feeling of love and respect for the doctor and see that justice is done.

Slip and falls, premises liability and products liability cases frequently require the use of qualified expert witnesses to demonstrate what the normal safety standards require. Then, in contrast, the expert points out the improper maintenance, unsafe construction, unsafe design or other physical shortcoming of the environment or product which forms the basis of the suit. Of course, the defendant would hire an expert witness also.

Sometimes cases of this nature are largely battles between the experts—and become a question of who appears to be the most qualified and most credible to the jurors.

Is a hospital required to have safe floors? The co-efficient of friction is an engineering term which compares the friction between a floor surface and a standard type of shoe sole material. A floor surface with a co-efficient closely approaching 1, feels like glue—you can't fall. A floor with a co-efficient of .1 would feel like smooth ice—you can't stand. To be safe a surface must have a co-efficient of .5 or more. In one case a hospital floor had a co-efficient of friction of .3. Several people had fallen and received injuries. The solution would have been to use a different wax and/or refrain from buffing it to such a high gloss. The hospital would not change its maintenance practices, preferring the slick and shiny surface because of its eye-appeal to potential consumers of health care. The hospital settled all its injury claims for paltry sums. Then, the hospital lost a $250,000 jury verdict. Other hospitals who were fortunate enough to prevail in slip and

"Unless you're able to prove fault, you have no cause of action."

fall litigation, continue to use the same floor care procedures. People are still falling and sustaining injuries. We can't make society safe from all problems, but hospitals, where elderly, infirm, and emotionally upset people are likely to be walking, should not knowingly have unsafe floors.

For all personal injury cases, once liability is nailed down and presented in a logical and persuasive format that the jury can understand, the next important task is proving damages.

C. DAMAGES

Damages are reflected in different ways. The first and most common form of damage is routinely referred to by insurance companies and personal injury lawyers as special damages, or in legalese: specials. Specials mean all out-of-pocket expenses resulting from the accident—even if those out-of-pocket expenses are not paid by the plaintiff.

Specials can include doctor bills, pharmacy bills, traveling expenses to get to the doctor's office, costs of psychiatric treatment, and loss of income from work. If the accident victim died, the loss of lifetime earnings would be specials but they must be proven by an economic expert. Even if a victim does not work outside the home, the victim has an economic value based on the cost to replace his or her services. If a person's lifetime earnings are permanently impaired, an economic expert can testify about the plaintiff's decreased earning capacity.

A spouse of an injured party can sue for loss of consortium (marital relations, emotional support and companionship). A parent or child of a deceased person can sue for loss of that person's companionship, service and financial support.

Proof of damages must be shown to the insurance adjuster, and if the case goes to trial, to the jury. Many people tend to lose medical bills, tend to forget about travel expenses to the doctor's office, physical therapy clinic and pharmacy, and over time, tend to forget the sheer intensity of the pain.

Legal assistants can assist in the preparation of the case by staying in close communication with the client, urging him to keep a diary of pain and suffering, keep a running log of medical-related travel expense, and by asking him to regularly forward copies of medical and pharmaceutical bills to the law office. If the evidence of damages is arranged in a logical sequence, the case can be more effectively demonstrated to the jury.

D. WHAT'S MY CASE WORTH?

One of the first questions a client asks a lawyer is: "What's my case worth?" It's a very tough question to answer and judges or juries often don't agree with the other's answer.

You just can't say to the nearest penny, sometimes not even to the nearest $100,000, what a tort case is worth. You can only guess. The guesses are based on experience and intuition. Here are some of the factors.

The settlement value of a personal injury case is almost always based on a multiple of the specials. Through careful accumulated work, you can take what originally seemed to be $10,000 in specials and come up with a legitimate $15,000 to $18,000 worth of damages. You might even raise your claim to the range of $30,000 to $50,000.

As a general rule, insurance companies consider three times the amount of the specials an acceptable award for pain and suffering. An attorney who can raise that value to five times the amount of the specials has done a great job for his client. Although insurance adjusters may claim to have no specific formula for settling cases, their basic goal is pay as little as they can get away with.

What is "fair settlement value?" When an individual is injured through the fault of another individual, the injured party has been forced to develop a product that can be sold in the courtroom. The victim most likely wishes that he was not even in that particular marketplace. The person with constant, lower backache from a rear-end collision might rather have his damaged spine surgically removed; have the defendant's healthy spine removed and transferred to his own body; and give the defendant the injured spine and make him live with a lifelong backache.

Since some injuries cannot be permanently repaired or undone, our legal system allows injured people to be paid a sum of money which compensates injured plaintiffs for all of their special damages, including their mental anguish, pain and suffering, and whatever other damages are proven.

Fair settlement value differs from one person to another. One person might feel that obtaining his out-of-pocket expenses would be a a satisfactory settlement value although another person might be willing to accept half of out-of-pocket as a compromise settlement value. Just as it takes an

---

"One of the first questions a client asks a lawyer is: 'What's my case worth?'"

---

experienced real estate broker or antique dealer to estimate the market value of a piece of land or an old vase, it takes someone familiar with the current market value of personal injuries to estimate the fair settlement value of a personal injury. Most general practice attorneys have a good idea of the market value of a personal injury claim.

Most of the attorneys who represent insurance companies are skilled. They have to be. If they lose too many cases, they get fired. They do a repeat business with one or many companies. All of them have experience, and most are good. Some of them are honest (That does not mean they won't cheat you; if they can, they will; it means if they give you their word, you can count on it.) Some of them are dishonest. That means their word is meaningless. Most are in between.

The attorneys who represent victims are different. Some have never tried a case at law. The best way to find out if a lawyer has tried a case before is to ask him, and then if he says yes, get some details. If you believe him, consider hiring him. If you don't believe him, forget him. There is no shortage of lawyers in this country.

An insurance adjuster who handles 2,000 to 3,000 files has as good of a grasp of fair market value as a personal injury attorney would, if not more; but it's not his job to be fair.

Texas and many other states have adopted Florida's "Stowers Doctrine" which provides for recovery against insurance companies which unreasonably refuse to settle a case for policy limits and a proven wrong. To implement this doctrine, the plaintiff must provide evidence to the opposing insurance company that there are damages exceeding the amount of the defendant's insurance policy—and then the plaintiff offers to settle for the full amount of the insurance policy. If the insurance company refuses, the case goes to trial.

If the jury agrees with the plaintiff and awards damages in excess of the policy, the defendant is then personally liable for the amount over the policy limit. However, the Stowers Doctrine then allows the plaintiff to release the defendant from his personal obligation, and allows the plaintiff to directly sue the insurance company for the amount over the policy.

In the first trial, no evidence could be introduced about the defendant's insurance policy. But the second trial would be different, and a bit easier. The plaintiff only must prove that he gave the insurance company the

"One of the legal assistant's task is to find out all of the insurance policies covering all of the defendents."

evidence, that he offered to settle for the amount of the policy and the insurance company refused, and that an amount in excess of the policy was awarded by the jury in the first trial.

Since jurors usually grant more favorable judgments against insurance companies, 18-wheelers, and obstetricians than other defendants, it's often valuable pre-trial technique to send the opposing counsel—who really works for the insurance company—a "Stowers" letter.

Suppose a plaintiff's claim is worth $100,000, but the defendant has only a $15,000 insurance policy. Should he settle for the $15,000? In most cases, the answer is "Yes." Why? Because when you go to trial there is always the possibility of losing. Also, when you accept a settlement, you know you'll get the insurance company's check. It could take a plaintiff years fighting an insurance company through the appeals court.

Suppose the jury awarded a plaintiff a $200,000 judgment. An enormous amount of time and energy could be spent defending the judgment on appeal. And if the judgment was upheld, years later you might get the $15,000 from the insurance company and the defendant would file bankruptcy and wipe out the other $185,000.

Sometimes there is more than one insurance policy involved. If a plaintiff was involved in an automobile accident in which the driver of the car wasn't the owner, and the plaintiff's claim exceeds the driver's insurance coverage, the owner's insurance company could be brought into the law suit. This is called "excess coverage." Most policies state that they will not cover anything in excess of the actual policies' limits. In a case such as the one described, the car owner's insurance company may involve the driver's insurance company, and both should pay.

One of the legal assistant's tasks is to find out all of the insurance policies covering all of the defendants.

To recover in a personal injury lawsuit, the defendant's negligence and the plaintiff's damages must be linked together in a proximate cause relationship. You must prove that the damages were caused by the accident which was caused by the defendant. This is usually proved through logical inference by showing a chain-of-events leading from one incident to the next.

Suppose an intoxicated driver of an 18-wheeler decides to use the side ramp of the freeway as a ski jump to see how high he can get into the air. He lands on top of the Plaintiff's car. Perhaps some insurance lawyer would argue that this was a necessary experiment in aerodynamics which will cut down the cost of transportation in the future and benefit mankind.

Suppose the plaintiff was an Olympic gymnastics champion who was safely driving with her seat belt fastened. She had never had a muscle strain, backache, or even a cold, before this incident. She had just been thoroughly x-rayed and tested and received a clean bill of health after winning her championship. Immediately after the accident, she was unable to move. The only thing she could do was scream at the top of her lungs. (Her vocal cords were injured so she could not speak, only scream.) After several hours of prying pieces of the 18-wheeler off her, paramedics transported her to the hospital where doctors determined that she would be a vegetable because shrapnel from the truck lodged in her brain, and every single bone, nerve and disk in her body was fragmented. Medical science would be able to keep her alive. She would not be able to respond to any stimuli (other than by screaming), but she would be completely aware of her environment and fully able to feel the agonizing pain. She lives in a state where the death penalty is imposed for mercy killing, and she is expected to live for 40 years in intensive care, praying every minute of the day for her life to end.

Her doctors will be able to state that in their professional opinions, her pain and suffering and medical bills are directly attributable to the injuries, and that those injuries are directly attributable to the accident which took place. They will not be able to testify from personal knowledge that the accident took place but only from reports that are given to them. This is a form of acceptable hearsay. In this extreme example, proving the proximate cause of the damages is relatively easy.

However, suppose that surgery revealed that the Olympic gymnast had a ruptured appendix. The doctor says he cannot correlate this ruptured appendix to the accident. The insurance attorney speculates that she would have died from the ruptured appendix. The doctor cannot swear under oath that she would not have died from the ruptured appendix if the accident had not happened. In fact, under vigorous cross-examination from the insurance attorney, the doctor might be willing to speculate that, in fact, this accident saved her life since she would not be in the hospital otherwise. If the jury became convinced that the ruptured appendix was a more significant problem facing the athlete than the accident was, the plaintiff's attorney would have a problem, even with this good a case. In all probability, the natural human sympathy of the jury and the natural feel for justice would overcome this ridiculous attempt to obviate the responsibility of the driver of the 18-wheeler for his actions (and the insurance company's liability to pay for their insured's misdeeds) and a huge verdict would be rendered in favor of the Plaintiff. A thousand and one factors, including the interaction of fault, damages, and a *causal nexus* between the two must be considered in estimating value.

E. TRIAL

The possibility of trial must be kept in mind; all evidence must be presentable and admissible in the event it ends up in court. The lawyers who settle all or most of their cases inevitably settle for less. If you play cards with someone for ten years and he bluffs on every hand, you call his bluff often.

If the case goes to trial, in order to get specials introduced, someone with professional knowledge must testify that the charges were incurred, that they are fair and reasonable for the area, and that they were necessary in order to treat the injury. The person doing this must be able to prove his claims from his medical or business records subject to the evidence rules of the jurisdiction. One of a legal assistant's tasks is to ensure that sufficient proof, in the proper form, is ready for presentation.

Pain, suffering and mental anguish are proven by testimony of the plaintiff's doctor, that injuries of this nature typically cause pain. The doctor may testify to his patient's verbal complaints to him. There can be other testimony by neighbors, friends, relatives, co-workers, and others who have knowledge of the plaintiff's specific pain, loss of former skills, and decline in his ability to function.

Of course the plaintiff himself is the best witness to his own mental anguish, pain, and suffering. Other methods of proving damages are through diaries, tapes, pictures, and eyewitness accounts. Frequently, the pain and suffering is proven at the same time that medical symptoms are proven.

When all the evidence on a personal injury trial has been presented and the jury is about to retire to decide a verdict, the court will instruct the jury on specific issues or procedures.

One instruction given in almost every jurisdiction is: "You are not to allow prejudice, passion, or sympathy to play a role in your verdict." The judge is asking you to be a cold and calculating computer arriving at an exact figure of dollars to compensate for the individual's pain and suffering and mental anguish. This is ridiculous. It can't be done. Evaluating human symptoms and suffering is a subjective task, and to suggest your emotions be left outside the courtroom is ludicrous.

Both parties to the suit will have given the judge certain questions for the jury to answer, called "special issues." The judge reads them to the jury as if he had prepared them (some judges do prepare them).

An example of a special issue for the jury (if liability is in question in an automobile accident) might be, "Assign a percentage of liability for causing the collision: Mary Smith ____%, John Jones ____%." Of course the plaintiff would hope that the defendant would be found fully liable. In most states, if the defendant is not found to be at least 51% liable, the plaintiff cannot recover anything.

Another special issue might be, "Indicate the dollar amount that would compensate Mary Smith for the following:

Lost wages ____
Lost future income ____
Services of Dr. Bones ____
Services of Dr. Muscles ____
Future medical care ____
Pain and suffering ____
Mental anguish ____."

During the closing arguments of a personal injury trial, the plaintiff's attorney will focus on the pain and suffering of his client (and, if necessary, re-affirm the defendant's liability). The insurance company attorney's task is to minimize the injuries in the juror's mind. He may agree that the grievously injured plaintiff "is in sad shape and we can all sympathize, but we must leave this sympathy out of the courtroom; it has no place here." Yet, the defense attorney might attempt to evoke juror's sympathy for the defendant as unlucky, saying, "Anyone could have an accident. You might have an accident on your way home from court."

While the plaintiff's attorney sits with his client in the silent courtroom, waiting for the jury to return its verdict, after he's done his best to put on an effective case, all he can do is pray that the jurors will exhibit wisdom and humanity as they fill in the blanks of the special issue questions.

"After criminal matters and divorce, personal injury is the most common category of litigation in America."

CHAPTER XXVI
CREDIT AND DEBT:

IS THERE LIFE AFTER DEBT?

"The Fair Credit Reporting Act provides that individuals may have access to their credit information, which is collected and reported by various credit bureaus that are networked throughout the country."

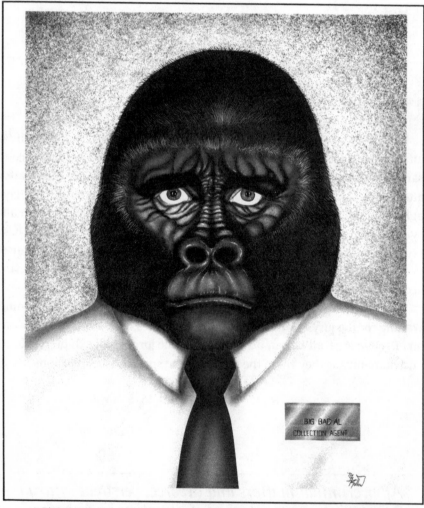

BIG BAD AL
COLLECTION AGENT

The Collection Agent: A big hairy animal without teeth or claws.

COLLECTION AGENT: A big hairy animal without teeth or claws.

While collection laws in the 50 states vary significantly, there are two very important federal laws that have jurisdiction over every state: the Fair Debt Collection Act and the Fair Credit Reporting Act. We will briefly review these statutes and examine this animal called a collection agent.

Like a vampire in a dark alley under the moonlight, this beast can be terrifying—but when exposed to full daylight, he's fundamentally, legally harmless.

The Fair Credit Reporting Act provides that individuals may have access to their credit information, which is collected and reported by various credit bureaus that are networked throughout the country. These credit bureaus exist for the convenience of merchants, real estate agents and lending institutions, to help them evaluate whether or not a person is an acceptable credit risk. These agencies only provide information to the merchants who financially support them as paid subscribers.

A major city might have several credit bureaus, some of which primarily work with retail merchants and automobile dealers, and others that cater especially to financial institutions or real estate brokers. Since the credit bureaus across the country share information, don't think that by moving from Florida to California you will leave a bad credit rating behind. It may continue to haunt you, since all these records are kept track of under your social security number.

The sort of information which is typically included in a credit report is the consumer and his wife's full name, address, place of business, number of years consumer and spouse have worked for current employers, past employers, social security numbers and names of other businesses that have extended credit to them, the amount of credit extended, the normal rate of payment of bills and whether or not the consumer has any judgments or liens against him or has had property foreclosed or has filed bankruptcy.

There are codes that indicate whether the consumer has been late paying any of his bill, and whether those payments have been 30, 60, 90 or more days late. There are codes that indicate if a debt has been referred to

"Since the credit bureaus across the country share information, don't think that by moving from Florida to California you will leave a bad credit rating behind. It may continue to haunt you, since all these records are kept track of under your social security number."

a collection agent or simply written off as a bad debt.

If a person has negative information on his credit report, he has a right to know what it is, and who has put it on. If a person is refused credit, he is entitled to know the reason why.

The credit bureaus can charge a reasonable fee, perhaps $20, for this information unless the consumer can show that he has been refused credit within the last 30 days—in which case the information will be provided at no cost.

If a consumer wants his attorney to have a copy of his credit report, a power of attorney must be drawn up authorizing this disclosure or the credit bureau should not release the information. Credit bureaus are also permitted to charge a fee for counseling when an employee of the credit bureau explains to the consumer the meaning of the various computer-generated entries on his credit report.

A consumer may submit a written statement to be included in his own credit report, to attempt to explain or mitigate some negative information that is there. Similar to the Freedom of Information Act, the Fair Credit Reporting act has time deadlines which must be complied with for disclosure of information to consumers.

A word of caution: there are numerous companies which advertise their services on television and magazines, boasting that they can clear up credit problems. Their fees vary from modest to exorbitant. Sometimes they promise to obtain major credit cards for their clients. Often, these are fly-by-night companies that will take a consumer's money and do nothing at all for them.

The promised MasterCard and VISA card, if obtainable at all, usually is on the basis of a line of credit charged against a bank account—for example, the consumer puts about $550 in the First Bank of Anywhere and is then issued a Mastercard with a $500 line of credit. Every time he uses the credit card, money would be subtracted from his account. That type of credit card—except for its value as identification or prestige—does not offer much immediate benefit to the consumer and probably could have been obtained by the consumer without the need of a company charging to arrange it. It does allow the consumer to re-establish credit. Some banks

"If a person has negative information on his credit report, he has a right to know what it is, and who has put it on. If a person is refused credit, he is entitled to know the reason why."

do it, some don't.

In dealing with a collection agent, bear in mind that he is simply that, an agent acting on behalf of someone else. You haven't made any deals with him at all. Most individual creditors have very limited collection procedures. In most states, the only way that money can be taken out of your bank account is through a court order. The IRS ignores this due process and gets away with it constantly. Banks also ignore this formality if they choose to seize the bounty from their own customer.

In most jurisdictions collection agents can't do anything except ask you for money. There are numerous tactics that these agents use. If one collection technique doesn't work, they'll try another. One tactic is to remind you that you owe them money, and ask you if you are going to be honest and pay it. Another method is to threaten you with legal prosecution. A third is just to threaten you with implied possibilities. Some collection agents threaten physical force. This is illegal, but not too long ago was not uncommon. You can file criminal charges or a civil suit—but in either case it is difficult to obtain sufficient proof to make your case stick. I recommend tape recorders.

Until the Fair Debt Collection Act was passed, most collection agents across the country didn't use their real names. Why? They didn't want the people they were threatening, harassing, and pushing around to come looking for them. The type of individual who worked as a collection agent was generally someone down on his luck who needed work or someone with some very nasty personal tendencies. These people tend to be migratory, moving from job to job.

When the Federal Fair Debt Collection Act was passed, collection agents were no longer allowed to use false names unless they filed these assumed names with the county in which they worked. Since you want to be dealing with another human being who is as exposed to you as you are to him, it is wise to tell the collection agent that you want to know his real name, social security number or other identifying characteristics. If he is using an assumed name, you want to know that, too.

Collection agents often make good IRS agents. There are many IRS agents who are nothing but collection agents with a bit of power. We can thank God and Congress for the Fair Debt Collection Act. Private collection agents do not have the power and authority of the IRS. There is no

> *"We can thank God and Congress for the Fair Debt Collection Act."*

debtor's prison in the United States—except for fathers who cannot afford the legal help and cannot afford child support payments, and some people who don't pay their taxes.

For the most part—except in jurisdictions where the Constitution is ignored—people in this country aren't put in jail for the non-payment of debts, at least, not legally. If you are put in jail for not paying a debt, you may have a very good civil rights action against the individuals who put you in jail.

The collection agents' tools are humiliation, embarrassment, fear, and crude psychology. You will not run into highly educated people doing collection agency work. You will run into some very smart manipulators and con artists. It's amazing how many collection agents go from collections to con artistry and back to collections when times get rough. There also seems to be an affinity between collection agents and high finance rip-off schemes. Bankers, it might be hard to believe, are actually several steps above collection agents.

If you owe somebody a debt, that person has the option of suing you. If the person can prove up the debt to the satisfaction of a judge or jury, a judgment will probably be issued against you. That judgment orders you to pay the debt. If you don't have the money, you can't obey the order. If you do have the money and are capable of hiding it, it is often very difficult to make you obey the order.

Once the judgment exists, the plaintiff must locate your money or property. If you have no money or property, you are what is called in the trade "judgment proof." If you can convince a creditor or their attorney that you are judgment proof, and that no matter how much money, time and effort they spend pursuing you, they will not collect any money— they will probably write you off as a lost cause.

Let's assume that a final judgment has been entered against you ordering you to pay money. Does that mean that you will immediately pay? No, it doesn't. If you don't have the money, and you don't own anything, you can't pay even if you wanted to.

Frequently, the people who end up with extremely unfair judgments against them are the very poorest people, the people who are completely down on their luck. They have so many problems that they are overwhelmed. They can't afford to hire an attorney and they don't know how

"If you owe somebody a debt, that person has the option of suing you."

to defend themselves. They don't file an answer, and whoever filed the lawsuit gets a default judgment against them that is unreasonable. Too often, the court awards attorneys fees that are unreasonable under the circumstances.

I know of a case where an elderly, single school teacher lost her entire life savings. A slip-shod home remodeler improperly performed some repairs on her home. He had received most of his fee in advance, but the woman indignantly refused to give him the remainder because his work did not meet city building code standards.

The builder sued her for the entire debt, without regard for the fact that she had paid him several thousand dollars. When the woman was served with the suit, she was bewildered and ignored it. A default judgment was taken against her.

A notice of the judgment sparked the woman into action. She retained an attorney who filed a motion for new trial. However, this attorney neglected to file an answer in the suit. A second default judgment was taken. Of course the school teacher was irate over the poor performance of her attorney. She hired a second attorney who, incredible as it may seem, committed the same error! He also filed a motion for new trial and got the default judgment set aside, but filed no answer. A third default judgment was taken against the woman.

Her bank account was garnished for the amount of the judgment—in excess of $4,000. Her only remedy now is a malpractice suit against her former attorneys to try and recover her actual financial damages and also recompense her mental anguish.

Once a collection matter turns into a lawsuit, ignoring the suit and allowing a default judgment to be taken against you is very dangerous. It's like the ostrich sticking its head in the sand and hoping that nothing will happen to it. While its neck is in the sand, someone may be carrying out an execution and cutting it off.

Contrary to what a collection agent may tell you and contrary to what workers in the credit and loan industries would have the populace believe, most of the people who do not pay debts on time are delinquent because of circumstances beyond their control. They got fired. Their company went out of business. They got wiped out in the stock market. Business schemes went awry. A family member went through a major cata-

---

"If you don't have the money and you don't own anything, you can't pay even if you wanted to."

---

strophic and unforseeable illness which ate up the family's money. Someone ended up in jail and the legal fees ate up the family's savings. An accident occurred for which their insurance company informed them they were not covered. The hard luck stories go on and on.

If your problem is in the hands of a collection agent, it is in the hands of someone who is usually working for a commission to get you to pay the money. The commission generally runs between 30 percent to 60 percent of the entire debt.

Collection agents also have another threat and that is to ruin your credit. The threat to ruin your credit is usually at this point not very honest. Everything that can be done to your credit has probably already been done. Generally an institution will report you to the credit bureau before it sends your file to a collection agent.

The collection agent who pretends to be an attorney is violating the Fair Debt Collection Act. The Fair Debt Collection Act specifically limits certain activities of collection agencies. Among the limitations are:

A) *They can only call between 8:00 a.m. and 9:00 p.m.*
B) *They are not allowed to call you at work*
C) *They are not allowed to discuss your account with anyone else, and*
D) *They are not allowed to be unnecessarily rude to you.*

The Fair Debt Collection Act concerns third party collection agents, and does not govern agents who work directly for the principal. What does this mean? Suppose you become delinquent in your monthly car payments to the bank. When an employee of the bank calls you to demand payment, he is not covered under the Fair Debt Collection Act.

If the bank gives up completely and turns the debt over to a private collection agent, then this agent is not a direct employee of the creditor, and is subject to the federal laws.

The collection agent almost always requests that the money be sent directly to him or her so that he can control it—or sometimes steal it. Remember, collection agents are not the most honest people in the world.

In fact, collection agents are sometimes flagrant in their own failure to pay their debts promptly and timely. Why? They know everything you

"Once a collection matter turns into a lawsuit, ignoring the suit and allowing a default judgment to be taken against you is very dangerous."

are reading in this chapter; furthermore, they begin to feel that the debtors they deal with on a daily basis have "gotten away with something," and they want to get away with something too. If you are a collection agent, you probably wouldn't want to be represented by the author of this book, and if your best friend is a collection agent, the author would recommend to you that you might get another best friend.

You are not required to talk to collection agents at all; you can hang up on them. As it is for any other human being, it's unnerving to a collection agent to be hung up on. Try it! You'll like their reaction. You gain nothing by talking to them. They gain nothing by being hung up on. After a few times of being hung up on, they may write you off.

There is also the possibility that a collection agent will have an arrangement with a law firm that works on a percentage of what it collects. If this is the case, the collection agent decides whether or not the person he is trying to collect from can pay the debt. If he decides that the debtor is solvent, but won't pay the debt without a lawsuit, he may refer it to the law firm with which he is associated.

There are attorneys who for a small fee—in the neighborhood of $150 per month—permit a collection agency to rubber stamp their name on their mass produced collection letters. When you get a collection letter on one of these attorney's letterheads in the mail, you may safely deduce that you are not dealing with the sharpest, most aggressive trial lawyer in the United States. He may be only a slight step above the collection agent.

A letter with an attorney's name on it seems more threatening than one from a mere collection agent. The letter may be the predecessor to a law suit. Usually, none of these private agencies can do anything or take any of your money without a court order. Most judges are reluctant to sign decrees ordering money to be taken from you prior to granting a final judgment which orders you to pay something. This rarely happens without political stroke, and few collection agencies have this kind of stroke.

The ultimate defense against a collection agent is bankruptcy. Most collection agents are disarmed by simply ignoring them. Rather than spending a long time on the telephone arguing with a collection agent, tell them you have no money, and if you did, you don't think you would send it to someone who had already damaged your credit.

Ask the collection agent to verify everything he says in writing. Tell

---

"You are not required to talk to collection agents at all;
you can hang up on them."

---

him that you have been reading about the lawsuits against collection agents for violating the Federal Fair Debt Collection Act. Has he ever been sued? Are the stories true? Is he following the law?

Ask the collection agent personal questions. Why did he or she get involved in such an insidious trade? How much does a collection agent make a month? Collection agents generally don't like to be put on the spot anymore than you like to be put on the spot.

A recent widow is a typical victim of collection agents. She doesn't know what she's going to do, and everybody has come pouncing on her. The whole pack of vultures—collection agents, IRS agents, and funeral directors know that the newly widowed are extremely vulnerable. They advance like the Charge of the Light Brigade. They have no fear and often no shame, unless directly confronted by a debtor who knows her rights or has a trustworthy attorney.

It is always a good idea to have everybody who communicates with you regarding any legal matter, send you, in writing, everything they've orally stated. It is also not a bad idea to hire an attorney—at a nominal cost—to simply take the collection agent's calls. When a collection agent threatens to turn you over to an attorney, ask for the attorney's name and phone number and tell the collection agent that you'll be happy to have your attorney talk with his attorney. However, suing you would be a waste of time.

The cost of an unlisted phone number may be a good investment. Of course, some collection agencies have illicit sources for obtaining unlisted phone numbers. If a collection agent harasses you at your unlisted phone number, scare him a bit. Tell him that in the event of a lawsuit, you will be inquiring as to what means he used to obtain your phone number.

Franklin Delano Roosevelt's words are probably better advice than any I have to offer, with regard to collection agents: "You have nothing to fear but fear itself."

The wisest money management rule is not to incur debts which you cannot cover. But the common human tendency to get over one's head in debt is the reason why our founding forefathers included "authority for bankruptcy" in the Constitution.

Personal credit is a valuable and helpful commodity, but quite frankly, cash can often be a more valuable commodity. A good name, without credit, might be better than a bad name with credit. I have, over the years, represented a score of decent, honest individuals who got caught in the downturn of the economy, devastated by a personal crisis, ground up to mincemeat in the litigation mill, or simply exercised abysmally poor judgment.

Sometimes what seems to be poor judgment can end up making that individual rich, and what seems to be good judgment can—through a change in circumstances beyond an individual's control—turn out to be the financial straw that breaks the genius' back.

A great deal has been said and written about what's called The American Dream—hard work leading to constant upward economic mobility. The doctrine does not acknowledge the possibility of failure if someone doesn't quit. Sometimes in the game of life, our Lord and Master simply takes people out of the game—a death or a catastrophic illness, a divorce, a child on drugs, a bank defaulting on all uninsured sums—all of these can take a winner out of the winner's circle and make him poor.

If you are among those of the American populace whose debts are greater than your assets, or if you are among that number who are being harassed by collection agents, don't let it get you down. Remember, if all fails, relief is just a filing away!

"Personal credit is a valuable and helpful commodity, but quite frankly, cash can often be a more valuable commodity. A good name, without credit, might be better than a bad name with credit."

CHAPTER XXVII

BANKRUPTCY:

RELIEF IS JUST A FILING AWAY

"Bankruptcy is a legitimate, constitutionally created protection that many righteous and law abiding people have used. It's also available for unscrupulous individuals who abuse the system and con their way out of paying their debts, while keeping substantial, ill-gotten fortunes hidden from the trustee and creditor."

A. HISTORICAL BACKGROUND

Bankruptcy, while not being *per se* a constitutional right, was provided for in the Constitution. Thomas Jefferson himself, exercised this option and declared bankruptcy. Pursuant to Article I, Section 8, Clause 4, the Constitution provides:

"The Congress shall have power to establish a uniform rule of naturalization, and uniform laws on the subject of bankruptcies throughout the United States..."

This chapter will provide a broad overview of a few important concepts of American bankruptcy.

All of the bankruptcy rules and regulations referred to in this chapter are current as of March, 1988, but may not reflect current law by the time this book gets to the reader's hands. Since local rules vary and are subject to change, if you are considering filing bankruptcy on your own, you should obtain a copy of your district court's local rules and up to date forms from a local stationery store. There are now form books and lawyers who will assist you in filing your own if you choose.

Early English laws provided for debtors' prison. If you couldn't pay your debts, you went to jail. Obviously in jail, it was very difficult to accumulate the wherewithal to pay your debts. For that reason, a lot of people died in debtor's prison.

The United States has never had a debtor's prison. The closest modern American parallel to debtor's prison is the jailing of fathers who are unable to pay court-ordered child support payments, and can't prove their inability to a judge's satisfaction. The ones who can afford to pay and simply don't want to pay are usually able to avoid the penalties of imprisonment for debt. There are other similar situations in the United States where citizens are jailed directly or indirectly (probation revocation for failure to pay court-ordered restitution) for failing to pay a debt.

Congress exercised its responsibility, under the Constitution, to prescribe uniform laws for bankruptcy, and it has done so in Title 11 of the United States Code.

The three areas of bankruptcy law which are most commonly utilized and which will be briefly surveyed here are Chapter 7, Chapter 13, and Chapter 11.

B. CHAPTER 7

When most people think of bankruptcy, they are thinking of Chapter 7, bankruptcy in its purest and simplest form. This provision of the bankruptcy code basically makes it possible for a debtor to turn all he owns, with certain exemptions, over to a bankruptcy trustee who will sell those possessions and pay what debts can be paid, and the debtor's slate is washed clean.

An individual or a company usually files a Chapter 7 bankruptcy when his debts far exceed his assets and the debtor believes there's no realistic hope of working out a repayment plan. The debtor wants his debts discharged—removed as if they had not existed—so that he can have a fresh start.

To do this the debtor discloses to the court a list of all his assets—such as real property, vehicles, clothes, furniture, office equipment, etc.—and supplies a list of all his creditors and his debts. This includes the names of the creditors, the date the debts were incurred, and the reason for incurring them. The debtor should also tell the court whether or not he disputes any debts.

A Chapter 7 bankruptcy has its limitations on both sides: While many

"An individual or a company usually files a Chapter 7 bankruptcy when his debts far exceed his assets and the debtor believes there's no realistic hope of working out a repayment plan."

debts cannot be discharged in the Chapter 7 bankruptcy, also many items of property are exempted from creditors. The exemptions, however, vary from state to state because the federal bankruptcy law—which provides its own exemptions—also allows each state to determine what exemptions can be claimed in that state.

1. EXEMPTIONS

What are exemptions? Example: Section 522 D of Title 11 of the U.S. Code determines the federal exemptions. If the state has no state exemptions, you are allowed to use the federal exemptions.

Readers should remember not only that the exemptions will naturally be different from state-to-state, but the exemptions are constantly being changed.

Currently, the federal rules exempt many things: Real estate that is used as your home up to a value of $7,500 and one motor vehicle up to a value of $1,200. You are also allowed to exempt all professional-prescribed health aids. Social Security benefits are exempt. Alimony or child support is exempt. Compensation you receive as a result of an injury is exempt. If you are receiving federal civil service retirement benefits, they are 100 percent exempt.

Federal rules also allow you to exempt 75 percent of your wages remaining after deductions required by law are subtracted, or 30 times the federal minimum hourly wage per week. Household jewelry up to $500 in value is exempt. You are allowed to exempt professional books or tools of your trade up to $750.

Compare that with the Texas system.

On your homestead, you are allowed to exempt up to 200 acres or a home worth any amount of money if the lot is worth $10,000 or less. This means you can have a $2 million home on a $10,000 lot, and it's completely exempt. There is a large exemption for home furnishings, family heirlooms, farming tools, dogs, cats and current wages of $30,000 per family or $15,000 for a single adult. Welfare benefits are completely exempt.

Texas legislators totally exempted the retirement benefits coming from the state's judicial retirement system, from the county and district

"...exemptions will naturally be different from state-to-state, but the exemptions are constantly being changed."

employees pension fund, and from the policemen and firemen pension system. The benefits that federal employees receive from their retirement system isn't exempted in Texas.

If you lived in Texas and owned a $1 million home on a $10,000 lot, you would most certainly elect to take the Texas exemptions. If you were a retired judge in Texas you would certainly choose to use the state's exemptions.

In Alabama you can exempt your homestead if it's valued at less than $5,000 and contains less than 168 acres. You are allowed to exempt all your clothing. You are allowed to keep your burial lot and your seat in a place of public worship. You are allowed to exempt all growing or unharvested crops.

In Alaska you are allowed to exempt $27,000 of the value on your homestead and $1,500 in household goods. You are allowed to exempt $1,500 on one motor vehicle not exceeding $10,000 in value.

In Arkansas, if you are a widow or a minor child, you exempt all of your homestead, plus future rents and profits from it for the life of the widow or the child. You can exempt your entire family graveyard, and your welfare benefits. Policemen, firemen and public school teachers are also allowed to exempt their retirement benefits. Arkansas laws also allow you to exempt one motor vehicle up to a value of $1,200. You can even exempt your wedding band including the diamonds if less than half a carat.

In California, you can exempt $45,000 for your homestead unless you're over 65, and then you're allowed a $55,000 exemption. All of your household belongings are exempt and $1,200 equity in a motor vehicle, and $2,500 worth of jewelry, heirlooms and works of art are exempt. All necessary personal, furnishings, provisions, wearing apparel, and personal effects are exempt. All public retirement benefits are exempt. A self-employed debtor with his own retirement benefits is allowed to exempt the amount needed to support himself and his dependents. If you're planning to declare bankruptcy later in life, it's better to work for the government than yourself.

As you can see from the above examples, each and every state's exemptions are different. For a complete and full guide on Chapter 7 and Chapter 13 bankruptcies, including some sample forms and a table of state and federal exemptions, I recommend the *Attorneys Handbook on Consumer Bankruptcy and Chapter 13*.[1]

Although one of the obvious goals of the Constitution was to keep bankruptcy procedures uniform throughout the 50 states, this brief review of several states' exemptions illustrates that the Constitution's intent is not being carried out. No two states have the same exemptions. How much you keep after filing your Chapter 7 bankruptcy depends on individual state's rules.

Filing a Chapter 7 bankruptcy does not automatically allow you to keep your exempt property. If there is a lien against that exempt property, the lien must be paid to keep your property. You must pay the bank or mortgage company who is financing your house, and you must pay the home improvement company that has a lien on your house for replacing the roof and adding a room last summer.

Also, if there is a lien against the motor vehicle, you must pay that lien if you want to keep the vehicle.

You may, of course, choose not to pay those debts, and they will be wiped out along with most of your other debts in the bankruptcy court. In that case, you would give up the secured property in order to wipe your debt out.

There is a difference between surrendering property under a Chapter 7, and merely having property foreclosed or repossessed. Without the protection of the bankruptcy court, a debtor can be sued for the amount of money left which is owed to a creditor after repossession and sale.

For example, suppose that outside of bankruptcy Peter Pauper had a $10,000 car repossessed after he had paid $1,000 on the loan. The finance company then sold the car to the highest bidder for $4,000. Peter Pauper still owes that $5,000 to the finance company, who could file suit against Peter for the $5,000.

However, if Peter Pauper had filed a Chapter 7 bankruptcy, the debt after the car was repossessed would be canceled. If he files bankruptcy before the car was repossessed, he could elect to keep the car and exempt the $1,000 value he's already paid, and keep up the payments on the car. If Peter filed chapter 7 and elected to surrender the car, he would be protected from being sued for any deficiency— even if it sold for less than he owed on it.

2. DISCHARGEABILITY VS. NON-DISCHARGEABILITY

If a debt is dischargeable, it means you will no longer owe on it if you qualify for bankruptcy. If the debt is nondischargeable you will still owe the debt when the bankruptcy proceeding is over. Almost all debts are dischargeable. According to various statutes, certain debts are classified as non-dischargeable.

You may not discharge (eliminate) a debt which you incurred as a result of a judgment for fraud, criminal conduct, or intentional tort (you can't deliberately injure someone, get a civil judgment against you, and then wipe the debt out through bankruptcy). Alimony and child support cannot be discharged in a bankruptcy court. Debts arising out of federal income tax returns that were filed within three years of the bankruptcy petition, cannot be discharged. One narrow category of income taxes can be discharged and in that case the taxes must be three years overdue, and you must have filed your tax return timely declaring the debt even though you were unable to pay.

The burden of proof of non-dischargeability is on the creditor who is complaining that the debtor's indebtedness to him should not be discharged. If the issue of non-dischargeability is not raised, or is not successfully proven, even a technically "non-dischargeable" debt may end up being discharged.

3. AUTOMATIC STAY

On the day your bankruptcy petition is filed, all civil actions involving monetary claims against you are stopped. If a foreclosure has been filed in state court against you, the court can no longer proceed on that action. If a finance company has filed an action against you because you are three months behind on your car payments, that action will be stopped. If your bank has filed an action against you because you haven't made a payment on your VISA account for several months, that action is also stopped. This includes the IRS.

The actual filing of the bankruptcy petition gives the debtor the protection granted by the automatic stay provisions of the federal law. When the bankruptcy is file-stamped and assigned a case number, you have the automatic stay. In some federal courts another stamp is placed on your petition specifically mentioning the automatic stay, and in other jurisdictions granting the stay is assumed. You do not have to specifically request

---

"If a debt is dischargeable it means you will no longer owe on it if you qualify for bankruptcy. If the debt is non-dischargeable you will still owe the debt when the bankruptcy proceeding is over."

---

the stay, and you don't have to get an order from the court to have the protection.

It's generally to a person's advantage, after filing a bankruptcy petition, to give creditors and any courts that have actions pending against you written notice that you have filed. This is particularly important if the debtor needed the protection of the court to stop an imminent action—such as a state court preparing to issue a garnishment of your wages or allowing the sale of your home in foreclosure. That written notice can be made in the form of a notice filed with the court declaring the date and case number of your bankruptcy petition. The Clerk of the Bankruptcy Court does, of course, send notice to all of the creditors, but often that notice comes too late to help the debtor in an emergency situation.

Anyone who violates the automatic stay is potentially liable to be punished by a federal judge for contempt of court and be fined or put in jail or both. Any creditor, including government agents, would be violating federal law if they continued actions against you contrary to the automatic stay.

You may file bankruptcy at any time as long as it is not for the purpose of deliberately defrauding your creditors and as long as you have not done so within the last seven years. Not paying creditors does not constitute defrauding them. Defrauding them is lying or hiding assets of which they are entitled to receive under bankruptcy laws.

4. CREDITORS' MEETING

Once you've filed bankruptcy, notices are sent to all your creditors. This is usually done within 30 days after you've filed your petition. Be careful to not omit any of the names and addresses of any of your creditors when you file your petition. If you do, the debt claimed by the omitted party will not be discharged.

When you prepare your bankruptcy petition, you should list creditors who claim you owe them money even if you dispute the debt or any portion of it. You simply list the claim as disputed. Some bankruptcy petition forms provide a space for declaring whether or not a debt is disputed. If there is no place, the debtor still makes note on the petition that the

"On the day your bankruptcy petition is filed, all civil actions involving monetary claims against you are stopped."

particular debt is disputed.

When you declare that a debt is disputed, you require the creditor to come into bankruptcy court and present evidence that you owe him the money. The overwhelming number of disputed claims are never fought— the creditors just give up. If you dispute the claim, they will have to either figure out how to proceed on their own or hire an attorney to go in and prove that you owe them the money.

The bankruptcy court and the trustee are there for the protection of honest debtors. As a general rule the odds are against the creditor in bankruptcy court, unless the debt is adequately secured by property which can be returned.

You elect what exemptions you are going to take. You then turn over all of your non-exempt assets to the bankruptcy trustee.

Next there is the meeting of the creditors. This is the moment where all your creditors may come and ask you questions while you are under oath. In a normal consumer bankruptcy, most creditors don't even show up. You are not precluded from any of your constitutional rights in this hearing.

The trustee takes over all of your non-exempt assets, if any, and arranges for the sale and distribution of the proceeds on a *pro rata* basis to the creditors. Part of the job of planning a bankruptcy is to attempt to honestly arrange your estate so that it is primarily exempt. Most personal bankruptcies report no non-exempt assets.

5. DISCHARGE

After the creditors' meeting, the sale of the debtor's assets by the trustee and distribution of the proceeds to the creditors, a discharge hearing is held, wherein the judge signs an order, discharging the debtor from his debt burden. Often, no one shows up for the discharge hearing, there's just a list of names read. In some crowded jurisdictions, there is no hearing, the discharge orders are simply sent through the mail, if the bankruptcy has not been contested.

In a Chapter 7, if no one has filed an objection to the debtor's discharge, and if the trustee is satisfied with the disposition of the estate, the slate is

"When you prepare your bankruptcy petition, you should list creditors who claim you owe them money even if you dispute the debt or any portion of it."

wiped clean of all remaining debts that were reported to the court.

But if the debtor has forgotten to list Uncle Henry's $100 loan, or the Mafia's $1,500 at 32 percent interest, compounded hourly, these debts are not discharged, and the debtor can expect further harassment. The biggest mistake the consumer makes in bankruptcy is not listing some of his creditors because, in anger, he feels the creditor isn't entitled to consideration.

A debtor may voluntarily elect to pay any debts he still wants to pay, by reaffirming them. For example, a debtor may reaffirm his debt for a car he is purchasing and promise to continue making his monthly payments— including catching up on arrears because he does not have many more payments to go, because he needs the transportation, or because he doesn't have cash or credit to buy another vehicle.

It is a good idea, generally, if you know you will be filing bankruptcy, to plan the filing date for a time when you will have used up all your cash and your non-exempt assets. You cannot, however, sell a non-exempt piece of property for $50,000, pay off your $50,000 homestead note the day before your bankruptcy, and expect to get away with it. I've seen some people do exactly that and not get caught, but it is not advisable and can place your bankruptcy proceeding in great jeopardy. There is also the possibility of criminal sanctions.

The bankruptcy courts are overloaded in some states and almost empty in others. There are very few people who aggressively go after the debtors in bankruptcy court. Local pockets of economic recession such as hit the northeast in the late 70s and Texas in the mid 80s, produce more bankruptcy filings in their particular jurisdiction.

I know people who will not file bankruptcy because they consider that it confers a social stigma and represents an admission of failure. Those people, over the years, carry huge debts on their shoulders as a constant reminder of the mistakes they have made or the bad fortune they have encountered. Sometimes, through hard work, they pay off all of the debts. Sometimes they do so through luck. When they succeed, they are due great congratulations.

"After the creditors' meeting, the sale of the debtor's assets by the trustee, and distribution of the proceeds to the creditors—a discharge hearing is held, wherein the judge signs an order, discharging the debtor from his debt burden."

Quite frequently, they simply go through life bearing a huge, unnecessary cross. Rather than having creditors who thank them for their honesty and integrity, their payments are so far behind that their credit is ruined, and the creditors call them deadbeats. On the other hand, when someone files bankruptcy people tend to be sympathetic and want to help. I make no value judgment, whatsoever.

Bankruptcy is a legitimate, constitutionally created protection that many righteous and law abiding people have used. It's also available for unscrupulous individuals who abuse the system and con their way out of paying their debts while keeping substantial, ill-gotten fortunes hidden from the trustee and creditors.

C. CHAPTER 13: THE WAGE EARNER PLAN

A Chapter 13 reorganization is substantially different from Chapter 7. To begin with, it's not considered straight bankruptcy although many creditors unfairly regard it as the same thing. A Chapter 13 bankruptcy is different inasmuch as the debtor says, "I am going to pay off my debts, I just need some time. I may be a few dollars short." Even the IRS is not immune to restructuring through Chapter 13.

A Chapter 13 proceeding includes the automatic stay, a meeting of the creditors, and a discharge just as in Chapter 7. However, between those events, some significant differences between the chapters are apparent.

Within 30 days of filing his petition, the debtor proposes a plan in which he expects to pay off all of his priority and secured debts and the largest possible portion of his or her dischargeable debts. The plan normally takes 36 months, but may go as long as 60 months.

When the Chapter 13 is filed, additional penalties and interest for non-payment of income tax immediately stop accruing. The debtor is still responsible for the penalties and interest which have built up before the date of filing. If the figures work out to show that the debtor can, over a period of 60 months, pay back the tax debt itself and the interest that accumulated before the bankruptcy petition was filed. The penalties can be treated as unsecured debts, and might be partially, or in some cases entirely, discharged.

"A Chapter 13 bankruptcy is different inasmuch as the debtor says, 'I am going to pay off my debts, I just need some time. I may be a few dollars short.'"

Secured debts must still be paid in full over the period of the plan. Unsecured creditors may receive no less than they would have in a Chapter 7 but over the period of the plan, these unsecured creditors may receive only a portion of their claim, and the rest is discharged.

Let's assume the debtor makes $1,100 in gross monthly salary, and, after withholding taxes, social security, and other bites out of his paycheck nets $800. Let's assume that the debtor owes $2,000 in secured debts, $1,000 in non-dischargeable priority debts, and $1,000 in unsecured dischargeable debts—such as debts to department stores, credit card companies and gasoline companies. Of the $2,000 in secured debts, $1,000 is for a car that has no value, the other $1,000 is for a car that is worth only $500.

The debtor chooses to give up one car by surrendering it to the noteholder. The debtor elects to keep the other car but will only pay $500 value on the car and will not have to pay the entire $1,000. The fair value of the car ($500) must be paid because the fair value would have to be paid under Chapter 7 to keep the car.

A debtor in Chapter 13 is required to pay as much money as he would have had to pay under a Chapter 7. However, the debtor gets to keep all the property that he is willing to pay on, *up to the value of the property*, not the debt on the property.

In a Chapter 13 bankruptcy, the debtor must file his plan showing how much he can pay each month on his debts. He does this by determining his take-home pay and deducting his normal living expenses. Whatever amount remains should be sufficient to—over a period of several years, for example—pay off the non-dischargeable debts.

This amount of money is then paid to the trustee each month, who in turn divides the money among the creditors who are in line to be paid off by the debtor's plan. In the event the debtor was unable to make the payments under the plan, the bankruptcy could be dismissed or it could be converted to a Chapter 7, and all non-exempt assets of the estate would be liquidated for the benefit of the creditors.

When all the creditors have been given notice, they must file a proof-of-claim. If the creditors do not file a proof-of-claim, their claim may be discharged—even without payment. This is the case in both Chapter 7 and Chapter 13. Creditors are required to file this proof-of-claim within 90 days after the first meeting of the creditors.

In the event a debtor doesn't agree to a particular claim in either a Chapter 13 or Chapter 7 bankruptcy, he has the option to fight it.

Since the outcome is uncertain, there's renewed impetus for negotiations and settlement. By this means, disputes with the IRS may be taken out of a prejudiced forum—the U.S. Tax Court, where the taxpayer seldom wins—and placed in a more neutral arena, where the debtor at least has a chance. Bankruptcy opens the door for negotiation, if there is a reasonable IRS agent involved (the author is using the word "reasonable" very loosely here).

D. CHAPTER 11

Chapter 11 is a reorganization plan frequently used by businesses that are faced with current, insurmountable debts, but are basically sound. How can they be sound with insurmountable debts? They can't pay now, but could over time with a little help and perhaps a void contract or two. Under a court-supervised plan, these entities have the opportunity to repay their debts over time and emerge strong and solvent, such as, Continental Airlines.

Although individual debtors in Chapter 7 and Chapter 13 bankruptcies sometimes represent themselves, normally only lawyers file Chapter 11 bankruptcies. Chapter 11 debtors are usually corporations. However, an individual with over $500,000 in assets can also file under Chapter 11 instead of Chapter 13 and he can legally represent himself, but that is probably rarer than solar eclipses at night.

A corporation cannot "represent itself," even if one individual controls the corporation. Filing Chapter 11 is thus an expensive option for a floundering business. Attorneys fees can be considerable. In addition, the filing fee is now $500 as compared to $90 for a Chapter 7 or Chapter 13 bankruptcy.

The owners of businesses in Chapter 11 normally continue to manage the business in the capacity of a debtor-in-possession. The business is supervised by an estate administrator to make sure it is run in a manner that protects the interest of the creditors. A trustee may be appointed if the debtors in possession demonstrate that they are dishonest or incompetent. Often agreements are entered into with a financial institution to be a source of funds to meet the business' day to day expenses—wages, utilities, etc.

"Chapter 11 is a reorganization plan frequently used by businesses that are faced with current, insurmountable debts, but are basically sound."

The 20 largest unsecured creditors together constitute the creditors' committee which, along with the estate administrator, has input into business decisions of the corporation in Chapter 11.

Chapter 11, like Chapter 13, requires the debtor to propose a plan by which the creditors can be fully or partly paid. However, far fewer Chapter 11 proceedings ever get to the plan and discharge stages. Very often, a business which really has no salvageable assets files a Chapter 11 as a stop-gap measure to delay the inevitable. It cannot meet its current expenses even when the past debts are dealt with by the bankruptcy. In such instances, dismissals and liquidations usually occur.

Individuals may have recourse to Chapter 11. This chapter is an option for an individual who has debts above the ceiling placed on Chapter 13—$350,000 for secured debts, $100,000 for unsecured. Under Chapter 11, repayment of a tax debt can be spread out over six years instead of a maximum of five. Chapter 11 also allows the substance of a secured debt such as a mortgage to be disputed and different terms to be worked out—whereas Chapter 13 just permits the same secured debt to be paid out, over time, but not re-negotiated.

E. OTHER CHAPTERS

There is a Chapter 9 which can be filed by insolvent municipalities.

Another Chapter was recently added to the bankruptcy code is Chapter 12—a bankruptcy proceeding uniquely designed for farmers. It takes into account the farmer's particular needs for credit, the seasonal nature of farm income, and other such special factors. It is, of course, deplorable that so many farmers have been forced into financial ruin by agri-business, mega-monopolies and inept government policies. The need to create an entire new bankruptcy chapter for farmers is a sad commentary on this nation's economic and social policies.

F. FORMS

Every federal bankruptcy court is actually an administrative division of a federal court. Most actions taken by a bankruptcy court can be chal-

"Although individual debtors in Chapter 7 and Chapter 13 bankruptcies sometimes represent themselves, only lawyers file may file Chapter 11 bankruptcies."

lenged by asking the appropriate federal judge to review the action.

Each federal court also has its own local rules and forms which must be used. It makes sense to call that court and ask them for their forms. A set of common bankruptcy forms and schedules can be purchased for about $10 to $15 from certain stationery stores; however, the court often requires certain additional local forms. These local forms and a pamphlet explaining local rules are usually supplied without cost from the clerk of the bankruptcy court.

One very important consideration in bankruptcy petitions is filling out the forms fully and completely. The task, in all probability, does not intellectually require the attention of an attorney, but a lot of people can't fill out their forms correctly, and a lot of good lawyers get their forms bounced.

In 1981 I filed my first bankruptcy petition representing a client in a Chapter 7 proceeding. Bankruptcy is considered by many a specialization in law. I decided I wanted to get involved in the lucrative bankruptcy business, and I accepted a bankruptcy case. I took the forms out of the package and filled them out scrupulously. I checked them over several times for errors and got together twice with the client.

I filed them and then attended the first meetings. There were about 30 attorneys in the courtroom at the time. The trustee bounced half of their petitions. Most of the attorneys considered themselves to be bankruptcy specialists. My amateur feat in filling out the forms on that particular day proved to be superior to the accomplishments of so-called experts. The forms are not complicated, yet they do demand painstaking accuracy.

G. THE TRUSTEE

The bankruptcy trustee is an individual appointed by the court to oversee the payment of the debts from the bankruptcy estate. Approximately ten percent of the bankruptcy estate is set aside for these administrative costs.

Some of the trustees are extremely competent and extremely knowledgeable in bankruptcy law. Some of them are stupid, lazy, and incompetent and are merely taking an easy payday, political appointment. As a general rule, the bigger the bankruptcy, the less competent the individual,

"The forms are not complicated, yet they do demand painstaking accuracy."

because the appointment is a juicier political plum.

Trustee drones who have to handle 1,000 bankruptcy cases and collect $500 or $1,000 from a 1,000 different people and retain 10 percent are generally hard-workers and have been appointed because of their intellectual capabilities and industrious work habits. The cases must be worked properly and this is not a job that handles itself. A good deal of the money the trustee takes in goes to pay his staff, often including competent legal assistants who do the nuts and bolts work.

Some of the best lawyers I've ever met are trustees. These trustees often have a staff of legal assistants working for them, without whom their offices could not function efficiently. The debtor or debtor's attorney who needs to communicate with the trustee is well advised to find out which person on the trustee's staff has been assigned to the particular case, and conduct all further business with that individual.

Most of the time, the debtor's attorney and the trustee see each other only in court. Other business is conducted between the attorney's legal assistants and the trustee's legal assistants. These people make the bankruptcy system work. At best they can be a debtor's best friend, at worst they can be inept, creating a lot of unnecessary work by letting justified causes be dismissed and filing 1,000 form motions to dismiss without reading to the files. The purpose is to get attention, which it does, but it also creates unnecessary work.

Then, there is the gentleman who is assigned one $40 million estate and collects $4 million, and who frequently hires his own attorney—even though he's an attorney himself—to represent him and actually do the work. More often than not, he is a political animal, uninterested in doing much more than receiving his fees.

H. CONTESTING A BANKRUPTCY DISCHARGE

In an earlier chapter, we reviewed the case of Ngo vs. Cho in which my client was taken advantage of by an unscrupulous building contractor and the affair spent several years in civil and criminal courts. The concluding chapter of the Ngo vs. Cho epic was in bankruptcy court.

Once my client Ngo won the judgment against Mr. Cho, he attempted to avoid paying this debt. We discovered that Mr. Cho had accounts in two different banks.

"Some of the best lawyers I've ever met are trustees."

Garnishment is a proceeding available to the prevailing party in a lawsuit, who has a final judgment. The holder of a judgment can apply for a Writ of Garnishment which allows him to demand money from banks where he believes the defendant has money. The suit for garnishment must be answered timely. If the named bank holds no money belonging to the defendant, all the bank needs to do is formally answer the suit and state that fact. The bank's liability is then over.

If a bank does not timely answer a garnishment action, even if the bank holds one penny of the defendant's money, a default judgment can be taken for the entire amount. We garnished both banks where we knew Ronald Cho had accounts. One bank failed to answer timely. We got a default judgment against one of Cho's banks for the entire $168,000 of the judgment. If we had won a default judgment against an individual who had not handled his legal affairs properly, the constable probably would have executed mercilessly on that person's non-exempt possessions.

However, banks, like government officials, are often given special privileges in our society. In Cho's case, the constable initially refused to execute against the bank. The bank's lawyer was a personal friend of his. A phone call saved the bank from immediate payment.

In violation of his oath of office, the constable granted the bank more time, and then the judge granted a temporary restraining order, stopping the execution of the judgment for ten days. A second law firm with connections to the judge was brought in. Their papers were poorly drafted and incorrectly sworn to, but the judge was friendly so they got their time out.

Next a bond was posted and it was clear they could win at least six months, maybe a year's delay and of course nothing in law is ever certain. I wanted to appeal and take that case through every appellate process available—while the judgment accrued interest at 10 percent a year. My client wanted to get some financial relief so his house could be made habitable.

The bank's lawyer, who knew his political connection was risky, wanted to settle. Ultimately, we settled for $35,000 cash. The bank agreed not to pursue Mr. Cho or to ask for any of their $35,000 back, so we still had our full $168,000 judgment against Mr. Cho, who at the time was not

"The holder of a judgment can apply for a Writ of Garnishment which allows him to demand money from banks where he believes the defendant has money."

bankrupt, and $35,000.

We then faced the question of the crooked constable. Favor or no favor, when he delayed the execution he cost us $133,000 cash. The constable had broken the law. I was angry and upset. My attorney friend wanted us to leave the constable out of any future litigation as part of the settlement. I refused.

However, with the bank released by our agreement it was possible the constable was also released. Finally, after discussing the whole matter with my client, I explained that I could not handle the case against the constable personally, (since I would be a major fact witness) and left it up to the client as to whether he wanted to pursue the matter with other counsel.

Mr. Cho then filed a Chapter 7 bankruptcy. At that point, we learned that he had lied about his other debts and obligations.

Mr. Cho had a restaurant. The restaurant had bought supplies and equipment on credit from a restaurant supply house. Mr. Cho reported to the bank that the equipment was paid in full and borrowed additional moneys from the bank with those items as security.

Mr. Cho took these additional funds and pumped them into some other properties. Reading the list of creditors in Mr. Cho's bankruptcy petition was like reading a confession of criminal fraud. I was amazed. It seemed that Mr. Cho had finally done himself in. His chickens had come home to roost, or had they? There were several banks listed as creditors. A bank had loaned money on equipment that had not been paid for. The restaurant equipment store had sold it on credit.

Apparently, subject to two liens, the equipment was now also gone— perhaps sold to a fourth party, perhaps used against debt. There were several important supply houses listed as creditors. There were several Chinese-Vietnamese names on the list: some had been friends and acquaintances; and others, business associates. Cho owed money to VISA and MasterCard. Mr. Cho had it all and borrowed it all.

The list of creditors also showed all of his prior attorneys whose bills he never intended paying. I noticed the name of my illustrious opponent in the trial court on the list. Mr. Cho had hired yet another attorney to file an appeal. When the appeal was about to be dismissed for failure to file a statement-of-facts timely, Mr. Cho dismissed his own appeal and opted to seek relief in the bankruptcy court.

By filing and then dismissing his appeal, Mr. Cho accomplished two things: A) He increased the judgment automatically by $10,000 (the amount the jury had awarded as an automatic extra legal fee in the event of an appeal) and B) Mr. Cho's incurred additional legal fees—although, of course, they would never be paid.

I told Cho's new attorney, "Don't get involved in this. Mr. Cho is going to cheat you. He's cheated everybody." The attorney, whose ego was getting in the way of his common sense, told me he'd been paid in advance. Apparently, he lied because his name was also listed on Mr. Cho's bankruptcy form as a creditor. What did Mr. Cho have to say about all these attorneys who had represented him? He said they were all crooks. Perhaps he was right. If it takes one to know one, I would have to admit that Mr. Cho would be an expert in that category.

The bankruptcy attorney turned out to be the most dishonest and sleazy of Mr. Cho's team. He was also the smartest. He actually did get money up front from his client: $3,000. Our office located a list of some of Mr. Cho's non-exempt (non- homestead) property. We had planned to go after it but were prevented from doing so by the automatic stay. However, one is not allowed to discharge a debt for fraud in bankruptcy court. The debtor is entitled to a hearing to determine whether or not he had committed fraud. It is expensive; it is time consuming and it is complicated.

My client, Mr. Ngo, was the only creditor who objected to Mr. Cho's discharge. The lawyers, the banks, the restaurant suppliers and the credit card companies, all lost 100 percent of the money Cho owed them. Even the bank—which had lost the $35,000 paid to us, plus probably $10,000 to $15,000 in legal fees with three law firms and an additional $25,000 debt for Mr. Cho's restaurant equipment—did not file an objection to the discharge.

Ultimately we settled out of court for a non-dischargeable $65,000 federal judgment which would be released, by agreement, upon the payment of $25,000 which would be paid out over three years, with monthly payments increasing by increments of $50 every six months—ranging from $200 to $350. At the end of the three years, the remainder of the $25,000 must be paid in one lump sum.

Mr. Cho's payments must be met timely every month, or we can execute immediately. Mr. Cho knows I will execute immediately and unpleasantly. Mr. Cho has remained current on his payments for approximately two years, and I expect him to continue to do so. He has manipulated every court in every way, shape, and form and was ultimately caught. Our total recovery (and even Mr. Cho's personal loss) is substantially higher than the original $15,000 settlement which Mr. Cho and his lawyers turned down.

As a result of litigation which forced Mr. Cho to take responsibility for his misdeeds, a former scoundrel has apparently undergone a transformation, becoming a trustworthy, productive member of society.

I. FROM A WHEELCHAIR TO THE STREETS AND BACK

I received a phone call from a West Texas oil field pipe salesman with a familiar tale of woe. The man had a powerful, commanding voice filled with strength and integrity, but he had no money. The IRS was demanding more money than he had or was likely to have, threatening to take his home, already taking more of his wages than he could lose and still fulfill his obligations in life, and sending him form letters which subtly implied the possibility of jail.

It was one of those cases I can only take a few of and still stay open—average middle class, IRS victim, no savings, a long distance to travel and facing a tough fight. I had finished five jury trials in four months and was facing six more in the next three; none appeared likely to settle. We had four appeals pending. We needed another legal assistant and another secretary but could not handle the cash flow necessary to hire them. Financially, we were carrying too many contingency fee, civil rights cases and cases for the deserving needy, so we couldn't take anything but cash up front.

The client would need $10,000 to $15,000 worth of work but was able to pay only a couple of hundred a month. I told him we would be unable to take his case, but after he insisted, I agreed to sell him an hour of my time to get a handle on his case. I've met clients who flew in from New York, California, Mexico, Hong Kong and other places to meet for an hour of uninterrupted private consultation and a no-nonsense review of their problems.

Telling someone to say nothing but rely on the Fifth Amendment or that he doesn't need a lawyer, or that he is being cheated, or that he is not being cheated can sometimes save thousands of dollars. There are a lot of lawyers who: A) Won't sell a single hour of their time and do some basic

---

"Law does not lend itself to exact answers, but, if a lawyer doesn't venture opinions, he doesn't answer questions."

research with the client present; B) Give away an hour to pitch for a large retainer promising personal attention and then after getting the money, never have anyone on staff return the client's phone calls and never send their clients copies of work done; C) Won't commit to any opinion at all.

Law does not lend itself to exact answers, but, if a lawyer doesn't venture opinions, he doesn't answer questions. Often, a single hour is all that is needed. Personalized attention can be economically paid through the utilization of legal assistants.

Sammy Lott arrived on time, driving his well-worn van ingeniously rigged with a semi-automated hydraulic lift on the the side door. The driver's seat was his own portable wheelchair! The steering wheel of the car had a specific device on it to allow Sammy to slip his weaker hand into a supporting device to aid him in steering.

Sammy had been injured in a car accident 13 years earlier, leaving him paralyzed from the neck down, without the use of his lower limbs, and only partial mobility in his hands. It's quite possible that inexpert medical care many years ago may have contributed to the overwhelming extent of his spinal cord injuries.

Gathering strength from God, Sammy miraculously rebuilt his life. His first heroic efforts were directed toward mobility. He needed a specially adapted form of transportation. The story of how he created his van, his wheelchair, and his success in the free market would fill another book.

The nuts and bolts of his life is that he's done it his way without government assistance; he's paid off his antique miracle van, supported two kids, had almost completely paid off his home and never looked back. Now, the IRS was stealing his income and metaphorically threatening to confiscate his wheelchair.

Sammy wanted to fight. He wanted a war. He was willing to go to jail if I could assure him his house could be sold and the money used to keep up his child support payments. When the IRS threatened to take his home, for the first time in his life, he was afraid. Would he be forced into not fulfilling all his obligations as a man? As a father? Could his kids visit him in prison? Would they want for anything?

I agreed to take his case. We negotiated the fee. I offered to take the case for free and somehow cover the out-of-pocket expenses myself. Sammy refused. I told him a man in a wheelchair, cast out into the streets is not a

---

"When the IRS threatened to take his home, for the first time in his life, he was afraid."

---

pretty sight. Sammy laughed. We negotiated for an entire hour. Both of us were tough. I wanted the good feeling that comes from making a sacrifice for a truly deserving and needy human being. Sammy wanted to maintain the pride he had earned all his life—a self-made man, a self-sufficient man who helped others, not needing their help.

In the end, we both compromised. I would still have to explain to my office manager another case without up-front money and with considerable up-front expenses. L.R. and I would both have to add more weekend working time for yet another non-profit case. We would both pray for the resources to hire another legal assistant.

Sammy would pay $25 a month for 20 months and try to cover our out-of-pocket expenses at some time in the future.

Sammy's case presented three questions: A) Did Sammy owe a debt to the IRS? B) Could he pay what he owed? C) Could we defeat or postpone the IRS claims?

Years earlier, Sammy had problems visiting an IRS agent because the building was not barrier-free, which means that a person in a wheelchair could not enter the building and get around inside without significant difficulty, if at all. Barrier-free construction does not just help wheelchair users but also older people, temporary disabled people on crutches, expectant mothers and those pushing baby carriages, cargo carriers, etc. Most cities and buildings just are not as sensitive to human needs.

The IRS agent didn't care. He simply charged penalties and interest and sent out nasty computer form letters. Sammy had been harassed for years by these friendly government bureaucrats.

One of Sammy's returns was lost by the IRS. No problem. They just charged him penalties for not filing. Agents failed to return his calls or respond to his letters. No problem. They sent more meaningless forms.

Over the years Sammy had learned to live with it until finally the IRS decided to unilaterally take most of his paycheck, literally starving him out, not leaving him enough wherewithal to eat and still pay the wages of his personal health care attendant—which his condition required.

Sammy's boss didn't mind if the IRS took most of his salary, after all Sammy still got his work done. Sammy was one of the best phone sales-

---

"Sammy had problems visiting an IRS agent because the building was not barrier-free, which means that a person in a wheelchair could not enter the building and get around inside without significant difficulty, if at all."

---

men in the business.

When Sammy came to my office he was at the brink of destitution. He asked if we could stop them from taking his next check. He didn't think he could survive the loss of one more check.

There were three possible approaches: A) Negotiate with the IRS as Sammy's former CPA had been doing for years, with the IRS escalating its demands at each visit. B) File for injunctive relief in federal court, asking the court to temporarily suspend its levy order. This was, theoretically, legally, on paper the best step to take, but, it was too slow. Sammy could starve. C) File for relief in the bankruptcy court.

Under federal bankruptcy law, when you file a petition, all non-criminal proceedings against the debtor stop. Legally, nothing can be done without the court's permission. Like the penalty watch stopping mid-circle in a sporting event or during a time out, the law requires everyone to back off and ask the bankruptcy court for permission to proceed.

Since Sammy was a wage earner with debts that appeared payable in a plan, he opted to file under Chapter 13. Did Sammy owe a debt? Yes, a small one. Could he pay his fair debt? Easily. Could he defeat or postpone the IRS claim? Postpone— yes. Defeat, most of the unsupported claim and all of the penalty—probably.

Our bankruptcy petition was filed, but the IRS continued to send nasty letters. We advised its agents that we would file for contempt of court proceedings if they continued their illegal contacts with a debtor in bankruptcy who was represented by an attorney.

Since Sammy Lott lived in Uvalde, Texas, his petition had to be filed in the Western District of Texas, Del Rio Division. Shortly thereafter, the last commercial airline offering plane service into Del Rio discontinued its route because the airline had been losing money on it. That meant that for each hearing set in Del Rio, I would have a day-long drive in each direction. I certainly could not afford two, non-paying days out of the office. I filed a motion for change of venue to the San Antonio division of the Western District. Our client's home was roughly halfway between Del Rio and San Antonio, east of the former, west of the latter.

If the motion had not been granted, we might have been forced to withdraw from the case.

The motion for a change of venue was granted. Fortunately, Sammy did not have to change trustees. David Morse, of Trustee Marion Olsen's office in San Antonio, was assigned to Sammy's case from the outset. He had not opposed the move. Throughout the case, he was extremely efficient and helpful; truly serving the cause of justice. He was in Sammy's corner from the start.

Time, distance, and accessibility are important factors in a law practice. There are a dozen cities around Houston that are only a short hop away by plane: Atlanta, Little Rock, Dallas, and Oklahoma City. I can get to some of them from an airport near my home in Katy. San Antonio is an hour away by air or three hours by car. Using the airlines in Katy and Houston, I have charted out paths to make large portions of the country very accessible in my practice.

Prior to the 1986 Texas oil-price slump, about 30 percent of my practice was concentrated in Texas. Afterward, it dropped to 10-20 percent.

All Sammy's creditors, except the IRS, tacitly approved his proposed plan by saying nothing. The IRS filed a proof of claim form demanding more. Sammy and I went to San Antonio to fight. They wanted him to pay penalties and interest and more, plus their ridiculous estimates of income from sources unknown and unimagined by rational minds.

Compared to a trial proceeding, the confirmation hearing is very simple. If the judge confirms the plan, the debtor proceeds under the court's protection for all debts incurred prior to the plan. If not, a new plan must be approved or the debtor will be thrown out of bankruptcy. Under the IRS proof of claim, Sammy would have no chance to pay. His income was too low. He could literally lose his home, car and wheel chair. No offer was made by the IRS to exempt any of these.

Our trustee announced the case and recommended adoption of the plan. I approached the bench and gave a brief summary of the dispute. The court, Bankruptcy Judge R. Glen Ayres, spent a few minutes reviewing the file and then confirmed the plan—firmly and in my opinion showing a bit of justified anger toward the IRS.

The IRS, relying totally on their proof of claim, did not appear at the confirmation hearing. The plan was confirmed, the court approved Sammy's schedule and version of debt, and threw out all of the IRS's penalties. Maybe no IRS agent showed up because they were too ashamed to face the judge or to face Sammy.

Sammy continued to faithfully make his monthly plan payments. We felt confident that his home and possessions were secure, but, on the recommendation of the trustee, we filed an objection to the IRS' proof of claim. We demanded proof from the IRS to substantiate the debt they claimed Sammy owed. The Justice Department attorney representing the IRS asked for a continuance of the hearing on our objection to the IRS proof of claim because she needed more time.

Finally certain figures were submitted by the IRS, along with a proposed order we were asked to sign. This proposed order provided for a debt lower than the IRS' original proof of claim, but beyond our client's ability to pay and considerably above what our client's accountant determined was owing. Of course, we did not agree.

The burden of proof was on the IRS to show a debt due. They set the case for a second hearing at the convenience of the IRS's attorney. I had the flu, but flew in on a rainy San Antonio day. Sammy drove his van and then faced the rainy weather in his electric wheelchair.

We were prepared to fight the IRS claim. No one showed up. Judge Ayres fined the IRS $600 in attorney's fees which I asked to be applied to Sammy's tax debt. Our plan was adopted and the objection to proof of claim granted.

The estimate of taxes due was reduced from approximately $30,000 to $1,500, with a credit.

The case was not over yet. The IRS asked for and received a new hearing and two appeals were filed—that's another story. However, the end of the story was a resounding victory for Sammy Lott, and another judge on my heroes list!

"Under federal bankruptcy law when you file a petition, all non-criminal proceedings against the debtor stop."

CHAPTER XXVIII

SOCIAL IN-SECURITY

"A lot of people believe the social security system to be one giant compulsory con with its ulterior motive being the government's desire to brand everyone with a social security number to function as a national identification number..."

Don't expect all of this to make sense. It doesn't. Don't expect this to be fair. It isn't. A lot of people believe the social security system to be one giant compulsory con with its ulterior motive being the government's desire to brand everyone with a social security number to function as a national identification number, which some regard as the Scriptural mark of the beast.[1]

One organization prints a "non-Social Security card" with number 000-00-0000. It's advantages over the genuine article are that it's free and it doesn't pretend to benefit you.

I recently represented a client who had been seriously injured due to the collapse of a faulty scaffold he had climbed while painting a house. At first, the owner and his insurance company claimed it was my client's fault.

In any event, my client had fallen the equivalent of three stories and had suffered a fractured spine. After surgery his doctors informed him that he would never be able to carry heavy paint cans, climb ladders or perform any sort of heavy labor. For a 43-year-old Mexican-American with only a moderate degree of fluency in English, a ninth-grade education, and no skills other than in his former career as a painter, this was devastating news.

He was the sole support of his family. He had one son in high school, hoping for a college education. He had four other young adult sons in their late teens and early twenties who still looked to him for assistance in

"One organization prints a "non-Social Security card" with number 000-00-0000. It's advantages over the genuine article are that it's free and it doesn't pretend to benefit you."

getting higher educational, vocational training, and general support as they tried to find their niche in the troubled economy of southeast Texas during the late eighties.

Our client was a loving grandfather to his married daughter's two small boys. He was blessed with a devoted wife who tended to his health and shared his anguish over his bleak-looking future. We sued the owner of the home, the building contractor and the maker of the defective scaffold.

We settled for $80,000 of a $100,000 policy on the house. A fast $80,000 without risk is worth more than a a slow $100,000 with risk and expenses. In terms of dollars it wasn't a lot for 30 more years of bad health and poor work ability, but in terms of the real world it was a fair deal the insurance company could live with, saving legal fees and future risks. It just wasn't enough to sustain our client and his family through the rest of his life.

Before he retained me to represent him on his personal injury case, my client had already applied for social security disability benefits and had been rejected. With the assistance of his family, he asked for a reconsideration of that decision, and it was still denied.

At this point, now that I was the family's attorney on the accident case, they asked me to represent them in the social security matter also.

I had to find out why our client had been denied benefits, and what could be done about it. He had paid his social security taxes for over 25 years—enough money at five percent interest to total almost $500,000 to Uncle Sugar—but he had received nothing.

Social security is basically an accident annuity pension/retirement plan that pays less per dollar than the worst insurance companies, and sells millions of policies because if you don't buy, and social security thinks you should, you can go to jail. The tables are not based on facts or probabilities, but laws—meaning political promises and political estimates.

The more you pay the more you are supposed to get, but A) After five years of bill payment (20 quarters) your account is filled to the maximum; and B) If you don't pay at all and aren't made to pay because you don't work you can apply for supplemental security and receive benefits from those who did pay for free. These benefits are often as great as those given to people who paid for 50 years, and under the right circumstances can be available to someone who never worked and never paid.

How does the program work? If an eligible worker gets hurt and can't work for over one year, theoretically, he is entitled to benefits. First, he must prove the disability will last at least one year. No matter how severe the injury is, if it lasts even one day short of a full year no benefits are paid.

The injury might be a broken back or a psychological trauma debilitating to such a degree that the individual can't work any more. If the eligible worker dies, his surviving spouse and children are entitled to certain benefits. Presumably, the date of the parent's death must be at least a year before the eligible child turns 18, or 23, if in college.

There is a four-step administrative procedure to follow and then if you are unhappy, you go to court and can appeal up to the U.S. Supreme Court.

STEP I. INITIAL DETERMINATION

In Step I, you fill out the forms and ask for money. Show you are disabled. Have your doctor prove it with tests and submit written reports. The doctor must show it all—your pain, your inability to work, problems tying your shoe, the end of marital bliss, headaches, pain from carrying the dishes into the kitchen.

If you don't complain, Doc can't write it down. If Doc doesn't write it down, even a broken back may be found to be an unimportant injury. If Doc hates people who get hurt and tells you that your broken neck and herniated disk is a minor problem a real man would learn to live with—leave Doc's office. He won't help you get social security benefits and he isn't overflowing with the milk of human kindness.

Your doctor needs to care about you and be on your side. He needs to understand that you wouldn't be applying for social security benefits you earned if you were not desperate. Read your physician's report before it goes to social security. If he made a mistake, ask him to fix it. If the report says you are six months pregnant and a hemophiliac with ingrown toenails and you are really a male longshoreman with disk problems and perfect blood—get it fixed.

You won't understand the entire report so ask questions. If there is no mention of your debilitating pain ask about it. There are two types of medical pain. Objective and subjective. Objective means the doctor can see it without asking you. Subjective means you have to tell Doc about it.

"There are two types of medical pain. Objective and subjective. Objective means the doctor can see it without asking you. Subjective means you have to tell Doc about it. "

Some social security people will open their hearts and help you, others hate you for interfering with their personal phone calls or a cigarette break. Whoever is assigned to your case as the claims representative is with you to the end. The claims representative decides yea or nay and sends it to be reviewed. The reviewer almost always agrees with the claims representative.

The longer lasting your injury—more than one year and one day—and the more severe, the better your chance of winning. In order to avoid paying you, the Social Security Administration will try to show that you are capable of working either in your former field or in some other endeavor. The greater your education and training, the better your chances of losing will be.

Can't lift 10 pounds, no education, former professional weight lifter, chief language—Polish, great difficulty in English? Age 55. Lifetime of disability. In life expectancy and fulfillment, you lose a lot of points, but for social security you hit the jackpot.

Do you need a lawyer at this stage? As a card carrying union man I'll probably get a lot of hate mail for this, but my honest opinion is "No." A friendly nurse or your high-school English teacher can help you with your forms.

The standard legal fee in social security matters is 25 percent of what the client receives from the date of disability until the day he receives the first dollar. If there is a permanent disability, no fee is due on future benefits. This arrangement is not absolutely mandatory. Depending on the agreement made with his attorney, a person could lose his case, and still have to pay his attorney a reasonable fee for his hourly work. However, the normal agreement is no disability money—no fee.

When a claimant is represented by an attorney, it is the policy of the Social Security Administration to withhold 25 percent of the benefits after they are awarded and then pay the rest directly to the claimant. However, to get this money, the lawyer must show he earned it, by showing his hourly work. If he doesn't prove that he is entitled to the fees, the money gets sent back to the claimant.

Unlike the situation in normal personal injury cases, the lawyer who represents a claimant for social security disability actually benefits from delay. Would he rather get 25 percent of two years' unpaid social security or 25 percent of one month's. Delay hurts the client and helps the attorney at the beginning stage. It is also likely that you can get the same benefit without the lawyer at this stage—only quicker.

To enhance your chances of obtaining payments, be sure that all of your income history is correctly reported under your social security number. Without a number you can't get the dollars. I won't try to convince you to use the system if you have deep conscientious objections to it, but if you don't, you lose the benefits you were forced to pay for and are entitled to, and you may become a burden on others. If you have reported your money under more than one social security number, at this point, you need to get them all together.

Advocate your position and find a good honest doctor who will advocate your position also. Be honest, but don't down-play your problems. The Social Security Administration will do that for you. If you and social security join in minimizing the impact of your disability, you probably will not get benefits.

If you receive benefits take them.

The Social Security Administration itself doesn't really make the *initial determination*. The claim is filed in the local office of the Social Security Administration which refers the claim to a state agency. A medical doctor and a somewhat trained medical layperson will review the claim papers as though they had seen you and render a decision—generally based solely on your doctor's report.

The decision will come back to you as though it were made by Social Security Administration on their paperwork. If you recover, and keep taking benefits to which you are no longer entitled, you may be required to make a refund in the future.

STEP II. ADMINISTRATIVE RECONSIDERATION

Hopefully you'll not need this step, but if you lose at the initial determination, you can ask for an administrative reconsideration. You should have received a letter telling you if you're dissatisfied, you can ask for a reconsideration.

New people are supposed to review it. Odds are, since they are rarely reconsidered, they are rarely reviewed. A certified letter and a personal visit won't hurt. Ask for your claims representative. If you can read and write well—and if you can't, you've accomplished a major feat getting this far again—you can do without an attorney up to this point unless you are very rich and if you are very rich what are you doing here?

At this point, everything is still being done in writing, by means of forms and doctors' records—there have been no oral hearings.

Remember the bottom line is: Do you have the ability to earn money?

Were there any prior medical findings that you might have failed to report, such as a veterans disability. Is the date of the onset of your disability correctly reported? Are all the other facts in evidence accurate?

Mistakes can be made. In the fractured spine case I've been discussing, on one of my client's hospital admission forms it said "compressed cervical strain" instead of "compressed fracture—cervical spine." As a claimant, you have the right to go the social security office and examine everything in your file.

Failure to attend to these details may be why you are at Step II now.

STEP III. ADMINISTRATIVE LAW JUDGE

You lost again. Actually, if you lose the initial determination, you will probably lose the reconsideration.

STEP III is an appeal to a Social Security Administrative judge. This is really a short, informal trial. Bring your tape recorder, and let the judge know you understand his recorder is the real record, but you want your own tape recording.

Bring a friend or someone experienced with administrative law. Many social security judges will allow non-lawyers to assist. Bring your witnesses as to disability, affidavits from doctors—the doctors themselves may be too expensive to bring to the hearing—spouses, kids, or anyone who can testify about your condition. Be careful, however, and don't waste the judge's time and repeat testimony through a dozen witnesses. Use affidavits when you can't get the witnesses there personally.

Administrative hearings don't require the legal niceties of court. Much of the so-called evidence is actually hearsay. After you've presented your witnesses and evidence, it's always valuable to remember and give the judge a summary of your case.

Your physical and mental abilities that remain intact after the disability are known as your Residual Function Capacity (R.F.C.). This includes how many pounds you can lift, whether you can bend or turn, how many hours of sitting or standing you can tolerate, whether or not there are any environmental factors you must be shielded from, and numerous similar items.

These assessments are made by your doctor, and the Social Security Administration may have arranged for you to be examined by a doctor designated by them. The Social Security Administration may have either or both a medical advisor or a vocational expert. One tells how hurt you are, the other might tell how good you are work-wise. These experts may help you. An honest vocational expert who testifies that you cannot do any lifting or real work might win your case for you.

You are on trial to get back some of the fortune you were compelled to put into the system. The judge may ask questions or listen to you or both. Each informal hearing is different because each judge is different. Informal or not, however, you are in an important trial.

If you don't hear from the judge two to four weeks later by letter giving you his decision, you should call or write.

You won. Good.

You lost. Bad. Go to STEP IV.

STEP IV. APPEALS COUNCIL

The next step is to appeal to the Appeals Council of the Social Security Administration. An attorney or someone trained in this area would be helpful at this point. You are asking for a review of the judge's decision, within 60 days of his ruling. You will usually lose.

Despite grievous injury, the administrative judge may rule that you are not disabled because there are other jobs you can do. It is appalling to realize what factors are NOT taken into account.

It does not matter if there are no local job openings in any of the suggested new careers that the vocational expert recommends—as long as there is such a job classification. Theoretically, a disabled painter from Texas could be declared ineligible for benefits if there was a job opening for blubber-burger shapers in Alaska and he could physically handle it, according to his RFC and the determination of the vocational expert!

It doesn't matter to the Social Security Administration that a destitute, unemployed worker with a family could not afford to move; nor does it matter that if he did move—a disabled individual would be leaving a network of extended family and friends whose support he has been relying on. There is no provision made by the Social Security Administration to provide even temporary help to the worker and his family while he is learning a new trade.

The wages that the disabled worker would receive in a theoretical new career do not have to equal his former earning capacity—the minimum wage is all that is required.

The Appeals Council is the last level of pure administrative law—from here, if you choose, you go into the real court room.

Within 60 days of losing at the Appeals Council level, you may appeal to federal district court by filing a complaint against the Social Security Administration. The trial court reviews the earlier case, without a jury, and decides if you were treated right. The odds are against you, but you are protected by an entire body of social security and administrative review cases. The trial court's decision may be appealed to the appropriate circuit court and then to the U.S. Supreme Court if necessary.

To appeal to the federal district court takes some ability with forms and research. It is not recommended for a non-lawyer. That doesn't mean a non-lawyer can't do it; he can. It just means it's not basic, first month, non-union, underground lawyer stuff.

In this chapter, I dealt with legal controversies and not basic retirement benefits. Social security retirement benefits amount to small monthly checks, based on money paid in and seldom are a source of litigation. However, if the government feels you owe money, this money is easily taken from those with the least ability to protest. A common source of friction is the government's claim that an elderly person earned too much in a given year, was overpaid by Social Security and now must give it back. Often the person who bears the brunt of this problem is a widow who does not get the lump sum death benefit when her husband dies because of an alleged past overpayment. If you are interested in obtaining facts on money you've paid and money you are to receive you can ask for it on a form SSA-7004. Write: Consumer Information Center Dept. 60, Pueblo, Colorado 81009. The form is called *"Pebes"* (Personal Earning and Benefit Estimate Statement).

"Social security is basically an accident annuity pension retirement plan that pays less per dollar than the worst insurance companies, and sells millions of policies because if you don't buy, and social security thinks you should, you can go to jail."

CHAPTER XXIX
WILLS AND PROBATE:

WHERE THERE'S NO WILL, THERE'S NO WAY

*"I advise my clients that it is as important for the
working class or middle-income person to have
a will as it is for the multi-millionaire."*

A. WHY HAVE A WILL

I am often asked to draft wills for my clients and their spouses. The preparation of a will is one of the more common services attorneys provide for the average person.

The most important reason for having a will is so that you, as an individual or a couple, decide where your money and property will go after you die, and who will be the guardian of your minor children (if any). If you have not made these decisions in a legally proper will, the state will step in with its guidelines and will determine these issues for you.

Of course, government being what it is, no one can honestly guarantee you freedom from state intrusion, especially after your death. For this reason, I advise my clients that it is as important for the working-class or middle-income person to have a will as it is for the multimillionaire.

Another factor in favor of having a will is the prevalence today of divorces and remarriages, creating a complex network of step-sibling, half-sibling and ex-in-laws who are blood relatives of some of your children but not others. A will allows you to specifically cite, by name and relationship, each person on whom you wish to bestow a monetary or specific bequest or endow with a position of trust (executor or guardian).

A will performs among other things two important functions:

1. Your loved ones are likely to be remembered as you want them to (subject to proper court treatment, no fights, and the extent of your estate).
2. You can decide who wraps things up, a person of great trust in your family or friendship circle (all again subject to proper court treatment and no fights).

Usually, there aren't fights, but the exception can wipe your estate out, even faster without a will. One client asked me, "What if I have no loved nswer was simple: "You don't need a will."

nless you want to donate your estate to a

her words, if you care what happens with

ı should leave a will.

drawing up of a will. The idea of having a

ble because it addresses the issue of their

younger people often like to ignore. Many

s. Some people set an appointment for their

someone they know has died, or after a life-

ra responsibility-marriage or the birth of a

poration forms, there are simple will forms.

fe and one child are often as follows:

he wife gets everything.

usband gets everything.

th husband and wife die simultaneously,— and "simultaneous" may be interpreted to mean if one did not outlive the other by say 30 days, why have the expense of two probates when the husband survived 24 hours longer than the wife after a car accident—the child gets everything.

I have devised an information form for my legal assistant to use with clients whose wills are being drawn up. This form is included in the Addendum.[1] Since considering one's will forces an individual to confront his own mortality, the information should be gathered with sensitivity; yet, even such questions as funeral plans, choices of cremation or burial, and place of internment need to be asked.

Not everyone includes that type of material in his will, but some wish to indicate a particular religious preference whose funeral custom they want followed, or they may wish to indicate a place of burial or other means of disposing their remains. Whether you hire an attorney on a flat fee, hourly or use a form book and do it yourself, filling out this will checklist sheet and outlining your objectives, should save you time and

---

"...considering one's will forces an individual to confront his own mortality..."

---

money.

If you hire a lawyer by the hour and start without having all the facts in order, you're wasting time and money. A lawyer can explain what a will may legally accomplish but the basic questions are: Who do you trust? Who do you love? Who is deserving of a bequest? These are not legal questions. You save time by first determining to whom you wish to leave your estate and with what variables, and then seek out an attorney for drafting the will according to your wishes.

When a husband and wife make their wills at the same time, the question arises as to whether or not the wills are contractual. If the wills are contractual, they are binding on the surviving spouse even after the death of the other. The surviving spouse is not permitted to change his or her will. These are generally not advisable. Life has so many variables that it is usually in the party's best interest to allow the surviving spouse to be able to change his or her will as circumstances change.

For example, consider Mr. and Mrs. Testator (this is based on a real situation—but the term "testator" means the one who is making the will). Mr. Testator, a man nearing 50, through his skill and industriousness, had accumulated a sizable amount of cash savings and property. He had two grown daughters from his first marriage living on their own. His will bequeaths a nominal sum to each. However, Mr. Testator had married a second time, to a woman almost 20 years his junior. That marriage produced two young sons, both under the age of seven. These youngsters are the second Mrs. Testator's only children.

Both of their wills leave everything to the surviving spouse. Mr. Testator's will, however, provides the bequest to his daughters and a life estate in some property for his parents, which after their deaths reverts to his heirs.

Each will says that in the event the spouse has pre-deceased the maker of the will, that the two young boys would be under the care of a guardian until reaching the age of 18. The boys, upon attaining maturity, will be equal beneficiaries of the estate. Provisions were made for the college education of each boy.

Problem: Mr. Testator wanted the wills to be contractual, so his second

"A lawyer can explain what a will may legally accomplish but the basic questions are: Who do you trust? Who do you love? Who is deserving of a bequest?"

wife couldn't change hers after he died. He could foresee a scenario in which he would die first and she would be the heir of all of his estate. He wanted to be sure that the fruits of his labors were still going to benefit his two sons and not some hypothetical other man or subsequent children born to his wife in some future marriage.

Mrs. Testator, on the other hand, did not want the wills to be contractual. She too, most likely, anticipated that she would outlive her husband. Perhaps she considered the possibility of a second marriage and having more children. In the event that she had another child or two, she would want to have the power to change her will to provide equally for her sons from her marriage to Mr. Testator and her new children. A contractual will would not permit her to do this.

The situation was resolved in favor of non-contractual wills, allowing young Mrs. Testator complete discretion with the estate after the death of her husband.

When I have couples who are signing their wills on the same day and who do not want their wills to be construed as contractual, I include a specific clause in each will that the will is not contractual.

The execution of a will should be a solemn ceremony. My custom is to have the clients come into our office conference room. We spread the documents out on a long table. Since I have prepared the will and may be called on to probate it some day, I am never a witness to my client's wills.

The Estate of Cash case, which appears later in this chapter, points out the inherent dangers when a lawyer wears more than one hat. An article to that effect, was published in the National Notary Association Magazine.[2]

I usually use friends of the testators or even neighbors in my office building as witnesses. If there is a fight, the witnesses will remember the ceremony and be able to testify the testator appeared to be of sound mind and said he understood the will.

The clients and witnesses initial each page. With computers, it's too easy to insert changes, otherwise. Each state has its own peculiar variations that are helpful and advisable.

"When a husband and wife make their wills at the same time, the question arises as to whether or not the wills are contractual."

B. HANDLING THE ESTATE OF A DECEASED

When someone dies, that person's property is distributed in one of the three manners: A) Intestacy; B) Testacy; or, C) Theft.

Intestacy means that that person left no will. Every one of the 50 states has a different formula for distributing the estate if the deceased left no will. There are so-called uniform probate codes used in many states, but most states who use them vary some of the rules, and each state's appellate and trial level courts are free to interpret them differently; therefore, for all practical purposes, each state is somewhat different.

In Texas, for example, suppose that a man dies without a will, leaving a wife and a child and a house. If the house was purchased during the marriage, it generally would be considered half his and half hers. Without a will, the deceased's husband's half would pass to the child rather than to the wife. If the deceased husband had been aware of the state's laws, he might have prepared a will specifically leaving his half to his wife.

The split inheritance causes many problems. In most cases, the husband prefers his widow to have the entire house. If she wishes to exercise control by selling it or transferring the title, she, generally, has to contend with both a court-appointed guardian of the minor and a court-appointed guardian of the minor's estate, both of whom would collect fees for determining whether it would be in the best interests of her child to sell the house.

Testacy means that a will has been left. The will in most states can distribute the estate in any manner that the testator wishes.

Less than half the people who die in the United States leave a will. A large portion of wills are not ever probated—that means recorded and taken to a probate court so the estate can be distributed as the deceased directed.

Even when wills are probated, the majority of the personal items are frequently not reported. Theft by surviving relatives is the way that many estates are handled. Wills frequently get lost. People who see great-grandmother's diamond wedding set sometimes decide to take it off great-grandmother's finger and pocket it. This is, of course, not legally permissible.

"When someone dies, that person's property is distributed in one of the three manners: A) Intestacy; B) Testacy; or, C) Theft."

C. PROBATE PROCEEDINGS

If there is a will, then it should be taken to the court. If there is not a will, then an administrator needs to be chosen to handle the estate. In Texas, the will generally names the person to handle the estate. This person is called—among other things—an executor or executrix or independent executor or independent executrix. The overwhelming majority of the work involved in handling the will can be done by a legal assistant. The clerks in probate court are often extremely helpful to individuals attempting to probate an estate without utilizing an attorney.

There are basically five steps in handling the estate:

First: The will is filed with the probate court. The will must be proven up. This involves the attorney, or the individual, going to the courthouse and proving that the testator is dead (a death certificate is sufficient; mere testimony usually is sufficient), and if relevant, that the document presented was the decedent's last will and testament and is now being submitted to the court.

If there is no will, it must simply be proven that the relative or person offering the estate has some standing to probate it. At that time, the court will generally appoint the executor named in the will to manage the will. Otherwise, the judge appoints an administrator; generally, someone who requests the right to be administrator—a child or next-of-kin, to manage the estate and grant letters testamentary.

These letters testamentary are the authority and power to handle the estate. A notice to all creditors of the estate must be published in a local newspaper within 30 days of the issuance of letters testamentary. This notice simply states that the testator has died, mentions the name of the executor, and provides an address where claims against the estate can be made.

Second: The estate usually must be inventoried. Frequently the inventory must accompany the probate. The inventory consists of a list of all the estate property of the estate and its approximate value. If the will is being contested and/or if the estate is substantial, the approximate value may

---

"Less than half the people who die in the United States leave a will. A large portion of wills are not ever probated—that means recorded and taken to a probate court so the estate can be distributed as the deceased directed."

---

have to be proven by an appraiser.

Third: Estate taxes must be paid to the federal government and the state government. Under current federal tax law all assets under $275,000 are exempt from federal taxation. There is a sliding scale determining the amount of taxes going up to $600,000. The state taxes vary from one state to another. Estate taxes must be paid and certificates should be obtained by the federal or state authorities that they have been paid, or that no taxes are due.

Fourth: The assets of the estate should be distributed and the estate closed.

Fifth: If the assets of the estate are not distributed according to the terms of the will, the beneficiaries may file a lawsuit. Frequently, specific items are not mentioned, and they are divided up by the executor according to the terms of the will or personal interpretation of the executor.

Every jurisdiction has its own forms for the purpose of probate. The majority of the work in most probates is putting together an inventory and filling out all of the proper papers. This can be done most effectively and inexpensively by a legal assistant.

D. THE ESTATE OF CASH

The Estate of Cash is included here because it is primarily a probate case, but, it also touches on civil trial law, and legal research, criminal law, and real estate law. The story has more than it's share of characters: judges, lawyers, clients and their enemies and of course, the jury. Portions of this case could have been told in other sections of this book, but that is the way with law in the real non-textbook world. People tend to have complex situations.

The estate of Raymond Cash, of course, did not exist until Cash died. How and why he died is important; some earlier background material is also necessary.

Our client in the case was Nathan White, a sharp, street wise black man with some junior college education and one of those ultra-honest big black Baptist wives who raise Nobel Prize winners, bake scrumptious biscuits,

"The Estate of Cash is included here because it is primarily a probate case, but, it also touches on civil trial law, legal research, criminal law and real estate law. "

belt—to children who miss school or door-to-

me into the office of Minns & Izen in 1977 look-
y. The law firm in 1977 was poor and barely
couple of trials under our collective belt. Our
been installed—it was a one-line, call-waiting
wife to loan me our card table and three metal
reception area. The office was two rooms large.
urns as receptionist and lawyer. The reception
rary home for our office equipment, which con-
high school typewriter. At a going out-of-busi-
rchased one large couch, one love seat, and one
brown vinyl for $199 and obtained at no cost an
randfather clock.
he big chair, all of this furniture graced the re-
firm's plush first impression.
nly furnishing in the lawyer room. No desk. We
rd. At this point in time, our firm was not pro-
pension plans for the two employees—we were
starving.

Mr. White qualified as a client. He was a warm, human body. I decided
if he had, as he claimed, $50 to pay a bonding company, he had $50 to pay
a lawyer. As a member of the country's most sacred private union sworn
to uphold the country's constitutional honor, could I fail to offer him the
bargain of a lifetime and re-direct him from the desire for a bond to the
desire for a lawyer? Of course not.

Never mind his problem. I was certain he needed our services, and I
knew we needed his money.

He had been picked up in Fort Bend County by a small city cop of another county and charged with an offense that did not exist in either
county or either city; four counts of improper loading of his pickup truck.
He was sentenced by a judge to pay an $800 fine or serve 30 days in jail—
it didn't matter that the judge's jurisdiction extended to maximum fines
of $200, *no* jail time. Mr. White had paid another lawyer $50 to represent
him, and without his permission, that lawyer had pled him guilty.

The case, itself, is worthy of a chapter in another book. We must unfortunately skip it and go to the end to pursue the Estate of Cash case. After
personal threats and what is best described as a war, my client, Nathan
White was found not guilty and the case was dismissed.

He paid for my time with the $50 check a bonding company would have gotten. If the check had cleared at the first deposit, I would have grossed about $.25 an hour. It didn't. It was put through what must be a record eight times before ultimately it cleared.

Mr. White, shortly, thereafter, stormed into our office wondering why we had taken the money out of his account. I'll never forget him gazing at Joe and me, saying: "You boys must think I'm made of money." That was our last encounter with Mr. White until the Estate of Cash case came along, years later.

Those years later, Mr. White stormed into the new law offices of Minns, Izen, Bradt and Associates, Inc. without an appointment. What we called our office then was a 2,000 square-foot office condominium on a busy freeway—we owned the office and shared the complex with various doctors, a pharmacist, and other white-collar professionals.

We had a full computer service—we were about five to ten years ahead of most small businesses with our own $17,000 computer that probably would only be worth $1,000 in today's computer-happy world—two full-time secretaries, a fourth full-time lawyer, a $40,000 library, a private shower, good furniture, a legal assistant and a part-time real estate examiner to help run our real estate title company.

Nathan White was told he would have to have an appointment, or he couldn't see me. He didn't really care. He was, although generally peaceful and very polite, a man who followed through on his decisions and who under the right set of circumstances was willing to face controversy with his shotgun, if necessary,

The Nathan White storm did not abate. He would not take no for an answer. He walked uninvited right into my office, dumped 50 pounds of legal papers on my desk, pulled out his wallet—flashing some cash—and carefully pulled out two 20s and a ten dollar bill and dropped it under my nose, one piece of currency at a time.

He explained: "Mr. Minns, you're expensive, but you're good. I'm hiring you for a new case. Here's $50 cash; go ahead; count it." It would have been hard not to count the three Federal Reserve notes as he dramatically displayed them.

At the time, all our new cases had to come with a $1,000 retainer, and the stockholders were considering jumping that fee to $5,000. We represented several international companies, three banks, and a dozen wealthy carpetbaggers from New York.

Mr. White, finally left, after re-pocketing his $50 and grabbing a handful of my business cards, and I felt I was rid of him. He refused to take his papers with him. I sent him a certified letter, giving him 30 days to pick them up, or I'd trash them. He didn't; I did. Izen pulled them out of the can—unknown to me—and saved them, or this story wouldn't be forthcoming.

A few days later, I got a telephone call from a real estate broker who wanted to speak to me in reference to Nathan White. "Raymond Cash", she told me, "had died."

So what, I thought. She continued. "He left everything in his will to his sister Erma Smith, his housekeeper, Henrietta Holman, and his brother." Okay, I thought, why is she telling me all of this, and what does that have to do with Nathan White.

She answered my unspoken question, voice rising in anger, "Nathan White says the will is no good, and that he runs the Cash Estate." I then interjected a question.

"So what? Why do you care, and why are you calling me?" "Easy," she explained her role, "The estate owns a half acre of commercial real estate. Ms. Smith hired me to sell it. Nathan is interfering."

My abnormal curiosity satisfied, having received my full quota of gossip, I moved to cut the conversation short: "What does any of this have to do with me?" I inquired.

"Why, you are Mr. White's lawyer."

"No, I am not." I denied.

"Yes, you are," she insisted.

"I do not and will not represent Mr. White," I re-affirmed.

"Yes, you do," she boldly asserted, now shouting and then with indignation, "he gave me your card."

The lady was getting me angry and pushing me into my adversary gear.

"How do you know who owns the property?" I cross examined her.

"I read the will," she answered.

"How do you interpret the will?" I pushed on.

"Nathan White, the son-in-law, was disinherited. The second will canceled the first will. Ms. Smith owns the land." She proudly showed off her legal talents.

"Did you tell all this to Ms. Smith and explain the meaning of all the terms to her?" I summarized what she was implying.

"Yes," she responded.

"Well Ma'am, I am going to have to report you to the Real Estate

Commission and the Unauthorized Practice of Law Committee of the State Bar of Texas for practicing law without a license. What's your full name and broker's license number?"

She hung up, pulled her sign off the property, and was never heard from again—by anyone I know. I did not turn her in. I'm not sure non-lawyers shouldn't be allowed to read wills, but I am sure I wanted to attack this self-righteous monster, who had abused me on the telephone, so I used my union power on her.

Was I delivered from the likes of this case? Not hardly. A few days later, a big, mean, black woman, heavy, tall and partly mustached, came pounding into my office. If Mr. White stormed in, she hurricaned in. "Why, are you interfering with my probate affairs?" she bellowed.

"I wasn't," I replied. I explained my total non-involvement and non-interest. She wouldn't buy it. She tossed a bunch of papers on my desk and with an arch of her powerful shoulders, indicated I should review them to be convinced. I was afraid not to and quite frankly, more than a little curious. I sped through about 40 papers, wills, probate forms, a title report, a police report on the death of Raymond Cash, a hospital report. A lot of interesting facts.

Raymond Cash, father of Nathan White's deceased wife (White had since re-married, the cause of his first wife's death was not indicated), had left his estate to his only living heir, James White, Nathan White's son.

Nathan White was named as the executor. Cash had been shot by his son-in-law with a shotgun and rushed to the hospital. The blind Cash and his mistress Holman, prior to his death, had gone to a will probate specialist, Frank Dobler, and executed a new Cash will, leaving out the Whites entirely.

Still, could this blind, sick, elderly man have been coerced into signing the second will? God only knows—well, God and maybe Cash and maybe many others—but the case still was weak. Throwing out wills is an uphill battle. Not one lawyer in a hundred has successfully thrown out a properly executed will in his or her career. It didn't matter. Why was I being compelled to get involved in this case? I didn't even represent Mr. White.

"Ms. Smith, I am going to have to ask you to leave. If you don't leave, I'll call the police. I do not, nor will I in the future, represent Mr. White. You've gotten me mixed up with someone else. Please spread the word." I thought that ended it. I was wrong.

Ms. Smith pulled a card out of her purse and slammed it down on my desk. "Oh, no you don't, lawyer Minns. I got your card, and where do you think I got it from?" I waited for the familiar answer—White's fingerprints were on the mauled, dirty evidence of my employment.

"Nathan gave me that card," she smirked. "And, who do you think gave it to him?" she ranted.

"Not I" said I, but it was too little, too late. She marched out with her papers and threatened to trounce me in court. She didn't believe me.

It was a few weeks later that probate expert Dobler called. He threatened to teach me a little law—he would ultimately perform on this threat, but not strictly according to the implications of his predictions—and to report me to the bar. I was doing a lot of things unethically, he said, but he would not spell them out to me.

Again, as if anyone would believe me, I told him that I did not represent Mr. White and had no intentions of doing so. Did he accept that?

"Young man, don't try that with me," Dobler admonished. "You are already in this over your head. In fact, you have only two weeks left to file a will contest even if you wanted to, the two-year statute of limitations will have passed. For the sake of your career and reputation, I strongly recommend against filing anything."

My head buzzed. Will contest?...Never heard of it. Two weeks left. Should I?...No.

"I can assure you, Mr. Dobler," for the last time, "I do not represent Mr. White."

"Son," he rebutted, "Do you know what I have in my hand right now?" I could guess, but preferred not to.

"No sir," I responded.

"Your very own business card. And do you know how I obtained it?"

"No, Sir."

"From your client, Mr. White."

Was I ready to accept mandatory White "slave labor?" No.

"Mr. Dobler," I fought for the last time, "White stole those cards. His use of them is unauthorized. I do not represent him."

A few days later, Mr. White "rained" in and reminded me that my partner had told him we only had a week left to file suit. He agreed if I would take the case, he would stop issuing my cards.

Joe and I rushed the petition through, pulling out all stops. Calling favors and purchasing tickets to the constables' barbecue—we got the papers served on the last possible day. Dobler, the will expert, sneered. He would not offer a dime to settle. The case, he surmised, was not even worth a small harassment fee. We would go to trial in two more years!

While preparing for trial, I tried to figure out why my client had shot his deceased father-in-law. I told White that if he didn't have a pretty good reason for having done so, he could kiss this case good-by.

White had a reason. His blind, father-in-law's mistress was trying to kill the elderly man. White had been trying to save Cash's life. Armed with his shotgun, at a risk to his own personal life, White attempted to enter the house to rescue his father-in-law. The evil mistress shoved the elderly man in front of the round of fire and he caught the shotgun blasts. At that point, not even thinking about his own safety, White rushed into the house and instructed people to call an ambulance to send the poor man to the hospital.

Apparently, they did so because Cash was hospitalized. His subsequent death may not have been directly caused by the shooting, but it certainly did nothing to improve his health.

I still was not certain whether or not we had a real good case. I later learned that my client had been charged with unlawful possession of firearms and had been convicted. The charge arose out of the Cash shooting incident. At the time, I hadn't thought to look it up.

The probate specialist, apparently knowing nothing about criminal law, hadn't thought to investigate it either. Knowing nothing about personal injuries, he made no investigation about the cause of Cash's death or about the deceased man's blindness and the cause of it. He did not inquire about the facts of the situation. So, we went to a jury trial without some facts. Actually you never have all the facts. There is always something critical left to find or learn, but you hope to have most of the critical facts.

I told the prospective jurors the case was all about this poor boy being cheated out of his inheritance. We all know that the natural recipients of your bounty would be your child or grandchild and not your mistress and not a sister whom you haven't seen in 25 years.

I asked the people in the audience if there was anybody there who had been cheated out of a will themselves. A sweet, 60-year-old Baptist, black woman stood up and answered, "I have. I was cheated." In *voir dire*, in a situation like this when you expect you have little chance to win, you take risks. I took a substantial risk. So I thought I would poison the well a little, and I asked her a question which she had no right to answer affirmatively, but asked anyway, "Were you cheated in the same way that this poor boy was cheated?" She answered, "Yes, that's exactly how I was cheated, and I believe that I was put here for a reason, to stop that from happening again." At this point, my favorable, potential juror had gone a little bit too far.

I was afraid she would be stricken for cause (taken off without forcing either side to use up a strike), so I asked her another question trying to mitigate her extreme statement so that my opponent would have to use a strike up on her. I said to her, "The judge will ask you to be fair and consider all of the evidence. If I fail to put on adequate evidence to prove my point, will you be able to listen unbiasedly, and come to a fair decision, even though this was a bad will and should be thrown out. Will you be able to consider all of the evidence?" Her answer: "No." We looked over at the probate expert who just sat there like he was in another world. Perhaps he had a hearing problem and had his hearing aid on "low." He was altogether uninterested in the *voir dire* questions and the examinations of prospective jurors.

We had already tried to negotiate a settlement with Mr. Probate Expert. He had turned down the offers, splitting the estate 50-50. He then turned down the offer splitting it 75-25 and finally, although my client was hard to convince, we offered a 90-10 split—that meant my client would take ten percent and the rest would go to the other people and the challenge of the second will would be over. No dice.

The great probate specialist was determined to teach us a lesson in law, and in fact, he did. Against my will we were about to play "bet the Cash estate."

The trial itself is worthy of a great deal more space than it is being given here, but I'll make a long story short for this book, and save the longer version.

Mr. Probate Expert did not ask the court to strike this woman for cause. Mr. Probate Expert did not strike her with one of his three strikes—in this probate court there were six jurors and each side got three strikes without the necessity of giving any reason—and she ended up on the jury.

I was so shocked that I was trying to figure out whether I had her mixed up with another woman, but no. My partner's file showed the same thing—our righteous bad-will-hater was on the jury. That woman became the foreperson of the jury. The will was thrown out.

When we got to trial the only witnesses he put on the stand were an elderly woman whose testimony was that she was friendly with the deceased Mr. Cash and was a suitable candidate for his inheritance, a banker who knew nothing about the case, and the deceased's brother, who received a bequest only under the second will.

Dobler, who wrote the will and notarized it, also attempted to testify.

We characterized this second will as unnatural because it cut out the grandson. We referred to it as the Dobler Will.

The estate had formerly included a lot of personal property in it: furniture, jewelry and cash, all of which had already been stolen from the estate. Only the real estate remained—a house on a half-acre of land located just off the freeway, having a fair market value of about $25,000. This was preserved, since it could not be stolen. Title had to be determined so that the house could be placed in the hands of the executor of the estate; he could sell it and, eventually, some of the proceeds would be used for the payment of our fee.

True to his words, the probate specialist had taught me a lot about law. He taught me how disastrous it is for an attorney who knows nothing about trying a case before a jury, to attempt a jury trial!

Most lawyers don't try cases and wouldn't know how if they were forced to. This is unfortunate. Every lawyer should try at least two or three cases so that he has some idea about the effect of what he does for a living, if it ends up in court.

Since almost everything a lawyer does is done on a presumption that it could end up in court, the absolute lack of any trial-related background is a distinct disadvantage to a lawyer.

Mr. Probate Expert didn't know anything about personal injuries, so he didn't examine the deceased's medical records. Because of his unfamiliarity with criminal law, it didn't occur to him to check my client's criminal record. Thus, he was not competent to prepare his case. He was not competent to support the will that he had originally drawn up. His knowledge on real estate was very limited. He had messed up the title to the real estate and had failed to get it sold out of our hands prior to the trial itself. He had been intractable in his negotiating posture, and had failed to realize that no matter what the case is, a 90 percent settlement is worth considering strongly. He should have taken that settlement offer.

If I were in Dobler's situation, I would have considered a 90 percent settlement offer acceptable, because as every lawyer who has been practicing litigation for more than three hours will tell you, anything is possible in a court of law.

In all probability, had the jury seen evidence that Nathan White had

"Every lawyer should try at least two or three cases so that he has some idea about the effect of what he does for a living, if it ends up in court."

pled guilty to a crime which was connected with the shooting of the decedent, they would have come to a different decision.

At least there would have been a five-to-one decision. I don't think anyone could have succeeded in getting the foreperson of the jury, our conscientious bad will hater, to vote against us under any circumstances. Mr. Dobler certainly had taught me some valuable lessons on how not to proceed.

Perhaps he learned something himself.

E. SOME SOLUTIONS

Probate laws are improving and getting a little simpler in many states, but like many areas of law, it's too little too late. Many states require an attachment to the will called a self proving affidavit. You and your witnesses sign the will, then sign again on the affidavit before a notary swearing basically the other signatures belong to who they say they do.

Many times, even with lawyers handling the proceeding, only the back sheet is signed. The document, then, does not constitute a valid will. If it's clearly the intention of the deceased and he made a clearly understandable mistake, isn't the law playing a silly game? In other words, as Dickens said, "Isn't the law an ass?"

For the standard will, "mutually husband to wife and back again, if both die, estate shared by children," a simple one-page form should be legislated with a few blanks and an option to use it. The clear intent of the deceased should control. Signing twice is ridiculous! Whoever decided that was nuts.

Probate without a will could also be improved. Who would rather leave half their community estate to a mother-in-law, instead of children from a prior marriage. Under some state guidelines, without a will it could happen.

Uncontested probate matters could be handled by mail on forms. Notaries could handle simple wills. The labor unions would of course raise the courtroom roofs. What about mistakes?

The answer: The courtrooms are full of mistakes anyway.

> *"Probate laws are improving and getting a little simpler in many states, but like many areas of law, it's too little too late."*

CHAPTER XXX

CONCLUSIONS AND OBSERVATIONS

*"The supreme authority in the
United States of America
is the individual soverign citizen."*

As Joy—one of the typists from outside my office staff, who worked on the original manuscript—was transcribing my tapes, from time to time she would laugh a little, and occasionally she would get downright mad. She often shared her impressions with me. As we were near the completion of the first rough draft of this manuscript, she approached me with the comment, "You're just making us angry; why aren't you giving us some solutions?" Several others read the draft who echoed her comment.

I could say, "give me a break." A lot of people spend thousands of dollars everyday to get a lot less information than you can get for very little in this book.

I could say that there are no solutions and leave it at that.

That wouldn't be true.

The truth is that there are some solutions. They are all difficult. They are all long shots. However, there are some interim solutions which are nearly sure shots.

NUMBER ONE: SOVEREIGN CITIZENS

As American citizens with a proud heritage, we can once again do what our parents and fore-parents have done repeatedly throughout our history: Challenge authority! The number one solution is to challenge government authority and reclaim our own! The supreme authority in the United States of America is the individual sovereign citizen. Government has attempted, as Thomas Jefferson and others repeatedly warned us it would, to take over that sovereignty. Too much respect for government is dangerous. I have a relative whose German passport and his parent's German passports were revoked in 1938 by the government. He left alone, sneaking out without a passport and now he runs a large business in Brazil. His parents kept trying to get passports—They were exterminated.

NUMBER TWO: THE JURY SYSTEM

If you are on a jury, you can effectively take back some of your rightful, constitutional authority. You can stand up to judges and other jurors who refuse to allow you to exercise your constitutional authorities and responsibilities. You can make known to your legislators, friends, and neighbors that you believe in the integrity of the jury system and that you want it strengthened rather than weakened. Legislators can endow juries with more power. Judges can voluntarily assume less power.

NUMBER THREE: INCOME TAX

A large number of patriotic citizens have been branded as criminals because of their various different methods of opposing federal income taxes. There will always be significant government force and power on our backs as long as our daily lives are monitored through the income tax reporting requirements.

There are those who think American society would be improved if we taxed all the millionaires and billionaires of the country 100 percent or everyone making more than $50,000 a year, all money over that amount, and distributed these funds equally among the population.

Proponents of such measures fail to understand that if you usurped the fortunes of every wealthy person in the United States of America and spread the money out, you'd be able to give every man, woman and child $10 or $15, and that would be the end of it. The money would be completely and fully disbursed without having done any significant good. Some people who had inherited wealth and who are intrinsically lazy, failing to improve their lot or do something of value, or who had stolen wealth would be disenfranchised. No one would lament their loss, except possibly people who work for the purpose of enriching their heirs.

However, the large majority of so-called wealthy people operate businesses which employ salaried workers. Owners of small to medium-sized companies, with from 5 to 200 employees, employ over half of the people in this country. These businessmen would also be disenfranchised

---

"You can make known to your legislators, friends, and neighbors that you believe in the integrity of the jury system and that you want it strengthened rather than weakened."

---

through financial ruin. Many members of the leisurely rich class promote much of our art, symphonies and important charities. They would be gone. Government would be asked to replace them. Massive unemployment would result across the country.

The real solution, is not to tax work at all. Just follow in the footsteps of our proud, strong fore-parents and eliminate income taxation altogether. This country grew rich and powerful on capitalism, and can do so again! Vote against income taxes. Speak up against them.

An income tax can never be fair. We need national sales or value added taxes.

NUMBER FOUR: PRIVACY

The new tax law and immigration act all combine to make the social security number a national identification number. To collect thousands and millions of new facts to put into new modern big-brother computers. Campaign against this. Government is collecting too much personal information on us.

NUMBER FIVE: CHILDREN'S EDUCATION:

Educate your children. Read to them. Talk to them. Encourage honesty and integrity. Encourage free thought and rebellion. Consider options and supplements to public education. If you have no options get involved with your local schools. The move toward more and more federally controlled education like day care and other national issues is a move toward more government control.

NUMBER SIX: SIMPLIFY THE LAW:

Study the law. Support reform to make it more comprehensible. Ask lots of questions. The law is unnecessarily complicated. Latin is beautiful and has an important role in the study of law, and history, and poetry, and languages, but it does not belong in statutes.

"The real solution, is not to tax work at all. Just follow in the footsteps of our proud, strong fore-parents and eliminate income taxation altogether. This country grew rich and powerful on capitalism, and can do so again!"

Many laws are drafted incoherently. Perhaps a good high school English teacher could be hired by each state legislative body and Congress to re-draft laws so they could be easily understood and unambiguous.

Probate, and divorce are unnecessary headaches. The law needs to be simplified and the role of lawyers severely limited. Wills can be modified and forms cleared to cover 90% of the people who want them. Divorces can be simplified, and lawyer involvment can be the exception rather than the norm. Routine divorces and probate of estates can be handled by facsimile machines over the phone and be made instantaneously effective, filling out a form and having a clerk file it.

NUMBER SEVEN: BREAK UP LEGAL MONOPOLIES:

Non-lawyers need to be given a greater role; paralegals, legal assistants and others need to be given the option of some type of adjunct membership to the union. A lot of incompetent, sometimes crazy, often criminal elements now compete with union member attorneys —as well as some very good people.

As a patron of lost causes I have spoken on the same platform with many. Some of the craziest, least competent were lawyers. Some of the best were not. People turn to them because of the union's bad reputation and monopoly price structures. If they were allowed to compete with or work with union members, the bar's stated reason for existence, the regulation of legal practitioners for the protection of the public would more likely be fulfilled.

Notaries and real estate brokers commit crimes, but they are also regulated. If we truly want regulation for the benefit of the public, we have to honor the laws of supply and demand, acknowledge the large underground source of legal assistance and give it access to the courts at the cost of supervision.

Lysander Spooner's rule of common sense should be adapted by the twentieth century American courts and legislatures.

If a law doesn't make any sense, it should be outlawed.

"If we truly want regulation for the benefit of the public, we have to honor the laws of supply and demand, acknowledge the large underground source of legal assistance and give it access to the courts at the cost of supervision."

ABOUT THE AUTHOR
1. Michael Louis Minns is duly licensed to practice
before the following courts:

Supreme Court of the United States of America *(Washington, D.C.)* 11/10/80

U.S. Court of Appeals for the Federal Circuit *(Washington, D.C.)* 10/01/82

U.S. Court of Appeals for the Third Circuit *(Philadelphia, Pennsylvania)* 11/19/84

U.S. Court of Appeals for the Fourth Circuit *(Richmond, Virginia)* 06/26/84

U.S. Court of Appeals for the Fifth Circuit *(New Orleans, Louisiana)* 07/24/78

U.S. Court of Appeals for the Sixth Circuit *(Cincinnati, Ohio)* 06/15/84

U.S. Court of Appeals for the Seventh Circuit *(Chicago, Illinois)* 02/24/84

U.S. Court of Appeals for the Eighth Circuit *(St. Louis, Missouri)* 10/28/83

U.S. Court of Appeals for the Ninth Circuit *(San Francisco, California)* 08/21/79

U.S. Court of Appeals for the Tenth Circuit *(Denver, Colorado)* 07/24/84

U.S. Court of Appeals for the Eleventh Circuit *(Atlanta, Georgia)* 12/08/83

U.S. Court of Appeals for the District of Columbia *(Washington, D.C.)* 02/07/85

U.S. District Court—Southern District of Texas 10/07/77

U.S. District Court—Northern District of Texas 09/21/83

U.S. District Court—Eastern District of Texas 10/02/84

U.S. District Court—Western District of Texas 08/24/87

U.S. District Court—Eastern and Western District of Arkansas 10/03/83

U.S. District Court—Northern District of New York 02/05/88

Supreme Court of Texas 06/10/77

U.S. Court of International Trade *(New York, New York)* 11/01/80

U.S. Court of Claims *(Washington, D.C.)* 09/26/77

U.S. Tax Court *(Washington, D.C.)* 08/25/77

U.S. Court of Military Appeals *(Washington, D.C.)* 04/12/85

U.S. District Court of the District of Hawaii *(Honolulu, Hawaii)* 04/30/87

U.S.District court of the District of Arizona *(Phoenix, Arizona)* 3/21/90

CHAPTER I. INTRODUCTION AND BACKGROUND

1. Constitution of the United States

We the People of the United States, in Order to form a more perfect union, establish Justice, insure domestic Tranquility, provide for the common defence, promote the general Welfare, and secure the Blessings of Liberty to ourselves and our Posterity, do ordain and establish this Constitution for the United States of America.

ARTICLE I.

SECTION 1. All legislative Powers herein granted shall be vested in a Congress of the United States, which shall consist of a Senate and House of Representatives.

SECTION 2. The House of Representatives shall be composed of Members chosen every second Year by the People of the several States, and the Electors in each State shall have the Qualifications requisite for Electors of the most numerous Branch of the State Legislature.

No person shall be a Representative who shall not have attained to the Age of twenty five Years, and been seven Years as a Citizen of the United States, and who shall not, when elected, be an Inhabitant of that State in which he shall be chosen.

Representatives and direct Taxes shall be apportioned among the several States which may be included within this Union, according to their respective Numbers, which shall be determined by adding to the whole Number of free Persons, including those bound to Service for a Term of Years, and excluding Indians not taxed, three fifths of all other Persons. The actual Enumeration shall be made within three Years after the first Meeting of the Congress of the United States, and within every subsequent Term of ten Years, in such Manner as they shall by Law direct. The Number of Representatives shall not exceed one for every thirty Thousand, but each State shall have at Least one Representative; and until such enumeration shall be made, the State of New Hampshire shall be entitled to chuse three, Massachusetts eight, Rhode-Island and Providence Plantations one, Connecticut five, New-York six, New Jersey four, Pennsylvania eight, Delaware one, Maryland six, Virginia ten, North Carolina five, South Carolina five, and Georgia three.

When vacancies happen in the Representation from any State, the Executive Authority thereof shall issue Writs of Election to fill such Vacancies.

The House of Representatives shall chuse their Speaker and other Officers; and shall have the sole Power of Impeachment.

SECTION 3. The Senate of the United States shall be composed of two Senators from each State, [chosen by the Legislature thereof,] for six Years,; and each Senator shall have one Vote.

Immediately after they shall be assembled in Consequence of the first Election, they shall be divided as equally as may be into three Classes. The Seats of the Senators of the first Class shall be vacated Expiration of the second Year, of the second Class at the Expiration of the fourth Year, and of the third Class at the Expiration of the sixth Year, so that one third may be chosen every second Year; [and if Vacancies happen by Resignation, or otherwise, during the Recess of the Legislature of any State, the Executive thereof may make temporary Appointments until the next Meeting of the Legislature, which shall then fill such Vacancies].

No Person shall be a Senator who shall not have attained to the Age of thirty Years, and been nine Years a Citizen of the United States, and who shall not, when elected, be an Inhabitant of that State for which he shall be chosen.

The Vice President of the United States shall be President of the Senate, but shall have no Vote, unless they be equally divided.

The Senate shall chuse their other Officers, and also a President pro tempore, in the Absence of the Vice President, or when he shall exercise the Office of President of the United States.

The Senate shall have the sole Power to try all Impeachments. When sitting for that Purpose, they shall be on Oath or Affirmation. When the President of the United States is tried, the Chief Justice shall preside: And no Person shall be convicted without the Concurrence of two thirds of the Members present.

Judgment in Cases of Impeachment shall not extend further than to removal from Office, and disqualification to hold and enjoy any Office of honor, Trust or Profit under the

United States: but the Party convicted shall nevertheless be liable and subject to Indictment, Trial, Judgment and Punishment, according to Law.

SECTION 4. The Times, Places and Manner of holding Elections for Senators and Representatives, shall be prescribed in each State by the Legislature thereof; but the Congress may at any time by Law make or alter such Regulations, except as to the Places of chusing Senators.

The Congress shall assemble at least once in every Year, and such Meeting shall [be on the first Monday in December,] unless they shall by Law appoint a different Day.

SECTION 5. Each House shall be the Judge of the Elections, Returns and Qualifications of its own Members, and a Majority of each shall constitute a Quorum to do Business; but a smaller Number may adjourn from day to day, and may be authorized to compel the Attendance of absent Members, in such Manner, and under such Penalties as each House may provide.

Each House may determine the Rules of its Proceedings, punish its Members for disorderly Behaviour, and, with the Concurrence of two thirds, expel a Member.

Each House shall keep a Journal of its Proceedings, and from time to time publish the same, excepting such Parts as may in their Judgment require Secrecy; and the Yeas and Nays of the Members of either House on any question shall, at the Desire of one fifth of those Present, be entered on the Journal.

Neither House, during the Session of Congress, shall, without the Consent of the other, adjourn for more than three days, nor to any other Place than that in which the two Houses shall be sitting.

SECTION. 6. The Senators and Representatives shall receive a Compensation for their Services, to be ascertained by Law, and paid out of the Treasury of the United States. They shall in all Cases, except Treason, Felony and Breach of the Peace, be privileged from Arrest during their Attendance at the Session of their respective Houses, and in going to and returning from the same; and for any Speech or Debate in either House, they shall not be questioned in any other Place.

No Senator or Representative shall, during the Time for which he was elected, be appointed to any civil Office under the Authority of the United States, which shall have been created, or the Emoluments whereof shall have been increased during such time; and no Person holding any Office under the United States, shall be a Member of either House during his Continuance in Office.

SECTION. 7. All Bills for raising Revenue shall originate in the House of Representatives; but the Senate may propose or concur with Amendments as on other Bills.

Every Bill which shall have passed the House of Representatives and the Senate, shall, before it become a Law, be presented to the President of the United States; If he approve he shall sign it, but if not he shall return it, with his Objections to that House in which it shall have originated, who shall enter the Objections at large on their Journal, and proceed to reconsider it. If after such Reconsideration two thirds of that House shall agree to pass the Bill, it shall be sent, together with the Objections, to the other House, by which it shall likewise be reconsidered, and if approved by two thirds of that House, it shall become a Law. But in all such Cases the Votes of both Houses shall be determined by yeas and Nays, and the Names of the Persons voting for and against the Bill shall be entered on the Journal of each House respectively. If any Bill shall not be returned by the President within ten Days (Sundays excepted) after it shall have been presented to him, the Same shall be a Law, in like Manner as if he had signed it, unless the Congress by their Adjournment prevent its Return, in which Case it shall not be a Law.

Every Order, Resolution, or Vote to which the Concurrence of the Senate and House of Representatives may be necessary (except on a question of Adjournment) shall be presented to the President of the United States; and before the Same shall take Effect, shall be approved by him, or being disapproved by him, shall be repassed by two third of the Senate and House of Representatives, according to the Rules and Limitations prescribed in the Case of a Bill.

SECTION. 8. The Congress shall have Power To lay and collect Taxes, Duties, Imposts and Excises, to pay the Debts and provide for the common Defence and general Welfare of the United States; but all Duties, Imposts and excises shall be uniform throughout the

United States;

To borrow Money on the credit of the United States;

To regulate Commerce with foreign Nations, and among the several States, and with the Indian Tribes;

To establish an uniform Rule of Naturalization, and uniform Laws on the subject of Bankruptcies throughout the United States;

To coin Money, regulate the Value thereof, and of foreign Coin, and fix the Standard of Weights and Measures;

To provide for the Punishment of counterfeiting the Securities and current Coin of the United States;

To establish Post Offices and post Roads;

To promote the Progress of Science and useful Arts, by securing for limited Times to Authors and Inventors the exclusive Right to their respective Writings and Discoveries;

To constitute Tribunals inferior to the supreme Court;

To define and punish Piracies and Felonies committed on the high Seas, and Offences against the Law of Nations;

To declare War, grant Letters of Marque and Reprisal, and make Rules concerning Captures on Land and Water;

To raise and support Armies, but no Appropriation of Money to that Use shall be for a longer Terms than two Years;

To provide and maintain a Navy;

To make Rules for the Government and Regulation of the land and naval Forces;

To provide for calling forth the Militia to execute the Laws of the Union, suppress Insurrections and repel Invasions;

To provide for organizing, arming, and disciplining, the Militia, and for governing such Part of them as may be employed in the Service of the United States, reserving to the States respectively, the Appointment of the Officers, and the Authority of training the Militia according to the discipline prescribed by Congress;

To exercise exclusive Legislation in all Cases whatsoever, over such District (not exceeding ten Miles square) as may, by Cession of particular States, and the Acceptance of Congress, become the Seat of the Government of the United States, and to exercise like Authority over all Places purchased by the Consent of the Legislature of the State in which the Same shall be, for the Erection of Forts, Magazines, Arsenals, dock-Yards, and other needful Buildings;—And

To make all Laws which shall be necessary and proper for carrying into Execution the foregoing Powers, and all other Powers vested by this Constitution in the Government of the United States, or in any Department or Officer thereof.

SECTION. 9. The Migration or Importation of such Persons as any of the States now existing shall think proper to admit, shall not be prohibited by the Congress prior to the Year one thousand eight hundred and eight, but a Tax or duty may be imposed on such Importation, not exceeding ten dollars for each Person.

The Privilege of the Writ of Habeas Corpus shall not be suspended, unless when in Cases of Rebellion or Invasion the public Safety may require it.

No Bill of Attainder or ex post facto Law shall be passed.

No Capitation, or other direct, Tax shall be laid, unless in Proportion to the Census or Enumeration herein before directed to be taken.

No Tax or Duty shall be laid on Articles exported from any State.

No Preference shall be given by any Regulation of Commerce or Revenue to the Ports of one State over those of another: nor shall Vessels bound to, or from, one State, be obliged to enter, clear, or pay Duties in another.

No Money shall be drawn from the Treasury, but in Consequence of Appropriations made by Law; and a regular Statement and Account of the Receipts and Expenditures of all public Money shall be published from time to time.

No Title of Nobility shall be granted by the United States: And no Person holding any Office of Profit or Trust under them, shall, without the Consent of the Congress, accept of any present, Emolument, Office, or Title, of any kind whatever, from any King, Prince, or foreign State.

SECTION. 10. No State shall enter into any Treaty, Alliance, or Confederation; grant Letters of Marque and Reprisal; coin Money; emit Bills of Credit; make any Thing but gold and silver Coin a Tender in Payment of Debts; pass any Bill of Attainder, ex post facto Law, or Law impairing the Obligation of Contracts, or grant any Title of Nobility.

No State shall, without the Consent of the Congress, lay any Imposts or Duties on Imports or Exports, except what may be absolutely necessary for executing it's inspection Laws: and the net Produce of all Duties and Imposts, laid by any State on Imports or Exports, shall be for the Use of the Treasury of the United States; and all such Laws shall be subject to the Revision and Controul of the Congress.

No State shall, without the Consent of Congress, lay any Duty of Tonnage, keep Troops, or Ships of War in time of Peace, enter into any Agreement or Compact with another State, or with a foreign Power, or engage in War, unless actually invaded, or in such imminent Danger as will not admit of delay.

ARTICLE II.

SECTION. 1. The executive Power shall be vested in a President of the United States of America. He shall hold his Office during the Term of four Years, and, together with the Vice President, chosen for the same Term, be elected, as follows

Each State shall appoint, in such Manner as the Legislature thereof may direct, a Number of Electors, equal to the whole Number of Senators and Representatives to which the State may be entitled in the Congress: but no Senator or Representative, or Person holding an Office of Trust or Profit under the United States, shall be appointed an Elector.

The Electors shall meet in their respective States, and vote by Ballot for two Persons, of whom one at least shall not be an Inhabitant of the same State with themselves. And they shall make a List of all the Persons voted for, and of the Number of Votes for each; which List they shall sign and certify, and transmit sealed to the Seat of the Government of the United States, directed to the President of the Senate. The President of the Senate shall, in the Presence of the Senate and House of Representatives, open all the Certificates, and the Votes shall then be counted. The Person having the greatest Number of Votes shall be the President, if such Number be a Majority of the whole Number of Electors appointed; and if there be more than one who have such Majority, and have an equal Number of Votes, then the House of Representatives shall immediately chuse by Ballot one of them for President; and if no Person have a Majority, then from the five highest on the List the said House shall in like Manner chuse the President. But in chusing the President, the Votes shall be taken by States, the Representation from each State having one Vote; A quorum for this Purpose shall consist of a Member or Members from two thirds of the States, and a Majority of all the States shall be necessary to a Choice. In every Case, after the Choice of the President, the Person having the greatest Number of Votes of the Electors shall be the Vice President. But if there should remain two or more who have equal Votes, the Senate shall chuse from them by Ballot the Vice President.

The Congress may determine the Time of chusing the Electors, and the Day on which they shall give their votes; which Day shall be the same throughout the United States.

No Person except a natural born Citizen, or a Citizen of the United States, at the time of the Adoption of this Constitution, shall be eligible to the Office of President; neither shall any Person be eligible to that Office who shall not have attained to the Age of thirty five Years, and been fourteen Years a Resident within the United States.

In Case of the Removal of the President from Office, or of his Death, Resignation, or Inability to discharge the Powers and Duties of the said Office, the Same shall devolve on the Vice President, and the Congress may by Law provide for the Case of Removal, Death, Resignation or Inability, both of the President and vice President, declaring what Officer shall then act as President, and such Officer shall act accordingly, until the Disability be removed, or a President shall be elected.

The President shall, at stated Times, receive for his Services, a Compensation, which shall neither be increased nor diminished during the Period for which he shall have been elected, and he shall not receive within that Period any other Emolument from the United States, or any of them.

Before he enter on the Execution of his Office, he shall take the following Oath or Affirmation:—"I do solemnly swear (or affirm) that I will faithfully execute the Office of

President of the United States, and will to the best of my Ability, preserve, protect and defend the Constitution of the United States."

SECTION. 2. The President shall be Commander in Chief of the Army and Navy of the United States, and of the Militia of the several States, when called into the actual Service of the United States; he may require the Opinion, in writing, of the principal Officer in each of the executive Departments, upon any Subject relating to the Duties of their respective Offices, and he shall have Power to grant Reprieves and Pardons for Offences against the United States, except in Cases of Impeachment.

He shall have Power, by and with the Advice and Consent of the Senate, to make Treaties, provided two thirds of the Senators present concur; and he shall nominate, and by and with the Advice and Consent of the Senate, shall appoint Ambassadors, other public Ministers and Consuls, Judges of the supreme Court, and all other Officers of the United States, whose Appointments are not herein otherwise provided for, and which shall be established by Law: but the Congress may by Law vest the Appointment of such inferior Officers, as they think proper, in the President alone, in the Courts of Law, or in the Heads of Departments.

The President shall have Power to fill up all Vacancies that may happen during the Recess of the Senate, by granting commissions which shall expire at the End of their next Session.

SECTION. 3. He shall from time to time give to the Congress Information of the State of the Union, and recommend to their Consideration such Measures as he shall judge necessary and expedient; he may, on extraordinary Occasions, convene both Houses, or either of them, and in Case of Disagreement between them, with Respect to the Time of Adjournment, he may adjourn them to such Time as he shall think proper; he shall receive Ambassadors and other public Ministers; he shall take Care that the Laws be faithfully executed, and shall Commission all the Officers of the United States.

SECTION. 4. The President, Vice President and all civil Officers of the United States, shall be removed from Office on Impeachment for, and Conviction of, Treason, Bribery, or other high Crimes and Misdemeanors.

ARTICLE. III.

SECTION. 1. The judicial Power of the United States, shall be vested in one supreme Court, and in such inferior courts as the Congress may from time to time ordain and establish. The Judges, both of the supreme and inferior Courts, shall hold their Offices during good Behaviour, and shall, at stated Times, receive for their Services, a Compensation, which shall not be diminished during their Continuance in Office.

SECTION. 2. The judicial Power shall extend to all Cases, in Law and Equity, arising under this Constitution, the Laws of the United States, and Treaties made, or which shall be made, under their Authority;—to all Cases affecting Ambassadors, other public Ministers and Consuls;—to all Cases of admiralty and maritime Jurisdiction;—to Controversies to which the United States shall be a Party;—to Controversies between two or more States;—between a State and Citizens of another State;—between Citizens of different States,—between Citizens of the same State claiming Lands under Grants of different States, and between a State, or the Citizens thereof, and foreign States, Citizens or Subjects.

In all Cases affecting Ambassadors, other public Ministers and Consuls, and those in which a State shall be Party, the supreme Court shall have original Jurisdiction. In all the other Cases before mentioned, the supreme Court shall have appellate Jurisdiction, both as to Law and Fact, with such Exceptions, and under such Regulations as the Congress shall make.

The Trial of all Crimes, except in Cases of Impeachment, shall be by Jury; and such Trial shall be held in the State where the said Crimes shall have been committed; but when not committed within any State, the Trial shall be at such Place or Places as the Congress may by Law have directed.

SECTION. 3. Treason against the United States, shall consist only in levying War against them, or in adhering to their Enemies, giving them Aid and Comfort. No person shall be convicted of Treason unless on the Testimony of two Witnesses to the same overt Act, or on Confession in open Court.

The Congress shall have Power to declare the Punishment of Treason, but no Attainder of Treason shall work Corruption of Blood, or Forfeiture except during the Life of the Person attainted.

ARTICLE. IV.

SECTION. 1. Full Faith and Credit shall be given in each State to the public Acts, Records, and judicial Proceedings of every other State. And the Congress may by general Laws prescribe the Manner in which such Acts, Records, and judicial Proceedings of every other State. And the Congress may by general Laws prescribe the Manner in which such Acts, Records and Proceedings shall be proved, and the Effect thereof.

SECTION. 2. The Citizens of each State shall be entitled to all Privileges and Immunities of Citizens in the several States.

A Person charged in any State with Treason, Felony, or other Crime, who shall flee from Justice, and be found in another State, shall on Demand of the executive Authority of the State from which he fled, be delivered up, to be removed to the State having Jurisdiction of the Crime.

No Person held to Service or Labour in one State, under the Laws thereof, escaping into another, shall, in Consequence of any Law or Regulation therein, be discharged from such Service or Labour, but shall be delivered up on Claim of the Party to whom such Service or Labour may be due.

SECTION. 3. New States may be admitted by the Congress into this Union; but no new State shall be formed or erected within the Jurisdiction of any other State; nor any State be formed by the Junction of two or more States, or Parts of States, without the Consent of the Legislatures of the States concerned as well as of the Congress.

The Congress shall have Power to dispose of and make all needful Rules and Regulations respecting the Territory or other Property belonging to the United States; and nothing in this Constitution shall be so construed as to Prejudice any Claims of the United States, or of any particular State.

SECTION. 4. The United States shall guarantee to every State in this Union a Republican Form of Government, and shall protect each of them against Invasion; and on Application of the Legislature, or of the Executive (when the Legislature cannot be convened) against domestic Violence.

ARTICLE. V.

The Congress, whenever two thirds of both Houses shall deem it necessary, shall propose Amendments to this Constitution, or, on the Application of the Legislatures of two thirds of the several States, shall call a Convention for proposing Amendments, which, in either Case, shall be valid to all Intents and Purposes, as Part of this Constitution, when ratified by the Legislatures of three fourths of the several States, or by Conventions in three fourths thereof, as the one or the other Mode of Ratification may be proposed by the Congress; Provided [that no Amendment which may be made prior to the Year One thousand eight hundred and eight shall in any Manner affect the first and fourth Clauses in the Ninth Section of the first Article; and] that no State, without its Consent, shall be deprived of its equal Suffrage in the Senate.

ARTICLE. VI.

All Debts contracted and Engagements entered into, before the Adoption of this Constitution, shall be as valid against the United States under this Constitution, as under the Confederation.

This Constitution, and the Laws of the United States which shall be made in Pursuance thereof; and all Treaties made, or which shall be made, under the Authority of the United States, shall be the supreme Law of the Land; and the Judges in every State shall be bound thereby, any Thing in the Constitution or Laws of any State to the Contrary notwithstanding.

The Senators and Representatives before mentioned, and the Members of the several State Legislatures, and all executive and judicial Officers, both of the United States and of the several States, shall be bound by Oath or Affirmation, to support this Constitution; but no religious Test shall ever be required as a Qualification to any Office or public Trust under the United States.

ARTICLE. VII.

The Ratification of the Conventions of nine States, shall be sufficient for the Establishment of this Constitution between the States so ratifying the Same.

DONE in Convention by the Unanimous Consent of the States present the Seventeenth Day of September in the Year of our Lord one thousand seven hundred and Eighty seven and of the Independence of the United States of America the Twelfth IN WITNESS whereof We have hereunto subscribed our Names.

GEO. WASHINGTON Presid. and deputy from Virginia.
[Signed also by the deputies of twelve States.]
New Hampshire. JOHN LANGDON, NICHOLAS GILMAN.
Massachusetts. NATHANIEL GORHAM, RUFUS KING.
Connecticut. WM. SAML. JOHNSON, ROGER SHERMAN.
New York. ALEXANDER HAMILTON
New Jersey. WIL: LIVINGSON, WM. PATERSON, DAVID
BREARLEY, JONA: DAYTON.
Pennsylvania. B FRANKLIN THOMAS MIFFLIN, ROB T. MORRIS,
GEO. CLYMER, THOS. FITZSIMONS, JARED INGERSOLL,
JAMES WILSON, GOUV MORRIS.
Delaware. GEO. READ, GUNNING BEDFORD, jun, JOHN
DICKINSON, RICHARD BASSETT. JACO: BROOM,
Maryland. JAMES MCHENRY, DAN OF ST. THOS. JENIFER,
DAN L. CARROLL.
Virginia JOHN BLAIR—JAMES MADISON JR.
North Carolina. WM. BLOUNT, RICH D. DOBBS SPAIGHT,
HU WILLIAMSON.
South Carolina. J. RUTLEDGE, CHARLES COTESWORTH
PINCKNEY, CHARLES PINCKNEY, PIERCE BUTLER.
Georgia. WILLIAM FEW, ABR BALDWIN.
Attest: WILLIAM JACKSON, Secretary

Ratification was completed on June 21, 1788.

The Constitution was subsequently ratified by Virginia, June 25, 1788; New York, July 26, 1788; North Carolina, November 21, 1789; Rhode Island, May 29, 1790; and Vermont, January 10, 1791.

CONSTITUTION OF THE UNITED STATES OF AMERICA, PROPOSED BY CONGRESS, AND RATIFIED BY THE LEGISLATURES OF THE SEVERAL STATES PURSUANT TO THE FIFTH ARTICLE OF THE ORIGINAL CONSTITUTION

ARTICLE [I]

Congress shall make no law respecting an establishment of religion, or prohibiting the free exercise thereof; or abridging the freedom of speech, or of the press; or the right of the people peaceably to assemble, and to petition the Government for a redress of grievances.

ARTICLE [II]

A well regulated Militia, being necessary to the security of a free State, the right of the people to keep and bear Arms, shall not be infringed.

ARTICLE [III]

No Soldier shall, in time of peace be quartered in any house, without the consent of the Owner, nor in time of war, but in a manner to be prescribed by law.

ARTICLE [IV]

The right of the people to be secure in their persons, houses, papers, and effects, against unreasonable searches and seizures, shall not be violated, and no Warrants shall issue, but upon probable cause, supported by Oath or affirmation, and particularly describing the place to be searched, and the persons or things to be seized.

ARTICLE [V]

No person shall be held to answer for a capital, or otherwise infamous crime, unless on a presentment or indictment of a Grand Jury, except in cases arising in the land or naval forces, or in the Militia, when in actual service in time of War or public danger; not shall any person be subject for the same offence to be twice put in jeopardy of life or limb; nor shall be compelled in any criminal case to be a witness against himself, nor be deprived of life, liberty, or property, without due process of law; nor shall private property be taken for public use without just compensation.

ARTICLE [VI]

In all criminal prosecutions, the accused shall enjoy the right to a speedy and public trial, by an impartial jury of the State and district wherein the crime shall have been committed, which district shall have been previously ascertained by law, and to be informed of the nature and cause of the accusation; to be confronted with the witnesses against him; to have compulsory process for obtaining Witnesses in his favor, and to have the assistance of counsel for his defence.

ARTICLE [VII]

In Suits at common law, where the value in controversy shall exceed twenty dollars, the right of trial by jury shall be preserved, and no fact tried by a jury, shall be otherwise reexamined in any Court of the United States, than according to the rules of the common law.

ARTICLE [VIII]

Excessive bail shall not be required, nor excessive fines imposed, nor cruel and unusual punishments inflicted.

ARTICLE [IX]

The enumeration in the Constitution, of certain rights, shall not be construed to deny or disparage others retained by the people.

ARTICLE [X]

The powers not delegated to the United States by the Constitution, nor prohibited by it to the States, are reserved to the States respectively, or to the people.

ARTICLE [XI]

The Judicial power of the United States shall not be construed to extend to any suit in law or equity, commenced or prosecuted against one of the United States by citizens of another State, or by Citizens or Subjects of any Foreign State.

ARTICLE [XII]

The electors shall meet in their respective states and vote by ballot for President and Vice-President, one of whom, at least, shall not be any inhabitant of the same state with themselves; they shall name in their ballots the person voted for as President, and in distinct ballots the person voted for as Vice-President, and they shall make distinct lists of all persons voted for as President, and of all persons voted for as Vice-President, and of the number of votes for each, which lists they shall sign and certify, and transmit sealed to the seat of the government of the United States, directed to the President of the Senate;—The President of the Senate shall, in the presence of the Senate and House of Representatives, open all the certificates and the votes shall then be counted;—The person having the greatest number of votes for President, shall be the President, if such number be a majority of the whole number of Electors appointed; and if no person have such majority, then from the persons having the highest numbers not exceeding three on the list of those voted for as President, the House of Representatives shall choose immediately, by ballot, the President. But in choosing the President, the votes shall be taken by states, the representation from each state having one vote; a quorum for this purpose shall consist of a member or members from two-thirds of the states, and a majority of all the states shall be necessary to a choice. [And if the House of Representatives shall not choose a President whenever the right of choice shall devolve upon them, before the fourth day of March next following, then the Vice-President shall act as President, as in the case of the death or other constitutional disability of the President.] The person having the greatest number of votes as Vice-President, shall be the Vice-President, if such number be a majority of the whole number of Electors appointed, and if no person have a majority, then from the two highest numbers on the list, the Senate shall choose the Vice-President; a quorum for the purpose shall consist of two-thirds of the whole number of Senators, and a majority of the whole number shall be necessary to a choice. But no person constitutionally ineligible to the office of President shall be eligible to that of Vice-President of the United States.

ARTICLE [XIII]

SECTION 1. Neither slavery nor involuntary servitude, except as a punishment for crime whereof the party shall have been duly convicted shall exist within the United States, or any place subject to their jurisdiction.

SECTION 2. Congress shall have power to enforce this article by appropriate legislation.

ARTICLE [XIV]

SECTION 1. All persons born or naturalized in the United States, and subject to the jurisdiction thereof, are citizens of the United States and of the State wherein they reside. No State shall make or enforce any law which shall abridge the privileges or immunities of citizens of the United States; nor shall any State deprive any person of life, liberty, or property, without due process of law; nor deny to any person within its jurisdiction the equal protection of the laws.

SECTION 2. Representatives shall be apportioned among the several States according to their respective numbers, counting the whole number of persons in each State, excluding Indians not taxed. But when the right to vote at any election for the choice of electors for President and Vice President of the United States, Representatives in Congress, and Executive and Judicial officers of a State, or the members of the Legislature thereof, is denied to any of the male inhabitants of such State, being twenty-one years of age, and citizens of the United States, or in ay way abridged, except for participation in rebellion, or other crime, the basis of representation therein shall be reduced in the proportion which the number of such male citizens shall bear to the whole number of male citizens twenty-one years of age in such State.

SECTION 3. No person shall be a Senator or Representative in Congress, or elector of President and Vice President, or hold any office, civil or military, under the United States, or under any State, who, having previously taken an oath, as a member of Congress, or as an officer of the United States, or as a member of any State legislature, or as an executive or judicial officer of any State, to support the Constitution of the United States, shall have engaged in insurrection or rebellion against he same, or given aid or comfort to the enemies thereof. But Congress may be a vote of two-thirds of each House remove such disability.

SECTION 4. The validity of the public debt of the United States, authorized by law, including debts incurred for payment of pensions and bounties for services in suppressing insurrection or rebellion, shall not be questioned. But neither the United States nor any State shall assume or pay any debt or obligation incurred in aid of insurrection or rebellion against the United States, or any claim for the loss or emancipation of any slave; but all such debts, obligations and claims shall be held illegal and void.

SECTION 5. The Congress shall have power to enforce, by appropriate legislation, the provisions of this article.

ARTICLE [XV]

SECTION 1. The right of citizens of the United States to vote shall not be denied or abridged by the United States or by any State on account of race, color, or previous condition of servitude.

SECTION 2. The Congress shall have power to enforce this article by appropriate legislation.

ARTICLE [XVI]

The Congress shall have power to lay and collect taxes on incomes, from whatever source derived, without apportionment among the several States, and without regard to any census or enumeration.

ARTICLE [XVII]

The Senate of the United States shall be composed of two Senators from each State, elected by the people thereof, for six years; and each Senator shall have one vote. The electors in each State shall have the qualifications requisite for electors of the most numerous branch of the State legislatures.

When vacancies happen in the representation of any State in the Senate, the executive authority of such State shall issue writs of election to fill such vacancies: Provided, That the legislature of any State may empower the executive thereof to make temporary appointments until the people fill the vacancies by election as the legislature may direct.

This amendment shall not be so construed as to affect the election or term of any Senator chosen before it becomes valid as part of the Constitution.

ARTICLE [XVIII]

SECTION 1. After one year from the ratification of this article the manufacture, sale, or transportation of intoxicating liquors within, the importation thereof into, or the exportaion thereof from the United States and all territory subject to the jurisdiction thereof for beverage purposes is hereby prohibited.

SECTION 2. The Congress and the several States shall have concurrent power to enforce this article by appropriate legislation.

SECTION 3. This article shall be inoperative unless it shall have been ratified as an amendment to the Constitution by the legislatures of the several States, as provided in the Constitution, within seven years from the date of the submission hereof to the States by the Congress.]

ARTICLE [XIX]

The right of citizens of the United States to vote shall not be denied or abridged by the United States or by any State on account of sex.

Congress shall have power to enforce this article by appropriate legislation.

ARTICLE [XX]

SECTION 1. The terms of the President and Vice President shall end at noon on the 20th day of January, and the terms of Senators and Representatives at noon on the 3d day of January, of the years in which such terms would have ended if this article had not been ratified; and the terms of their successor shall then begin.

SECTION 2. The Congress shall assemble at least once in every year, and such meeting shall begin at noon on the 3d day of January, unless they shall by law appoint a different day.

SECTION 3. If, at the time fixed for the beginning of the term of the President, the President elect shall have died, the Vice President elect shall become President. If a President shall not have been chosen before the time fixed for the beginning of his term, of if the President elect shall have failed to qualify, then the Vice President elect shall act as President until a President shall have qualified; and the Congress may by law provide for the case wherein neither a President elect nor a Vice President elect shall have qualified,

declaring who shall then act as President, or the manner in which one who is to act shall be selected, and such person shall act accordingly until a President or Vice President shall have qualified.

SECTION 4. The Congress may be law provide for the case of the death of any of the persons from whom the House of Representatives may choose a President whenever the right of choice shall have devolved upon them, and for the case of the death of any of the persons from whom the Senate may choose a Vice President whenever the right of choice shall have devolved upon them.

SECTION 5. Sections 1 and 2 shall take effect on the 15th day of October following the ratification of this article.

SECTION 6. This article shall be inoperative unless it shall have been ratified as an amendment to the Constitution by the legislatures of three-fourths of the several States within seven years from the date of its submission.

ARTICLE [XXI]

SECTION 1. The eighteenth article of amendment to the Constitution of the United States is hereby repealed.

SECTION 2. The transportation or importation into any State, Territory, or possession of the United States for delivery or use therein of intoxicating liquors, in violation of the laws thereof, is hereby prohibited.

SECTION 3. This article shall be inoperative unless it shall have been ratified as an amendment to the Constitution by conventions in the several States, as provided in the Constitution, within seven years from the date of the submission hereof to the States by the

Congress.

ARTICLE [XXII]

SECTION 1. No person shall be elected to the office of the President more than twice, and no person who has held the office of President, or acted as President, for more than two years of a term to which some other person was elected President shall be elected to the office of the President more than once. But this Article shall not apply to any person holding the office of President when this Article was proposed by the Congress, and shall not prevent any person who may be holding the office of President, or acting as President, during the term within which this Article becomes operative from holding the office of President or acting as President during the remainder of such term.

SECTION 2. This article shall be inoperative unless it shall have been ratified as an amendment to the Constitution by the legislatures of three-fourths of the several States within seven years from the date of its submission to the States by the Congress.

ARTICLE [XXIII]

SECTION 1. The District constituting the seat of Government of the United States shall appoint in such manner as the Congress may direct:

A number of electors of President and Vice President equal to the whole number of Senators and Representatives in Congress to which the District would be entitled if it were a State, but in no event more than the least populous State; they shall be in addition to those appointed by the States, but they shall be considered, for the purposes of the election of President and Vice President, to be electors appointed by a State; and they shall meet in the District and perform such duties as provided by the twelfth article of amendment.

SECTION 2. The Congress shall have power to enforce this article by appropriate legislation.

ARTICLE [XXIV]

SECTION 1. The right of citizens of the United States to vote in any primary or other election for President or Vice President, for electors for President or Vice President, or for Senator or Representative in Congress, shall not be denied or abridged by the United States or any State by reason of failure to pay any poll tax or other tax.

SECTION 2. The Congress shall have power to enforce this article by appropriate legislation.

ARTICLE [XXV]

SECTION 1. In case of the removal of the President from office or of his death or resignation, the Vice President shall become President.

SECTION 2. Whenever there is a vacancy in the office of the Vice President, the President shall nominate a Vice President who shall take office upon confirmation by a majority vote of both Houses of Congress.

SECTION 3. Whenever the President transmits to the President pro tempore of the Senate and the Speaker of the House of Representatives his written declaration that he is unable to discharge the powers and duties of his office, and until he transmits to them a written declaration to the contrary, such powers and duties shall be discharged by the Vice President as Acting President.

SECTION 4. Whenever the Vice President and a majority of either the principal officers of the executive departments or of such other body as Congress may be law provide, transmit to the President pro tempore of the Senate and the Speaker of the House of Representatives their written declaration that the President is unable to discharge the powers and duties of his office, the Vice President shall immediately assume the powers and duties of the office as Acting President.

Thereafter, when the President transmits to the President pro tempore of the Senate and the Speaker of the House of Representatives his written declaration that no inability exists, he shall resume the powers and duties of his office unless the Vice President and a majority of either the principal officers of the executive department or of such other body as Congress may be law provide, transmit within four days to the resident pro tempore of the Senate and the Speaker of the House of Representatives their written declaration that the President is unable to discharge the powers and duties of his office. Thereupon Congress shall decide the issue, assembling within forty eight hours for that purpose if not in session. If the Congress, within twenty-one days after receipt of the latter written declaration, or, if required to assemble, determines by two-thirds vote of both Houses that the President is unable to discharge the powers and duties of his office, the Vice President shall continue to discharge the same as Acting President; otherwise, the President shall resume the powers and duties of his office.

ARTICLE [XXVI]

SECTION 1. The right of citizens of the United States, who are eighteen years of age or older, to vote shall not be denied or abridged by the United States or by any State on account of age.

SECTION 2. The Congress shall have power to enforce this article by appropriate legislation.

☆☆

NOTE TO READERS: The original eighteenth century spelling of the following words has been preserved in the text of the Constitution: defence (defense), chuse, chousing (choose, choosing), encreased (increased), offence (offense), controul (control), behaviour (behavior) and labour (labor). It was also customary in 1787 to capitalize more nouns than are currently capitalized in modern usage.

☆☆

[2] Paul des Fosses is the author of *The Internal Revenue Service—An Agency Out of Control*, published by Freedom News Journal in cooperation with the National Coalition of I.R.S. Whistleblowers, 1985.

CHAPTER II. THE AMERICAN JURY: A HISTORICAL PERSPECTIVE

[1] Hammurabi's Code was a precursor to most modern, western justice systems. Hammurabi was a Babylonian who carved out an empire in Mesopotamia in 1700 B.C., and gained fame for establishing a uniform code of laws which proclaimed the state as the authority to enforce the law, set strict punishments for offenses and categorized crimes according to severity.

Hammurabi's purpose in enacting this code was "to cause justice to prevail in the land, to destroy the wicked and the evil, to prevent the strong from oppressing the weak...and to further the welfare of the people"

The code was carved on s stone pillar crowned with a statue of the Babylonian god of justice, Shamesh.

Source: Beers, Burton K., Professor of History, North Carolina State University, *World History, Patterns of Civilization*, Prentice-Hall, Englewod CLiffs, New Jersey, 1984.

[2] The Ten Commandments are found in Exodus 20: 1—18

Source: *The New English Bible*, Oxford University Press, New York, 1979.

[3] Exodus 1:11, 13, 14

"So they (the Israelites) were made to work in gangs with officers set over them to break their spirit with heavy labor...

So they (the Egyptians) treated their Israeli slaves with ruthless severity, and made life bitter for them with cruel servitude, setting them to work on clay and brick-making, and all sorts of work in the fields. In short they made ruthless use of them as slaves in every kind of hard labor."

Source: *The New English Bible* (see Footnote 2)

[4] Exodus 21: 2

"When you buy a Hebrew slave, he shall be your slave for six years, but in the seventh year he shall go free and pay nothing."

[5] Exodus 21: 23—25

"Whenever hurt is done, you shall give life for life, eye for eye, tooth for tooth, hand for hand, foot for foot, burn for burn, bruise for bruise, wound for wound."

6. "Vengeance (justice) is mine, sayeth the Lord, I will repay"
Romans 12:19. Hebrews 10:30
Source: *The New English Bible,* Oxford University Press, New York, 1979.

7. Job 42: 10

"So the Lord restored Job's fortune and doubled all his possessions."
Source: *The New English Bible* (see Footnote 2)

8. Plato, "The Apology", *Dialogues of Plato,* translated by Jowett, edited by .D. Kaplan, Washington Square Press Inc., New York, 1950.

9. Spooner, Lysander, *An Essay on the Trial By Jury,* originally published by John P. Jewett and Company, Boston, 1852.

10. Ibid.

11. Foucoult, Nichel, *Discipline and Punishment: The Birth of the Prison* Vantage Press

12. Ibid.

13. Ibid.

14. Ibid.

15. Ibid.

16. Ibid.

17. Ibid.

18. Ibid.

19. Ibid.

20. Ibid.

21. Ibid.

22. Ibid.

23. Ibid.

24. Ibid.

25. Jefferson, Thomas, *Five Thousand Quotations for All Occasions,* edited by Lewis C. Henry, Doubleday & Co., Inc., New York, 1952.

26. Jefferson, Thomas, Ibid.

27. Spooner, (see Footnote 9) and Finkelman, Paul, *Slavery in the Courtroom,* 1985, Washington D.C., 1985, Published by Paul Finkelman

28. Finkelman, Paul *Slavery in the Courtroom* (see Footnote 25)

29. John Jay, first Chief Justice of the United States Supreme Court, upheld the jurors' right to judge both the facts AND THE LAW, *State of Georgia vs. Brailsford,* 3 Dall. 1 (1794)

30. Holmes, Oliver Wendell, as quoted in and *U.S. vs. Moylan,* 417 F 2d. 1002. 9th Cir. (1969) and in *U.S. vs. Dougherty* 473 F 2d 1113, 1139 (1972).

31. Spooner, Lysander, *An Essay on the Trial By Jury,* See Footnote 9

32. Ibid.

33. Foucoult, Michel, *Discipline and Punishment: The Birth of the Prison,* Vantage Press.

34. Spooner, Lysander, *An Essay on the Trial By Jury,* See Footnote 8.

35. Kafka, Franz, *The Trial* translated by Willa and Edwin Muir, Vintage Books Division of Random House, New York, 1937.

36. Orwell, George, *1984,* Signet Classics, New York, 1949.

37. Spooner, Lysander, *An Essay on the Trial By Jury,* See Footnote 8

38. Ibid.

39. Ibid.

40. Ibid.

41. Ibid.

42. In 1980, the Justice Times of Clinton, Arkansas published a pocket sized educational cartoon book entitled "Kings and Queens of the Jury" in which American jurors are depicted as sovereigns, complete with crowns, and in which prospective jurors are urged to exert the ancient right of judging the law, as well as the facts.

43. Excerpt from Appellant's Brief, Cause No. 14-86-00455-CV, Fourteenth Supreme Judicial District of Texas, on appeal from the 127th Judicial District of Texas, Harris County,

page 13:

"If the Appellee, William Henry Neill, has no punitive damages assessed against him to send a message about how strongly the Courts and juries disapprove of an inebriated driver who leaves the scene of an accident, we are tacitly endorsing such behavior and passively granting permission for others to 'go and do likewise.' The court specifically erred on this point by granting a directed verdict in favor of the Defendant Neill on the issues of gross negligence and punitive damages."

[44.] Excerpt from Appellant's Petition for Rehearing to the Fourteenth Supreme Judicial District of Texas, Cause No. 14- 86-00455-CV (see Footnote 43 for further details); pages 3 and 4)

"In the opinion of this Honorable Court on the issue of negligent entrustment, this Honorable Court fails to mention the fact that the driver had, by his own admission, been twice convicted of driving while intoxicated. A certified copy of Defendant's conviction for D.W.I. was entered on Plaintiff's Exhibit Nine (9). Pages two hundred thirty eight (238) through two hundred forty (240) of the Statement of Facts are attached hereto as Exhibit "A".

This evidence was not considered by this Court in its review of the case. On page four (4) of its opinion, (attached hereto as Exhibit "B"), this Court states:

"There is no evidence of any traffic violation or traffic accidents prior to November 29, 1982. There is no evidence that Neill had driven while intoxicated in the past."

This Honorable Court further fails to acknowledge what is in fact fundamental law in the State of Texas, that drinking is as a matter or law, improper in conjunction with vehicle control and responsibility. Drinking, in and of itself, impairs judgment and in and of itself, constitutes gross negligence when operating a vehicle. It was foreseeable that an alcoholic who had not conquered his sickness would drink and drive. It was foreseeable that an alcoholic who had been twice convicted of driving while intoxicated would again drink and drive. This foreseeable precluded the lending of the car to the Appellee by a responsible car owner. The act of lending him the car was not responsible. The fact that he admitted that he made no inquiry into the record of the individual was not responsible."

[45.] Spooner, Lysander, *Trial By Jury*, (see Footnote 9)

[46.] Ibid.

[47.] Houston Chronicle, August 11, 1988

[48.] Spooner, Lysander, *Trial by Jury*, (see Footnote 9).

[49.] Ibid.

[50.] *Blacks' Law Dictionary* Fourth Edition, West Publishing Co., St. Paul, Minn. 1951.

[51.] The United States Supreme Court in *Branzburg vs. Hayes*, 92 S. Ct. 2646 at 2660, note 23, 1972, determined that the Fourteenth Amendment did not include indictment by Grnad Jury for infamous crimes as a part of due process guaranteed to state criminal defendants.

CHAPTER III. HERE COMES THE JUDGE

[1.] Neely, Richard, *How Courts Govern America*, Yale University Press, New Haven, Conn. 1981

[2.] Ibid.

[3.] Dershowitz, Alan M., *The Best Defense*, First Vintage Books Edition, 1982.

[4.] Thomas Jefferson, *Five Thousand Quotations for All Occasions*, edited by Lewis C. Henry, Doubleday & Co., Inc., New York, 1952.

[5.] Alan Dershowitz is a Professor at Harvard Law School and the author of *The Best Defense* (see Footnote 3).

[6.] Neely, Richard, *How Courts Govern America* (see Footnote 1)

[7.] On June 23, 1986, Time Magazine published an article which discussed Daniel Manion's scant qualifications for the federal appellate bench, and carried a cartoon which showed senators reaching into a barrel labeled "Reagan Nominations to Federal Judiciary," with the caption, "The ones at the bottom are awfully far gone." The thrust of the article was that Reagan was making his appointments from among those who shared his conservative political outlook, regardless of their qualifications.

[8.] The September, 1986 issue of *The American Spectator* carried an article by Thomas Sowell, discussing the impending recall election of Supreme Court Chief Justice Rose Bird, whose attitude, particularly toward the death penalty, differed markedly from that of her constituents.

[9.] Houston Post, April 9, 1986

[10.] de Toqueville, Alexis, *Democracy in America,* translated by Henry Reeve in 1840, revised by Francis Bowen in 1862, published by Vintage Books, a division of Random House, New York, 1945.

CHAPTER IV.

[1.] During the federal harboring trial of the Udeys, Ginters and Arthur Russell, in the fall of 1983, and the state capital murder case of Norma Ginter, (both of which are fully discussed in Chapter XI B) Minns' opinions were quoted frequently in Little Rock, Arkansas newspapers, *The Arkansas Democrat* and *The Arkansas Gazette* and also in the *Commercial Appeal* from Memphis, Tennessee.

In December, 1985 and January and February, 1986 both the *Houston Chronicle* and the *Houston Post* contained accounts of the verbal warfare exchanged between Minns and his opponents in litigation which followed the dramatic execution of a judgment which closed the President and First Lady Health Club Chain for several days. A further aspect of this case is discussed in Chapter III C.

[2.] Swift, Jonathan *Gulliver's Travels* originally written in 1727, Norton Critical Edition of Jonathan Swift's Gulliver's Travels published by W.W. Norton & Company, New York, 1970.

[3.] Robert Ringer's "Winning Through Intimidation" actually doesn't tell his readers how to intimidate. It tells them how to defend against intimidation. this self published book is a masterpiece of simplicity. Misconstruing it has become part of our American Culture, and I have deliberately done so in this chapter to make a point.

SAMPLE TIME SLIP

DATE	LAWYERS INITIALS	CLIENT'S NAME	MATTER OR FILE NUMBER	TIME STARTED	TIME ENDED	TOTAL TIME	$ AMOUNT

TIME SLIP
Description of Work Performed

[4.] H.A.L.T. stands for Help Abolish Legal Tyranny. The organization maintains an office at 1319 F Street, N.W., Suite 300, Washington, D.C. 20004.

[5.] On August 11, 1986, *Time* Magazine published an article about the high starting salaries (such as $65,000 annually) paid to new associates at some of the nation's largest lawfirms. These positions were described as a "gilded cage" however, because of the high pressure and insecurity.

CHAPTER V. PRACTITIONERS ON THE FRONTIER

[1.] An attorney who is licensed elsewhere, but NOT LICENSED in a particular jurisdiction in which he wishes to represent a client on a particular case may file a MOTION TO APPEAR PRO HAC VICE (meaning for this occasion only). The Motion would normally set forth those areas where the attorney is licensed in good standing, a statement that a particular party wishes to retain him, an assurance that local rules will be obeyed, and, if applicable, a statement that the attorney wishes to initiate the process of becoming licensed in that jurisdiction.

A typical motion for Pro Hac Vice follows:

UNITED STATES DISTRICT COURT
DISTRICT OF ALASKA

UNITED STATES OF AMERICA   *
VS.   *   CASE NO. 88-XXX-CR
XXXXXX X XXXXX   *

REQUEST FOR PERMISSION TO APPEAR PRO HAC VICTO THE HONORABLE JUDGE OF SAID COURT:

COMES NOW, Michael Louis Minns, attorney for the Defendant, Xxxxxx X. Xxxxx, in the above-referenced cause of action, and requests permission of this Honorable Court to appear pro hac vice in this matter in the District of Alaska.

I.

Xxxxxx X Xxxxx, Defendant herein, contacted me for the purpose of retaining my services regard to his defense against the charges of willfully failing to file income tax returns for the years 1981, 1982 and 1983 in this matter.

III.

I am an attorney whose place of business is in Houston, Texas and whose residence is in Katy, Texas, Harris County, in the Southern District of Texas.

IV.

Attached hereto as Exhibit "A" is a list of the Courts in which the undersigned is licensed, and the dates of admission to each Court. The undersigned is a member in good standing of the State Bar of Texas and is licensed to practice law by the Supreme Court of the State of Texas. The undersigned is in good standing as a member of the bar of the Southern District of Texas. The undersigned is licensed to practice before the Ninth Circuit Court of Appeals.

V.

The office of the undersigned has requested a copy of the Local Rules for the District of Alaska. Upon receipt of them, the undersigned will endeavor to become familiar with them and to abide by same.

WHEREFORE PREMISES CONSIDERED, the undersigned respectfully requests permission to appear pro hac vice in this matter.

Respectfully submitted,

MICHAEL LOUIS MINNS, P.L.C.

[2.] CONWAY BOGUE VS. TRANS AMERICAN, 312 Pacifica 2nd 998, 1957

[3.] The "Magic Divorce Questions"

On these questions, you can lead the witness and (yourself) since no one is objecting. Leading means suggesting the answer in the questions itself.

Question 1: Were you and your wife married on the _____ day of _____, 19____?
Magic Answer—Yes.

Question 2: Did you and your wife cease to live together as husband or wife on or about the ____ day of _____, 19____?
Magic Answer—Yes.

Question 3: Is there currently a child being expected to be born from this union?
Magic Answer—No.

Question 4: Have you and your spouse agreed to divide all the property and does the divorce order reflect as agreed and is the agreement fair?
Magic Answer—Yes.

Question 5: Have you tried to reconcile but found that the marriage is irreconcilable and are you asking for a divorce because of insupportability of the marriage between you?
Magic Answer—Yes.

Question 6: Have you lived in this county for the six month period preceding the filing of this divorce?
Magic Answer—Yes.

Question 7: (Only if you have existing children). Have you and your spouse come to an agreement regarding the custody and support of your children which you believe is in the best interest of the children and incorporated that into your proposed divorce decree? This tough question might require reading a few extra times but it's worth the effort to save $400.00 or more, because attorneys often significantly increase the fee if children are involved even if it there is very little extra work.

Magic Answer—(Close your eyes and guess on this one, then open them to see if you were right). Answer—Yes.

4. de Tocqueville, Alexsis H., *Democracy in America,* translated by Henry Reeve in 1840 and revised by Francis Bowen in 1862, more recently published by Vintage Books, a Division of Random House, New York, 1945.

CHAPTER VI. CIVIL OR CRIMINAL?

1. Pastor Everett Sileven was jailed for 120 days on a "contempt" charge stemming from a dispute over licensing his church school. While incarcerated, he wrote *Pastor Sileven's Jail Writings,* published by Daniels Publishing Co., Orlando, Florida, 1983.

CHAPTER VII. ANATOMY OF A CIVIL LAWSUIT

1. A Typical Personal Injury Petition

PRUDENCE B. CAREFUL	*	IN THE DISTRICT COURT OF
VS.	*	HARRIS COUNTY, TEXAS
RUTH LESLIE RIPSNORTER	*	_____ JUDICIAL DISTRICT

PLAINTIFF'S ORIGINAL PETITION

TO THE HONORABLE JUDGE OF SAID COURT

COMES NOW, Prudence B. Careful, herein called Plaintiff, complaining of Ruth Leslie Ripsnorter, herein called Defendant, and for cause of action would show this Court the following:

I.

Plaintiff is a resident of Harris County, Texas.

II.

Defendant Ruth Leslie Ripsnorter is a resident of Harris County, Texas and may be served at 1530 Rotten Apple Lane, Houston, Texas.

III.

All the actions complained of in this petition occurred in Houston, Harris County, Texas.

III.

On or about the 25th day of March, 1988, the Defendant, while driving her vehicle, struck a vehicle driven by the Plaintiff herein, while Plaintiff was stopped for a red light at the intersection of Preston and Fannin, Houston, Texas 77002.

IV.

The Plaintiff's vehicle was being operated in a reasonable and prudent manner under the circumstances.

V.

The proximate cause of the collision was the neglience of the Defendant. The Defendant Ruth Leslie Ripsnorter failed to keep a proper distance between the vehicle she was driving and the Plaintiff's vehicle; failed to drive at a proper speed under the circumstances; failed to keep a proper look-out in front of her; failed to turn to the right or to the left to avoid an accident; failed to properly apply her brakes, and as a result of these and other failures, collided with the Plaintiff's vehicle, proximately causing the accident complained of herein, and proximately causing the injuries sustained by the Plaintiff and of which the Plaintiff complains herein.

VI.

As a direct and proximate cause of the collision which took place as a direct and proximate result of the negligence of the Defendant, the Plaintiff was substantially injured. The Plaintiff, Prudence B. Careful, sustained injuries to her back and neck.

VII.

The Plaintiff incurred reasonable and necessary medical expenses, and in all medical probability will continue to incur medical expenses in the future in an amount in excess of the jurisdictional limits of this court.

VIII.

The Plaintiff, Prudence B. Careful, was injured in the way of lost time from work. Plaintiff has suffered diminished earning capacity. Plaintiff has endured pain and suffering, mental anguish, and other proximately caused damages in the amount of an amount in excess of the jurisdictional limits of this court.

WHEREFORE PREMISES CONSIDERED Plaintiff prays this Honorable Court grant judgment against the Defendant, for damages as recited in this Petition, plus costs of court and any and all other damages or relief which this Court may find just and proper under law and equity.

Respectfully submitted,
John Q. Barrister,
100 Legal Eagle Road
Houston. Texas 77000
(713) 555-0000
State Bar No. 0000000

2. Typical Plaintiffs' Personal Injury Interrogatories

PRUDENCE B. CAREFUL	*	IN THE DISTRICT COURT OF
VS.	*	HARRIS COUNTY, TEXAS
RUTH LESLIE RIPSNORTER	*	_____ JUDICIAL DISTRICT

1. Who is answering these Interrogatories on behalf of—Ruth Leslie Ripsnorter?

A. What is your full legal name?

2. Do you use any other names such as alias names, assumed names or nicknames? Answer YES or NO.

3. If your answer to Question 2 was YES, state the names.

4. What is your Social Security Number?

5. What is your driver's license number and what state issued it?

6. On the date (herein called date) which is given as the date for the collision which is the subject of this lawsuit, did you own or operate a motor vehicle? Answer YES or NO.

7. If your answer to Question 6 was YES:

A) State the model, year, type, vehicle identification number of every motor vehicle you own.

If your answer to Question 6 was YES or NO:

B) State the model, year, type, vehicle identification number of the motor vehicle you were operating, if any, on the date of the collision which is the subject of this lawsuit (or if you were not operating one, the name of the individual or individuals who were with regard to the collision which is the subject of this law suit), and the name and address of the owner of that vehicle.

8. On the herein referenced date, were you involved in a collision or accident? Answer YES or NO.

9. Describe to the best of your ability the events that led to the collision or accident, the collision or accident itself, and the results of that collision. Identify any and all vehicles involved by make, year and model. Name and identify to the best of your ability all persons involved in the accident, directly or collaterally, and their role therein, including the names, addresses and phone numbers of all persons in each vehicle involved, specifying which vehicle they were in.

10. Has a suit ever been filed against you for a vehicle related injury? Answer YES or NO.

11. If you have answered Question 10 YES, state the name of the Plaintiff, cause number and Court number of the suit, the county where the suit was filed and the disposition of the suit.

12. Was the vehicle owned or operated by you on tghe date of collision insured? Answer YES or NO.

13. If the answer to question 12 was YES, state the policy limits, the name of the insurance company and in whose name the policy is held.

14. (A) If you will, without a Motion for Production, attach a copy of your policy to your answers. If you will not, state you will not.

15. Give the following information on every person directly or collaterally involved in the collision which is the subject of this lawsuit:

A) Name

Relationship to the accident.

E) Relationship to either Plaintiff and/or Defendant

16. Give the following information on every person not named in Question 14 who witnessed or may have witnessed the accident or may be called as a witness in trial to the accident including but not limited to any and all expert witnesses and medical witnesses that you are aware of:

A) Name

B) Birthdate

C) Address

D) Relationship to the accident

E) Relationship to either Plaintiff and/or Defendant

17. State the name, address and location, and the telephone number of each person who you expect to call as an *expert witness* at the trial of this cause, stating the subject matter on which the expert is expected to testify, the substance of fact and opinions to which the expert is expected to testify and a summary of the grounds for each opinion. Also, please attach to your Answers to these Interrogatories a copy of the reports, including factual observations and opinions, of all experts who will be called as witnesses upon the trial of this cause.

18. Did you receive any personal injury as a result of the collision which is the subject of this lawsuit? Answer YES or NO.

19. If you have answered YES to Question 16, give a detailed explanation of that injury.

20. Have any photographs or videotape recordings been taken regarding this accident, (including vehicles and scene) or the injuries claimed; if so, please state the date when each picture was made, the subject matter of each photograph or videotape, who has custody of each photograph or videotape recordings, and please attach a xerox copy of each photograph to your Answers

21. State in detail exactly how, when and where the accident happened, including weather and road conditions, and draw a diagram of the accident

22. If you saw the Plaintiff's vehicle prior to the impact, state what you saw with respect to the vehicle, its location, any movements made by it, and any other relevant evidence pertaining to that vehicle.

23. If you had conversation with, or overheard conversation by the Plaintiff, state exactly what you heard and when they occurred. If not, state that you have not.

> Respectfully submitted,
> John Q. Barrister

3. A typical Motion to Compel:

PRUDENCE B. CAREFUL	*	IN THE DISTRICT COURT OF
VS.	*	HARRIS COUNTY, TEXAS
RUTH LESLIE RIPSNORTER	*	_____ JUDICIAL DISTRICT

TO THE HONORABLE JUDGE OF SAID COURT:

COMES NOW Prudence B. Careful, Plaintiff herein, by and through her attorney, and files this Motion to Compel Answers to Interrogatories and in support of same would show this Honorable Court the following:

I.

On the 7th day of February, 1989, Plaintiff served interrogatories upon Defendant Ruth Leslie Ripsnorter. Attached hereto as Exhibit "A" is a copy of the file stamped interrogatories. Attached hereto as Exhibit "B" is a copy of the Certified Mail green card showing that said interrogatories were received in the office of Defendant's attorney, Gustaf Guts, of the lawfirm of Guy and Guts, on the 9th day of February, 1989.

II.

Pursuant to Texas Rules of Civil procedure, a response to Plaintiff's interrogatories was due within thirty (30) days of Defendant's receipt of same. As of the current date, March 27, 1989, said interrogatories have not been answered, nor has there been any communication from the lawfirm of Guy and Guts regarding said answers.

III.

Plaintiff requires discovery in order to prosecute her case against the Defendant. Plaintiff requests that this Court enter an order compelling Defendant to answer her interrogatories within thirty (30) days or her pleadings will be stricken. Plaintiff incurred attorneys fees for the preparation of this motion. Plaintiff requests that attorneys fees in the amount of TWO HUNDRED FIFTY DOLLARS ($250.00) be taxed against the Defendant.

WHEREFORE PREMISES CONSIDERED, Plaintiff requests that this Court order Defendant Ruth Leslie Ripsnorter to answer interrogatories on or before the 27th day of April, 1989, with the sanction of striking her pleadings in the event that she does not do so. Plaintiff further requests that this Court award the sum of TWO HUNDRED FIFTY DOLLARS in attorneys' fees, payable within thirty (30) days, for which the Defendant and the lawfirm of Guy and Guts shall be jointly and severally liable.

> Respectfully submitted,
> John Q. Barrister
> 100 Legal Eagle Road
> Houston, Texas 77000
> (713) 555-0000
> State Bar No. 00000000

The accompanying ORDER would have the same CAPTION and would leave blanks for the Judge to fill in all the appropriate dates, and the amount of the attorneys fees awarded (if any).

PRUDENCE B. CAREFUL	*	IN THE DISTRICT COURT OF
VS.	*	HARRIS COUNTY, TEXAS
RUTH LESLIE RIPSNORTER	*	_____ JUDICIAL DISTRICT

On the _____ day of _____, 1989. came on to be heard Plaintiff's Motion to Compel Answers to Interrogatories. Good cause having been shown, the Court is of the opinion that the same should be granted. Accordingly, it is hereby

ORDERED, ADJUDGED and DECREED that the Defendant, Ruth Leslie Ripsnorter, shall file her Answers to Interrogatories on or before the _____ day of _____, 1989. Failure of the Defendant to do so will result in her pleadings being stricken. It is further

ORDERED, ADJUDGED and DECREED that the Defendant, Ruth Leslie Ripsnorter, and the lawfirm of Guy and Guts pay to the Plaintiff, and her attorney, John Q. Barrister, the sum of _____ on or before the _____ day of _____, 1989.

SIGNED this _____ day of _____, 1989.

_____
JUDGE PRESIDING

CHAPTER IX. CRIMINAL LAW

[1] The famous "Miranda warning" comes from Miranda vs. Arizona, 384 U.S. 436 (1966), and includes the familiar words:

"You have the right to remain silent. Anything you say can and will be held against you in a court of law. You have the right to an attorney. If you can't afford an attorney, one will be appointed for you."

[2] Foucoult, Michel, *Discipline and Punishment: The Birth of the Prison*, Vantage Press.

[3] Neely, Richard, *How Courts Govern America*, Yale University Press, New Havenm Conn., 1981.

[4] Paine, Thomas, *Five Thousand Quotations for All Occasions*, edited by Lewis C. Henry, Doubledy & Co., Inc., New York, 1952.

[5] The Supreme Court ruled that the Fourteenth Amendment requirement of due process did not demand that an appeal be available, *National Union of Marine Cooks and Stewards vs. Arnold*, 348 U.S. 37 (1954)

[6.] The Supreme Court also held that even in criminal proceedings, the appellate process was not mandatory, *Ross vs. Moffit* 417 U.S. 600 (1974). Also valuable for further reading on this subject is "Appellate Justice: A Crisis in Virginia", 57 Virginia Law Review, 3.121 (1981)

CHAPTER X. HABEAS CORPUS

[1.] *Black's Law Dictionary,* Fourth Edition, West Publishing Co., St. Paul, Minnn., 1951.

[2.] *Corpus Juris Secundum*

[3.] Ibid.

[4.] Constitution of the United States of America, Article I, Section 9, Clause 2 (See Chapter II, Footnote 1)

[5.] *Corpus Juris Secundum*

CHAPTER XI. CIVIL RIGHTS

[1.] *Bell vs. The City of Milwaukee,* 746 F 2d 1205 7th Cir. (1984).

[2.] Dickens, Charles *Bleak House,* first published in book form in 1853; reprinted by Riverside Press, Cambridge Massachusetts, 1956.

[3.] Turner, Capstan and Lower, A. J., *There Was a Man—Kahl,* Sozo Publishing Co., 1985

[4.] This statement occurred during Dero Downing's cross- examination at a hearing in the capital murder case against Leonard and Norma Ginter; *Arkansas vs. Ginter* CR-83-37, in which Michael Minns represented the Ginters. The incident is also reported in Chapter XVIII of *There Was a M—Kahl* (see Footnote 3)

Downing: I'm not an experienced arson investigator.

Minns: Why did you use the word "arson"? Isn't arson a criminal offense as opposed to just setting a fire? There are legal ways to do it, and illegal.

At that point, an objection by prosecutor Stallcup was sustained by Judge Ponder.

[5.] *The Justice Times,* a patriot newspaper published in Clinton, Arkansas, printed a special issue in July, 1983, bearing the headline, "Kahlgate Kover-up Expose'", and featuring the story of how the Ginters' neighbor Ray Wade and New York Times Reporter Jim Barden found the charred, severed foot of the alleged Gordon Kahl in the rubble of the Ginter home, one month after the incident.

[6.] This letter addressed to the Editor of *Newsweek* was written by Michael Louis Minns in response to *Newsweek's* article, *"Violence on the Right",* which was published on March 4, 1985.

"Dear Editor:

I am extremely disappointed with your March 4, 1985 article "Violence on the Right". Newsweek seems destined to join *"Time"* as a news periodical unworthy of the public's respect.

The well written but incredibly inaccurate yellow journalism, (as in yellow fire), is frightening. The article clearly attacks the First Amendment (as in right to peaceably assemble and the Court interpreted right to freedom from guilt by association). You have branded "tax protesters" with the Nazi's, the Klu Klux Klan and the Posse Comitatus. (Remember our forefathers were tax protesters and the President of the United States is a tax protester).

I would appreciate it if you would either retract or reexamine portions of your article regarding "Gordon Kahl".

First: He was not as you claim, a "tax evader". Tax evasion is a serious Federal Felony punishable by five (5) years in jail. Intentional knowing dishonesty is required. Kahl was a "non-filer", a Federal Misdemeanor punishable by one (1) year in jail. You are guilty if you willfully fail to file by April 15, midnight each year. Dishonesty is not a necessary element. Kahl was in my opinion, a religious fanatic who was also fanatically honest.

Fourth: The issue of the identity of the corpse called Kahl is not finally determined. In the trial Court, Judge Waters ruled that the intentional burning of the Ginter home was not relevant and could not be brought before the jury. The Supreme Court of the United States is reviewing the trial. If they reverse the trial court's decision, new evidence will be available.

Fifth: The Ginter's concrete "Bunker" home was an earth home with large windows. It was not as defensible as a more typical modern home would be.

Sixth: Everything was in ashes. The rounds of ammunition were blasting caps used to clear stumps on the Ginter farm and 22 Caliber shells. (Mr. Ginter did own a 22 rifle which was confiscated when he was "captured".)

As a Jewish attorney who tries to represent people I believe in, I am no supporter of any of the groups you lumped together in your article. I am however, a strong supporter of the First Amendment, not just the portion that protects Newsweek but the rest of it that Newsweek seems uninterested in protecting.

Norma Ginter was convicted of harboring Gordon Kahl. (I did not represent her in that case, but did represent Irene and Ed Udey). She was wholly and completely innocent. She was convicted by a loud press which intimidated a brain-washed jury and linked her erroneously with every nut-fringe group in the United States.

The right of existence for these groups is important to continue our national divergent character and must be supported to protect our First Amendment rights of press and free association; but joining them should be optional. The press forced Norma Ginter and Irene Udey (found not guilty) and Ed Udey (found guilty but on appeal to U.S. Supreme Court) to "join" groups (many of which they did not even know existed) by being associated with them in the press.

I did represent Norma in *Arkansas vs. Ginter*, in which she was unjustly accused of the murder of Sheriff Gene Matthews and spent seven (7) months in jail without bond. After eighteen (18) months of hearings, the case against her was dismissed.

Judging from your article, there seems to be a rash of "accidental" F.B.I. fires around the country. As most competent Arson investigators will tell you, and as Roy Paul of the Houston Fire Department and Floyd McDonald, the chemist who analyzed the samples of the Ginter residence procured by Paul know—these "accidental" fires are sometimes the result of Arson.

With the hiring of new F.B.I. agents recently announced, I advise my clients to raise their fire insurance coverage."

CHAPTER XII. FREEDOM OF INFORMATION ACT/PRIVACY ACT

1. Sample Freedom of Information Act/Privacy Act letter:

YOUR LETTERHEAD
(NAME, ADDRESS)

DATE
FULL NAME & ADDRESS
OF THE AGENCY FROM
WHOM THE INFORMATION
IS BEING SOUGHT
ATTN: NAME of person responsible for the file (if known) OR
         CUSTODIAN OF THE RECORDS
Dear Sir or Madam:

Pursuant to the Freedom of Information Act, 5 U.S.C. 552 and the Privacy Act, 5 U.S.C. 552 (a), the following information is requested:

(DESCRIBE THE INFORMATION SOUGHT AS EXPLICITLY AS POSSIBLE—INCLUDING DATES AND IDENTIFYING NUMBERS—SOCIAL SECURITY NUMBER, MILITARY SERIAL NUMBER ETC.)

I await your reply within the statutory time period.

Yours truly,

YOUR SIGNATURE

An excellent source for further reading on this subject is:

Franklin, Justin D, and Bouchard, Robert E., *Guidebook to the Freedom of Information and Privacy Acts*, Second Edition, Clark Boardman Co., New York, 1987.

CHAPTER XIII. RESEARCH

[1] Sample pages of a published case, showing headnotes (*U.S. vs. Udey* 748 F2d 1231, Eighth Circuit, 1984).

[2] A sample page of Shepard's Citations (including citations to the U.S. vs. Udey case, see Footnote 2 to this Chapter).

[3] The legal research firm the author occasionally uses (and there are many others) is: United Law Search, 2651 East 21st Street, Suite 525, Tulsa, OK 74114.

CHAPTER XIV. INCOME TAX

[1] On April 15, 1986, the Houston Post carried a major article entitled "Tattling to the Taxman"

[2] *Pollock vs. Farmers' Loan & Trust Co.*, 158 U.S. 601 (1895)

The Supreme Court ruled that a direct income tax was unconstitutional.

[3] Neely, Richard, *How Courts Govern America*, Yale University Press, New Haven, Connecticut, 1981.

[4] Beard, Henry and Cerf, Christopher, *The Pentagon Catalog*, Workman Publishing Company, New York, N.Y. 1986.

The Pentagon Catalog is amusing, with its illustrations and advertisements for $700.00 toilet seats and $2,000 wrenches, but the joke is on us, the taxpayers, whose hard-earned money is being shamefully wasted.

On June 17, 1988, the Houston Chronicle printed a front page article entitled, "Fraud called 'way of life' at Pentagon"

[5] Chappell, Robert, *Secrets of Offshore Tax Havens*, ABM Publishing Co., 1985.

[6] Benson, Bill and Beckman, M.J. "Red," *The Law that Never Was Volume I* Published by Constitutional Research Association, South Holland, Ilinois, 1985. In 1986, Bill Benson came out with Volume II of *The Law that Never Was*.

[7] Sherman, Roger, *Caveat Against Injustice*, Spencer Judd, Publishers, Sewanee, Tenn.

[8] *United States vs. Sullivan* 274 U.S. 259.

[9] Chappell, Robert, *Secrets of Offshore Tax Havens*. see Footnote 5

[10] Des Fosses, Paul, *The Internal Revenue Service: An Agency Out of Control*, published by Freedom News Journal in cooperation with the National Coalition of I.R.S. Whistleblowers, 1985.

[11] Ibid.

[12] Bastiat, Frederic, *The Law*, translated by Dean Russell, copyright 1950. Foundation for Economic Education.

[13] Ibid.

[14] Ibid.

[15] Ibid.

[16] Ibid.

[17] Ibid.

[18] Ibid.

[19] Chappell, Robert, *Secrets of Offshore Tax Havens* See Footnote 5.

[20] Ibid.

[21] Ibid.

[22] A front page article in the Arkansas Gazette, (Little Rock, Arkansas) May 1, 1988 proclaimed, "Tax shelter dispute sets of chicken war."

[23] The Houston Chronicle for April 24, 1988 carried a front page article declaring "Tax reform bill packed with loopholes for rich.

[25] The Anchorage Daily News, March 29, 1988, announced "Chugach posts $18.3 million profit" and sub-titled the article "Native corporation benefits from sale of losses, fish processing plants."

CHAPTER XV. THE INSURANCE CON

1. Sample pages of a published case, showing headnotes
(*U.S. vs. Udey* 748 F2d 1231, Eighth Circuit, 1984).

UNITED STATES v. UDEY   **1231**
Cite as 748 F.2d 1231 (1984)

where a jury meets prevailing standards of impartiality]. [M]any existing standards of acceptability tolerate considerable knowledge of the case and even an opinion on the merits on the part of the prospective juror. And even under a more restrictive standard, there will remain the problem of obtaining accurate answers on *voir dire*—is the juror consciously or subconsciously harboring prejudice against the accused resulting from widespread news coverage in the community? Thus if change of venue * * * [is] to be of value, [it] should not turn on the results of the *voir dire*; rather [it] should constitute [an] independent [remedy] designed to assure fair trial when news coverage has raised substantial doubts about the effectiveness of the *voir dire* standing alone.

American Bar Association Project on Standards for Criminal Justice, *Standards Relating to Fair Trial and Free Press* 127 (1968).

"Substantial doubts" have been raised about the effectiveness of the voir dire examinations as a barometer of jury impartiality in this case. Under any standard of review, the district court wrongly failed to grant the defendants' request for a change of venue. In the exercise of this court's supervisory powers, the defendants' convictions should be vacated and a new trial should be granted in a district remote from that of North Dakota.

A: Yes.
Q: Has anything that you have heard or read about this case in following these reports caused you to form an opinion as to the innocence or guilt of any of the defendants in the case?
    *   *   *   *   *   *
A: Yes, sir. It's a very strong opinion.
    *   *   *   *   *   *
Q: You feel if you were selected as a juror in the case it would be very difficult for you to set aside or disregard the opinion that you have formed?
A: Yes, sir.
Id. at 171–72.
Each of the chosen jurors also was exposed to the extensive news coverage. Several of the jurors actually subscribed to the *Forum*. One of the selected jurors admitted that at an earlier date his "mind [was] pretty well set," *id.*, at 91, although he did not claim to have any opinion at the time of the voir dire examination. Anoth-

UNITED STATES of America, Appellee,

v.

Ed UDEY, Appellant.

UNITED STATES of America, Appellee,

v.

Arthur H. RUSSELL, Appellant.

UNITED STATES of America, Appellee,

v.

Leonard G. GINTER, Appellant.

UNITED STATES of America, Appellee,

v.

Norma GINTER, Appellant.

Nos. 83–2615, 83–2632, 83–2654, 83–2655.

United States Court of Appeals,
Eighth Circuit.

Submitted May 14, 1984.

Decided Nov. 7, 1984.

Rehearing Denied in Nos. 83–2654,
83–2655 Dec. 28, 1984.

Rehearing En Banc Denied in Nos.
83–2615, 83–2632 Dec. 28, 1984.

Defendants were convicted in the United States District Court for the Western

er selected juror also testified that he had formed an opinion, albeit "nothing that I would consider a strong opinion." Transcript of Proceeding, Vol. III, at 165.
The majority's statement that only 27% of the jurors attributed their partiality to media coverage is misleading. The majority admits that of the 114 original venirepersons, twenty-eight were excused before voir dire on the basis of hardship. Another venireperson was excused for hardship later in the proceeding and four others were never considered. Seventy-eight prospective jurors actually underwent voir dire. Thirty-nine, or one-half, were excused as potentially partial due to pretrial publicity or knowledge of persons involved in the prosecution. This statistic should be a factor considered in an evaluation of defendants' request for a change of venue. Indeed, even if the analysis was limited to a review of the voir dire examinations, a 50% partiality rate sufficiently demonstrated the need for a change of venue in this case.

1. Sample pages of a published case, showing headnotes
(*U.S. vs. Udey* 748 F2d 1231, Eighth Circuit, 1984).

1232   748 FEDERAL REPORTER, 2d SERIES

District of Arkansas, H. Franklin Waters, Chief Judge, of conspiracy to harbor and conceal fugitive, and of substantive offense of harboring and concealing fugitive, and they appealed. The Court of Appeals, Ross, Circuit Judge, held that: (1) evidence was sufficient to support conviction; (2) sentence did not violate double jeopardy; (3) affidavit in support of search warrant was sufficient to establish probable cause to believe that fugitive was at defendant's residence; (4) incriminatory statements were properly admitted; (5) District Court did not err in refusing defendants' motion for counsel of their choice in order to obtain someone who shared their belief about this country's tax laws; (6) defendants' allegedly exculpatory statements to police were not admissible; and (7) District Court did not abuse its discretion in imposing five-year sentence.

Affirmed.

Lay, Chief Judge, concurred in part and dissented in part and filed opinion.

Lay, Chief Judge, Heaney, Bright and McMillian, Circuit Judges, dissented from denial of rehearing and filed opinion.

1. Criminal Law ⬤77

In order to support conviction of harboring and concealing a fugitive, Government was required to establish that defendants knew that federal warrant had been issued for fugitive arrests; defendants harbored or concealed fugitive; and defendants intended to prevent fugitive's discovery and arrest. 18 U.S.C.A. § 1071.

2. Conspiracy ⬤28(3)

Knowledge of federal warrant for fugitive's arrest is essential element of conspiracy to harbor or conceal fugitive. 18 U.S.C.A. § 371.

3. Conspiracy ⬤47(3)

Knowledge of existence of warrant for fugitive's arrest, an essential element of conspiracy to harbor or conceal fugitive, can be established by evidence from which jury can properly infer knowledge and guilt beyond reasonable doubt. 18 U.S.C.A. § 371.

4. Conspiracy ⬤28(3)

In order to establish conspiracy to harbor or conceal fugitive, Government had to prove: defendants entered into agreement; agreement had as its objective a violation of the laws; and that one of those in agreement committed an act in furtherance of the objective. 18 U.S.C.A. § 371.

5. Conspiracy ⬤47(1)

Once existence of conspiracy is established, even slight evidence connecting a particular defendant to conspiracy may be substantial and therefore sufficient proof of defendant's involvement in scheme. 18 U.S.C.A. § 371.

6. Criminal Law ⬤77

Evidence that defendant concealed fugitive was sufficient to support conviction for harboring and concealing fugitive, where evidence overwhelmingly established that defendant knew federal warrant had been issued for fugitive's arrest, and with this knowledge, defendant allowed fugitive to stay in his home. 18 U.S.C.A. § 1071.

7. Criminal Law ⬤77

Evidence of defendant's knowledge of existence of warrant for fugitive's arrest was sufficient to support conviction of harboring and concealing fugitive, based upon defendant's involvement in plan to move fugitive from one residence to another in attempt to avoid Federal Bureau of Investigation. 18 U.S.C.A. § 1071.

8. Criminal Law ⬤199

Double jeopardy clause protects against multiple punishments for greater and lesser included offenses. U.S.C.A. Const.Amend. 5.

9. Criminal Law ⬤200(6)

Defendant does not receive double punishment when he is convicted and sentenced for substantive offense, and for conspiring to commit offense. U.S.C.A. Const. Amend. 5.

10. Criminal Law ⬤200(6)

Sentence for conspiracy to harbor and conceal fugitive and for substantive crime did not violate double jeopardy, since it was

1. Sample pages of a published case, showing headnotes
(*U.S. vs. Udey* 748 F2d 1231, Eighth Circuit, 1984).

UNITED STATES v. UDEY

1233

Cite as 748 F.2d 1231 (1984)

not necessary to prove substantive offense in order to prove conspiracy, and proof of conspiracy was not necessary to conviction of substantive crime charge. 18 U.S.C.A. § 1071; U.S.C.A. Const.Amend. 5.

11. Searches and Seizures ⟋3.6(3)

Affidavit in support of search warrant was sufficient to establish probable cause to believe that fugitive was at defendants' residence, where informant's tip that fugitive was with given group of people in particular type of car was corroborated by aerial surveillance of defendants' home where car was in fact seen.

12. Criminal Law ⟋394.4(10)

Even if search warrant was invalid, evidence discovered during initial entry into defendants' home was lawfully seized, where shooting began inside residence when one defendant asked for search warrant, at which time house became scene of crime committed in officers' presence.

13. Criminal Law ⟋1169.1(8)

Even if search warrant was improvidently issued, admission of shotgun discovered day after shoot-out was harmless error beyond reasonable doubt, where plain-view discovery of corpse subsequently identified as that of the fugitive and his rifle provided sufficient evidence upon which to support defendants' convictions for conspiracy to harbor and conceal fugitive, and for substantive offense. 18 U.S.C.A. §§ 371, 1071; Fed.Rules Cr.Proc. Rule 52(a), 18 U.S.C.A.

14. Criminal Law ⟋1036.1(1)

Issue was not properly preserved for appeal because no objection was made at trial to admission of testimony. Fed.Rules Evid. Rule 103, 28 U.S.C.A.

15. Criminal Law ⟋1036.1(5)

Defendants' claim that their initial responses to law enforcement officers' questions regarding presence of others in their home should have been suppressed as they were not informed of their *Miranda* rights did not amount to plain error. Fed.Rules Cr.Proc. Rule 52(b), 18 U.S.C.A.

16. Criminal Law ⟋414

District court's determination that defendant had never requested counsel, and that her initial request to remain silent was tentative and equivocal, so that subsequent police-initiated conversations did not contravene defendant's constitutional rights, was not factually nor legally erroneous.

17. Criminal Law ⟋112.1(4)

Test to be employed when examining propriety of resumption of questioning after right to remain silent has been invoked is whether defendant's right to cut off questioning has been scrupulously honored.

18. Criminal Law ⟋412.1(4)

Factors employed in determining propriety of resumption of questioning after right to remain silent has been invoked include: whether police immediately ceased interrogation upon defendant's request; whether they resumed questioning only after passage of significant period of time and provided fresh *Miranda* warnings; and whether they restricted later interrogation to crime that had not been subject of first interrogation.

19. Criminal Law ⟋412.2(3)

Statement defendant made to law enforcement authorities at time of his arrest was voluntarily made by him after he had been informed of his *Miranda* rights.

20. Criminal Law ⟋469

Admission or exclusion of expert testimony is matter within sound discretion of district court.

21. Criminal Law ⟋469

District court did not abuse its discretion in excluding proffered testimony of arson investigator and chemical analyst which would have shown that government agents intentionally destroyed fingerprint evidence of burned body taken from residence, where testimony did not appear to have been germane to any issue in prosecution for conspiring to hire and conceal fugitive and for substantive offense. 18 U.S.C.A. §§ 371, 1071.

1. Sample pages of a published case, showing headnotes
(*U.S. vs. Udey* 748 F2d 1231, Eighth Circuit, 1984).

1234   748 FEDERAL REPORTER, 2d SERIES

22. Criminal Law ⟶611.10(1)

District court did not err in refusing defendants' motion for counsel of their choice in order to obtain someone who shared their belief about this country's tax laws.

23. Criminal Law ⟶412(5)

Testimony of law enforcement officers as to certain exculpatory comments defendant had made to officers after defendants' arrest was not admissible under hearsay exception for statement of declarant's then-existing state of mind or emotion, since defendant's existing state of mind or emotion on date allegedly exculpatory statement was made was not relevant to charges in indictment which concerned defense two days earlier. Fed.Rules Evid. Rules 401, 803(3), 28 U.S.C.A.

24. Criminal Law ⟶412(5)

There was no claim of privilege or ruling by court establishing defendants' unavailability as witnesses as required for admission of their allegedly exculpatory statements as declarations against interest; furthermore, offers of proof failed to establish that statements were inculpatory. Fed.Rules Evid. Rule 804(a)(1), (b)(3), 28 U.S.C.A.

25. Criminal Law ⟶1169.12

Given overwhelming evidence in case, any error committed by exclusion of defendants' statements was harmless beyond reasonable doubt. Fed.Rules Cr.Proc. Rule 52(a), 18 U.S.C.A.

26. Criminal Law ⟶1208.3(2)

Sentence within statutory limits is generally not disturbed.

27. Criminal Law ⟶1147

Absent abuse of discretion, court of appeals will not substitute its judgment for sentencing discretion committed solely to district court.

28. Criminal Law ⟶77

District court did not abuse its discretion in imposing five-year sentence on conviction for conspiracy to harbor and conceal fugitive and for substantive offense, to run concurrently. 18 U.S.C.A. § 1071.

Charles Karr, Fort Smith, Ark., Joe A. Izen, Houston, Tex., and Michael L. Minns, Katy, Tex., for appellant.

Larry R. McCord, Asst. U.S. Atty., Fort Smith, Ark., for appellee.

Before LAY, Chief Judge, ROSS and FAGG, Circuit Judges.

ROSS, Circuit Judge.

The appellants, Edwin C. Udey, Arthur H. Russell, Leonard Ginter, and Norma Ginter, were indicted for conspiring to harbor and conceal a fugitive, and for the substantive offense of harboring and concealing a fugitive. They were tried by a jury and convicted on each count. The district court[1] sentenced Udey to five years imprisonment on each count with the sentences to run concurrently. Russell was sentenced to five years on each count, but the period of actual incarceration was to be six months followed by four years probation in lieu of the remainder of the term which was suspended. Leonard Ginter received a sentence of five years on each count with the sentences to run concurrently. Norma Ginter was sentenced to five years on each count, but the sentence was suspended and a five year probation term was imposed instead. The defendants appeal their convictions under 28 U.S.C. § 1291 (West Supp.1984). For the reasons stated herein we affirm the convictions.

I. FACTS

On February 13, 1983, a shootout occurred in Medina, North Dakota, which resulted in the death of two United States Marshals.[2] The following day a magistrate

---

1. The Honorable H. Franklin Waters, Chief Judge, United States District Court, Western District of Missouri.

2. The details of the Medina shootout, and the events leading to the search for Gordon Kahl, are discussed at length in *United States v. Faul,* 748 F.2d 1204 (8th Cir. 1984).

2. A sample page of Shepard's Citations (including citations to the U.S. vs. Udey case, see Footnote 2 to this Chapter).

Vol. 748   FEDERAL REPORTER, 2d SERIES

Cir. 7
f768F2d'824
f768F2d²824
Cir. 8
788F2d'1367
788F2d²1369
Cir. 11
775F2d'1465

-965-
US cert den
in105SC2324
in471US1100
Cir. 5
764F2d⁷1115

-972-
Cir. 2
786F2d⁵71
f623FS⁵718
Cir. 4
d766F2d⁸859
Cir. 5
769F2d⁵256
d774F2d
['1284
d774F2d
[³1285
780F2d'518
810F2d⁵493
Cir. 7
782F2d⁶1389
785F2d⁶592
Cir. 9
767F2d⁶610
770F2d832
800F2d⁵880

-975-
Cir. 2
f615FS³1203
Cir. 8
d627FS'755

-979-
US cert den
in105SC2049
in471US1020

-982-
Cir. 5
807F2d¹²417
Ark
290Ark402
720SW297
84Æ1073s

-996-
Cir. 5
786F2d²1313

-999-
Cir. 5
810F2d⁵532

-1001-
US cert den
in105SC1845
in470US1085

-1006-
77ÆF237n

-1011-
Cir. 1
775F2d449
Cir. 5
788F2d'1151
Cir. 9
763F2d'1073

-1015-
s778F2d1127
Cir. 5
779F2d'1101
796F2d⁴64
Cir. 8
810F2d²762
Utah
709P2d319

-1023-
Cir. 4
110FRD''98
Cir. 5
762F2d
['²1302
772F2d1209
j772F2d1215
789F2d340

-1027-
cc754F2d
[1262
Cir. 5
767F2d'85
771F2d'873
777F2d⁵1025
805F2d⁵1170
813F2d'58
606FS961
Cir. 11
791F2d1547
791F2d¹548

-1037-
92LÆ46
92LÆ347
92LÆ'447
106SC2766
106SC³2767
106SC⁴2767
54USLW
[4882
54USLW
[4883
Cir. 5
772F2d¹³149
636FS1131
636FS³1133
636FS⁴1133
636FS⁵1134
Cir. 9
647FS³1009
647FS⁴1009
647FS⁷1014
Cir. 11
j787F2d1534
640FS¹³1353
640FS¹¹356
645FS575

-1049-
s799F2d1079
Cir. 2
777F2d⁸89
777F2d⁷89

Cir. 5
794F2d⁸977
Cir. 6
f799F2d1108
Tex
706SW796

-1055-
Cir. 3
628FS⁷918
Cir. 5
807F2d'1233
Cir. 6
791F2d²452
DC
503A2d1236
Mass
395Mas446
480NÆ1002

-1058-
Cir. D.C.
627FS⁸1523
627FS⁸1525
106FRD⁸407
Cir. 7
614FS²214
Cir. 8
627FS1236
627FS³1237
627FS⁸1238
Cir. 11
f629FS'1032
629FS⁸1033
629FS¹²1033
NY
133NYM838
510NYS2d
[431

-1077-
Cir. 5
779F2d²262
798F2d³134
809F2d³1052
Cir. 8
638FS²279
638FS³279
Cir. 10
645FS⁸804
645FS³805
645FS⁴805
Cir. 10
e812F2d²662
621FS954

-1083-
s617FS869
Cir. 1
653FS'63
Cir. 4
762F2d356
Cir. 6
f772F2d²283
Cir. 7
648FS²813

-1087-
Cir. 4
622FS³357
Cir. 5
628FS⁴427
Cir. 6
768F2d²103

790F2d⁷520
791F2d²57
791F2d⁰57
803F2d³266
d811F2d⁴317
j811F2d321
Cir. 7
769F2d²1217
769F2d¹1221
609S³902
Cir. 8
f771F2d⁴1166
650FS³298
Mich
424Mch682
424Mch708
385NW589
385NW601
24ÆF808s

-1091-
Cir. 4
780F2d⁴433
Cir. 6
766F2d1004
630FS⁸1105
10LÆ1243s

-1097-
Cir. 3
632FS⁷361
f632FS'362
Cir. 4
774F2d75
Cir. 6
771F2d⁸954
644FS⁷219

-1103-
Cir. 4
49BRW'297
49BRW²297
49BRW³297
49BRW⁷297
Cir. 6
f780F2d'588
f780F2d²588
618FS⁸1240
59BRW²593
Cir. 8
616FS⁸1210
q65BRW151
Cir. 10
66BRW⁴557

-1109-
Cir. 6
764F2d1189
j764F2d1194
798F2d'897
84TCt735
86TCt562
86TCt583

-1112-
US cert den
in105SC2357
in471US1116
Cir. 4
785F2d⁶435
Cir. 6
769F2d⁷361
806F2d641
808F2d'445

808F2d⁸445
j811F2d305
Cir. 7
812F2d⁷378

-1124-
Cir. 6
653FS⁴1216

-1142-
j881F2d688
j106SC675
j54USLW
[4098
Cir. D.C.
641FS''374
Cir. 2
780F2d¹⁵209
780F2d²²209
650FS⁷141
Cir. 6
639FS¹⁰594
Cir. 7
777F2d1279
e777F2d⁸1280
784F2d797
799F2d
[²²1174
607FS⁴537
610FS34
612FS⁴254
614FS⁴529
615FS¹³343
615FS⁴891
615FS⁴899
616FS⁴468
617FS⁴598
622FS⁴974
628FS⁴960
631FS⁴796
634FS⁴49
634FS⁴828
634FS¹⁶828
637FS⁴503
637FS⁴620
644FS⁴977
646FS594
646FS⁶922
650FS203
652FS⁴232
Cir. 8
769F2d503
780F2d
[¹⁹1428
Cir. 10
776F2d⁴912
642FS⁹176
41Æ1021s
51Æ111s

-1151-
US cert den
in105SC1397
in470US1029
Cir. 3
f638FS⁴261
Cir. 7
787F2d¹⁰88

-1158-
Cir. 7
774F2d'810
774F2d²811

791F2d²503
801F2d²954
809F2d²396
631FS604
f631FS'605

-1161-
Cir. 7
786F2d⁵278
j801F2d923
811F2d1063
610FS³1188
Cir. Fed.
812F2d⁴1391

-1177-
Cir. 6
f626FS²1074
Cir. 7
769F2d⁴398
771F2d⁶991
773F2d1163
776F2d⁷737
787F2d⁷221
792F2d'79
792F2d¹653
792F2d703
796F2d⁷220
798F2d⁶245
609FS1018
631FS'220
631FS²220
70BRW⁶541
654FS'873

-1186-
US cert den
in106SC94
Cir. 4
637FS²967
Cir. 7
761F2d375
615FS⁵178

-1199-
Cir. 2
785F2d⁵387
Cir. 7
773F2d²168
776F2d⁵690
652FS446

-1204-
Cir. 10
US cert den
in105SC3500
in105SC3501
in472US1027
Cir. 11
770F2d729
793F2d¹⁸947
793F2d¹⁸952
801F2d⁴312
813F2d155
625FS1351
RI
517A2d241
10LÆ1243s

-1231-
US cert den
in105SC3477
in105SC3478
in472US1017

Cir. 8
785F2d'⁴618
788F2d
[²⁰1338
Ark
289Ark134
709SW814
Nebr
224Neb894
402NW270
60ÆF524s

-1246-
Cir. 8
628FS807
Cir. 8
f760F2d201
760F2d³210
760F2d⁸874
626FS²863
627FS²347
627FS³347
107FRD⁴212
107FRD⁵212
372NW894
401NW713
SD
368NW591
368NW595

-1249-
Cir. 8
804F2d⁴490
812F2d416

-1254-
Cir. 8
770F2d¹105
d106FRD'218
1ÆF922s

-1258-
US cert den
in106SC61
US reh den
in106SC547
Cir. 2
771F2d18
f610FS392
638FS1570
Cir. 3
619FS416
Cir. 8
800F2d⁴755
109FRD32
Cir. 9
795F2d790
Cir. 11
f762F2d'919
775F2d⁵1424
775F2d⁴1425

-1265-
Cir. 8
765F2d'739
780F2d1361

-1269-
Cir. 8
777F2d⁶408

-1275-
Cir. 8
777F2d¹1329

788F2d'489

-1278-
US cert den
in106SC75
Cir. 1
789F2d959
Cir. 2
617FS936
Cir. 5
638FS³1395
638FS⁴1395
Cir. 7
776F2d²³695
Cir. 8
632FS⁸941
Cir. 9
763F2d⁴1046
770F2d²⁰830
772F2d588
774F2d⁴974
774F2d⁹974
782F2d²818
782F2d¹⁵821
783F2d³1404
783F2d⁴1406
783F2d⁵1406
784F2d²⁰998
784F2d
[¹⁶1365
786F2d1455
789F2d¹²753
789F2d¹⁵753
789F2d
[¹⁶1433
790F2d
[²⁰1447
794F2d¹1354
794F2d²1355
j794F2d1358
795F2d²⁴754
795F2d'772
797F2d¹1471
797F2d²1471
797F2d
[¹⁵1475
799F2d
[¹⁷1298
800F2d'963
800F2d²963
800F2d¹1454
800F2d
[¹²1454
626FS85
25Æ1149s
34Æ16s

-1304-
Cir. 9
802F2d⁴330
611FS⁹580
620FS²12

-1308-
s107SC1442
s55USLW
[4379
Cir. D.C.
606FS'1090
606FS²1093
c607FS¹1285
Cir. 3
614FS'394
Continued

378

[1.] *Houston Chronicle*, March 23, 1988, reporting Texas Attorney General Jim Mattox's findings that the PROFITS of property/casualty insurance companies, after taxes, increased from $2.1 BILLION in 1985, to $13.1 BILLION in 1986 and $13.7 BILLION in 1987.

2. Statistics gathered by the National Trial Lawyers Association, and published in the May, 1986 issue of their magazine *"Trial."*

3. The *Houston Chronicle* reported that on March 23, 1988, the state attorney generals of Texas, New York, California, Massachusetts, West Virginia, Alabama, Minnesota and Wisconsin filed anti-trust suits against more than thirty major insurance companies: Aetna Casualty and Surety, Cigna Corp., Fireman's Fund, Hartford Fire, Liberty Mutual, St. Paul Fire and Marine, the Travelers Insurance Co., SF&G Corp., ISO, Allstate, Kemper Reinsurance, Continental Reinsurance, Mercantile & General Reinsurance, North American Reinsurance, Winterthur Swiss Insurance, and others, for conspiring to artificially constrict the insurance market in order to raise prices and by artificially creating a "crisis" atmosphere to bring about favorable legislation and for other deceptive practices.

CHAPTER XVI. THE BANKING SCAM

[1.] All four (4) Gospels include an account of the incident where Jesus Christ drove the moneychangers out of the Temple in Jerusalem, the event is often referred to as "the cleansing of the Temple":

Matthew 21:12-13

"Jesus entered the temple area and drove out all who were buying and selling there. He overturned the tables of the money changers and the benches of those selling doves. "It 's written', he said to them, 'My house will be called a house of prayer, but you are making it a den of robbers.'"

The other accounts of this incident are found in:

Mark 11:15-17

Luke 19:45-46

John 2:14-16

Source: The Holy Bible, New International Version

Zondervan Bible Publishers, Grand Rapids, Michigan, 1987.

[2.] Thomas Jefferson—as quoted in *Five Thousand Quotations for All Occasions*, Edited by Lewis C. Henru, Doubleday & Co., Inc., New York, 1945.

[3.] The Federal Reserve Board enacted a new rule to control the practice of excessive "check holding." As of September 1, 1988, banks must make available the next day all deposits of cashier's checks, certified checks and government checks. Local checks will have 3 business days to clear. Out of state checks will have 7 business days to clear. Source: Houston Chronicle, May 12, 1988.

[4.] Michael Louis Minns vs. Commonwealth Mortgage et al,

Cause No. 85-12954, 165th Judicial District, Harris County

CHAPTER XVII. REAL ESTATE

[1.] Sun Tzu, *The Art of War*, 500 B.C. translated by Samuel B. Griffith, Oxford University Press, London, Oxford, New York, 1971.

[2.] An example of a Warranty Deed

WARRANTY DEED

THE STATE OF TEXAS

KNOW ALL MEN BY THESE PRESENTS:

COUNTY OF HARRIS

That SIGMUND SELLER and his wife SYVIA SELLER of the County of Harris and State of Texas for and in consideration of the sum of TEN DOLLARS and other valuable consideration to the undersigned paid by the grantees herein named, the receipt of which is hereby acknowledged, have GRANTED, SOLD AND CONVEYED, and by these presents do GRANT, SELL AND CONVEY unto BERTRAM BUYER and his wife BERNIECE BUYER of the County of Harris and State of Texas, all of the following described real property in Harris County, Texas, to-wit:

Block 5, Lot 3, Section 2 Happydale Subdivision, as recorded in the map records of Harris County, Texas.

TO HAVE AND TO HOLD the above described premises, together with all and singular the rights and appurtenances thereto in anywise belonging, unto the said grantees, their heirs and assigns forever; and Grantors do hereby bind their heirs, executors and administrators to WARRANT AND FOREVER DEFEND all and singular the said premises unto the said grantee, heirs and assigns, against every person whomsoever lawfully claiming or to claim the same or any part thereof.

EXECUTED this day of , A.D. 19___

THE STATE OF TEXAS
COUNTY OF

(Acknowledgment)

THE STATE OF TEXAS
COUNTY OF

Before me, the undersigned authority, on this day personally appeared SIGNUMD SELLER, known to me to be the person whose name is subscribed to the foregoing instrument, and acknowledged to me that he executed the same for the purposes and consideration therein expressed.

Given under my hand and seal of office on this the 15th day of January , 1989.

Notary Public in and for the
State of Texas

My commission expires: Notary's Printed Name:

SYLVIA SELLER would sign a similar notary acknowledgment.

[3.] An example of a Quitclaim Deed

QUITCLAIM DEED

THE STATE OF TEXAS

KNOW ALL MEN BY THESE PRESENTS:

COUNTY OF HARRIS

That QUINCY QUITMAN of the County of Harris, State of Texas, for and in consideration of the sum of TEN DOLLARS in hand paid by the grantee herein named, the receipt of which is hereby acknowledged, have QUITCLAIMED, and by these presents do QUITCLAIM unto CLARENCE CLAIMER of the County of Harris, State of Texas, all of his right, title and interest in and to the following described real property situated in County, Texas, to-wit:

Block 6. Lot 4, Section 5 of the Bubbling Brook Forest Subdivision as recorded in the map records of Harris County, Texas.

TO HAVE AND TO HOLD all of his right, title and interest in and to the above described property and premises unto the said grantee, his heirs and assigns forever, so that neither Grantor, nor his heirs, legal representatives or assigns shall have, claim or demand any right or title to the aforesaid property, premises or appurtenances or any part thereof.

EXECUTED this 20th day of March, 1989.

(QUINCY QUITMAN's signature would need to be acknowledged by a Notary)

[4.] An example of a promissory note:

PROMISSORY NOTE

$40,000.00   Houston, Texas,   January 10, 1989

FOR VALUE RECEIVED, after date, without grace, in the manner, on the dates, and in the amounts so herein stipulated, the undersigned, DUDLEY DEBTOR, promises to pay to the order of

PATRICK PAYEE the sum of TEN THOUSAND DOLLARS ($40,000) in Lawful money of the United States of America, which shall be legal tender, in payment of all debts and dues, public and private, at the time of payment, and to pay interest thereon from date until maturity at the rate of 10% per annum, payable as stipulated herein.

This note is payable as follows, to-wit:
Ten Thousand Dollars ($10,000.00) on the 10th day of July, 1989.
Ten Thousand Dollars ($10,000.00) on the 10th day of January, 1990.
Ten Thousand Dollars ($10,000.00) on the 10th day of July, 1990.
Ten Thousand Dollars (10,000.00) plus all interest accrued on the 10th day of January, 1991.

It is agreed that time is of the essence of this agreement, and that in the event of default in the payment of any installment of principal or interest when due, the holder of this note may declare the entirety of the note evidenced hereby, immediately due and payable without notice, and failure to exercise said option shall not constitute a waiver on part of the holder of the right to exercise the same at any other time.

In the event of default in the making of any payment herein provided, either of principal or interest, or in the event the entirety of said note evidenced hereby is declared due, interest shall accrue at the rate of 10% per annum from such time.

The undersigned hereby agrees to pay all expenses incurred, including an additional 10% on the amount of principal and interest hereof as attorney's fees, all of which shall become a part of the principal hereof, if this note is placed in the hands of an attorney for collection, or if collected by suit or through any probate, bankruptcy or any other legal proceedings.

Each maker, surety, and endorser waives demand, grace, notice, presentment for payment, and protest and agrees and consents that this note and the liens securing its payment, may be renewed, and the time of payment extended without notice, and without releasing any of the parties.

The payment of this note is secured by
Real Property owned by Dudley Debtor, known as Lot 5, Block 2, of the Dwelling Place Subdivision, Houston, Texas.

5. An example of a Deed of Trust:

THE STATE OF TEXAS
KNOW ALL MEN BY THESE PRESENTS: COUNTY OF
That I, _____ Dudley Debtor_____ of _____Harris_____ County, Texas, hereinafter called Grantors (whether one or more) for the purpose of securing the indebtness hereinafter described, and in consideration of the sum of TEN DOLLARS ($10.00) to us in hand paid by the Trustee hereinafter named, the receipt of which is hereby acknowledged, and for the further consideration of the uses, purposes and trusts hereinafter set forth, have granted, sold and conveyed, and by these presents do grant, sell and convey unto Bertram Bankboy_____, Trustee of ___Harris_____ County, Texas, and his substitutes or successors, all of the following described property situated in _____Harris_____ County, Texas, to-wit:
Lot 5, Block 2 of the Dwelling Place Subdivision, Houston, Texas.

TO HAVE AND TO HOLD the above described property, together with the rights, privileges and appurtenances thereto belonging unto the said Trustee, and to his substitutes or successors forever. And Grantors do hereby bind themselves, their heirs, executors, administrators and assigns to warrant and forever defend the said premises unto the said Trustee, his substitutes or successors and assigns forever, against the claim, or claims, of all persons claiming or to claim the same or any part thereof.

This conveyance, however, is made in TRUST to secure payment of that certain promissory note of even date herewith in the principal sum of FORTY THOUSAND DOLLARS ($40,000.00) executed by Grantors,   payable to the order of ____Patrick Payee_____ in the City of   Houston_____, Harris_____ County, Texas as follows, to-wit:
Ten Thousand Dollars ($10,000.00) on the 10th day of July, 1989.
Ten Thousand Dollars ($10,000.00) on the 10th day of January, 1990.

Ten Thousand Dollars ($10,000.00) on the 10th day of July, 1990.

Ten Thousand Dollars ($10.000.00) plus all interest accrued on the 10th day of January, 1991.

Bearing interest as therein stipulated, providing for acceleration of maturity and for Attorney's fees;

Should Grantors do and perform all of the convenants and agreements herein contained, and make prompt payment of said indebtedness as the same shall become due and payable, then this conveyance shall become null and void and of no further force and effect, and shall be released at the expense of Grantors, by the holder thereof, hereinafter called Beneficiary (whether one or more).

Grantors covenant and agree as follows:

That they are lawfully seized of said property, and have the right to convey the same; that said property is free from all liens and encumbrances, except as herein provided.

To protect the title and possession of said property and to pay when due all taxes and assessments now existing or hereafter levied or assessed upon said property, or the interest therein created by this Deed of Trust, and to preserve and maintain the lien hereby created as a first and prior lien on said property including any improvements hereafter made a part of the realty.

To keep the improvements on said property in good repair and condition, and not to permit or commit any waste thereof; to keep said buildings occupied so as not to impair the insurance carried thereon.

To insure and keep insured all improvements now or hereafter created upon said property against loss or damage by fire and windstorn, and any other hazard or hazards as may be reasonably required from time to time by Beneficiary during the term of the indebtedness hereby secured, to the extent of the original amount of the indebtedness hereby secured, or to the extent of the full insurable value of said improvements, whichever is the lesser, in such form and with such Insurance Company or Companies as may be approved by Beneficiary, and to deliver to Beneficiary the policies of such insurance having attached to said policies such mortgage indemnity clause as Beneficiary shall direct; to deliver renewals of such policies to Beneficiary at least ten (10) days before any such insurance policies shall expire; any proceeds which Beneficiary may receive under any such policy, or policies, may be applied by Beneficiary, at his option, to reduce the indebtedness hereby secured, whether then matured or to mature in the future, and in such manner as Beneficiary may elect, or Beneficiary may permit Grantors to use said proceeds to repair or replace all improvements damaged or destroyed and covered by said policy.

That in the event Grantors shall fail to keep the improvements on the property hereby conveyed in good repair and condition, or to pay promptly when due all taxes and assessments, as aforesaid, or to preserve the prior lien of this Deed of Trust on said property, or to keep the buildings and improvements insured, as aforesaid, or to deliver the policy, or policies, of insurance or the renewal thereof to Beneficiary, as aforesaid, then Beneficiary may, at his option, but without being required to do so, make such repairs, pay such taxes and assessments, purchase any tax title thereon, remove any prior liens, and prosecute or defend any suits in relation to the preservation of the prior lien of this Deed of Trust on said property, or insure and keep insured the improvements thereon in an amount not to exceed that above stipulated; that any sums which may be so paid out by Beneficiary and all sums paid for insurance premiums, as aforesaid, including the costs, expenses and Attorney fees paid in any suit affecting said property when necessary to protect the lien hereof shall bear interest from the dates of such payments at ten per cent (10%) per annum, and shall be paid by Grantors to Beneficiary upon demand, at the same place at which the above described note is payable, and shall be deemed a part of the debt hereby secured and recoverable as such in all respects.

That in the event of default in the payment of any installment, principal or interest, of the note hereby secured, in accordance with the terms thereof, or of a breach of any of the covenants herein contained to be performed by Grantors, then and in any of such events Beneficiary may elect, Grantors hereby expressly waiving presentment and demand for payment, to declare the entire principal indebtedness hereby secured with all interest accrued thereon and all other sums hereby secured immediately due and payable, and in the event of default in the payment of said indebtedness when due or declared due, it shall thereupon, or at any time thereafter, be the duty of the Trustee, or his successor or substitute as hereinafter provided, at the request of Beneficiary, (which request is hereby conclusively presumed) to enforce this trust; and after advertising the time, place and terms of the sale of the above described and conveyed property, then subject to the lien hereof, for at least twenty- one (21) days preceding the date of sale by posting written or printed notice thereof at the Courthouse door of the county where said real property is situated, which notice may be posted by the Trustee acting, or by any person acting for him, and the Beneficiary (the holder of the indebtedness secured hereby) has, at least twenty-one (21) days preceding the date of sale, served written or printed notice of the proposed sale by certified mail on each debtor obligated to pay the indebtedness secured by this Deed of Trust according to the records of Beneficiary, by the deposit of such notice, enclosed in a postpaid wrapper, properly addressed to such debtor at debtor's most recent address as shown by the records of Beneficiary, in a post office or official depository under the care and custody of the United States Postal Service, and sell the above described property, then subject to the lien hereof, at public auction in accordance with such notice at the Courthouse door of the county where such real property, then subject to the lien hereof, is situated (provided where said real property, then subject to the lien hereof, is situated in more than one county the notice to be posted as herein provided shall be posted at the Courthouse door of each of such counties where said real property is situated, and said above described and conveyed property, then subject to the lien hereof, may be sold at the Courthouse door of any one of such counties, and the notices so posted shall designate the county where the property will be sold), on the first Tuesday in any month between the hours of ten o'clock A.M. and four o'clock P.M., to the highest bidder for cash, selling all of the property as an entirety or in such parcels as the Trustee acting may elect, and make due conveyance to the Purchaser, or Purchasers, with general warranty binding Grantors, their heirs and assigns; and out of the money arising from such sale, the Trustee acting shall pay first, all the expenses of advertising the sale and making the conveyance, including a commission of five per cent (5%) to himself, which commission shall be due and owing in addition to the Attorney's fees provided for in said note, and then to Beneficiary the full amount of principal, interest, Attorney's fees and other charges due and unpaid on said note and all other indebtedness secured hereby, rendering the balance of the sales price, if any, to Grantors, their heirs or assigns; and the recitals in the conveyance to the Purchaser or Purchasers shall be full and conclusive evidence of the truth of the matters therein stated, and all prerequisites to said sale shall be presumed to have been performed, and such sale and conveyance shall be conclusive against Grantors, their heirs and assigns.

It is agreed that in the event a foreclosure hereunder should be commenced by the Trustee, or his substitute or successor, Beneficiary may at any time before the sale of said property direct the said Trustee to abandon the sale, and may then institute suit for the collection of said note, and for the foreclosure of this Deed of Trust lien; it is further agreed that if Beneficiary should institute a suit for the collection thereof, and for a foreclosure of this Deed of Trust lien, that he may at any time before the entry of a final judgment in said suit dismiss the same, and require the Trustee, his substitute or successor to sell the property in accordance with the provisions of this Deed of Trust.

Beneficiary shall have the right to purchase at any sale of the property, being the highest bidder and to have the amount for which such property is sold credited on the debt then owing.

Beneficiary in any event is hereby authorized to appoint a substitute trustee, or a successor trustee, to act instead of the Trustee named herein without other formality than the designation in writing of a substitute or successor trustee; and the authority hereby conferred shall extend to the appointment of other successor and substitute trustees successively until the indebtedness hereby secured has been paid in full, or until said property is sold hereunder, and each substitute and successor trustee shall succeed to all of the rights and powers of the original trustee named herein.

In the event any sale is made of the above described property, or any portion thereof, under the terms of this Deed of Trust, Grantors, their heirs and assigns, shall forthwith upon the making of such sale surrender and deliver possession of the property so sold to the Purchaser at such sale, and in the event of their failure to do so they shall thereupon from and after the making of such sale be and continue as tenants at will of such Purchaser, and in the event of their failure to surrender possession of said property upon demand, the Purchaser, his heirs or assigns, shall be entitled to institute and maintain an action for forcible detainer of said property in the Justice of the Peace Court in the Justice Precinct in which such property, or any part thereof, is situated.

It is agreed that the lien hereby created shall take precedence over and be a prior lien to any other lien of any character whether vendor's, materialmen's or mechanic's lien hereafter created on the above described property, and in the event the proceeds of the indebtedness secured hereby as set forth herein are used to pay off and satisfy any liens heretofore existing on said property, then Beneficiary is, and shall be, subrogated to all of the rights, liens and remedies of the holders of the indebtedness so paid.

It is further agreed that if Grantors, their heirs or assigns, while the owner of the hereinabove described property, should commit an act of bankruptcy, or authorize the filing of a voluntary petition in bankruptcy, or should an act of bankruptcy be committed and involuntary proceedings instituted or threatened, or should the property hereinable described be taken over by a Receiver for Grantors, their heirs or assigns, the note hereinabove described shall, at the option of Beneficiary, immediately become due and payable, and the acting Trustee may then proceed to sell the same under the provisions of this Deed of Trust.

As further security for the payment of the hereinabove described indebtedness, Grantors hereby transfer, assign, and convey unto Beneficiary all rents issuing or to hereafter issue from said real property, and in the event of any default in the payment of said note or hereunder, Beneficiary, his agents and representatives, is hereby authorized, at his option, to collect said rents, or if such property is vacant to rent the same and collect the rents, and apply the same, less the reasonable costs and expenses of collection thereof, to the payment of said indebtedness, whether then matured or to mature in the future, and in such manner as Beneficiary may elect. Beneficiary shall not be, in any event or circumstances, liable or responsible for failure to collect, or exercise diligence in the collection of, any such sums.

It is agreed that an extension, or extensions, may be made at the time of payment of all, or any part, of the indebtedness secured hereby, and that any part of the above described real property may be released from this lien without altering or affecting the priority of the lien created by this Deed of Trust in favor of any junior encumbrancer, mortgagee or purchaser, or any person acquiring an interest in the property hereby conveyed, or any part thereof; it being the intention of the parties hereto to preserve this lien on the property herein described and all improvements thereon, and that may be hereafter constructed thereon, first and superior to any liens that may be placed thereon, or that may be fixed, given or imposed by law thereon after the execution of this instrument notwithstanding any such extension of the time of payment, or the release of a portion of said property from this lien.

In the event any portion of the indebtedness hereinabove described cannot be lawfully secured by this Deed of Trust lien on said real property, it is agreed that the first payments made on said indebtedness shall be applied to the discharge of that portion of said indebtedness.

Beneficiary shall be entitled to receive any and all sums which may become payable to Grantors for the condemnation of the hereinabove described real property, or any part thereof, for public or quasi-public use, or by virtue of private sale in lieu thereof, and any sums which may be awarded or become payable to Grantors for damages caused by public works or construction on or near the said property. All such sums are hereby assigned to Beneficiary, who may, after deducting therefrom all expenses actually incurred, including attorney's fees, release same to Grantors or apply the same to the reduction of the indebtedness hereby secured, whether then matured or to mature in the future, or on any money obligation hereunder, as and in such manner as Beneficiary may elect. Beneficiary shall not be, in any event or circumstances, liable or responsible for failure to collect, or exercise diligence in the collection of, any such sums.

Nothing herein or in said note contained shall ever entitle Beneficiary, upon the arising of any contingency whatsoever, to receive or collect interest in excess of the highest rate allowed by the laws of the State of Texas on the principal indebtedness hereby secured or on any money obligation hereunder and in no event shall Grantors be obligated to pay interest thereon in excess of such rate.

If this Deed of Trust is executed by only one person or by a corporation the plural reference to Grantors shall be held to include the singular and all of the covenants and agreements herein undertaken to be performed by and the rights conferred upon the respective Grantors named herein, shall be binding upon and inure to the benefit of not only said parties respectively but also their respective heirs, executors, administrators, grantees, successors and assigns.

Grantors expressly represent that this Deed of Trust and the Note hereby secured are given for the following purpose, to-wit:

To secure that certain promissory note EXECUTED this 10th day of January, 1989.

(THE NOTARIZED SIGNATURE OF DUDLEY DEBTOR WOULD BE REQUIRED)

CHAPTER XVIII. NOTARIES

[1.] This proposal was discussed in a spring, 1988 issue of the *The National Notary*, a educational news magazine for members of the National Notary Association, Canoga Park, California, written to acquaint notaries with the latest developments and legislation in their field.

[2.] Excerpt from the deposition of Harvey Baum, taken in Cause No. 85-38597 November 1, 1985, page 91, lines 3—25. Lines labeled Q are questions by Michael Minns. Lines labeled A are Harvey Baum's answers.

Q Were you suspicious at all that a woman would sell her homestead to you without any other place to go?

A A lot of people sell their homes.

Q How many homesteads have you purchased in the last ten years from people who had no other means of purchasing a home?

A Can we take that back to about 15 years?

Q All right. Go ahead.

A And instead of saying homes, maybe it would be a home that they lived there but they were— as an upstairs, that they rented out or something or maybe it was divided up.

Q All right. How many of these have you —

A Many.

Q Over a hundred or under a hundred?

A Going back 15 years to about 1970 is what it would be.

Q All right.

A Is that correct?

Q Is that as far back as you can go?

A Well, why don't we go back to about 1967?

Q All right. How many?

A Lots of them. I would say probably 50.

[3.] *Downer vs. Aquamarine* 701 S.W. 2d 238 (1985), a landmark ruling by the Texas Supreme Court indicating that repeated, flagrant abuse of the discovery process will not be tolerated.

CHAPTER XIX. CORPORATIONS

[1.] CORPORATION DATA SHEET

#1 Name (first choice, alternate choices)

A _____

B _____

C _____

#2 Term—Perpetual or Limited _____

#3 Purpose—Specific or General

#4 No. of Shares _____

Par value _____

#5 Registered Agent _____

Address _____

Address _____

#6 Directors: No. _____ <u>Addresses</u>

A _____

B _____

C _____

D _____

Optional: The shareholders shall not have the pre-emptive right to subscribe to any issue of shares or securities of this corporation.

#7 <u>Offices / Officers</u>

President_____

Vice-President _____

Secretary _____

Treasurer _____

Chairman of the Board _____

#8 Initial Issuance of Stock

A _____

B _____

C _____

D _____

CHAPTER XX. POWER OF ATTORNEY

1. POWER OF ATTORNEY

STATE OF TEXAS

                *   KNOW ALL MEN BY THESE PRESENTS THAT

COUNTY OF HARRIS   *

I, Mr. William A. Traveler, grant and convey to my son, Mr. John J. Traveler:

All of my personal, legal, business and financial affairs during the months of June, July and August, 1989, while William A. Traveler and Sarah B. Traveler will be traveling.

In my name, place and stead and to the same extent that I would do so if present. I hereby put all persons and entities on notice that this Power of Attorney is applicable from the date of the undersigned's signature until August 31, 1989, unless otherwise extended, in writing, by me."

This Power of Attorney shall allow my son, Mr. John J. Traveler, to execute on my behalf any and all documents necessary to bring about the desired result.

SIGNED on this the 31st day of May, 1988.

_____

William A. Traveler

(William Traveler's signature would need to be notarized).

CHAPTER XXII. PUBLIC EDUCATION

1. *Houston Post,* April, 19, 1986.

2. *Houton Chronicle,* July 11, 1988: The U.S. Department of Education's Center for Statistics reported that the sum of $4,263.00 is spent on each child's education, annually.

3. Sileven, Everett *Pastor Sileven's Jail Writings* Daniels Publishing Co., Orland FLorida, 1983

4. Ibid.

5. Turano, Frank *A Need to Be Free*

6. Ibid.

7. Ralph Waldo Emerson, as quoted in Frank Turano's *A Need to Be Free.*

8. Turano, Frank, *Need to Be Free.*

9. Ibid.

10. *Five Thousand Quotations for All Occasions,* Edited by Lewis C. Henry, Doubleday & Co., Inc., Nw York, 1945.

11. Albert Einstein, as quoted in Frank Turano's *A Need to Be Free.*

CHAPTER XXIII. AMERICAN DIVORCE

1. The Final Judgment in Cause No. 56-752-A In the Matter of the Marriage of Martha M.

Izen and Joe Alfred Izen and in the Interest of Price and Thomas Izen; Martha Macklin Izen, Petitioner, Joe Alfred Izen, Jr., Respondent, Karen Cooley, Co- Respondent. *(see page 622)*

2. Judge Stansbury's Findings of Fact and Conclusions of Law in the above referenced case *(see page 623)*.

CHAPTER XXIV. THE SHRINK IN LAW

1. *Houston Post*, August 31, 1986: Six percent of psychiatrists in the United States admit to having sexual relations with their patients, according to a voluntary survey sent to 5,574 randomly selected psychiatrists. One quarter of them responded with the data recorded above. An article addressing this phenomenon was published in the American Journal of Psychiatry, September, 1986.

2. Rothblatt, Henry B. *Handling Health Practitioner Cases,* published by The Lawyers Cooperative Publishing Company, Rochester, N.Y., 1983 This excellent volume devotes a whole chapter to discussing lawsuits involving mental health practitioners and other physcians accused of sexually taking advantage of their patients. 3. *U.S. vs.McBride* 20 Fed Rules Evid. Serv. 204, Second Circuit (1986).

3In this case, the judgment of a trial court which refused to admit mental health testimony on the basis that "psychiatry is still in its infancy" was reversed by the Second Circuit Court of Appeals which cited in its opinion *Ake vs. Oklahoma* 105 S.Ct. 1087, (1985) in support of the profession:

"Psychiatrists ideally assist lay jurors who generally have no training in psychiatric matters, to make a sensible and educated determination about the mental condition of the Defendant at the time of the offense."

These cases were quoted by the author in his Brief to the Fifth Circuit Court of appeals on United States of America vs. Leland Ray Williams, No. 86-2557, November 19, 1986.

CHAPTER XXVII. BANKRUPTCY

1. Williamson, John H., *The Attorney's Handbook on Consumer Bankruptcy and Chapter 13* Argyle Publishing Company, Lakewood, Colorado, 1988, updated annually.

CHAPTER XXVIII. SOCIAL INSECURITY

1. Revelation 13: 16—18

...it (the beast) caused everyone, great and small, rich and poor, slave and free to be branded with a mark on his right hand or forehead, and no one was allowed to buy or sell unless he bore this beast's mark, either name or number. (Here is the key; and anyone who has intelligence may work out the number of the beast. The number represents a man's name, and the numerical value of its letters is six hundred and sixty six).

Source: The *New English Bible*, Oxford University Press, New York, 1979.

CHAPTER XXIX. WILLS AND PROBATE

1Instructions: Fill out to the best of your ability. If you have questions, write them down so you won't forget. If you run out of room go on to the back and add pages.

1. State your full legal name.

2. State every nickname by which you are commonly or customarily called.

3. A) State the name of your current spouse, his/her birthdate, name of all of your current children and their date of birth, and who they reside with.

Spouse—_____

Children—_____

3. B) Grandchildren, if any. If not applicable, put "not applicable."

_____

3. C) State who you would want to be the Guardian of any minor children in the event your spouse did not survive you. State who you would want to actually have custody of your children. State who you would want to be a Trustee of any Trust set up for your children.

4. State the name of any past spouses and their residence and whether or not they have children. If this is not applicable put "not applicable".

5. Give a description of all of your personal property. Personal property is everything other than real estate.

A) Personal jewelry—_____

_____

value—_____ debt—_____
B) Personal clothing—_____

_____

value—_____ debt—_____
C) Personal furniture— _____

_____

value—_____ debt—_____
D) Stocks and bonds—_____

_____

value—_____ debt—_____
E) Certificates of deposits—_____

_____

value—_____ debt—_____
F) Businesses or interests in businesses—_____

_____

value—_____ debt—_____
G) Interests in partnerships other than real estate—_____

_____

value—_____ debt—_____
H) Vehicles—_____

_____

value—_____ debt—_____
I) Life insurance policies— _____

_____

value—_____ debt—_____

J) Real Property—Real property is real estate. It means dirt and anything permanently affixed to it. Your home if you own it.

1) List each and every parcel of real estate you own, the legal description if you know it, (this can be found from your deed) the address, the approximate value, and the approximate debt against it.

2) List the names of each and every partnership which owns real estate in which you are a partner, the name of the partnership, the amount of money invested in the partnership, the approximate value of the holding, the percentage of the total holding, your percentage and the approximate value of your percentage and the personal liability (exposure) in which you have on it. Are there any restrictions to passing to interest in a Will?

6. State your birthdate.

7. State your social security number, social security of your current spouse if any.

8. In order to have a will, you must have an executor or an executrix. This is the person who is responsible for taking your will to the probate court and handling your affairs after you are dead. If you are married, the most common choice for executor or executrix is your spouse. However, you are under no obligation to use your spouse. In the event that your number one choice cannot be the executor or executrix or your estate, you should have alternative choices. Therefore, in the following blanks numbered 1-4 fill in the name, address, and relationship to you, if any, of persons in order of your preference to serve as your executor.

1) _____
2) _____
3) _____
4) _____

9. Texas law requires a bond on the executor unless you state otherwise. If you have the bond, it will cost extra money and cost extra time and trouble. You have the option to have an Independent executor or executrix who has very little court supervision and does not have to post a bond. Most of the wills in the State of Texas have an independent executor or executrix. State your option either for independent or against.

10. Who do you want to receive your property? In the space below indicate your first choice to inherit, and in the even that person dies before you do, choose two (2) alternates. For example, you may wish for your spouse to inherit everything, and in the event of your spouse's death you would want your estate divided equally between your children. Simply indicate who you want to inherit from you, and what you want them to receive. If some of the beneficiaries (this means people who inherit from you) are minors or for any other reason you do not wish them to receive the money immediately upon your death then state this and give instructions at what age you want them to receive the money or under what circumstances. The money can be given in different steps i.e. age 25 one-half, age 35 one-half. Do not consider what the law is. Decide exactly what you want. Do not put a ham string on your imagination. It is quite likely that your plan can be reduced to a legal will. Most can. A provision in the will can be made for some other person or entity to control the money for a certain period of time or property. If you have several options put them down and we will discuss them when you come into the office.

Express yourself as clearly and simply as you can. Do not attempt to use legal words unless you are certain you know what they mean. Write down your questions.

11. Occasionally a major disaster strikes and all members of the family die. If you wish to consider this and what to do with your money in this event, come up with some ideas.

12. Occasionally a husband and wife will die in the same accident but one will linger on for some time. This is not advantageous if the wife or husband inherits from the other because it can cause the estate to go through two probates. It is customary to put in the will that the spouse must survive his/her spouse by a minimum amount of 30 days (or 60, the length of time is up to you) before inheriting from the other spouse. Consider this and write down your wishes.

13. A will can be made contractual or noncontractual. Generally noncontractual is preferred. If the will is contractual, the surviving spouse cannot write a new will that deviates from the contractual agreement of the deceased spouse. This can limit them substantially.

14. A will is not the place to put personal messages. Nevertheless, I have a form paragraph which I use and you may wish to put in some ideas at the top of your will, if you do so reduce them to writing here and we will discuss them later.

15. State any funeral or burial instructions. State if you would wish to donate organs from your body.

[2] An article written by Michael Louis Minns, entitled *To Be or Not to Be*, addressed the broader issue of the impropriety of attorneys wearing the "hats: of both attorney and notary, and also described the specific problems that can arise when an attorney is a witness on a client's will or other document which the attorney might be called upon to uphold in court. This article was printed in the February, 1987 National Notary Association Viewpoint, a bi-monthly news magazine for N.N.A. members.

1. The Final Judgment in Cause No. 56-752-A In the Matter of the Marriage of Martha M. Izen and Joe Alfred Izen and in the Interest of Price and Thomas Izen; Martha Macklin Izen, Petitioner, Joe Alfred Izen, Jr., Respondent, Karen Cooley, Co- Respondent.

CASE NO. 56,752-A

MARTHA M. IZEN	*	IN THE DISTRICT COURT OF
VS.	*	FORT BEND COUNTY, T E X A S
KAREN LEE COOLEY	*	328TH JUDICIAL DISTRICT

FINAL JUDGMENT

On the 15th day of December, 1987, came to be heard the Motion for Sanctions of Petitioner, Karen Lee Cooley, against Respondent, Martha M. Izen, re-set from November 4, 1987. Final Order granting said sanctions was signed on December 16, 1987. On the 16th day of February, 1988, Martha Izen's Motion for New Trial was granted.

By agreement of the parties, this case was resubmitted to this Court on submission:

The Court having read the pleadings of both parties, and reviewed the entire record, finds in favor of the Defendant/Petitioner, Karen Lee cooley, and awards sanctions against Martha M. Izen in the amount of $ 4,000 .

ACCORDINGLY, IT IS ORDERED that Martha M. Izen pay to Karen Lee Cooley the sum of $ 4,000 00 . bearing interest from this date at TEN PERCENT (10%) per annum until fully satisfied.

IT IS FURTHER ORDERED that Martha M. Izen pay all costs of court, including costs of severance.

IT IS FURTHER ORDERED that any relief not granted with regard to this cause of action, (Martha M. Izen vs. Karen Lee Cooley, Cause no. 56,752-A, severed from Cause no. 56,752), is hereby denied.

FOR WHICH LET EXECUTION LIE.

SIGNED on this the 15 day of March , 1988.

_____
Presiding Judge

STATE OF TEXAS
COUNTY OF FORT BEND
I, OLORY KETHLERS, District Clerk of Fort Bend, County, Texas, do hereby certify that the foregoing is a true and correct copy of the original record now in my lawful custody and posted in ___ years of record in
Vol._____ _____ ____, Minutes of said court, on tus ___ ___ office.
Witness my hand and seal of office at Richmond, Texas, this 16 day of March , 1988

OLORY KETHLERS
District Clerk
Fort Bend County, Texas
By _____ Deputy

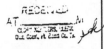

CAUSE NO. 56,752-A

MARTHA M. IZEN   *   IN THE DISTRICT COURT OF

VS.   *   FORT BEND COUNTY, T E X A S

KAREN COOLEY   *   328TH JUDICIAL DISTRICT

CONCLUSIONS OF FACT AND LAW

FINDINGS OF FACT

A divorce action was filed by Martha Izen against Joe A. Izen, Jr. in 1987. Karen Cooley was named by Martha Izen as Co-Respondent.

Karen Cooley set the deposition with a subpoena duces tecum of Martha Izen on April 14, 1987 with twelve (12) days' notice. The day before, April 13, 1987, Martha Izen filed a Motion for Protection without alleging proper grounds and without giving the requisite three (3) days notice.

The Court denied same and ordered the deposition to take place and ordered production.

Martha Izen did not appear for the deposition, disobeying the Court order. Cooley filed a Motion to Compel.

The Court ordered compliance a second time.

Martha Izen was deposed but did not produce the Court ordered items, disobeying the Court's orders a second time. She stated her private investigator had the missing items. Her attorney, John F. Nichols stated to opposing counsel in the deposition record that Martha Izen had no duty to inquire of her agent for the Court ordered production.

She subsequently inquired of her agent, some production was

1

made by the agent but the key item of inquiry, a tape with alleged incriminating evidence, .was not produced. At the re-setting of Martha Izen's deposition, she retracted her earlier remark and stated the tape had been in her possession at all times, specifically a tape which was now erased.

A second Motion for Sanctions concerning this conduct was filed and held for further consideration. The motion was not granted.

Martha Izen, on the 29th day of September, 1987, conducted, through her attorney John Nichols and/or Warren Cole, his associate, the deposition of Joe A. Izen, Jr. without giving notice to Karen Cooley or her attorney, Michael Louis Minns.

Following the filing of a third Motion for Sanctions by Karen Cooley, in relationship to this conduct concerning discovery, Martha Izen filed a non-suit.

This Court subsequently severed this action from the divorce and maintained jurisdiction for the purposes of ruling on the pending sanctions motions.

From a review of the didacted discovery presented to this Court, the Petition of Martha Izen against Karen Cooley appears to have been frivolous, but the Court does not make any finding of facts with regard to the merits of said suit. The Court merely finds that Karen Cooley was the successful party, since the cause of action against her was dismissed.

Karen Cooley incurred substantial legal fees defending herself. The file and pleadings and evidence before the Court show almost all of that was incurred with regard to discovery efforts, sanctions hearings, and protective motions which

2

demonstrated conduct by Martha Izen, the Court finds to have been abusive. Martha Izen asked for no sanctions to be levied. Karen Cooley has asked for sanctions in the amount of ELEVEN THOUSAND FIVE HUNDRED AND NO/100 DOLLARS ($11,500.00). The Court found, in light of prior rulings and dispositions, reasonable sanctions for the pending motion to be FOUR THOUSAND AND NO/100 DOLLARS ($4,000.00) and so ruled on March 15, 1988.

CONCLUSIONS OF LAW

The Court concludes that Martha Izen violated the rules of discovery on several occasions and disobeyed Court orders causing Karen Cooley to incur substantial attorney's fees. The Court finds sanctions under Rule 215 to be justified.

The Court concludes that costs should be taxed against Martha Izen pursuant to Rule 131. 10

The Court concludes Martha Izen violated Rule 21(a). 10

SIGNED this the 20 day of April, 1988.

_____
Judge Presiding

ROUTED TO COURT

FILED

1988 APR 20 PM 3: 46

Glory Ketelers

CLERK DISTRICT COURT
FORT BEND CO., TX

3

Free. When is free really free? Free is when all you have to pay for is a stamp (for the postcard).

A short follow-up memo will be written bringing you up to date on some of the cases in this book. It will be mailed to you free. (We pay for the stamp). A few additional insights will be offered. There will be no charge. All you have to do is fill out the postcard, put a stamp on it, and put it in a mail box.

Why this offer?

Gopher has other books it wants to sell. If you like <u>The Underground Lawyer</u>, we hope you will continue to look for other Gopher publications. Plans are also underway to make a third edition of "The Underground Lawyer." Your comments concerning errors you may have found or ideas you may have would be appreciated. Even one word like —good or bad helps.

Gopher Publications, Inc.® is a Texas Corporation with mailing address at **870 Mason Road, Suite 104-813, Katy, Texas 77450.**

For information on distribution rights call **(713) 461-6700**.